# Dictionary of Social Work

# COLLINS EDUCATIONAL

# Dictionary of
# Social Work

Principal editors:
**Martin Thomas and John Pierson,**
*Staffordshire University*

Contributing editors:
Anne Worrall, *University of Keele*
Jim Radcliffe, *Staffordshire University*
Sue Wainwright, *University of Birmingham*

Collins Educational
*An Imprint of HarperCollinsPublishers*

© Martin Thomas, John Pierson and Collins Educational 1995

Published by Collins Educational Ltd
An imprint of HarperCollins*Publishers*
77–85 Fulham Palace Road
Hammersmith
London
W6 8JB

First published in 1995
Reprinted 1995

British Library Cataloguing in Publication Data is available on request from the British Library.

ISBN 000 322 3310

Typeset by Harper Phototypesetters Limited, Northampton
Printed in Great Britain by HarperCollins Manufacturing, Glasgow

# Contributors

Specialist contributors

Helen Barnes, *Staffordshire University*
Jennifer Bradley, *Staffordshire University*
Judith Cavet, *Staffordshire University*
David Clark-Carter, *Staffordshire University*
Anthony Esgate, *Staffordshire University*
Jo Hutt, *Staffordshire University*
Pauline James, *Staffordshire University*
David Jary, *Staffordshire University*
Julia Jary, *Staffordshire University*
Marie Lebacq, *Staffordshire University*
Elizabeth Meins, *Staffordshire University*
Bernard Moss, *Staffordshire University*
Adrian Randall, *City of Birmingham, Welfare Rights and Money Advice Unit*
Alison Read, *Staffordshire University*
Joan Smith, *Staffordshire University*
Pauline Stuart, *Barnabas Drug Advice Project, Macclesfield*
Ben Whitney, *Staffordshire Education Department*
Nevil Wyatt, *Staffordshire University*

# Acknowledgements

Our considerable gratitude goes to Joan Deakin and Jackie Clewlow, who typed the manuscript with accuracy and considerable good grace while the writers and editors fretted and stormed. We would also like to thank our editors at HarperCollins, Emma Dunlop and Patrick McNeill, for all their help, guidance and support. Finally, our thanks go to Miles Litvinoff who copy-edited the entire manuscript and in doing so made many improvements.

Martin Thomas and John Pierson,
*Staffordshire University, Division of Social Work,*
*September 1994.*

# Using the Dictionary

We intend the *Dictionary* to be used by a wide range of people in a number of different occupations, as well as by those studying in the field of social care and social work. To facilitate this, we have tried to define and explain terms in as straightforward and concise a way as possible and to have each term defined so as to stand on its own. We have, however, included within most entries one or more cross-references; it is desirable for the reader to follow these in order to reach a full understanding of the subject under discussion. Wherever appropriate, we have discussed the related implications for social work and social care practice under the individual entry. Thus readers will not find a separate entry for 'social work with older people' but will find that information under **older people**.

Entries are arranged in strictly alphabetical order, treating all words in the entry as a continuous word; thus the **Children Act 1989** precedes **child support**.

Entries in the *Dictionary* are written on up to three different levels: (1) all entries have a short definition of the term; (2) many entries consist of the short definition plus a longer summary of what the term refers to, usually of up to half a page; (3) still others consist of the short definition, the summary and a more detailed discussion of the topic, of about two pages. We should like to point out that length of entry does not necessarily indicate its relative significance.

Where appropriate, further reading is cited below the entry.

*Dedication*

**Martin Thomas:**
*to Kate, Carl, Clare, Daniel and Madeleine*

**John Pierson:**
*to Sally, Alice, Orrin and Miriam.*

# A

**able-bodiedism** an assumption that being non-disabled is an ideal state and that disabled people must accept an inferior status to non-disabled people. This is often coupled with a tendency to produce an environment unsuited to the needs of disabled people.

**abortion** the loss of a foetus through planned termination or miscarriage. In lay person's terms, 'abortion' applies to the termination of an unwanted or unplanned pregnancy. This became legal in 1967 in England, Scotland and Wales but remains illegal elsewhere in the British Isles. Abortion is legal up to twenty-four weeks into pregnancy (later in exceptional circumstances). The majority of abortions are carried out in the first twelve weeks of pregnancy, either by the NATIONAL HEALTH SERVICE (or its agents) at no cost to the individual, or at a clinic or private hospital where the patient bears the expense. Over half the women seeking abortions are not able to get NHS treatment, according to the British Pregnancy Advisory Service, whose clinics charge a non-profit-making fee to cover cost of treatment. For an abortion to be legal under the Abortion Act 1967, two doctors must agree on the grounds, including: risk to the life of the woman; risk to her own or her existing children's physical or mental health; and risk of abnormality to the foetus. In emergencies, abortions can be carried out to save the woman's life or to prevent permanent injury. If the woman is under 16 years old, the doctor will usually need her parents' consent; however, doctors can use discretion and make exceptions if the young woman refuses to give the information.

The two main methods of abortion are by vacuum aspiration (suction) and the 'abortion pill'. Both are available to day patients, and major complications as a result of abortions are rare. Although most women feel physically fine within a day or two, some feel emotionally 'low' after an abortion. The effects of an unplanned pregnancy are many and varied, and women therefore react differently to their abortion. The range of emotions may include relief, euphoria, depression, grief, anger, sadness, guilt and numbness – all appropriate responses to a difficult life crisis. Severe DEPRESSION after abortion is rare but most likely to affect women who are very young, lonely or unsupported, or those who have a late abortion or a history of depression. Women facing unplanned pregnancy may need the opportunity to talk to someone who understands, such as a pre-abortion counsellor. Women who find it difficult to come to terms with their abortion – perhaps because they have been pressured into having it – may benefit from the time and support offered by post-abortion counselling.

Although abortion is legal, some people oppose it for religious or moral reasons. Some disability groups also object to the criteria for abortions of 'abnormality to the foetus', because they believe this devalues the existence and life experiences of disabled people. They argue that more resources should be made available to disabled people and their carers in society so that women do not feel that abortion is the only option. Pro-choice groups, on the other hand, argue that it is essential for abortion to remain legal if we are not to return to the days of back-street abortions and self-induced methods of ending unplanned pregnancies.

**abuse**  intentional, purposeful acts, or acts of omission, leading to a person being hurt, injured or killed. Attention has focused mainly on CHILD ABUSE, more recently on ELDER ABUSE and abuse of people with mental health problems or learning disabilities. 'Spouse abuse' is more commonly referred to as DOMESTIC VIOLENCE.

Particular environments can be abusing (for example, to be a child in any society where there is violent conflict or extreme poverty). However, abuse in most industrialized societies is thought of as a non-accidental act perpetrated by an individual, family or group, or as something that an individual, family or group fails to prevent. Individuals are therefore held to be responsible, although mitigating circumstances related to abusing environments may be accepted. While most accounts now distinguish between PHYSICAL, EMOTIONAL and SEXUAL abuse, different forms of abuse may overlap or interact with each other. Physical abuse is likely to be accompanied by emotional abuse; sexual abuse is likely also to involve emotional abuse; emotional abuse can occur independently of the other two forms. Historically, physical abuse was the first to be recognized. Social work services and public awareness have focused on this form of abuse for some decades. The 'discovery' of sexual abuse is relatively recent in Britain, but it has attracted considerable attention in the last ten years. Emotional abuse is the most likely form to pass unrecognized unless associated with other forms.

Definitions of abuse are highly value-laden, and for this reason attempts to define abuse are usually couched in fairly general terms. In relation to physical abuse, for example, when does the physical chastisement of a child constitute abuse? Or in relation to neglect (acts of omission), to what extent must a child's development be impaired for the situation to be considered unsatisfactory and to warrant intervention? Some cultures are very indulgent of their children – among the Turks, emotional abuse is said to take place if young children are forced to sleep alone – while others require considerable emotional control at an early age. Sexual abuse is frequently couched in terms of a more mature person in some sense exploiting a dependent and developmentally immature person in a sexual act that they perhaps do not fully understand and could not give informed consent to. How understanding and informed consent are to be interpreted are clearly matters of delicacy. Some societies define the age of sexual consent as low as 12, others as high as 18.

Definitions of abuse may simply utilize a medical model, listing injuries or deficits in relation to behaviour that cannot be explained by natural events or accidents. Or they may emphasize the circumstances in which care and protection outside the family will be required. Some definitions take a more general approach, seeking to describe the difference between the optimal development of children and their actual achievement. Others try to give shape to the needs they believe all children have and then ask what it is about a particular child that prevents the fulfilment of those needs. These attempts at definitions have helped to establish a substantial consensus that appears to 'fit' most children in most circumstances; but for many children in certain situations the problem of interpretation will be difficult.

The search for predictors of abusive behaviour has been long and, so far, inconclusive. Research has concentrated both on groups of factors (explanations rooted in environmental issues, in family dysfunction, in parental characteristics and in the children themselves) and on combinations of what might be precipitating factors. No single explanation or apparent combination of explanations has to date revealed reliable predictors of who will and who will not abuse others. Clearly there are combinations of factors whereby the incidence of abuse increases. For example, people living in poverty, with debt, poorly housed and who are inexperienced parents, have a poor marital relationship and have a demanding child to look after are more likely to abuse their child than a couple who do not experience these difficulties. But not all couples in these adverse circumstances will abuse their children; indeed, most will not.

Abuse in all its forms is to be found in most societies where research has been completed and in all social classes. As to its incidence, there have been widely varying estimates of the extent of sexual and physical abuse. Sources of information are confined to current cases of substantiated abuse and adult survivors who are willing to reveal their experiences. The former source overlooks undetected abuse and the latter those unwilling to share their histories with researchers; both are probably substantial groups. (See also CHILD PROTECTION, RITUAL ABUSE.)

**acceptance**   the process of perceiving and working with a service user based upon an accurate notion of who and what they are. This is not to approve of a service user's behaviour, but to recognize the 'real' person and their actual circumstances.

Acceptance involves recognizing the humanness in every person, however heinous their previous or current behaviour. The central purpose of this principle of social work is thought to be therapeutic because, first, the worker can see the person without any illusions about them and, second, the person can feel that they are so recognized and therefore that it is unnecessary to adopt or maintain defences or masquerades. Acceptance clearly does not imply approval. (See also ETHICAL CODE, VALUES.)

**access (1) (disability)**   the capacity of public amenities and buildings to be used by disabled people with the same degree of ease as non-disabled people. Access is seen as a key issue in the successful integration of disabled people in society. Some local authorities have access committees and access officers.

**access (2) (education)**   the opportunity of attaining awards for people who can demonstrate the required competence. Access courses are designed to help people lacking formal qualification gain entry to further and higher education by enabling them to demonstrate their competence through a recognized course of study.

**accommodation**   a family support service in which a child is cared for
away from home for twenty-four hours or more by mutual agreement
between parents and local authority.

Accommodation is part of the wider range of services that a local authority
can offer to families and parents. In using it, parents do not lose their
PARENTAL RESPONSIBILITY, nor are they placing their child 'in care'. The use of
accommodation should not be taken as a sign of parental inadequacy. Under
section 20 of the CHILDREN ACT the local authority has a duty to provide
accommodation to any child in need who appears to require it, either
because the child is lost or abandoned, or because there is no one with
parental responsibility, or because the person who has been caring for the
child is prevented for any reason from providing suitable accommodation
or care. As a service to families, accommodation can be used flexibly to
include short-term and RESPITE CARE or longer periods when a child has to
live away from home for whatever reason. Even where a child is abused,
social workers should explore the possibility of accommodating that child
on a voluntary basis.

Parents (or others with parental responsibility) retain control over the use
of this service. A local authority may not provide accommodation for a child
if a person holding parental responsibility (usually a parent) objects and is
at the same time willing and able to provide accommodation themselves or
to arrange to have it provided. The only occasion when this power of 'veto'
does not apply is if a person with a RESIDENCE ORDER for the child agrees to
the child being accommodated. In this case, the parent without the residence
order could not veto the child's being accommodated. Any person with
parental responsibility (usually a parent) may remove the child at any time;
the Act does not require notice of any kind – although how and when a child
is to be removed from accommodation would be covered in the written
agreement that must accompany any placement. The Act also requires prior
consultation with the child. A young person 16 years and over may consent
to accommodation against parental wishes. (See LOOKED AFTER.)

**accountability**   the principle and process of ensuring that public-sector
officials and elected representatives are responsible for their actions.

Liberal democracies must ensure that civil servants and other appointed
officials are accountable to the people whose interests they are intended to
serve. Accountability is the idea that office-holders must not abuse their
positions for corrupt or irresponsible purposes. Accountability is also meant
to guarantee that decisions and policies made on behalf of the public by its
elected representatives are in the public interest and are actually carried out.
Traditionally this has meant that most bureaucracies are based on a rigid
hierarchy, with rules and regulations to ensure that officials comply with
policy decisions and that their actions are recorded in detail. Accountability
flows upwards, to ministers in central government and to the full council at
local level, and this results in a tendency for decision-making also to flow
upwards.

In the case of social workers and other professional officers, accountability
operates in two additional ways. First, it may flow downwards to the client or user

of the service. Officials may therefore see their actions as determined by their relationship with and responsibility to the individual client, since they are an advocate for that person's interests. As a result, they may sometimes find themselves in conflict with the more traditional form of accountability, which operates upwards in the social services department within which they are employed. Second, social workers and other professionals may identify a further form of accountability, towards their profession: the need to behave in an acceptable professional manner, particularly in their relationship with other social work colleagues and in relation to other professional groups, such as the Probation Service and the police. This threefold process of accountability creates a permanent source of tension for social workers, as well as a framework for understanding their roles in their work.

P. Day and R. Klein, *Accountabilities: Five Public Services*, London: Tavistock, 1987.

**adaptive behaviour**  an individual's behaviour that accords with social norms and sustains that person in looking after themselves or others.

**addiction**  describes when an individual uses a substance (legal or illegal) regularly and has developed a dependence on it. Addiction often harms the individual, their family and society. Because the term is value-laden, the alternative term DRUG 'use' is often preferred.

**additional pension**  see STATE EARNINGS-RELATED PENSION SCHEME.

**adjudication**  hearings conducted by prison governors when prisoners are charged with breaching prison discipline. Governors may award up to twenty-eight additional days in prison. Serious offences can be referred to the police and dealt with by outside courts (see PRISON).

**administration order**  an order secured through the county court to deal with debts that an individual cannot manage. Debtors pay weekly or monthly to the court whatever they can afford; the court pays each creditor a small sum in proportion to their claim on the debt.

The order is especially useful to people who have a large number of creditors and are being actively pursued for payment. In order to qualify for the administration order the consumer must already have had one judgement debt against them from the county court or High Court, and their total debt to all creditors must not exceed £5,000. Administration orders are technically simple to obtain and have advantages in managing multiple debt that has got out of control; the consumer has only to remember to pay a fixed amount to the court at regular intervals. Once the order has been given by the court, creditors may not trouble the debtor, however little is being paid to them. The disadvantage to the consumer is that their name will be added to a list held in the county court, which will make it difficult or impossible for them to obtain further credit until the total debt is cleared, which in some cases takes many years.

**adoption**  the process through which the legal relationship between a child and their birth parents is severed and a new legal relationship established with their adoptive parents.

Adoption was introduced into English law in 1926 to clarify the position of children brought up by adults other than their own parents, in particular to ease concerns that such children would be taken back by their parents. Until that year it was impossible to transfer PARENTAL RIGHTS permanently, although in practice *de facto* adoptions did occur. Adoption creates a new legal relationship nearly identical to that between a child and their natural parents. When a child is adopted, all the powers, duties and rights of the natural parents in relation to them cease and are transferred to the adopting parents.

Social workers' views about adoption were traditionally dominated by the intention of creating a completely new family for the adopted child, with no ties to the old one. The objective was to provide a permanent, secure and loving home for children whose parents were unable or unwilling to look after them. The common image of an adoption involved placing an infant with a childless couple who were complete strangers to the child's parents. The natural parents did not know the identity of the adopters and lost all right to see the child. To avoid stigma for the child, and to protect mothers of non-marital children, secrecy concerning the child's origins was strictly maintained throughout childhood and beyond. In this view, adoption was supposed to provide permanent security for children in public care who otherwise might have drifted from one foster home or children's home to another.

This perspective is changing. Studies confirm that the secrecy surrounding adoption has often led to confusion and unhappiness for adopted people. Lack of information about their natural parents and the mystery surrounding their family background often produced distrust and bitterness as the adopted child grew older. Consequently the law was changed, making it possible for adopted people aged 18 and over to obtain access to their birth records and to search for their natural parents if they wished. Moreover, the value of continuing CONTACT between natural parents and the adopted child is recognized as helping to clarify confusion over identity and to stabilize the adoption placement. The old view is also changing because the number of babies placed for adoption has fallen dramatically with the advent of widespread birth control and less social disapproval of 'illegitimacy'. Adoption is increasingly used to secure a family for older children with SPECIAL NEEDS who may require considerable care that their parents are unable or unwilling to provide. Local authorities may pay adoption allowances in such cases. Step-parents have also used adoption in greater numbers to secure parental responsibility for a child of their new partner.

Social workers have a number of tasks during the adoption process. They must obtain consent from the child's natural parents, explaining to them the effect of the adoption on their parental rights. They must also explain what each stage of the process involves. Such work may be extremely fraught, since parents may change their mind several times. Sometimes when parents refuse permission and the local authority concludes that adoption is the only long-term arrangement able to promote the welfare of a child in its care, the social worker has to persuade the court to dispense with parental consent (see ADOPTION HEARING).

Social workers must also gather information and write detailed reports. For example, because a child may only be placed for adoption by an ADOPTION AGENCY after a properly constituted ADOPTION PANEL has met to consider the decision, a social worker has to provide the panel with a report based on a range of information concerning the natural parents, the child and the adopting parents. Such reports involve considerable skill in the presentation of information based on lengthy interviews on often sensitive topics – for example, about when the prospective adopters would propose to reveal to the child the fact of their adoption. Other tasks include SUPERVISION of the child placed for adoption but not yet adopted, and going to court on behalf of the adoption agency to explain why this irrevocable step needs to be taken.

The passage of the CHILDREN ACT has triggered a review and white paper on adoption law. A court can already make a CONTACT ORDER, under section 8 of the Act, in favour of the natural parents at the same time as making an adoption order (see OPEN ADOPTION). In the future, it is likely that the court will also have to be convinced that making an adoption order will be better for the child than not doing so or making another order such as a RESIDENCE ORDER. The white paper has also placed greater emphasis on the child's wishes. For children of 12 years or older the court may not grant an order unless the child has agreed to the adoption or is incapable of giving agreement. The white paper also proposes that due consideration must be given to parental wishes and feelings, and to factors of race, religion, culture and linguistic background. Parents will have the right to put their views to the adoption panel and be allocated their own social worker. Under the proposed changes in adoption law, parental agreement will normally be given to a particular adoption placement and not simply to adoption in principle. (Where good practice exists, this procedure is already well established.) (See also PERMANENCY PLANNING.)

J. Thorburn, *Child Placement: Principles and Practice*, Aldershot: Arena, 2nd edn, 1994.

**adoption agency**   an organization approved by the Secretary of State at the Department of Health to undertake adoption services. Local authorities and diocesan adoption societies are both examples of adoption agencies.

One of the main tasks of an adoption agency is to oversee arrangements for the adoption of children. This includes selecting prospective adoptive parents, placing and supervising children for adoption and providing post-adoption services such as counselling for birth parents who have had children adopted.

**adoption contact register**   a national register of names of people adopted as children and willing to be contacted by their birth parents or other relatives. The register also lists the names of parents and relatives wishing to contact their children, who were adopted and have reached 18 years of age.

The function of the register is to facilitate contact between both sides of the original family. The setting up of the register is further recognition that the secrecy that used to surround adoption, and the finality of the separation that occurred between adopted children and their parents, often caused distress to both sides, and in the case of the child led to confusion as to their identity and background.

G. Stafford, *Where to Find Adoption Records*, London: British Agencies for Adoption and Fostering, 1985.

**adoption hearing** the proceedings in court that determine whether a particular child is to be adopted. Applications by prospective parents for an ADOPTION ORDER are heard in magistrates' or county courts and are always in private.

Information placed before the courts at an adoption hearing is strictly confidential. If the natural parents of the child have not given their consent to the adoption the hearing is usually in two parts. First, the court considers whether grounds exist for overriding the requirement for each parent to agree to the adoption. Under the Adoption Act 1976 this can be done, for example, if the child has been persistently ill-treated and their return home is unlikely, if parents withhold agreement unreasonably or if one or both are incapable of giving agreement. The legal representatives of the agency, the child's GUARDIAN *AD LITEM* and the child's parents are represented and place their arguments before the court; the prospective adopting parents are not in court at this stage. The second stage follows if the court decides to dispense with parents' consent. (Alternatively, if both parents have given their consent, the hearing starts at this point.) In this second stage the court then focuses on the merits of the application and whether the adoption is in the child's best interests. The would-be adoptive parents – who may be a single person or indeed a lesbian or gay couple – are usually in court at this stage, and the natural parents are not.

Social workers may be called to give evidence in support of the application at either stage of an adoption hearing, if the child has been in the care of the local authority and adoption is seen as the best way to secure a permanent home for them. Social workers' evidence is often crucial to the outcome, so command of the facts and circumstances of the case, and the reasoning behind the application, is essential. In reaching any decision the court's first consideration is the need to safeguard and promote the welfare of the child throughout their childhood, that is, until they reach 18. Social workers' arguments to the court must bear this long-term perspective in mind. The court will also take into account the wishes and feelings of the child if it is practical to do so. The child's wishes in the matter are set to become even more influential following the reform of adoption that will require a child of 12 years or older giving their consent if the adoption is to go ahead.

**adoption order** a court order that transfers legal responsibility for a child from their birth family to the adoptive family.

Following an adoption order, all the rights, duties and responsibilities of the natural parents in relation to the child cease and are assumed by the adoptive parents. In some cases courts will also order that some form of CONTACT between the child and their birth parents should continue.

**adoption panel** the panel constituted by each ADOPTION AGENCY that authorizes the decision to place a child for adoption by that agency.

In deciding whether a child should be placed for adoption, the panel considers whether the adoption is in that child's best interests and whether a particular child should be placed with particular adoptive parents. Panels also decide whether individual applicants should be approved as prospective adoptive parents. Would-be adopters may include single people or a gay or lesbian couple. The panel is made up of lay members such as doctors, local councillors and parents and is usually chaired by a senior member of the adoption agency itself. The panel officially makes only advisory judgements, with final decisions left to the agency; but its decisions are almost always respected in practice.

**adult education**  facilities, both formal and informal, to help people beyond school-leaving age (and normally older than 18 in Britain) acquire new knowledge, skills and aptitudes.

There are strong connections between adult education and COMMUNITY WORK, some of whose activities might be regarded as educational in the wider sense. A community group working together to develop a detailed understanding of the welfare benefits system, for example, for individual participants (such as claimants) is clearly engaging in an educational exercise. The acquisition of social skills is often an objective for community groups. Social workers may have the task of helping people to change so that they are able to do something that previously they could not. Helping a father or mother acquire parenting skills could be an objective for a social worker or a nursery worker. Through demonstration, counselling and encouragement such a worker could be said to be involved in informal adult education.

**adult training centre (ATC)**  a traditional day service setting for adults with learning disabilities, commonly provided by social services departments.

Historically, typical adult training centres sought to attract work on contract from local firms, which was carried out within the training centres by supervised groups of service users. This approach has been largely abandoned, partly because of difficulties in attracting suitable tasks, but chiefly because such work was widely criticized as unstimulating and financially unrewarding for service users. The title 'adult training centre' persists in some areas but has been widely superseded by 'social education centre', a term that emphasizes the educational focus of some day services for people with learning disability. Such services are, however, still criticized for segregating people with learning disability from the rest of society and congregating them into large groups. Some centres endeavour to take service users into local COMMUNITY-based facilities, such as shops and leisure centres, on an industrial basis, but such initiatives are constrained by limited resources in this often underfunded area of provision. Some alternatives to day centres exist, notably in the form of initiatives to develop supported employment opportunities for people with LEARNING DISABILITY, and there is evidence that many people with learning disability would like real work. Other alternatives focus on the use of community resources by people with learning disability on an individual basis, according to their needs and preference.

**adversarial process**  a type of legal proceedings whereby the court hears the opposing legal arguments of both sides before reaching judgement.

Because each side attempts to undermine the argument of the other, adversarial process can prove a destructive experience for all parties. The resulting bitterness can make negotiation and reconciliation difficult, particularly in family matters. Moves to soften the consequences of the adversarial process have played an important part in recent family law reform.

**advice** the process by which people with expert knowledge, or with considerable experience of a problem and its potential solutions, indicate how a problem might be solved or eased.

Advisers are found in many guises. They include advice centre workers, solicitors, social workers, youth workers, probation officers, general medical practitioners and specialists working in particular fields, such as AIDS counsellors, consumer advisers and child guidance workers. In addition, advice can be offered by people who have experienced a certain problem or still experience it. In this context, SELF-HELP can be the method of working among those who have the same difficulties, with professional advisers expressly excluded from the process.

**advice services or centres** services or centres located within the statutory sector or the voluntary sector that seek to offer either general or specialized ADVICE for people with problems.

Advice services have grown significantly in recent decades, and most provision is in the voluntary sector. The best-known advice organization is the Citizen's Advice Bureaux, each of whose bureaux is staffed by at least one paid organizer and trained volunteers; this model of staff organization and service delivery is commonly found in the voluntary sector. The CAB has developed expertise in relation to welfare rights, debt, consumer problems, housing, employment, and personal and family difficulties. Specialist voluntary advice and counselling services – tending to focus on a single issue such as homelessness, rape crisis, immigration, welfare rights, mental health problems, conciliation or marriage guidance – exist in most British cities and towns. In addition, some local authorities have built up networks of neighbourhood offices offering advice on housing, social services, environmental services, public health, and so on. This form of local authority provision, particularly when integrated into the major service-providing departments, helps users perceive services as accessible; it can facilitate useful preventive work on problems that might otherwise become more serious; and such centres may also devote resources to take up campaigns in relation to welfare benefits, home insulation, secure homes in localities where burglary is a major issue, and other similar matters.

Studies have often made use of advice services as centres for the systematic collection of information about problems faced by residents within a particular locality. Such information has subsequently been used to trigger community action or at least to encourage a collective approach to community problem-solving. Advice-giving, because it is essentially a one-to-one, individual process, can be limited in its objectives. However, a whole housing estate complaining together about a problem – say, damp dwellings – will be more powerful in relation to a reluctant local authority than the same individuals complaining separately.

Democracy is said to depend heavily on good information about the law and individual rights. Advice services can act as a major source of useful and disinterested information for citizens – information that will help solve or ease problems, as well as encouraging participation in social and political life. With these objectives in mind, some advice and counselling services seek consciously to develop the social skills of service users, so that they can tackle the problem themselves next time. In this sense, advice-giving can become an educational process regardless of whether it is dispensed by professionals or by 'amateurs' on a self-help basis.

**advocacy** the representation of service users' interests in order to improve their situation.

In the case of SELF-ADVOCACY a service user acts as an advocate for themselves or on behalf of others, typically after gaining confidence through meeting in a group with other service users who also wish to assert their needs and views. In one-to-one advocacy an independent person helps to represent the views of a service user who needs assistance in putting forward their views. The most widely publicized form of this type is known as CITIZEN ADVOCACY, whereby an unpaid lay person develops a relationship with a service user and becomes familiar with their wishes in order to act as a spokesperson for them. Social workers sometimes see themselves as advocates for service users, but to be completely effective advocates must be independent of the service to which representations are being made. The need for independent advocacy is becoming recognized in law and in policy documents. Sections 1 and 2 of the DISABLED PERSONS (SERVICES, CONSULT-ATION AND REPRESENTATION) ACT 1986 set out the rights of authorized representatives of disabled people but have yet to be implemented. Government guidelines regarding care management and assessment recognize that service users should have independent advocacy available to them, although this is limited by resources.

K. Simons, *'Sticking Up for Yourself'*, York: Joseph Rowntree Foundation, 1993.

**age appropriateness** the notion that people with LEARNING DISABILITY should dress, behave, take part in activities and be treated in ways suitable to their chronological age. This notion is often associated with NORMALIZATION.

The principle of age appropriateness suggests, for example, that adults with learning disability should not play with children's toys, although the toys might be apparently suited to their developmental level. The rationale for this approach is that such behaviour is at odds with social norms, is undignified and is unlikely to gain respect from other people.

**ageing** the process of physically growing older, usually associated with chronological age but not always identical.

Problems of defining ageing are rooted in the linking of *time* with *development*, when there is considerable diversity between time and development in human populations. Ageing as a variable is most frequently used to explain other phenomena, for example patterns of physiological and behavioural change in people, but ageing is itself much affected by social conditions and by the regard with which people are held. Thus older people may be old in years but vigorous in behaviour, whereas others because of major difficulties in their lives may be 'old before their time'. People with learning disabilities may also have difficulties behaving in an AGE-APPROPRIATE manner, although contemporary social work practice encourages age-related treatment of such people. In other contexts, ageing may have gender dimensions – for example, that girls mature more quickly than boys and that women live longer.

**ageism** a prejudicial approach towards people that implies inferiority on the basis of age.

Ageism generally refers to discriminatory behaviour towards OLDER PEOPLE, containing erroneous beliefs about a lessening of competences and worth in them. Ageism encompasses a set of ATTITUDES that assume and maintain powerlessness in old people. It is used to legitimate the 'rearranging' of power relationships between people who are young and old, which results in older people being alienated from other social groups. Ageism is apparent in the 'splitting' of images of older people – for example, perceiving them as a 'burden', contrasting with images of 'kindly' grandparents. In Britain there is no legal ban on age DISCRIMINATION in employment advertising. Substantial differences exist in the attitudes to older people from one society to another, some clearly venerating and valuing old people, while others perceive them as economically unproductive and thus as a burden. ANTI-DISCRIMINATORY PRACTICE includes countering ageist attitudes.

**agency** the general term used to denote any organization that provides a social or welfare service, whether a local authority, a voluntary organization or a private organization.

**agency agreements** local agreements between organizations providing services and those organizations purchasing them.

In agency agreements, service providers undertake to provide a specific service in a given locality for a specified period of time. Typically such agreements will be between a local authority as purchaser and a voluntary or private agency providing, for example, home care to older people in that area.

**aggression** action or an ATTITUDE intended to impair, injure or destroy another person's or group's physical or psychological well-being (see also VIOLENCE).

**aids and adaptations** means by which people with DISABILITIES are helped to live more independently or comfortably in their own home.

LOCAL AUTHORITIES have a duty placed upon them under section 2 of the CHRONICALLY SICK AND DISABLED PERSONS ACT 1970 to assist people who are sick or disabled in respect of aids and adaptations for their homes. Capital spending for adaptations is also available from various local authority housing department funds. Assessments of need are usually undertaken by OCCUPATIONAL THERAPISTS. Aids include a wide range of items such as commodes, handrails, bathmats, ramps and mobility aids. Sometimes major alterations to homes are undertaken to aid independent living; for example, a ground-floor bathroom or bedroom might be built as an extension to a house for a person who can no longer climb stairs. Some aids are provided by health services too. Much provision under the 1970 Act is now means-tested.

**alcohol**   a colourless liquid that acts as a central nervous system depressant and sedative, taken by mouth, usually in the form of beer, wine or spirits. Alcohol is a legal substance, although it cannot legally be sold to people under the age of 18.

Alcohol in moderation does not appear to have harmful effects. The suggested weekly maximum is 14 units for a woman and 21 for a man – one unit is a glass of wine, a measure of spirits or half a pint of ordinary-strength beer. If this level is increased on a regular basis, both psychological and physical ADDICTION are a possibility. Short-term effects include a reduction in anxiety and tension, drowsiness, increased confidence and impairment of judgement, depending on how much is consumed. The physical harm that can result from excessive alcohol use includes liver and heart disease, high blood pressure, strokes, stomach ulcers and dementia. Pregnant women run the risk of foetal abnormalities, and low birth weight and mental retardation of the infant. It is important to monitor the progress of infants of mothers with an excessive alcohol intake both before and after birth, applying the normal criteria for good parenting, and liaising where necessary with other professionals. It is an offence to be in charge of a vehicle while 'unfit to drive through drink or DRUGS'.

**alcohol hallucinosis**   a psychotic frame of mind often accompanied by auditory hallucinations (hearing voices). Feelings of fear and persecution are also common. This is frequently a symptom of withdrawal in acute drinkers who suddenly give up or reduce intake.

**alcoholism**   the extreme psychological and physical ADDICTION resulting from the consumption of excessive ALCOHOL over a lengthy period of time.

Alcoholism is commonly defined as a chronic illness characterized by depression of the central nervous system and liver damage. Other medical effects may include stomach and heart problems, peripheral neuropathies and auditory hallucinations. Alcoholism can also result in psychological and social difficulties, with friends and relatives becoming increasingly frustrated by their inability to affect any change in the alcoholic's behaviour. It is important for them to know whom to approach for help when the alcoholic is at the stage of wanting such assistance. Usually a general medical practitioner will be able to provide direct help or referral to a specialist agency. As alcoholism is physically addictive, withdrawal will result if supplies are abruptly stopped; withdrawal symptoms include sweating, trembling, hallucination, nervous system dysfunction and seizures. The extreme form of alcohol withdrawal is known as delirium tremens. When a person is in this state, confrontation is best avoided – a calm, quiet approach is preferable, with talking through problems or attempts at relaxation if appropriate. There is considerable debate as to whether alcoholism is inherited or environmental; it often runs in families.

**alcohol psychosis** a group of mental disorders resulting from the excessive use of alcohol, such as delirium tremens, Korsakow syndrome and acute hallucinosis. In such cases dysfunction or damage to the brain will be present.

**allocation** the process whereby tasks are distributed among workers within a social work team. This process is undertaken sometimes within team meetings, sometimes with individual team members on an *ad hoc* basis and sometimes by a combination of both practices.

Allocation within team meetings has the advantage of conveying to all workers what each is undertaking in relation to the quantity and range of cases and to other kinds of work. Such a system may help build or develop teams by giving members information about how the team is functioning. Knowledge of colleagues' work can facilitate the sharing of tasks. Clearly some work, such as dealing with emergencies, must be allocated quickly by team managers. Allocation should be closely related to WORKLOAD MANAGEMENT and SUPERVISION to determine that work is being done well and that workers are not overwhelmed by the quantity and the demands of their tasks.

**almoner** a term, no longer in use, for a medical social worker.

Stemming originally from voluntary work sponsored by the Charity Organization Society in the nineteenth century (probably the most important voluntary organization in the early formation of social work as an occupation), almoners became key elements in the delivery of social work services in hospital settings. The word lost currency in the 1960s in the wake of generic training for all branches of social work.

**Alzheimer's disease** an organic age-associated disorder typified by progressive brain degeneration.

Age of onset is usually between 50 and 60 years. The disorder is commoner in women than in men and affects 6 per cent of people aged over 65. The average duration of the disease is two to five years, but at the extremes durations can vary between three months and twenty-five years.

Typically Alzheimer's disease shows a number of changes in brain tissue: degeneration of the ends of nerve cells and the formation of 'tangles' in the fibres of nerve cells. Post-mortem examination shows widespread brain atrophy. The disease affects a broad range of mental and physical functions; memory loss and recall difficulties occur; and learning, perception, attention and recognition are all impaired. Rapid forgetting is evident. Disorientation, dementia and confusion are usually present. Aphasia (loss of words), agnosia (not recognizing objects), irritability, overactivity and stereotyped movements are all characteristic. Changes in mood – depression, apathy and lethargy – may be observed. In the final stages, before death, there is profound emaciation. Key practice issues in work with people suffering from Alzheimer's disease include support to CARERS and balancing the sufferer's rights against the very tangible risks that their behaviour might entail. (See also REMINISCENCE THERAPY, DEMENTIA.)

I. Stuart-Hamilton, *The Psychology of Ageing*, London: Jessica Kingsley, 1991.

**amphetamine**   a chemically produced illegal stimulant that has the effect of increasing levels of energy and stamina with an accompanying loss of interest in food and sleep; also known as 'speed' or 'whiz'.

Amphetamine has the appearance of an off-white powder. Purity can be as low as 4 per cent, and it may be mixed with any look-alike substance to give bulk. It is commonly sniffed up the nose through a tube, or sometimes injected. As a powder it is a class B DRUG, with penalties ranging from a CAUTION to five years' imprisonment and unlimited fine for possession, and up to fourteen years' imprisonment plus unlimited fine for supply. When injected it is a class A drug with correspondingly higher penalties. Long-term effects can include PARANOIA and PSYCHOSIS.

**anabolic steroids**   a group of hormones occurring naturally in the body that are responsible for developing and controlling the reproductive system. Synthetic anabolic steroids are taken (orally or by injection) to increase strength and muscle.

Anabolic steroids are prescription-only medicines. They are not controlled under the MISUSE OF DRUGS ACT 1971; it is not illegal to possess them for personal use, although it is an offence to sell them. There is a large illegal market in steroids, and some of those sold are fakes. Side effects can vary from an interruption of normal growth to interference with the reproductive system in both males and females. Other effects may include kidney and liver abnormalities, and heart and behavioural problems.

**anal dilatation**   a medical diagnosis that observes whether the involuntary muscles controlling the sphincter are open.

As the sphincter is normally closed, a sphincter that is open can be an indicator that the child has been sexually abused. The diagnosis was used extensively by the paediatricians involved in diagnosing the children thought to have been abused in Cleveland (see CLEVELAND INQUIRY). The subsequent inquiry concluded that while anal dilatation suggested that penetrative SEXUAL ABUSE could have occurred, its presence was not in itself sufficient to make a certain diagnosis.

**anal phase**   see PSYCHOANALYSIS.

**anatomical dolls**   dolls with male and female genitals and body hair, sometimes used by social workers, child psychologists and police when interviewing children thought to have been sexually abused.

Playing with anatomical dolls gives the child a way of showing what may have happened to them, which they might find difficult to put into words. The use of such dolls has been criticized as providing unreliable information, since their use cannot establish with certainty whether the child has been abused or not. Even if a child uses the dolls to portray an abusive act, much additional corroborating evidence is required before a case can be put to court either for a protective order on the child or for a criminal prosecution of an alleged abuser.

**angel dust**   see PCP.

**anger management**   see VIOLENCE.

**anorexia nervosa**   a condition of self-induced weight loss, characterized by exaggerated fears of growing fat and the denial of hunger.

Anorexia often leads to malnutrition and the cessation of menstruation. The condition is most common in adolescent females, often persisting into adulthood. It has also been identified in young males. Medical models of anorexia define it as psychiatric illness; feminist explanations suggest that anorectic behaviour develops as a symptom of women's oppressed position in patriarchal society.

**Antabuse (Disulfiram)**   a prescribed drug used as a deterrent to ALCOHOL for people with drinking problems who are trying to abstain.

If a person consumes alcohol while taking Antabuse, disturbance of the nervous system may lead to unconsciousness and even a psychotic reaction. Drowsiness, skin rash and headaches are also a possibility. People being prescribed the drug should carry a card indicating both this and the person to contact in an emergency.

**anti-discriminatory practice**   a term used widely in social and probation work, and in social work training, to describe how workers take account of structural disadvantage and seek to reduce individual and institutional DISCRIMINATION particularly on grounds of race, gender, disability, social class and sexual orientation.

In the CRIMINAL JUSTICE SYSTEM the main concerns of anti-discriminatory practice are the over-representation of black people in prison and the inappropriate treatment of female offenders. In both cases it is argued that sentences and professional workers display discriminatory attitudes based on stereotypical views of black people and women who commit crimes. In an attempt to minimize inaccurate portrayals of such defendants, probation officers often engage in 'gatekeeping' exercises when writing PRE-SENTENCE REPORTS. They read drafts of colleagues' reports and advise each other on the likely effects of particular words or phrases. Concern about discrimination in the criminal justice system led the government to include a section (s. 95) in the CRIMINAL JUSTICE ACT 1991 requiring the Home Secretary to publish information annually that enables people administering the system to avoid discrimination 'on the ground of race or sex or any other improper ground'. Critics point out that the drafting of the section makes this optional, because the Home Secretary has the incongruous alternative option of publishing information to assist administrators 'to become aware of the financial implications of their decisions'.

*Racial discrimination.* Black people – of both Afro-Caribbean and Asian origin – are more likely than whites to live in high-crime areas and appear to be involved disproportionately in the criminal justice system as offenders and victims. Relative to their numbers in the general population, black people, especially Afro-Caribbeans, are over-represented in prison; in 1990, 16 per cent of the male and 26 per cent of the female prison population was non-white. By contrast, the proportion of black people working in criminal justice is very low.

Do black people commit more crime than whites? Generations of white Britons have blamed 'foreigners' with 'alien cultures' for crime and public disorder. No objective evidence can be found to support racist arguments such as that young black people grow up without respect for 'British' ways; nor even to justify the apparently 'reasonable' view that black people commit more crime than whites because of the discrimination and deprivations they experience.

There is evidence, however, that black people attract more attention and suspicion from the police than white people, being more likely to be stopped, searched and arrested, especially if they are Afro-Caribbeans. Young black people may be less likely than their white counterparts to receive a CAUTION and no further action; and interaction between police and non-white ethnic minorities may be influenced by a police 'canteen culture' of racist banter and stereotyping. As defendants, blacks are more likely than whites to be committed to Crown Court for trial. This is often their own choice, because they deny the offence and hope for fairer treatment from a jury. If they are found guilty, however, they are likely to receive a harsher sentence than in a magistrates' court (see CRIMINAL COURTS). Recent evidence suggests that at least some of the difference between the number of black men in the overall population and the number in prison can be accounted for by differential sentencing of black and white defendants. Black men are less likely than whites to be given community punishments such as PROBATION ORDERS and COMMUNITY SERVICE ORDERS. Studies suggest that black people experience discrimination inside the prison system in relation to allocation to open prison, accommodation and work. Prisons are required to have a race relations management group to monitor accommodation and work allocation, diet and religious provision for ethnic minorities and incidents that may be racially motivated.

*Gender discrimination.* Women comprise less than a fifth of known offenders in most years. Some explain this in terms of men being genetically more aggressive and inclined towards deviant behaviour; others argue that females are socialized to be more conforming. As adults looking after home and children, women may have less opportunity to commit crimes than men, and they are more likely to seek medical or psychiatric help than to turn to crime. Women's liberation was expected by some to mean more women committing more serious, violent crime; but, although more women are committing crime in terms of numbers, it is generally less serious than that committed by men.

Women criminals have been depicted as biologically or mentally *abnormal*, often as 'more masculine' than 'normal' women. An alternative view is that they commit crime because they suffer from pre-menstrual tension, menopause or postnatal depression. Others argue that women criminals tend to be sexually promiscuous or emotionally unbalanced. There is no evidence to support these explanations as general theories. It is also said that women who commit crimes do so largely because they are poor; and numerous women in prison have been in care as children and find that they cannot look after themselves as adults. They may be homeless or have drug or alcohol problems. Women who commit violent crimes frequently do so after years of abuse.

While it may appear that female offenders are treated more leniently by the police and courts than males, if a woman gets a 'light' sentence it is usually because her offence is not very serious. Occasionally a woman gets off 'lightly' because a magistrate thinks she is a good wife and mother. Magistrates may also think that it is a kindness to put a woman on probation, giving her someone to talk to; unfortunately, once on probation she is more likely to go to prison if she reoffends. Men get more chances to do community service or to go to day activities in a PROBATION CENTRE, while women more often get sent to hospital for psychiatric reports. There is contradictory evidence that some women get heavier sentences than they should because magistrates think they have failed to behave like 'proper' women. Unmarried or divorced women, those with children in care and black women appear to get heavier sentences, being punished for who they are rather than for what they have done. Nearly a third of women in prison are black, a vastly disproportionate figure. Some of these are drugs couriers who will be deported when they finish their sentence and perhaps imprisoned again in their country of origin; but many black women in prison were born in Britain and commit the same offences as white women. There is evidence that they are treated harshly by criminal courts, although perhaps less so than black men.

The criminal justice system has been described as 'male-dominated' and insensitive to women's needs; most occupations in the system appear to have poor equal opportunities records. Even so, it does not necessarily follow that an increase in women working in criminal justice will lead to improvements. Although 45 per cent of magistrates are women, their social background and deference to male colleagues may make them more, not less, judgemental towards women defendants.

*Social class discrimination.* Discrimination in the criminal justice system on the grounds of SOCIAL CLASS has arguably been both overwhelming and taken for granted. The vast majority of defendants are from the working or unemployed classes, and some writers argue the existence of a largely criminal UNDERCLASS of poor, unemployed, homeless people with unstable family relationships. The first National Prison Survey (1991) indicated that people with these background characteristics are over-represented in prison. Critics respond that people in every class commit crime, with crime committed by the very rich often damaging society most. The fact that lower-class crime is most stigmatized is itself a form of discrimination.

Discriminatory practices can be demonstrated in almost every aspect of social life within Britain and not just within the CRIMINAL JUSTICE SYSTEM. Similarly, disability, sexual orientation, age and, in some locations, religious convictions can seriously inhibit people's life chances.

Anti-discriminatory practice involves recognizing this structural oppression and seeking to combat it. Monitoring of all social work processes with regard to oppressed groups will provide critical information about patterns of discrimination. Recruitment of people in greater numbers from such groups to positions of power within social welfare systems may help their cause, provided they are not required to work with discriminatory policies. (See also, entries on ANTI-RACIST PRACTICE, DISABILITY, SEXUAL ORIENTATION, AGEISM and SOCIAL CLASS).

N. Thompson, *Anti-Discriminatory Practice*, Basingstoke: Macmillan, 1993.

**anti-oppression**   attempts to confront or resist injustice or the abuse of power. Anti-oppression can refer to either individual or personal experiences and to structural arrangements.

There appears to be, as yet, no agreed definition of anti-oppressive work, as distinct from ANTI-DISCRIMINATORY PRACTICE or from the desire to promote EQUAL OPPORTUNITIES. Many writers use these terms uncritically and interchangeably. Some writers have, however, begun to suggest that anti-discriminatory practice might usefully be defined as work designed to address specific, legally defined injustices. Anti-oppressive practice might then be agreed to mean wider social analyses that begin to challenge structures and thereby help people challenge individual aspects of oppression. These may well be useful distinctions but they are not widely understood in this way and do not have wide currency.

**anti-poverty strategy**   strategy of the kind developed during the 1980s and 1990s by metropolitan district authorities to provide a corporate focus for council services, and often to try to redress increasing divisions between rich and poor by enhancing opportunities for lower-income individuals and groups.

Elements of an anti-poverty strategy may include programmes to increase the take-up of local and national benefits, to prevent debt and, where debt occurs, to promote sensitive collection and recovery procedures. Local authorities may examine their own services with a view to making them more relevant and accessible to people on low incomes and ensuring that charging policies for services do not form an additional barrier or exacerbate an individual's poverty. Authorities have also sought to influence and intervene with other organizations whose policies affect low-income groups, such as the utilities (water, gas, electricity, telephone), the NATIONAL HEALTH SERVICE and mortgage lenders. Anti-poverty work may also embrace activities in the field of business development, job creation and training. All anti-poverty work will have a strong theme of equality, since the economic disadvantage experienced by women, black and ethnic-minority people and people with disabilities is reflected in both a need for, and difficulties in, accessing services. (See also POVERTY.)

**anti-psychiatry**   the term given to a cluster of theories that regard MENTAL ILLNESS as a myth, and psychiatric diagnosis and treatment as oppressive to the individual.

Anti-psychiatry theories emerged in the 1960s as a reaction against the view that mental illness was no different from physical illness and that, with a period of hospitalization and appropriate medication, the sufferer could be expected to recover and return to a normal life. This MEDICAL MODEL came under increasing attack from a number of sources at a time when the rights of the individual over the social group were regarded as of supreme value.

There were a number of strands to anti-psychiatry. The first and most influential was associated with the work of R.D. Laing, who saw the family as the source of mental illness. He regarded the family as oppressive, denying the needs of the person who became ill in the interests of holding the family together. This led to the person developing a 'false self' to meet the expectations of the family, and madness resulted as an entirely understandable confusion between the 'false self' and the individual's 'true self'. A second strand held that mental illness was a label created by society for people who posed a threat to its norms, and was particularly reserved for those who were low in status and had little power in resisting the label attached to them. Once individuals were labelled mentally ill, other people behaved towards them on the basis of the expectation associated with that label (see LABELLING THEORY). A third strand, associated with the work of Thomas Szasz, regarded mental illness as a myth created by those elements in society that sought to interfere with the individual, notably the state and its institutions, of which psychiatry was one. Diagnosis of mental illness and its 'treatment' had the effect of creating dependency and undermining self-reliance. Szasz attacked the notion that a psychiatric diagnosis allowed a person, such as an offender, to claim diminished responsibility because of an alleged mental impairment. The real nature of mental illness was nothing more than failure to cope with 'problems in living'. People with such problems should seek consultation on a fee-paying basis to strengthen their independence and responsibility.

On the central issue – that mental illness is a myth, a label, a concoction of society – anti-psychiatry is today widely regarded as wrong. Mental illness involves such a complex interaction of factors and can be so devastating in its impact both on the sufferer and on those around them as to make it impossible to dismiss it in such a way. However, anti-psychiatry did contribute to the growing realization that mental illness cannot be understood as an exclusively medical phenomenon, and that there is a crucial social component to recovery. In Britain, the closure of large mental hospitals and community care policies are two outcomes of this new consensus. Most importantly, those who have suffered mental distress have begun to organize in their own advocacy group (SURVIVORS), with an emphasis on SELF-HELP.

**anti-racism**    attempts to confront and eradicate any view that encourages a belief that one ethnic group is biologically superior to another ethnic group.

RACISM can take many forms. Racist attitudes can be personally held views or they can be the result of official policies or, in some circumstances, both. A social work or social welfare organization seriously wishing to confront racism must develop policies and practices that work at both the personal and institutional levels. Racist acts by staff should be clearly denoted as serious matters for both disciplinary and grievance procedures. Comprehensive training programmes accompanied by induction packages for new staff should convey to all employees the commitment of the organization to the eradication of racism in staff relationships and employment practices. In relation to issues of service delivery, particular policies are required to consider the anti-racist issues. For example, if it can be demonstrated that more black juveniles receive custodial sentences than white offenders for comparable offences, then appropriate anti-racist practice might usefully include ethnic monitoring of all the critical decision-making processes, the development of triggers to ensure that people in the justice system are aware of the potential problems, the recruitment of more black people to the justice system, the addition of black advisers' views to reports and many other possibilities. Broadly the same processes could also be incorporated into work in the field of MENTAL HEALTH, to ensure an anti-racist stance. In other circumstances, it is the underuse of social work and social welfare facilities that is notable in relation to ethnic minorities. Examples include the use of facilities for people with learning disabilities and for older people. In these circumstances, dialogue with ethnic-minority communities about their needs, explanations of the functions of particular services, the provision of good INFORMATION for ethnic minorities in appropriate languages and the employment of ethnic-minority workers can all be part of a committed anti-racist strategy.

In sum, anti-racism starts from an assumption that Britain is a racist society. Progress has been made in some areas but has been very uneven, and in some quarters the patterns of DISCRIMINATION remain remarkably persistent. Any social work practice must therefore be rooted in a recognition and acceptance of racism. Such recognition is the first necessary step towards an effective anti-racist strategy. Policies that confront both employment practices and issues of service delivery have then to be developed. It seems likely that an organization that is serious about anti-racism will attempt to make policy in both areas, and the one will undoubtedly inform the other. (See also ANTI-DISCRIMINATORY PRACTICE, EQUAL OPPORTUNITIES POLICIES, ETHNICALLY SENSITIVE PRACTICE, RACE RELATIONS ACT 1976, TRANS-RACIAL ADOPTION.)

L. Dominelli, *Anti-Racist Social Work*, Basingstoke: Macmillan, 1988.

**anti-sexism**   any attempts to confront and deal with beliefs, policies or ideologies that explicitly or implicitly suggest the superiority of men over women or, more unusually, women over men. In practice, SEXISM invariably concerns negative stereotypical views of women, which tend both to encourage DISCRIMINATION against women and broadly to devalue them.

Attempts to explain sexism have been routed principally in two theories: first, the analysis of capitalism and of women's role within it (as part of the reserve army of labour and as mothers of a future labour force); second, in the analysis of patriarchy (that is, the belief that men universally dominate and oppress women). There have been some analyses that attempt a synthesis of these two perspectives. Anti-sexist tactics and strategies take very different forms, depending on the perspective(s) chosen. For example, if the capitalist mode of production is regarded as the major explanation for women's oppression, there would seem to be the possibility of alliances between all oppressed people, including black people, women and working-class men. If patriarchy is the adopted explanation, then clearly women need to become confident and strong in their own right before attempting to work with, or take on, the men. A mixture of tactics may be appropriate, according to circumstances.

Within social work, there are many examples of sexism, both in the employment practices of social work agencies and in services. Systematic discrimination occurs within agencies to create organizations that have a predominantly female workforce and management weighted very heavily in favour of men. In relation to service delivery, social workers still seem unable to perceive women as other than CARERS or mothers; and they still apparently overlook, institutionally, women's very clear needs in relation to, for example, VIOLENCE at the hands of men.

> At root, anti-sexist practice within social work agencies requires a clear analysis of the dynamics of women's oppression in particular situations; it requires the devising of a range of policies and practices by women (with perhaps the support of 'enlightened men') and mechanisms whereby women can begin to influence and take on the policy-making processes. Some social work agencies have indeed developed women's support groups; and some professional organizations have established groups to encourage women's perspectives. These are important beginnings, but interest and support groups need to move into the next stage of developing policy and frameworks for practice in their own right. Although the legal framework will help (the SEX DISCRIMINATION ACT 1975, the EQUAL PAY ACT 1970, and so on), it has proved fairly marginal to women in Britain over the last two decades. Bolder anti-oppressive strategy is required, and clearly women must take the initiative, since men show little inclination to surrender their positions of privilege.
>
> J. Phillipson, *Practising Equality: Women, Men and Social Work*, London: Central Council for Education and Training in Social Work, 1992.

**anxiety** a high level of fear, tension and sense of imminent danger. Anxiety involves both subjective feelings and bodily reactions that are uncomfortable and distressing.

People in different cultures or different social groupings in Western culture may emphasize one or other aspect of anxiety. For example, people from traditional cultures, older white people, men, and people in lower socio-economic groups often experience physical rather than emotional discomfort. The overlap in meaning between anxiety as a 'normal' response and anxiety as a 'problem' and even a MENTAL ILLNESS (as defined by the medical profession) has important implications. On the one hand, the similarity in the two experiences enables the social worker to understand anxiety as a mental health problem; on the other, there may be little acknowledgement of the difficulties of the sufferer of severe anxiety on the part of workers or the person's relatives and friends if it is regarded as no more than an everyday experience that has been allowed to get out of proportion. It may not then be seen as a 'legitimate' problem requiring help. Where people experience only the physical symptoms, they may not be given a 'diagnosis' of anxiety by a general practitioner, so the worker may not be fully aware of the problem.

> Anxiety involves reactions that anyone may experience in a threatening situation. The subjective experience is one of fear, dread, apprehension, panic and physiological reactions, including palpitations, gastric upsets, headaches, lack of concentration and faintness. When anxiety takes the form of a NEUROSIS, such reactions are experienced for much of the time in the absence of immediately and obviously threatening stimuli. However, this may be either a reaction to an

ongoing long-term situation – perhaps relationship difficulties, or conflicting obligations that are not clearly visible as threatening – or a prolonged reaction to past problems or threatening experiences. The former type can be understood within the framework of stress, while the latter may attract the medical diagnosis of neurosis, or 'minor psychiatric disorder' – in which case the person could be referred to the psychiatric services (see PSYCHIATRY).

Whether anxiety takes the form of stress or a 'neurosis', the consequences can be serious. Accidents are a danger, because of lack of concentration, and young children can similarly be put at physical risk. Tension leads to irritation, family conflict and disturbed relations with children; physical exhaustion and discomfort may also prevent the person from fulfilling role expectations. Besides resentment on the part of spouses or partners, this may lead to employment difficulties and to condemnation from relatives and friends, because of lack of recognition of the anxiety as a legitimate 'illness'.

Oppressed groups may experience anxiety as a result of their greater exposure to threat. Social services clients are particularly likely to be members of such groups, most of whom are in poverty, and the majority do indeed suffer the mental health problems of anxiety and DEPRESSION. Typically these people will be women (twice as likely as men to suffer anxiety), and usually the referral problem will be children and family difficulties, or caring for a disabled relative. It is important to understand how the referral difficulties may have caused and/or result from the woman's anxiety and to provide help with that problem, as well as with the anxiety itself. Black people and members of other ethnic-minority groups are likely to experience anxiety in response to RACISM – although white professionals may not recognize this.

The psychodynamic approach is a helpful method of both assessing the extent of the person's anxiety and the problems and situations giving rise to it, along with establishing a valuing relationship. A good relationship with the client is essential to minimize communication barriers; in addition, where the client suffers from anxiety, such a relationship is understood in psychodynamic theory to reduce this stress, thus enabling them to become more effectively involved in the intervention process.

The medical approach involves use of medication (see DRUGS) to block the physical symptoms of anxiety, in the belief that this will relieve the subjective feelings. While ideally this should perhaps form part of a bio-psychosocial approach, women are particularly likely to be prescribed medication by general practitioners without referral to other professionals. A psychological approach, using BEHAVIOUR MODIFICATION and COGNITIVE-BEHAVIOURAL THERAPY, centres on the anxiety management group.

The FEMINIST approach to anxiety understands it as a natural response to women's powerlessness in their relationships with male partners; to the stressful tasks of caring for dependent people; to their socialized inability to be effectively assertive; and to financial pressures (women, particularly black women, are poorer than men). Intervention here would seek to help the woman – as a member of a group of other women with similar experiences, or through one-to-one discussion with the (female) worker – develop an understanding that the roots of these problems lie in society. This is regarded as the basis on which the woman can start to take control of her life, perhaps developing skills such as assertiveness, through assertiveness training, and thereby relieving the anxiety at its source.

Anxiety becomes prolonged if there are long-term practical problems and conflicts in relationships, which is often the case with social services clients. Such people may be referred to the psychiatric services. With this group, assistance with the practical difficulties, alongside more direct medical and other intervention, can help relieve the anxiety; MULTIDISCIPLINARY teamwork is therefore important (see PSYCHOSES). Additionally, conflict in relationships can often result from long-term anxiety, because of the failure to fulfil role expectations, and the worker can assist by providing practical help and enhancing understanding in the family of the person's difficulties. This can be achieved in families of different cultures through an appropriate understanding of and respect for the family's expectations, values and beliefs.

**appeal (1)**   the process whereby a defendant can complain about and seek remedy for a court decision that they consider unjust.

In criminal cases in England and Wales, appeals against conviction or sentence in a magistrates' court are heard in a Crown Court, and appeals against decisions made in a Crown Court are heard in the Court of Appeal (Criminal Division) or, finally, the House of Lords. A Crown Court has the power to increase as well as reduce a sentence, but the Court of Appeal does not have this power. However, a sentence may be increased by the Court of Appeal if it has been referred by the Attorney General as being unduly lenient, although this is not (technically) an appeal (see CRIMINAL COURTS). In civil cases, appeals are dealt with in the HIGH COURT and the Court of Appeal (Civil Division) (see CIVIL PROCEEDINGS, FAMILY PROCEEDINGS).

**appeal (2)**   the act of a claimant asking for a decision made by the Department of Social Security to be looked at again.

There is a right of appeal to an independent tribunal against most social security claims decisions. However, the introduction of the SOCIAL FUND in 1988 eroded this principle. Some decisions, particularly on DISABILITY questions, must be reviewed before appeal. Other decisions are made by the secretary of state and have no formal appeal rights. Appeals should be made in writing within three months of the original claim decision and sent to the Benefits Agency office of the Department of Social Security where the decision was made; from there they are forwarded to the Independent Tribunal Service that administers SOCIAL SECURITY APPEAL TRIBUNALS and DISABILITY APPEAL TRIBUNALS. The appeal letter may be brief, but if more detail is given the adjudication officer may change the decision without going to tribunal. Appeals may be accepted outside the three-month time limit if the claimant has some special reason for being late. There is a further right of appeal from a tribunal decision to a SOCIAL SECURITY COMMISSIONER, open to both the claimant and the adjudication officer. The commissioner will uphold an appeal only if the tribunal is shown to have made an 'error of law', and will not normally re-examine the facts of a case.

**applicable amount**   the amount of money a person or family is allowed on INCOME SUPPORT. Applicable amounts are also used in the calculation of other means-tested benefits, notably HOUSING BENEFIT and COUNCIL TAX BENEFIT.

**approved probation hostel**   a hostel approved by the secretary of state as a place of residence for offenders either on BAIL or as a condition of a PROBATION ORDER. Hostels may be managed by the Probation Service or by a voluntary organization.

**approved social worker**   the specially qualified social worker who must by law be involved in the decision to detain a person compulsorily in psychiatric hospital.

The approved social worker (ASW) has overall responsibility for coordinating the ASSESSMENT of a person who, because of severe mental illness, may require compulsory admission to psychiatric hospital under the MENTAL HEALTH ACT 1983. Such an assessment will consider first and foremost whether the person's mental illness poses risks to their own health and safety or to that of other members of the family or public. Before a decision is reached, many factors must be taken into account, including the nature of the mental illness, any behaviour disorders the person is showing, the person's own views as to what should happen, the effectiveness of any proposed treatment and the impact on the person of compulsory admission. To obtain the information needed to make this decision, the ASW must interview the person in a suitable manner. The code of practice for the Mental Health Act places considerable emphasis on the manner in which this crucial interview is conducted. It should, for example, be with the person on their own unless doing so presents a risk of physical harm to the social worker. It should not take place through a window or closed door. Every effort should be made to facilitate the communication of the person by providing an interpreter if the person is deaf or if English is not their first language. If the person is sedated or unresponsive the ASW should make attempts to get their views through interviewing others who might be familiar with them. The views of the nearest relative must also be obtained but are not binding on the ASW. Often the ASW acts as the applicant for the compulsory admission of the person involved, although not in cases where the nearest relative has decided to do so.

The decision to admit a person compulsorily to psychiatric hospital can be finely balanced and is never taken lightly. It is always made jointly with a consultant psychiatrist or general practitioner and therefore depends on the mutual goodwill and respect between these various professionals. The decision depends, in part, on whether the person is judged to be in need of psychiatric assessment or treatment in hospital, a decision which rests largely with the consultant psychiatrist. If the decision is taken to admit the person compulsorily to psychiatric hospital, the ASW is responsible for assembling the documentation and making arrangements to transport that person to hospital in a manner that takes their needs and wishes into account. Transport is often by ambulance and never by the ASW acting as lone driver.

The work of the ASW is frequently conducted in an atmosphere of crisis; it can be the focus of pressure from other professionals, such as general practitioners and psychiatrists, who, from the perspective of their medical training, may believe that hospital presents a quick solution to problems posed by a person's difficult behaviour. For the same reason, the ASW may come under pressure from family members to act one way or another. Nevertheless the ASW has to retain a clear view of what their role and function are. They must try to strike a balance between what might be best for the person in the short run, when protective considerations may predominate, and what is best in the longer run, when considerations of a person's social effectiveness and autonomy – which could be undermined by a period of hospitalization – are important.

ASWs are usually members of social work teams specializing in mental health. As such, they will share the work of that team, which includes assessments under the NATIONAL HEALTH SERVICE AND COMMUNITY CARE ACT of people with varying degrees of mental illness, and arranging the services that provide support and assistance in their day-to-day life. This may include purchasing a place at a local day centre for adults with mental distress, arranging for a COMMUNITY PSYCHIATRIC NURSE to provide fortnightly injections of a prescribed medication, and regular visits to check on progress. The work can also involve running special groups that teach participants SOCIAL SKILLS TRAINING or ASSERTIVENESS. ASWs also have a vital preventive role, in working to develop strategies and policies locally for improving services to people with mental illness. This can include, for example, working to establish facilities such as day centres that can help support an individual sufficiently so that periods of hospitalization are not necessary, explaining the nature of mental illness to other professionals and to groups of carers, and improving communication with hospitals and medical personnel.
*Mental Health Act Code of Practice*, 2nd ed., London: HMSO, 1993.

**area child protection committee**  the joint forum for developing, monitoring and reviewing CHILD PROTECTION policies in a given area.

Area child protection committees were first established in 1974 as a way of coordinating policies and practices between those bodies primarily involved in child protection work. Senior representatives from the medical profession, the social services, the police and major voluntary organizations all sit on these committees.

**arm's length inspection unit**  a team of inspectors usually established by a local authority social services department to undertake inspection of its own residential homes and those of the voluntary and private organizations in its locality.

The 1989 white paper *Caring for People* made it a requirement for social services departments to establish independent inspection units. These were to be created at 'arm's length' from the day-to-day management of the local authorities' own residential provision. In addition, each inspectorate was to report directly to the director of social services, as a way of giving it the authority and status to carry out its task. A concern expressed by the white paper was that the owners of private homes had expressed a belief that local authorities were applying stricter guidelines to the running of homes in the non-state sector than to those provided by social services departments. In order to overcome this concern, the government proposed that the units should include people from outside the state sector, including people who had owned or managed private residential homes, or former state-sector employees not associated with the local authority. The government also emphasized the need to involve the non-state sector in determining the organization and management of the unit, the aim being to reduce the potential for a conflict of interest in the way the units carried out their duties. Those in the private and voluntary sectors who would be subject to inspection would also have to be involved in discussions about the process of inspection. This unit would then be engaged in inspecting the local authorities' own residential provision and applying the same standards to all the homes visited.

Some social services departments had already embarked on the task of developing new inspection systems prior to the legislation, but this gave them an added incentive. In some authorities, the inspection units are engaged in examining and disseminating best practice rather than taking a straightforward inspection role. This is in line with the white paper's emphasis on the inspection units' assessment of the quality of service and the impact on clients' quality of life.

> *Caring for People: Community Care in the Next Decade and Beyond*, London: HMSO, 1989.

**assertiveness**   behaviours and thoughts that have at their root a concern to establish interests or RIGHTS either of oneself or of others.

Many people experience difficulties in social situations that arise directly from lack of assertiveness. This might mean that, in a work setting for example, a person is assigned too much work, too little work or inappropriate work – all situations that are individually and organizationally counterproductive – and they feel unable to seek to alter the situation. In such cases, the non-assertive person denies their own rights. Assertion strategies encompass a set of rights that people should attempt to develop into verbal and non-verbal strategies of stating their position. Some of these rights are: the right to state one's own needs and set one's own priorities, and for those needs and priorities to be considered as important as others; the right to be treated with respect as a capable human being; the right to express one's feelings, opinions and values; the right to make mistakes and to change one's mind; the right not to understand something and to seek information; the right to ask for what one wants; and the right to refuse responsibility for others.

> It is important to maintain a distinction between assertion and AGGRESSION. The former can be learned; the latter, which involves the denial of rights to others, needs to be unlearned. There are many assertiveness exercises that people can practice, such as to practice saying 'no', to role-play worrying situations or to re-enact past events in new ways. The objective of such skill development is to act assertively and to feel good about oneself and others. An assertive person maintains good eye contact with others, sits comfortably and talks in a strong, steady voice, giving clear messages and responding actively to the other person.
>
> C.L. Cooper, R.D. Cooper and L.H. Eaker, *Living with Stress*, London: Penguin, 1988.

**assessment**   the process by which judgements are made about an individual or family and their environment, in deciding what their NEEDS are.

Social workers have in the past regarded assessment as their exclusive professional task, akin to a medical or psychiatric diagnosis. The wide scope of social work assessments – covering many dimensions of a person's life, such as state of mind, family relationships, physical capabilities, housing conditions, and income in relation to basic needs – involves too many complex variables for diagnostic certainty to be achievable. Moreover, the new emphasis on clients' PARTICIPATION in their own assessment means that assessment is no longer under exclusive professional control. Practitioners have therefore come to recognize that assessment is a continuous process, mixing professional appraisal and client viewpoint, and reflecting the VALUES of both. An assessment contains at least four elements: *description*, for example of a client's living conditions or the nature of family relationships; *explanation*, suggesting possible causes and probable consequences; *identification*, for example of problems to be resolved or an individual's or family's strengths or weaknesses; and *evaluation*, for example how a person's needs might most effectively be met.

The objective of most assessments is to discover to what extent a child, an adult or a whole family is in need. This requires the social worker, almost always with the client's consent, to gather important information about the client's recent past, health, social contacts, capacity to look after themselves, strengths, the degree of safety in their present circumstances, and the resources at their disposal. The kind of assessment undertaken depends on who the client or user is and what problems they wish to address or others would wish to address on their behalf. One of the common assessment tasks is to decide whether a child is in need, since a local authority can arrange services for children and their family only if this applies. This may require only a brief assessment to determine whether, for example, the child might have needs that can be met by a funded place at a playgroup. Such an assessment could occur quickly, informally and with the involvement of the whole family, soon after that family contacted the social services.

But a child's needs may also be complex, and the scale of services more significant. For a child who may be LOOKED AFTER by the local authority, an assessment may have to take into account a multiplicity of factors. A team at the University of Bristol has developed the best available child assessment charts, covering health, education, identity, family and social relationships, social presentation and emotional and behavioural development. Using the charts designed for specific age ranges both ensures a thorough collection of information and at the same time highlights where action should be taken to produce favourable developmental outcomes for the child as they develop.

Black practitioners and social work academics in the United States and Britain have developed an assessment approach that specifically takes into account environmental pressures and historical considerations in assessing a family (see BLACK PERSPECTIVE). They have been concerned to reverse prevalent notions within the social work profession of stereotypical weaknesses in black families and have accordingly developed a framework that looks at family strengths in coping with the racist environment in which black people live. It has been suggested that the following factors be included in the assessment of a black family: *the person* – what specific life-cycle tasks does each child and adult in the family face, and to what extent does the black experience influence these tasks?; *the environment* – what are the stresses, demands, rewards and attitudes in the family's environment?; *the family* – what is the nature of the relationships within the family and of its coping strategies, particularly when confronted with demands from an antagonistic culture of the white majority?

When assessing the needs of adults who may require COMMUNITY CARE services, such as older people or people with LEARNING DISABILITIES, the Department of Health has explicitly outlined the steps through which every assessment should progress. First, the scope of every assessment should be individually negotiated with the individual concerned. Second, it should take place in a setting where the interviewee feels most comfortable. Third, practitioners should ensure that users understand what is involved in the assessment process, the timescale, the possible outcomes and what authority or powers the practitioner holds. Fourth, the practitioner must define the cause of any difficulty, since without this it will be difficult to select the appropriate service to meet the defined need. The DoH makes a crucial distinction between using assessment as an instrument of social support and using it for social control – the former offering 'choices to the user', while the latter 'imposes solutions'.

Two trends are evident in the current development of assessments. The first is the increasing participation of the user, carer and their families in their own assessment. To enhance participation, individuals need more information about services and whether or not they might be eligible for them. This is precisely the kind of information that social service agencies would not make publicly available in the past. Individuals being assessed also require appropriate ways of expressing their point of view and having influence on the assessment decision. This is a particularly important for people with a DISABILITY or for whom English is not the first language. The second trend is the increasing emphasis on MULTIDISCIPLINARY assessment. The task of a social worker often requires the coordination of vast amounts of information, with their consent, on many aspects of a person's life, including health care, income, housing, mobility, social contacts and mental health. Such information can be obtained only from other professionals and is almost always recorded on lengthy assessment sheets or computerized records. (See also NEEDS-LED ASSESSMENT, SIMPLE ASSESSMENT.)

V. Coulshed, *Social Work Practice: An Introduction*, Basingstoke: Macmillan, 1991; University of Bristol, School of Applied Social Studies, *Looking after Children: Assessment and Action Record*, London: HMSO, 1991.

**assessment centre**   a residential establishment where children are placed for a specified length of time so that an ASSESSMENT can take place. The assessment usually includes such factors as family relationships, health, behaviour and educational attainments, aiming to produce a plan for the child's future.

The concept of the assessment centre has come under increasing attack. Research has indicated that to remove a child from home only for the purposes of assessment gives a distorted picture of the child – separated from their natural surroundings – and at the same time increases the likelihood that contact with home will be weakened. Further, since the assessment process is dominated by psychologists, social workers and senior child-care staff, at such centres little scope is left for the PARTICIPATION of the child or other family members in the process.

**Association of Black Probation Officers**   a nationwide group of black members of the PROBATION SERVICE who believe that all those involved in the CRIMINAL JUSTICE SYSTEM should provide an ANTI-DISCRIMINATORY service to all clients in Britain's multiracial society.

The association seeks to contribute a BLACK PERSPECTIVE to professional issues and service delivery. A network for black probation officers is maintained to support individual professionals, especially if they are isolated from black colleagues in their day-to-day practice. It is also interested in promoting ethnically sensitive services and a rigorous ANTI-RACIST perspective in a system that members firmly believe to be both racist and discriminatory. Practical activity includes direct contributions to social work training courses and to the wider debate on criminal justice issues.

**Association of Black Social Workers and Allied Professions (ABSWAP)** an interest and pressure group launched in 1983 to support black professionals in social work and related occupations and to attempt to enhance the quality of social work services to ethnic-minority communities.

The group reported a growing sense of frustration, anger and humiliation at the treatment of black professionals and black communities that led directly to the formation of the group. ABSWAP was particularly critical of prevailing child placement policies of some local authorities. The inaugural theme for the group consequently was 'black children in care'. The founding of ABSWAP was significant for the construction and development of a new black consciousness in social work. (See also ANTI-RACISM, BLACK PERSPECTIVE, TRANS-RACIAL ADOPTION.)

**Association of County Councils** a national association of representatives from the English and Welsh counties intended to represent the view of counties to central government. The association was formed in 1973 as a result of the reorganization of local government.

The association superseded the County Councils' Association, which had been established in 1889. Its objectives include the promotion of the interests of its membership, the initiation of action on issues of concern to the membership and the dissemination of information to its membership on these issues. The association also has as its aim the creation of a single organization to represent the views of all local authorities in England and Wales rather than just the counties. For most of its existence the association has been dominated by Conservative-controlled authorities, and this has been a factor in obstructing the achievement of the latter aim, because the other associations representing local authorities, such as the Association of Metropolitan Authorities, have more frequently been controlled by Labour Party representatives.

**Association of Directors of Social Services** an umbrella organization bringing together the directors of all the SOCIAL SERVICES DEPARTMENTS in England, Wales and Northern Ireland.

Membership of the association is strictly limited to directors of social services departments. Its major role is to act as a forum for heads of departments to exchange ideas and develop policy initiatives at a national level. The association's other roles include: consultation with civil servants, ministers and opposition spokespersons on social services issues; to meet regularly with other professional and managerial groups to discuss common issues of concern; to provide information to members and facilitate research initiatives; to give evidence to relevant parliamentary select committees; and to provide information to the press and other media.

**Association of Directors of Social Work** an organization representing the directors of social work departments in Scotland.

The association's activities are comparable with those of the ASSOCIATION OF DIRECTORS OF SOCIAL SERVICES. However, the social work departments of the nine regions and two island authorities in Scotland also have responsibilities associated with probation, court services and parole. This gives directors of social work a wider area of concerns than that of their English, Welsh and Northern Ireland counterparts.

**Association of Metropolitan Authorities** an umbrella organization representing the views of the metropolitan district councils to central government.

Membership of the association is open to the London boroughs, the City of London Corporation and the metropolitan districts, that is, those districts that control all services within the geographical areas previously designated metropolitan counties. (Metropolitan counties were abolished along with the Greater London Council in 1986 and included Merseyside, Greater Manchester, West Midlands, Tyne and Wear, South Yorkshire and West Yorkshire.) Corporate membership is also open to those authorities run jointly by metropolitan districts, such as the police authorities, fire and civil defence authorities and transport authorities in the metropolitan areas. The objects of the association include: to protect and promote the interests of its membership, particularly in relation to new or proposed legislation; to provide a forum for discussion on matters of common interest, enabling the development of joint views for negotiating with government; and to provide central services for the membership, such as legal services and information resources.

**asylum** a safe refuge offering shelter and support for distressed or vulnerable individuals.

Originally the word 'asylum' was used to describe the large mental hospitals built during the nineteenth century, often in isolated rural surroundings, which were intended by mental health reformers of the day to provide a refuge for people with MENTAL ILLNESS. At the time, such institutions were regarded as a distinct improvement in conditions, since individuals with a mental illness had often been imprisoned or committed to madhouses as incurable. In the nineteenth century punitive regimes were replaced by some provision of amenities and attempts at treatment. Over a period of time, however, the concept of asylum acquired strongly negative qualities in the public mind as a result of the physical remoteness of the large mental hospitals, their sheer size and the fact that they housed great numbers of demoralized patients for very long periods of time. The notion of asylum as a total institution, which stripped people of their identity and autonomy, became prevalent in social work thinking largely through the work of Irving Goffman. The concept of asylum acquired positive meaning once more in the 1960s, when it was used to signify small places of refuge where individuals suffering mental distress could live without loss of identity and autonomy while being supported by a few close relationships formed within that small community. In this new meaning, the building, often an ordinary house, became a retreat where a person could go in crisis to escape the pressures of their circumstances.

E. Goffman, *Asylum*, Harmondsworth: Pelican, 1961.

**attachment** a long-lasting emotional bond between two individuals, involving their seeking proximity to each other and having pleasure in each other's company. Typically attachment is developed by infants towards their principal care-givers, but it may also characterize feelings between other people, or between a person and some object.

While in adults the term 'love' would be appropriate, 'attachment' is usually reserved for the bond between infants – human and animal – and their care-givers, usually the mother. Close proximity of infant and care-giver ensures that the former's biological needs are met and that both partners build up trust and satisfaction through a close social relationship. Such is the importance of an early relationship of this kind that biologists have suggested that the conditions for its formation must be innate. For example, newly hatched ducklings will follow the first moving object to which they are exposed – a phenomenon called 'imprinting'. Some child psychiatrists have suggested that the responses of a baby to their mother, such as smiling, are human examples of imprinting. Both psychologists and psychiatrists have modified their viewpoints in recent years, taking into account evidence that some mutual instrumental learning is also involved in mother–infant interaction. Mothers 'reinforce' the behaviours they enjoy from their babies, and these behaviours, in turn, reinforce mothers' care-giving.

Whatever the relative importance of innate and learned factors in the development of attachment, its significance is universally acknowledged. Infants who are securely attached are more confident in exploring their environment, using their mother as a base. They are also more confident in responding to the overtures of strangers, again using their mother as a secure base. It has been suggested that babies who have not built up secure attachments in early life are more at risk of emotional disorders in later life than securely attached infants; also that parents who have not had an opportunity to form strong attachments to their children are more likely to abuse them.

Social workers must be careful not to interpret attachment as something that happens once and for all to newborn babies. Such an interpretation has been used to justify the permanent removal of children from families where separation between infant and care-giver (usually the mother) took place, for example as a result of that person's hospitalization, or where the infant's care-giver did not form a close relationship with the infant in the first weeks of life. This narrow conception of attachment viewed children as unable to form attachments either later in their childhood or to more that one person. Such was the importance that social workers placed on attachment that rating scales were devised to help them judge the quality of attachments formed between particular children and their care-givers.

Recent research conducted by psychologists now suggests that attachment is a continuous process that passes through different phases, so that if there is disruption, even early on in the relationship between mother and child, this does not mean that attachment will not take place at all. Social workers have also learned to use the concept more flexibly, as one of many aspects they consider when forming a view of the strength of relationship between a child and their parents.

H. Bee, *The Developing Child*, New York: HarperCollins, 1992; W. Sluckin, M. Herbert and A. Sluckin, *Maternal Bonding*, Oxford: Blackwell, 1983.

**attendance centre order**    a sentence for YOUNG OFFENDERS aged between 10 and 20. Offenders attend a local centre run by the police, usually at weekends, and undertake a programme of physical education and work. Orders last for 12 to 36 hours, depending on age and nature of offence.

**attitude**    a habitual way of responding to, or thinking about, people, groups and objects in a generally favourable or unfavourable manner.

Attitudes influence both a person's behaviour and the way they interact with the world around them. Attitudes are mental states that carry evaluative elements and behavioural tendencies; they provide ready explanations for social events and as a consequence may assist in the management of ANXIETY. Attitudes may be understood as mental short cuts in the processing of information, providing a framework that permits a person to make a rapid assessment of social events based on earlier experiences. Stored in memory, attitudes influence behaviour only when recalled by situations. Whatever their strength, attitudes remain undisclosed if no situation occurs for their translation into behaviour. Attitudes are developed by a person from peer-group influences, direct experience, early learning, the media, membership of social groups and social interaction; once acquired, attitudes interact with each other and with beliefs that are already part of the person's mental processes. Attitudes seem to be most strongly held when they have been acquired by repeated experiences.

Attitudes have two components: the way an event is perceived, and feelings about the event. They may vary in the intensity in which these components are present and in the intensity with which each attitude is held. A person is likely to hold several attitudes towards a person, object or event, with a corresponding choice of behaviours and actions. It is possible for a person to have one attitude and yet behave in a manner that suggests another. People may hold contradictory attitudes and as a result may experience the emotional and intellectual discomfort known as cognitive dissonance. A person may be motivated to resolve this conflict by changing or modifying their attitudes. Similarly, if a person is compelled to behave in a way that conflicts with held attitudes, then those attitudes may change.

People hold central attitudes or beliefs about such things as freedom, equality and the challenging of oppression, with such attitudes interacting closely with behaviour. Attitudes are fundamental in the way a person understands and interprets the social world, linking the person into social groups. Hence attitudes may carry social rewards or punishments for individuals, by ensuring membership of or exclusion from social groups.

Attitudes and attitude change are key aspects of social work. They can be the root of a problem – for example, in racist or sexist behaviour, or in a negative view of one family member by another that is wholly unjustified. Determining precisely the nature of people's attitudes and the willingness or ability of people to change them is central to the social work task. (See also ABLE-BODIEDISM, RACISM, SEXISM, STEREOTYPE.)

**audit**  the annual examination of the financial accounts of an organization aimed at independently establishing the probity of its records and expenditure. Audit is particularly important in public-sector organizations, where expenditure involves the use of public money; it is therefore related to the public ACCOUNTABILITY of such organizations.

In local government, annual audits are performed by auditors contracted by or working directly for the AUDIT COMMISSION. This is an independent organization established by the government to examine the accounts of local government and more recently the National Health Service, to establish whether these bodies have spent money economically and efficiently. The accounts of the authorities have to be published in an annual report, and the auditor can refuse to sign the accounts if they believe these accounts do not reflect the true situation or if there are doubts concerning particular areas of expenditure. More recently, the government has expanded the role of the audit to cover the effectiveness of local government spending. This has brought the Audit Commission and the role of the audit into a more sensitive area of study. The concern with 'value for money' has led the commission to expand the role of the audit to include the identification of ways in which local authorities can make policy implementation more effective. However, there have been doubts as to whether this is an appropriate role for the audit, given that there may be several political perspectives on what constitutes effectiveness.

**Audit Commission**  a central government agency whose task is to AUDIT the activities of local authorities and the National Health Service on the basis of economy, efficiency and effectiveness.

Established under the Local Government Finance Act 1982 and operational in 1983, the commission took over from the District Audit Service responsibility for approving the accounts of local authorities for their annual reports. At first its remit was concerned with ensuring that the accounts had been appropriately drawn up, that there was evidence of probity in financial dealings and that spending was in line with statute. In addition, it was to provide advice on economy and efficiency in the provision of services. However, this remit has since been widened and now includes another element in 'value for money' auditing: effectiveness. This has led the commission into a wider role of providing more direct guidance to authorities on the management of services. In doing so, it has sometimes challenged the methods employed by service professionals in service provision. The commission should not, however, be seen as a mouthpiece for central government policy; it has at times been highly critical of government, most notably with regard to the way the block grant system of local government finance was operated and how this mitigated against appropriate levels of planning for services.

In the area of personal social services and social work activities the Audit Commission has produced major reports that are central to the development of government policy on care. The most significant such document was probably *Making a Reality of Community Care* (1986); this pointed out the lack of progress in implementing COMMUNITY CARE, conflicts in planning arrangements between local authorities and health authorities, and the anomaly of the social security system promoting residential rather than community care. In addition, the report recommended that an independent inquiry be established, which led to the GRIFFITHS REPORT and the subsequent white paper, *Caring for People*. Other reports have looked into services for older people, housing the homeless and the provision of community care for adults with learning disabilities.

Of particular note has been the role of the Audit Commission in drawing up PERFORMANCE MEASURES for a variety of local authority services, including the personal social services. These general reports are promoted very effectively as guidance to all local authorities, but much of the groundwork emerges from more specific investigations by the district auditors into individual authorities. Working within guidelines from the commission, the district audit team may be made up of commission employees or private-sector firms. The results of these investigations are open to the public and may be widely disseminated.

While the Audit Commission has done important work, the extension of its remit to cover the issue of effectiveness has been open to criticism. Issues of effectiveness involve more contentious areas of management and service delivery that may overlap with policy decisions. These, it can be argued, are more legitimately the concern of elected representatives. Further, the fact that issues are perceived from an accounting viewpoint also results in a particular managerial perspective that may be challenged by other professionals and from alternative political positions.

Audit Commission, *Managing the Cascade of Change*, London: HMSO, 1992.

**authoritarian personality** a person who is extremely deferential or obedient towards authority figures and hostile to others perceived as unlike themselves. The authoritarian PERSONALITY may not see themselves as accountable for their own actions but may consider themselves to be under the direction of others.

In explaining the authoritarian personality, psychologists have argued that the usual balance of discipline and self-expression afforded to a child by their parents is disturbed when the child is reared in a harsh disciplinary regime associated with close conformity to social rules. The consequences are that the appropriate expression of childhood aggression is directed away from parents to alternative targets to avoid the punishment incurred through directing it at parents.

**aversive stimulus** an event or physical sensation that a person finds unpleasant and that therefore acts as a punishment.

BEHAVIOUR MODIFICATION programmes occasionally stipulate that an aversive stimulus should immediately follow an unwanted behaviour by an individual that the therapist or social worker wishes to diminish. In the past, such stimuli have included the administration of electric shocks, ammonia vapours and lemon juice. More recently behaviourists have emphasized more natural forms, such as expressions of disapproval. Many behaviourists now discard all aversive stimuli as manipulative and counterproductive, and devise wholly non-aversive programmes with the individuals concerned and their families.

# *B*

**backdating** the making of a backdated payment of social security benefit, in the rare cases where this is possible. Most benefits are paid only from the date a claim is made.

Although there are a few exceptions, such as CHILD BENEFIT and RETIREMENT PENSION, that can be backdated automatically for specified periods, benefits can generally be backdated only if 'the claimant shows continuous good cause for the failure to claim earlier'. Ignorance alone is not good cause, since there is a general duty on claimants to find out about their rights to benefits. 'Good cause' means some fact or facts that in the circumstances would probably have caused a reasonable person to act or fail to act as the claimant did. People who made inquiries but were misinformed or accidentally misled will be able to show good cause even if the inquiry did not relate to the benefit in question. People who did not make inquiries may show good cause if their mistaken belief that they could not claim earlier is 'reasonably held' – for example, entitlement arose because of a change in the law or a particularly obscure rule.

**bail** the system by which courts release an alleged offender pending their trial. Bail may be unconditional or subject to sureties and/or specified residence. The term also applies to the money used as security binding the released person to appear in court and forfeited if they do not appear.

The Bail Act 1976 requires bail to be granted unless there is reason to believe that the alleged offender will fail to appear for trial or will reoffend or interfere with witnesses. The term 'police bail' refers to the process of releasing a person following charge at a police station, prior to court appearance. (See also REMAND.)

**bail hostel** accommodation provided by the PROBATION SERVICE and some organizations in the VOLUNTARY SECTOR to enable homeless offenders to be remanded on BAIL rather than be sent to PRISON while awaiting trial (see also APPROVED PROBATION HOSTEL, REMAND).

**bankruptcy**    a formal legal process, usually undertaken in the county court (the High Court in London), whereby a person without the means to meet their normal financial commitments and debts has their financial affairs taken over by an appointee of the court.

Although the term has fearful connotations, bankruptcy can be a way of handling a complex and difficult financial situation. It is available to people who owe more than £750, although in practice most people filing for bankruptcy owe substantially more. The major advantages of choosing bankruptcy include: the facility of dealing with all creditors at the same time; paying much less to a creditor than would otherwise be necessary (because creditors have to recognize the court's intervention and cannot pursue the debt beyond this, although the rights of people with secured debts are unaffected); removing the anxiety from an uncertain situation; and gaining the chance of a fresh start. The disadvantages may include: the loss of valuable assets (apart from those thought necessary for day-to-day living); loss of the ability to get credit; loss of office in the case of people in public service (such as local councillors, Members of Parliament and magistrates); and the possible loss of home and future business activity. The process can be expensive, and most bankrupts feel at least embarrassment at the involvement of officialdom in their lives. (See also ADMINISTRATION ORDER, INSOLVENCY, MONEY ADVICE.)

**barbiturate**    a manufactured depressant DRUG used to sedate or induce sleep and commonly misused for its intoxicating effects. Barbiturates are available in tablets, suppositories, solutions or capsules and can be taken by mouth or injected.

All barbiturates are class B prescription-only drugs under the MISUSE OF DRUGS ACT 1971. Unauthorized production, possession or supply of the drug is an offence. Effects include relaxation and sedation depending on the size of the dose, although ANXIETY and DEPRESSION may result. Toxic overdose is a serious possibility, especially if the effect is compounded by ALCOHOL.

**Barclay Report**    the report published in 1982 by the committee set up by the government to examine the state of social work and chaired by Peter Barclay. The report's formal title was *Social Workers: Their Role and Tasks.*

The Barclay Report provided a valuable analysis of what social workers actually did in their work, showing that CARE PLANNING had become a major component. The report stressed the importance of RESIDENTIAL CARE at a time when it had fallen from favour among professionals, and it used the phrase 'the continuum of care' to describe the evolving community-based and residential options open to people needing care. Among the report's recommendations it called for less bureaucratic service organizations and for the devolution of decision-making to team level. It further urged the development of a more grass-roots-level COMMUNITY SOCIAL WORK to strengthen CLIENTS' own networks as a key resource.

**baseline**   a record of the frequency in which an individual engages in a particular kind of behaviour before any programme of help begins.

Obtaining this record usually depends on some form of direct observation – such as reports from the CLIENT themselves, from other family members or by the general practitioner – in which the results have been recorded at timed intervals. Keeping track of the number of tantrums a child has during a week is an example. Such a record is used to help measure subsequent progress after intervention begins and almost always forms part of a BEHAVIOURAL ASSESSMENT.

**battered baby**   the term first used by paediatricians in the 1960s to indicate that an infant had been injured by their parents or by other adults.

Before the 1960s the medical profession did not recognize that deliberate injury to infants was occurring. As a result, doctors were often unable to account for multiple injuries suffered by some children, such as old unexplained fractures. The term was a first step in the recognition of CHILD ABUSE as a widespread problem and of its many forms. (See ABUSE, EMOTIONAL ABUSE, PHYSICAL ABUSE, SEXUAL ABUSE.)

**battered wife**   see DOMESTIC VIOLENCE.

**bed and breakfast**   a form of temporary accommodation for families considered to be homeless by local authorities.

Under the HOUSING (HOMELESS PERSONS) ACT 1977, local authority housing departments became responsible for HOMELESSNESS, which was defined principally as the situation of people with dependent children, together with certain other vulnerable groups. As the stock of public housing has decreased over the period since 1979, homelessness figures have risen dramatically. In these circumstances local authorities have been driven to use temporary accommodation, although 'temporary' can mean up to several years. Bed and breakfast in boarding houses and hotels has constituted a major part of this provision. Families are typically confined to one room and required to vacate their room during daylight hours. Standards in this private sector are variable but have included quite sordid establishments. There is increasing evidence that women and ethnic minorities are disproportionately offered this kind of accommodation. In 1990, 30,000 households (approximately 100,000 people) were living in temporary accommodation.

M. Miller, *Bed and Breakfast*, London: Women's Press, 1990.

**behavioural assessment**   observation and detailed recording of the behaviour of a person, with the aim of understanding why they engage in it.

A behavioural ASSESSMENT begins with an exploration of problems. In doing this, it is important to acquire as much information as possible regarding the behaviour that is considered difficult. The aim is to describe a selected behaviour in as much detail as possible: what it is, who is doing it, the conditions under which it occurs and whether it is to be increased or decreased. Behavioural assessment avoids vague formulations and judgemental statements, such as: 'He is badly behaved.' Instead, the assessment should include specific and descriptive statements, such as: 'The boy scatters the pots and pans over the kitchen floor approximately four or five evenings a week.' It is critical to establish a BASELINE – the number of times a person engages in the particular problem behaviour before any intervention is organized. The final element of a behavioural assessment is FUNCTIONAL ANALYSIS, which attempts to discover the purpose that the behaviour serves for the individual who engages in it. As with other forms of social work assessment, it is acknowledged that the person being assessed, their family members and other people such as carers must take part to the fullest extent possible in the assessment and be a party to any decisions taken.

**behaviourism**   a theoretical approach to explaining human development and activity, the central belief of which is that behaviour is the outcome of learning.

Behaviourism is a school of PSYCHOLOGY that considers humans as biological organisms reacting to stimuli in the environment. It argues that internal states such as thoughts, intentions and feeling are not observable and replicable, hence not amenable to scientific analysis, nor the data of a valid science, preferring instead to study human behaviour in terms of stimulus and observable response. (See also BEHAVIOUR MODIFICATION.)

**behaviour modification**   a method of teaching people to change their behaviour by the systematic use of reinforcements and, infrequently, low-level forms of punishment. It is based on LEARNING THEORY.

In general, behaviour modification programmes aim to reduce unwanted behaviour – such as tantrums, acts of self-mutilation or dependency on alcohol – and to increase positive or socially appropriate behaviour in its place. Several points are fundamental to behaviour modification: (1) all behaviour, even extreme problem-behaviour, is viewed as serving a purpose for the individual who engages in it; (2) strong emphasis is placed on defining problems in terms of behaviour that can be observed rather than looking for psychological roots of a problem in the person's past; (3) the CLIENT can learn other, more effective behaviours; (4) the behaviour to be reduced, along with the behaviour to be increased, must be measurable, since measurement is the best indicator of the extent to which a problem is being resolved. The simplest way to increase particular behaviours, according to learning theory, is to reward, or reinforce, the person engaging in that behaviour. A reinforcer can be something tangible, such as toys, trips, preferred activities or preferred foods, or intangible, such as attention, praise, a hug, personal satisfaction or increased effectiveness in completing a task. However, a reinforcer is particular to an individual and may not resemble a typical reward; one cannot assume that what acts as a reinforcer for one person will do so for another. For example, for some children a reprimand acts as a reinforcement rather than a punishment and increases rather than decreases the possibility that the behaviour that caused the reprimand will happen again. So behaviourists define a reinforcer as anything that increases the likelihood that the behaviour in question will be performed again.

Part of any effective behaviour modification programme relies on discovering what it is that acts as a reinforcer for each individual. Once identified, any reinforcement should be made immediately after the selected behaviour occurred, and should be applied consistently and with conviction. The approach can be particularly effective in working with children with behaviour problems. For example, the parents and teachers of a 7-year-old boy report that he is unable to sit still for more than a few seconds. Because of this it has been impossible to teach him to read, to sit for meals or to use the toilet. They agree that teaching him to sit still is the target behaviour, since other activities will follow from that. They further agree to teach the boy to sit still for one minute and listen to instructions. Reinforcers are chosen that are attractive enough to override the boy's continuous motion. In a room free of other distractions, the boy is asked to sit down and is then held and seated on a chair. Immediately he is praised and given a crisp and a cuddle. The process continues in short sessions of no more than ten minutes with some ten to twenty attempts at the task, each similarly reinforced.

Behaviourists have also used punishments following unwanted behaviour. These have tended to fall into one of four categories; physical punishments, reprimands, TIME OUT and 'response costs' whereby the person who engages in unwanted behaviour loses a specified reinforcer. However, punishments are used less and less as behaviourists realize that they both present considerable ethical dilemmas and are much less effective than reinforcement. Only time out is used with any frequency, particularly in work with children. In behaviourist language it means 'time out from positive reinforcement' and involves removal of the child to a neutral space for no more than two to three minutes where they receive no stimulation or reinforcement, social or otherwise, but can still be kept in view. Parents of children with behaviour problems are often taught how to administer time out rather than to use physical punishment or shouted verbal reprimands.

The use of reinforcers and punishers has attracted much criticism from non-behaviourists, since their use seems to imply a mechanical and crude view of human nature. Bestowing reinforcers creates an imbalance of power that can be used for ends other than changing behaviour. For example, in the 1950s and 1960s token economies were introduced into wards in mental hospitals. This system allowed patients to 'earn' tokens for specified behaviours, the tokens being redeemable in terms of specific goods or privileges. In fact, token economies often encouraged psychiatric nurses to act as behavioural engineers and had more to do with controlling the patient population than with teaching more effective behaviour to individuals. Behaviourists now acknowledge that the techniques were often employed by undertrained staff and used for purposes other than what they were designed for. The use of punishments, such as electric shocks, ammonia vapours and prolonged tickling, has left a legacy that behaviour modification has found hard to live down.

Behaviour modification has proved particularly effective with people with learning disabilities and with children with conduct disorders. It has also been used in treating people with addictions and in assisting people to cope with specific anxieties such as fear of open spaces (agoraphobia).

B. Sheldon, *Behaviour Modification*, London: Tavistock, 1982.

**behaviour therapy**    the treatment of a psychological disorder by altering a person's perception of the consequences of a certain type of behaviour. Behaviour therapy is based on the theories of BEHAVIOURISM, which states that certain types of behaviour (such as phobias) can be acquired as maladaptive learning responses. The types of treatment that can be described as behaviour therapy are diverse, including systematic DESENSITIZATION and MODELLING.

**Benefits Agency**    the executive agency of the DEPARTMENT OF SOCIAL SECURITY, responsible for the adjudication and payment of social security benefits.

**bereavement**    the LOSS of a close and personally significant relationship, whether with a relative or a friend, through death.

Reactions to bereavement may take a number of forms: shock, disbelief, pain, depression, sadness, relief and even possible euphoria. Grief and MOURNING – respectively the emotional response and the expression of that response – are an integral part of the experience of personal loss; yet bereavement may also evoke relief, because of the ending of suffering or an unsatisfactory relationship. Bereaved people may feel socially isolated and even suicidal. Often preoccupied with thoughts of the dead person, or concerned to keep their memory alive, the bereaved person may lose their appetite, suffer from disturbed sleep – in which dreams of the lost loved one may occur – and engage in aggressive activity.

Bereavement reactions may be complex and contradictory, as are the range of theoretical explanations for bereavement experiences. Illness models talk in terms of the symptoms and management of bereavement. Biological explanations for grief identify changes in cardiovascular and immune system functioning and point to the enhanced activity of respiratory, endocrine and autonomic systems during acute grieving. PSYCHODYNAMIC models of bereavement reactions focus on the removal of libido (life energy) from the lost person or object and its attachment to someone or something new. This explanation views the transferring of life energy as slow and painful, offering insight into why bereavement is a lengthy process.

ATTACHMENT theories suggest that a person's attachments to others are mediated by instinctive responses and that loss of an attachment figure precipitates crying, longing, searching, withdrawal, apathy and anxiety in attempts to recover the lost person. Bereavement is a period of social transition. As a major event in the survivor's life, death causes a rearrangement of social roles, activities and assumptions about the social world. A person's concepts of self and the way they locate themselves in the social world are profoundly disrupted by the death of a significant individual. Shifts in social position, status and role for the survivor, plus the loss of the 'validating' person, precipitate thoughts of loss of self. All models of bereavement suggest that the survivor experiences a reorganization of links to the dead person and to the environment in which the dead person had a significant position.

Four tasks have been identified for people in bereavement: acceptance of the death; experience of the loss; adjustment to the loss; and the investment in new relationships and activities. Awareness of cultural diversity in bereavement reactions is also growing. Social workers offering appropriate help during bereavement may lessen the timescale of mourning. Effective work with the bereaved should view bereavement as a social as well as an emotional experience, and see recovery in terms of social relationships, meaning and the construction of new opportunities. Bereavement work means offering a genuine, accepting, supportive and flexible relationship to an individual who is experiencing pain, bewilderment and meaninglessness. Grief work aims to facilitate the ending of relationships with the deceased and to free the bereaved person so that they can invest in other life activities and relationships. This is not easy, since the bereaved person's self-understanding is rooted in their relationship to the dead person, and it may appear to the survivor that they are required to reject that person. For example, the bereaved child will find it difficult to invest in a step-parent relationship because their self-concept stems from their relationship with the dead parent.

The social worker needs to listen to the survivor as they painfully attempt to describe a social world in which the dead person cannot be regained. It may be appropriate to stimulate discussion, to 'give permission' that, in a death-denying society, talk of the impact and meaning of the death is acceptable and to be encouraged. Social work should aim to enable the bereaved to locate the dead person in their past.

T. Philpot, *Last Things: Social Work with the Dying and Bereaved*, Wallington: Community Care / Reed Business Publishing, 1989.

**Beveridge Report** the official report of the wartime committee on social insurance chaired by W.H. Beveridge. Entitled *Social Insurance and Allied Services* and published in 1942, it is still regarded as providing the foundation for the modern welfare state.

Beveridge identified five major problems to be tackled in postwar Britain: 'want, disease, ignorance, squalor and idleness'. The report sought to address the first of these by introducing a comprehensive system of income maintenance. The report recommended the introduction of a social insurance scheme to cover loss of income resulting from unemployment, sickness and retirement. Benefits were to be paid at a flat rate, regardless of other forms of income, and were to be financed by flat-rate insurance contributions. Additional amounts were payable for dependants, mainly wives and children. The scheme also proposed the introduction of maternity grants and widows benefits based on a husband's contributions, and death grants and maternity benefits for women who had paid contributions in their own right. Benefits were to be paid at a subsistence level. Although Beveridge intended the scheme to cover the majority of situations in which someone was unable to work, he recognized that there would be a need for a system of means-tested social assistance to provide a safety-net for people whose circumstances were not covered by the insurance scheme (see NATIONAL ASSISTANCE).

From the outset, Beveridge was clear that his social security scheme could succeed only if it was supported by other related areas of policy. He therefore recommended the introduction of child allowances to be paid for the second and subsequent child where parents were in work but to include the first child where the parents were in receipt of an insurance benefit. These allowances were intended to eliminate family poverty without undermining incentives to work or causing wage inflation. The system was to be further underpinned by a system of comprehensive health care and the avoidance of mass unemployment.

The Beveridge proposals were accepted almost without change with the passing of the Family Allowances Act 1945, the National Insurance Act 1946 and the National Assistance Act 1948. There were, however, a number of significant departures from the plan that had implications for its success and can still be felt today. First, the government rejected the proposal that the retirement pension should be phased in over a period of twenty years but allowed individuals to claim much earlier. The resulting loss in revenue meant that the levels of all benefits were much lower than Beveridge had envisaged. Second, entitlement to unemployment benefit was limited to one year rather than being paid indefinitely. Third, Beveridge's plan for a scheme of benefits to be paid on separation was rejected totally. The implications of these changes were that far more people were dependent on means-tested National Assistance than Beveridge anticipated. The low rates of insurance benefits meant that many people had to claim national assistance to cover their housing costs. Beveridge also made assumptions about the nature of family life and the position of married women in society that meant that their needs were inadequately catered for, while the growth and continued existence of high rates of unemployment have also exposed weaknesses in the plan. Failure to address the needs of LONE PARENT FAMILIES and people with sickness and disability who never work has also meant that these groups remain disadvantaged today. Reform since 1945 has attempted to fill some of these gaps but within the framework set by Beveridge.

**black market**    a term used commonly to describe the means by which DRUGS, and other items, are bought and sold illegally. Black market transactions are often associated with organized criminal activity.

Drugs sold on the black market may be either legal substances, such as METHADONE and tranquillizers, or illegal ones, such as CANNABIS and HEROIN. Some people have argued that drug use should be legalized, thus abolishing black markets and associated crime; most policy-makers, however, feel that this would be a retrograde step. (See also SUBSTANCE MISUSE.)

**black perspective**    a view of issues that contains and reflects the reality of the experience of black people in Britain.

In Britain in the 1970s and 1980s many black commentators argued that the experiences of black people was not being heard or sought in relation to policy formation in the social welfare and justice systems. Often black history was not acknowledged at all, rendering black people marginal or anonymous even where (as in Liverpool) they have formed part of the community for a very long time. More recently, black activists have been able to demonstrate that black people's concerns were not being recorded, let alone acted upon. The term 'black perspective' incorporates and acknowledges the different experiences and needs of black people living in Britain; fundamentally, it includes bringing black people's knowledge, aspirations, analysis and developments to bear on issues faced by black communities and individuals, and also illuminating them for white communities. A key part of this process is to dislodge white people from positions where they apparently speak for black people. The black perspective is motivated by a sense of current injustice for black people in Britain.

One of the key issues concerning the black perspective relates to how it is to be determined and expressed in social and political life. Does there need to be, for example, black representation in key political and policy-formation processes? Within a social work context, should there be black workers' groups invited to give a black perspective on all issues, or should the 'normal' democratic representational procedures be relied on to deliver a black view? How, in effect, is the 'tyranny of the majority' to be avoided and how can weight be given to minority views? (See also ETHNOCENTRISM, RACISM.)

B. Ahmed, *Black Perspectives in Social Work*, Birmingham: Venture Press, 1990.

**Black Report**   the official report, published in 1980, of the investigative committee that looked into the persistence of inequalities in HEALTH in Britain since the Second World War.

The committee that compiled the report was chaired by Sir Douglas Black, then president of the Royal College of Physicians. The government repudiated the report and refused to endorse its recommendations; indeed, by circulating only a limited number of copies, it sought to strangle debate. The report indicated strong associations between SOCIAL CLASS and health, with reference to both mortality and illness. For example, the death rate for unskilled workers (class 5) was nearly twice that for the highest social class (class 1), and for particular diseases the gap was significantly wider. Social classes were seen as having differential access to health services, with the poorest sections of the population using such services appreciably less than better-off people. The committee decided that poor health was strongly correlated with low income, unemployment, low educational achievement and poor housing. Although some of its recommendations were about the organization of health services – for example, more resources to be allocated to preventive medicine – the farthest-reaching proposals concerned ANTI-POVERTY STRATEGIES and, by implication, a measure of redistribution in relation to wealth.

**blind and partially sighted**   the legal definition of blindness in the United Kingdom, used to determine BLINDNESS REGISTRATION, is 'so blind as to be unable to perform work for which eyesight is essential'.

A person may be considered 'blind' if they can see only the top line on a Snellen test chart at a prescribed distance. This is known as 3/60 vision and means that a person can see at 3 metres what a normally sighted person sees at 60 metres. A person with more vision, up to 6/60, may be registered as blind if they have a restricted field of vision. There is no legal definition of partial sight, but the accepted description for registration purposes is 'substantially and permanently handicapped by defective vision caused by "congenital defect" or illness or injury'. A partially sighted person may be able to read the top letter on the Snellen test chart at the normal distance but may have a very limited field of vision; or they may have reduced distance vision but a full field of vision. Clinical measurements of blindness and partial sight do not necessarily indicate what an individual can do effectively in everyday life. Visual functioning can be affected by variables such as print size and quality, lighting, contrast of items, personality, health and other people's reaction.

It is estimated that there are approximately 300,000 blind people and 457,000 partially sighted people in Great Britain aged 16 and over, of whom only 25 per cent are registered with SOCIAL SERVICES DEPARTMENTS. AGEING accounts for the greatest incidence of visual DISABILITIES in Great Britain. The Royal National Institute for the Blind estimates that 90 per cent of registered blind and partially sighted people are aged 60 or over. The majority of people registered as blind retain some usable vision, and only 18 per cent have light perception or less.

**blindness registration**  registers of BLIND AND PARTIALLY SIGHTED people, resident within the area served by a department, kept by SOCIAL SERVICES DEPARTMENTS (or their designated agents).

Blindness registers are distinct from registers of disabled people. Registration was first introduced with the Blind Persons Act 1920 as a means of monitoring earlier entitlements of blind people to the retirement or old-age pension. Registration is voluntary, and non-registration should not exclude blind or partially sighted people from receipt of welfare or educational services, including STATEMENTING. Registration may be a requirement for receipt of some financial and welfare benefits, employment training services and services from some voluntary organizations for visually disabled people. Registration is conditional upon medical certification by a consultant ophthalmologist (see BLINDNESS for criteria). Certification and registration represent a significant life event for the individual and their CARERS, so receipt of the registration form should be followed by the immediate provision of information about services and assessment for eligibility.

**Bliss symbol communication system**  a means of communication for people who have limited speech and hand functions.

The Bliss symbols, set out on a board, are based on meaning rather than words and therefore do not rely on reading skills. They are used by people who can indicate by means of hand, fingers, eye gaze, pointer or electronics. The written word can be presented with the symbol, so the 'listener' does not need to know the symbols.

M.P. Lindsey, *Dictionary of Mental Handicap*, London: Routledge, 1989.

**Braille**  a system of embossed scripts that has been universally adopted by BLIND people so that they might read; named after its inventor Louis Braille.

There are two levels of Braille: Grade One, in which every word is fully spelt out, and Grade Two, in which contractions are used to express frequently recurring groups of letters and words. Only a small percentage of registered blind people are Braille users.

**breach proceedings**  proceedings whereby an offender placed on PROBATION or ordered to undertake COMMUNITY SERVICE who fails to meet the requirements of their order may be returned to court.

The court may deal with the breach in a number of ways, for example by imposing a fine or sending the offender to prison.

**British Association of Social Workers (BASW)** the main professional body representing the interests of social workers in Britain.

The British Association of Social Workers is a relatively new professional association, having been founded in 1970. This was the result of a fairly long period of discussion between various social services associations under the auspices of the Standing Conference of Social Workers, established in 1963. Prior to 1970 social workers were organized in associations based on client or functionally related areas. These included the Association of Child Care Officers, the Association of Family Case Workers and the Institute of Medical Social Workers. The move towards a single professional association was stimulated by the recommendations of the SEEBOHM Committee for comprehensive social services departments in local authorities, and by the trend towards generic social work rather than client-based approaches.

BASW now has a membership of approximately 9,000 professional social workers and in 1992 established a set of core purposes. According to its annual review for 1993, these purposes are: to promote and provide a focus for social work activities throughout the United Kingdom and through the International Federation of Social Workers; to promote rights, participation and partnership in the practice and development of social work services with the people who use them; to promote anti-oppressive policies and practice, and equality of opportunity, in social work activity and in the affairs of the association; to lobby and liaise on social policy and campaign to influence government and others; to promote BASW membership and local, regional and national activities; to promote the BASW code of ethics; to provide support services, advice and representation to all BASW members; and to develop and support staff care policies.

As the main representative body for social workers, the association plays an important part in the development and scrutiny of policy issues. It actively responds to policy proposals and guidelines emerging from the DEPARTMENT OF HEALTH and other government departments, and is regularly invited to give evidence before parliamentary select committees. BASW also employs a parliamentary adviser to brief Members of Parliament and Members of the Lords on social work issues. These pressure group activities are in addition to the association's role in supporting members in their relations with employers.

**British Crime Survey** a survey carried out by Home Office researchers by interviewing a sample of 10,000 adults about their experiences as victims of crime. There have been four surveys, in 1982, 1984, 1988 and 1992. They provide an index of crime to compare with official CRIMINAL STATISTICS recorded by the police.

**British Sign Language (BSL)** the term used to describe one of the languages of the DEAF COMMUNITY.

British Sign Language is one of several natural human languages produced in a visual/gestural medium. The language user, the signer, makes gestures including movements of the hands, arms, eyes, face, head and body, which are watched and decoded by the other participants in the communication. If we do not know the significant types of patterning within the gesturing activity of the signer, we cannot decode, and hence understand, the linguistic information imparted by the signer.

M. Brennan, M.D. Colville and L. Lawson, *Words in Hands*, 1980.

**budgeting loan**   a repayable loan from the SOCIAL FUND that people can apply for after getting INCOME SUPPORT for twenty-six weeks. Such loans can be paid to assist with important intermittent expenses for which it is difficult to budget.

The maximum loan that can be made is fixed by law at £1,000. The amount that will be offered depends on the applicant's need, budget, stated priorities and 'ability to repay' within eighteen months. The loan will be reduced by the value of any capital over £500 that the applicant has (or £1,000 if the person is aged 60 or over). Repayments are deducted from income support and other benefits at rates up to 15 per cent of the applicant's APPLICABLE AMOUNT. Repayment rates are not set by law and can be varied at the beginning or during the repayment period. A second loan can be given before the first one is repaid, but the Social Fund officer is likely to restrict the amount offered, having regard to the repayment guidelines. In 1992/3 over 80 per cent of the money loaned was for furniture and household items.

**bulimia**   an eating disorder involving periodic bouts of bingeing and dieting. Attempts to lose weight can include self-induced vomiting, going without food for lengthy periods and the excessive use of laxatives and dieting pills.

The condition seems to be particularly associated with women. Treatment includes trying to help women develop more positive views of themselves and to resist, as feminists see it, oppressive stereotypes of women's bodies.

**bullying**   the harassment, intimidation or abuse of a child by one or more other children in school or elsewhere.

Bullying can include name-calling, racist and sexually motivated ABUSE, AGGRESSION, extortion and actual violent conduct. Surveys suggest that large numbers of children are subject to various forms of bullying at school and that primary schools as well as secondary schools have high rates of bullying. Some schools have developed anti-bullying policies, and it would appear that those working most effectively have involved pupils directly in their devising and implementation. Research also suggests that a straightforward victim–bully dichotomy is simplistic, because victims can also be bullies in other contexts. There is a strong association between bullying and non-attendance at school.

**burnout**   an outcome of prolonged exposure to stress characterized by DEPRESSION, apathy, chronic tiredness, poor health and, frequently, SUBSTANCE MISUSE.

Burnout may be further characterized by diminished attention, forgetfulness, poor concentration and poor MOTIVATION for task achievement. For social workers, burnout may result from a conflation of long working hours, particularly in residential care, little control over the work environment and inefficient or absent support systems, both professional and personal. Burnout at work is an occupational hazard for social workers and may result in heightened absenteeism or even premature leaving of the job. Key signs and symptoms of job stress and worker burnout in human services have been noted as follows: high resistance to going to work, accompanied by a sense of failure; negativism about self and the environment; postponing service-user contacts and resisting service-user phone calls and office visits; increasingly going by the book; avoiding discussion of work with colleagues; loss of positive feelings towards service users; clock-watching; feeling immobilized; and blaming service users. Resistance to change and rigid thinking may be present, and the person may experience sleep disorders.

C. Cherniss, *Staff Burnout: Job Stress in the Human Services*, London: Sage, 1980.

# C

**cannabis or marijuana**  an illegal DRUG derived from the plant *Cannabis sativa* that grows in many parts of the world.

Any part of the cannabis plant may be used. It may be loose, looking rather like green tea, compressed into a block or, strongest of all, oil. It can be smoked, crumpled into a cigarette or through a water pipe, inhaled or put into food and drink. Cannabis is classified as a class B drug under the MISUSE OF DRUGS ACT 1971; penalties for possession and supply range from a fine to fourteen years' imprisonment, depending on the severity of the offence. Immediate effects of cannabis use include decreased blood pressure, increased pulse rate, dry mouth, increased appetite, a feeling of relaxation and a sense of well-being and heightened awareness. Ability to drive or operate machinery may be impaired. With high doses or long-term use some psychological effects such as PARANOIA or mild PSYCHOSIS may result. The drug has many nicknames, including 'weed', 'draw', 'grass', 'pot', 'ganja', 'bush', 'hash' and 'dope'.

**care component**  part of DISABILITY LIVING ALLOWANCE.

**care management**  the process of identifying the social and health care needs of individuals in the community, together with the planning and delivery of integrated programmes designed to meet those needs.

Care management, or case management as it is often called, evolved in the 1970s in the United States, where services are provided across numerous health and welfare organizations and the need for coordination is especially pressing. The concept was introduced into Britain in the 1980s in the form of pilot projects in certain health authorities, and was subsequently given prominence by the Department of Health as the most effective way of overseeing individual CARE PLANS for people in the community. It has become popular because it seems to meet two different requirements: the effective coordination of services, and the containment of costs. Care management is a means to coordinate health and social care services to a named CLIENT; without such coordination, services from different providers with differently trained staff would be fragmented and not suited to the needs of the client.

The range of care management functions, undertaken by a care manager or case manager, varies with the agency and client group involved. There are, however, a number of functions in common. First is the initial ASSESSMENT OF NEED, involving service user, carer and other professionals, who reach agreement, with the care manager, on how needs will be met. Second is the drawing up of a plan, also agreed by all parties. Third is the negotiation of agreements, or contracts, with organizations providing the required services. Fourth is the monitoring of the plan through regular CASE REVIEWS to ascertain whether the agreed services are having the desired effect and, if not, to see how far the person's needs may have changed and require different services.

The aim of care management is to help stimulate a wider choice of services from both the statutory and the independent sectors. The interests and responsibilities of the care manager and associates who purchase the service are separate from those who provide it. The former are able to offer a NEEDS-LED ASSESSMENT and then to commission the services that the assessment has identified. But care management also includes responsibilities for cost containment, and local budgets will not necessarily cover the purchase of whatever services are required. As a result, there is considerable disagreement over how an individual's need that cannot be met should be recorded, if at all (see UNMET NEED).

Department of Health, Social Services Inspectorate and Scottish Office Social Work Services Group, *Care Management and Assessment: Practitioners' Guide*, London: HMSO, 1991.

**care order**   a court order under sections 31 and 33 of the CHILDREN ACT directing a local authority to take into care a child named in the order. Only the local authority or the National Society for the Prevention of Cruelty to Children, as an 'authorized person', may apply for a care order.

For a care order to be made, the applicant must convince the court that the child is suffering, or likely to suffer, SIGNIFICANT HARM, and that this harm can be attributed to a standard of care falling below what a parent could be reasonably expected to provide, or to the child's being beyond parental control. The applicant must also show the court how the care order will benefit the child, by outlining a plan for the child and showing why other alternatives, such as providing support services to the family, will not work. Once an order is obtained, the local authority acquires PARENTAL RESPONSIBILITY for the child, who then passes into its care, although the necessity continues for parents and local authority to work in PARTNERSHIP. A care order lasts until the child is 18, unless the order is discharged earlier by a court. An order cannot be made on a young person who is 17 or who is

16 and married. Applying for a care order is an extremely serious step that should only be taken after other alternatives such as support services have failed.

> The court will reserve the care order for the most serious cases where the probability of significant harm to the child's health or development is high and the willingness of parents to cooperate is low. Such an order does not give the local authority the power to do whatever it likes with the child, and parents do not lose their parental responsibility. The authority may restrict the parents' exercise of their responsibility only when it is satisfied that this is necessary to safeguard or promote the child's welfare. Other sections of the Children Act require joint planning and decision-making with parents, as well as consultation with the child before a placement is made with FOSTER CARERS or in a CHILDREN'S HOME. Throughout the duration of a care order the child's circumstances must be regularly reviewed to evaluate whether the plan for the child is working. The parents and others important to the child should be able to visit at reasonable intervals or have other forms of CONTACT with the child. Parents, the child or the local authority may appeal against a decision to the HIGH COURT or apply for a discharge of a care order.

> Department of Health, *Guidance to the Children Act, Vol. 1: Court Orders*, London: HMSO, 1991.

**care plan** a written statement specifying the objectives for the future agreed between practitioners and users and their carers or family, and outlining the means by which those objectives are to be met.

Historically social work placed little emphasis on planning, and in particular on written plans; instead, it tended to put faith in the strength of relationships between CLIENT and practitioner and in the latter's counselling skills as the primary means by which obstacles and difficulties, often primarily of an emotional nature, for the client would be overcome. Plans, certainly written plans, were not deemed necessary for such CASEWORK objectives. Even as social workers became more involved in protective work with children, child-care plans, if they existed at all, were rudimentary. This lack of planning was critically highlighted in a summary of research published by the Department of Health in 1986 as a chief reason why children were often the subject of erratic decision-making by local authorities.

The DoH now requires local authorities to draw up substantial plans for adults who receive their services under COMMUNITY CARE arrangements and for children who are being LOOKED AFTER by the authority. For adults such a plan would usually begin with a statement of what the person's needs are, following ASSESSMENT. Although there is no one prescribed format for care plans for either adults or children, DoH guidance for both the CHILDREN ACT and the NATIONAL HEALTH SERVICE AND COMMUNITY CARE ACT has laid down what should be included in such plans. For children being looked after by the local authority, the DoH, in conjunction with Bristol University, has developed an effective and comprehensive format now widely in use.

> School of Applied Social Studies and Department of Health, *Looking after Children: Assessment and Action Record*, London: HMSO, 1991.

**carer**   a person – often but not always a relative – responsible for looking
after another person who cannot look after themselves in some or all
respects. Care is likely to take place in domestic settings and to be
largely without monetary reward.

The term describes a range of relationships whereby one person cares for
another, sometimes solely, sometimes in conjunction with others. The level
of dependence of the cared-for person varies enormously, from people
largely able to look after themselves – except for, say, shopping – to others
requiring almost constant attendance. Care involves a wide range of
physically and emotionally tiring activities: bathing, assistance with
toileting, help with personal hygiene, feeding, containment, home nursing,
the management of personal finances, and organizing or liaising with health
and social services. The care given may or may not be supplemented with
DOMICILIARY and DAY CARE services provided by social welfare and health
agencies. There are an estimated 6 million carers in Britain, of whom 1.7
million live in the same home as the cared-for person; 1.4 million spend
more than twenty hours a week in caring activities. Research suggests that
at least 70 per cent of carers are women, the remainder being men and
children. Caring often imposes a financial cost for such items as extra
heating, lighting and laundry. A limited number of carers are able to claim
welfare benefits in recognition of their caring duties, but most are ineligible
for help from the state. To care for someone means, in many instances,
giving up the chance of paid employment; such 'opportunity costs' are
incalculable.

The NATIONAL HEALTH SERVICE AND COMMUNITY CARE ACT has for the first time
officially recognized the needs of carers. The white paper preceding the Act, the
Act itself and subsequent government guidelines have made it clear that statutory
service providers must do everything reasonably possible to assist and support
carers. Further, there is an understanding that the needs of cared-for people and
of carers may differ or even conflict; in these circumstances separate ASSESSMENT
OF NEED is perceived as a requirement.

There are difficulties with the words 'care' and 'carer'. Both assume or imply
that the domestic environment is a place of warm or loving reciprocal
relationships between kin. Such connotations can disguise the feelings of duty and
obligation that may be involved, as well as the considerable levels of stressful
work. Carers usually provide care because of a pre-existing relationship with the
cared-for person; such relationships may contain a range of emotions from
hostility (including ELDER ABUSE) to affection, and from satisfaction to guilt.
Feminist arguments indicate that assumptions about the loving nature of caring
may be exploitative of carers in general and coercive in relation to people who are
reluctant to undertake the task. It is suggested that a distinction can usefully be
made between 'caring for' and 'caring about'; the former implies the labour
involved, while the latter acknowledges the love or affection. A key anti-
oppressive task for social and health service workers is to create a climate in which
it is possible for the potential carer to reveal feelings about the extent to which
they are willing, if at all, to undertake caring tasks and responsibilities.

Carers' support groups have burgeoned in the last few decades. Sometimes such groups are supported directly by social workers and by financial help from statutory sources; other such groups are organized on a SELF-HELP basis. There is no doubt that current statutory provision for vulnerable people rests upon the assumption that families and relatives will undertake the bulk of caring activities. The relief provided to carers under considerable stress is often negligible. Local authority assessments of carers' needs are heavily influenced by available resources, such as day care centres, rather than by the actual needs of the individual carer. With more women working and with the increasing divorce rate – hence a potential loss of the daughter-in-law as carer – the assumptions held by the statutory services will have to be adjusted if current provision is to be maintained, if not improved.

**Care Sector Consortium** the national committee representing all sectors of the caring professions, including probation and social work, responsible for overseeing the development of competencies that care staff have to demonstrate in order to qualify for one of the NATIONAL VOCATIONAL QUALIFICATIONS.

**case conference** a formal meeting of representatives from different professions called to decide a course of action in relation to a particular person or family with whom they have been working.

Case conferences are often used where the CLIENT concerned is in some degree of risk and there are a number of professionals involved with that person. Each case conference has a formal agenda, with a chairperson to manage proceedings. Its purpose is to exchange information, to discuss plans of action and to coordinate services in relation to the particular client or family. Typically, there may be from six to ten professionals present at a case conference, all of whom should have direct dealings with the service user(s) concerned. Wherever possible, the conference should include members of the client's family or indeed the client themselves. Workers attending may include the health visitor, the social worker and the social worker's line manager, who may well be the chair of the conference. Case conferences are particularly important in CHILD PROTECTION work, where representatives from the police and the local education authority are also usually present, as well as the child's doctor. Parents of the child concerned are frequently present for some of the conference, although this is still a new practice and many authorities have been slow to include parents in any decision-making. The chief task of a child protection case conference is to decide whether to place the name of the child on the CHILD PROTECTION REGISTER after considering the child's circumstances and weighing the risks. Such conferences also may decide what course of action should be taken in relation to the child (for example, whether the social services department should apply for a CARE ORDER); but such decisions are only recommendations and not binding on the individual agencies participating in the conference.

*Working Together Under the Children Act,* London: HMSO, 1991.

**case history** a historical account of a person and their family, emphasizing significant events or factors that appear to 'explain' the individual's or family problems. Some social welfare agencies prefer the term 'social history'. Health authorities use the term 'medical case records'.

Trends in relation to the RECORDING of case records have sometimes stressed full case histories, at other times brief notes on the individual and the family background. The consensus until the late 1960s, influenced by therapeutic models of social work practice, was to keep full case histories. Since then recording has become relatively brief and focused. However, recent research sponsored by the Department of Health has been critical of the lack of family background information in relation to children in care. For long-term cases at least, the current practice is to keep fuller accounts of case histories. Major practice dilemmas concern the keeping of records and the issue of access. Regarding the former, the concern is whether records should be kept for each individual in a family and whether there should be a family file. With the latter the issue is who should have access to the records and whether information might be kept confidential.

**caseload management**    a system for monitoring cases allocated to a social worker, adviser or counsellor. The concept is allied to the notion of WORKLOAD MANAGEMENT, which differs only in that its primary concern is all work and not purely CASEWORK.

Caseload management entails the supervision of cases to ensure that workers deliver a good service. A supervisor will be concerned about the quantity and range of a practitioner's work. A caseload should be appropriate to the worker's experience, skills and interests, and it should take account of the morale of the practitioner and any personal stress they may be experiencing. An undiluted caseload of challenging or distressing cases consistently allocated to somebody under pressure is likely to lead eventually to a poor service and a less effective worker.

**case review/system**    a process by which work by social welfare workers is reassessed, taking stock of work done since the case was opened or since the last review. If new problems emerge or earlier plans have proved unhelpful, a new plan should emerge from the review.

A case review is a key event in a piece of long-term CASEWORK. Reviews offer an opportunity for a further appraisal of the effectiveness of work undertaken to date and a chance to devise and implement new plans if necessary. They should prevent drift in casework and ensure that long-term work continues to have a focus. Long-term goals can usefully be broken down into shorter-term objectives. Like case conferences, reviews should involve as far as possible all concerned parties, including the focal person and their family, unless there are exceptional reasons for exclusion. The spirit of user involvement in social work currently makes such PARTICIPATION more likely. The case review system determines the frequency with which cases are to be looked at anew. Some systems have fixed intervals between reviews; others are more flexible, with the interval decided according to the merits of the case. Review system can have other functions, including the collection of critical data about an organization's work.

**casework**   a way that social workers, advisers and counsellors work with individual people and families.

The term was widely used among social workers in the 1950s and 1960s, when all casework was thought to entail the giving of support to the person or 'ego' and/or seeking to help them achieve insight into problems and effect permanent change. The work could be undertaken in families or with individuals. Social work as therapy, with the social worker as therapist, was the model, influenced by PSYCHOANALYSIS. The problems experienced by the person or family were considered amenable to the influence of the social worker (therapist), and external factors (such as poor housing or debts) were regarded as less important in unravelling the difficulties. Casework later came to include additional aspects, such as liaising with other organizations with whom the service user had a problem. For the worker to act as an advocate was seen as consistent with casework, as was MEDIATION and the giving of technical advice. Thus casework came to acquire a wider meaning, although it was still regarded as work with individuals and families. It also came to be seen as one form of social work among many, including GROUPWORK and COMMUNITY WORK. Problems might now be solved or eased by non-therapeutic methods or combinations of methods.

The RADICAL SOCIAL WORK movement of the 1970s was extremely critical of the casework method, which it perceived as rooted in the belief that problems were to be explained by personal or individual failure rather than by wider social causes, such as unemployment, poor housing and poverty. Casework was thought to actively inhibit the service user from understanding the structural origins of their problem. However, a radical form of casework is currently considered possible, with individual work in a variety of guises now deemed necessary in some circumstances (such as feminist COUNSELLING in relation to domestic violence or rape) as a prelude to understanding wider issues. Casework in this sense has a secure place in social work, ADVICE and counselling practice, although it no longer has its former monopoly.

J. G. Barber, *Beyond Casework*, Basingstoke: Macmillan, 1991.

**catharsis**   the revealing and re-experiencing of unresolved emotions that accompanied past traumatic events, in order to bring them to resolution.

The process of catharsis assumes that past traumatic events and the feelings engendered by them have not been resolved and that unresolved emotions are affecting current behaviour, thoughts or feelings. Catharsis occurs where the re-experiencing of past events and associated emotions leads to a resolution of the person's difficulties (see CRISIS INTERVENTION).

**caution**   an alternative to charge and prosecution. The POLICE may caution an offender who admits committing an offence and gives consent to being cautioned. A formal caution is usually given to a YOUNG PERSON committing a first or minor offence but may be used for an adult where appropriate.

**centile charts**   charts on which the growth in height and weight of individual children is plotted and compared with national averages.

Children tend to grow at a regular rate, and this simple fact is used to assist in recognizing when a child has suffered some disturbance. Depending on their weight and height at birth, a child should proceed to grow along a recognized curve or centile, which is simply the average for a child of similar height and weight at birth. But a child may stop growing in some way when emotionally upset over a long period of time, inadequately fed or ill. An unexplained change in the rate of growth can be a sign of the child's FAILURE TO THRIVE. To be of use, the charts require regular measurement of the child in question. Young infants are usually measured by HEALTH VISITORS at specific intervals. School-age children for whom there might be concern can be monitored by the school doctor. Social workers often use this information to help them decide whether a child is being abused or not.

**Certificate in Social Service (CSS)**   introduced in 1977 as a qualification separate from, but equal to, the CERTIFICATE OF QUALIFICATION IN SOCIAL WORK (CQSW), largely for residential and day care staff working in social services.

In 1988, after much debate, the Central Council for Education and Training in Social Work decided that the CSS should be considered a formal social work qualification with the same professional standing as the CQSW. The CSS programme was based on close cooperation between the educational institutions, where the teaching took place, and the work setting of the student; this element influenced the design of the DIPLOMA IN SOCIAL WORK, which eventually replaced the CSS in the early 1990s.

**Certificate of Qualification in Social Work (CQSW)**   the first general social work qualification, introduced in 1971 and offered by a number of colleges and university social work departments until it was phased out in the early 1990s.

The CQSW curriculum reflected the commitment to GENERIC social work that the SEEBOHM REPORT had called for in 1968. Over time, the CQSW was thought to be insufficiently responsive to the work that practitioners actually did, and it was superseded by the DIPLOMA IN SOCIAL WORK.

**chaining**   a method of teaching a person a new skill or activity by breaking it down into small steps or behaviours and reinforcing the mastery of each part until the entire chain is learned and the skill or activity can be performed.

Chaining is frequently used in work with people with LEARNING DISABILITIES who need to learn ordinary skills of day-to-day living, such as dressing themselves, eating with utensils, shopping or using public transport.

**challenging behaviour**   behaviour displayed by some people with LEARNING DISABILITY that is dangerous to themselves or other people, or is sufficiently unacceptable to significantly limit their opportunities for going out into public places.

In the past, admission to hospital was seen as the appropriate course for people with challenging behaviour. With indications that service users with challenging behaviour progress best in community rather than hospital settings, and in environments that are responsive to their needs and wants, current policies emphasize the need to keep such people in the community. Staff should be adequate in numbers, appropriately trained and properly supported. BEHAVIOUR MODIFICATION can be effective in producing a reduction in challenging behaviour, although in some programmes interventions have been unacceptably punitive. Other interventions include the use of psychotropic drugs, methods encouraging relaxation and attempts to improve the person's communication skills. Specialist support teams are being set up in some parts of the country, but a single additional resource in each area may be an insufficient answer. Demands on community-based services for people with challenging behaviour will probably increase in the coming years, although research in the North-West of England suggests that existing services will be unable to cope with larger numbers. There is evidence that parents often need regular relief from the demands of caring, but that respite and other services are inadequate.

P. Harris, 'Aggressive behaviour by people with learning disabilities', in D. Robbins (ed.), *Community Care: Findings from Department of Health Funded Research 1988–92*, London: HMSO, 1993.

**charging policy**   the policy followed by a LOCAL AUTHORITY with regard to charges for its services. Authorities have significant discretion in this area.

In the field of social services, charges for RESIDENTIAL CARE are controlled by statute. By contrast, charges for DOMICILIARY SERVICES are governed by the Health and Social Services and Social Security Adjudication Act 1983, of which section 17 allows an authority 'to recover such charge (if any) for a service they consider reasonable'. A reasonable charge relates to the cost of providing the service and to the means of the service user. Although this is a matter for individual consideration in each case, authorities will sensibly devise a charging policy that provides an immediate assessment in the majority of cases. Authorities concerned with ANTI-POVERTY issues generally devise a policy compatible with the rules of MEANS-TESTED BENEFITS to ensure that charges do not form a barrier to service use.

**charity**   a non-profit-making organization registered with the Charities Commission that seeks to dispense services and sometimes grants to people in need.

Charities have different practices and different terms of reference. Some deal directly with potential recipients of their services and/or grants; others deal with intermediaries such as social workers; yet others work only through other organizations. Some charities are extremely modest, with very specific objectives within perhaps a very small area. Others are immensely rich, with wide terms of reference and perhaps serving an area as large as the whole of Britain. Many VOLUNTARY organizations are also charities.

Social workers and others working in social welfare are often employees or members of management committees of, or VOLUNTEERS with, charities. More frequently, perhaps, social workers make appeals to charities on behalf of service users in need. Many workers feel uneasy about this practice, especially if the need arises from poverty or disability. This unease rests upon the view that, first, the state ought to meet these basic needs and, second, the kinds of account of CLIENTS' difficulties that charities find persuasive smack of the 'deserving poor'. Some also make the point that the use of charitable funds or services inhibits the realization of a more just society, because ideas of charity and of discretion obscure the need for basic rights in relation to, for example, an adequate income for all or the ability of a disabled person to participate in society on equal terms with able-bodied people. Workers prepared to appeal to charities on behalf of people in need argue that present problems need present solutions and that they wish to deal with a problem immediately in order to enhance people's LIFE CHANCES.

**chasing the dragon**   refers to the way HEROIN is 'smoked'. The powder is heated, invariably on foil, and the fumes are inhaled through a small tube. The heroin forms an oil that 'runs' in a line, hence the term.

**child abuse**   physical or psychological harm done to a child through deliberate act or neglect.

Social workers have to work with several forms of child ABUSE. PHYSICAL ABUSE is the intentional use of physical force to hurt, injure or kill a child. Social workers are not expected to diagnose with certainty whether a child has been abused or not, but they are expected to be alert to suspected cases of abuse so that they can initiate a CHILD PROTECTION INVESTIGATION. To do this, they require some familiarity with injuries that might have been deliberately inflicted (often called 'non-accidental' injuries) on a child. Some knowledge of the difference in bruising between accidental and non-accidental injury assists in this recognition. The former usually occurs where bone is close to the skin such as the forehead, shins or knees. The latter is more frequently present on soft parts of the body, such as the cheeks, buttocks, upper legs and mouth. Bruises caused by an adult slapping or grabbing a child often leave a distinctive mark, such as several finger bruises. Burns, particularly cigarette burns and scalds from hot liquids, and frequent fractures are other injuries deliberately inflicted. Social workers also encounter children harmed through neglect: the persistent lack of attention paid to the child's needs by its parents or care-givers. Preschool children are most vulnerable to neglect, which can take the form of injury through repeated accidents, for example burning a hand in an unguarded fire, or of weight loss, or of abnormally slow growth rates (see FAILURE TO THRIVE). Social workers also work with children who have been sexually abused. Child SEXUAL ABUSE can take several forms: exposure such as the viewing of sexual acts, pornography and exhibitionism; molestation, that is, the fondling of genitals, either the child's or the adult's; sexual intercourse – oral, vaginal, or anal – without the use of force and over a period of time; and rape, that is, intercourse achieved by use of force.

Although the injuries to an abused child can be extreme, detection of abuse is rarely easy and is usually achieved only by a pooling of knowledge and expertise from both professionals and lay people. Health visitors, preschool playgroup assistants, teachers, general practitioners, and medical staff at hospital emergency units, as well as paediatricians, social workers and police, all play important roles in this task. Often the child's own willingness to speak to someone confidentially about the abuse happening to them, or the observations of a non-abusing parent, are critical to detection. Children's account of the experience of abuse has in the past been treated sceptically by many child-care professionals; but it is now commonly recognized that children often do tell the truth, and each child's account is taken seriously. The social worker's task is to assemble all the information and opinion. Frequently a child protection CASE CONFERENCE, attended by professionals and others who work with the child, as well as by the child's parents, will be held to appraise precisely the nature of the abuse that has taken place.

There has been some attempt to develop 'indicators', factors that when present in a child's life might suggest an increased likelihood of abuse of that child. Such indicators usually include a young (teenage) mother without supports, an infant who was premature or of low birth weight, a previous history of violence in the family, alcoholism, and one parent who was abused as a child. Indicators have been heavily criticized by feminist practitioners as apparently laying the responsibility for abuse with the mothering of the child and ignoring the fact that the great majority of abusers, particularly child sex abusers, are male. Others have argued that heavy emphasis on child abuse and child protection has seriously skewed the nature of social work, which has become excessively cautious and defensive as a result, relying more on compulsory legal action than on the development of preventive and support services for families. It is important to underscore that the incidence of child murders has fallen dramatically since 1973 in the United Kingdom, with the biggest drop among infants. For all the publicized failures of SOCIAL SERVICES DEPARTMENTS to protect certain children, children are relatively more protected now than twenty years ago.

H. Owen and J. Pritchard (eds), *Good Practice in Child Protection: A Manual for Professionals*, London: Jessica Kingsly, 1994.

**child abuse inquiries**   public inquiries held to examine why particular children were assaulted or killed when a SOCIAL SERVICES DEPARTMENT was involved in the case.

There have been a number of major inquiries as to why children have been harmed or killed by adults in the family, while the children were either under the direct supervision of social workers or known to a social services department. Some of the inquiries investigated the way certain CHILDREN'S HOMES systematically abused children in their care, such as those in Leicestershire, Staffordshire and North Wales. Others examined the cases of children killed by parents, step-parents and partners in the family, and why social workers and other professionals failed to protect them even when their circumstances were familiar to those professionals. This second group includes the inquiries into the deaths of Kimberly Carlisle, Jasmine Beckford, Lucy Gates and Tyra Henley. Each inquiry in this group published detailed reports that gave precise accounts of what happened, including the day-to-day actions of the social workers involved and their immediate line management. They often made stinging criticisms of the conduct of both social workers and their departments. Both the hearings and the reports themselves were extensively covered in the media, partly because of the distressing nature of the children's deaths, and partly because of the heavy criticisms directed at the way the professionals working with the children failed to take sufficient protective action in time. A third group of inquiries dealt with instances where social services departments were deemed to have overreacted and removed children from families unnecessarily (see CLEVELAND INQUIRY, CLYDE REPORT).

> The inquiries were usually conducted along quasi-judicial lines, either formally or informally, with a prominent barrister or judge overseeing the accumulation of evidence and testimony and writing the report. Most of the reports offered important recommendations regarding changes in the law, social work practice and communication between professional agencies. In general, the reports focused on the particular circumstances of the family concerned and paid little attention to the effects of environmental disadvantage on the family and on the behaviour of the abuser. The inquiry into the death of Tyra Henley was a notable exception, as it also looked at the impact of poor housing conditions on the family. The inquiries also concentrated on the family as recipients of a service, so that many of the recommendations have to do with improving inter-agency communication as a means of enhancing that service rather than with wider issues of social policy.
>
> Department of Health, *Child Abuse: A Study of Inquiry Reports 1980–1989*, London: HMSO, 1991.

**child assessment order**   an order under section 43 of the CHILDREN ACT requiring any person in a position to do so to produce the child named in the order for ASSESSMENT.

To obtain a child assessment order, the local authority must convince the court in full hearing that the child is suffering or is likely to suffer SIGNIFICANT HARM, that assessment of the child is necessary in order to establish whether that harm has occurred, and that the required assessment would not take place without the order being made. If the court grants the order, it can also direct where, when and how the assessment will take place. Only very rarely will the assessment involve the child in an overnight stay away from home. Effectively, the child can refuse to undergo the arranged assessment, since the Children Act allows children of sufficient age and understanding to refuse medical or psychiatric examination.

**child benefit**   a benefit paid in respect of a child aged under 16, or under 19 and in full-time non-advanced education, to a person with whom the child lives or who contributes to the child's maintenance to the value of the benefit.

Where two people would qualify for child benefit, special rules prioritize between claimants. It is a non-MEANS-TESTED, non-contributory benefit and is the best example of a universal benefit. People seeking to curtail public expenditure argue that child benefit is poorly TARGETED, because with a TAKE-UP rate of nearly 100 per cent (unlike means-tested benefits) it is paid to all families regardless of need. Its defenders regard it, however, as an important expression of society's collective responsibility to maintain and encourage the family, and see it as an effective way to support all children in low- and middle-income families.

**child-care worker**  a person employed in a CHILDREN'S HOME to undertake direct care of children living there.

The work of a child-care worker may include eating with the child at meal times, seeing that the child is ready for school, taking the child to doctor's appointments, playing games, talking about problems, building relationships, and giving information to other professionals about aspects of the child's life. As a designated post, child-care worker ranks below residential social worker in most staffing structures.

**child guidance**  a service for school-aged children with emotional, behavioural or educational problems (or some combination of these problems). The service is provided by education departments of LOCAL AUTHORITIES, although such services often work in close collaboration with SOCIAL SERVICES DEPARTMENTS.

Child guidance clinics provide MULTIDISCIPLINARY teams of social workers and EDUCATIONAL PSYCHOLOGISTS with access to psychiatric services. REFERRALS are usually from general practitioners, schools or social services departments, although other routes are possible. Clinics often offer FAMILY THERAPY services too, given that many problems of children are located within families rather than solely in the children themselves.

**child-minder**  a person who looks after children for reward, in domestic premises, usually their own home, during the day. Child-minders must be registered with, and approved by, the LOCAL AUTHORITY under the CHILDREN ACT.

Child-minders – almost always women, often with children of their own – look after preschool and school-age children up to the age of 8. The local authority will inspect the premises for safety and to see that it provides a stimulating environment. A good child-minder will play with the child, provide intellectual stimulation, companionship, food and warmth, and take the child on excursions. Child-minders and parents should work in collaboration to ensure agreement in all important matters affecting the child, as well as a clear understanding regarding fees, hours of attendance and sickness and holiday arrangements. Child-minders are expected to share with parents any important information about the child that they pick up while with the child. They may be deregistered by their authority if the care they give is seriously inadequate with regard to the child's racial origins or religious or cultural needs; the authority can provide training on these and related matters. The extent to which child-minders may discipline children in their charge has become a hotly debated issue, with one minder taking her local authority to court to establish her right to smack a badly behaved child. The importance of child minding as a family support service has been underscored by the Children Act's emphasis on day care for children in need.

**child protection** action taken by social workers and others to safeguard children from harm inflicted deliberately or through neglect.

Child protection is the general term for the measures, steps and procedures taken when a child is reported to have been abused. Although social workers play a lead role in individual cases, steps to protect a child are almost always the result of intensive collaboration between SOCIAL SERVICES DEPARTMENTS – including management – doctors and paediatricians, health visitors and police. Generally, the more complicated the case, and the graver the injury to the child, the more intensive is the collaboration among professionals. There are a number of stages involved in child protection work: investigation, ASSESSMENT, legal action (if required) to ensure the child's safety, and devising a plan to safeguard the child's welfare. The investigation must be carried out by a social worker from the local authority social services department after it receives a REFERRAL or has cause for suspicion. Such referrals come from doctors, teachers or playgroup assistants, but can also come from neighbours or members of the child's family. Under section 47 of the CHILDREN ACT a local authority must investigate each such case if it has reasonable cause to believe that the child is suffering, or is likely to suffer, SIGNIFICANT HARM; the authority is obliged to make a report on its findings. Even this early stage of the work poses difficult decisions for social workers, since to begin such an investigation means accumulating information on the child and their family and to begin discussions with the child's parents about the alleged ABUSE. Most families find such an investigation intrusive, so a decision to begin investigation has to be taken carefully.

The aim of any CHILD PROTECTION INVESTIGATION is to judge whether or not immediate action must be taken to protect the child. Because speed is essential, only basic information can be gathered. This information includes obtaining the child's views about the situation, interviewing the child where appropriate and exploring with the parents the circumstances in which the alleged abuse took place. Other information is obtained from professionals already working with the child or family. The decision to take immediate action such as an EMERGENCY PROTECTION ORDER will be based on the nature of the cause for concern and the parents' reaction to it; the child's age or vulnerability; the knowledge of, and whereabouts of, an alleged perpetrator; past knowledge of the family; and the capacities of the parents. Obtaining such information can take place in a tense, or even hostile, atmosphere and requires social workers to be skilful in their interviewing techniques, careful in their recording of the information and calm in the face of considerable pressure.

Following the investigation the social worker has several courses of action: to take no further action at all (which is the outcome in the great majority of referrals); to offer the family some supporting service such as a place at a FAMILY CENTRE; to call a child protection CASE CONFERENCE in order to get a multidisciplinary view; or removal of the child for their own protection. Where there are grounds to remove the child compulsorily for their own protection, and a longer-term plan has to be developed for the child's future (for example, should the child be returned home?), the social worker undertakes a full assessment regarding the child's vulnerability.

It is also sometimes necessary to undertake a full child protection assessment without a preceding investigation, in cases where child-care professionals have concern for the child but there has been no specific event to trigger an investigation. A full assessment has to be carefully arranged, since it involves a number of other professionals and must cover a vast range of information. The information required is specified in the guidelines from the Department of Health called *Protecting Children: A Guide for Social Workers Undertaking a Comprehensive Assessment*. It includes the nature of the abuse – whether physical harm, neglect, sexual or emotional abuse; the child's behaviour and any emotional problems; aspects of routine care such as feeding, toileting and sleeping; and the relationship between the parents, as well as their individual capacities for caring for their child. The outcome of the assessment must be recorded carefully and in a way that all participants can understand.

The full assessment is an essential part of a child protection plan, which will identify the various contributions that each professional agency will make to the child, their family and the abuser. It will make clear what is expected of the child's parents, such as bringing an infant to a health clinic for regular weighing, or visiting their child regularly before the child returns home. The Children Act requires that, whenever a child has to be removed from home, it is preferable to place them with close family members in order to facilitate their return home and to maintain family ties in the meantime.

Child protection work can also involve working long-term with the family of the abused child. This may involve specifying in a written agreement the plan for the child's return, and how the family will specifically work to safeguard the child's welfare, plus arrangements for monitoring such as attending a family centre. This work may involve the social worker in providing family support services or guidance to the family on matters of discipline. It can also entail arranging for more specialist work to be undertaken with the abuser, such as techniques for controlling anger or containing sexual impulses.

No aspect of social work has caused more controversy with the public or stress for practitioners themselves than child protection. Collaborative work is essential at every stage, and particular care is needed to ensure good communication between the various professionals involved in the case and within the social services management team. Often the social worker takes an important role in seeing that this is done. Social workers are selected for child protection work on the basis of a range of skills and experience that enable them to gather information and make decisions under extreme pressure, to work with parents and other family members following physical assault by those same people, to present testimony to court and to record their interviews and decisions meticulously.

H. Owen and J. Pritchard (eds), *Good Practice in Child Protection: A Manual for Professionals*, London: Jessica Kingsly, 1993.

**child protection investigation** a legal obligation on local authorities, under section 47 of the CHILDREN ACT, to investigate where they suspect a child is suffering or might suffer SIGNIFICANT HARM and to assess the needs of the child and the family, including the likelihood of harm and the need for protection.

Suspected cases of CHILD ABUSE remain among the most contentious areas of involvement for social workers. The nature of CHILD PROTECTION investigations is made more difficult by the complexities of working with other agencies, including the police and the legal system. The competence with which the investigation stage is handled will crucially influence the overall effectiveness of subsequent work. High standards of cooperation with other agencies are needed, and these are best promoted by clear and detailed procedures to guide investigation. The essential feature of this stage is the assessment of whether there is an immediate risk to the child. A first requirement, therefore, must be speedy action to see, examine and, where appropriate, interview the child. The child's perspective and views about the situation should be sought and understood. Parents and carers will equally need to be seen and interviewed, and the social worker is responsible for exploring the circumstances of the alleged or suspected abuse with them, in addition to explaining to them the reasons for concern about the child and the responsibility and powers of the local authority.

Research into child protection investigations has highlighted that even initially hostile and uncooperative parents prefer openness, honesty and a social worker who shows concern and listens to their point of view. Such basic principles are an essential requirement in helping parents engage in a relationship with professionals focused on concerns about their child or children. Initial decisions about immediate action to protect the child are likely to be based on limited information. In consultation with management and others with knowledge in the professional network, the social worker is likely to base such decisions on the nature of the cause for concern and the reaction of the parents to it; the child's age or vulnerability; knowledge, and whereabouts, of an alleged perpetrator; past knowledge of the family and parental personalities; and the current initial assessment of the parents.

Although the police will wish to ensure that all appropriate steps are taken for the protection of the child, the primary responsibility for this will fall to the social services department. Because the functions of each agency are different in the investigation of an allegation of child abuse, it is essential that methods of joint working are established, agreed and put into effect in the local area child protection committee procedural handbook. This should cover consultation, how inquiries will be pursued and the arrangements for obtaining court orders and removing the child if necessary.

Apart from possessing good investigative and recording skills, the social worker needs to be a good listener, to be calm and in control and to avoid jumping to conclusions.

Department of Health, *Protecting Children: A Guide for Social Workers Undertaking a Comprehensive Assessment*, London: HMSO, 1988.

**child protection register**   the central list of all children in an area who have been considered by a CASE CONFERENCE to be likely to suffer SIGNIFICANT HARM or who have actually suffered or are suspected of having suffered significant harm.

It is the sole responsibility of a child protection case conference to register (or deregister) particular children. The register is usually kept by the local SOCIAL SERVICES DEPARTMENT, which is able to respond quickly to bona-fide queries, for example from a doctor, as to whether a child is on the register or not. The purpose of the register is to alert other professionals that the child listed has already been discussed by a case conference and may well be receiving services.

**child refuge**  see CHILDREN'S HOME.

**Children Act 1989**  the single most important piece of legislation concerning children passed this century, providing a wide-ranging framework of responsibilities and duties for parents, courts and local authorities for safeguarding and promoting the welfare of children.

The Act came into effect in October 1991. Its central principle is that children are best looked after within their own family, with both parents playing a full part. The concept of PARENTAL RESPONSIBILITY, which replaces the notion of PARENTAL RIGHTS over children, reflects this. Both parents, if married, have parental responsibility for their child automatically and both retain it should they divorce or the LOCAL AUTHORITY looks after the child for a period of time. Unmarried fathers acquire parental responsibility either through a court order or by agreement with the child's mother. The Act places a primary duty on the local authority to promote the upbringing of children in need by their families as long as this is consistent with their welfare. Children in need are defined as those whose development and health would be impaired if they did not receive support services or who are disabled. To carry out this duty the authority must identify children in need in their area and offer a range of support services to them, including nursery places, child minding, family aides, home help and laundry services, and ACCOMMODATION either in a CHILDREN'S HOME or in FOSTER CARE. Other services include financial help in exceptional circumstances, guidance and counselling, holiday arrangements and cultural or educational activities. The authority is not expected to provide all such services itself and may assist VOLUNTARY-SECTOR organizations in providing them. Family members other than the child may be the recipient of these services as long as it can be established that provision of service will assist the child in need to remain with their family. For example, an adolescent who shoulders a large role in caring for a younger sibling with a severe physical disability may be supported in this through regular leisure opportunities arranged by the authority.

To ask for support services is not a sign of parental inadequacy and should be agreed on the basis of PARTNERSHIP between parents and local authority. Services, including accommodation, are provided after negotiation and agreement with parents in order to help them to meet their responsibilities towards their children, rather than as a substitute for them. The family's racial origin and cultural and linguistic background are considerations that the authority must take into account when making plans with parents for their children.

The Act recognises, however, that support services are not always enough to protect the child from harm. For instance, parents may be uncooperative and refuse services, or the child may be subject to abuse by a parent or another person in the household. In such cases the local authority can apply to the courts to take further action under one of several orders. A SUPERVISION ORDER places the child under the responsibility of a social worker or a probation officer who has the power to lay down certain requirements for the child or young person to follow. A CHILD ASSESSMENT ORDER requires the parents to cooperate in the assessment of their child. Alternatively the local education authority may apply for an EDUCATION SUPERVISION ORDER to help ensure school attendance.

In more extreme cases the local authority may apply for a CARE ORDER. To obtain a care order it must convince the court that the child is suffering, or is likely to suffer, SIGNIFICANT HARM because of a lack of reasonable standard of parental care or because the child is beyond control. In addition, the authority must demonstrate to the court that making an order will be better for the child than not making it, by explaining the plans it has in mind for the child in question. Although the grounds for a care order are exactly the same as for a supervision order, the courts will in practice grant a care order only in the most serious circumstances where other alternatives have been tried and have failed to safeguard the child from significant harm. A care order lasts until the child is 18 years of age, unless discharged earlier, and more importantly gives the local authority parental responsibility and with it decision-making powers over the plan for the child.

Not only does the Act govern court proceedings between local authority and parents, it also introduces new orders for use in disputes between parents over their children. The Act does not use the concept of custody of the child, which often resulted in a bitter contest between parents, but provides four orders that take their name from the section of the Act in which they appear: SECTION 8 ORDERS. Each of the four orders is intended to resolve disputes over practical arrangements concerning the child, such as who is to see the child and where the child is to live, and to encourage both parents of the child to work out these arrangements between them. The two most important of these are the RESIDENCE ORDER, which designates with whom the child is to live, and the CONTACT ORDER, which establishes the frequency of contact between the child and parents or others in the family (see also PROHIBITED STEPS ORDER, SPECIFIC ISSUE ORDER). The courts have great flexibility in using these orders in both matrimonial and care proceedings. For a child subject to care proceedings the court may decide to combine a residence order, to a grandparent for instance, with a supervision order to the local authority, instead of granting a care order. Children are also able to apply for these orders and have done so in well-publicized cases where they wish to separate from one or both of their parents.

When a child is involved in any FAMILY PROCEEDINGS, that is, proceedings for care or supervision order or matrimonial proceedings, the Act stipulates that the child's welfare is the court's paramount consideration. To underscore this the WELFARE CHECKLIST lists a number of factors that the court must bear in mind when making a decision on the case before it.

Whether a child is accommodated with the agreement of the parents or subject to a care order made by the courts, the Act considers that child as LOOKED AFTER by the local authority, which then has the responsibility of placing the child with FOSTER CARERS or in a CHILDREN'S HOME. For any child being looked after, the authority must try to place the child as near to home as possible and to consult the child about the placement decision. If the child is accommodated by agreement with the parents, the arrangements must be covered by a WRITTEN AGREEMENT covering such matters as the continuing role of the parents in the life of the accommodated child and when the placement will end. The authority must still attempt to work in partnership with the parents of any child it is looking after; but it is recognized that after contested care proceedings, for example, parents may continue to dispute the local authority's plans for their child. In exceptional circumstances the local authority may limit the parents' exercise of parental responsibility in relation to their child as long as that child is subject to a care order. Detailed regulations covering plans, written agreements and reviews for children looked after by the authority are covered in the Arrangements for Placement of Children Regulations accompanying the Act.

The Act also sets out how the local authority, the police or the National Society for the Prevention of Cruelty to Children should respond when they believe that a child may need emergency protection. Where the local authority has reasonable cause to suspect that a child is suffering from significant harm it has a duty to investigate the child's circumstances. The objective of that inquiry is to enable the authority to decide whether it should make an EMERGENCY PROTECTION ORDER or take any other action under the Act, such as offering support services to the family in question. The emergency protection order should be taken only in extremely urgent cases, where the child's safety is under immediate threat. The order allows the authority either to remove the child from home or other place of danger, or to retain the child in a safe place, such as a hospital, for a maximum of eight days, with a possible extension of up to seven days in exceptional circumstances.

Taken together, the major reforms initiated by the Children Act make a sharp break with past child-care law and practice. The Act seeks to avoid bringing children before the court; but if this has to happen, it ensures that the child's voice is heard and that parents have an opportunity to be represented at every stage. More importantly, it underpins the importance of the parents' point of view in planning for children in need with the local authority. Making this partnership work, often in the most difficult and stressful circumstances, is the most important challenge the Act presents.

Department of Health, *An Introduction to the Children Act*, London: HMSO, 1989.

**children's hearing**   a lay citizens' panel convened in Scotland to decide what should happen to a YOUNG OFFENDER.

Children's hearings were set up in Scotland in the 1960s at a time of concern over rising rates of juvenile crime, most of which involved trivial offences. Juvenile courts were by no means universal in Scotland as they were in England, and this gave the chance to try a progressive and innovative arrangement. The thinking behind their establishment was that young people who came before the courts were simply showing symptoms of neglect, ill-treatment or family problems. Law breaking was thus a facet of the more common problem of deprivation. The needs of juvenile petty criminals and deprived children were broadly the same; and the hearings were, and are, a way of working out non-punitive alternatives to what was at that time, and is now, available in the youth justice system. Children's hearing are concerned only with what response or plan there should be for the child or young person after they have admitted an offence or after the offence has been proven in the sheriff's court. The hearing applies to young offenders aged from 8 (the age of criminal responsibility in Scotland) to 16. It is usually attended by the child and their parents, the social worker and members of the panel. The hearing can impose a SUPERVISION ORDER, including a residential requirement, and retains continuing jurisdiction in the case, allowing it to review each case annually. It has no powers to impose a punitive order; for example, it cannot fine the young person or their parents, impose a custodial sentence or even send the case to the sheriff's court for sentence. (See also KILBRANDON REPORT, REPORTER.)

**children's home**   a residential unit providing 24-hour care for children and young people.

The Department of Health guidance on the CHILDREN ACT refers to several different types of children's home: (1) community homes maintained, controlled and assisted by the LOCAL AUTHORITY; (2) homes run by VOLUNTARY-SECTOR organizations; (3) registered children's homes run by private organizations; (4) independent schools accommodating between four and fifty boarding pupils and not approved under the Education Act 1981. The Children Act further defines a children's home as a place providing care and accommodation for more than three children.

Each home must register under the Act and issue a statement of purpose and function describing what the home sets out to do for children and the manner in which care is provided. There is a diversity of services offered by children's homes, including emergency PLACEMENT, short-term or respite placement, bridging placements (for example, between a child's own home and a foster placement), SECURE ACCOMMODATION and long-term placements that may incorporate some therapeutic provision. Increasingly, children's homes are aiming to meet specific needs of children at particular phases of their lives, such as preparing children for long-term foster care or helping young people to prepare for living on their own.

It is legally possible for some voluntary children's homes or registered children's homes to apply to the Secretary of State for Health for a certificate that allows them to provide a refuge for children who appear to be at risk of harm. This exempts the home from offences under the Children Act such as harbouring or abducting children. The significance of such status lies in the fact that it recognizes that some young people do require a legitimate breathing space where refuge workers can help them return to parents or local authority care or to sort out some other arrangements if appropriate.

**children's rights**   claims to treatment, benefits or protection made by, or on behalf of, children on the basis of law, code of practice or declaration.

Historically children had no RIGHTS separate from their parents or guardian. They were viewed as property of their father, who enjoyed complete freedom in how he raised them. Fathers always gained custody in courts when disputes arose. Increased concern over poverty and extreme examples of neglect in the late nineteenth century began to produce a change in the law to permit legal intervention in family life to prevent the worst excesses of cruelty. For the first time courts could award mothers custody of their children. The National Society for the Prevention of Cruelty to Children was established in 1882 – ironically, some years after the first animal protection legislation.

Children still lacked recognizable rights at this time, however, mainly because of the prevailing view of them as immature and self-centred and requiring strict discipline. To confer political and social rights on children was held to be unfair, burdening them with responsibilities they could not cope with. This view endured for many years, even among professionals working with children. During the last twenty years, however, a vigorous and expanding discussion of the nature of children's rights has had increasing impact on the law, on parents and on professionals working with children. The debate has changed with the realization that children have significant capacities for decision-making and self-expression, combined with arguments that children should be able to decide some things for themselves, or at least express their opinion on key decisions taken on their behalf.

There are three broad areas of children's rights: rights to protection and safeguarding their welfare; rights that give greater choice and autonomy; and procedural rights through which children have a say in decisions affecting them. The first area is now largely enshrined in the CHILDREN ACT. Measures developed in the wake of the CLEVELAND INQUIRY balance the need to protect the child with some of the problems found in child abuse investigations, when children were often kept away from home for a lengthy period and with no contact with their parents.

Considerable changes have also occurred recently in relation to children's rights to decide things for themselves. The House of Lords ruling in GILLICK v. *West Norfolk Health Authority* implied that the child's capacity to make decisions was not tied to a specific age, and that if the child sufficiently understood the issues they should be able to contribute to decisions affecting them, and in certain matters have their wishes prevail. The Lords ruling in the Gillick case directly influenced the drafting of the Children Act, in which, for example, children have the right to withhold their consent regarding medical or psychiatric examination or social work ASSESSMENT, even when they are being checked for possible signs of abuse. Children may begin certain legal proceedings on their own initiative, such as applying for a discharge of a CARE ORDER. They can also initiate complaints about services that they are receiving from the local authority, including the quality of residential care if they are in a children's home. Perhaps most importantly, if they are to be LOOKED AFTER by the local authority, that authority must find out the child's wishes and feelings about any possible PLACEMENT and give them due consideration.

Other positive rights for children have been established in relation to education and health. Children have the right to see their school records, the power to take action over discriminatory practices and policies, and the right to free medical and dental checks through schools of the local education authority. Schools may no longer use corporal punishment as a method of discipline.

Many children's rights activists believe that such rights as outlined above are too narrow and are only the start. There are still many areas of a child's life in which they think a child should have a far greater say, such as schooling. In particular, they consider that children of 12 and over have far greater powers of understanding and judgement for choosing courses of action than hitherto recognized. In addition, there are a number of positive rights, such as the right to health, to a safe environment, to adequate play areas and preschool services, and to a standard of living adequate for their physical, mental and social development, that have still to be won for children.

**children's rights officer**  an officer, appointed by the local authority, whose job is to ensure that children and young people with whom the authority is working are able to exercise their RIGHTS and seek redress if necessary.

Local authorities have laid increasing emphasis on the rights of children in their care, particularly after numerous recent examples of physical and mental cruelty at the hands of staff to children in residential care. The rights in question may relate to confidentiality of personal information, consultation in decisions affecting them, contributions to CASE REVIEWS and CASE CONFERENCES and access to information so that they can make informed choices about their future.

**child rescue philosophy**  a set of attitudes originating in the nineteenth century that emphasized the importance of removing neglected, abused or delinquent children from their families and immediate environment because these were regarded as a source of dangerous influence on the child's attitudes and behaviour.

The extreme form of the philosophy was embodied in the early twentieth-century policy followed by some national children's charities of having children in their care transported to Canada or Australia to start a new life. But long after this Draconian practice was ended, the belief persisted that home influences adversely affected the child in care. Such attitudes and practice were shared to some extent by local authority social workers who, intentionally or unintentionally, facilitated permanent separation of children in care from their families through long periods in care without a plan to reunite the family and infrequent child–parent visits. Parents had few effective powers in law to reverse local authority decisions. One of the principal aims of the CHILDREN ACT was to overcome the legacy of this perspective by requiring more frequent contact between children in care and their parents.

**child's special allowance**  a benefit paid in respect of children to a woman who cannot get WIDOWED MOTHERS ALLOWANCE because she divorced before her ex-husband died. It was abolished in 1987 and is paid only to women who qualified before that year.

**child support**  the policy of ensuring that both parents, in particular absent fathers, contribute to the financial maintenance of their child or children.

The Child Support Act 1991 introduced radical changes in the area of child maintenance following relationship breakdown. The Act introduced a standard formula to assess how much the 'absent' parent should pay and established a new executive agency of the Department of Social Security, the CHILD SUPPORT AGENCY, to assess, collect and enforce these payments. The assessment formula is relatively complex, since it seeks to balance the needs of the children and the parent with care against the needs of the absent parent and any second family. A large number of complaints by absent parents over the first few months resulted in some amendment to further protect their income. Even after these changes the formula has produced figures several times higher than those previously awarded by the courts.

The Child Support Agency (CSA) has to rely on the parent with care providing information to help trace the absent parent. To encourage this cooperation in cases where the parent with care is in receipt of benefit, a reduction lasting up to eighteen months may be made if she, or rarely he, does not provide appropriate help. The requirement to cooperate will be waived if there is a risk of the parent with care or any child suffering harm or undue distress. Although there is no widespread evidence of the use of the benefit deduction, it is feared that it might lead some mothers to cooperate inappropriately and put themselves into danger. When the Child Support Act came into effect, changes were made in the rules for means-tested benefits to enhance work incentives. However, for the majority of LONE-PARENT FAMILIES who remain on INCOME SUPPORT there is no gain in the new arrangements.

The CSA will eventually assess maintenance in nearly all cases where the courts would have been involved in marital proceedings. It started taking on work from April 1993. Initially it has handled all new cases where maintenance cannot be agreed that would previously have gone to court. It is also taking on and reassessing existing maintenance arrangements where the parent with care makes a new or renewal claim for income support, FAMILY CREDIT or DISABILITY WORKING ALLOWANCE. Between April 1993 and April 1996 the agency will take on and reassess existing maintenance arrangements where the parent with care already gets income support; and between April 1996 and April 1997 people with existing maintenance orders (on 5 April 1993) will be able to apply to the agency. Court orders and voluntary agreements need not be disturbed unless one party seeks to vary a court order or the parent with care claims income support, family credit or disability working allowance. Voluntary agreements are likely to be less stable in the future, because the services of the CSA will be relatively accessible. Although increased payments under the agency's assessment will sometimes be phased in over eighteen months, the assessment takes no other account of previous maintenance agreements. 'Clean break' agreements, where in the past (typically) the absent parent transferred equity in a home to the parent with care, would be ill-advised in the future, because the child support assessment will take no account of such transactions.

Although the British public largely accepts the idea of PARENTAL RESPONSIBILITY for child maintenance, the government's motivation for change is almost certainly to limit the level of social security expenditure. In 1991 there were about 1.3 million lone-parent families, with 2.2 million children, of which 70 per cent were in receipt of income support. In the 1990s the NEW RIGHT has depicted single parents as threatening family values and responsible for the rising crime rate while consuming a huge proportion of welfare resources. This thesis tends to ignore the facts that most single parents are separated and divorced and will eventually form new long-term relationships, and that most single parents do not stay on income support for more than a few years, because they return to work when their children are at school.

**Child Support Agency**   see CHILD SUPPORT.

**chill out**   the process whereby a DRUGS user 'cools off', sometimes in a special room, quietly allowing the effects of the drugs to wear off. The term is associated with 'raves' and with drugs such as ECSTASY, LSD and AMPHETAMINE.

**Chronically Sick and Disabled Persons Act 1970**   the first major piece of legislation giving comprehensive coverage to issues of DISABILITY and heralded as a 'charter for the disabled'. The Act was implemented in 1972 in Scotland and in 1978 in Northern Ireland.

With the exception of the Blind Person's Act 1920 and the Disabled Persons (Employment) Acts of 1944 and 1958, most help offered to disabled citizens before the 1970s was provided by legislation that had not been framed with disabled people in mind. The emphasis of the 1970 Act was on provision of welfare services to disabled people living in their own homes. This reflected the growing view that residential care was inappropriate in most cases. The Act therefore concerns itself very little with residential facilities. There are thirty substantive clauses, the most significant of which require local authorities to inform themselves of the numbers and needs of disabled people in their area and to inform such people of available services. The Act also lists services that should be provided for people whose needs have been assessed, and these services include practical help and adaptations within the home, such as radio, television or recreational facilities, meals at home or some other appropriate facility, and a telephone, together with any special equipment needed to use it; and, outside the home, recreational and educational facilities and practical help so that people with disabilities can make use of such facilities (for example, transport).

> Due to a tight parliamentary schedule and an impending general election, a number of compromises were made in the framing of the Act, leading to subsequent ambiguities of interpretation. The resourcing was similarly hindered by the ambiguous wording of the money order resolution. As a result, many local authorities failed to comply with the Act, which therefore failed to live up to its early promise. Despite its shortcomings, however, the Act is still regarded as a significant piece of legislation in that it attempts to address disability as an issue of human RIGHTS. It moved the focus from disability conceived as a tragedy and a problem for the individual (see MEDICAL MODEL) towards a view of disability where society has a collective responsibility to deal with the problems of integration of disabled people into the mainstream. The influence of the Act can be seen in later legislation, and many of the clauses excluded from the original Act were subsequently developed in the DISABLED PERSONS (SERVICES, CONSULTATION AND REPRESENTATION) ACT 1986, the CHILDREN ACT 1989 and the NATIONAL HEALTH SERVICE AND COMMUNITY CARE ACT 1990.

**citizen advocacy**   the process whereby one person acts as representative of, or advocate for, another, vulnerable person (often referred to as the 'partner') to safeguard their legal and human rights. Citizen advocates are usually VOLUNTEERS.

Citizen ADVOCACY schemes are usually run by a coordinator, who finds and matches advocates and partners. The aspiration is that the relationship between the two will be long-term. It may involve problem-solving aspects and social and emotional aspects. Citizen advocacy schemes are set up typically for people with DISABILITIES, generally for people with learning disability and, less frequently, for people with MENTAL HEALTH PROBLEMS.

K. Butler and A. Forrest, 'Power to the people', in L. Winn (ed.), *Citizen Advocacy for People with Disabilities*, London: Kings Fund Centre, 1990.

**citizenship**  legal, social and political status conferred by a state on individuals in which certain RIGHTS, duties and obligations are placed on both the state and the citizen.

In effect, citizenship is legal membership in a nation state. It emerged as a concept in the seventeenth and eighteenth centuries with the consolidation of strong centralized state authorities in Europe and in the wake of the English, French and American revolutions, which called into question the limits of that authority in relation to individuals. Citizenship was underpinned by the idea that states should be founded on the will of the people, involving a contract of mutual rights and responsibilities.

One of the most influential interpretations of citizenship has been that of T.H. Marshall, who broadly linked citizenship with the acquisition of rights over the last three or four hundred years: legal rights, such as the right to property and freedom from arbitrary arrest; political rights such as the right to assembly and to vote; and social rights such as health care and welfare benefits. In Marshall's view, citizenship in our own time has come to include economic welfare and security for each citizen as well as the right to live life according to the standards prevailing in the society.

A number of factors have undermined Marshall's progressive conception of citizenship. Much of it was based on the presumed permanence of a thriving welfare state providing a range of entitlements and a safety net for the poorest. Financial limits placed on welfare spending and the widespread retrenchment of the welfare state have called into question the inevitability of this conception of citizenship. The political philosophy of the NEW RIGHT, which emphasizes responsibilities rather than rights and believes in the MARKET as a way of allocating services, has also introduced new elements into discussions of citizenship. Additionally, both the feminist and ecology movements imply that certain moral duties for the individual should be balanced against rights. Hence citizenship is not now defined purely in terms of rights but includes a greater elaboration of duties.

M. Roche, *Rethinking Citizenship: Welfare, Ideology and Change in Modern Society*, Cambridge: Polity Press, 1992.

**civil proceedings**  court proceedings that do not involve criminal matters.

The HIGH COURT deals with many aspects of civil law, but the civil proceedings most relevant to social workers and probation officers are those relating to FAMILY PROCEEDINGS under the CHILDREN ACT and those relating to DOMESTIC VIOLENCE. Most civil proceedings start in a magistrates' court or county court; they may be referred to the High Court or the Court of Appeal

(Civil Division) on appeal. (See also FAMILY COURT WELFARE SERVICE, WELFARE REPORT.)

**classical conditioning** the process of transferring the automatic response of the nervous system to one stimulus to a different stimulus, by repeated associations.

The process of classical conditioning involves a basic technique for adapting reflexes, which are part of the nervous system. For example, a squirt of lemon juice in the mouth will stimulate salivation; if the lemon juice is squirted into a person's mouth on a number of occasions at the same time as a bell is sounded, salivation will occur at the sound of the bell alone. Classical conditioning describes this process as the pairing of an unconditioned stimulus (lemon juice) with a neutral stimulus (the bell) to produce a conditioned response (salivation). Salivation at the lemon juice alone would be an unconditioned response. The discovery and terminology of classical conditioning are credited to the Russian psychologist Ivan Pavlov. The technique is used in BEHAVIOUR MODIFICATION.

**Cleveland Inquiry** the judicial inquiry set up by the government to examine how certain suspected cases of child SEXUAL ABUSE were dealt with in Cleveland in 1987. The inquiry was headed by Lord Justice Butler-Sloss, whose 1988 report was praised for its analysis, balance and advocacy of reforms.

Between February and July 1987, 121 children were diagnosed by two consultant paediatricians in Cleveland as having been sexually abused. The paediatricians relied heavily on a method of diagnosis called ANAL DILATATION. The majority of the children were compulsorily removed from home or kept in hospital under court orders. The crisis became heated and aroused national debate when parents began to complain vigorously about the allegations of abuse levelled at them and about the way they and their children were treated: removal of children without prior notice, restrictions on their visiting the children, lack of consultation and information, and the impossibility of appeal. The involvement of the local Member of Parliament on the parents' side highlighted a breakdown in confidence in the local social services department. The report principally recommended that in future cases of suspected abuse the child should not be subjected to repeated medical examinations, and that interviews with children should not use probing or confrontational methods; the Cleveland children investigated had been subject to both. Butler-Sloss considered the examinations and interviews with the children a form of abuse itself and reminded practitioners that 'the child is a person and not an object of concern'.

> Lord Justice Butler-Sloss, *Report of the Inquiry into Child Abuse in Cleveland*, London: HMSO, 1988.

**client** a term used to designate a person receiving a social service.

The word 'client' was originally intended to convey an emphasis on the quality of relationship between the individual recipient of a service and their social worker, home carer, occupational therapist or other social services professional. It was also intended to avoid any connotation of a patient in need of treatment. The term applied equally to those who sought out and those who were compelled by law to submit to a service. Thus probationers, adolescents on supervision order and parents whose children were compulsorily removed could all be referred to as clients, as could an older person requiring short-term care.

From the beginning, the word 'client' acquired a meaning opposite to the way other professions used it, such as in law or architecture, where the relationship with the client is based on a contractual obligation to provide specialist service for a fee. In social work the relationship was intended to be based on empathy, warmth and understanding freely given on the part of the social worker. Problems in using the term gradually multiplied, however. In the 1970s, when SYSTEMS theory first made an impact on social work thinking, the client could be seen as more than one person. The first question for a practitioner to ask was, who is the client? Often it became clear that more than one client was involved in a given case, each with individual, even competing, objectives. It made more sense to speak of the 'client system' – the person, family, group, organization or community that engaged the services of the worker and was the presumed beneficiary of the services. Also at that time, the first studies were published of clients' views on the quality of services; it was a measure of how little the client actually counted in social work thinking that this had not been done before. From these studies the general conclusion emerged that while clients valued the quality of relationship they also wanted help with practical and material problems. Modest as these conclusions seem now, they were a challenge to the long-held view that the helping relationship itself was of primary importance and that environmental problems were secondary.

RADICAL SOCIAL WORK also began to highlight the class element common to social services clients and that economic disadvantage played a powerful role in shaping their 'problems'. The picture of the client that emerged was of a powerless, unwilling, but dependent recipient shaped by social and economic forces beyond their control. The word in its original meaning hardly did justice to the real nature of the relationship between the social services professional and the receiver of a service. However, the term continued in use, if only for the practical reason that alternatives were unsatisfactory. The BARCLAY REPORT (1982) decided on 'client' and specifically rejected the alternative term 'service user' because it did not carry the notion that social work is a personal service to meet individual needs, still less that some who receive services are subject to measures of control. The universal use of the term has come under fresh pressures from the perspectives of PARTNERSHIP and EMPOWERMENT theory, which have served notice that people receiving services will no longer be passive recipients but are joint participants in arranging those services. The word 'user' has been adopted primarily by ADVOCACY and SELF-HELP groups, particularly in the fields of mental health, disability, learning disability and child-care, in their message that there is a chasm between the quality of services offered and what people expect of those services. The pressure is having effect, and 'user' is increasingly being taken up by professionals inside the service.

Something of a division of terms has emerged. 'Service user' describes those who are voluntarily in touch with services, and 'client' those who under law are compelled to receive a service. A disabled person asking for a home care service is a user; the parents of a child taken into compulsory care are a client. Thus 'client' has come full circle; originally coined to destigmatize, it is now increasingly linked to those who have little choice but to be the target of intervention.

S. Croft and P. Beresford, *Citizen Involvement: A Practical Guide for Change*, Basingstoke: Macmillan, 1993.

**client system**    the immediate social and family SYSTEM of which the CLIENT is part.

Because all parts of the client system are interrelated, there may be more than one person asking to be considered as a client within that system. The intention of analysing a client system is to see how the relationships inside it are shaped by other parts of that system. A client's 'problems' may arise as a result of the way the system functions as a whole, rather than be the result of one person's behaviour. This can be particularly true in families, and it forms the basis of FAMILY THERAPY. The social worker may intervene within the system to improve aspects of support for the client or to try to change the way the system responds to the client. In the terminology of the 'unitary method', if the social worker intervenes within the client system it also becomes the TARGET SYSTEM.

**closed-end question**    a question used in an INTERVIEW framed in such a way as to require a specific answer. Such a question does not encourage the client to respond more fully with their own opinions, information or feelings.

Principles of good practice suggest that closed-end questions are used only occasionally, especially when interviewing a child who may have been abused.

**Clyde Report**    the report of the inquiry conducted by James Clyde into the removal of a number of children from their families on Orkney in February 1991.

Although the children concerned were removed by teams of social workers and police, both the manner of their removal, which occurred during 'DAWN RAIDS', and the nature of the allegations against the parents of the children – namely, that they were engaged in ORGANIZED SEXUAL ABUSE – caused fierce national controversy. The Clyde Report made nearly 200 recommendations, many of which focused on how child protection orders should be enforced more sensitively and with greater safeguards for the families concerned.

J. Clyde, *The Report of the Inquiry into the Removal of Children from Orkney in February 1991*, Edinburgh: HMSO, 1992.

**cocaine (cocaine hydrochloride)**    a stimulant DRUG extracted from the leaves of the South American coca bush and taken in the form of a crystalline white powder. Cocaine is invariably of uncertain purity, due to being mixed with other substances, and is usually sniffed or injected.

Also known as 'coke', 'snow' and 'charlie', cocaine is a class A drug under the MISUSE OF DRUGS ACT 1971, with penalties for production, possession and supply ranging from a fine to life imprisonment. When taken, its effects are almost immediate, especially with INJECTING. It can be extremely addictive psychologically, with repeated doses needed to maintain the 'high' effect. Short-term effects include euphoria and excitability, increased heart and pulse rate, decreased appetite, sweating and a dry mouth. Regular users may experience all these effects together with insomnia, diarrhoea, exhaustion and in some cases extreme ANXIETY leading to PARANOIA and PSYCHOSIS.

**code of ethics**   see ETHICAL CODE.

**cognitive-behavioural therapy**   a form of therapy that aims to change the way people think about themselves and their environment.

The approach, which grew out of BEHAVIOUR THERAPY, stresses that thought patterns are crucial to the way a person views their own behaviour. Changing such thought patterns is important to the resolution of problems such as DEPRESSION. In the main, the therapy aims to replace long-entrenched thoughts with a more positive appraisal of given situations, using techniques such as keeping a record of thoughts and learning to interrupt certain lines of thinking that reinforce depression. Other techniques concentrate on learning ANGER MANAGEMENT, for example in the case of parents of young children with behavioural difficulties. The approach marked a break with behaviour therapy which placed relatively little importance on the mind as a source of change, and it has had some success in treating people with emotional disorders such as depression.

M. Scott, *A Cognitive Behavioural Approach to Clients' Problems*, London: Tavistock, 1989.

**cohabitation**   two adults living together in the same domestic unit. The couple may be in a heterosexual or a homosexual relationship.

Cohabitation is for many heterosexual couples a stage before marriage; in 1988, 48 per cent of women marrying for the first time had lived with their husband before marrying. A minority of couples cohabit without subsequently ratifying the relationship legally. Such long-term cohabitation is more frequent among the poorest sections of the population. In some important areas cohabiting couples have different rights from those of married couples – for example, in relation to tenancies, INJUNCTIONS and welfare benefits. Whether someone is cohabiting or not is a key issue in relation to the calculation of welfare benefits, and social workers and advice workers often become embroiled in such disputes. Many agencies too still seem unable to deal with unmarried parents with different names; schools, for example, sometimes deal insensitively with unmarried parents.

**cold turkey**   the abrupt cessation of use of a DRUG by a regular user and the suffering of WITHDRAWAL symptoms without the use of another substance to dull the pain.

**cold weather payments**   payments from the regulated SOCIAL FUND to cover extra domestic heating costs during exceptionally cold weather.

Cold weather payments can be made to a person receiving INCOME SUPPORT that includes any pensioner's premium, the disability premium, the severe disability premium or the disabled child premium, or an amount for a child aged under 5. Payment will be made for any period of seven consecutive days when the average of the mean daily temperature is freezing or below. A cold weather payment should be paid automatically when temperature conditions dictate. It is worth £6 for a week (1994/5).

**combination order**   a new sentence introduced by the CRIMINAL JUSTICE ACT 1991, whereby courts may combine a period of community service, between 40 and 100 hours, with a period of supervision, between twelve months and three years.

**commissioner**   see PURCHASER.

**Commission for Racial Equality**   the body established by the RACE RELATIONS ACT 1976 with primary responsibility for the elimination of racial DISCRIMINATION, the promotion of 'equality of opportunity and good relations between people of different racial groups' and keeping the workings of the 1976 Act under review.

The CRE has the power to carry out formal investigations into any circumstances covered by the Act where racial discrimination is suspected. Such investigations can require organizations to produce information. If the CRE decides that discrimination has occurred it can produce reports and make recommendations. The major mechanism for this process is the issuing of 'non-discrimination notices', which spell out in what manner the person or organization has contravened the law and gives instruction about the changes required to bring any policy or practice into line with legal requirements. Other major areas of work for the CRE include the publication of investigations and suggestions for good practice, as well as much advice and counselling to individuals. The CRE has attracted considerable criticism, especially on the part of radical blacks who maintain that the British approach to eliminating racial discrimination lacks vigour and commitment. Its defenders hold that the CRE is constrained by being part of the government and by the limited powers conferred upon it by the 1976 Act. Researches, however, are consistent in their findings that little progress has been made in the last two decades in eliminating racial discrimination in Britain.

**communication**   the giving or exchange of INFORMATION through a variety of media.

In social work and social welfare agencies, effective communication is important in several contexts. First, all organizations should provide quality information about services and processes in relation to their own functions. Second, workers need to be aware of language and to avoid unnecessarily obscure technical or professional terms (jargon). Third, particular groups have their own communication needs: for example, BLIND people, DEAF people, members of ethnic minorities whose first language is not English, and people with severe DISABILITIES whose communication skills are affected. Fourth, agencies working together need to develop effective channels for communication to enhance collaboration. Fifth, LISTENING skills are an important part of interpersonal communication. (See also BRAILLE, BRITISH SIGN LANGUAGE, LOW-VISION AIDS, MOON.)

**community**  a term used by sociologists to describe social relationships within groups or territorial boundaries.

Many writers in the social sciences have sought to analyse the concept of community, offering numerous definitions. It has been suggested that attempts to make sense of the concept can be broadly grouped into three sets of meanings; community as geographical locality; community as a collection of relationships and interrelationships; and community describing particular qualities to relationships. Among social welfare workers the tendency is to use the term in all three senses simultaneously, as when community or social workers speak of developing community resources, for example. Such statements are based upon a contentious belief that to have community is better than not to have it. Rural communities in this context are thought to be more supportive than urban communities, where relationships are seen as more contractual and anonymous. In sum, there is prescription in the use of the term as well as description. Other writers have thought of community in a negative way as denoting the parochial and a set of confining and constraining relationships. Thus there is ambiguity in the values apparently underpinning the idea of COMMUNITY CARE, for example; the idea suggests both responsibility for primary caring relationships and the placing of intolerable burdens on families and especially women as principal carers.

P. Worsley, *New Introductory Sociology*, London: Penguin, 3rd edn, 1992.

**community care**  the provision of care services and social support for people living in the COMMUNITY, usually their own home.

The term 'community care' is used to describe a range of care services provided for people in NEED who continue to live in the community. Usually this means that the person remains in their own home, but sometimes they live in a house or flat shared by others who have similar needs. The objective of providing such services is to enable a person to continue to live in familiar surroundings rather than in an institution such as a hospital or residential home. The services most commonly associated with community care are personalized services such as meals on wheels and assistance with bathing, but they also include those provided nearby and outside the home, such as at DAY CARE centres. Other services linked to community care are those that enable a person to develop social, leisure or educational interest. Still other services focus on the needs of CARERS, such as arranging for the cared-for person to spend a few days in RESIDENTIAL CARE so that the carer has time to themselves. The term 'community care' was first used in the 1960s to describe the policy of relocating people from psychiatric hospitals into less institutionalized surroundings; it is now used in relation to all adult clients of social services, such as people with learning disabilities and older people. In this sense the term is now used very loosely to describe any policy or service designed to help people stay out of institutional care, including residential homes and hospitals. (See also CARE MANAGEMENT, DOMICILIARY SERVICES, NATIONAL HEALTH SERVICE AND COMMUNITY CARE ACT.)

Audit Commission, *The Community Revolution: Personal Services and Community Care*, London: HMSO, 1992.

**community care grant**   a payment (not a loan) from the SOCIAL FUND that a person receiving INCOME SUPPORT can apply for to help with a one-off expense.

The law outlines five circumstances where payment of a community care grant may be made, subject to the Social Fund's local budget and stated priorities: to help a person re-establish themselves in the community following a stay in institutional or residential care; to help a person remain in the community rather than enter institutional or residential care; to ease exceptional pressure on a person or their family; to allow a person to care for a prisoner or young offender on home leave; to pay travelling expenses in specified circumstances, including visits to seriously ill relatives and attendance at funerals, and to ease domestic crises. These circumstances have the force of law. Guidance provided in the *Social Fund Guide*, although not legally binding on the Social Fund officer, lists 'priority groups' and 'priority items', concentrating on people deemed vulnerable by age or ill-health; however, 'absence of guidance applying to a particular circumstance, item or service does not mean that help should be refused'. A community care grant will be reduced by the value of any capital over £500 (£1,000 if aged 60 or over) that the applicant has. The majority of payments are made to young families with children for basic household items.

**community care plans**   three-year plans produced by SOCIAL SERVICES DEPARTMENTS, covering community care provision in their area.

The NATIONAL HEALTH SERVICE AND COMMUNITY CARE ACT established the requirement for local authorities to produce community care plans. The aim, according to the 1989 white paper *Caring for People*, was to increase public accountability by requiring local authorities to publish their proposals for future provision. These plans should also involve other core agencies, including health authorities, housing authorities, and the voluntary and private sectors. The aim is to ensure that plans made by the various agencies involved in community care do not conflict with each other. According to the government, plans should cover a three-year period and include issues such as the development of the local authority's own services, what services are to be purchased from the private and voluntary sectors, proposals for individual case management and the development of complaints procedures. In addition, plans are published, to ensure improvements in the public accountability of local authority services, and it is emphasized that they should be written in an accessible manner.

The approach recommended by the 1989 white paper in the development of community care plans is that they cover such issues as: assessment of NEED in the local authority population; strategic objectives for the service; the development of information systems; systems for purchasing services; plans for improvements in domiciliary care; and coordination with other agencies. The DEPARTMENT OF HEALTH has an important role to play in the planning process in that all community care plans require its approval to establish that they are in line with national government policy. Critics have therefore contended that, while there is an emphasis on decentralizing services to ensure flexibility and tailor services to individual needs, in reality there is a much greater degree of centralization involved through a more interventionist DoH and a more powerful Social Services Inspectorate.

**community care worker** a person in a social services department who undertakes relatively simple ASSESSMENTS of adults, such as frail older people or people with a learning disability, who may require services under the NATIONAL HEALTH SERVICE AND COMMUNITY CARE ACT.

The community care worker is usually a member of a FIELDWORK team, does not hold a social work qualification and will have some limited authority to negotiate and purchase services for a client, such as day care, up to a preset limit.

**community development projects** a series of experimental projects set up by the Home Office in 1969 in an attempt to tackle multiple deprivation in both inner-city areas and areas of rural poverty.

Community development projects (CDPs) involved the use of some additional resources to help improve infrastructure – for example, modernizing housing stock, improving pupil–teacher ratios in primary schools, and providing resource centres to assist people in relation to welfare benefits advice and job creation. However, the central focus was an attempt to mobilize communities to solve their own problems through community action (see COMMUNITY WORK) and SELF-HELP. The researchers evaluating the CDPs found virtues in locally based initiatives but considered that improvements to communities and neighbourhoods would always be seriously constrained by wider economic and political forces, such as local industrial decline, rising unemployment or a decrease in the value of state benefits. The final reports were critical of government policies that sought to tackle poverty solely through local activity. Subsequently, sociologists and others have criticized the lack of attention given to the role of women in community initiatives and, in the case of a few projects, the influence of RACISM on community relations. The Home Office in effect abandoned this approach to the alleviation of poverty in the mid-1970s.

**community drug team** a MULTIDISCIPLINARY team situated in the COMMUNITY, away from a hospital setting, and dealing with any aspect of illegal DRUGS – sometimes also with solvents and minor tranquillizers – ranging from the giving of advice and treatment to the training of professionals.

Community drug teams (CDTs) serve a designated area, usually corresponding to the boundaries of the health district. They sprang up in the 1970s and grew in number from 20 in 1982 to 287 in 1992. Teams may comprise both paid professional members of staff as well as VOLUNTEERS, their size usually depending on the actual or perceived extent of drug use and misuse in the district. A common mix for CDTs is a combination of general medical practitioner or consultant, one or more community psychiatric nurses, secretary, administrator, OUTREACH worker, social worker or probation office, youth worker and volunteers (often ex-users). Because of the mix in professionals, such teams are referred to as multidisciplinary.

Depending on the size of the team, roles often overlap. A social worker would be expected to take the lead in issues involving child-care issues, the NATIONAL HEALTH SERVICE AND COMMUNITY CARE ACT and welfare/housing benefits, as well as having a caseload of their own. As the major objective is to serve a designated community, home visits are offered, and outreach sessions may be held in other parts of the district.

**community health councils**   locally nominated bodies representing the views of the local community on health service issues.

Established in 1974 with the restructuring of the NATIONAL HEALTH SERVICE following the NHS Act 1973, there are approximately 200 community health councils in England and Wales, normally one for each district health authority. In Scotland their role is taken by local health councils. Members of the community health councils are from the LOCAL AUTHORITY, both councillors and officers, representatives from voluntary organizations and nominees from the regional health authority. While they provide a forum for the expression of community views, their role is limited, more by the fact that their recommendations do not have to be implemented than by the fact of their members being nominees rather than directly elected. However, they are an important source of information and comment to health service administrators and have proved relatively influential, given the constraints noted above.

**community psychiatric nurse (CPN)**   a person employed by the NATIONAL HEALTH SERVICE to work with people with MENTAL HEALTH PROBLEMS in the COMMUNITY.

Community psychiatric nurses have traditionally worked with any person in the community referred by the psychiatric services. In practice, this can include people attending a psychiatric hospital or a psychiatric wing of a general hospital as outpatients, people attending community mental health facilities, or people in their own home. More recent developments have included a limited number of attachments to general practitioners' surgeries. The work of CPNs can be varied, ranging from administering medication to long-term mentally ill people to counselling around problems of living. With people suffering neuroses, CPNs are often involved in conducting anxiety- and stress-management groups; in the case of people with long-term psychoses, domiciliary visits for monitoring and assessment purposes constitute a major role. Joint work with social workers is increasingly common, both in community mental health teams and in joint care planning for psychiatric patients who are to be discharged into the community and have problems of accommodation, income or social supports.

**community sentence**   a collective term introduced by the CRIMINAL JUSTICE ACT 1991 to describe the tier of sentences between financial penalties and CUSTODIAL SENTENCES. (The fourth and lowest tier of sentences is that of absolute and conditional DISCHARGES.)

Prior to the Criminal Justice Act, community sentences were known as 'alternatives to custody'. The change of terminology implies a change of philosophy, removing prison from its central position in sentencing policy. A community sentence is defined as 'a restriction on liberty that consists of one or more community orders'. The following community orders are available: ATTENDANCE CENTRE ORDER, COMBINATION ORDER, COMMUNITY SERVICE ORDER, CURFEW ORDER, PROBATION ORDER, SUPERVISION ORDER. Some community orders require the consent of the offender (probation, comm-unity service, combination and curfew). The court obtains this information through a PRE-SENTENCE REPORT written by a probation officer. If an offender fails to meet the requirements of a community sentence, they will be subjected to BREACH PROCEEDINGS, which will involve them in being returned to court for a review and possible change of sentence (including imprisonment).

> Courts may impose a community sentence if they believe that the offences before them are 'serious enough' to warrant it. The concept of 'seriousness' has proved difficult to define and interpret; it may best be described as an equation that balances 'aggravating' and 'mitigating' factors relating to the offence. For example, the seriousness of an offence of theft may be aggravated if it constituted a breach of trust, involved a large sum or was theft from a vulnerable (such as an elderly) victim. The seriousness may be mitigated if the theft involved a small sum, had little impact on the victim or was the result of desperation. In addition to factors relating directly to the offence, the court may take account of other mitigating factors such as previous good character, addictions, age, health, reparation, and signs of reform or settling down. A court's choice of community sentence will depend on its suitability for the offender and on the commensurability of the restriction of liberty with the seriousness of the offence.
>
> D. Gilyeat, *A Companion Guide to Offence Seriousness*, Ilkley: Owen Wells, 1993.

**community service order**  a COMMUNITY SENTENCE under the CRIMINAL JUSTICE ACT 1991 under which an offender aged 16 or over is required to do unpaid supervised work for between 40 and 240 hours. The order should usually be completed within twelve months.

A community service order may be combined with other sentences; when combined with a PROBATION ORDER it is known as a COMBINATION ORDER. The community service order was introduced as a sentencing option in the Criminal Justice Act 1972. It was originally intended as a direct alternative to custody, in an attempt to relieve prison overcrowding, but it soon became a sentence in its own right in practice. It has proved popular with courts, and in 1991 a total of 29,500 orders were made (compared with 34,300 probation orders). Community service orders are administered and supervised by the PROBATION SERVICE and governed by NATIONAL STANDARDS. Offenders work on projects, individually or in groups, ranging from manual work such as painting and decorating to work with a higher 'social' content, such as assisting in the care of children or elderly people. The work has to be carried out to a satisfactory standard, and a strict check is kept on attendance and time-keeping. If an offender fails to meet the requirements, they are subjected to BREACH PROCEEDINGS, which involve being returned to court for a review and possible change of sentence (including imprisonment).

As a sentence, the community service order has several clear advantages in the eyes of both the offender and the court. Courts view it as a cost-effective, punitive sentence with a deterrent effect but also as symbolizing reparation and, by instilling a work discipline, as involving rehabilitative effects (see PRINCIPLES OF SENTENCING). From the offender's viewpoint, it is less damaging and disruptive than prison, enabling the offender to 'make amends' and increasing self-esteem through the achievement of 'a job well done'. However, critics of such orders express concern that, rather than receiving the help they need, offenders, who may be among the most disadvantaged people in society, are required to make additional sacrifices by working for nothing. They argue that such work reinforces the prejudices of politicians and sentencers who believe that criminals should be sentenced to 'hard labour' of the 'rock-breaking' kind for its own sake, regardless of any benefits to the offender. There is also concern that community service is undertaken overwhelmingly by male offenders and that it has an image of machismo which makes it appear unsuitable for female offenders. Steps are being taken within the probation service to remedy this, including employing more female project supervisors, providing child-care facilities and reimbursing child-minding fees. Some adverse media publicity has invoked criticism of community service schemes for allowing convicted criminals to work for members of the public, some of whom (such as children and elderly people) may be vulnerable. Yet recent research indicates that there is a high level of satisfaction among recipients of community service, many of whom would be willing to make use of the service again.

G. McIvor, 'Community service by offenders: how much does the community benefit?', *Research on Social Work Practice*, vol. 3, no. 4, 1993, pp. 385–403.

**community social work**  an approach to social work that seeks to promote or maintain COMMUNITY-based supports for people already providing care to CLIENTS.

The concept was first put forward in the BARCLAY REPORT, which recognized that the bulk of care for clients in Britain is provided by individual people, most often family members, who have their own resources and sources of support. Community social work's objective was to ensure that these informal sources of support were in good shape and where a client did not have a network of supports or resources to call upon to help develop one. As outlined in the Barclay Report, community social work begins with the problem affecting an individual or group and then seeks to support and promote the local networks of formal and informal relationships to help resolve those problems. Its style of working was decentralized and local, relying on people's own initiatives and capacities to do what in an earlier time social work itself would have tried to do (but less satisfactorily) with clients. Community social work required social workers to see their clients not just as family members but as part of a wider social network and to focus upon the links that exist in practice or could potentially be developed for that client. These links were to be based on family networks, neighbourhood contacts and interests shared between people, such as having a common problem to deal with. While community social work achieved only limited formal recognition, most notably within PATCH teams, it did have influence in the sense that social workers now pay considerably more attention to the support systems around families, carers and clients. The planned involvement of family members in care and in coordinating neighbours and volunteers to provide care, buttressed by certain services such as DAY CARE and short-term RESIDENTIAL CARE, reflects something of what community social work was intended to achieve.

Barclay Committee, *Social Workers: Their Role and Tasks*, London: Bedford Square Press, 1982.

**community work** a wide-ranging set of practices that seek to improve people's quality of life in particular geographical localities or neighbourhoods.

Some people see COMMUNITY work as an alternative to social work, with attempts to help individuals and families with problems focused on work with them and the communities of which they are a part. Experiments in the 1970s and 1980s in Britain witnessed attempts to solve, through collective work, individual and family problems that had hitherto received individual attention. Instead of being treated as separate cases, families were invited to join community groups concerned with problems commonly experienced in the locality. Attempts were also made to improve the quality of life by upgrading housing stock and increasing income with benefit take-up campaigns, and through energy conservation programmes and community SELF-HELP activity. Although such experiments demonstrated that individual and family problems recede with collective approaches to problem-solving, this strategy is no longer encouraged, because current dominant ideology tends to locate problems within families themselves. Other forms of community work are perceived as complementary to the activity of social work. Thus work with offenders in the community and community groups to help with the development of parenting skills or with particular problems or activities – such as carers' support groups and playgroups – can be seen as enhancing the quality of life. Many such activities may be run or supported by social workers.

Terms such as 'community development' and 'community action' suggest additional dimensions to the community work role. The former has roots in a movement to encourage better living standards in colonial societies, especially after the Second World War, when literacy programmes and schemes to broadly promote citizenship were prominent. Since then 'community development' has been loosely applied to activities promoting the generation of community contacts where there are none or where they are poorly developed, such as in new towns or in areas where people do not linger (hard-to-let estates, for example). The term 'community action' has been used rather more specifically to describe attempts to secure additional resources for a locality, to achieve a measure of political participation for marginalized groups or perhaps to defeat some proposal thought to be against the interests of those living within the locality. Hence groups have campaigned to have high-rise blocks of flats demolished because they were damp, expensive to heat and inappropriate for young families. Others – various ethnic groups, for example – have sought to secure regular consultative meetings with politicians who in their view have not responded to their needs. Yet others have worked collectively to prevent, say, the building of a highway through the neighbourhood. The achievement of change or, paradoxically, its prevention are usually the focus of community action.

The central practice issue in relation to community work concerns power in many contexts. Community needs or problems have to be determined, and a key issue is, by whom? Are they to be shaped by professionals, or should the community itself determine what is most important? There are clearly degrees of control in relation to levels of participation by communities. Public meetings about a community concern can be used to help communities shape their demands and devise potential solutions; they can also be used to control or divert a community through the pretence of consultation without the intention of listening. Similarly, some experiments have denied a role for professionals in any form. For example, community or residents' associations have simply been given sums of money, usually by local government, to promote community activity. What the money is used for is seen as the concern of the community, and so long as it is not used inappropriately such community groups are left to their own devices. Other possibilities include the community worker as catalyst. In these circumstances community workers initiate activity through, perhaps, the arrangements of public meetings. Their concern might then be to help shape initial direction for community activity in a disinterested way and then to act purely as adviser as required by the community or to disengage entirely from subsequent activity. There have been many instances, however, where those paying for community work services, often the local authority, become dissatisfied with the outcomes of such services. Much community action, for example, can be critical of local authorities and their policies which can present the community worker with conflicts that are not easily resolved. Such conflicts of interest can arise in both the statutory and voluntary sectors if the funding originates in local or central government.

A. Twelvetrees, *Community Work*, Basingstoke: Macmillan, 1987.

**compensation payments**   a semi-formal scheme of the DEPARTMENT OF SOCIAL SECURITY for dealing with compensation for delays in benefit payments. Compensation is made if payment of a benefit claim is delayed by six months or more and the benefit owed was at least £50.

**complaint and complaints procedure**   a grievance or accusation, and a formal mechanism for hearing the complaint and making recommendations.

Both the CHILDREN ACT (section 26) and the NATIONAL HEALTH SERVICE AND COMMUNITY CARE ACT (chapter 6 of the policy guidance on COMMUNITY CARE) require LOCAL AUTHORITIES to establish complaints procedures. Complaints are construed widely to include comments on the way a particular case is being handled, rather than simply a negative view of events. With adult services, complainants may include users and their carers and representatives; for children's services, complainants can include the child or their parent, a person who has PARENTAL RESPONSIBILITY for a child, a foster parent or, finally, any person considered by the local authority to have a legitimate interest in the welfare of the child.

The policy guidelines recommend that a senior officer in any SOCIAL SERVICES DEPARTMENT be given overall responsibility for the complaints procedure. All staff, however, need to be committed to the policy in order to deal with complaints effectively at an early stage or to help complainants shape up a formal complaint if the difficulty cannot be resolved informally. Leaflets in various media need to be devised (for example, for the BLIND, for members of ethnic minorities and for children), and careful thought needs to be given to distribution. Procedures with clear timescales must be established, and the whole operation must be closely monitored, with annual reporting of the nature of the complaints and the quality of the organization's response to them. It is also recommended that all authorities have a designated complaints officer and some independent member on the complaints committee. Random inspections of services and the use of lay visitors can help ensure that staff operate the scheme positively. Any formal complaint should receive a written answer within a few weeks, including a decision about the validity of the complaint and, if justified, any remedial or compensatory action proposed. Another possible channel for complaints is to use the Parliamentary Commissioner (Ombudsman), who has responsibility for investigation of any alleged maladministration on the part of a local or POLICE authority. The police also have their own internal mechanisms for dealing with complaints by the public, including by people in custody.

Department of Health, Right to Complain: Practice Guidance on Complaints Procedures in Social Service Departments, London: HMSO, 1991.

**compulsory competitive tendering**  the statutory requirement for LOCAL AUTHORITIES to put specified services out to tender to open up competition with the private sector.

Competitive tendering is not a new phenomenon for local authorities. In areas of major capital expenditure, such as road maintenance and school building, local authorities have mainly used the private sector in a competitive bidding system. However, in the 1980s a number of Conservative local authorities expanded the use of competitive tendering to areas that more traditionally had been directly provided by the authorities themselves, notably refuse collection, street cleansing and cleaning in schools. The Local Government Planning and Land Act 1980 had introduced the requirement that direct labour organizations operate on a more competitive basis and that they had to have a rate of return of 5 per cent on overall operating costs. By the mid-1980s competitive tendering in these areas had become an important source of financial saving and a challenge to public-sector trade unions in a number of authorities. However, it has been argued that there were also a number of problems encountered in areas such as quality of services provided and conditions of employment.

The approach was identified as a way of introducing a greater level of competitive behaviour in local authorities and opening up services to private-sector activity. Lobbying from various think-tanks, such as the Adam Smith Institute, and from commercial interests reinforced the government's support for increased competitive tendering. Consequently, after the 1987 general election the government expanded the area of services subject to competitive tendering and enforced this through the Local Government Act 1989. This legislation requires local authorities to tender for services, including cleaning, catering, refuse collection and the management of leisure facilities. More recent proposals extend competitive tendering to white-collar jobs within local authorities, including some legal services and personnel matters, notably recruitment of some staff. At present there are no plans for such legislation to cover social services, although the financial incentives to utilize the private and voluntary sectors for services may have a similar impact.

K. Ascher, *The Politics of Privatization*, Basingstoke: Macmillan, 1987.

**conciliation**   see FAMILY MEDIATION.

**concurrent jurisdiction**   the competence of two or more courts at different levels of the court system to hear the same case.

The concept of concurrent jurisdiction is relevant to proceedings involving children under the CHILDREN ACT whereby an application for a care order may be sought from either a FAMILY PROCEEDINGS COURT, where proceedings will be heard by MAGISTRATES, or a county court, where the proceedings will be heard by a judge. The decision as to which court a particular case should go is generally taken by the clerk to the family proceedings court; most cases will start there. More complex cases will go to the county court.

**conditional response**   now usually referred to as 'conditioned response'. See CLASSICAL CONDITIONING, OPERANT CONDITIONING.

**conditioning**   any form of learning about the dependence of one event on the occurrence of another. See CLASSICAL CONDITIONING.

**conduct disorders**   a term used in behavioural PSYCHOLOGY to refer to a broad range of serious and persistent antisocial behaviours in children that result in significant impairment of a child's everyday functioning to the point that the behaviours are considered unmanageable by parents, care-givers, teachers or others in the child's life.

Estimates vary as to the numbers of children who show conduct disorders – which include hitting, setting fires, stealing, truancy and running away – and range from 4 per cent to 10 per cent of the child population. But among those children referred to clinical services for help, the proportion may be as high as 50 per cent. There is widespread agreement that conduct disorders are becoming more prevalent and are creating a need for specialist services in education, clinical psychology and social services that far exceeds available staff and resources.

Conduct disorders in children have proven difficult to change, and studies of some children have shown a link with problems in later life. However, certain approaches focusing on the child's behaviour or on the behaviour of that child's parents or other care-givers have begun to indicate some hopeful ways of tackling the problem. One of these is parent training, where the parents of the child are taught to observe and identify behaviours in new ways and in particular to reward sociable behaviours and to avoid the unwitting rewarding of antisocial behaviours by shouting, counter-aggression and escalation of conflict.

**confidentiality**   the safeguarding of privacy in relation to INFORMATION about service users.

Social welfare agencies are much concerned about issues of access to CLIENT information. There are several senses in which confidentiality is an issue.

First, service users are concerned that information about them is not freely shared with third parties. Second, workers may wish to protect the identity of people who help to reveal, say, CHILD ABUSE or some other criminal offence. Third, there may be information on social work or other files to which access by the service user is denied. Fourth, information divulged to a worker by a service user may not in some circumstances be kept confidential.

> Many of the issues surrounding confidentiality are complex in practice. Information about a service user is in practice often shared with other agencies with welfare issues as the justification. Thus a case of alleged child abuse may involve a social worker in inquiries with the family doctor or HEALTH VISITOR or at the child's school. Should such inquiries be initiated only with parental permission (which may be withheld)? Or are the interests of a possibly abused child sufficient to override such concerns? Similarly, should there be a confidential section on social work files to which the service user has no access, because such information may be upsetting to the focal person or involve sensitive material about third parties? Finally, can a social worker ever guarantee confidentiality when such information may concern their statutory duties?

**constant attendance allowance**   paid as part of the INDUSTRIAL INJURIES SCHEME to people needing personal care.

**contact**   the different means by which a child keeps in touch with family members when away from home.

A child living away from home, for example in local authority care, or not living with one of their parents following separation or divorce, can maintain links with people such as parents, siblings and grandparents in a variety of ways, including visits, telephone calls, cards, letters and gifts. Maintaining contact between a child being LOOKED AFTER by the local authority is a matter of great importance to social workers. Research has shown that the consistency and degree of contact between a child in care and their parents is one of the best indicators as to whether the child will return home successfully or not. Because of this key finding, the CHILDREN ACT pays a great deal of attention to contact.

> The Children Act, section 34, requires children subject to a CARE ORDER to have 'reasonable contact' with their parents or other member(s) of the family as long as this is in the welfare of the child. The Act does not define what is 'reasonable' but leaves this to the parties concerned to work out, including the child, if old enough, the parents and other important family members. The Act also lays a general duty on social workers to facilitate contact between children whenever they are away from home, a duty that must receive the social worker's priority. Facilitating contact is not always easy; difficulties in the parent–child relationship, distance to the child's placement, and resistance of the child's foster carers are all factors that can adversely affect the frequency of contact. Nevertheless, social workers are expected to commit considerable resources, in terms of their own time or in offering to pay fares, to ensure that contact comes about. The frequency of contact and how it will be undertaken form an essential part of any CARE PLAN for a child. Only if the welfare of the child is jeopardized may the local authority ask the court

for a CONTACT DIRECTION, restricting contact or even terminating it altogether. Similarly, parents may ask the court for such a direction for increasing contact. (See also CONTACT ORDER, REUNIFICATION.)

Family Rights Group, *Promoting Links: Keeping Children and Families in Touch*, London: FRG, 1986.

**contact direction** stipulation by a court regarding the degree of CONTACT to take place between a child in the care of the LOCAL AUTHORITY and other members of the family.

Under section 34 of the CHILDREN ACT the court making a CARE ORDER may also specify the degree of contact that the child may have with those who have PARENTAL RESPONSIBILITY for them. It may do this at the time the care order is made or at any time afterwards. Any party to the proceedings may ask the court for such a direction. This includes a local authority that wishes to terminate all contact between a child in its care and their parents, or a parent of a child in care who wishes to visit their child more frequently. If no such direction is made, the Children Act assumes that 'reasonable contact' will take place between the child in care and their parents.

**contact order** a court order under section 8 of the CHILDREN ACT determining the frequency and kind of CONTACT that a child will have with a parent or others with PARENTAL RESPONSIBILITY for the child.

Contact orders are generally used to settle differences of opinion as to how often the child should see one or the other of the parents in matrimonial disputes. An order can also be used in relation to a child who goes to live with other members of their family, such as grandparents, including a child who might otherwise have come into local authority care. The order should not be confused with a CONTACT DIRECTION made by a court to regulate contact between a child in local authority care and their parents or other family members.

**contributions** sums of money paid by people in employment to fund the NATIONAL INSURANCE scheme.

There are four different classes of contribution, three of which give rise to benefit entitlement. Class 1 contributions are earnings-related and paid by employed earners; they give entitlement to all short- and long-term benefits. Class 2 contributions are flat-rate contributions paid by self-employed people; they give entitlement to all benefits except unemployment benefit. Class 3 contributions are voluntary flat-rate contributions that give entitlement only to widows benefit and retirement pension. Class 4 contributions are profit-related, paid by self-employed earners, and do not give entitlement to benefit. Until 1977 married women could choose to pay a reduced class 1 or no class 2 contribution, with no entitlement to benefit. Not all contributions are actually paid; credited contributions, which help to satisfy the qualifying conditions for benefits, are given in a variety of circumstances, for example to people who are unemployed and signing on as available for work or who are incapable of work. Home responsibility protection can help people qualify for retirement pension. It reduces the number of years a person has to contribute by disregarding years spent bringing up children or caring for adults with disabilities.

**contributory benefits**   benefits entitlement to which depends on National Insurance CONTRIBUTIONS as well as on a person's circumstances.

The main contributory benefits are INVALIDITY BENEFIT, RETIREMENT PENSION, UNEMPLOYMENT BENEFIT and WIDOWS BENEFIT. Retirement pension is the most significant of all benefits, paid to nearly 10 million people at a cost of £25 billion or one-third of the total social security budget. (See also SOCIAL SECURITY.)

**councils of voluntary service**   the major coordinating bodies for VOLUNTARY-SECTOR organizations within particular geographical areas. Some rural areas are able to sustain a council, but predominantly they are located in large towns and cities. Most such councils receive their funding from local authorities.

Following the publication of the Wolfenden Report on the future of voluntary organizations in 1974, many councils of voluntary service were established. These either replaced the former councils of social service or were entirely new creations. Their functions include the development of voluntary activity in the locality, often through the provision of volunteer bureaux to recruit VOLUNTEERS to affiliated organizations; the provision of information about local conditions and needs; the coordination of effort and policy among voluntary bodies; and sometimes the direct delivery of services to the public and to voluntary organizations (for example, printing and distribution of newsletters, or training of volunteers including management committee members). Councils of voluntary service have in recent years been active in opposing cuts in public expenditure. Given that many voluntary organizations work with vulnerable and marginalized groups, the councils are in a unique position to offer opinion about how such groups are faring in relation to government policy. The councils have also been particularly active in promoting harmonious race relations.

**council tax**   the local tax, based on the worth of an individual's housing, whose revenue helps fund local services.

The council tax was introduced in April 1993 to replace the community charge (poll tax). It is a hybrid of the earlier system of domestic rates and the community charge, and possibly more complicated than either to administer. Domestic properties are divided into one of eight bands according to their value defined by the Inland Revenue and Valuation Service, and the tax payable varies according to the value. Properties in the highest band incur three times as much council tax as properties in the lowest band. The full tax on a property is payable if two adults live there. Some properties are exempt: for example, unfurnished properties awaiting sale (for six months) and dwellings where all the residents are students.

If anyone living in a property has a DISABILITY, the council tax may be reduced to that paid by the valuation band below. It is also reduced if there is a second bathroom, second kitchen or some other room used mainly for the special needs of the person with a disability (for example, a downstairs bedroom). If there is only one adult or no one living in the property the tax payable is reduced to 75 or 50 per cent respectively of the full bill. Certain people are not counted towards the number of adults in a dwelling, such as people who are severely mentally impaired, students, people on youth training schemes, some carers and people detained in hospital or prison. Bills can be further reduced by COUNCIL TAX BENEFIT, which can be claimed by the person liable to pay the tax.

Most councils like to have the tax paid in monthly instalments from April to January. This is the minimum arrangement that must be offered, but weekly or fortnightly payments over the whole twelve months are also legal. Council tax law includes detailed regulations about enforcement and recovery. If an instalment is missed, the council must first send a reminder. If payment is still not made within fourteen days, the council can apply for a LIABILITY ORDER in the magistrates' court. A liability order allows the council to collect by using attachment of earnings orders or distraint. Most councils will still be prepared to make an arrangement before using these methods, unless previous arrangements have failed without good reason. The ultimate sanction for non-payment is imprisonment.

**council tax benefit**   a benefit that provides help towards the payment of COUNCIL TAX. It is administered by the local authority charging the tax and is credited against the account of the person liable to pay.

Council tax benefit can take two forms. Main council tax benefit depends on the income and circumstances of the person liable to pay council tax. SECOND ADULT REBATE depends only on the income and circumstances of other adults in the household. Only one of these will be paid – whichever is higher. Main council tax benefit cannot be paid to anyone who has more than £16,000 in capital. Capital between £3,000 and £16,000 is deemed to produce an income of £1 per week for every £250 or part thereof. People receiving income support get council tax benefit to cover the full liability, subject only to non-dependant deductions. As income increases above this level, the benefit is reduced at the rate of 20p in £1. The second adult rebate can be claimed where the liable person has no partner. If all the other adults are on a low income, the rebate given is of up to 25 per cent.

**counselling**   the process whereby a trained professional gives another person support and guidance in an individual or group setting.

Counselling provides one form of assistance when a person experiences stress in their life, due to traumatic life events such as unemployment or bereavement, or due to the effects of general circumstances – for example, an unhappy marriage, poverty or housing problems. Counselling may also involve ADVICE-giving, as in careers guidance or Citizens Advice Bureau work. However, despite the breadth of use of the term, the core of its current meaning is the enabling of the counselled person to take control of their own life through greater understanding and a realistic assessment of their current emotional and interpersonal experience. Counselling is a rapidly expanding field and is becoming professionalized. The British Association of Counselling approves and accredits courses that meet the standard requirements.

Although Freud's 'talking cure' (see PSYCHOANALYSIS) set the stage for the development of counselling, the crucial theorist is Carl Rogers, who introduced client-centred therapy as a method. He believed that the counselled person is helped primarily through the quality of the relationship with the counsellor, who must provide the three 'core conditions' of empathy, genuineness and unconditional positive regard. However, some counselling methods are more directive; for example, COGNITIVE-BEHAVIOURAL methods aim to shape thinking behaviour towards greater realism, while the PSYCHODYNAMIC APPROACH proceeds by looking to childhood experience to explain current emotional states and the resolution of these problems through CATHARSIS. Evaluation studies of counselling suggest that these diverse theoretical approaches and their associated methodologies have preferred application in different client groups and at different stages of the counselling process. An eclectic approach is therefore often preferred by practising counsellors. (See LISTENING, PERSON-CENTRED COUNSELLING.)

J. McLeod, *Introduction to Counselling*, Buckingham: Open University Press, 1993.

**crack** COCAINE (cocaine hydrochloride), a stimulant, that has been dissolved in water and heated with a chemical reagent. The result is small lumps of 'freebase' cocaine ('rocks') that are smoked in pipes, on tinfoil like HEROIN or in cigarettes.

Also known as 'rock', 'freebase' or 'base', crack is, like cocaine, a class A DRUG under the MISUSE OF DRUGS ACT 1971. It carries severe penalties for production, possession or supply, varying from a fine to life imprisonment. The effects of crack are almost immediate, producing an intense but brief high. The desire to repeat the experience can become compulsive, making the substance psychologically addictive (see ADDICTION). Repeated use can lead to paranoia, hallucinations and psychosis.

**credit union** a group of people, with a common bond, who save money together in order to build up sufficient funds to make low-interest loans available to participants in the union. Credit unions in Britain are governed by the Credit Union Act 1979.

The credit union movement is long-established and international; popular and successful unions exist, for example, in Ireland, the Caribbean and South Asia. Poor people often do not have access to 'mainstream' credit facilities, because credit agencies such as banks and loan and insurance companies will not lend to them. Facilities that are available to them – such as local moneylenders – invariably charge very high rates of interest or operate other constraints, such as the requirement that goods are purchased from certain stores.

Credit unions must comprise people who have a 'common bond' – for example, who all live in the same neighbourhood, belong to the same church or work for the same company. Members save and, once a personal target and a collective target are reached, can borrow. Loans are usually modest, and rates of interest low; in Britain, interest rates must not exceed 1 per cent per month (APR 12.6 per cent). Credit unions have grown significantly over the last ten years.

**crime** see THEORIES OF CRIME AND DEVIANCE.

**crime prevention**   a very broad term covering a range of activities, from education to high-technology security, all aimed at reducing crime.

A distinction can be made between individual and social crime prevention and between primary and secondary prevention. Primary individual prevention involves work with individuals identified as 'at risk' of offending or victimization; this work is mainly educational. Secondary individual prevention involves risk reduction and delinquency management work with offenders (for example, the work of the PROBATION SERVICE and YOUTH WORKERS). Primary social prevention involves COMMUNITY WORK and anything aimed at ameliorating social problems. Secondary social prevention involves 'situational crime prevention' work in high-delinquency areas; this might entail general improvements to the environment, such as better street lighting, or specific improvements intended to deter criminals – 'target hardening' that usually involves the use of hardware such as locks and/or installation of surveillance technology. The philosophy underlying situational crime prevention is that the police alone cannot solve crime; responsible citizens must play their part; professional knowledge and community commitment should go hand in hand. Critics argue that situational crime prevention is a cosmetic exercise, enabling the government to blame the victim for crime, and achieving nothing without other improvements to community life and to the effectiveness of the police and the criminal justice system.

R. Harris, *Crime, Criminal Justice and the Probation Service*, London: Routledge, 1992.

**criminal courts**   courts dealing with the prosecution of people for breaking the criminal law. They deal with behaviour considered harmful to society as a whole, as opposed to civil courts, which deal with legal disputes between one private interest (individual or body) and another.

The main criminal courts in England and Wales are MAGISTRATES' courts and Crown Courts. Magistrates' courts deal with almost 98 per cent of criminal cases. They hear the facts of a case, make decisions about guilt or innocence and give sentences. Magistrates are ordinary members of the public, appointed by the Lord Chancellor, with the power to impose any sentence up to the laid-down maximum for the offence; the maximum prison sentence they can impose is six months for one offence or a total of twelve months for more than one offence (see Magistrates Court Act 1980). If magistrates consider an offence to require greater punishment than they have powers to inflict, they must commit the defendant to the Crown Court. Some offences – 'summary offences' such as minor assault and criminal damage – can be dealt with only in magistrates' courts, whereas very serious indictable offences (such as murder, rape and robbery) can be dealt with only by the Crown Court. Most are triable either way, allowing the defendant or magistrates to decide whether to be dealt with in the magistrates' court or by jury in the Crown Court (the latter usually because they believe they have a better chance of acquittal). The appeal process starts at the Crown Courts, hearing appeals from the magistrates' courts, and may proceed to the Court of Appeal, the High Court and the House of Lords.

The process whereby an offender comes to court is complicated. A person arrested by the POLICE who admits to committing an offence may receive a formal CAUTION, with matters being taken no further. If they deny committing the offence, or if the offence is considered too serious for a caution, the police report the matter to the CROWN PROSECUTION SERVICE, which decides whether or not to prosecute. The police may release the accused person on BAIL to appear later at court, or simply agree to send them a summons; or they may keep the person in custody at a police station, in which case they must take the person to court within seventy-two hours or as soon as possible, so that magistrates can give legal permission for the person to be detained (see REMAND). The accused person may be transferred to a remand prison until their case can be dealt with.

Magistrates' courts are local courts, open to the public, and have existed in one form or another for over 600 years. They cover 550 small geographical areas known as petty sessional divisions. There are around 29,500 lay magistrates (or justices of the peace), who sit in threes, known as 'benches'. They undergo basic training but are not legally qualified; they have legal advisers and court administrators known as justices' clerks. In very busy courts, there may also be a stipendiary magistrate, a professional lawyer who sits alone and usually works more quickly than lay magistrates, although with the same powers. There are 70 to 80 stipendiary magistrates. Magistrates sometimes adjourn a case for up to three to four weeks in order to obtain PRE-SENTENCE REPORTS or medical reports on a defendant before passing sentence. There are separate magistrates' courts for young people under 18 years of age, known as YOUTH COURTS, where proceedings tend to be less formal, and members of the public are excluded; the press are admitted but may not publish defendants' names or addresses.

The right to trial by jury is seen as a fundamental constitutional right in England and Wales, though there has been a debate about restricting this right in order to reduce the burden on Crown Courts and the subsequent delays in bringing cases to trial. Crown Courts have existed only since 1972, when they replaced the old quarter sessions and assize courts. There are 90 to 100 Crown Courts in England and Wales. Depending on the seriousness of the offence, the Crown Court is presided over by a High Court judge (for the most serious), a circuit judge (most cases) or a part-time recorder, all former experienced barristers. Like magistrates' courts, Crown Courts are open to the public. If a defendant pleads not guilty, the decision about their guilt or innocence is made by a jury of twelve lay people selected at random, after they have heard all the evidence from the prosecution and defence lawyers and the witnesses. After the jury has delivered its verdict, it plays no further part in the proceedings; it cannot influence the sentence, which is the responsibility of the presiding judge.

The Crown Court acts as an appeal court against both conviction and sentence in the magistrates' court. It can impose any sentence that could have been imposed by the magistrates, whether harsher or more lenient than the original sentence. In 1991 there were 19,000 appeals against conviction or sentence at magistrates' courts.

The Court of Appeal has two divisions: the Criminal Division, headed by the Lord Chief Justice, which hears appeals from the Crown Courts, and the Civil Division, headed by the Master of the Rolls, which hears appeals from the county and high courts. There are twenty-seven lords justices of appeal. All appeals against conviction and sentence passed in the Crown Courts are heard by the Court of Appeal (6,700 in 1991); it does not hear witnesses but considers only written material. It also has the role of interpreting the law if it is unclear and setting precedents to be followed by the lower courts. Unlike the Crown Court, the Court of Appeal cannot impose a more severe sentence than was originally imposed. A sentence can be increased if it has been referred by the Attorney General as being unduly lenient, although this is not technically an appeal. Other courts may be involved in the appeal process. Where a point of law is at issue in a magistrates' court, the Queen's Bench Division of the High Court hears the appeal. The highest court of appeal in the country is the House of Lords or, more accurately, the nine or ten law lords who sit in panels of five to hear cases granted leave to appeal by the Court of Appeal.

Although there is no written British constitution, there is a basic assumption that the criminal courts are independent of Parliament and local government and not subject to political influence. Critics of the criminal justice system dispute its independence; and a more modern view is that, while decisions in relation to individual cases must remain independent, there is joint responsibility – or interdependence – for ensuring a just and effective system.

M. Berlins and C. Dyer, *The Law Machine*, London: Penguin, 1990.

**Criminal Justice Act 1991** an Act that came into force in October 1992, aiming to provide a new coherent sentencing framework based on the principle of JUST DESERTS, with only the most serious offences being punished with imprisonment.

Under the Act, less serious offences were to be dealt with by means of three categories of disposal other than imprisonment: DISCHARGES (for most minor offences); financial penalties; and COMMUNITY SENTENCES. Due to early vociferous criticism of the Act, especially from sentencers, amendments were made by August 1993 that some people argue have undermined the whole philosophy of the Act. The background to the Act was a growing concern with overcrowding in PRISONS and a related belief that alternative, non-custodial sentences were viewed by sentencers as being 'soft options'. It was accepted that some offenders were being sent to prison unnecessarily and some were being sent for too long. Attention was increasingly being paid to adopting appropriate criteria for custody, especially in the juvenile court. There was also a recognition that sentencing lacked consistency and that this was unjust. Evidence was growing that black people and women might experience DISCRIMINATION in the courts. Finally, there was dissatisfaction that courts appeared to make insufficient distinction between violent and sexual offences against the person and offences against property. The government set out its views in the green paper *Punishment, Custody and the Community* (1988) and the white paper *Crime, Justice and Protecting the Public* (1990), which preceded the Act.

The Act is based on six key principles. First, sentences should reflect the seriousness of the offences committed ('proportionality'), with custody reserved for only the most serious offences. The Act required a court to focus primarily on the seriousness of the offence before it and to send the defendant to prison only if that offence and, if appropriate, one other associated offence were so serious that only such a sentence could be justified (section 1). This was intended to prevent courts from sending someone to prison for a number of minor offences, none of which in itself warranted imprisonment. However, this section was amended by later legislation to allow a court to take account of the overall seriousness of all the offences before it. The Act also prevented courts giving too much consideration to previous convictions, unless the circumstances of those offences shed light on features of the current offence that make it more serious (section 29). This section was intended to restrict the powers of a court to send someone to prison for repeatedly committing minor offences, but courts found it difficult to interpret, and in August 1993 it was amended to allow courts to revert to their former practice of taking previous convictions into account (section 66). The same amendment allows courts to consider offences committed while on BAIL to be regarded as more serious than would otherwise be the case. Besides problems relating to numbers of offences and previous convictions, courts have experienced difficulty in defining the concept of seriousness. The Act allows courts to take account of aggravating and mitigating factors, but the achievement of consistency in assessing seriousness remains elusive.

The second principle is that a sharper distinction should be drawn between property offences and offences against the person. This reflects the government's concern that people committing violent and sexual offences should be dealt with particularly severely. Courts are therefore permitted to consider the need to protect the public from serious harm when deciding the length of prison sentences for these offences.

Third, community sentences stand in their own right and should not be seen as alternatives to custody. This principle refutes a popular misbelief of the 1980s that most offenders deserved to go to prison, and that if they were given a non-custodial sentence they were being 'let off' with a 'soft' alternative. The Act recognizes that community sentences (ATTENDANCE CENTRE ORDERS, COMBINATION ORDERS, COMMUNITY SERVICE ORDERS, CURFEW ORDERS, PROBATION ORDERS and SUPERVISION ORDERS) constitute a sentencing band in their own right, providing a particular degree of restriction on liberty commensurate with a particular level of offence seriousness.

Fourth, young people should be dealt with in a way that takes account of their maturity and stage of development. The Act replaces the juvenile court (which dealt with offenders aged 10 to 16) with the YOUTH COURT (offenders aged 10 to 17). At the same time, it allows courts to impose certain adult sentences (combination order, community service order, probation order) on 16- and 17-year-olds. This means that courts may treat 16- and 17-year-olds as either juveniles or adults, depending on their maturity and stage of development. Little guidance has been given to courts to help them define and assess maturity objectively, and there is concern that the concept may result in prejudiced judgements of teenagers' circumstances and abilities.

Fifth, the intention of the court should be properly reflected in the way a prison sentence is served. The Act introduces a clearly defined system of EARLY RELEASE for prisoners, replacing the much-criticized PAROLE system. The Act abolishes automatic remission after two-thirds of the sentence and discretionary parole after one-third (or six months, whichever is the longer). Instead, it provides that half of all sentences must be served in custody. Thereafter, there is a system of automatic release (with or without licence conditions) during which time a prisoner may be recalled to prison if they reoffend. Parole remains an option for only a few long-term prisoners.

Sixth, the criminal justice system should be administered efficiently and without discrimination. The Act contains a significant new provision (section 95) for monitoring the criminal justice system to ensure 'value for money' and the absence of discrimination on the ground of race or sex or any other improper ground. To these ends, the secretary of state is required to publish relevant information annually. Cynics have pointed out the incongruous coupling of discrimination issues with concerns about financial implications.

The Act made two further major changes, one of which has since been revoked. The introduction of UNIT FINES was intended to force courts to give systematic consideration to offenders' means when imposing fines, recognizing that the same fine could be insignificant for a rich person while causing devastating hardship for a poor person. Due to a series of wildly anomalous decisions by magistrates, who claimed the Act gave them no choice, the unit fine was abolished in 1993, and courts are now simply exhorted to 'consider the offender's means' when imposing a fine. The Act also replaced the SOCIAL INQUIRY REPORTS (SIRs) prepared by the Probation Service with PRE-SENTENCE REPORTS (PSRs). Such reports provide courts with information about the offender to assist in sentencing; but, while SIRs focused primarily on social and personal information relating to the offender's welfare, PSRs are required to focus more clearly on the offence and to include only information relevant to that. Probation officers are also no longer allowed to make professional sentencing recommendations, but must instead discuss proposals for suitable options, making clear that the final decision rests with the court (as, of course, it always has done).

Home Office, *Crime Justice and Protecting the Public*, London: HMSO, 1990; A. Jones, B. Kroll, J. Pitts, P. Smith and J. Weise, *The Probation Handbook*, Harlow: Longman, 1992.

**criminal justice system**  see CRIMINAL JUSTICE ACT 1991, POLICE AND CRIMINAL EVIDENCE ACT 1984, PRISON, PROBATION SERVICE, JUVENILE/YOUTH JUSTICE.

**criminal proceedings**  the process whereby a person suspected of having committed a criminal offence is dealt with by the CRIMINAL JUSTICE SYSTEM.

The process starts with arrest and charge by the POLICE but then passes through a number of stages with alternative outcomes available at each stage. For example, a person who admits to committing a minor offence may simply receive a police CAUTION. Even if the police wish to proceed further, the CROWN PROSECUTION SERVICE may decide that it is not in the public interest to pursue a prosecution. If a person is prosecuted, it may take some time for the case against them to be prepared, and for them to prepare their defence. During this time they will be on REMAND, either on BAIL or in custody. All criminal proceedings start in the MAGISTRATES' court, and many are dealt with there. However, defendants may elect to go, or magistrates may commit a defendant, to the Crown Court for either trial by jury or sentence. If a defendant wishes to appeal against conviction or sentence, they will go to the Crown Court (for a decision in the magistrates' court), to the Court of Appeal (for a decision in the Crown Court) or to the House of Lords. Permission, however, is required for appeals to the House of Lords. (see CRIMINAL COURTS).

**criminal statistics**  a term usually referring to offences recorded by the POLICE, although it may be used more broadly to cover any statistics relating to criminal justice.

Criminal statistics refer only to *known* crimes, and this makes them problematic. A great deal of crime is never recorded, and the way crimes are recorded changes over time. Therefore, criminal statistics can only be a reflection of the processes of recording crime, not an accurate picture of crime itself. Of recent years, the BRITISH CRIME SURVEY has provided an alternative method of finding out about the prevalence of crime, and this information is now seen as complementing official police statistics.

There are a number of explanations for the misleading nature of criminal statistics. First, VICTIMS do not always report crimes to the police. This may be because they are unaware of the crime, because they consider it too trivial, because they are afraid, because they know the offender or because they do not think the police can or will do anything. Second, the police may not record the reported crime. This may be because they do not believe the complainant or because the complaint is not clear. It may also be because the police think it unlikely that they will be able to do anything – the chances of the crime being 'cleared up' (that is, of an arrest being made) may seem very low. The police have wide discretion about recording crime, and their practices change over time. Apparent rises in a particular crime (for example, DOMESTIC VIOLENCE) may be due more to public campaigns that have encouraged women to report this crime, and to policies that have instructed the police to take such reports more seriously, than to any increase in the crime itself. Despite these criticisms, criminal statistics are important because they influence the way that people perceive crime, and this, in turn, affects their behaviour and the criminal justice policies they demand from the government.

**criminology**  the academic discipline that provides and analyses explanations of offending and the place of crime in society, as well as evaluating criminal justice policy and practice.

Criminologists vary in the emphasis they place on different perspectives on crime. Those favouring psychological perspectives are concerned primarily with the individual or group MOTIVATIONS and attitudes of criminals and criminal justice personnel, especially sentencers. Those favouring sociological perspectives focus on the social, political and economic conditions that give rise to particular patterns of crime and particular official and media responses to it. Those favouring socio-legal perspectives examine the social and political influences on the making and implementation of criminal law, as well as its impact and consequences. (See also CRIMINAL STATISTICS, PRINCIPLES OF SENTENCING, THEORIES OF CRIME AND DEVIANCE.)

**crisis intervention**  an attempt to understand the nature of episodes that people find extremely difficult or impossible to handle, and to understand how services might be organized to help people through such events.

Crises are precipitated by hazardous events, which may be a single catastrophe or a series of mishaps. They may be brought about by something external to the person, or by something that appears to be rooted in them (although on further investigation an external cause may be revealed, such as an earlier trauma or crisis). The same hazardous event may bring about a crisis for some people but not for others – although some events (for example, the unexpected death of a loved one) bring about a state of crisis in most individuals. The hazardous event is likely to disturb the person's 'balance' and arouse feelings of extreme vulnerability. Most people attempt to deal with such difficulties by employing their usual coping mechanisms; if these coping mechanisms do not help, the person may employ rarely used, emergency methods as a measure of desperation. If the problem persists and cannot be alleviated or avoided, the person is likely to enter a period of acute discomfort. This period is thought to be the state of active crisis. The interval between the onset of a crisis and its resolution will vary, but the active state of crisis is unlikely to last more than four to six weeks.

> As individuals experience a crisis, and during the early stages of conflict resolution, they are especially amenable to help. They may even embrace help that they have earlier rejected. Minimal, focused effort at this time, because of emotional accessibility, may bring about substantial change in the person. As the person recovers, new 'ego sets' and adaptive styles may be learned that may enable the person to cope with future crises. Complete, rather than partial, recovery seems to be dependent upon a 'correct' understanding of the event. Thus a woman who has been raped needs to understand that she was in no way responsible for the event and that she has been a victim of a man's abuse of power. Services dealing with crises have to be able to give the time to help people through these events. Intensive support is required, and services need to be organized so that an appropriate response is possible. Rape crisis centres and women's refuges, for example, are in some measure organized in the expectation of crises, but other services clearly are not. Children are often rescued from abusive situations, yet services are rarely mobilized to help them cope with their crises in the aftermath.
>
> K. O'Hagan, 'Crisis Intervention: Changing Perspectives' in C. Harvey and T. Philpot, eds., *Practising Social Work*, London: Routledge, 1994.

**crisis loans**   repayable loans from the SOCIAL FUND towards expenses in an emergency if this is the only means to prevent serious damage or risk to health or safety.

People can apply for a crisis loan of up to £1,000, whether or not they receive INCOME SUPPORT. Loans are most commonly used to provide living expenses for short periods; nearly half the expenditure is on this. Benefit agency staff often decline to give people application forms, advising them that it is not worth their applying, and for this reason the success rate of applications exceeds 80 per cent.

**Crown Prosecution Service**   the national service of lawyers with responsibility for deciding whether a case should be brought to court and for conducting the prosecution in court.

The functions of the Crown Prosecution Service were formally carried out by the POLICE and include making recommendations about remanding defendants on BAIL or in custody. The service may decide to discontinue a prosecution if it considers that there is insufficient evidence or that it would not be in the public interest to continue.

**culture of poverty** a term devised and developed by sociologists and anthropologists to describe the existence of poor people, with the suggestion that people living in long-term POVERTY develop a particular way of life, passing on that way of life to future generations. The term is closely allied to the idea of a CYCLE OF DEPRIVATION.

The anthropologist most closely associated with the idea of a culture of poverty is Oscar Lewis. He believed that his researches in both developing and advanced capitalist societies revealed a complex culture of interlocking behaviours, beliefs and attitudes that characterize poor people. Thus a strong present time orientation, the cult of machismo, matriarchal family structures and a sense of fatalism all appeared to be widespread features of the lives of poor people. Additionally, the inability of the poor to become involved in institutions such as trade unions, political parties and 'normal' economic activity was thought to add to their marginality and to confirm their membership of an UNDERCLASS. Lewis has been criticized because there is a sense in which he seems to blame the poor for their own poverty. If culture is a set of responses for coping with immediate circumstances, the critical issue is how much those attitudes and values rooted in the experience of poverty may prevent a person or community from responding to improved circumstances. Lewis has it that the culture of poverty will inhibit ANTI-POVERTY STRATEGIES, whereas others have argued that if life chances are significantly improved for poor people they will quickly respond.

Many professionals working in social welfare have been dismayed at what they perceive as the inability of the poor to respond to help offered. Others take the view that social welfare workers, in the main, have little to offer poor people in relation to an improvement in LIFE CHANCES. On the contrary, most social welfare workers, they argue, endorse the status quo and in that respect become agents of social control. COMMUNITY DEVELOPMENT PROJECTS, designed to improve the lot of poor communities, have been criticized because they do not acknowledge the importance of structural inequality and therefore must be regarded as superficial. Although the idea of the culture of poverty is perceived as flawed by its critics, its influence is still acknowledged as substantial. Many social workers probably see at least some individuals, families and communities in terms that imply a view of poverty consistent with that of Oscar Lewis.

D. Moynihan, ed., *On Understanding Poverty*, New York: Basic Books, 1968.

**curfew order** a new sentence introduced by the CRIMINAL JUSTICE ACT 1991, whereby courts may require any offender aged over 16 to remain for a specified period, between two and twelve hours per day, in a specified place, for up to six months.

Experiments have taken place to monitor curfews electronically. 'Night restrictions', which serve a similar purpose, have been available to juvenile courts as conditions of supervision orders since 1969 but have rarely been used, because of the difficulties of enforcement.

**custodial sentence**    a sentence of imprisonment.

In the past, the term covered detention centres, borstals and youth custody centres for YOUNG OFFENDERS, as well as adult PRISONS. These institutions have now been integrated and are referred to generically as YOUNG OFFENDER INSTITUTIONS. There are many offences that can, in law, attract a custodial sentence, and these are referred to as 'imprisonable offences'. This does not mean that a person convicted of such an offence is bound to be sent to prison. With the exception of murder (for which a LIFE SENTENCE of imprisonment is mandatory), all offences can be dealt with by non-custodial measures such as fines or COMMUNITY SENTENCES.

> Under the CRIMINAL JUSTICE ACT 1991 (amended in 1993), courts must justify any sentence of imprisonment by stating that one or more of the following grounds applies: the offence or offences before the court are so serious that only a prison sentence is appropriate; the offence is violent or sexual, and the public must be protected from serious harm from the defendant; the defendant has refused to consent to a community sentence. In most cases, the crucial factor in deciding whether or not prison is justified is the seriousness of the offence, but defining and assessing seriousness are difficult and controversial. The extent to which courts take account of previous convictions is also a matter of discretion, resulting in wide variations in sentencing practice.
>
> The length of a prison sentence is also a matter for the court's discretion. Maximum sentences are laid down in law for every offence, but these are not often relevant in routine sentencing, because maximum sentences are used very sparingly. However, the length of time that an offender spends in prison will not be the same as their stated sentence and could be as little as half of that sentence. Under arrangements for EARLY RELEASE, at least half of a sentence must be served in prison, but the remainder may be served in the COMMUNITY, sometimes under supervision. During that time, however, the offender is 'at risk' of being returned to prison to serve the remainder of their sentence if any further offence is committed.

**custodianship**    the legal category introduced by the now repealed Children Act 1975 as a kind of halfway stage between fostering a child long-term and adopting that child.

Parents who had been fostering a child for three years and more could, with the agreement of the local authority, apply for custodianship. This provided the foster parents with a greater sense of security in relation to the child, since under custodianship the child could not be removed from that placement. Step-parents were also expected to apply for custodianship rather than adopt. There was, however, considerable delay in implementing the provision for custodianship in the 1975 Act, and in the event only a small number of applications were made. Custodianship has now disappeared with the repeal of the entire Children Act 1975; its nearest equivalent in the CHILDREN ACT 1989 is the RESIDENCE ORDER.

**cycle of deprivation**    an explanation for the persistence of POVERTY that focuses upon how attitudes, values and behaviours are passed on from one generation to the next, mainly through the family but also perhaps through communities.

The notion of the cycle of deprivation achieved considerable political prominence at the hands of Keith Joseph, Minister for Social Services, in 1972. It is closely linked to the theory of the CULTURE OF POVERTY developed in the 1960s by, among others, the North American writer Oscar Lewis. Governments in Britain and the United States, particularly in the 1960s and 1970s, were influenced by ideas that have roots in the concept of a cycle of deprivation. Attempts to tackle urban poverty, especially in inner-city areas, have often focused upon early education (for example, Educational Priority Areas, pre-school provision and the US Headstart programme) in an attempt to improve the LIFE CHANCES of young children from poor homes. Despite promising beginnings, such children often seemed to be constrained by their backgrounds. Critics have argued that wider forces such as SOCIAL CLASS, RACISM and GENDER stratification (and indeed capitalism in general) could not be so easily 'defeated'. It is now widely accepted that COMMUNITY DEVELOPMENT PROJECTS have a role to play to raise the morale of depressed areas, but the gains will be limited by wider forces in society.

# D

**dangerousness**   the potential to cause physical or psychological harm to others. The term is used in the courts in the offender sections of the MENTAL HEALTH ACT 1983, referring to some people who are convicted of an offence and are also mentally disordered (see MENTALLY DISORDERED OFFENDERS).

If the court considers, on psychiatric evidence, that a person is 'dangerous', they will be sent to a special hospital offering secure psychiatric provision. They will also be placed on a restriction order under the Mental Health Act, which means that they are to be detained until they are considered by psychiatrists to be no longer dangerous. The concept is used also in relation to families or individuals who may be abusing children. 'Dangerous families' are those where the pattern of interaction between partners, the degree of VIOLENCE and conflict, or the presence of an unstable and aggressive individual exposes the children of that family to physical harm. Social workers try to gauge the potential for causing physical or psychological harm in the behaviour of both individuals and families (see RISK ANALYSIS). They do this in a number of situations, such as with an older person who may have been assaulted, a child who may have been sexually abused or a psychiatric patient who may attack others. Social work has attempted to gauge the dangerousness of an abuser more accurately by developing 'indicators' such as psychological portraits of child abusers and of partners who collude with the abusive acts.

The concept of dangerousness has many critics. In relation to working with children in particular, such critics have pointed out that focusing on dangerousness reflects a drift from a rehabilitative model of child-care work to a more coercive way of working. The social work role becomes more narrowly protective by swiftly distinguishing and removing children from the truly dangerous families as opposed to those that are not so dangerous, with which children are safe. In working with people defined as 'dangerous' by the courts or other professionals, practitioners need to be aware of the public STEREOTYPES of dangerousness – how these are based on images of wild animals and of badness fixed in the person's character. These can lead to perceptions of the person's character being wildly exaggerated, which results in the worker feeling extremely anxious. This in turn makes the building of a relationship or the carrying out of social work tasks such as ASSESSMENT highly quite fraught.

N. Parton, *Governing the Family: Child Care, Child Protection and the State*, Basingstoke: Macmillan, 1991.

**Data Protection Act 1984**   legislation designed to restrict the possibility of individuals being harmed by the abuse of personal data or information and to enable the United Kingdom to satisfy the Council of Europe Convention.

The Act gives people (data subjects) the right to know what is being stored about them on computers, and aims to protect the individual by laying certain duties on organizations (data users) who keep information on computer. There are eight principles that data users must follow: (1) information must be collected and used fairly and lawfully; (2) data users must register the purpose for which information is held; (3) the information cannot be used or disclosed except for those purposes; (4) data users can hold only information that is relevant to their purposes and cannot hold more than is needed; (5) the information held must be accurate and, where necessary, up to date; (6) the information held must be kept no longer than necessary for those purposes; (7) the information must be accessible to individuals and correctable or erasable if appropriate; (8) data users must have appropriate security against unauthorized access, disclosure or destruction and against accidental loss or destruction. The Act gives individuals who are 'data subjects' five rights: (1) to know if any organization keeps information about them on computer; (2) to see a copy of the information, except if this is being held to safeguard national security, to prevent or detect a crime, to catch or prosecute offenders or to assess or collect tax or duty; (3) to make a complaint to the Data Protection Registrar if a person does not like the way a data user is collecting or using personal information about them; (4) to have inaccurate records erased or corrected; (5) to claim compensation through the courts if the person has been hurt by the loss or destruction of personal data, through an improper disclosure or because of inaccuracy.

**'dawn raid'**   the compulsory removal of a child or children, believed to be abused, from their family by police and social workers in the early morning before the family is awake.

The intention is to forestall any warning of the action and as a result to ensure the presence of the child or children on the premises. Following removal of children in this manner in Orkney in 1991, both the CLYDE REPORT and the DEPARTMENT OF HEALTH advised that in the timing of a child's removal the prime consideration must be the welfare of that child.

**day care**   a variety of caring facilities for people in need who are still living predominantly in their own home.

Day care facilities have been devised for virtually all client groups where people are regarded as at risk. Such facilities may focus upon rehabilitation, monitoring, or respite care to give CARERS a break or to supplement their efforts or as a social focus for isolated and vulnerable people. Programmes of work in day care centres reflect these differing objectives. Some facilities are specialized, for example ADULT TRAINING CENTRES for people with LEARNING DISABILITY; others may be multi-purpose, where there is an attempt to meet the needs of all client groups. Many facilities that have residential provision as their major focus also have day care services too, for example residential homes for old people. Day care is seen as a very important part of COMMUNITY CARE provision.

**deaf-blind**   a term referring to people who either are born deaf-blind, are born deaf and become blind, are born blind and become deaf or become deaf-blind through increasing age, accident or illness.

Such people are said to have 'dual sensory disability'. There is no legal definition and no overall legislation dealing with the needs of deaf-blind people. They are usually included in categories of either blind or deaf and sometimes registered with local authorities as blind. In 1989 it was estimated that the deaf-blind population in the United Kingdom numbered at least 11,000 people. Social services departments play a leading role in providing services to deaf-blind people and often employ workers skilled in communication methods such as the deaf-blind manual alphabet. Other departments may at times be the lead agencies, for example local education or health authorities.

**deaf/Deaf people**   deaf – the audiological condition of not hearing; Deaf – people who identify themselves as part of a linguistic and cultural minority group. (The convention of lower- and upper-case d/D is increasingly used in the United States and Britain to make this distinction.)

A construction of deafness from the perspective of Deaf people, based on their experiences in a predominantly 'hearing' society, is in the early stages of articulation. This perspective describes a group of people who share a common language, that is, sign language (see BRITISH SIGN LANGUAGE), and whose culture is historically created and transmitted across generations. Being Deaf usually means the person has a hearing loss, but the degree of loss is not in itself a criteria for being Deaf. There is also the common notion of deafness as a sensory impairment, that is, lack of hearing. This view of deafness as a physical deficit has dominated most professional discourses (such as medical, audiological, educational and welfare services) and lay discourses (such as film and fiction). Deafness is seen as a deviation from the so-called 'normal healthy state', and emphasis is placed on normalization and cure. In psychology, deafness has been seen as a defining characteristic of a deaf person. The two main models of deafness are therefore the clinical/pathological model, which focuses predominantly on audiological factors, and the cultural model, which emphasizes social factors.

Social work with Deaf people has its origins in the missions or welfare societies that were established for social and religious purposes throughout Britain during the nineteenth century. In common with many social welfare services, the missions were church-based organizations concerned with the religious and moral affairs of Deaf people. These organizations were developed initially by people who had some contact with Deaf people but were rarely Deaf themselves. Their motivation was compassion, charitable concern and a response to Deaf people's desire to meet together. As the societies developed and became more complex, they became the centre for social, educational and vocational activity for Deaf people. A person, usually male, was appointed to carry the responsibility of organizing activities and fund-raising. This person was the missioner, the predecessor of the social worker with Deaf people. The work of the missioners included visiting and advising, job-finding and interpreting, while at the same time managing and organizing the society. They concentrated on adult Deaf people who were users of sign language. In the 1920s in-service training was offered to people working in the societies, a large part of which was the development of sign language and interpreting skills. The missioner was involved in the daily life of Deaf people, available day and night for preaching or interpreting at church services, and interpreting at job interviews and doctors' appointments. They had the opportunity to develop sign language skills and understand Deaf culture in a way that is perhaps unavailable to some present-day social workers with Deaf people. Some Deaf people view the time of the missioner positively, as they had ready access to sources of help, while others see it as a time of oppression when the missioner's involvement in so many aspects of Deaf people's lives created dependency on the mission.

The services of the missions constitute almost the only welfare service provision for adult Deaf people for over a century. The first statutory funding became available in 1933, and services became mandatory in 1960 following the Younghusband Report in 1959. From this time, local authorities took a more direct interest in the welfare of Deaf people, by funding either their own services or those of a voluntary agency.

The majority of social workers with Deaf people are employed by local authorities offering direct services, and a minority of workers are located in voluntary organizations that provide services on behalf of their local authority. Despite reports highlighting the need for skilled workers, social workers with Deaf people are less likely than their generic colleagues to have a social work qualification. Even more rarely do they have the dual qualification of basic social work and a post- qualifying certificate in the specialism. Only a small percentage of social workers have the requisite signing skills to practise as recommended by the Social Services Inspectorate report *Say It Again* (1988). In some local authorities there are no services at all, with posts vacant or filled by unqualified people. About 20 per cent of social workers with Deaf people are deaf themselves. It has been argued that section 11 funding (Local Government Act 1966) could be used to ensure that posts are designed for Deaf people themselves to work with their own community group. Yet this would require a shift in thinking on the part of the policy-makers towards the view of Deaf people as a cultural minority group rather than as disabled (that is, dependent). Similarly, the numbers of black social workers with Deaf people and black Deaf social workers are small. The city of Bradford has been referred to as an example of emerging good practice; it employs an Asian social worker to work with Asian deaf families. Overall, however, there has been a decline in the provision of specialist social workers employed to work with Deaf people, as there has been a move towards setting up separate interpreting services and employing technical officers to deal with environmental equipment.

Social services departments provide services to all 'hearing-impaired' people, which includes people who are audiologically deaf but do not identify with Deaf culture. Greater emphasis may be placed on their actual hearing loss, adjustment to it or management of it when referral is made to social services. Some local authorities and their agents' services for Deaf people are provided by social workers with Deaf people (SWDPs), who have particular information and knowledge about deafness. Others are not; this results in a distinction between service providers who are employed to work bilingually and transculturally with people from a minority group – that is, Deaf people – and mainstream social workers who, with information and appropriate communication skills, work with people whose hearing is 'impaired', that is, deaf people. Both Deaf and deaf people do share, however, experiences of oppression and DISCRIMINATION in a society that seeks to 'normalize' those who are seen as 'deficient' (see DISABILITY, IMPAIRMENT).

Social workers with Deaf people have inherited the role of missioner, and whether they should or should not interpret is probably the single biggest issue of debate in services to Deaf people. That interpreters are required is not in question, but responsibility for the funding and provision of such services is. Where the social worker with Deaf people works in isolation, is a 'hearing' person and has sign language skills, they have often been expected, by the employing body and by Deaf service users in that area, to carry the interpreting role. Some have done this willingly and have not accepted the argument that a social work role is, in the main, in conflict with that of an interpreter. For example, interpreters follow a code of practice that includes not offering personal opinions or advice and keeping all matters confidential, which would be inappropriate for a social worker to adhere to. It has been argued that combining the social work and interpreting roles actually oppresses Deaf people by denying their rights of 'self-determination, independence, choice and equality'. Some local authorities, responding to opinion from both service user groups and some service providers, recognizing the need for separate interpreting services and are acting accordingly. The provision of equipment for daily living has been another task that social workers with Deaf people have traditionally undertaken. It is an important service in terms of quality of life for service users, but because of the high demand, it is also very time-consuming. In many areas, this is now being undertaken by technical officers as part of the overall service offered to Deaf people.

Some social workers with Deaf people argue that, without the demands of interpreting and assessing for equipment, they could concentrate on areas of work that have, in some areas, been neglected and require a high standard of social work skill, a sound understanding of Deaf culture and British Sign Language and a commitment to anti-oppressive practice. These areas of work include sexual abuse of deaf children, working with Deaf people with mental health problems, and working with Deaf-blind people and those with other disabilities. In common with other social workers in the mainstream, some social workers with Deaf people are concerned at what they see to be the decline in preventive work. Some local authorities have responded to this in a positive way by creating a development worker's post and appointed a Deaf person to this position to work in partnership with service users, as part of their commitment to services that value Deaf people's skills, resources and lifestyles.

So far reference has predominantly been made to Deaf people – those who, regardless of their degree or age of onset of hearing loss, identify with Deaf culture and use British Sign Language. Such people are frequently referred to in social services departments as 'profoundly, pre-lingually deaf' or 'deaf without speech'. These categorizations are misleading and often inaccurate, but they reflect the model of deafness predominating in service provision, namely the medical model of deafness as a deficit rather than the recognition of Deaf people as a minority group. As service users, Deaf people may present the same range of problems as other service users, including child-care issues, debt or housing problems, and mental ill-health, which are not directly related to their 'hearing loss' but will be influenced by the fact that they are from a minority group in a society that does not widely recognize sign language and devalues the experience of Deaf people.

Although Deaf people share experiences around 'being Deaf', the Deaf 'community' also reflects the wide variety of human beliefs, lifestyles and attitudes. Deaf people are therefore all ages and ethnic origins, male, female, gay/lesbian, bisexual, heterosexual and mentally or physically disabled. Prejudice is evident in the Deaf community as in any other, and some Deaf people are marginalized and have different experiences of using social services. For example, from a study of the experiences of both Deaf/deaf people from ethnic-minority groups it was concluded that black Deaf people are isolated and generally receive poor services. Other reports suggest the same is also true for Deaf-blind people (see DEAF-BLIND).

Deaf people are not often born into Deaf culture but rather they acquire it, as the majority of Deaf people have hearing parents and families. As such, it is difficult to describe a deaf child as culturally Deaf before they have developed their self-identity as a Deaf person by mixing with other Deaf people, using sign language, etc. Given the general lack of awareness about Deaf issues, parents sometimes find it difficult to take on board the idea that their child will become a Deaf adult. Also, the place of sign language and the role of Deaf people in the education of deaf children are an ongoing controversial debate that again highlights the different ways of understanding deafness. These issues have influenced the provision of social work services to deaf children and their families.

S. Gregory and G. Hartley (eds), *Constructing Deafness*, London: Open University, 1991 in conjunction with Pinter.

**death instinct**  an unconscious wish for personal destruction directed either towards other people (murderous intent) or, more usually, towards oneself (suicidal intent).

**debt advice**  see MONEY ADVICE.

**decentralization**  the transfer of staff out from social services headquarters to local and COMMUNITY-level offices.

Decentralization has become an increasingly important approach to the delivery of social services by local authorities. The aim is to establish a closer link between officials and the local community they serve. The main services affected by decentralization are those of housing and social services, although some authorities are experimenting with a wider range of services. The introduction of decentralization has been associated mainly with Liberal Democrat local authorities and Labour authorities, particularly those of the Left. It has been noted that decentralization has been principally of three kinds: *departmental* decentralization, in which departments are reorganized into neighbourhood or community-level teams; *corporate* decentralization, where a range of services are decentralized into what are often termed 'mini-town halls', with the aim of providing almost the full range of services at community level in easy reach of local people; and *political* decentralization, where local-level committees of elected representatives are also devolved to advise the neighbourhood offices. With the latter approach, the aim is to provide a political reform that encourages local groups to become more involved and to increase levels of participation; emphasis is often placed on those groups who are most often excluded from the traditional networks of representation, including the disabled, ethnic-minority groups and women.

While decentralization approaches have sometimes proved very successful, they have also resulted in opposition. In particular, corporate and political decentralization has proved to be expensive, and in periods of financial constraint there has been some retrenchment. Costs have been high because of a number of factors: first, there is a need for training as junior officers are given greater responsibility; second, there is some capital cost in setting up neighbourhood offices; third, the relative success in the area of housing has led to an increase in demand from the public for services. However, departmental decentralization in the provision of social services has been maintained, as the development of community care has often been seen as more effective within a decentralized structure. Also, many senior managers have seen the devolution of some day-to-day management responsibilities as a way of freeing themselves to concentrate on more strategic planning of services. In addition, the AUDIT COMMISSION is promoting decentralization as a way of challenging entrenched power structures within local authority SOCIAL SERVICES DEPARTMENTS. The Audit Commission has argued that these vested interests mitigate against the interests of service users; in particular, the commission sees the need for budgets to be devolved so that decisions on the level of service provided for an individual can be made as close to the client as possible.

H. Elcock, 'Local government', in D. Farnham and S. Horton (eds), *Managing the New Public Services*, Basingstoke: Macmillan, 1993.

**decriminalization**   the removal of a socially deviant act (see DEVIANCE) from the orbit of the criminal law.

An example of decriminalization is homosexuality between consenting adults, which ceased to be classified as a crime in 1967. The term may be used in the strictly legal sense of removing an act from the list of crimes, or it may be used less formally to imply a change of attitude within the CRIMINAL JUSTICE SYSTEM resulting in certain offences and offenders being treated increasingly leniently. This has applied to trivial offences committed by very young juveniles and also appears to be happening in relation to DRUG users (though not suppliers), where fewer and fewer are being brought to court each year. It has long been argued by some that offences relating to prostitution should be decriminalized; prostitution itself is not a crime, but such activities as soliciting and living on the earnings of a prostitute are crimes. Decriminalization is not the same as legalization, since the latter implies legislation that actively regulates the actions in question (for example, licensing brothels).

**deferred sentence**   a decision by a court to postpone sentencing for up to six months to enable a defendant to demonstrate their motivation to reform – for example, by obtaining employment, responding to treatment or making other constructive changes to their life.

**deinstitutionalization**   the policy of moving residents in large care institutions such as mental hospitals to places of smaller scale in the community such as shared flats, foster families or independent living.

The policy gathered support after research indicated that living in large institutions led to passive and dependent behaviour on the part of many residents. The policy has been criticized on the grounds that people have been poorly prepared for living in the community. Critics cite evidence that people who have previously lived in large children's homes or mental hospitals make up a disproportionate number of homeless people, for example.

**dementia**   a progressive and irreversible decline in intellectual abilities, usually of gradual onset, affecting all areas of the brain. The disorder is usually associated with old age.

Five per cent of people aged over 65 years are severely demented, and 20 per cent of those over 85 show symptoms from mild to severe. Dementia can also appear in middle-aged people, where it results in more rapid deterioration. Indications of dementia are impairment in short- and long-term memory and in judgement, and inability to learn new information, to remember past personal information or facts of common knowledge, to perform routine or basic tasks, or to make and carry out plans. In addition, there may be significant changes of personality and major disorientation in time and place. There are differences in the degree of symptoms, however. Those with mild dementia have some impairment of social activities, although the individual retains adequate control over tasks associated with daily living. Sufferers of moderate dementia require some supervision of daily tasks, while the activity of those with severe dementia is so impaired as to require constant supervision or institutional care.

> ALZHEIMER'S DISEASE is the principal, but not the only, cause of dementia, accounting for some 55 per cent of all cases. Other causes include minor strokes, degenerative disorders such as Parkinson's disease, ALCOHOL toxicity, head injuries and infections of the central nervous system. Whatever the cause, the condition results in emotional, motor and behaviour problems which often require interdisciplinary care from both health and social services, including the services of consultant geriatrician, community psychiatric nurse, social worker and domiciliary carers. Assessment of need under the NATIONAL HEALTH SERVICE AND COMMUNITY CARE ACT is interdisciplinary and must involve the service user and their carers to the fullest extent possible.
>
> Care of people with dementia should take account of the clinical features presented, the personality prior to outset and any subsequent changes, accompanying medical conditions and the psychosocial pressures on the person and carers. Dementia may be accompanied by anxiety, sleeplessness, agitation, paranoia, depression and apathy. While medication may relieve some symptoms, careful assessment should identify whether any of these relate to a monotonous environment. Sufficient levels of stimulation in the person's immediate environment have proved to be a critical factor in maintaining optimal mental functioning.
>
> M. Marshall (ed.), *Working with People with Dementia*, Birmingham: Venture Press, 1990.

**denial**   a powerful defence mechanism that protects the personality from anxiety or guilt by ignoring or refusing to accept the validity of unacceptable thoughts, emotions or wishes.

The concept of denial has its origins in PSYCHOANALYSIS but is often used in a much looser way by social workers, who have in the past – sometimes unfairly – labelled a client's refusal to accept their point of view as denial.

**Department of Health (DoH)**   the main central government department responsible for personal social services and policies affecting social work.

The DoH was created in 1986 with the dismantling of the Department of Health and Social Security. Its responsibilities include the NATIONAL HEALTH SERVICE community care policy, implementation of major parts of the CHILDREN ACT, the operation of the SOCIAL SERVICES INSPECTORATE and health promotion. As with all other central government departments, the DoH is headed by a secretary of state, who sits in the cabinet as a senior minister; this cabinet minister is accountable to Parliament for the policy of the DoH and sits on the government's front bench. Legally and constitutionally subordinate to the secretary of state are a group of ministers responsible for aspects of the department, served by a group of senior civil servants who provide advice on health and social services policy and manage the department's business. Within the department, there is a National Health Service Management Executive and a National Health Service Policy Board. These are responsible for NHS organization and policy matters and report directly to the secretary of state through the NHS chief executive.

In respect of social work activities, the Secretary of State for Health has been given important powers under the NATIONAL HEALTH SERVICE AND COMMUNITY CARE ACT and the Children Act. The first requires all local authority social services departments to develop community care plans, which have to be submitted for approval to the secretary of state. The second has given the secretary of state power to have DoH officials enter and inspect all premises where children are kept under the Act, and the children in these premises. The department also communicates policy guidance to local authority social services through a series of circulars and ministers' letters. These follow up on points of detail to clarify aspects of government legislation but do not necessarily have the same force as Acts of Parliament. However, they are influential and allow the government to work towards national standards in the application of legislation. The use of other agencies including the Social Services Inspectorate and the Health Advisory Service also helps to communicate policy guidance to providers, as well as furnishing the department with information on the response from providers to legislation.

Ministers respond to questions on policy on the floor of the House of Commons as well as through a spokesperson in the House of Lords. Both ministers and civil servants respond to parliamentary questioning in front of PARLIAMENTARY SELECT COMMITTEES. The DoH will also work closely with other departments on the development of aspects of policy, notably with the DEPARTMENT OF SOCIAL SECURITY on issues relating to benefit systems. At the same time, the department will often be in competition with other departments for resources from the Treasury to try to pay for new and continuing policies.

**Department of Health and Social Services, Northern Ireland** the department responsible for health, social services and social security within the province of Northern Ireland.

This department coordinates all health and personal social services work in association with four boards. It is headed by a junior minister, who in turn is responsible to the Secretary of State for Northern Ireland. The Northern Ireland Office is itself seen as temporary, having been established in 1971 when direct rule from London began. The explicit intention is that at some stage control will return to the devolved government of the province. According to the official expenditure plans in 1993, the Health and Personal Social Services wing of the department is responsible for hospital and community health services, personal social services for the most vulnerable members of the community, family health services, centrally financed services for training and research, and administrative support. The Health and Personal Social Services wing is divided into a series of policy divisions covering the development of policy and legislation across a wide range of services. These divisions include the Health Policy Division, Family and Child Care Division, Social and Community Division, Client Groups, Social Legislation and the Strategy and Intelligence Group.

Department of Health and Social Services, Northern Ireland, *Northern Ireland Expenditure Plans and Priorities*, London: HMSO, 1993.

**Department of Social Security (DSS)** the main central government department responsible for policy on welfare benefits and their supply to clients.

Formerly part of the Department of Health and Social Security, the DSS operates through many local and regional offices to supply benefits to claimants throughout the country. In addition, it is responsible for all state pension schemes and for the collection of National Insurance contributions. Consequently, this department is one of the largest spenders of government money and has one of the largest workforces.

Major changes in the organization of the DSS have resulted from the implementation of a report by the Cabinet Office Efficiency Unit, *Improving Management in Government: The Next Steps* (1986). This report argued that government departments were too large and that ministers could not effectively manage such large organizations, particularly as their main concerns were with policy-making. In addition, the report argued that there was a need to make departments more efficient through the development of agencies that could be run on more businesslike lines, headed by a management team and a chief executive. The aim of the government is to move between 75 and 90 per cent of all civil servants into agencies by assessing the work of departments and identifying those areas of work that are coherent executive activities rather than policy-making areas.

In the case of the DSS, it was found to have three major areas of activity that could be given agency status. These are now the Social Security Benefits Agency, the Social Security Contributions Agency and the Information Technology Services Agency. Each of these agencies works within a policy framework document that provides details of the areas of responsibility allocated by the parent department to the agency and the relationship to the DSS and its ministers. These include the following remit for the Benefits Agency: 'The function of the Agency is the administration of social security benefits and other services . . . including the handling of claims, reviews and appeals, and arranging payment. It must do this in accordance with the law and any directions from the Secretary of State' (*Framework Document*, 1991 p. 4).

As a result of these changes, responsibility for day-to-day management issues now lies with the chief executive of each agency and not with the secretary of state. Appeals and complaints should now be directed to the chief executive rather than to the secretary of state, and the chief executive also reports directly to the Parliamentary Select Committee on Health and Social Security. This has raised concern in Parliament about the accountability of these agencies to Parliament and to the electorate. Whether these changes will lead to an improved service for claimants, without continual interference from ministers in day-to-day management issues, is still a debatable point. The introduction of the Citizen's Charter in the local offices of the Benefits Agency is also aimed at improving the service by publicizing targets, including waiting times for interviews and maximum delays in receiving benefits. These agencies were introduced in April 1991, and it is too early to make any firm judgement on their performance.

**dependence**  a term that, when applied to DRUG use and misuse, means the user experiencing a compulsion to use the drug again. Dependence usually develops only after regular use of a drug.

There are two types of dependence: psychological dependence, which involves a strong desire to repeat the experience for the effect, and a feeling that the user cannot cope without the drug; and physical dependence, which occurs when the body becomes so accustomed to receiving regular amounts of the drug that unpleasant WITHDRAWAL symptoms (sweats, cramps, diarrhoea, and so on) are experienced if the drug is not taken. All drugs can be psychologically addictive (see ADDICTION), but only some physically so, the main ones belonging to the OPIATE family (such as heroin, methadone, morphine and opium).

**depressant**   a DRUG that slows down the workings of the body and brain. While depressants usually have the effect of relaxing the body, they do not, as the name might suggest, lead to depression. Such drugs include ALCOHOL, BARBITURATES, benzodiazepines and OPIATES. When used over a period of time, they may produce both physical and psychological DEPENDENCE.

**depression**   feelings of hopelessness, sadness, tearfulness and intense ANXIETY.

Depression is the most common of all psychiatric disorders, with a high reported incidence throughout the population, of between 10 per cent and 15 per cent. It is twice as common in women as in men and is more prevalent in lower socioeconomic groups. Depression affects people in different ways. A person suffering from depression can feel sadness, low self-esteem, hopelessness or something more extreme, such as feelings of total despair, complete worthlessness, intense guilt and constant irritability. Tasks require extra effort; thinking becomes more difficult; and thoughts can centre on SUICIDE or by preoccupied with fears of serious illness. Speech and particularly physical movements can be slowed drastically, while at the same time the sufferer is tense and restless, with pronounced interruption to sleep patterns. Depression is frequently classified as *endogenous*, which means arising from within, when it seems to have no specific cause, or *reactive*, when it is a result of specific events, such as bereavement, in a person's life. Reactive depression is generally viewed as the milder form, from which the sufferer may recover spontaneously over a period of time.

The causes of depression are much debated. Certain social and economic factors have been highlighted. In a famous study in the late 1970s it was noted that of 500 women in an inner London suburb some 33 per cent experienced some degree of depression. Against a background of bad housing and unsatisfactory marriages, the authors noted four vulnerability factors: (1) three or more children aged under 14 living at home; (2) lack of an intimate or confiding relationship; (3) loss of mother in childhood; (4) lack of employment outside the home. Certain psychological explanations have also been advanced, centring on the concept of LEARNED HELPLESSNESS – certain individuals believe that they have no control over their environment and that any effort on their part is bound to be ineffective. This state of mind leads people to view problems in their lives as the product of long-standing personal inadequacies and not as the result of specific situations that can be resolved.

Many people who are depressed are diagnosed as such by a medical practitioner, including their own general practitioner, and receive some form of medication such as anti-depressants or major or minor tranquillizers. But in many cases, social work practitioners and counsellors are able to offer assistance that enhances personal effectiveness. This has proven particularly so in the case of assertiveness training, often provided for a group of depressed people, in which people are encouraged to express their opinions and feelings in a direct and appropriate way. Social workers have also been effective in running all-women groups, which often provide a therapeutic and support element as well as some ASSERTIVENESS TRAINING. Conversely, practitioner and sufferer may decide that individual COUNSELLING, particularly grief counselling, is the most effective way to help the person find an alternative response to the loss that they have suffered and to which the depression is a reaction.

A. Corob, *Working with Depressed Women*, Aldershot: Gower, 1987.

**desensitization**  a principal component of BEHAVIOUR THERAPY, involving the gradual substitution of a relaxed response for an anxious response in relation to an event, object or thought that a person finds anxiety-provoking.

Desensitization is usually achieved by combining relaxation techniques with visualized images of the thing that is feared. The technique is often used in relation to PHOBIAS such as fear of open places or flying.

**detention**  usually refers to the process of being held in a police station under the provisions of the POLICE AND CRIMINAL EVIDENCE ACT 1984. The term may also be used in relation to CUSTODIAL SENTENCES, especially in a YOUNG OFFENDER INSTITUTION.

**detention centre**  a penal institution designed for short custodial sentences for YOUNG OFFENDERS.

Set up in 1948, detention centres provided a strict, military-type regime for predominantly male offenders aged 14 to 21 years for a maximum of six months. The term was abolished by the Criminal Justice Act 1988, and existing establishments were integrated into the YOUNG OFFENDER INSTITUTION system.

**deterrence**  the philosophy of sentencing that emphasizes the aim of deterring people from committing crime.

There are two elements in this principle: individual and general deterrence. Individual deterrence refers to measures intended to impress on the offender that the personal consequences of their actions in the form of the punishment received make it 'not worth' committing crime again. General deterrence refers to measures intended to set an example for other people in the hope of deterring them from committing crime. (See PRINCIPLES OF SENTENCING.)

**detoxification**  the process whereby a person dependent on DRUGS stops using the substance to the point that the body no longer requires it. This may be done at home or in a drug unit or hospital and implies physical discomfort as the body adjusts to the absence of the drug.

**deviance**  a sociological term referring to behaviour perceived to deviate from socially constructed and accepted norms and role expectations. It may also be described as social 'rule-breaking' or a breach of social order.

Deviant behaviour need not be criminal (for example, mentally ill people are often classified as deviant), but explanations or THEORIES OF CRIME are frequently regarded as specific examples of more general theories of deviance. Deviance tends to be studied in two ways: as an objective reality or as a subjective experience. Those who view deviance as an objective phenomenon argue that there is widespread consensus on norms and values in society and that this basic agreement makes it relatively easy to identify deviants. Standard negative sanctions can then be imposed, and this act of punishment or control reaffirms for the group that it is bound by a set of common values and norms. Those who view deviance as a subjective experience are concerned with its social definition. They are concerned to examine how particular people are identified and set apart and what the consequences are both for such people (in terms of developing a deviant identity) and for those who impose the label of deviance.

**Diploma in Social Work**  the basic qualification for social workers in Britain. The regulations for the diploma were issued by the Central Council for Education and Training in Social Work (CCETSW) in 1989, and the first of the new programmes came into existence in 1990. All previous qualifying courses (both Certificate of Social Service and Certificate of Qualification in Social Work) must change to the diploma by 1995.

The Dip.SW was developed as a result of a number of concerns about previous qualifying courses in social work. First, earlier courses were perceived as uneven in quality; second, they were of unequal length, which many felt could not be justified; third, many courses were no longer relevant to the needs of current social work practice; and fourth, few courses were able to deliver the ANTI-DISCRIMINATORY and ANTI-RACIST dimensions thought to be central to contemporary problems. The new arrangements were to establish social work programmes rather than courses; such programmes were to be collaborative enterprises between colleges and employers. The collaboration was to encourage much closer relationships between college teaching and practice. All key functions in the delivery of programmes were to be shared by academics and social work agencies. Given the parallel proposals to improve practice teaching, the overall experience for students was likely to be closer to the expectations and hopes of employers.

The regulations still permit substantial variations in programme delivery. College-based and employment-based routes are still permissible. Flexible provision in relation to credit transfers between colleges, the accreditation of prior learning and possibly distance-learning packages are all to be encouraged. Most importantly, the regulations require all programmes to address requirements in relation to core skills, VALUES and knowledge. In this respect CCETSW has clarified its thinking about the needs of social work in the latter part of the twentieth century. CCETSW hopes that a greater degree of consensus about what competence in social work means has resulted from the new qualification. Nevertheless the diploma is to be reviewed yet again in the course of 1994.

Central Council for Education and Training in Social Work, *Requirements for the Diploma in Social Work*, London: CCETSW Paper 30, 1990.

**direct payment** deductions from an individual's INCOME SUPPORT and paid to a third party, made in a variety of circumstances.

Mortgage interest payments are now always made direct to the lender. Deductions can also be made for other housing costs, rent arrears, fuel debts and consumption, water charges, council tax and community charge (poll tax) arrears, unpaid fines, costs and compensation orders, and child support payments. There are some limitations on the amount that can be deducted from a person's benefit without their consent. Because of these limitations debts are prioritized in the order shown above. Apart from council tax and community charge arrears, these deductions can also be made from unemployment, sickness or invalidity benefit, retirement pension or severe disablement allowance where these are combined with income support.

**disability** increasingly recognized as a form of social oppression resulting from an environment unsuited to the needs of impaired people; hence recently defined as 'the disadvantage or restriction of activity caused by contemporary social organization which takes no or little account of people who have impairments and thus excludes them from activities'.

The above definition reflects the view that disability is socially constructed and contrasts with the approach of the World Health Organization, which has adopted a classification known as the International Classification of Impairments, Disabilities and Handicaps; this defines disability as 'any restriction or lack (resulting from an impairment) of ability to perform an activity in the manner or within the range considered normal for a human being'. This definition, still widely used, has been criticized for several reasons, most notably by some disabled people, who regard it as underemphasizing the restrictions imposed on disabled people by society and overemphasizing the individual and dubious notions of normality. The social model of disability dismisses the view that disability is either a medical phenomenon or a tragedy that befalls some individuals. It regards disability as a social construction resulting in physical and attitudinal barriers to disabled people's full participation in society. Within this framework, attention has been drawn to the compounded experiences of oppression of some disabled people – for example, disabled women and black and ethnic-minority disabled people. The presence of such people in society and their contribution to it have been largely ignored until recently, as has their need for appropriate services. Although the majority of disabled adults are female, disabled women have generally been treated as invisible and placed under unacknowledged stress by this and other factors, including the particular pressure on women in Western society to conform to unrealistic stereotypes of female beauty.

The physical environment frequently denies equality of opportunity to disabled people, as do public attitudes. Anti-discriminatory legislation is widely acknowledged to be required to remedy this situation. Legal entitlement to service provision is derived from a number of Acts of Parliament – see, for example, the CHILDREN ACT, the CHRONICALLY SICK AND DISABLED PERSONS ACT 1970, the DISABLED PERSONS (SERVICES, CONSULTATION AND REPRESENTATION) ACT 1986 and the NATIONAL HEALTH SERVICE AND COMMUNITY CARE ACT – but eligibility under these laws still draws on the NATIONAL ASSISTANCE Act 1948. Section 29 of this act refers to 'the blind and partially sighted, the deaf and hard of hearing, the dumb, persons who suffer from any mental disorder, and other persons who are substantially or permanently handicapped by illness, injury, or congenital deformity'. Registers of disabled people, both adult and children, exist, but many disabled people are not registered.

Social work with disabled people should be informed by the social model of disability. The emphasis should be upon ensuring the maximum degree of autonomy and choice for disabled service users. This is true both for social workers who are service providers and for those who act as purchasers of services. The importance of the availability of full information for service users cannot be overstated. Especially relevant is information about service users' rights, including welfare benefits. The welfare rights of disabled people are a complex field, and service users may need expert advice. Take-up rates are often less than satisfactory, even for basic allowances such as DISABILITY LIVING ALLOWANCE (a benefit for disabled people) and INVALID CARE ALLOWANCE (a benefit payable to carers of people in receipt of disability living allowance). Useful relevant advice is available from disability rights handbooks, which are updated annually.

Social workers must work and plan services on a multi-agency basis collaboratively with other professionals. Among these professionals are OCCUPATIONAL THERAPISTS, who can make available relevant AIDS AND ADAPTATIONS. Social workers who are responsible for purchasing services and for coordinating packages of care require the ability to ascertain the needs and wishes of potential service users and the skill to negotiate with service providers to meet those needs and wishes. The emphasis must be upon maximum empowerment for disabled service users. This is also true of disabled children, who are recognized as 'children in need' under the Children Act. Under this legislation disabled children are eligible for services that should minimize their disability and permit them to lead as normal a life as possible. The philosophy of 'children first' is well established in this field, emphasizing the need to consider a disabled child's needs primarily from the point of view of the child rather than with emphasis upon their disability. In accordance with this view, very few disabled children live in permanent residential care; the vast majority live with their family or in a substitute family. In working with disabled children and their families, social workers should recognize the expertise of parents and other care-givers. They must also bear in mind that abuse of disabled children is probably more prevalent than abuse of non-disabled children.

Social work services for disabled children are usually provided from children and family teams. Social workers in this field need expertise in child-care plus the knowledge and skills outlined above as necessary for working with disabled adults. In addition, for disabled people of all ages the value of peer support should not be overlooked.

A. Stevens, *Disability Issues: Developing Anti-Discriminatory Practice*, London: Central Council for Education and Training in Social Work, 1991.

**disability appeal tribunal**   a tribunal that hears appeals against decisions of ADJUDICATION officers on DISABILITY benefits claims. Such tribunals are independent of the Department of Social Security.

Benefits within the remit of disability appeal tribunals include DISABILITY LIVING ALLOWANCE, attendance allowance, DISABILITY WORKING ALLOWANCE, industrial disablement benefit and SEVERE DISABLEMENT ALLOWANCE. Each has three members: the chairperson, who is a lawyer, one member who is a medical practitioner and the other who 'is experienced in the needs of people with disabilities either in a professional or voluntary capacity or because they have a disability themselves'. An adjudication officer from the Department of Social Security is usually present to explain the department's decision. The claimant or their representative has an opportunity to explain their case. The chances of success are greatly increased if the claimant attends. To win disputes about disability questions the collection of favourable medical evidence may be important.

**disability living allowance** a benefit paid to people with severe disabilities who need help looking after themselves or supervision to avoid danger, or who have difficulty with outdoor mobility. It includes a CARE COMPONENT, paid at three different rates, and a MOBILITY COMPONENT, paid at two different rates.

The benefit was introduced in 1992, for people aged under 65, replacing attendance allowance and MOBILITY ALLOWANCE. People of 65 or over can still claim attendance allowance. The higher-rate care component is paid to people who need frequent attention with bodily functions or continual supervision to avoid danger during the day and night. It is also paid to people who are terminally ill. The middle rate is paid to people needing frequent attention or continual supervision during the day or the night. The lower rate is paid to people needing attention for a significant part of the day or who are aged 16 or over but cannot prepare themselves a cooked meal. The higher-rate mobility component is paid to people aged 5 or over who are physically disabled and unable or virtually unable to walk, or for whom the effort needed is likely to seriously effect their health. The lower rate is paid to people with physical or mental disabilities who need guidance or supervision from another person to get about out of doors. Disability living allowance is a non-contributory and non-means-tested benefit. It acts as a passport to higher rates of INCOME SUPPORT but is not taken into account as income for any means-tested benefits. A claim for disability living allowance includes a long self-assessment form. This was envisaged as a great improvement on the previous, often unsatisfactory medical examinations. In practice the form has proved contentious and difficult for people to use.

**disability working allowance** a means-tested benefit paid to a person who works sixteen hours or more each week and is at a 'disadvantage in getting a job' because of their disability.

The amount paid depends on the number of people in the claimant's family (if any), the age of any children and the family income, including earnings. Disability working allowance cannot be paid to anyone who has more than £8,000 in capital. Capital between £3,000 and £8,000 is deemed to produce an income of £1 per week for every £250 or part thereof and is taken into account in determining the level of benefit. Disability working allowance was introduced in 1992. It is a completely new benefit, designed to encourage and enable people who are partly incapacitated to take employment. By the end of its first year only 2,800 people in the whole of Britain were receiving this benefit.

**Disabled Persons (Services, Consultation and Representation) Act 1986** an Act whereby it was intended to bring about improvements for people with learning disability, physical disability and mental health problems as regards assessment, representation, consultation and service coordination.

Only certain sections of the Act have been implemented. Section 4 places a clear duty on social services departments to decide whether the needs of a disabled person require services to be provided under the CHRONICALLY SICK AND DISABLED PERSONS ACT 1970. Sections 5 and 6 require local authorities to identify and assess disabled school-leavers. Local education authorities refer disabled children to the social services department so that an ASSESSMENT can take place as to whether the children are likely to be disabled in adult terms. Section 8 requires carers' ability to care to be taken into account. Section 9 requires the provision of information about services, while under section 10 organizations of disabled people must be consulted when people with knowledge of disability are appointed to public bodies or organizations. Individual programme plans (IPPs) are regular reviews for people with learning disability. Their aim is to enable a MULTIDISCIPLINARY workforce to develop with a service user a prioritized list of objectives designed to meet the user's identified needs. The response of service users to IPPs and to meetings associated with them is mixed. Some service users feel they offer them a chance to put their views forward, but others have expressed more negative views, sometimes noting lack of any resultant change and a non-participative mode of operation.

**disabled students allowance** an additional allowance payable to disabled students who are on degree or degree-level courses, to enable them to purchase non-medical personal assistance and special equipment. Such assistance might include, for example, note-takers, and special equipment might include personal computers.

**discharge** a sentence following a conviction in a criminal court. An absolute discharge involves no further action and is imposed only for very minor offences; a conditional discharge involves no further action, provided the defendant does not reoffend within a specified period up to a maximum of three years.

**disclosure** when a child tells or otherwise represents that they have been sexually abused.

Setting the right conditions for interview in which a child may say that they have been sexually abused is among the most difficult of all social work skills, for which considerable training is required. The child may be in distress and reluctant to say that perhaps their father or some other trusted adult abused them in some way. Talking about this may take some time and require a number of different forms of communication, such as drawings or play. At the same time, the social worker may be working with police officers to gather evidence for a criminal investigation that involves technical equipment such as video. Some social workers and paediatricians have been criticized for conducting 'disclosure interviews' with children, on the grounds that because they have assumed that abuse has happened they are encouraging, even pressurizing, the child to provide this admission. This presumption then heavily influences their style of questioning and at its worst can lead to prolonged and insistent questioning until the 'right' answer is obtained therefore the term 'disclosure interview' is no longer used. The recent MEMORANDUM OF GOOD PRACTICE issued by the government makes it clear that interviewing styles based on the presumption that the child will disclose eventually are impermissible.

> Department of Health and Home Office, *Memorandum of Good Practice*, London: HMSO, 1992.

**discrimination**  see ABLE-BODIEDISM, ANTI-DISCRIMINATORY PRACTICE, EQUAL PAY ACT 1970, FAIR EMPLOYMENT COMMISSION, GENDER, HOMOSEXUALITY, RACISM, SEXISM.

**district nurse**  a registered nurse employed by a district health authority or NATIONAL HEALTH SERVICE trust to provide nursing care in patients' homes, health centres and general practitioners' premises.

**divorce**  the legally sanctioned dissolution of a marriage, often preceded by a period of separation that may also be legally ratified.

Approximately one in three marriages ends in divorce, and second marriages are twice as likely to fail as first marriages. In relation to children, about one child in twenty experiences their parents' divorce by age 5, and one child in five by age 16. Attitudes to divorce have changed significantly over the last few decades. The Divorce Reform Act 1969 made it possible to divorce without the 'matrimonial offence'. Social stigma in relation to divorced people has also clearly diminished. Problems of adjustment to divorce for all parties remain, however, and for many the difficulties are profound. Researchers have distinguished many elements to a divorce in terms of social and personal dimensions. First, there is the emotional separation and uncoupling; second, the issue of child custody and parenting arrangements; third, the settling of material issues, including maintenance and the disposal of property; fourth, the rearrangement of social, community and official relationships; and, finally, in the wake of all these issues, adjustments for the divorced pair.

> Children's reactions to the separation and divorce of their parents encompass a wide range of responses. At worst a child's fundamental stability can be upset for a long period or, in extreme cases, permanently. Many children yearn for the non-custodial parent, harbour unrealistic hopes for a reconciliation and have their school performance and ability to sustain robust peer relationships substantially impaired. Other children seem to make successful adjustments after a period of anxiety, grief and, often, anger. Variation in children's success or otherwise in

making adjustments seems to be reflected in variables such as the child's age and understanding, the parents' relationship before and after separation, continuity of other things like school, having to adjust to a parent's new partner and perhaps their children, and the child's attitude to the custodial and non-custodial parent. Social workers and others can become involved at many points in attempts to deal with a failing marriage and in subsequent separation. If the decision to separate has been made, the role of the conciliator (see CONCILIATION) or mediator and the divorce court welfare functions become very important.

J. Wallerstein and J. Kelly, *Surviving the Breakup*, London: Grant McIntyre, 1980.

**dole**   to be 'on the dole' means claiming benefit as unemployed.

A person who is on the dole signs on as unemployed at the Employment Service office. They may be getting unemployment benefit or income support or unemployment benefit topped up by income support.

**domestic violence**   a term that usually refers to the physical, sexual, emotional and mental ABUSE of women by male partners or ex-partners.

The term and its definition are controversial. Some people feel that the word 'domestic' implies a cosiness that detracts from the seriousness of the VIOLENCE and prefer the term 'partner abuse'. Terms such as 'marital violence', 'spouse abuse' and 'battered wives' imply that the couple involved must be married. It has also been pointed out that the term 'battered wives' or 'battered women' diverts attention from violent husbands or men. Although the 1988 British Crime Survey shows that the people most likely to be victims of violent assault are young men, it also shows that women are particularly at risk of sexual assault and domestic violence. Over 60 per cent of offences against women occur indoors (compared with 40 per cent against men), and around half of the incidents of violence against women reported to the police are committed by male partners. Because many women are afraid of reporting such incidents to the police, the true figure may be much higher. The same is also true for offences of rape, of which about 4,000 were recorded in 1991, although changes in police attitudes and practices have resulted in an increase in reporting. Of these reported rapes, about one-third were committed by strangers and two-thirds by intimate or casual acquaintances.

Violence within the family takes many forms, including CHILD ABUSE and ELDER ABUSE, besides violence to women. Domestic violence is now perceived as pervasive, present in many societies and in all social classes, and a common phenomenon. A study of a particular locality in the city of Leeds revealed that the majority of women had to contend with intimidatory or violent behaviour, both in the home and in the community, in the course of a year. Because domestic violence takes place in the privacy of the home, it is difficult to establish its prevalence, but it is generally accepted as being far more widespread than most people would like to think, and it is not confined to any particular social class or group.

Many different explanations are offered for domestic violence. Some people argue that men are by nature aggressive and will instinctively react violently if they feel threatened or thwarted by their partner's behaviour. Others argue that violence occurs when couples are incompatible or suffer from excessive stress in their lives. A further explanation attributes violence to the pathology or abnormality of particular men or to the provocation or masochism of particular women. Although all of these explanations may apply in individual situations, many people feel that none of them is sufficient to account for domestic violence as such a widespread feature of society. A feminist perspective would argue that domestic violence is the product of the power that men have over women and of their need to maintain their dominant position by controlling women. Thus violence, the threat of violence or the potential for violence is said to characterize all sexual relationships.

Many women endure domestic violence without seeking any remedy, often because they are afraid of the consequences for their children if they were to leave. Those who seek to change their situation have rights in both civil and criminal law. In civil law, a woman may apply to court for either a non-molestation order (to prevent a man molesting or harassing her), an OUSTER ORDER (to get him removed from the family home) or a RE-ENTRY ORDER (allowing her back into the home, for example if she has fled to a women's refuge). In criminal law, the man may be arrested for assault.

In the past, the police have been notoriously reluctant to intervene in 'domestics', but official attitudes have changed greatly, and the police are now encouraged to treat domestic violence like any other form of violence they encounter.

Much of the increasing political awareness and public attention now given to domestic violence is the result of the work of the WOMEN'S AID movement, which has successfully combined direct provision of refuges with active campaigning, political lobbying and research. As a social problem, the 'battering of women' came into the public domain in Britain in the 1960s with the establishment of Chiswick Women's Aid, a hostel for women who wished to get away from violent partners. Since that time the women's aid movement has grown substantially, leading to the development of a network of refuges around the country. There is now some public and political recognition of the problem of domestic violence.

Despite these developments there is in some social welfare and justice circles a concern about the adequacy of services for women (and their children) who have experienced violence in the home. Services continue to be fragmented, with very patchy provision across the country; no agency has overall responsibility for helping women and children who face these problems. There is some evidence to suggest that men who are violent to women may also be violent to children. Similarly there is increasing recognition that violence in the home is emotionally damaging to children as well as to women. For these reasons many people feel that social services departments, in conjunction with the police, should assume responsibility for the problem. Help for women from this source, however, remains very uneven, which is clear evidence for some of institutional sexism.

The social work tasks include securing the immediate and future safety of a woman and her children, enabling the woman to make considered decisions about her future and helping both woman and children to recover from the trauma of violence. In this context there are many practical and legal problems that may have to be considered, including the custody of children, issues of income and shelter, and long-term protection from a man intent on further violence (see also INJUNCTIONS).

J. Hamer and S. Saunders, *Well-Founded Fear*, London: Hutchinson, 1984.

**domiciliary services**   any social welfare or health provision taken to the recipient in their own home.

The justification for such services are many and include: the idea of 'aftercare' for those who are still vulnerable after discharge from hospital; provision for those who could not reasonably get to a service based in a hospital or in the community such as a person with a disability; and provision for somebody in a frail state wishing to stay within their own home, rather than being cared for elsewhere. Such services include COMMUNITY PSYCHIATRIC NURSES, family aides, HEALTH VISITORS and HOME HELPS (or COMMUNITY CARE WORKERS). Domiciliary services are related in intent to the idea of OUTREACH. Similarly, many believe that the success of community care will in part depend on the comprehensiveness or otherwise of domiciliary services.

**drug**   a chemical substance that alters an individual's emotional and/or psychological state, physical state and/or behaviour. Different drugs have different effects on people. Some are legal, sold over the counter or by prescription only; others are illegal. (See SUBSTANCE MISUSE.)

**drug or alcohol dependency**   a condition of DEPENDENCE for which a court making a PROBATION ORDER can include a condition that requires an offender to undertake treatment (resident or non-resident) at an appropriate institution. The requirement is not confined to offenders convicted directly of drug- or alcohol-related crime.

**drugs**   see MISUSE OF DRUGS ACT 1971.

**due process**   dealing with an alleged offender through strict adherence to the rules of legal proceedings rather than using authorized discretion to divert them to informal or therapeutic disposals.

The term tends to be associated with 'just deserts' or retributive PRINCIPLES OF SENTENCING but is usually interpreted positively by its advocates as entailing the provision of legal protection for the defendant. In contrast, the use of discretion and rehabilitative approaches is regarded as potentially discriminatory. Due process was a feature of the reforms of the juvenile justice system in the 1980s, resulting from a concern that 'welfare-oriented' approaches had, ironically, led to the incarceration of undue numbers of YOUNG OFFENDERS. Critics of due process argue that its inflexibility can be discriminatory by failing to take account of individual circumstances and needs.

**dying**   the sudden or gradual cessation of all physiological and mental processes in a person. Recovery of function is not possible.

This definition of dying, simple and clear, could cause offence to many people, because Western societies have traditionally been death-denying societies. Reluctance to employ direct language to describe death – the use of such euphemisms and metaphors as 'going to heaven', 'going to God' and 'falling asleep' – may indicate people's feelings about dying. People may change the subject or joke, or consider talking of dying morbid. Often a dying person is denied the opportunity to talk about what is one of the most significant events of their lives. Dying people may feel isolated from their carers.

The reluctance to deal openly with death and discussion of death makes it difficult for people who are dying to express their needs in personally meaningful ways. In her work on the subject, Elizabeth Kubler-Ross notes that a patient dying of cancer in a hospital was prevented from saying how good it felt to be dying; the care she received, the relief from pain, the new friendships with hospital staff and the acceptance of the fact of death by Kubler-Ross all helped ensure that for her dying was a peaceful, shared and comfortable experience. The reluctance towards, or taboo against, discussion of dying means that many people do not receive the support and help they need, as in the case of a nurse who when dying was permitted to share feelings with others only by writing them down.

Many people have difficulties when the fact of a person's dying needs to be communicated to the dying person themselves and to others. It has been suggested that this is linked to the fear of dying that most people have and to the belief that others have the same fear. Although there may be a fear of dying in most people, possibly shared by people who 'manage' death professionally (such as medical personnel), it has often been argued that the experience of dying should be shared. Many people when told initially that they are dying may deny or ignore the information. Working effectively with dying people requires a recognition of social taboos on talk about dying, together with a willingness for a worker to break that taboo if a dying person desires it. Working with the dying means offering an accepting and supportive relationship, responding honestly to cues that the dying person may give as to the direction they wish discussions to take.

E. Kubler-Ross, *On Death and Dying,* London: Routledge & Kegan Paul, 1970.

# E

**early release**    arrangements for early release from PRISON under the CRIMINAL JUSTICE ACT 1991, replacing previous arrangements for remission (a term that has been abolished) and PAROLE (which is now available only in limited circumstances).

There are three principles underlying the arrangements. First, at least half of the stated length of a CUSTODIAL SENTENCE must be served in prison. Second, the remainder of the sentence may be served in the community, with or without supervision by a probation officer. Third, during the time in the community, the offender is 'at risk' of being returned to prison to serve the remainder of the sentence if any further offence is committed. The exact nature of the release arrangements depends primarily on the length of the original sentence. Short sentences (under twelve months) attract automatic unconditional release at the halfway point and do not involve any supervision. Medium sentences (of one to four years) attract automatic conditional release at the halfway point that involves a period of supervision. Long sentences (over four years) can attract discretionary conditional release (formerly parole) at the halfway point and automatic conditional release at the two-thirds point, both of which involve supervision. There are a few exceptions to these provisions, including YOUNG OFFENDERS (who always receive supervision after release) and life-sentence prisoners (for whom the process of release is very complicated).

**earnings disregards**   those parts of earned income that do not count in full when a person's income is calculated for purposes of INCOME SUPPORT, HOUSING BENEFIT or COUNCIL TAX BENEFIT.

Earnings disregards are intended to cover some work-related expenses but usually not child-care. The level of disregard varies according to the claimant's circumstances.

**eating disorders**   see ANOREXIA, BULIMIA.

**ecological approach**   a perspective in social work that emphasizes the adaptive and reciprocal relationship between people and their environment.

The central concept of the ecological approach (sometimes called the 'life model') is the 'goodness of fit' between people and their environment. The approach focuses on the adaptations that individuals achieve in relation to their environment over their life span and also on the degree to which they can change or shape that environment. Although offering a general and often abstract model, the approach has the merit of highlighting the connection between a person's needs, problems and goals, on the one hand, and the characteristics of the social, economic and physical environments in which they live, on the other. It notes that the 'transactions' between people and their environment are reciprocal; they act on and affect each other. Transactions are said to be adaptive when a person's development, achievements, needs and well-being are promoted and met by the environment – the family, work organizations, and political and economic structures; transactions are maladaptive when they generate tension and antagonism, creating a relationship between person and environment characterized by conflict, loss and stress.

In practice, the ecological model focuses on the impact of life transitions, such as puberty, on the individual; on those elements in the person's environment that either cause stress or are supportive; and on the processes by which the individual interacts with that environment. Social work assessments following the ecological model tend to identify any life transitions that the client may be undergoing (which often call for a new kind of adaptation to their environment), sources of stress and the person's 'life space' in which they arise – family, work and physical environment. Further, the ecological approach seeks to clarify what actions the client should undertake in order to regain an adaptive relationship with their environment. Like all variants of the SYSTEMS APPROACH, the ecological model has been criticized for seeming to imply that the individual must adapt to their environment. Adherents emphasize, however, that social work intervention based on it often attempts to rearrange elements of the client's environment rather than have the client passively adapt.

C. Germain and A. Gitterman, *The Life Model of Social Work Practice*, New York: Columbia University Press, 1980.

**ecomap** a diagram used by a variety of social welfare workers to describe the focal person's social situation. It could typically include family or kin (see GENOGRAM) but also significant others.

In many situations significant or influential people can come from outside the family, such as a teacher or family friend. Some problems are now seen as at least partly soluble by mobilizing potential helpers from outside the family (see NETWORK CONFERENCE).

**EC Social Security Directive 79/7** a directive setting out the then European Community's (now European Union's) objective for sex equality in social security.

The directive states that 'there shall be no DISCRIMINATION on grounds of sex either directly or indirectly by reference in particular to marital or family status'. Member states were supposed to abolish discriminatory laws and practices by 1985. The directive applies to the 'working population', but this includes people whose work is interrupted by ill-health or involuntary unemployment, people who are retired and people looking for work. Women who give up work to care for children are not covered, but women who gave up work to care for a person with a DISABILITY are; it was action in the European Court that forced the United Kingdom government to extend INVALID CARE ALLOWANCE to married women (excluded until 1986). Benefits covered include those relating to sickness, invalidity, old age, unemployment and industrial injury. INCOME SUPPORT paid, for example, to an unemployed person is covered, but HOUSING BENEFIT and FAMILY CREDIT are not.

**Ecstasy** an illicitly produced DRUG exhibiting characteristics of both AMPHETAMINE and LSD.

Methylenedioxymethylamphetamine is the full chemical name of Ecstasy, but it has many nicknames including 'E', 'Adam', 'love doves', 'disco biscuits' and 'hamburgers'. It is available in either tablet or capsule form, and the exact composition is usually variable and unpredictable. It is usually swallowed but may be snorted, smoked or injected. Ecstasy is a class A drug under the MISUSE OF DRUGS ACT 1971, and penalties for possession, production and supply vary from a fine to life imprisonment.

**Education Act 1944** a major reforming piece of legislation that still underpins the general structure of primary, secondary and tertiary education in Britain.

Section 36 of the Act defines the basic duty of a parent to ensure that their child is properly educated according to their age, ability, aptitude and any special educational needs they may have, either at a school or 'otherwise'. Although education is compulsory, attending a school is not.

**Education Act 1981** arising from the Warnock Report (1978), the 1981 Act made a number of important changes for children with SPECIAL EDUCATIONAL NEEDS.

A key principle of the Act is that disabled children have a right to be educated in mainstream school where it is 'compatible with the efficient use of resources'. In addition, the Act requires that children should be educated according to their 'special educational needs' and not according to their DISABILITY. The Act makes provision for the assessment of special educational needs (see STATEMENTING), gives parents the right to be involved in the assessment and recognizes their value as partners in the educational process.

The Act contains three key definitions: learning difficulty, special educational needs and special educational provision. Central to the Act is a definition of special educational needs as defined by Warnock: 'In broad terms special educational need is likely to take the form of the need for one or more of the following: (i) The provision of special means of access to the curriculum through specific equipment, facilities or resources, modification of the physical environment or specialist teaching techniques. (ii) The provision of a special or modified curriculum. (iii) Particular attention to the social structure and emotional climate in which education takes place.'

It is now recognized that 'special educational needs' is a relative concept, describing a continuum from greater to less need. Warnock intended that 'gifted children' should be included on this continuum, but the Act is rarely interpreted to include exceptionally able children. As a result of the Act, fewer children are segregated and educated in special schools. There have been a number of difficulties in implementing the Act. First, the lack of national guidelines has meant that services are patchy and variable across the country. The Warnock Report and the subsequent Act were framed at a time when the national economy was relatively strong and school rolls were falling. Warnock wrongly assumed that the funding for education would remain at the current level and that moneys saved by falling rolls would automatically fund the extra resources required to support children with special educational needs. Many educationalists fear that the recent introduction of Standard Assessment Tests and publication of 'league tables' of school results will cause schools to be more selective about accepting children with special educational needs, or that such children will be denied access to the full curriculum.

**Education Act 1993** a major piece of legislation concerned with provisions relating to grant-maintained schools, SPECIAL EDUCATIONAL NEEDS and school attendance.

The Act set up the funding agency for schools that is designed to take over financial responsibilities from any local education authority for which 75 five per cent of the schools in its area (either primary or secondary) are grant-maintained. The Act also abolished previous requirements relating to the inspection of smaller residential schools.

**educational maintenance allowance** cash payments made by local education authorities to children or young people who stay at school beyond the statutory minimum leaving age. Although most authorities make some provision, grants are usually small.

**educational psychologist**   a teacher with additional qualifications in psychology, responsible for assessing and supporting children with SPECIAL EDUCATIONAL NEEDS, the vast majority of whom attend mainstream schools.

Educational psychologists devise packages to assist learning, support parents and facilitate behaviour change. If provision within school is not meeting a child's needs, they draw up a 'statement' outlining in more detail what kind of provision the child requires, including any need for alternative special school.

**education clothing grants**   discretionary schemes still operated by some local education authorities for assisting parents with the costs of school clothing.

Many local education authorities have no such provision at all, whereas others have delegated funds to schools as part of local financial management. It is unlikely that the DEPARTMENT OF SOCIAL SECURITY BENEFITS AGENCY will give grants for school clothing to claimants, although it may make loans for coats or footwear. Where local education authorities do operate a scheme, application is usually via the education social worker or education welfare service. Some schools operate second-hand school clothing schemes.

**education social work (education welfare)**   one of the oldest forms of public welfare provision, dating back at least to the Education Act 1870 and the extension of compulsory education through local 'school boards'.

Under these arrangements, the 'attendance officer' was responsible for identifying children in their area who were not registered at any school or receiving education in some other way, and establishing whether they should be enrolled. Much of this work involved seeking to assist children who could not attend school through poverty, supervising children who were at work and protecting children found to be at risk.

The traditional perception of the role of attendance officers as based essentially around enforcement does not do justice to what were quite sophisticated attempts to approach the work from a 'welfare' perspective. Although the failure of parents to ensure that children are 'properly educated' has always been an offence, contemporary commentators noted that even by the turn of the century these officials were acting as 'the children's friend and the parents' adviser', rather than relying too much on their power to prosecute. With the provision of financial assistance for meals at schools from 1902, as well as the administration of charitable funds for clothing and footwear, the welfare of children at school formed a much wider agenda than simply forcing children to attend. With the Children Act 1948 much of this wider responsibility passed to the children's committees; and since then education social work has tended to be seen as of lower status than other forms of local authority provision. The major focus has continued to be school attendance (CHILDREN ACT, section 36, EDUCATION ACT

1993, Part IV, EDUCATION SUPERVISION ORDERS), although education social workers (ESWs) and education welfare officers (EWOs) also have a statutory duty for regulating child employment (Children and Young Persons Act 1933 and local bylaws), administering educational welfare benefits, assisting children with SPECIAL EDUCATIONAL NEEDS and participating in CHILD PROTECTION procedures.

With the current debate about the future of local education authorities, their declining role in managing schools, and the growing emphasis on delegating resources to local schools, education social work faces an uncertain future. The Ralphs Report of 1973 highlighted the nature of the tasks as substantially the same as other forms of social work, but few authorities have integrated the service into social services departments, and local education authorities have been reluctant to resource the service adequately. There are about 2,800 officers employed by LEAs (for a school population of about 8 million), usually working a patch system based on one, two or more high schools and their pyramid primaries. About 20 per cent of staff hold social work qualifications, though opportunities for training and career development tend to be increasingly limited.

However, there has never been a more urgent need for the welfare of children at school to be safeguarded. In an increasingly competitive environment, children who find it difficult to attend school regularly, or who have behavioural and emotional problems, are at considerable risk of being denied education. ESWs and EWOs act as agents on behalf of children and parents in ensuring that they are given access to educational opportunity, including the growing numbers of children being permanently excluded from school. They act as go-between in facilitating partnership between schools and parents and, since the Children Act, will increasingly be seeking to work by negotiation and agreement wherever possible.

**education supervision order**   provision under the CHILDREN ACT (section 36) whereby a local education authority (LEA) may apply to the FAMILY PROCEEDINGS COURT to have a child who is not being 'properly educated' placed under the LEA's supervision, initially for one year; the order may be extended for up to three years.

This provision replaced the sections of the Children and Young Persons Act 1966 that gave LEAs the power to initiate care proceedings on the grounds of irregular educational attendance. Education supervision order applications are 'family proceedings' and so subject to all the other relevant parts of the Children Act. They are not punitive, nor designed to force children into school. They are primarily intended to provide a structure within which the supervisor, normally from the EDUCATION SOCIAL WORK services, can 'advise, assist and befriend' the child and give 'direction' to both child and parent. Parents persistently failing to follow directions may be committing an offence; a child in such a position must be referred to the social services department for assessment of whether other services or orders are required to promote and safeguard their welfare. The order gives the LEA power to make certain decisions about the child's education, such as choice of school. There is a statutory duty on the supervisor to consult the parent and (the only example in educational law) the child before issuing directions. Not all LEAs have made use of the order being successful in order to satisfy the 'no order' principle of section 1(5) of the Children Act.

**education welfare**   see EDUCATION SOCIAL WORK.

**elder abuse**   the mistreatment of an older person, either continuously and systematically or as a single incident.

Elder ABUSE usually occurs in the context of long-standing relationships, often, though not always, at the hands of the person who has the main care of the older person. It is also known to have occurred in residential institutions. Both older women and men may experience abuse. Abuse takes many forms, but psychological distress is always a feature of it. The abused person experiences hopelessness, fear, anxiety, insecurity and loss of self-respect. Abuse may lead to confusion in an older person, which may in turn lead to further abuse. Elder abuse manifests in a number of ways, and older people may encounter any one or several types of abuse: *physical* abuse, such as hitting, burning, restraint, injury, forcible feeding, the withholding or overdosing of medication, and confinement to bed; *psychological and emotional abuse*, such as shouting, harsh language, threats, ridicule, swearing, ignoring, rejecting and isolation; *financial abuse*, such as stealing or exploitation of property, values and assets, misappropriation of the pension or bank book, and denying money for personal use; *sexual abuse*, such as assault, rape and coercion into sexual activity without consent; *neglect*, such as abandonment, starvation, preventing or not enabling access to needed public services, and neglect of hygiene routines; *neighbourhood abuse*, such as harassment and scapegoating; and *domestic violence*, such as a long-standing history of violence in a relation that has become increasingly dangerous because of the frailty of older age. Abuse usually occurs in a domestic setting, which makes the incidence difficult to identify, and research has usually focused on abuse within families. However, abuse can occur in hospital, day care, nursing homes and care homes. The abuser is likely to be known to the abused person, perhaps as daughter, granddaughter, daughter-in-law, son, grandson or son-in-law – the most likely abuser being the main carer. Frequently such situations are reflections of desperation on the part of care-givers, who often feel quite hopeless. Although abuse may be taking place, it is often mixed with other, more positive feelings for the cared-for person, and in these circumstances the abuser may indeed feel that they have failed as carer.

The causes of abuse are various. Ageist attitudes disempower old people, and physical and/or mental disability may result in loss of respect and render the person vulnerable to abuse. Abuse may be a spontaneous response to a stressful situation or may arise from long-standing difficult domestic interactions. Sons and daughters may resent caring for a formerly dominant parent and retaliate for past suffering.

Carers may be sadistic, gaining pleasure from the abuse – something that has been seen in both domestic and institutional environments. Carers may be overwhelmed by what seems an unending burden, exacerbated by social isolation, loss of control and resultant depression. Carers may be angry and frustrated at the high levels of dependency of the old person. They may additionally experience feelings of revulsion at the person soiling, vomiting or eating rubbish. Bizarre behaviour may occur, notably if dementia is present, raising anxiety throughout a household. Family members may also resent the changes brought about by the need to care for an old person.

Legal protection is available through both criminal and civil courts if a person is able and willing to take action. Both physical and sexual abuse could lead to criminal action on the basis of actual harm to the person under the Offences Against the Person Act 1861. The restriction of a person's movements may be actionable under the tort of false imprisonment, and where financial abuse occurs prosecutions for theft and/or fraud can take place. It is possible to bring an action for negligence where it can be proved that the carer has a duty of care and that duty has been broken. All such actions require that the older person, or possibly their advocate, will make the appropriate complaints. In practice, this is very rare, as older people are unwilling to risk offending family members and possibly jeopardizing the limited amounts of care that they have. Both the National Assistance Act 1948 and the Mental Health Act 1983 allow for an old person to be removed from home if mentally ill and considered to be neglected or ill-treated. Certain forms of abuse may also be remedied under the Domestic Violence and Matrimonial Proceedings Acts and the Sexual Offences Acts.

P. Decalmer and F. Glendenning, eds, *The Mistreatment of Elderly People*, London: Sage, 1993.

**elderly mentally infirm**  describes OLDER PEOPLE who, because of mental impairment, experience forgetfulness, disorientation, loss of speech and understanding, and an inability to recognize familiar others.

Social behaviour may be disturbed and show itself in verbal abuse, aggression and wandering. Physical activities such as toileting, dressing and walking may be difficult. Elderly mentally infirm people may have any combination of these problems in varying degrees of severity. They may exhibit different symptoms at different times, but these will be particularly evident if a person is in unfamiliar surroundings.

**electro-convulsive therapy (ECT)**  a treatment used in PSYCHIATRY, especially for people with acute DEPRESSION, whereby electrical currents are passed through the brain. The intention is to produce a convulsion. Patients are sedated during the process.

ECT treatments are still widespread, although used less frequently than before, principally because of the greater use of drugs in the treatment of MENTAL ILLNESS. The therapy is controversial; although it is thought to be useful in the alleviation of affective disorders, how and why it helps some patients remain a mystery. Many critics point to ECT's inappropriate use in the past and to its harmful side effects, which can include memory loss and disorientation.

**electronic monitoring**  an experimental system used to track people, introduced briefly in 1989, involving the 'tagging' of defendants on BAIL.

Despite much publicity, electronic monitoring was used very little by courts and was subject to serious technical problems. The CRIMINAL JUSTICE ACT 1991 allows for its use to be extended to sentenced offenders on curfew orders, but there are no plans currently for its implementation.

**emergency duty team**    a team of local authority social workers providing social work services when offices are closed overnight and during holidays.

Generally the team covers a large geographical area such as an entire county and responds only in urgent situations. These critical situations include when a person may have to be detained in mental hospital or a child may have to be removed from their parents to avoid further abuse. Members of the team are experienced practitioners skilled in working with psychiatrists and the police, who will frequently be present when they are called out.

**emergency protection order**    an order under section 44 of the CHILDREN ACT allowing a local authority social worker (or a National Society for the Prevention of Cruelty to Children officer) to remove a child from their parents or other adults, or to retain the child in a safe place such as a hospital, if they have reasonable cause to believe that the child is likely to suffer SIGNIFICANT HARM.

The order may also be applied for if the social worker is unreasonably denied access to a child who is likely to suffer significant harm. It is usually obtained by the worker's application before a magistrate without other parties to the case such as the child's parents present (see EX-PARTE). The application must outline the circumstances in detail, including why the child is likely to suffer significant harm. If the social worker thinks that they may be refused entry to the home where the child is living, they can ask the court for a warrant to enter the premises and for a police officer to assist in this.

The order lasts for eight days, with a possible seven-day extension in exceptional circumstances. During this time the local authority must decide on the course of action it is to take, such as returning the child home or preventing the child from going home by asking the court for a CARE ORDER. If at any time while the order is in force the authority thinks it is safe to return the child home, it must do so. Parents, the child or anyone with whom the child was living before the order was made may apply for a discharge of the order after seventy-two hours, if the original order were made ex-parte. As long as the order is in force, parents and their representatives enjoy reasonable CONTACT with the child, unless the court has made a specific direction to the contrary. One of the main objectives of the Children Act is to ensure that local authorities remove children only when this is necessary in order to protect life and limb. In this it has succeeded; the number of emergency protection orders taken by authorities has fallen significantly compared with emergency removals of children under previous child-care law. Department of Health guidance says that authorities should try to secure the child's safety through other measures, if at all possible, such as providing FAMILY SUPPORT SERVICES.

Department of Health, *Guidance to the Children Act, Vol. 1: Court Orders*, London: HMSO, 1991.

**emotional abuse**    a term used rather loosely by many writers to describe negative psychological effects on people resulting from the damaging behaviour of others.

Emotional ABUSE can be a result of physical or sexual abuse, or it can be a consequence of other behaviours rooted in sustained unpleasant and unhappy transactions between two or more people. In social work most recent attention on this issue has focused upon children, although emotional abuse can relate to relationships within whole families, or specifically to vulnerable elders and to marital and partner relationships. Some writers prefer the term 'psychological abuse', because they regard emotional reactions as properly the province of psychology. Others differentiate between matters pertaining to the mind as against issues of feelings or emotions. Clinical psychologists would regard the distinction as unsustainable, arguing that feelings and emotions are the concern of psychology and provide crucial evidence of personal adjustment or maladjustment. The distinction, in their view, possibly originates in a confusion about means and ends. Physical, sexual or emotional abuse can all, singly or in combinations, lead to psychological maladjustment. Different forms of abuse (means) may result in psychological problems.

Whatever term is used, there is some consensus about the kind of behaviour that can be described as emotionally abusing. Intimidating behaviour, deprivation of a carer or loved one, loneliness and isolation, withholding approval or a consistent negative response, constant refusal to recognize someone's needs or worth, and the encouragement of negative or antisocial behaviour can all be usefully cited. Physical and sexual abuse can be emotionally damaging too. To have been physically or sexually assaulted, and perhaps to live in fear of it happening again, is almost certainly to experience at least some of the circumstances described above. The severity of the abuse depends upon a number of factors, including its duration, the age and maturity of the abused and the degree of power exercised by the abuser.

In relation to children, it is comparatively rare for social welfare agencies to intervene on the basis of emotional abuse alone. Even with children who are clearly very unhappy and are displaying major indicators of psychological disturbance, the chances of compulsory intervention are slight, unless sexual or physical abuse is present too. Explanations for this worrying situation are varied. The problem of proof seems to be more elusive than for sexual or physical abuse, partly because there are competing psychologies of human development. Social workers and health professionals are not at ease in this field even where they are sure that emotional abuse is visible and substantial. Some critics have suggested that there has been a fundamental failure to recognize the emotional abuse involved in removing children from their homes as a result of, for example, physical abuse – further evidence, perhaps, of social workers' inability to handle emotional issues with confidence. Others have suggested that, whereas sexual and physical abuse can be understood by the public, emotional abuse is difficult to comprehend. Intervention by SOCIAL SERVICES DEPARTMENTS, already viewed critically by the world at large, would almost certainly not have public support. In the meantime, many children are being irreparably damaged because their abuse is not being heeded. (See also CHILD PROTECTION, PHYSICAL ABUSE SEXUAL ABUSE.)

K. O'Hagan, *Emotional and Psychological Abuse of Children*, Buckingham: Open University Press, 1993.

**employment of children** part-time employment of school-aged children. Employment of children is subject to regulation and inspection, being illegal unless the child is registered with the local education authority and an employment licence is issued by the education welfare service.

The primary legislation affecting child employment, the Children and Young Persons Act 1933, is badly in need of reform and is supplemented by local authority bylaws. These regulations cover all employment in any undertaking carried on for profit, whether or not the child is paid. Consequently, jobs such as babysitting and washing neighbours' cars are exempt, but newspaper delivery, shop work, waitressing, and so on, must all be licensed. No child can work at all under the age of 13, before 7.00 a.m. or after 7.00 p.m., or on Sundays except for two hours between 7.00 and 11.00 a.m. No child can work more than two hours on a school day, and not more than one hour before school. Thirteen- and 14-year-olds can work up to five hours on a Saturday; 15- and 16-year-olds can work up to eight hours, provided they have an hour's break. Local bylaws may impose further restrictions, and no child can be employed in a factory, in a commercial kitchen or doing anything dangerous. Prosecutions are rare, and few local authorities are able to regulate employment adequately. Some have more thorough registration systems than others or employ specialist officers to work directly with schools, children and employers. The growth of Sunday trading will inevitably lead to a considerable increase in the illegal employment of children. A review of the needs of children at work was not included in the CHILDREN ACT.

**Employment Protection (Consolidation) Act 1978** an Act of Parliament that spells out some of the statutory provisions in relation to pregnant women and employment rights.

The Act makes it illegal to dismiss a pregnant woman before her maternity leave is due, unless it can be demonstrated that she was prevented from doing her job by virtue of the pregnancy or, in some limited circumstances, it was illegal for her as a pregnant woman to continue her job. In the latter case, it will still be illegal to dismiss her if suitable alternative work is available. If an employer attempts to prevent a woman from returning to work after pregnancy, such an action should be treated as unfair dismissal. The Act also allows reasonable time off for antenatal care. Finally the Act spells out a woman's rights in relation to the kind and status of a job she returns to after pregnancy (normally the same kind and status of job). Many unscrupulous employers seek to disguise their real motives by dismissing workers for other reasons, for which workers cannot in many circumstances appeal.

**empowerment theory** theory concerned with how people may gain collective control over their lives, so as to achieve their interests as a group, and a method by which social workers seek to enhance the power of people who lack it.

Empowerment can refer to user PARTICIPATION in services and to the SELF-HELP movement generally, in which groups take action on their own behalf, either in cooperation with, or independently of, the statutory services. However, the term is most frequently associated with a more radical approach that has as its aim change in society; anti-racism and FEMINISM are the best-known examples. Radical empowerment theory is related to the RADICAL SOCIAL WORK theories of the 1970s, which regard the oppression of some groups by others in society as central to an understanding of the client's need and position. However, where the latter theories focused more upon the material disadvantages suffered as a result of oppression, empowerment theory is more concerned with the suppression and devaluation of the members of oppressed groups as people.

Relying on the humanist notion that action arises from the awareness that people have of their needs, value and capacities, empowerment theory regards the dominant groups in society as suppressing a true awareness of these realities in the consciousness of oppressed groups. This is done in order to prevent the latter from taking action against the dominant groups, which would naturally follow if they had a true picture of their situation. In place of a true awareness, oppressed groups are taught to denigrate themselves and misperceive their needs in ways that will motivate them to act in the interests of the dominant groups. For example, workers in Latin America were reported as seeing themselves as helpless to act in their own right and dependent upon powerful groups to provide for their needs, a position placing them totally at the disposal of the latter.

Women and black people are both regarded in empowerment theory as oppressed groups in society. Women are taught to meet men's needs at the expense of their own, and have not been given the skills and confidence to act in their own right; black people are negatively valued, and this denies them resources, skills and confidence. Both groups are thus disempowered, both in their subjective view of themselves, which leads them to blame themselves for their problems, and in their objective control over resources.

Such problems present themselves to the social worker (and to the client) as personal problems of poor self-confidence and incapacity, but empowerment theory shows how they actually derive from the powerlessness of the client's position as a member of an oppressed group. The aim of social work intervention in response to this is to understand the real reasons for these problems, inherent in the power structure of society, and then to act collectively to change society to one that is more humane. A key social work method in this approach is consciousness-raising, which involves increasing people's understanding of how their apparently 'personal' problems are the result of oppression and are thus shared by all members of the oppressed group. Consciousness-raising is believed to be most effective in groups where the shared nature of the problem makes for increased understanding. Women and black people as workers or clients will therefore be empowered primarily by engaging in groups with other women and black people respectively who share their oppression.

The anti-racist approach sees the main objective for white social workers as changing their consciousness as oppressors to an understanding of what they are doing to black people and developing collective responses to white racism. The role for male social workers in relation to the oppression of women would follow similar principles. Once consciousness is raised, it is assumed that the new understandings will compel actions. Oppressed groups will seek to change society; and social workers will 'take sides' against racism and sexism and concentrate their efforts on social and political change.

As members of the dominant groups in society, social workers need to relinquish their monopoly of power and use it to enable oppressed clients to take control of their situation and act in their own right. This means maintaining an egalitarian, power-sharing relationship on a one-to-one basis and where possible linking up the individual to a group of people with common concerns. Such groups are far more empowering – through their greater ability to provide support, articulate awareness and resource action – than a hierarchical relationship with a social worker. The practitioner's role is also to empower these groups and relevant organizations (such as black voluntary organization) by providing appropriate resources, seeking funding and working alongside them for legislative and policy changes. More concretely, it has been proposed that social workers should share all information with users and improve information systems; involve other professionals and non-professionals only with the agreement of service users; share organizational power and avoid social work strategies that place the service user on the receiving end of power and control; develop 'exchange' ways of working, with the worker acknowledging and using feedback from the service user; and allow service users to make visible the processes of oppression that impact in their relationship.

B. Ahmad, *Black Perspectives in Social Work*, Birmingham: Venture Press, 1990.

**enabling authority**  the concept of local authorities providing an environment that enables consumers of services to exercise choice and encourages the development of the private and voluntary sectors.

The term 'enabling authority' has been coined by the Conservative government to identify the direction in which it would like to see local authorities go. The term is applied to local authorities in general but may be seen to have particular relevance to the provision of personal social services. Conservative thinking has had within it a traditional suspicion of the state, and Conservative Prime Ministers since the war have frequently spoken in favour of 'rolling back the state'. Under Mrs Thatcher and Mr Major this has included the aim of reducing important aspects of local government activity, such as their role in housing provision and education. However, the emphasis has been on the way such an approach could increase choice for consumers of services. In line with ideas associated with 'public choice' theory, some Conservatives have argued that the increasing role of the state in the provision of services, including welfare services, has forced out or substantially reduced provision by the private and voluntary sectors. Consequently, client groups have become increasingly dependent on state provision, which has usually meant local authority services. The aim has been to reverse this trend through the introduction of a MIXED ECONOMY OF CARE that will increase the role of the voluntary and private sectors and increase choice.

The concept of the enabling authority is that local authorities should assist this process and provide an environment that encourages the development of the private and voluntary sectors. Consequently, the role of local authorities should no longer be that of the primary or sole provider, but rather that of ensuring that the services are available in their area, no matter from what source. The enabling authority should be more of a regulator and purchaser of services, through contracts and contract enforcement, than the direct provider of services such as residential accommodation or home helps. Such a change of role will result in the reduction of local authority services and may also lead to a changed role for many officers, including social workers. The development of care managers (see CARE MANAGE-MENT) who will act as purchasers may well change the relationship between social workers, their clients and the providers of the service purchased. The government believes that this will encourage the enabling authority to increase choice for users of services and improve the service provided. In-house providers will no longer be able to rest on the security that their local authority will continue to use the service they provide. Recent reports by the SOCIAL SERVICES INSPECTORATE have been critical of local authorities that in their view have actively discouraged the provision of services by the private sector. The financial incentives included in the NATIONAL HEALTH SERVICE AND COMMUNITY CARE ACT will encourage much greater use of the voluntary and private sectors by local authorities, in line with the concept of the enabling authority. Further encouragement is provided by the AUDIT COMMISSION in its management advice to local authorities.

G. Wistow, M. Knapp, B. Hardy, C. Allen, *Social Care in a Mixed Economy*, Buckingham: Open University Press, 1994.

**encopresis**   refers to the passing of normal stools in inappropriate places by a child who has sensation and control.

This is a British definition; in the United States definitions tend to be broader. Treatment, which may be available from hospital paediatric clinics, from CHILD GUIDANCE clinics and more rarely from specialist clinics, often entails a package of measures. These may include a behavioural approach plus social work support for the family concerned, as well as dietary and medical means. Relapse is relatively common, but there is also evidence that some children improve without intervention. It has been suggested that there is an increased risk of PHYSICAL ABUSE in some affected families.

A. Buchanan, in collaboration with G. Clayden, *Children Who Soil*, Chichester: Wiley, 1992.

**enhanced benefit**   a discretionary increase in the amount of HOUSING BENEFIT or COUNCIL TAX BENEFIT paid by local authorities to a person whose circumstances are exceptional but who is not already entitled to full benefit. Benefit can be increased up to the full eligible rent or full council tax.

Although local authorities have wide discretion under this regulation, expenditure is not subsidized and must be limited to 0.1 per cent of total benefit expenditure. It nevertheless provides significant potential to help some people who do not receive full benefit.

**enuresis**   involuntary wetting during the day or at night by non-disabled children aged 5 years or over.

Enuresis has been more specifically defined as the 'involuntary discharge of urine by day or night or by both, in a child aged 5 years or older, in the absence of congenital or acquired defects of the nervous system or urinary tract'. Nocturnal enuresis is more common than diurnal (daytime) enuresis;

the former is more common in boys, the latter in girls. Contributory factors may include a family history, delayed physical maturation, stressful life events and urinary tract infections. The effect of enuresis may be to produce tension in child–parent relationships, loss of confidence in an affected child and a curtailment of a child's social life. Associated practical problems include increased washing, cleaning and financial costs. There is some evidence that toileting problems may lead to PHYSICAL ABUSE. Treatment programmes should be tailored to a child's individual needs, which should be established by a detailed assessment including a medical examination. It is important that an affected child is encouraged to be an active participant in any measures adopted. Methods of intervention are frequently behavioural, including star charts, bladder training and use of an alarm system. However, other measures, including drugs, are used on occasions.

C. Blackwell, *A Guide to the Treatment of Enuresis for Professionals*, Bristol: Enuresis Resource and Information Centre, 1989.

**Equal Opportunities Commission**    an official body created as a result of the SEX DISCRIMINATION ACT 1975 with primary responsibility to eradicate gender DISCRIMINATION in Britain.

The duties of the Equal Opportunities Commission are to enforce the law in relation to the Sex Discrimination Act and the EQUAL PAY ACT 1970. In this respect, the commission has the power to investigate any case of alleged discrimination. In some circumstances it can require organizations to provide information, even if they are reluctant to give it. Where discrimination is proved, the commission can issue a non-discrimination notice, requiring the organization to mend its ways in some defined respect. The commission also helps individuals in some legal cases, especially where there is an important point of principle or perhaps a significant test case. Individual advice and counselling are a major area of work, as is the provision of information and educational programmes.

**equal opportunities policies**    statements of intended practices adopted by organizations to confront DISCRIMINATION in relation to both the employment of staff and the delivery of services.

Equal opportunities policies are usually prefaced by a guiding statement of principle. Usually such statements indicate which groups are recognized by the organization as experiencing discrimination within the wider society. Thus GENDER, 'RACE', marital status, DISABILITY and religious commitments are invariably found in such statements. Age, ex-offenders, SOCIAL CLASS or social status, and sexual orientation or preference are mentioned less often, especially the latter.

A survey of social services departments undertaken by the COMMISSION FOR RACIAL EQUALITY in 1989 revealed that of a sample of 116 departments only 24 (21 per cent) appeared to have any kind of written equal opportunities policy document. Forty per cent of departments did not respond at all; the remainder reported that work was being done or gave explanations for their lack of progress. The Commission for Racial Equality had chosen areas where there are significant ethnic minorities. Local authorities run by the Conservative Party in Britain are unlikely to mention sexual orientation in their equal opportunities statements. They believe that such an inclusion would run counter to clause 28 of the Local Government Act 1988, which states that local authority services 'shall not promote the teaching of the acceptability of HOMOSEXUALITY as a pretended family relationship'. In relation to employment practices, some social welfare employers operate procedures that are perhaps more rigorous than they once were. Thus, job descriptions, person specifications, interview schedules and formal decision-making procedures have been adopted as good practice by many organizations. The willingness of organizations to adopt additional procedures to address revealed discrimination within their organization is much more limited. Monitoring of applications, the effectiveness of targeted advertising, appointments, promotions and uptake of training opportunities are indicators of organizations' willingness to identify problems and to take POSITIVE ACTION to address them.

All organizations ought to be able to present annual reports in which they can specify progress made in relation to agreed policy targets. For example, a report should be able to indicate how many employees with disabilities are currently part of the workforce, what efforts have been made over the last year to increase the numbers of disabled workers (if indeed this had been an acknowledged problem in the previous year), an evaluation of those efforts and finally an action plan for the forthcoming year. The organization's plan should include all groups experiencing discrimination.

With reference to issues of severe delivery, social welfare organizations' performance has been very uneven. A full and comprehensive equal opportunities policy should contain an analysis of ANTI-DISCRIMINATORY measures needed with every client (service user) group. Thus with older people, as a client group, the needs of black elders, elders with disabilities, poor elders, elders of particular religious commitments and gay/lesbian elders, for example, should all be separately identified. Where little is known about a particular group's needs, plans should be devised to collect critical information. Also, action plans need to be drawn up to address aprticular policy objectives. An example will serve to illustrate this sequence. It may be noted, as a result of monitoring processes, that no black elders use social service DAY CARE facilities, and it is not known why this is so. A plan to consult with black community organizations is devised; offers are made to arrange visits to day care centres for individuals, families and community groups; critical information leaflets are translated into the appropriate languages, and efforts are made to highlight the services with other key social welfare personnel such as doctors and other support health workers. Such a process shows the link between reviews of policies, monitoring and planning. Sometimes, however, it is possible to have policies in place; but an organization may make little progress in relation to anti-discriminatory practice. Researchers have sought to understand this problem by looking at the organization's culture or climate. Where people are actually involved and committed to policies they are more likely to work in practice. In this respect, it is likely that a commitment to equal opportunities in relation to service delivery will enhance an organization's commitment to equal opportunities in employment practices. An organization that actually employs disabled people, has women in senior positions and has black people at all levels is more likely to deliver services that promote equal opportunities.

A. E. M. Holmes and W. E. Painter, *Employment Law*, Oxford: Blackstone Press, 1991.

**Equal Pay Act 1970**  an Act of Parliament that seeks to deal with DISCRIMINATION against women specifically in relation to pay.

Under the Act a woman is entitled to the same pay when she does work that is the same or very broadly the same as that undertaken by a man. Subsequent legislation has included the provision of equal pay for work of equal value. Employers have over a very long period of time sought to exploit women by giving them lower pay and inferior conditions of work to men. Justifications – or, more accurately, rationalizations – for this behaviour have included the excuses that women work only for pin money, that they are temporary employees only and that men are breadwinners. Since many women work on a part-time basis, other dubious practices have limited the payment of bonuses to full-time workers only. Some employers have women do virtually the same job as men in most respects but have used the minor differences between men's and women's jobs to justify major differences in pay. Under the legislation women can ask for a job evaluation exercise to determine the value of their job in terms of some agreed criteria about responsibility and skill. Although not without their difficulties, such exercises have helped women in some important cases. Despite the legislation the EQUAL OPPORTUNITIES COMMISSION estimates that women still earn significantly less than men in comparable jobs across the whole occupational spectrum.

**ethical code**  a body of guiding principles for professional organizations to set the standard for good practice in relation to service delivery, client and professional relationships, and relationships between the professional and other occupational groups.

The British Association of Social Workers has produced a code of ethics that has become influential within the occupation, regardless of whether practitioners are members of the association or not. The guiding principles of the code emphasize the 'value and dignity of every human being' and the need 'to encourage the self-realization of each individual person with due regard to the interests of others'. A further principle requires social workers to make efforts 'to relieve and prevent hardship and suffering'. There is an obligation for individual practitioners to develop and improve their skills, and this process requires 'the constant evaluation of methods and policies in light of changing circumstances'. Additionally, 'the worker has the right and duty to bring to the attention of those in power, and of the general public, ways in which the activities of government, society or agencies, create or contribute to hardship'. Finally, 'while they work', this must 'be balanced against their professional responsibility to their client'.

These guiding principles underpin principles of practice that urge workers to 'contribute to the formulation and implementation of policies . . . for the benefit of all sections of the community; to respect their clients as individuals . . . and to ensure that their dignity, individuality, rights and responsibility shall be safeguarded; they will not act selectively towards clients out of prejudice, on the grounds of disability, beliefs or contribution to society . . . nor will they deny those differences which will shape the nature of clients' needs and will ensure any personal help is offered within an acceptable personal and cultural context; they will help their clients increase the range of choices open to them and their powers to make decisions; they will not reject their clients ... even if obliged to protect themselves or to acknowledge an inability to help them; they will give precedence to their own professional responsibility over their personal interest; they accept responsibility for the continuing development of their skills; they recognize the need to collaborate with others in the interest of their clients; in making any public statements or undertaking any public activities they will make clear whether they are acting in a personal capacity or on behalf of the organization; they will help clients to obtain all those services to which they are entitled ... to ensure that these services are ethnically and culturally appropriate and ... that an appropriate diversity of services will be promoted; they will recognize that information clearly entrusted for one purpose should not be used without sanction for another ... they will divulge such confidential information only with the consent of the client (or informant) except where there is clear evidence of danger to the client, worker, other persons in the community or in other circumstances judged exceptional; they will work for the creation and maintenance in employing agencies of conditions which enable workers to accept the obligations of this code.' This ethical code is comparable to those of other professions – indeed, may be more comprehensive than many – and is similar to those of other social work bodies in other countries. Both the statement of principles and the practice principles are seen as having the appropriate clarity and yet acknowledging that the problems of implementing principles in practice can sometimes be complex and far from easy.

**ethnically sensitive practice**    social work practice based on a recognition of the cultural traditions of a particular group of people, including family patterns, lifestyles, language and culture.

The problem for social work practice is that services may often be undertaken with scant knowledge or understanding of minority client groups, as the ASSOCIATION OF BLACK SOCIAL WORKERS AND ALLIED PROFESSIONS has argued with regard to black and other ethnic-minority communities. Some commentators hold that the provision of an ethnically sensitive service is not simply a matter of adjusting social work practice to take into account cultural differences, with the applicants being the passive beneficiaries, but should instead be a two-way process, with black families actively involved in and contributing to the social work service offered. The notions of 'ethnicity by consent' and 'compulsory ethnicity' have been used to distinguish between individuals' differing abilities to reject or adopt a specific ethnic identity. Compulsory ethnicity refers to the institutionalization of ethnic identification as a basis for the assertion of collective claims concerning the distribution of scarce resources. Additionally, many clients have interpreted the cultural pluralist approach of social services departments as an attempt to impose a form of compulsory ethnicity, with efforts to provide a more 'ethnically sensitive service' serving as a further instrument of oppression rather than redressing the balance of past injustices. The provision of an ethnically sensitive service should be seen not as 'extra' or 'special' but as a basic client entitlement.

Northern Curriculum Development Project, *Setting the Context for Change*, Leeds: CCETSW, 1991.

**ethnocentrism** a generalized attitude of mistrust towards cultures, communities or groups other than one's own. Such an attitude is usually based upon a view that one's own group or culture is superior in moral and social terms. Thus the values of one's own culture come to be regarded as the legitimate standard, and the beliefs, customs and standards of all other groups are scaled and rated accordingly.

The classic study *The Authoritarian Personality* (1950) perceived ethnocentrism as associated with other characteristics such as a general lack of flexibility, conservatism and paternalism to the point of embracing anti-democratic sentiments. The study originally focused on the nature of anti-Semitism but clearly revealed the more general characteristics of bigotry, prejudice and RACISM; hence the concept of the ethnocentric personality.

T. Adorno, E. Frenkel-Brunswick, D. Levinson and R. Sanford, *The Authoritarian Personality*, New York: Harper, 1950.

**Eurocentrism** a form of ETHNOCENTRISM that involves understanding and interpreting the world exclusively, or nearly so, through the experiences and perspectives of (white) Europeans.

A Eurocentric perspective – which by implication places Europe at the centre of the world – may be detected in such apparently 'objective' activities as the presentation and interpretation of historical events, and definitions of 'correct' methods of child rearing and organizing family life. Eurocentric textbooks, teaching methods and underlying philosophies reinforce negative perceptions of many non-European peoples and fail to inform about the diversity and strength of the many cultures, languages, ethnic communities and religions that enrich and make positive contributions to human society.

**European Community funding** The provision of finance for services and economic development from the European Union.

The European Union (EU; European Community prior to the enactment of the Maastricht Treaty) provides a series of grants to various services and projects under a range of different headings. These cover issues such as education, social policies, and urban and regional economic development.

The most significant areas are covered by grants under the European Regional Development Fund (ERDF) and the European Social Fund (ESF). The ERDF supports infrastructure projects and productive investment, including urban improvements. The ESF is concerned with training and employment measures for the long-term unemployed and young people. Both these are designated as structural funds and aim to counter the effects of industrial decline and unemployment. They are also concerned with helping in the promotion of rural development and promoting new ideas for changing agricultural structures. Other important EU initiatives include funds such as now and horizon. Now is an initiative concerned with equal opportunities for women, including financial aid for employment assistance in the creation of new businesses and cooperatives run by women; financial assistance may also be available for training advice and the development of child care facilities. Horizon is a similar initiative aimed at people with disabilities. The aim of this programme is to prevent people with disabilities being marginalized in society; it provides financial support for the development of information exchange networks concerning good practice in respect of disability, vocational training, and funding for small businesses and cooperatives run by people with disabilities.

CIFPA Chartered Institute of Public Finance and Accounting, *Europe: A Guide for Public Authorities*, London: CIFPA, 1992.

**eviction**  the process by which people living in a dwelling, legally or illegally, are required to give up possession of the property.

Grounds for eviction include rent or mortgage arrears, illegal occupation of the property and unacceptable behaviour. In some circumstances a property may have to be sold to release capital to pay off a debt. Social work tasks, involving helping a tenant or owner-occupier attempt to retain tenancy or ownership of the dwelling, may entail advocacy with landlords, building societies and the courts. With problems concerned with rent or mortgage arrears, the central objective is to come to an arrangement that is considered feasible and manageable by landlord or building society, tenant or owner, and, if involved, the courts. A critical component of this problem can sometimes be that tenants run the risk of being labelled INTENTIONALLY HOMELESS. If a family is so labelled, the local authority is not required to rehouse them. In relation to alleged unacceptable behaviour, the social worker's or housing adviser's task may be to challenge the accuracy of the evidence. Hostile landlords sometimes manufacture evidence if they wish to have occupancy of the property for their own purposes – perhaps to increase rents, or because of their racial or sexual harassment of the tenant. Harassment and unlawful evictions are criminal offences and should be preventable under the Protection from Eviction Act 1977 (amended by the Housing Act 1988).

**evidence**  written documents, verbal statements or exhibits presented in court to support or refute accusations against an alleged offender.

There are strict legal rules governing what is and what is not admissible as evidence. Several notable miscarriages of justice have hinged on the inadmissibility of confessions believed to have been made under duress. It was to counter such allegations that the POLICE AND CRIMINAL EVIDENCE ACT 1984 was passed, requiring the police to record interviews of suspects. The CRIMINAL JUSTICE ACT 1991 recognizes the particular problems faced by child victims and witnesses in giving evidence, and it makes provision for children to give evidence to courts on video tape recordings in certain circumstances.

**exceptionally severe disablement allowance**  benefit paid as part of the INDUSTRIAL INJURIES SCHEME to some people needing personal care.

**excess benefit**  the term used to describe overpaid COUNCIL TAX BENEFIT (see OVERPAYMENT).

**excess income**  the amount by which a person's income exceeds their APPLICABLE AMOUNT for purposes of calculating the HOUSING BENEFIT and COUNCIL TAX BENEFIT paid to them.

Maximum housing benefit and council tax benefit are paid to a person whose income is less than their applicable amount. If their income exceeds their applicable amount, then the two benefits are reduced by 65 per cent and 20 per cent respectively of this excess income.

**exclusion from school** the correct term for what is usually called 'expulsion' or 'suspension'. A child is officially prevented from attending school usually following unacceptable behaviour.

Since the EDUCATION ACT 1993 there are two types of exclusion from school: fixed-term (which can amount to no more than fifteen days per term) and permanent. Schools are expected to make every effort to resolve problems without resorting to exclusion, including assessment for special education provision and involvement of parents and specialist agencies. Parents (not children) have a right to make representations to the school's governing body and the local education authority before permanent exclusion is confirmed. (In grant-maintained or self-governing schools there is no appeal to the LEA.) It is not legal for a school simply to remove a child's name from the register (unless their whereabouts are unknown), though many operate such informal procedures, denying parents the right to appeal and possibly leaving the child without provision. This strategy also enables the school to retain the financial allowance it has received for the child, which passes to a subsequent provider if the child is permanently excluded. There are early indications that as schools opt out from local authority control, and become grant-maintained or self-governing, they are more likely to exclude children.

**ex-parte hearing** literally means 'without the parties' and is the legal phrase for a court hearing that is held without all the parties to the case present.

Social workers are most likely to come across ex-parte hearings when applying for an EMERGENCY PROTECTION ORDER in relation to child-care issues or an INJUNCTION in relation to the problem of DOMESTIC VIOLENCE. With the first example, these can be heard ex-parte, without the parents or the child present, and usually involve a single magistrate, the magistrate's clerk and the social worker on the case. The aim of such a hearing is speed, since time may be short to protect the child concerned; ex-parte hearings can be organized quickly and sometimes occur in a magistrate's own home if out of hours. In cases of domestic violence the term is used where one party, usually the woman, seeks an injunction to prevent something happening. The injunction will be in force without the defendant being present and until such time as a full hearing can be arranged.

**expert witness** a person who, by virtue of training, qualification or experience, is regarded by a court as capable of supplying expert opinion in criminal or civil proceedings.

The chief function of an expert witness is not to support one side or the other in contested hearings but to make their knowledge and judgement available to the court so that it is able to reach the best decision. In an application for a CARE ORDER for a child that is opposed by the child's parents, a psychologist or paediatrician often appears as an expert witness to help the court decide what solution is best for the child's welfare.

**extended sentence** previously known as 'preventive detention', a power formerly held by the Crown Court to impose an extended term of imprisonment on a persistent offender who was convicted of an imprisonable offence.

Extended sentencing was abolished by the CRIMINAL JUSTICE ACT 1991 in line with its principle that punishment should be proportionate to current, not past, offences.

**extinction** in psychology, the term for the gradual cessation of previously conditioned reflexes when the pairing of the mental stimulus and the conditioned stimulus is discontinued. See CLASSICAL CONDITIONING.

**extroversion–introversion** a description of personality characteristics based on certain kinds of personality tests. Extroversion describes a personality type more concerned with external reality that with inner feelings, and introversion its opposite.

The extrovert dimension embodies TRAITS of sociability, impulsiveness, assertiveness and sensation-seeking, while the introvert dimension describes the opposite traits of lack of sociability, anxiety and social withdrawal. Although the extroversion–introversion dimension is a means of describing and categorizing personality traits, it does not explain why people are this way. However, some trait theorists think that heredity plays an important part in shaping the personality in this way.

# F

**failure to thrive** the term applied to children who are not receiving adequate nutrition for normal growth.

One common form of measuring whether a child is failing to thrive is through CENTILE CHARTS that plot the child's weight, head size and height against national averages. If a child falls below the third centile in one or more of these for a period of time, this is an indication of its failure to thrive. Certain factors in a child's background are associated with, but not the cause of, failure to thrive. These are POVERTY, which may severely restrict the child's diet, social isolation of a parent, and the child's having severe behavioural problems. Failure to thrive is rarely the product of deliberate parental neglect. Support for the parents is usually given in the form of guidance on diet from HEALTH VISITORS and doctors. In extreme cases, brief periods of hospitalization or ACCOMMODATION help the child to gain weight and size.

**Fair Employment Commission** established by the Fair Employment (Northern Ireland) Act 1989 with the primary duty to eliminate DISCRIMINATION in Northern Ireland in relation to the employment of Catholics and Protestants.

Employers in Northern Ireland, depending upon their size, are required to undertake various procedures to encourage fair employment. They have to register with the commission and are expected to monitor their workforce and regularly review all practices concerned with recruitment, training and promotion. If employers are found to be discriminatory in their practices they can be required to take affirmative action by setting targets within specified time limits. Comparatively substantial financial penalties – fines of up to £30,000 – and economic sanctions may be used against organizations that do not make reasonable progress or are found to be discriminatory in their policies and practices; for example, government grants may be denied to such organizations, and government may not purchase goods and services from them. Many commentators have compared provision in Northern Ireland to eliminate discrimination with the relatively ineffective powers and sanctions of the COMMISSION FOR RACIAL EQUALITY.

**family assistance order** an order under Section 16 of the CHILDREN ACT, available in matrimonial disputes involving children and where the court may be considering a SECTION 8 ORDER, that allows the court to appoint a probation officer or local authority social worker to advise, assist and befriend any person named in the order.

The aim of the family assistance order is to provide short-term help in the resolution of conflict between parents or to help overcome problems associated with their separation or divorce. The work is often undertaken with the parents rather than with the child, although the court's main concern in making the order is the child's welfare. The order lasts for six months and may be made only with the consent of every person named in the order (other than a child).

**family centre** a unit run by either a local authority or a voluntary organization that works with both children and their parents to achieve such objectives as teaching improved parenting skills or reducing family conflict.

Family centres provide a safe environment in which to show parents how to play with their children and build a more positive relationship with them. They may be intensively therapeutic or more in the nature of local drop-in centres. Centres run by large voluntary organizations or local authorities generally work with the families of children who have suffered some ABUSE or severe emotional disturbance. Local authority family centres are often former day nurseries, but some have overnight accommodation for use in family crises.

  T. Smith, 'Family Centres, Children in Need and the Children Act', in J. Gibbons, ed., *The Children Act 1989 and Family Support: Principles into Practice*, London: HMSO, 1992.

**family court** a single court in which all family matters would be dealt with, that is, both PRIVATE LAW and public law matters relating to the family, including ADOPTION and CARE proceedings.

Such a court does not exist in Great Britain and Northern Ireland, despite persistent calls by law reformers for over twenty years to reform the court structure to enable all family matters to be dealt with by a specialist system of family courts. The CHILDREN ACT established a compromise position in England and Wales. Family matters are currently dealt with through the following tiers: magistrates' domestic courts, known as FAMILY PROCEEDINGS COURTS, designated county courts and the Family Division of the High Court. It is possible to transfer cases between the tiers, provided specified criteria are met, such as sufficient complexity of case. Unfortunately the administrative systems of the courts remain fragmented; an Interdepartmental Working Party has been appointed to monitor the changes to the court structure. It is possible that a system of family courts may be eventually introduced, but this is unlikely to happen in a period of economic stringency.

**Family Court Welfare Service**   the non-criminal branch of the PROBATION SERVICE, dealing primarily with arrangements for children of separating or divorcing parents, within the family proceedings framework established by the CHILDREN ACT.

Previously known as matrimonial work, civil work or divorce court welfare, this has been a traditional aspect of probation officers' work. Historically, officers provided a social work service to all magistrates' courts, including the 'domestic' court, which dealt with matters of matrimonial discord. Officers were involved extensively in matrimonial reconciliation and in providing welfare reports in respect of the children of separated parents. With the reform of DIVORCE law under the Matrimonial Causes Act 1973, the role of the divorce court welfare officer in the county court became more clearly defined. Before granting a divorce, the court must be satisfied about the arrangements for any children of a marriage. This often involves obtaining a welfare report, especially if the parents are in dispute about the arrangements.

During the 1970s divorce court welfare officers were expected to make recommendations to the court about which parent a child should live with (custody, now residence) and how often they should see their other parent (access, now contact). This meant that officers frequently had to make judgements about the relative merits of each parent. This tended to exacerbate any hostility between the parents and placed unfair pressure on children to ally themselves with one or other parent. By the 1980s this adversarial approach gave way to a method of working known as conciliation or FAMILY MEDIATION. The principles of conciliation are based on the belief that parenting continues beyond divorce and that parents have a responsibility to reach an agreement about arrangements for children wherever possible. Conciliators (often working in pairs) act as professional mediators and facilitators at a voluntary meeting where both parents are present. The task of the conciliator is to report to the court when an agreement has been reached, or to identify the points of disagreement. As conciliation has developed, it has been seen increasingly as a specialized area of work within the

Probation Service, and many people would now like to see the Family Court Welfare Service as a completely separate service. A 1991 government green paper proposing changes in divorce law suggested a significantly enhanced role for family mediation and conciliation services.

**family credit**  a means-tested benefit paid to a person who works sixteen hours or more each week and has a dependent child or children.

The amount of family credit paid depends on the number and age of the children and on the family income including earnings. It cannot be paid to anyone who has more than £8,000 in capital. Capital between £3,000 and £8,000 is deemed to produce an income of £1 per week for every £250 or part thereof and is taken into account when determining the level of benefit. Family credit was introduced in 1988, replacing a similar benefit, family income supplement, but it is far more generous. It was estimated that 800,000 families would qualify, but despite extensive advertising the take-up remains at about 60 per cent, with some 500,000 families claiming family credit. Although it pays relatively large amounts of benefit, family credit is taken into account as income when calculating HOUSING BENEFIT and COUNCIL TAX BENEFIT. This means that for many tenants the overall gain is not that substantial.

If the objective of family credit is to encourage people to take low-paid employment, possibly working less than full-time, the crucial test is whether they are better off on family credit than on INCOME SUPPORT. For many claimants the loss of FREE SCHOOL MEALS, combined with the cost of child-care, means they are not better off. In addition, the scheme provides no help with housing costs, which means that low-income owner-occupiers can receive help with their mortgage only by remaining on income support.

**family group conference**  a meeting of the extended family and adults significant to a child who it is thought may have been abused.

Such a conference or meeting is called together to work out a plan to protect the child, if this is what is required, and is given powers and responsibility to make the necessary plans to protect the child. In New Zealand, where the concept originated, the family group conference has replaced the CHILD PROTECTION CASE CONFERENCE and thus marks a significant reallocation of power between professionals and family members. The group conference takes place in two stages: during the first stage, the family meets together to develop its own plans to protect the child; in the second stage, social workers or other professionals are called in to provide advice or to help secure resources. Although the concept is viewed with some suspicion by social work professionals in Britain, because it accords the family considerable new powers and status to make decisions, it is gaining adherents as a way to develop protection plans that both are effective and tend to include arrangements for keeping the child within the extended family.

P. Marsh and J. Triseliotis, *Prevention and Reunification in Child Care*, London: Batsford, 1993.

**family mediation**  a non-adversarial method of helping divorcing or separated couples make decisions about the custody of children, issues of access and parenting, property and maintenance.

The central idea in family mediation is the promotion of a settlement or an attempt to reduce the intensity of conflict. Family mediation or conciliation has arisen partly from dissatisfaction with the adversarial approach to DIVORCE, separation and child custody issues. This system seemed to encourage conflict and bad feeling between parents, if only as a means to an end. Such experiences often seemed to sour relationships between parents, even where they appeared willing to work together. Other sources for this developing method of conflict resolution included a need to devise ways for parents to talk to each other, where they had lost the habit, had never had it or were so tied up in their own feelings that they could not see their children's needs. Many divorcing parents began to recognize that a relationship might be over, but parenting and PARENTAL RESPONSIBILITY remain.

> Family conciliation – this term seemed to be preferred in the early years – services began to develop in several different ways. Some services began to be offered by the divorce court welfare section of the PROBATION SERVICE. Sometimes mediation was in court, possibly at the instigation of a judge and often fairly brief. More recently, more leisurely methods have been employed by the service. In some parts of the country, the voluntary sector has made the running, usually with alternative models of mediation. To be outside the judicial or court system seemed to be an important point to some. Other differences were that some voluntary services had two mediators working together (often a man and a woman), that sessions might be spread over several weeks, that an incremental view of seeking agreements was sometimes adopted (protagonists trying to re-establish trust might try out an idea to see if it worked before coming back for further sessions), and that some might involve children too. There have been other theoretical and procedural differences, but all family mediation services have as their objective a wish that parents maintain their relationship with their children (unless it is seen not to be in the children's interests) and that they secure, through negotiation, something as close as possible to a feasible and practicable plan that has the welfare of the children as the major focus. A government green paper issued in 1993 has proposed compulsory mediation in the context of a reformed divorce law.
>
> L. Parkinson, *Conciliation in Separation and Divorce*, Beckenham: Croom Helm, 1986.

**family proceedings**   a group of court proceedings involving disputes about children.

Family proceedings are defined under the CHILDREN ACT as including most proceedings that originate in that Act, such as those for CARE ORDERS, SUPERVISION ORDERS and SECTION 8 ORDERS. They also include proceedings under other laws such as divorce proceedings, adoption proceedings and INJUNCTION and non-molestation proceedings between married or unmarried couples. By designating this range of proceedings in this way, the Children Act allows courts greater flexibility in dealing with cases before it. (See FAMILY PROCEEDINGS COURT.)

**family proceedings court**   created under the CHILDREN ACT, this court deals with non-criminal matters relating to children, such as care proceedings, adoption, child protection, and residence and contact following divorce (see CRIMINAL COURTS).

**family therapy**   a range of techniques and strategies for helping families resolve relationship problems, attain goals and function more harmoniously.

There are many variants of family therapy. Most of them work on the central premise that relationships between family members can become rigid, so that behaviour between members tends to repeat compulsively a familiar destructive pattern. This pattern may involve blaming or scapegoating a particular member of the family or coercive behaviours such as shouting, physical ABUSE, isolation and withdrawal. Such patterns are a kind of 'solution'; the family survives, but in a way that prevents further development, and often at immense cost to the individuals. The central insight of family therapy is drawn from the SYSTEMS APPROACH, namely that relations between family members are circular; how each member behaves affects the way everyone else behaves, and vice versa. An oft-cited example is where a parent continually criticizes an adolescent, who withdraws from family life, but who then elicits more criticism, only to withdraw even more. The therapist or social worker begins with the assumption that no one is to blame. The therapist's role is to provide an outside view of the way the family interacts as a whole and to try to minimize the 'blame games' that inevitably occur in a family deeply at odds with itself. Maintaining a position of neutrality, the therapist explores with the whole family how to achieve a different overall pattern and how to view behaviours more positively. By doing so, the therapist enables the family to change attitudes, viewpoints and behaviour.

M. Preston-Shoot and D. Agass, *Making Sense of Social Work*, Basingstoke: Macmillan, 1990.

**feedback**   written or verbal comment given to others about how well they performed a particular task.

The term originally came from SYSTEMS theory, where it referred to part of a system's output being 'fed back' into the system itself, which was then able to evaluate it and undertake necessary modifications to improve its output. 'Feedback' is now used much more generally to include any comment or judgement given to a person or group of people.

**feminism**   see FEMINIST SOCIAL WORK.

**feminist social work**   a diversity of social work approaches that have as their common element recognition of women's oppression and the aim of overcoming its effects.

Feminism regards all aspects of social relations as shaped by the great inequality of power held by men over women in all aspects of life: in the family, in the professions, in politics, in work and employing organizations, in purchasing power and in community institutions. Feminist social work begins with this fundamental perspective and develops a practice that attempts to address this inequality. When women social workers are working with women as clients it adopts strategies of EMPOWERMENT. This often places it at odds with the traditional role of social work, which seeks to control difficult or poorly adapting individuals or to regulate families in difficulty. A significant part of feminist social work takes place in the small local organizations that have developed as responses to male violence: rape crisis centres, women's refuges, incest survivors' groups among others.

> Feminist social work places heavy emphasis on the role that the oppression of women plays in creating the very problems that social work deals with. One notable example is in the field of child SEXUAL ABUSE, where much of the conventional analysis from both inside and outside social work assigned the 'cause' to distorted family relationships and implicitly blamed poor mothering. Conventional analysis ignored the fact that by far the greater number of abusers were men and that this rested on the extreme differences of power held by men and others in the family. This analysis applied to much of social work with children, where the content of case records, court reports and CASE CONFERENCES blamed women as individually poor mothers rather than focusing on poverty and lack of material resources. Feminist social workers have also looked more closely at the behaviour of the male abuser, have called attention to the secrecy that male abusers demand and have called for protective solutions that remove the abuser, rather than the child, from the family. One of the major concerns of feminist social work is the inequality based on gender within social services organizations themselves, particularly in the management structures of those organizations, which are dominated by men, although women form some 80 per cent of employees overall. How to structure management jobs so that they are more appealing to women, as well as allowing more flexible working arrangements including part-time and job share, are objectives that feminists have at least succeeded in having social services organizations discuss, if not put into practice.

> A. Hudson *et al.*, 'Practising feminist approaches', in C. Hanvey and T. Philpot (eds), *Practising Social Work*, London: Routledge, 1994.

**fieldwork**    social work undertaken in the COMMUNITY, most frequently in people's homes, with an office as administrative centre.

Field social work is the principal way of organizing local authority social work. Other ways of organizing, such as RESIDENTIAL WORK and HOSPITAL SOCIAL WORK, are not nearly as common. Field social workers are invariably based in teams at a local authority social services office. From there they undertake the many administrative tasks associated with social work, such as recording and writing reports for court and developing CARE PLANS. They often also see clients at the office, meeting in rooms specially designated for INTERVIEWING. The defining element of fieldwork, however, is precisely that some of the social work tasks are undertaken 'in the field', in the homes and neighbourhoods where clients live. There are many different kinds of fieldworkers; they may be specialist, such as those working only with children and their families or with adults with LEARNING DISABILITIES, or they may be generic, that is, general social workers with different groups of clients on their caseload. Over the last twenty years and more since the SEEBOHM REPORT, the trend in fieldwork has been steadily in the direction of specialist teams.

> Because fieldworkers visit service users in their own homes, as opposed to undertaking social work tasks only in the office or in a residential or day care

establishment, they have a number of difficult roles to merge. On the one hand, they are entering the user's personal space and property, and should do so with the same respect and consideration as anyone would (for example, only after making an appointment first, unless there are overriding issues of protecting a child). On the other hand, they are also local government officers, with authority and legal powers, charged with undertaking certain tasks and responsibilities. Fieldworkers carry out the main functions of social work such as ASSESSMENT, care planning, arranging family support services, ADVOCACY and COUNSELLING within this difficult framework. Issues of the fieldworker's personal safety also increasingly arise.

J. Hillman and M. Mackenzie, *Understanding Field Social Work*, Birmingham: Ventura Press, 1993.

**Finer Report**  an official report on LONE-PARENT FAMILIES in Britain that appeared in 1974, collecting and presenting much statistical data and reviewing a number of issues, including social security, income, housing, employment and child-care.

Shortly before the Finer Report was published, roughly 10 per cent of all families with dependent children were single-parent families, and of these only 16 per cent were headed by men. Of the women, approximately 190,000 were deserted or separated, 120,000 divorced, 120,000 widowed and 90,000 unmarried. Single-parent families were clearly growing as a proportion of all families with dependent children. The association between single-parent families and poverty was noted in the report. Statistical evidence revealed that two-parent families were consistently better off. LONE-PARENT FAMILIES were much more likely to be dependent on welfare benefits, with both less opportunity to work and discouragement from the benefits system, which clawed back most of any part-time earnings.

The Finer Report recognized the value of part-time work for single parents, not only because of a potential increase in income (if the benefits system could be reformed to encourage such efforts), but also as a boost to morale and confidence for the parents, to combat social isolation and to increase the chances of full-time work in later life. It recommended that any maintenance payable to families by estranged partners should be paid to social security offices and not through the courts. Such a system would at least ensure a regular income for parents and children, while the Department of Social Security could pursue reluctant fathers. Other reforms were to make it easier for women to take over tenancies of properties and to make it easier for women to stay in the matrimonial home.

Perhaps the most important outcome of the report was public recognition of the stress of constant and unrelieved child-care. Children too were thought to suffer in comparison with their two-parented contemporaries, partly because of relative material deprivation and partly because of psychological stresses in relation to the loss of a father, the pains of divorce, bereavement and other factors. The report recommended better counselling services, an increase in nursery provision both in the public sector and with workplace nurseries, and after-school provision for older children. Most of these recommendations were not implemented.

Finer Committee, *Report of the Committee on One-Parent Families*, London: HMSO, 1974.

**flashback**   a repetition of an experience resulting from the use of certain hallucinatory DRUGS, such as LSD and 'magic mushrooms', some time, even months, after the actual use. Although vivid, flashbacks are usually of short duration and rarely dangerous.

**foetal alcohol syndrome**   a congenital abnormality in a newborn infant resulting from a high maternal intake of ALCOHOL. Defects can include limb and craniofacial abnormalities, cardiovascular defects and growth retardation.

**forensic psychiatry**   a psychiatric specialism concerned with the assessment and treatment of mentally disordered offenders. It works at the interface between PSYCHIATRY and the criminal law, advising courts, lawyers, prisons and probation officers on the links between MENTAL ILLNESS and offending.

**foster care**   the placement of a child with a family or lone carer who is able to offer the child full-time day-to-day care in place of the child's natural parents.

There are many possible fostering arrangements, all regulated by the CHILDREN ACT. A child may be placed in foster care by their parent, by anyone with PARENTAL RESPONSIBILITY for the child or by the local authority where the child is normally resident. The child may be privately fostered or may be placed with local authority foster carers.

Foster care usually refers to a placement with local authority foster carers, who are recruited and trained by local authorities. Financial maintenance of the child is through a fostering allowance paid by the local authority to foster carers at a locally set scale of payment. Foster care is the preferred way of providing care and nurture for children who need to be LOOKED AFTER by a local authority, because it provides family-based as opposed to institutionally based care.

Private fostering is arranged between the child's parent (or an adult with parental responsibility) and the private foster carer, who is not a relative of the child. The private foster carer is responsible for the day-to-day care of the child. The placement must be of twenty-eight days or more in duration. The child's parents and the foster carers have a legal duty to notify the local authority where the foster carer lives and that the arrangement is proposed. The local authority has a duty to satisfy itself that the arrangements are satisfactory and that the private foster carer is suitable. The child's parent remains responsible for safeguarding and promoting the child's welfare, retaining financial responsibility for the child and reaching an agreement with the private foster carer on the issue of maintenance. In certain circumstances the private foster carer can claim child benefit. The regulations concerning private fostering are covered in *The Children Act Regulations and Guidance, Vol. 8.*

The development of foster care has enabled local authorities to develop flexible patterns of care for the children they look after. There are different kinds of local authority foster placements, as follows.

(1) *Short-term placements*. The child is placed with foster carers who take care of them on a short-term basis until long-term plans are made for the child. The range of goals for a short-term placement can include 'shared' or relief fostering, holiday fostering, emergency protection, assessment of needs, a bridge to a long-term placement and pre-adoptive fostering. There is no universally agreed duration for short-term placements, which can last from days to months, depending on the child's situation. Research indicates that short-term foster placements become long-term placements with variable success. It is generally agreed that it is poor practice to let a short-term placement drift into a *de facto* long-term placement with no agreed long-term plan.

(2) *Bridging or link placements*. These are used when a child's long-term placement has broken down or the short-term foster carers cannot continue to look after the child, and a long-term placement has yet to be found. Some children are placed in bridging placements after a period in residential care. The task then is to help the child to readjust to family life. The duration of the bridging placement varies according to the child's situation and the speed at which suitable long-term carers are identified for the child.

(3) *Long-term placements*. The child is placed with foster carers on a planned long-term basis; this is sometimes referred to as a permanent foster placement. The intention is that the child will live with their foster family until they are ready to live independently. It is an alternative to adoption for some children, taking into account factors such as the child's age, any special needs, the level of ongoing contact with family of origin and the child's wishes. Studies indicate that long-term fostering is less successful than adoption. It is recognized in current child-care practice that children need a sense of permanence and a sense of identity if their developmental needs are to be met. A sense of permanence is more difficult to achieve in long-term foster placements, because the foster carers do not acquire parental responsibility for the child, and a sense of insecurity may result from the involvement of the social worker in supervising the placement and in the way reviews and medicals are carried out.

(4) *Respite or shared care*. This arrangement involves the day-to-day care of the child being shared between the family of origin and foster carers. This kind of placement may be offered if the child has special needs or if the quality of the care available at home can be enhanced. It enables the child and the family to have regular breaks from each other and provides the child with additional caring relationships outside the family. It is good practice to ensure that the same respite foster carers look after the child on each occasion and that respite care is offered on a planned, predictable basis rather than only in response to a crisis. Specialist placements are designed to meet the needs of a child with specified special needs in accordance with a scheme set up by a local authority or voluntary agency to provide a family-based alternative to residential care. Each scheme recruits foster carers to look after children who are deemed hard to place by reasons of their age, disability or behaviour. Foster carers involved in these schemes receive special training and are often referred to as 'professional foster carers'. They are paid enhanced fostering allowances in recognition of the skills they offer and the additional costs incurred in caring for children with such special needs.

(5) *Fostering with a view to adoption*. A child may be placed with foster carers who are recruited as prospective adopters. This enables the placement to be tried before

a decision is taken to make an adoption order. It is possible for short-term or long-term foster carers to apply to adopt their foster child. In these instances, the foster carers have to be reassessed as prospective adopters by an ADOPTION AGENCY (usually the child's local authority).

(6) *Foster placements with relatives*. A child who is unable to live with their birth parent may be placed with an extended family member. A relative can become a local-authority-approved foster carer for a particular child. The local authority has the same legal obligations in respect of a child fostered by a relative as to any child in a local authority foster placement. This includes the payment of a fostering allowance. Research suggests that long-term placements with relatives are among the most successful for children. Relatives can care for a child without the need for them to become approved foster carers. The local authority has the discretion to provide financial support under section 17 of the Children Act or through payment of a RESIDENCE ORDER allowance if the relative acquires a residence order under the Act.

A number of important regulations govern the placing of children by the local authority with foster carers. The foster carers will already have to be approved by the authority. This process usually involves lengthy discussions as to what the responsibilities of fostering are and why they want to become foster carers. Approval may be given only in relation to a particular child. Foster carers are expected to meet the full range of day-to-day needs of the child placed with them, such as supporting the child's progress through school or undertaking all health and developmental checks. Matching the child with an appropriate family is also an important social work task. There is strong evidence to show that a child's identity is best preserved when the foster carers share the same ethnic and cultural origins as the child. As a result many authorities have policies stipulating some 'race' placements wherever possible and actively engage in recruiting foster carers to reflect the diversity of the community they serve.

J. Thoburn, *Child Placement: Principles and Practice*, Aldershot: Arena, 1994.

**frail elderly**　OLDER PEOPLE who by reason of physical or mental impairment are more than usually vulnerable to trauma.

Trauma affecting the frail elderly may be *social*, for example loneliness or suffering physical abuse; it may be *physical*, as a result of disease, accident or environmental effects; or it may be *psychological*, such as confusion and DEPRESSION.

**free association**　a technique used in PSYCHOTHERAPY to 'uncover' the cause of presenting behaviours, thoughts and feelings, by encouraging the patient to relax within the consulting environment and to say whatever comes into their mind.

The technique assumes that behaviour is determined by unconscious processes. The therapist encourages the patient to confide in them and to explore the contents of their unconscious mind – however unrelated to current events, trivial or shocking this may be – while the therapist offers an interpretation of the material revealed by the patient. The aim is to affect current behaviours by 'uncovering' the effects of early years' traumas on the patient's adult functioning.

**freebasing** refers to the illicit manufacture of the DRUG crack by heating a solution of COCAINE with a chemical, producing hard 'rocks' of varying size. The term also describes the smoking of the resulting substance.

**free prescriptions** refers to the availability of free drugs on prescription to a number of different targeted groups.

People entitled to free prescriptions include those getting INCOME SUPPORT or FAMILY CREDIT; people aged under 16, or under 19 and in full-time education; women over 60 and men 65 or over; pregnant women and those who have given birth within the last twelve months; and people suffering from listed conditions, including epilepsy, colostomy and diabetes. It is also possible to obtain an exemption certificate on the grounds of low income. (See also HEALTH BENEFITS.)

**free school meals** arrangement whereby children whose parents receive INCOME SUPPORT are entitled to a midday meal at school free of charge (Education Act 1980).

Not all schools make a hot meal available under this arrangement, but they must provide a sandwich lunch as an alternative. Application needs to be made through the local education authority's EDUCATION SOCIAL WORK or education welfare service. The 1980 Act abolished the requirement to provide free milk, making it discretionary. Free meals cannot be given to parents receiving benefits other than income support.

**Freudian slip** an act (usually verbal) that is out of place with the context and conveys meaning opposite to that intended. Such slips were thought by Freud to indicate an occasional success of the unconscious processes to subvert the ego and superego (see PSYCHOANALYSIS).

As an example of a Freudian slip consider the statement: 'It is with pleasure that I announce the retirement of . . . ', instead of 'It is with sadness that I announce the retirement of . . . '.

**functional analysis** a way of analysing the purpose of a particular behaviour, developed within BEHAVIOUR MODIFICATION.

Much behaviour that is considered abnormal does in fact serve a purpose for the person who engages in it, but it is not always easy to discover what the purpose of a particular behaviour is. Functional analysis begins by closely defining what behaviour is to be analysed. The practitioner or carer, or the client themselves, notes carefully what happened before the person engaged in that behaviour (the *antecedents*) and what happened as a result of that behaviour (the *consequences*). The information is usually logged on an ABC (*a*ntecedents, *b*ehaviour, *c*onsequences) chart, which logs time, antecedent, behaviour and consequences in parallel columns. In practice, the observer's recording often begins when the behaviour is observed. The consequences are noted with a view to isolating those that act as *reinforcement*, such as gaining of attention or relief from a task. The last step usually is to try to recall the antecedents – what was happening before the behaviour took place.

From a behavioural point of view, all behaviour, even seemingly destructive behaviour, that is repeated must be receiving reinforcement and must therefore serve some purpose for the person who engages in it. The point of functional analysis is to understand how the behaviour is reinforced and how it is triggered in the first place. For example, a young adult with LEARNING DISABILITY regularly throws tantrums (behaviour) at the training centre that they attend. Observation indicates that the tantrums frequently happen after they have been asked to undertake a complex task for which they have not been trained (antecedent) and result in them having the task taken from them (consequence).

**funeral expenses payment**    a payment from the regulated SOCIAL FUND to which there is a legal entitlement if the applicant is receiving INCOME SUPPORT, FAMILY CREDIT, DISABILITY WORKING ALLOWANCE, HOUSING BENEFIT or COUNCIL TAX BENEFIT and has responsibility for a funeral held in the United Kingdom.

The regulations allow for the cost of a modest funeral. The payment is reduced by the value of any capital over £500 (£1,000 if the person is aged 60 or over) that the applicant has, and it is recovered from the deceased's estate, if any.

# G

**gatekeeping**    the controlling of access to services, so that, out of all those people who seek the service, only those who most require it will receive it. The assumption is that many more people will ask for the service than can be provided for.

**gay**    see HOMOSEXUALITY.

**gender**    the social and psychological characteristics attributed to men and women.

Social scientists maintain that, whereas sex is determined by biology or anatomy, gender is determined by social processes that can vary significantly between social groups and historically within societies. SOCIALIZATION is regarded as the key process by which gender characteristics are conveyed to individuals, a process that can be much influenced by social class, membership of ethnic groups and other factors. There is still a substantial debate concerning the issue of whether there are any biological bases to behaviour that are rooted in biological differences between the sexes. For example, does a woman as child bearer have a biological predisposition also to nurture that is different from that of a man? Most social scientists now believe that such behaviour is a matter of social expectation, pointing to major differences between societies with regard to parenting.

**general practitioner** a qualified and registered doctor who holds a contract with a family health service authority to provide general medical services to the public.

General practitioners work from a district health authority health centre or from a surgery owned by their practice. They are independently contracted by the NATIONAL HEALTH SERVICE and receive a fee based on the number of people registered with them. Since 1991 some general practitioners have opted to become fund holders; this allows them to purchase certain health services such as hospital beds from the district health authorities or NHS hospital trusts. General practitioners often refer patients to the social services department of the local authority for COMMUNITY CARE and are often involved in the multidisciplinary ASSESSMENT of needs. As such they are important colleagues of social workers and social care professionals.

**generic** general, unspecialized; a generic social work service deals with all or most client groups and their problems, as do generic workers.

In the pre-SEEBOHM period, social work training courses and social work services were specialized. The profession distinguished between work in the child-care field, in mental health and in welfare (the latter dealing in the main with people with disabilities and old people). During the 1960s and earlier, some practitioners and commentators stressed the common elements to these branches of social work and called for both common training and a unified service. With the establishment of SOCIAL SERVICES DEPARTMENTS, generic services replaced specialized provision as the dominant model in England and Wales (in Scotland, the PROBATION SERVICE was also added). Generic services are now much less common. In the 1980s they came to be viewed as uneven in their responses to different client groups. Priorities for generic teams seemed always to be statutory child-care and emergency mental health work, with other service users receiving comparatively short shrift. Many social services departments have now restructured into adult services and children's services, in effect encouraging specialisms again. A few departments have retained INTAKE TEAMS where generic workers handle all initial work for a short period before passing it on to specialist teams. Another reason for the demise of genericism is continued growth in the range of duties that social workers are expected to discharge. Professional training courses can no longer pretend to be other than basic, with many specialist skills added as a result of post-qualifying or advanced training. The advent of COMMUNITY CARE work is also significantly changing the focus of some parts of social work, stressing MULTIDISCIPLINARY activity and new roles in the PURCHASER/PROVIDER SPLIT. It is unlikely that genericism will re-emerge unless the social work role contracts or, as in many European countries, education and training are considerably extended.

**genetic counselling** a medical service providing information to potential parents about the likelihood of their conceiving a disabled child.

People referred for genetic COUNSELLING are those with a disability or who have a close relative who is disabled. Information about the probability of certain conditions occurring or recurring can be offered. This form of counselling is likely to play an increasing part in medical practice.

**genogram**   a diagram used by social workers, mediators and therapists to describe the family tree.

The convention is to depict females with circles and males with squares, with a cross through the square or circle if the person is deceased. Horizontal lines indicate marriage or a cohabiting relationship. A vertical line with squares and circles beneath describes the children of a relationship. Additional information can be added, such as dates of birth, marriage or cohabitation, divorce or separation, deaths, major illnesses and other critical events. Problematic relationships can be indicated with wavy lines. Such visual representations of families can help in the ASSESSMENT of family problems, because significant events and relationships can be described briefly on one piece of paper. Genograms are especially useful in LIFE STORY BOOKS to indicate to children something about their background when they have lost touch with their birth family (see also ECOMAP).

**geriatrics**   the branch of medicine concerned with the health or ill-health of OLDER PEOPLE.

The Royal College of Physicians recognized geriatrics as a specialist area of medicine in 1977. The distinguishing aspects of geriatric care are accurate diagnosis, careful identification of problems, judicious medical intervention and the management of sickness in old age through multi-agency care teams.

**gerontology**   the MULTIDISCIPLINARY study of the ageing of OLDER PEOPLE.

Gerontology embraces biological, psychological and social theories in its understanding of the older person. Biological theories suggest that changes occur in the older adult's ability to adapt and interact with their environment. Psychological theories focus on older adults' self-concepts, and sociological theories examine the nature of the older adult's social relationships and of the position of older people in society.

**Gestalt**   a whole; a good configuration; a German term that is difficult to translate, and thus has entered English usage.

The original Gestalt psychologists, working in the early decades of the twentieth century, argued that reducing perceptual phenomena to simple elements loses the meaning of the total configuration; that is, the whole is greater than the sum of its parts. They formulated laws, such as that items that are similar and items that are close together tend to group, and that wholes that have a part missing will still be perceived as wholes. The essence of this perspective is that the appropriate level of analysis is holistic, whereas a reductionist analysis is generally inappropriate. If this argument is transferred from physical perceptual phenomena to the perception of people and their relationships, the individual is seen as a complex whole, existing in the present context, but composed of past and present influences, plus plans and aspirations for the future. It is also evident that the emphasis could be on patterns of behaviour, perhaps at the level of the family rather than the individual, and the individual will be seen as part of a network of wider social relationships.

Gestalt PSYCHOLOGY was used in the 1940s and 1950s as the theoretical basis to develop Gestalt therapy. With an emphasis on the 'person as a whole', driving towards greater fulfilment through becoming more complete, or self-actualized, this therapy was very much part of the larger movement termed the 'third force' in psychology – the humanistic movement – which developed as a counterbalance to psychoanalysis and behaviourism. The Gestalt therapy of its most celebrated practitioner and advocate, Fritz Perls, aims to assist the individual to complete those aspects of themselves that seem incomplete and restrict their personal growth. There may be 'unfinished business' with a parent or sibling as a hangover from the past; there may be a current situation that does not 'make sense', and clarification may come through action or understanding. The form of therapy may be individual or groupwork. It is primarily aimed at helping those involved to become aware of themselves as functioning organisms – a psyche and a body that form a whole. This awareness must include the context of this functioning organism, that is, social and cultural pressures that influence and are influenced by it. These features – of holism and of the total 'field' – are the essence of Gestalt theory and form the underpinning of Gestalt therapy. The actual methodology may vary among practitioners but is humanistic in that it recognizes self-actualization as a basic drive, and self-healing as a possibility.

The social worker may find this a useful theoretical position in that it emphasizes the necessity of seeing the person as a unique whole, but also as part of the sociocultural context. Therapeutic insights may be gained by considering how clients may have interpreted past experiences inappropriately through their effort to make a Gestalt (for example, if a child is abused, they 'make sense' of this by feeling responsible or guilty). A new, more appropriate understanding is necessary for the individual to move on from current problems resulting from this.

**Gillick competent**   the term used to describe a child under 16 years old who is deemed legally competent – that is, has sufficient understanding – to consent to all forms of medical treatment, including psychological assessment.

The term originated from the decision in the 1986 case of *Gillick* v. *West Norfolk Area Health Authority*, in which Mrs Victoria Gillick tried to show that it was illegal to offer contraceptive treatment to her daughter, who was under 16, without her parents' consent. The House of Lords decided that a child under 16 could consent to medical treatment, provided they could demonstrate 'sufficient understanding to make informed decisions'. The ability to consent is still linked to chronological age in the sense that the Law Lords recognized that competence was a developing capacity but that the rate of development between children varied. The decision about whether a child is competent is decided by the doctor responsible for treatment. If a child is deemed to be 'Gillick competent', the doctor can treat the child without the consent or knowledge of their parents.

The principle of Gillick competence has been incorporated into the CHILDREN ACT. A child who is subject to a CHILD ASSESSMENT ORDER, an

EMERGENCY PROTECTION ORDER, an INTERIM CARE ORDER or a SUPERVISION ORDER can refuse to submit to a medical or psychiatric examination or other assessment if they are able to demonstrate sufficient understanding to make an informed decision. This applies even if the examination has been ordered by a court. Further case decisions since the Children Act came into force have made the issue of consent less clear cut, however. A person with PARENTAL RESPONSIBILITY, or the High Court in exercising its powers, can override a child's refusal to consent to treatment, including where the child is over 16 years of age, provided the decision is deemed to be in the child's best interest.

**graduated pension**  an additional pension paid with RETIREMENT PENSION. The scheme operated between 1961 and 1975 and pays limited benefits to people who contributed during that period.

**Griffiths Report**  the government report on COMMUNITY CARE policy, written by Sir Roy Griffiths and published in 1988.

Griffiths had been asked by the DEPARTMENT OF HEALTH to undertake an overview of community care policy at a time when, on the one hand, the social security system was encouraging large numbers of older people in particular to enter residential care and, on the other, large psychiatric hospitals were discharging long-stay patients into the community prior to closure. Griffiths recommended that the local authority SOCIAL SERVICES DEPARTMENT act as designer, organizer and purchaser of community care services for all client groups. To do this it should develop local plans based on its assessment of community care needs, in wide consultation with the health authority and private and voluntary organizations. The report also recommended that the local authority social services department be responsible for assessing an individual's needs and arranging the purchase of whatever services were required – domiciliary, day or residential care. But the local authority would not be the primary provider of such services; Griffiths's intention was to stimulate the supply of services from the voluntary and private sectors, and his separation of the PURCHASER/PROVIDER functions was one of the report's most influential proposals. Many of the key reforms proposed in the report were later enacted in the NATIONAL HEALTH SERVICE AND COMMUNITY CARE ACT.

Sir R. Griffiths, *Community Care: Agenda for Action*, London: Department of Health/HMSO, 1988.

**group home**  a very broad term to indicate a type of service provision utilizing ordinary houses and other domestic settings to provide a home for small numbers of service users.

Commonly the term is used for homes for groups of about four people, but it has also been employed to describe accommodation for considerably larger groups. This pattern of service provision is often used for people with LEARNING DISABILITY and people with MENTAL HEALTH PROBLEMS. Staffing levels vary according to the need of service users and may range from no permanent staff at all to staff being on duty at all times.

**groupwork**  a range of activities, including a method of social work intervention, that can enable individuals and groups to develop problem-solving skills to address both their own concerns and those of members of the wider COMMUNITY (see also FAMILY THERAPY).

Evaluation of the groupwork method in social work relies predominantly on subjective accounts of group members' experiences and on observations of group leaders or facilitators. Such accounts seem to point to the potential effectiveness of working with groups in all areas of social work, statutory and voluntary, field and residential. Although it is widely accepted that individual behaviour and attitudes are influenced by groups, it does not automatically follow that groups formed by social workers will achieve their aims. However, it is appropriate to look at the possible advantages and disadvantages of this method, and at the skills and knowledge required by workers who may wish to include groupwork in their repertoire of responses to problems presented by service users.

A way of classifying the different models of groupwork is by looking at the aims of groups under broad headings such as the following: alleviating isolation; promoting social learning and maturation; preparing for an approaching crisis or other life change; solving or clarifying problems at the personal/familial level; solving or clarifying problems in the members' environment; and achieving insight. In practice, groups may combine these aims, or start with one and develop into another during the life of the group.

Models of groupwork are influenced by theories from a range of disciplines, such as sociology, social psychology and criminology, that have contributed to our understanding of behaviour in groups. These theoretical frameworks inform the worker's practice and influence and shape the methods used in groupwork. Values are also important, in that they affect how the social worker plans and facilitates groups. Groupwork practice is never value-neutral, so workers need to be clear about their own values and the principles on which they base their practice. For example, in the 'self-directed' groupwork model, which emphasizes ANTI-DISCRIMINATORY PRACTICE and empowerment, five practice principles may be outlined: (1) all people have skills, understanding and ability; (2) people have rights; (3) the problems that service users face are complex, and responses to them need to reflect this; (4) practice can effectively be built on the knowledge that people acting collectively can be powerful; (5) practise what you preach. An essential part to planning when using this model is the worker's recognition of these principles. Whatever model or approach groupworkers choose to use, they need to consider the difficulties and circumstances of individual group members and their public and political context, rather than having a narrow focus on just one of these areas.

What are some of the possible advantages and disadvantages of using groupwork? Groups cannot offer exclusive individual attention. This can be positive, however, for some service users who find a one-to-one relationship too intense and are therefore more comfortable in a group setting. Being able to put aside personal considerations at times may be necessary, since members will need to work cooperatively to achieve the aims of the group. Any benefits of groupwork may not be immediately apparent, because it takes time for a collection of people to start to function as a group. Confidentiality can be difficult to maintain; information about individuals is often shared with other group members, who may not be bound by a professional ethic. In groupwork, the roles of client and worker are not clear cut – members may develop skills of leadership, for example – and so it can be a democratic, participatory and empowering method of social work.

For groupwork to be anti-discriminatory in practice, leaders or facilitators need to be prepared to challenge oppression on the grounds of age, gender, race, sexual orientation, class and disability. This means that workers and co-workers will have explored and defined their own values before planning a group and thought in advance about how issues are going to be dealt with. A worker's commitment to anti-oppressive practice will involve them in learning about lifestyles different to their own and about the way DISCRIMINATION impacts on people's lives. In practice, this can mean having to make some difficult decisions about whether a group should proceed at all if crucial questions around the group's racial and gender mix or access requirements cannot be adequately addressed. Further essential considerations for groupwork practice are supervision or consultation, recording and evaluation. Each of these issues needs to be looked at in some depth, and all groupwork publications stress their importance.

Overall, groupwork is demanding on a worker and requires a great deal of commitment in terms of time and effort to plan and resource any initiative. As groupwork is more 'visible' than individual work, and the worker is more exposed as a person, this may increase their level of anxiety. However, working with groups of people in ways that develop their potential can be a rewarding experience.

M. Preston-Shoot, *Effective Groupwork*, Basingstoke: Macmillan, 1987.

**guardian *ad litem*** a trained social worker selected from a local panel to provide independent social work opinion to a court about what is best for a child's welfare during proceedings for an ADOPTION ORDER, a CARE ORDER, an EMERGENCY PROTECTION ORDER or a SUPERVISION ORDER.

The guardian *ad litem* makes a full assessment of each case by interviewing the child and their family, as well as any professionals such as health visitors and teachers who are involved with the child. They also have access to records kept about the child. On the basis of this assessment they reach a decision about what they think best serves the child's welfare. At all times they represent the child, and if necessary they instruct a solicitor on the child's behalf. The management of local panels of guardians *ad litem* in each area is the responsibility of a voluntary organization or of the local authority itself. In every case individual guardians *ad litem* retain complete independence from their authority in reaching their decisions.

Department of Health, *The Children Act Guidance and Regulations, vol. 7 Guardians Ad Litem and Other Court Related Issues*, London, HMSO, 1991.

**guardians allowance** a benefit paid to a person looking after a child who is effectively orphaned, that is, where both parents have died or one has died and the other is in prison or cannot be found.

**guardianship** a legal arrangement whereby one person looks after the affairs of another who cannot act for themselves. Guardianship is based on the common law concept of *parens patriae* (literally 'the state or parent', whereby a guardian looked after and cared for those who could not attend to their own needs.

Within the current legislative framework of England and Wales, 'guardianship' has two distinct meanings, one in relation to children and the other, less commonly, in relation to adults who are incapacitated in some way. Guardianship in respect of children is governed by the CHILDREN ACT. The effect of guardianship is that the person or people appointed as the child's guardian(s) acquire PARENTAL RESPONSIBILITY for the child. A person may apply to the court to be appointed as a child's guardian if the child has no living parent with parental responsibility or if a RESIDENCE ORDER has been made with respect to a child in favour of a parent or guardian who died while the order was in force. The court's decision concerning the appointment of a guardian must be in the child's best interest. A parent with parental responsibility or a guardian can appoint an individual to be a child's guardian in the event of their death without recourse to court, provided the appointment is made in writing.

Guardianship in respect of adults is governed by section 47 of the NATIONAL ASSISTANCE Act 1948 where the person in need suffers from 'grave chronic disease' or is 'aged, infirm or physically incapacitated', and by sections 7–10 and 37 of the MENTAL HEALTH ACT 1983 where the person in need suffers from a MENTAL DISORDER. The powers of guardianship in respect of adults are more limited than those in relation to children. If the criteria laid down in the National Assistance Act are fulfilled, a local authority may apply to a court for an order to remove the person from the place where they live to a suitable hospital or other premises. This provision is intended to be used where an adult is unable physically to care for themselves or is not receiving adequate care from someone else and so is living in insanitary conditions. The provision under the Mental Health Act is intended to enable any mentally disordered person aged 16 or over to receive COMMUNITY CARE where it cannot be provided without the use of compulsory powers. Technically, this may be used where the person has either a mental illness or a learning disability; but due to the definition of mental impairment in the Act, the latter group are largely excluded.

The powers of guardianship in this context can restrict the liberty of the person to ensure that various forms of treatment, social support, training, occupation or education are undertaken. A guardian cannot, however, consent to medical treatment on behalf of a person. Guardianship can be granted by application to the local authority by an approved social worker or a nearest relative supported by the written opinion of two registered medical practitioners. The local authority or a private citizen may be appointed as the guardian. Courts in criminal proceedings may, in certain circumstances, make guardianship orders as an alternative to a penal disposal for offenders who are mentally disordered at the time of the sentence. Guardianship in relation to adults is rarely used; some commentators argue that this is largely due to the resource implications involved and the limitations imposed on the powers of the guardian.

Millington, *Guardianship and the Mental Health Act 1983*, Norwich: University of East Anglia, Social Work Monographs, 1989.

# H

**halfway house**   an alternative name for a residential facility that offers a stepping stone between a long- or longer-stay institution and living in the COMMUNITY.

Halfway houses are usually designed for alcoholics or other drug abusers, for people with MENTAL HEALTH PROBLEMS and occasionally for ex-prisoners. Such facilities offer a measure of support for people who have experienced a long period of institutional living (where most decisions have been made for them), as a prelude to living unsupported in the community. Halfway houses may help to prepare people for a more independent lifestyle or offer a measure of supervision to those who perhaps cannot yet be fully trusted. (See HOSTEL.)

**hallucination**   a false perception of the senses that occurs in the absence of any external stimulus. Simple hallucinations may take the form of noises such as buzzing, banging or sounds of shuffling, while complex hallucinations involve a combination of sounds such as voices or music.

Auditory hallucinations are commonly experienced as voices that may convey a message or may be unintelligible. Such voices, if intelligible, are experienced as directing the person to do something or as 'running commentary' in which the person's activities are discussed. Visual hallucinations are commonly experienced in the form of people, objects or animals, symbols or flashes of light. Tactile hallucinations are experienced sensations of touch such as the feeling of insects crawling on the skin or of another person's fingers touching the body.

**hallucinogens**   DRUGS such as LSD and 'magic mushrooms' that when taken have the short-term effect of altering perception and causing hallucinations.

The experience of hallucinogens can be either pleasant or confusing and frightening. In certain people the experience can trigger a psychotic episode.

**handicap**   a term, meaning DISABILITY or disadvantage, that is rejected by many disabled people, who regard it as pejorative.

The World Health Organization utilizes the term as part of its International Classification of Impairment, Disabilities and Handicaps to indicate 'a disadvantage for a given individual, resulting from an impairment or disability, that limits or prevents the fulfilments of a role (depending on age, sex and social and cultural factors) for that individual'. The advantage of the WHO's definitions is that they label states of health rather than people; however, these definitions have been rejected by the disabled people movement because of their medical focus. A recent publication by the Central Council for Education and Training in Social Work stated that a group working on disability issues and ANTI-DISCRIMINATORY PRACTICE did not use the word 'handicap' because disabled people are uncomfortable with the term, which has connotations of burden or limitation.

**harassment** see VIOLENCE.

**harm minimization** a term employed in relation to the use of (mainly illegal) substances to mean reducing the social, medical, legal and psychological harm surrounding the taking of such DRUGS.

When taken under medical supervision diamorphine HEROIN), for example, will not cause any harm to the body and may be used safely over a considerable period of time. However, in its illegal state it is likely to be mixed with adulterants that can be harmful, especially if injected. It is expensive, which often leads the user to indulge in criminal activities, with all the social and psychological consequences this can entail. COMMUNITY DRUG TEAMS often prescribe METHADONE as a substitute for heroin, thus enabling the user to stabilise their life, avoid the BLACK MARKET and use their drug of ADDICTION safely. If the user is INJECTING, a supply of clean needles/syringes is made available, to reduce as far as possible the harm surrounding their drug use.

**health** in medical terms, the absence of illness.

On the basis of the MEDICAL MODEL, illness can be regarded both as an individual phenomenon and as something that occurs naturally. Illness can of course be induced by people, as with SUBSTANCE MISUSE, but in the main, according to this view, biology provides the best explanation for illness. Using the social or environmental model, health is seen in the context of particular societies. Thus, nineteenth-century Britain gave rise to particular epidemics because of problems of sanitation, poor diet and poverty. The social model does not entirely reject biological explanations, for even in the healthiest societies people grow old. This model, however, has to be supplemented by an appreciation of wider forces, including the physical environment and social relationships.

These differing definitions of health have major repercussions for the way health services and social services are organized. If the medical model is adopted, then the means of treatment are primarily drugs and surgery. If the social definition is used, then health becomes the concern of a wide range of people other than medical staff. The BLACK REPORT, reflecting upon different patterns of mortality and illness in Britain in relation to SOCIAL CLASS, came to the conclusion that ANTI-POVERTY STRATEGIES were more important than putting more resources into health provision and reorganizing such services.

Sociologists have revealed interesting connections between health and other factors. Unemployment and ill-health appear to be strongly associated, although this association is not a simple one. Poverty is often also a feature of unemployment, whereas in other circumstances (such as early retirement) unemployment can be viewed positively if there is no hardship. In terms of access, the poorer sections of the population clearly use health services less than the better off. People from ethnic minorities see themselves as poorly served by the NATIONAL HEALTH SERVICE, particularly in relation to MENTAL HEALTH. Although many health workers are from ethnic minorities, they rarely have power over decision-making or the development of policy. Similarly, the major critique of the health and social services from a feminist perspective is that it has a mainly female workforce and yet mostly male management. The assertion is that women's problems have been unnecessarily 'medicalized' and that the process is a form of control exercised by men over women.

**Health Advisory Service (HAS)** an independent agency of the DEPARTMENT OF HEALTH concerned with all aspects of the organization of the NATIONAL HEALTH SERVICE.

Established in 1969, the HAS frequently works with the SOCIAL SERVICES INSPECTORATE (SSI) in looking at services for specific client groups, evaluating those services and providing advice on improving them. HAS advice includes considering issues of patient care organization and management, education and training, and cooperation between agencies, particularly in joint planning of services. As with the SSI, the role of the HAS is both to disseminate good practice and to provide a monitoring service to government on the impact of service provision on users. However, unlike the SSI the HAS is independent of the Department of Health and is headed by a clinician or other medical specialist, not by a civil servant; staffing is largely made up of professionals working for the HAS on a temporary basis. In relation to social work, the main role of the HAS is to collaborate with the SSI in promoting effective cooperation between health authorities and social services departments, which is of particular importance in relation to the development of COMMUNITY CARE. In 1986 the HAS also established the Drug Advisory Service, to help advise district health authorities on the development of services for drug users in their area. The HAS has fought hard to maintain its independent status and sees itself not as an inspectorate but rather as a professional consultancy. Its ability to maintain this level of independence is a reflection of the greater power of clinicians as a profession when compared to social workers, and their determination to maintain professional and clinical freedom; in order to gain the cooperation of clinicians, the HAS emphasized its advisory role and the idea of professionals in dialogue, rather than appearing as a mouthpiece for the Department of Health.

P. Day and R. Klein, *Inspecting the Inspectorates*, York: Rowntree Trust, 1990.

**health benefits** benefits associated with the NATIONAL HEALTH SERVICE, including free prescriptions, free dental treatment, free eye tests, vouchers towards glasses, fares to hospital appointments, wigs and fabric supports, free milk tokens and free vitamins.

Free milk tokens and free vitamins are available to expectant mothers and children under 5 getting INCOME SUPPORT. The other benefits listed are available to people on income support and FAMILY CREDIT and to others on low incomes who satisfy a separate means test that is similar to, but marginally more generous than, that for income support. Under this low-income scheme, people can qualify for partial help towards dental treatment, eye tests, glasses, fares to hospital, wigs and fabric supports, as well as being eligible for free services. Although all the other services can be provided completely free, since the introduction of the 'vouchers for glasses' scheme many income support claimants find it impossible to obtain glasses without contributing to the cost themselves. People who want to apply for help under the means test can get forms at local Department of Social Security offices. People who are passported by income support or family credit can apply for the free service directly to the pharmacist, dentist, optician or hospital.

**health visitor**   a registered nurse who is also qualified to provide regular home health check-ups at specified intervals for infants and young children.

Health visitors are generally employed by a district health authority and based at a health centre or general practitioner's surgery. They are often viewed as a source of support, advice and guidance in the care and upbringing of children; and because of this they may play an important role in assessing whether a child has been abused or neglected. Most district health authorities also employ GERIATRIC health visitors, whose principal concern is the care and welfare of older people in their own homes.

**Hemineverin (chormethiazole)**   a non-benzodiazepine, non-BARBITURATE sleeping drug also used in the treatment of acute ALCOHOL WITHDRAWAL symptoms.

To minimize the risk of DEPENDENCE, Hemineverin should ideally be given short-term and under inpatient supervision. Short-term adverse effects can include headache, gastro-intestinal problems, irritation of the eyes, sneezing and confusion.

**hepatitis B**   a blood-borne and sexually transmitted infection common among DRUG injectors.

Although the routes of transmission for hepatitis B are similar to those of HIV (human immunodeficiency virus), it can also be spread by saliva. It is more infectious than HIV. Hepatitis B attacks cells in the liver, where it reproduces. Symptoms may not appear for up to six months, and then the body's immune system may be successful in preventing further progression. However, in approximately 10 per cent of people the virus will persist, and the individual will be at risk of developing cirrhosis or cancer of the liver. As many as 60 per cent or more of drug users, especially injectors, may test positive to the antibodies to the virus. Unlike with HIV, it is possible to be vaccinated against hepatitis B, and general practitioners will provide this service to high-risk groups, including certain drug users. People consuming excessive amounts of ALCOHOL are also more vulnerable to the risk of contracting hepatitis.

**heroin**   a sedative DRUG processed from the opium derivative morphine; opium grows mainly in the Middle East and Far East. Heroin is also known as 'smack', 'H', 'scag' and 'junk'.

Heroin in its pure pharmaceutical and legal form is a white powder called diamorphine that is used to alleviate extreme pain. By the time illegal heroin reaches the streets it is very low in purity and has been adulterated with other similar looking substances. It is a brownish, off-white powder usually sold in small 'wraps' of paper. Street heroin is either smoked ('CHASING THE DRAGON') or INJECTED. Both routes can lead to physical and psychological ADDICTION. Injectors also run the risk of infections such as septicaemia, abscesses, HEPATITIS B and HIV. Heroin is a class A drug and attracts the most severe penalties under the MISUSE OF DRUGS ACT 1971, ranging from a fine for possession to life imprisonment for supply.

> The effects of taking heroin on a regular basis are wider ranging than the actual physical effects on the body. Physical effects include a slowing down of the body's activities, such as breathing and heart rate. Those new to the drug usually experience nausea as well as varying states of 'intoxication'. The initial 'high' is a feeling that users try to repeat, but TOLERANCE to the drug builds up, and more is increasingly required to give the same effect. After the initial feeling wears off, varying degrees of sedation follow ('nodding off'), which may culminate in an overdose if too much is taken or if the purity is higher than expected. Because the drug is expensive and tolerance increases, funding the habit can become a problem, with all the social and legal implications that may follow. Users who are addicted to heroin may be offered a METHADONE prescription by their general practitioner or COMMUNITY DRUG TEAM as a way of stabilizing their life. Giving up a heroin addiction, as with any other entrenched habit, is not easy and entails DETOXIFICATION. Some users decide to go on to a RESIDENTIAL REHABILITATION house to complete the process of staying off.

**High Court**   a collective term for three different divisions of court with different functions: Queen's Bench Division, Family Division and Chancery Division.

The largest division of the High Court, the Queen's Bench, is concerned with civil disputes involving more money than can be dealt with in the county court. It also has a general role of protection against the abuse of power, so that it is concerned with a range of matters such as libel, habeas corpus (issuing writs for the release of someone unlawfully detained) and the judicial review of government and local authority decisions. It can also deal with appeals from magistrates' courts where points of law are involved. The Family Division is concerned with disputes about children and family property, covering matters relating to divorce, ADOPTION and wardship (see FAMILY COURT WELFARE, WELFARE REPORT). The Chancery Division deals mainly with matters of taxation, wills and company disputes (see CRIMINAL COURTS).

**HIV/AIDS**   HIV (human immunodeficiency virus) is the virus that may lead to AIDS (acquired immunodeficiency syndrome). HIV damages the body's defence (immune) system, making it more vulnerable to the effects of opportunistic infections.

The HIV virus is spread by an interchange of bodily fluids, which must pass from an infected person into the body of an uninfected person before it can spread. The behaviour most likely to affect this interchange is penetrative sexual intercourse and the sharing of needles and other drug-using equipment. The virus may also be passed from an infected mother to her unborn child or to the child at the time of birth. At the present time there is no vaccination to prevent the virus, nor any cure should AIDS result, although infections can often be successfully treated. It is good practice in any working environment to cover up cuts and to clean up any body fluids wearing disposable gloves. The HIV antibody test shows whether or not the body has developed antibodies to the virus; if it has, this means the body at some time has been infected by HIV. However, it may take up to three months for the antibodies to develop after the virus has been contracted, so ideally two tests with 'safe' behaviour in between are necessary.

> There are many pros and cons around the decision of whether to be HIV tested or not, and any person considering having a test should receive both pre- and post-test COUNSELLING. It is not legal to take a named sample of blood for testing without informed consent. Genito-urinary clinics handle the issues sensitively; they carry out testing and are under no obligation, unlike general practitioners, to divulge information about any specific patient. Prisoners and drug-related offenders are particularly vulnerable to contracting HIV/AIDS. The Prison Service has consistently refused to issue condoms to prisoners, except on home leave, or to countenance needle exchange schemes, despite the prevalence of homosexuality and drug taking in prisons.

**home help**   a person who undertakes domestic tasks, such as cooking, cleaning and shopping, for people unable to do such things for themselves by reason of DISABILITY, illness or the affects of ageing.

A home help is usually available from a private or voluntary agency, or from a SOCIAL SERVICES DEPARTMENT. Their assistance is often only obtainable through a REFERRAL. Home helps are also known as community care workers.

**homelessness**   the condition of being without a home or shelter or of living in circumstances wholly inappropriate to social and personal needs.

Definitions of homelessness, and consequently estimations of the extent of homelessness, have varied widely in Britain. Official registers are unreliable, because many people do not bother to report themselves in need of housing. Statistics reflect only those people who are accepted as homeless by housing departments of local authorities. Those not in priority categories will not report themselves as homeless, because they believe that local authorities cannot help them. Others despair of lengthy waiting lists, often accepting poor-quality accommodation in the private sector. Official statistics therefore grossly underestimate the extent of the problem. Some analysts would add to the homeless list all those who are in inappropriate accommodation, that is, people living in HOSTELS, in BED AND BREAKFAST accommodation or in overcrowded conditions. If all these arguments are accepted, then homelessness in Britain must be seen as a major problem and one that has been growing rapidly in recent years. In practice housing department officials often offer homeless people 'temporary' accommodation, although this frequently means long periods in unsatisfactory dwellings.

> Associations between homelessness and other social problems are now well established. Educational attainment for children of homeless families often

suffers, because children find it difficult to adjust to new schools even if a school can be found to accept them. HEALTH for the whole family can be fundamentally affected both by low morale and through an unwillingness of general practitioners to accept short-term patients. There are also strong associations with chronic UNEMPLOYMENT. These additional difficulties seem in part a problem of access to social and welfare services, because homeless families are vulnerable and because services are often unable to deal with their needs. Once a family is permanently housed, often in the least popular local authority housing stock, these additional problems often follow such families, particularly if their period of homelessness was lengthy. Feelings of being powerless and marginal while homeless seem to be common, especially where people have been housed temporarily away from their communities of origin and their support networks. Oppressed groups such as single parents (mostly women) and ethnic minorities, not surprisingly, figure prominently among the homeless.

J. Greve and E. Currie, *Homeless in Britain*, Housing Research Findings No. 10, York: Joseph Rowntree Foundation, 1990.

**Home Life** the code of practice for residential care produced by a working party appointed by the Centre for Policy on Ageing at the direction of the then Department of Health and Social Security.

The code, first published in 1984, was intended to assist local authorities in carrying out their registration and INSPECTION duties with regard to private and voluntary RESIDENTIAL CARE homes for all client groups (except most children's homes) under the REGISTERED HOMES ACT 1984. It placed great emphasis on recognizing the individuality of each resident by encouraging trial stays, retaining personal possessions and clothing, and providing private rooms, access to records and a chance to pursue individual activities. While the standards that *Home Life* urged are far more accepted now than they were ten years ago, there has been no revision of it; it remains a widely used set of standards for local authority, voluntary and private homes.

Centre for Policy on Ageing, *Home Life: a Code of Practice for Residential Care*, London: 1984.

**Home Office** the central government department with overall responsibility for the work of the PROBATION SERVICE through its Criminal Justice and Constitutional Department.

The Home Office provides 80 per cent of the funding for the Probation Service (the remaining 20 per cent comes from local authorities). It also approves appointments of deputy chief probation officers and chief probation officers; other appointments are made by local PROBATION BOARDS (formerly probation committees). The Home Office sponsors students to train as probation officers and finances student training units to provide practice placements. Until the 1980s it adopted a *laissez-faire* approach to the oversight of the fifty-six Probation Service areas, relying on circulars, letters to chief probation officers and periodic inspections by HM Inspectorate of Probation. However, in 1984 it produced the *Statement of National Objectives and Priorities* for the service, whose very production – although its content was not particularly controversial – indicated an increasingly centralized management ethos. Since then the Home Office has sought to impose a clear policy framework on the service and has become increasingly preoccupied with issues of 'value for money'. The publication of national standards was intended to establish quality-control mechanisms in respect of professional practice, and a publication entitled *Organizing Supervision and Punishment in the Community: A Decision Document* (1991) set out the Home Office's plans for the service's future organization. In 1992 the Probation Training Unit was established to oversee training and staff development within the whole service.

**homophobia**   an intensely negative feeling about homosexuals and HOMOSEXUALITY.

Homophobia may be an irrational fear and possibly a deep-seated hatred of homosexuals and of what is perceived as their lifestyles. It is thought to be widespread in society, although for most people the feeling is relatively dormant, brought occasionally to life by anti-homosexual jokes. It is rare for people to be involved in active anti-homosexual politics or campaigns. Some have argued that homophobia may be evidence of repressed or latent homosexuality.

**homosexuality**   sexual attraction to a person, or people, of the same sex. In everyday practice, the term has come to mean sexual relationships between men, with the comparable term 'lesbianism' for relationships between women.

In the following discussion, homosexuality is taken to refer to both men and women. Estimates in Britain and the United States are that at least 10 per cent of the population is homosexual. There is considerable disagreement among scientists and social scientists as to whether homosexuality is a result of SOCIALIZATION, genetics or perhaps some combination of the two. This debate is related to issues of value and of DISCRIMINATION. Homosexuality is regarded by many as a problem to be 'treated'; others see it as a legitimate form of sexuality. On the one hand, many have an abhorrence for homosexuality to the point of HOMOPHOBIA, likening it to paedophilia and perceiving it as essentially evil. Others, by contrast, perceive it to be as 'normal' as heterosexuality. Some sympathizers argue that sexuality is socially constructed upon a biological entity (men and women) that is generally sensuous in impulse – what Freud called 'polymorphous sexuality'. Society shapes our sexuality into two genders, so it is argued, but this shaping is, to some extent, arbitrary.

These arguments have been used to underpin not only value positions but also laws and policies in the justice and welfare fields. Thus critics of homosexuality would have such relationships identified as not only evil but illegal – requiring, in some circumstances, both 'treatment' and punishment. Most US states, for example, still regard particular acts in same-sex relationships as either a misdemeanour or a felony. Much Christian teaching has it that homosexuality is a sin. Those who perceive homosexuality as a 'natural' or legitimate form of sexuality would wish to develop the rights of gays and lesbians so that they are comparable to those of heterosexual people. Such rights would not only concern the age of consent to sexual activity but also address current discriminatory practices in many areas of social and public life. In Britain the age of consent to homosexual activity has recently been lowered, although it is still higher than for heterosexual activity. In the 1970s both the American Psychiatric Association and the World Health Organization removed homosexuality from the list of behavioural 'disorders'. Regardless of how people evaluate evidence of the legitimacy or otherwise of homosexuality, many take the 'liberal' view that what consenting adults do with each other is an issue of personal liberty rather than one of morality or legality. According to this view, as long as people are not hurt, the issue is one of personal choice.

In social welfare and social work activity, there are many value concerns. Under the Local Government Act 1988, homosexuality must not be promoted as a legitimate family form through local government services. Some have interpreted this clause to mean that all services for gay and lesbian people should be closed down. Others have sought to ignore the Act. The national picture is therefore uneven. Social workers have to deal with these issues in a variety of contexts. Counselling young people who are in care or being accommodated by local authorities; applications to foster or adopt children by gays and lesbians, either as single people or as couples; requests for housing (including sheltered accommodation) from homosexual couples; requests for residential accommodation from homosexual elders; dealing with partners when a gay or lesbian person is dying: social workers of all persuasions have to deal with all these areas of practice. The evidence is that practice varies substantially. Within social work training courses the treatment of homosexual issues is also extremely variable. US research has indicated that social workers may well be more homophobic than psychiatrists and psychologists and only marginally less so than the general public. The profession has yet to decide on the nature of ANTI-DISCRIMINATORY PRACTICE in this area of work and on how social workers should demonstrate their commitment to it.

**hospice care**  an approach to working with DYING people that combines medical interventions for symptom relief with concern for the emotional and psychological well-being of the dying and those about to be bereaved.

Hospice care in Britain began in the 1960s with the opening of St Christopher's Hospice in South London. Dame Cicely Saunders, a nurse and social worker, is credited with the early development of the hospice movement. Her approach was not a departure from medical modes of working with terminally ill people but an attempt to view the dying person in a holistic way, acknowledging their broad spectrum of psychological, emotional and medical needs. The modern hospice movement now offers active total care (palliative care) to dying people whose disease no longer responds to curative intervention; it is an approach that enables dying people to live with dignity until death. The hospice offers palliative care in a number of ways. Residential inpatient units offer short- or long-term care and pain management. The day hospice, usually found within residential units, offers a wide variety of activity and care to the dying person. Home care approaches offer the dying person and their relatives advice, support, care and pain control in the person's own home. Home care teams may be based in the hospice or at a hospital. More recently, hospitals have been developing support care teams to bring hospice palliative care principles to the needs of dying people in hospital.

**hospital social work**   social work services conducted in hospital and allied settings.

Although terminology varies between authorities and institutions, the label has tended to replace the competing term 'medical social work' and has displaced entirely the now defunct ALMONER. The probable reason for the demise of the term 'medical social work' is the rejection, at least in some quarters, of the MEDICAL MODEL as the predominant explanation for social problems experienced by users of social work services. The generalized movement suggesting the social construction of problems is preferred in many medical settings. Hospital social workers are present in the whole range of hospitals and clinics and increasingly in other settings such as HOSPICES and community mental health teams. A wide range of specialisms are developing in relation to particular areas of practice – for example, mental health, older people (including the elderly mentally infirm), people with DISABILITIES stemming from traumatic events like accidents or strokes, patients with kidney failure, people with HIV/AIDS, DRUG abuse, profound learning or physical disability, and children with behavioural difficulties.

> Although much of the work undertaken by hospital social workers is within the institution, a considerable proportion can be within the community. Thus helping discharged patients to adjust to life in the community can be a major objective; similarly, work, say, in relation to mentally ill people to prevent their readmission to hospital might be a substantial part of a social worker's brief; work in relation to people with sexually transmitted diseases can be primarily located within the community; and so on. A large part of hospital social work is conducted in teams of a MULTIDISCIPLINARY nature, with nurses, psychologists, doctors, health visitors, social workers and others often required to work together. A key issue is the extent to which such professionals are able to work together with equal status, or whether the medical hierarchy dominates both the teams and the way problems are framed.

**hostel**   a residential unit that offers a measure of support, supervision or, sometimes, protection.

Hostel facilities are often a HALFWAY HOUSE between a long-stay institution and 'normal' community living; or they may be designed to help vulnerable people live more independently and thus at some later stage effect a move into community living. They may offer both supervision and support to ex-offenders without family support, especially after a long prison sentence. Such facilities are often appropriate to those on PAROLE and where a conviction has included an offence against the person. Hostel accommodation, together with a PROBATION ORDER, is also increasingly offered to sex offenders as an alternative to imprisonment as part of a rigorous regime of 're-education'. Supervision and support are also pertinent to people with mental health problems, either as a temporary measure to reintroduce them into the community or, conceivably, to prevent admission to hospital, or as a long-term placement for those who cannot manage alone. Other vulnerable groups, including OLDER PEOPLE (see SHELTERED ACCOMMODATION), people with LEARNING DISABILITIES (see GROUP HOME), children LEAVING CARE, alcoholics 'drying out' and HOMELESS people or families (as a prelude to finding more settled and secure accommodation), have all benefited from hostel accommodation of varying kinds. Hostels differ in terms of social work support, which is provided intensively on the premises in some cases, and more distantly in others, with workers visiting from time to time. (See also BAIL HOSTEL.)

**housing associations**   range of non-profit organizations involved in the building and maintenance of housing.

Housing associations are organized in a variety of ways reflected in their status, which can range from that of a friendly society through to charitable companies under the Charities Act. Under the changing legislation of the 1980s housing associations have expanded to become an increasingly important part of public housing provision. As a result of this expansion, they are responsible for approximately a third of all newly built housing. This has been largely due to the way central government has aimed to reduce the role of the local housing authorities in providing and managing public-sector housing. This change has also allowed central government to have greater direct control over the housing programme, bypassing local authorities. In 1964 the government established the Housing Corporation as an agency for financing housing associations. Through the Housing Corporation the government can channel funds through a system of deficit loans that allow housing associations to engage in building new housing without being dependent on raising finance through more commercial channels such as the banks.

As housing associations have increased their role in providing new housing, they have also established themselves as a major provider of accommodation for people emerging out of long-stay hospitals. SOCIAL SERVICES DEPARTMENTS have worked with housing associations in the development of new forms of sheltered accommodation, often maintaining allocation rights in return for contracts with housing associations. This has enabled social services departments and health authorities to develop new initiatives, particularly in areas where the district housing authority is a limited supplier or in response to the government's emphasis on non-statutory provision.

P. Malpass and A. Murie, *Housing Policy and Practice*, Basingstoke: Macmillan, 1987.

**housing authorities**   the housing departments of local district councils, primarily responsible for the management of council housing stock.

Housing authorities are involved in the provision of public-sector housing, as both builders and managers. Within the metropolitan areas they are part of the metropolitan district council alongside SOCIAL SERVICES DEPARTMENTS. This has allowed for some close working relationships to develop; and in some authorities, including Tower Hamlets in London and St Helens in Merseyside, there has been a move towards the integration of these services as a response to the demands of COMMUNITY CARE. However, local authority housing provision has come under severe strain since 1979, when the new Conservative government introduced a range of financial and statutory controls on housing finance. Most important was the introduction of a statutory right to buy in the Housing Act 1980, which resulted in approximately one and a quarter million sales of council dwellings by 1988. The financial benefit to local authorities from the sale of council dwellings has been restricted due to capital controls on the use of receipts from sales. These and other controls have led to a fall in capital spending on housing of approximately 46 per cent in real terms between 1976/7 and 1987/8.

The government introduced its controls on housing finance with the stated objective of reducing the role of the state in providing public housing. The aim was to increase the role of the Housing Corporation and HOUSING ASSOCIATIONS in public housing and to provide more incentives for the private sector both in owner-occupation and in rented accommodation. Additionally, the government has introduced measures to ensure that local authority housing is provided at a price closer to its market value. Local authorities' housing revenue accounts can no longer be subsidized from other sources; therefore, management, repair and maintenance costs must come out of the rents charged. This has inevitably resulted in an increase in rents in recent years and consequently a major increase in HOUSING BENEFIT payments as tenants find rents outstripping their ability to pay.

Critics have argued that the introduction of the right to buy, allied to controls on capital spending, has resulted in a reduction in the housing stock available to local authorities for housing the poor. This has given rise to an increase in the number of cases of homelessness and the use of BED AND BREAKFAST accommodation to try to resolve the problem.

With all these financial pressures, some local housing authorities have concentrated more on providing SHELTERED ACCOMMODATION. The approach adopted involves the use of wardens and introduces an element of care into the service. This led to the publication of a response to the GRIFFITHS REPORT by the housing authorities of the largest non-metropolitan English city councils, including Bristol and Stoke-on-Trent, who argued against Griffiths's view that housing authorities should concentrate on the 'bricks and mortar' aspects of housing management and instead emphasized their welfare role in caring for tenants. However, with the changes in government policy stressing the role of housing associations as providers of public housing, social services frequently see these as partners in providing accommodation for clients rather than the district housing authorities.

**housing benefit** a generic term describing benefits that provide help towards the payment of rent, administered by district councils. Rent allowance is a cash payment to tenants of private landlords or housing associations; rent rebate is a credit against a local authority tenant's rent account.

Housing benefit cannot be paid to anyone who has more than £16,000 in capital. Capital between £3,000 and £16,000 is deemed to produce an income of £1 per week for every £250 or part thereof. People receiving INCOME SUPPORT get maximum housing benefit. As income increases above this level, benefit is reduced at the rate of 65p per £1. The maximum housing benefit is equal to the claimant's full rent but subject to certain deductions, including deductions for heating charges and for non-dependent adults, who are expected to contribute towards housing costs, and deductions if the rent is restricted. Rules allow benefit administrators to restrict rent if the accommodation is unreasonably expensive or unnecessarily large; but some protection against these measures is provided for claimants aged 60 and above, for the long-term sick and for those with dependent children (see MARKET RENT, RENT RESTRICTION). Housing benefit expenditure is substantially subsidized by central government. However, in areas where the authority has discretion – for example, to pay high rents, not to recover overpayments and to backdate benefit – the subsidy is reduced. This encourages authorities to be less generous in the exercise of their discretion.

**housing benefit review board**   a board consisting of at least three elected councillors from the local authority paying HOUSING BENEFIT and COUNCIL TAX BENEFIT, that hears disputes about entitlement to these benefits.

The review board's decisions can be challenged by JUDICIAL REVIEW in the HIGH COURT (or Court of Session in Scotland).

**housing grants**   MEANS-TESTED grants administered by the local authority and available for the renovation, repair, improvement and adaptation of dwellings.

Renovation grants are mandatory if they are necessary to make a house fit for human habitation. Discretionary renovation grants are available for repairs and, for example, to provide insulation, space heating and satisfactory internal arrangements. Disabled facilities grants are mandatory if they are necessary to meet the needs of an occupier who has a disability. This would include, for example, work to facilitate access to the dwelling or rooms within it, to improve any heating systems, to provide or adapt toilet and washing facilities and to facilitate cooking by the person with a disability. Discretionary grants are available for other work to make the dwelling suitable for the person with a disability. Renovation grants and disabled facility grants are subject to the same means test, which is based on that for INCOME SUPPORT, but with a flat-rate addition for housing costs and no capital cut-off. If income is less than the APPLICABLE AMOUNT, the grant covers the full approved cost up to £50,000. If income is more than the applicable amount, the EXCESS INCOME is multiplied by set amounts to calculate the applicant's contribution. This contribution is supposed to represent the amount of a loan that they could afford to repay with that excess income over ten years if an owner, or five years if a tenant. Multiple means-testing is necessary if more than one person or family has an interest in the property. Minor works grants are available for owner-occupiers and private tenants to cover thermal insulation and security measures, repairs and adaptations for people aged 60 or over, and so on. The maximum grant is £1,080 (1994) for any one application. They can be paid to anyone getting income support, family credit, disability working allowance, housing benefit or council tax benefit.

**Housing (Homeless Persons) Act 1977**   legislation that gave local authorities in Britain a duty to help homeless people with a priority need.

Priority need is interpreted under the Act as HOMELESSNESS as a result of a disaster (such as a fire), somebody who is pregnant, somebody who has dependent children, and vulnerable people. People deemed INTENTIONALLY HOMELESS are not regarded as a priority. Homelessness is defined as a person's having no accommodation that they have a right to occupy, or if they have such accommodation it is too dangerous for them to occupy it; they occupy emergency accommodation; the family is living apart because the accommodation is unsuitable for them; the dwelling is of such a poor standard that they could not reasonably be asked to live in it; or they have been illegally evicted and cannot regain possession of the dwelling. Potential homelessness is defined as a situation where one of the above conditions will apply within the next twenty-eight days.

Much depends upon how local authorities interpret the conditions outlined above, and there is in practice considerable variation from one authority to another. The idea of vulnerability in particular is used sympathetically by some authorities; but the majority, in the face of dwindling public housing stock, have little to offer ex-prisoners, the mentally ill and young people LEAVING CARE. Much of the 1977 Act has been subsequently incorporated into the Housing Act 1985. This Act issued a code of guidance that gives a generous view of local authorities' obligations in relation to vulnerable groups, but the code is not binding. The social worker's and housing advice worker's task of trying to secure accommodation for vulnerable people may find the code helpful.

**housing problems** a wide range of difficulties concerning accommodation or shelter or its lack (see HOMELESSNESS). Social workers and advice workers, among others, spend an increasing amount of time assisting people with such problems.

Housing problems can generally be divided into issues of homelessness, inappropriate accommodation, the conditions of dwellings, tenancy and financial difficulties. A distinction is often drawn between a shelter and a home. The function of a shelter is to provide protection from the elements, whereas a home should provide privacy and seclusion for individuals and families to express themselves in a manner reflecting the society of which they are a part. A home is thus a basic requirement without which people cannot adequately function in relation to the other principal social roles (for example, work and raising a family).

A major focus for work in this field is with vulnerable groups who may lack even basic shelter or, more often, where available accommodation does not meet their needs. Thus, young people LEAVING CARE, people discharged from PRISON, women fleeing DOMESTIC VIOLENCE and people returning to the community from long-stay institutions, especially hospitals, all have accommodation needs that, if not met, are likely to cause serious difficulties in their lives. Sometimes vulnerable people cannot live independently, and a measure of support is needed for them to be sustained in the community. Thus, people with LEARNING DISABILITY may live in small groups (GROUP HOMES), with or without paid helpers on the premises, depending upon the degree of support needed. Similarly, young people leaving care frequently find it difficult to survive without guidance and support from social workers and counsellors. The same might be said of people with mental health problems (see HALFWAY HOUSE, HOSTEL). A major area of work is now the modification of dwellings with AIDS AND ADAPTATIONS (see also OCCUPATIONAL THERAPY) to help people with health problems and physical disabilities remain in their own home. Other kinds of work undertaken by social workers in this field include helping tenants with rent-related problems. Poor people often find it difficult to meet their financial commitments, and in these circumstances the prevention of EVICTION can become a focus for work (see also BED AND BREAKFAST). Getting landlords to repair their properties is also a concern, and this applies to both the private and the public sector. In these circumstances, individual complaints may not be listened to by the landlord, and either legal remedies will have to be found or tenants with similar difficulties might work with COMMUNITY WORKERS collectively to put pressure upon reluctant landlords. People living in the poorest housing stock and those who are homeless are also very likely to be among the most oppressed groups in society. In addition to the particular groups identified above, there are strong associations between housing poverty and women, ethnic minorities, the unemployed and poor people in general.

G. Stewart and J. Stewart, *Social Work and Housing*, Basingstoke: Macmillan, 1993.

**human development**   the process of change that occurs throughout the human life cycle.

In terms of developmental PSYCHOLOGY, humans develop abilities in four domains: cognitive, social, linguistic and emotional. Development in the linguistic and cognitive domains is completed first. In terms of learning their native language, practically all children are accomplished speakers by the time they reach 4 years of age. In terms of cognitive development, all basic mental operations are acquired in the early years of life; a person's IQ is relatively stable after the age of 18. Cognitive and linguistic development is still able to occur throughout the life cycle, however. Social development is an ongoing process, involving how we attain and maintain a concept of self, whether we are introverted or extroverted, whether we perform well in groups and have leadership qualities, whether we need company or are content to be alone. All of these qualities have their basis in childhood but are shaped by life events. The development of an under-standing of emotions does not appear to begin until middle childhood, and problems with interpreting emotions persist throughout the life course. The developments that occur in these four domains do not occur in isolation, and changes in each separate domain can have profound effects on the other three.

Human development can begin before the infant is born or even conceived. The foetus can detect sounds from the outside world and is affected by the mother's emotions as well as by physical agents such as drugs, alcohol or HIV. Parental expectation before conception may affect human development – for example, the desire for a child of a certain sex, with a high IQ, a special gift or the willingness to pursue a specific career. The study of human development also considers the process of ageing, dementia and so-called abnormal development, such as cogenital deafness/blindness, autism and schizophrenia.

**hysteria**   a mental disorder that results in the appearance of some physical ailment that has no physical cause.

The psychological characteristics of hysteria are said to include attention-seeking and manipulation of situations to achieve emotional gratification, along with a denial by the person that they are doing this. Symptoms include physical ailments such as the loss of function of a limb or sense organ, combined with the absence of any detectable physical cause of such symptoms. The term 'hysteria' is derogatory in its connotations because it has been used to describe behaviour that is devalued in Western male-oriented society, which values independence and 'rationality': that is, behaviour involving the supposed expression of dependency needs in an unconscious, irrational way. Selfish motives are imputed to this behaviour; the subject may be believed to be unconsciously feigning physical illness to gain gratification, and in fact the borderline drawn between malingering (conscious manipulation) and hysteria may be thin.

Apparent pretence to any 'illness' including suicide attempts, may be diagnosed as hysteria. It has been suggested that there are different cultural forms of expression of this condition, such as suicide attempts in white females and 'pseudo-epileptic fits' in Pakistani females. Women and black people have been traditionally regarded by Western society as closer to 'nature', with less rational control over the 'passions', than men and white people; consequently women, particularly women from ethnic-minority groups, are most likely to be given this diagnosis. As a very pejorative diagnosis, it serves to devalue members of these groups further, while men given the diagnosis are regarded as 'effeminate'. Feminist therapists therefore reject the diagnosis as referring to any real state experienced by women. Hysteria can also be misdiagnosed by Western psychiatrists when, for example, women from other cultures follow certain culturally required expectations in their behaviour.

The traditional psychodynamic explanation for hysteria is one of repression. The person cannot face a particular conflict or anxiety and thus represses it; it then becomes unconscious and reappears as a physical complaint. Alternative explanations of the behaviour are offered by feminist psychotherapists, who consider that the behaviour associated with 'hysteria' may be the result of excessive ANXIETY, arising when there is loss of support that was depended on; mourning has not been properly worked through, because the woman has been socialized to attend to the needs of others, and thus is repressed. The emphasis here is on the pain of the loss, rather than, as in the traditional psychodynamic view, on the person's failure to face it. Child SEXUAL ABUSE may give rise to hysteria in later years through repression of the trauma it involves. Social workers may prevent such problems as far as possible by addressing the losses that women clients may suffer rather than giving their needs a lower priority than those of the children or adults they are caring for. Women in midlife may be particularly at risk. Similar help can be given to anyone already suffering hysteria; studies report improvements in the symptoms of people who have had a worker who cares for and values them and who can help them gently to look at their past or present relationships. The worker needs to be aware that men can suffer hysteria too, despite inhibiting cultural expectations.

There is a tendency for women to be given drug treatment only for hysteria, especially women from black and other ethnic-minority groups. Social workers are in a position, with other mental health professionals, to try to address the person's emotional needs, usually in combination, perhaps with a medical approach. However, care should be taken, if deeper work with the person's past experiences and pain is required, that this is carried out in a fully structured and 'safe' therapeutic relationship, either by the worker or via a referral elsewhere (see PSYCHODYNAMIC APPROACH). With people from different cultures to that of the worker, a culturally sensitive, ANTI-OPPRESSIVE approach to helping – usually involving partnership with organizations working within the person's culture – and/or transcultural counselling is necessary. It is also important to consider the possibility that the person's physical complaints may have a real physical base; here ADVOCACY and/or liaison with the medical practitioner may be required.

# *I*

**impairment**   any mental, sensory or physical characteristic or functioning of an individual that is seen, in medical terms, as deviating from the norm. For example, good sight is the norm, and impairment is to have less than good sight.

Impairment can be temporary or permanent and can be caused by illness, trauma or age. Impairment includes the loss of a limb or part of a limb, or defective limbs, organs or body mechanisms. People with impairments have historically occupied an inferior status in society and continue to be excluded from participation in the mainstream of social activities. This restriction of activity in the social, economic and physical environments is a form of social oppression.

**incapacity benefit**   a planned new contributory but taxable benefit, announced by the government in November 1993 as a replacement for SICKNESS BENEFIT and INVALIDITY BENEFIT, to be introduced in April 1995.

Incapacity benefit will be paid at two rates: the lower rate for the first fifty-two weeks and a higher rate thereafter. Incapacity for the first twenty-eight weeks at least will be based on statements by the claimant's general practitioner. After this, claimants will be required to complete a questionnaire about their dysfunctions and to obtain a statement from their doctor confirming their disabling conditions. The questionnaire will be assessed using a pre-set scoring system. If the score exceeds a certain threshold, benefit will continue in payment. It is expected that 5 per cent of current invalidity benefit recipients will lose their entitlement.

**income support**   a MEANS-TESTED BENEFIT paid to people who are not working or who work less than sixteen hours in a week.

To receive income support, most claimants, apart from pensioners and single parents, must either sign on as available for work or provide a medical certificate showing incapacity for work. Income support cannot be paid to anyone who has more than £8,000 in capital. Capital between £3,000 and £8,000 is deemed to produce an income of £1 per week for every £250 or part thereof and is taken into account by Department of Social Security officers when they determine the level of benefit for each claimant. An individual's needs under income support are called the APPLICABLE AMOUNT, which is made up of three elements: personal allowances, set at fixed rates for adults and children in the family; PREMIUMS, designed to provide extra money for particular groups of claimants, such as pensioners, people with disabilities, carers, families and LONE PARENTS; and housing costs for home owners, including interest payments for mortgages and home improvement loans. The amount paid to the claimant is the difference between the applicable amount and their income, with certain types of income disregarded.

Income support is frequently used to top up other benefits such as RETIREMENT PENSION, UNEMPLOYMENT BENEFIT and SICKNESS BENEFIT. Receipt of income support acts as a passport to HEALTH BENEFITS, HOUSING BENEFIT, COUNCIL TAX BENEFIT, FREE SCHOOL MEALS and LEGAL AID. Income support claimants can also make claims on the SOCIAL FUND. Income support was introduced in 1988 to replace SUPPLEMENTARY BENEFIT. Although the number of recipients was initially lower than for supplementary benefit, it has risen steadily, reaching 5.7 million in Britain by February 1993. Including adult and child dependants this represents 9.9 million people (about 20 per cent of the population) living on income support. Thirty-two per cent of recipients are aged 60 or over, 32 per cent are unemployed, 19 per cent are lone parents, and 8 per cent are long-term sick or disabled.

**incontinence**  an inability to control bladder or bowels in socially acceptable ways.

Incontinence may be due to a wide range of physical, emotional and environmental causes and is a common phenomenon that may be temporary or permanent. Its incidence may be underestimated, because people affected by it are reluctant to seek help because of the STIGMA attached. Many health authorities now employ incontinence advisers, nurses specializing in this area of work who may supply relevant equipment. (See also ENCOPRESIS, ENURESIS.)

**independent living**  the aspiration of many disabled people to live as autonomously as possible in a non-institutional setting of their choice.

'Centres for independent living' (CILs) exist in North America and in some areas of Britain. Run by disabled people, they offer advice and support.

**Independent Living Fund**  an independent trust set up by central government in 1988, in response to criticism following the abolition of the domestic assistance addition paid with SUPPLEMENTARY BENEFIT, to give people with severe DISABILITIES financial help to remain living in their own homes.

The fund established its own criteria for awards and generated an unexpected demand for assistance. Criteria were progressively narrowed, but despite this over 20,000 people were receiving help by the time the fund closed in 1993. The wider responsibilities for funding COMMUNITY CARE taken on by local authorities in 1993 cut across the fund. Existing recipients are assured of continued, and if necessary increased, payments under the Independent Living (Extension) Fund. People can get help from the new Independent Living (1993) Fund only if the local authority already provides domiciliary services valued at £200 per week or more. The 1993 fund, like its predecessor, will give money to purchase personal care and domestic assistance that are necessary for independent living. The applicant must be aged between 16 and 66, receiving DISABILITY LIVING ALLOWANCE with the higher-rate CARE COMPONENT and have capital of less than £8,000.

**independent sector**  providers of a service from the private, voluntary and not-for-profit sectors. Such providers are independent of the state, principally of the local authority.

**individual racism**  a form of RACISM that occurs when (usually) a white person treats (usually) a black person unfairly because of their racial or ethnic origins.

Acts of individual racism appear to their perpetrators to confirm their underlying belief that black people are inferior to white people in relation to culture, intellect, beliefs and lifestyles. This racist ideology was developed by white people in the seventeenth and eighteenth centuries and was given credence/legitimacy by pseudo-scientists, historians, literary people, religious and missionary bodies, academics, politicians and workers in the media who supported the belief that physical criteria determine intellectual and other abilities. The core of individual racism consists of people acting as though ideas about 'race' are valid criteria for differentiating among human beings, yet there is wide support for the view that there is no adequate biological basis for believing in 'race' as a legitimate, scientifically proven term. Racism is not, however, simply individual prejudice but rather a reflection of discriminatory structures and institutional practices. The net effect of this is that racism is built into social structures and dominant social institutions. (See ANTI-DISCRIMINATORY PRACTICE.)

N. Thompson, *Anti-Discriminatory Practice*, Basingstoke: Macmillan, 1993.

**Industrial Injuries Scheme**  a government scheme that provides benefits to employees who suffer personal injury through an accident arising out of and in the course of work, or who contract a prescribed disease or prescribed injury while working.

The scheme has been hugely eroded since 1983. Disablement benefit is paid to compensate people who suffer a 'loss of physical or mental faculty', sometimes expressed as an ability to enjoy life. This means it can take account of the effects of trauma and disfigurement as well as inability to do things. It is normally paid only if the disablement is assessed as 14 per cent or more. Disablement benefit awards are often provisional in the first place. Final awards may be for a fixed period or for life. If the disability increases, because of a deterioration in the condition or because of the interaction of some other condition, an award can be reviewed on the grounds of unforeseen aggravation. REDUCED EARNINGS ALLOWANCE can be claimed only if the accident happened or the disease began before October 1990, when it was abolished. Reduced earnings allowance is extra benefit to provide some compensation for a person who cannot earn as much as they could before the accident or disease. It can be paid provided that disablement is assessed at 1 per cent. RETIREMENT ALLOWANCE replaces reduced earnings allowance when people retire but is paid at a much lower rate.

**information** in social work, knowledge that may be acquired or transmitted about services and about legal and social work processes.

There is increasing recognition of the importance of good information about a wide range of services and transactions in social welfare organizations. The CHILDREN ACT, for example, requires that SOCIAL SERVICES DEPARTMENTS publicize their services to children in need, and often the relevant information includes details about voluntary provision where the voluntary sector works closely with the statutory services. The NATIONAL HEALTH SERVICE AND COMMUNITY CARE ACT has a requirement that COMMUNITY CARE PLANS are published for public consumption and consultation.

Organizations need an information strategy to inform potential users of all services. The strategy should include an analysis of the most likely points of contact with particular client groups and an appreciation of the forms of communication most suitable to their needs. For example, a leaflet for children might have to be written in a different way from one designed for young people or adults. Similarly, DEAF and BLIND people have very particular needs. Social work processes and clients' and parents' rights could also usefully be described in written or another appropriate form. When, for example, an EMERGENCY PROTECTION ORDER is served, parents need to be able to understand what has happened or, if invited to a CASE CONFERENCE, they need to know what might happen. Similarly, service users or their representatives will benefit from information about sources of help, if they are in dispute with social welfare agencies, or about how to make a complaint. Some agencies have made considerable progress in the development of information services, although others have not. (See also RECORDING.)

**initial interview** the first attempt by a worker in a welfare agency to assess a potential service user's problems and the appropriateness of the agency's services for this person.

Considerable attention has been given to the issue of who becomes a service user and who does not. One of the important issues here is the quality of first contact with an agency. This first contact is sometimes with reception staff and sometimes with the duty officer. It is clear that the service user must feel some measure of welcome and interest on the part of the agency and, in many circumstances, that the agency can be trusted. With sensitive problems of a personal nature, such trust and confidence have to be established very quickly. Failure in this regard may result in the service user withdrawing from the service even when they patently need it. Features associated with effective initial interviews seem to be clarity of INFORMATION about the agency's services, an inviting atmosphere, and an ability on the part of the worker to listen attentively and to clarify and summarize at intervals the nature of the problems as they emerge from the interview. How the agency can help, perhaps in conjunction with other services, and the service user's willingness to receive the service (where this is optional) need to be determined. (See also REFERRAL.)

B. Compton and B. Galaway, *Social Work Processes 4th ed.*, Belmont, California: Wadsworth, 1989.

**injecting**   the introduction of a substance into the body, usually by means of a syringe; often the preferred method for those using illegal DRUGS.

There are different forms of injecting: intravenous, that is, into the vein; intramuscular, into the muscles; and subcutaneous or 'skin-popping', just under the surface of the skin. Needles and syringes are available in different sizes and may usually be obtained free by using a SYRINGE EXCHANGE scheme. Injecting can be an unsafe practice and, drug users who inject run the risk of septicaemia, abscesses, HEPATITIS and HIV. In extreme situations, such as in prison, other objects may be adapted for use as syringes.

**injunction**   a court order that prohibits particular behaviour.

A judge or magistrate may issue an injunction order under the Domestic Proceedings and Magistrates' Court Act 1978 or the Domestic Violence and Matrimonial Proceedings Act 1976. The former Act gives protection to married people only, but the latter has wider-ranging powers for married or unmarried couples. Orders might prohibit the harassment or molestation of a woman by a man who has been violent towards her. An injunction order can be obtained without the respondent being present (EX-PARTE), and it can have the power of arrest attached to it, so that if the person concerned ignores it the police will arrest them.

**insight**   a new understanding of the root or origins of a problem or situation.

Insight may be gained when new information comes to light or old information is 'rearranged' to give new significance to familiar aspects. Insight is thought necessary before some problems can be solved or before people are able to 'move on' or make necessary adjustments to their lives. Historically, the idea of insight is strongly associated with PSYCHOANALYSIS, where it had the very specific meaning of discovering the influence of childhood experiences upon adult difficulties. In current usage, among social workers and counsellors, the word is employed more loosely to denote an understanding of something and it is seen to apply to both recipients of services and workers. In this more generic usage of the term, experience of class, race and gender is considered especially important, although other, more personal factors can also be critical.

**insolvency**   a situation where a person lacks the financial means to meet debts and other obligations and does not have any prospect of meeting them.

Insolvency arises from many situations, including the failure of businesses, the overcommitment of resources and substantially changed circumstances.

People who consult MONEY ADVICE agencies such as Citizen's Advice Bureaux are often, although not exclusively, from the poorer sections of society. Among them, sustained poverty or unforeseen changes, such as redundancy, illness or the failure of a marriage or cohabiting relationship, are the major causes of insolvency. There are various strategies for dealing with insolvency. Informal negotiations with creditors are one; the others are ADMINISTRATION ORDERS and BANKRUPTCY.

**inspection** in social work, defined by the Department of Health as 'a process of external examination intended to establish whether a service is managed and provided in conformity with expected standards'.

Nationally the SOCIAL SERVICES INSPECTORATE (SSI) is the chief regulatory body in social work (see also AUDIT COMMISSION). The government plans to introduce overall inspections of individual social services departments that will involve collaboration between the SSI and the Audit Commission. At a local level, residential and other social work services are inspected by personnel employed by local authorities. Under the REGISTERED HOMES ACT 1984, local authorities have a duty to register and inspect residential homes provided by the independent sector. The NATIONAL HEALTH SERVICE AND COMMUNITY CARE ACT requires that they also inspect local authority residential homes 'even-handedly', that is, on the same terms as independent homes. At their discretion local authorities may also inspect other social work services that they provide.

Since 1991 local authorities have been required to operate special units for inspection, which must have a degree of independence and operate at arm's length from the general activities of the social services department. Most inspection units report to the social services committee through the director of social services, but exceptions to this exist. In addition, under the CHILDREN ACT inspection and registration duties exist for local authorities with regard to safeguarding and promoting the welfare of children who may be living away from home or receiving child minding or day care services. Inspection functions have expanded rapidly in recent years, and this trend is continuing. For example, there are plans under the Registered Homes (Amendment) Act 1991 to register all residential homes, including those with fewer than three beds, as well as adult placement schemes. There is variation in the operation of inspection units, but all are required to prepare an annual report describing their work. They are also required to pay particular attention to ANTI-DISCRIMINATORY and EQUAL OPPORTUNITIES issues. In addition, the government has signalled a requirement to involve lay people in their inspections. As part of the same trend, the Social Services Inspectorate now includes lay people in its social services inspections.

Department of Health and Social Services Inspectorate, *Inspecting for Quality: Guidance on Practice for Inspection Units*, London: HMSO, 1991.

**instinct** an innate, biological mechanism motivating behaviour.

The behaviour of lower animals tends to be dependent on instinct, and this can be seen in the stereotyped behaviours of nest-building, courting and mating rituals, sparring, and the cooperative behaviour of insects living in communities. Human behaviour is less dependent on innate mechanisms because the cortical development of the human brain allows for much learning as the result of experience. There is debate about the extent to which human behaviour is instinctually based (for example, the presence of a 'maternal instinct'). Humans do have biological drives, which are necessary for survival, such as eating and drinking; but it is inappropriate to regard any common behaviour as instinctive, for example a competitive instinct, since it is not known if there is a biological basis. Freud regarded instincts as the key motivators of behaviour, nominating sex and aggression as primary. He saw these as complementary: sex, the life instinct, Eros; and aggression, the death instinct, Thanatos. These instincts reside in the id and are unconscious. Eros involves all behaviours leading towards survival, so it is not synonymous with the sex drive, although this is central to it. Eros is creative, in contrast to Thanatos, which is destructive. Behaviours associated with Eros are life-enhancing and pleasure-seeking, while Thanatos is associated not only with aggression but with denial, particularly of pleasure, and the negation of development. (See also PSYCHOANALYSIS.)

Social workers within the PSYCHODYNAMIC tradition may find the place of instincts within personality dynamics conceptually useful. The adult personality, according to psychodynamic theory, is the result of the child's experiences in learning to deal with the libido and with aggressive instincts. In general, however, it is important to be cautious about the assumptions of biological determination, since this provides only a partial explanation, excuses the person of responsibility and reduces the possibility of change. The human brain allows for profound effects of experience in forming behaviour, not only in the early years, but through the LIFE COURSE. Any behaviour, whether problematic or not, is the result of hereditary and environmental factors interacting. For example, it would be unwise to attribute adult aggression solely to an aggressive instinct, to frustrations in childhood or even to the observation of aggressive acts in childhood; there will also be contextual factors involved. (See also NATURE–NURTURE DEBATE, VIOLENCE.)

**intake team**  a group of social workers who take on and work with all problems submitted to a social work agency for a limited period of time.

An intake worker might work with a family or individual for up to three months, although in some cases the work may be handed over to specialists much sooner after the intake worker has completed the emergency work. Such workers are normally GENERIC, prepared to work with the full range of problems; but, although they are not specialists, intake workers are usually relatively experienced. Many SOCIAL SERVICES DEPARTMENTS in the 1970s and 1980s had intake teams to handle initial assessments. As specialisms began to reappear (usually divided between children's teams and adult teams), intake teams were often disbanded and replaced by a duty function, sometimes run by a single individual, sometimes on a rota basis staffed by workers from the specialist teams. Emergency duty teams covering weekends and out-of-office hours are all, in a sense, intake teams.

**intelligence testing**  forms of testing that are intended to measure people's cognitive abilities.

The first documented attempts at intelligence testing were made by the French psychologist Alfred Binet, who had been asked by the French government to devise a means of identifying those children who would not be able to cope with standard schooling. Binet assembled a number of tasks, such as digit span (the capacity to memorize a series of numbers), and introduced the term 'mental age' (MA) to refer to the level of performance expected of a child at a given chronological age (CA). Later the intelligence quotient (IQ) was devised, based on the formula: $IQ = MA \div CA \times 100$. Thus, a child of average intelligence should have an IQ of 100.

The practice of intelligence testing has been controversial for a number of reasons. First, theorists have disagreed about what constitutes intelligence and therefore about what should be contained in a test of intelligence. Second, different theorists have come to varying conclusions about whether intelligence is a single ability or a constellation of abilities; those who hold the latter view have argued that a single score, IQ, does not do justice to the complexity of intelligence. Most tests in use today contain items that assess three abilities; verbal, numerical and spatial. More recently, cognitive psychologist have argued from an information-processing perspective that a test of intelligence should deal with each of the processes involved in reasoning. A further source of controversy has been the use of intelligence testing to compare the intelligence of different 'races'. Related to this is dispute over whether IQ is a measure of potential or of achievement; if the latter is the case, then it must be affected by experience. This has prompted the devising of 'culture-fair' tests that are meant to remove the effects of experience. Intelligence tests have also been devised for use with special groups, such as non-verbal tests for DEAF people and versions of Binet's original test for use with BLIND people. Intelligence testing is sometimes used by employers to select candidates for jobs. This seems appropriate only when the job requires the sort of skills measured by IQ tests, such as computer programming. The most appropriate use of intelligence tests is by clinical and educational psychologists as a diagnostic tool to identify the particular 'weaknesses' in an individual's reasoning.

S.J. Gould, *The Mismeasure of Man*, London: Penguin, 1981.

**intentionally homeless**   describes a person identified by a local authority as having made themselves HOMELESS by virtue of unacceptable behaviour or by giving up accommodation that might reasonably have been kept.

If a local authority has decided that an applicant for public housing is intentionally homeless, it is not required to offer that person permanent housing, although in some circumstances (if the person is in priority need) temporary accommodation may be offered. The usual criteria applied by councils in such decisions include substantial rent arrears, unneighbourly conduct and the misuse of property. They may also decide that a person is intentionally homeless if they believe that the person has left the property without sufficient cause, as in the case of a woman who is not experiencing domestic violence. There are often major differences between housing authorities in their interpretations of the criteria and in their willingness to use the appropriate legislation. The social worker's and housing advice worker's task is often to challenge a local authority's decision and the alleged evidence upon which such a decision has been made. Since evidence from a tenant's past behaviour, often over many years, may be cited, the task of helping such tenants can be complex.

**inter-country adoption**   the ADOPTION of babies and very young children from other countries.

The Department of Health's white paper *Adoption: The Future* (1993) highlighted a dramatic increase in inter-country adoptions and acknowledged the problems that British couples face who wished to adopt children from countries whose adoption orders the United Kingdom does not recognize. Such countries included Romania, other Eastern European countries and countries in Central and South America. The interest in adopting children from Eastern Europe in particular was stimulated by harrowing reports of orphaned and abandoned children in institutions that emerged after the collapse of the Communist regimes. Additionally, a general decline in the numbers of babies and very young children available for adoption in Britain helped stimulate a general interest in adoption from overseas.

When a child is adopted from a country with which the UK has no bilateral arrangement, the process is especially complex. Without mutual recognition of adoption orders, adoptive parents must obtain an adoption order in the British courts even if an adoption order has already been successfully granted in the sending country. Separate entry clearance for the child is required from the British immigration authorities, which is sought by the adopting parents through the British embassy in the sending country. An assessment of the applicant parents by their local authority is sent by the Department of Health to the London embassy of the sending country, which is then required to send it on to the appropriate authorities in that country. The government has recognized that such arrangements are complicated for all concerned and often lead to delays and uncertainties in settling the adoptive status of the child, and also that such arrangements have not been wholly successful in preventing very young children from being brought into Britain without proper regularization of their legal and immigration status and the child-care processes in their countries of origin. However, as a general principle, the government considers that mutual recognition of adoption orders, practices and procedures is a desirable objective wherever it can realistically and safely be achieved. It has therefore participated fully and actively in the Hague Conference on Inter-Country Adoption, which completed its work in May 1993 by drawing up a Convention on International Cooperation in Inter-Country Adoption. The convention is consistent with the United Nations Convention on the Rights of the Child (which the UK ratified in 1991) and the 1986 UN Declaration on Social and Legal Principles Relating to the Protection and Welfare of Children with Special Reference to Foster Placement and Adoptional Nationally and Internationally.

The principles underlying the Hague convention of 1993 include: inter-country adoptions should take place only after the best interests of the child have been properly assessed and in circumstances that protect the child's fundamental rights; birth parents or others responsible for consenting to adoptions should understand what they are consenting to and its implications, should be objectively counselled and should not be offered financial or other inducements; agencies acting in inter-country adoptions should be suitably staffed and scrutinized; no one should derive improper financial gain from adoption; adoptive parents should be carefully and objectively assessed for their suitability. The convention envisages that inter-country adoptions would be known as 'convention adoptions' and that there will be an established central authority and accredited bodies to oversee transmission of the required documentation and proper authorization.

As a result of the British government's intention to ratify the Hague convention, a change in the law governing adoption is necessary, and it intends to seek the necessary legislation through a new Adoption Bill. Through this legislation the government intends to clarify the role of local authorities, which it is envisaged will have a statutory duty to provide or arrange for inter-country adoption assessments, and an explicit power to make a monetary charge. Additionally, local authorities will be required to make balanced and objective assessments consistent with the principles of the convention and of domestic adoption policy and free from any prejudice against the principle of inter-country adoption. In particular, the government intends that in due course it should become a criminal offence to bring a child into the UK without having obtained the proper authorization. It also proposes that people who bring children into the country without entry clearance should, subject to their means, be liable for costs if it becomes necessary for the local authority to look after that child.

**interim care or supervision order**    an order made under the CHILDREN ACT for a limited duration.

A court may make an interim CARE ORDER or an interim SUPERVISION ORDER when hearing an application for either, if it decides to adjourn the proceedings. To make an interim order the court must be satisfied that there are reasonable grounds for believing that the child in question is suffering or likely to suffer SIGNIFICANT HARM. This is a less stringent test than for a full care or supervision order, which requires proof that the child is actually suffering or likely to suffer significant harm. The making of an interim order should not prejudice a final hearing on the full order, although in practice it is hard to ignore the fact that a previous hearing has already found reasonable grounds for such an order. Interim orders when first made can last up to eight weeks and thereafter up to periods of four weeks.

The whole aim of interim orders is to provide further flexibility to the court in settling the outcomes of care or supervision proceedings. They provide a short-term legal intervention into a family's life if the situation warrants it. The powers given the local authority are the same as under a full order but they are of limited duration. The court determines how long the order is to last and may give directions to the local authority to carry out a medical or psychiatric examination or other ASSESSMENT with the child's consent. In the main, interim orders are used to follow a period of emergency protection for a child, particularly if the authority has not yet completed inquiries. If the authority thinks that direct supervision of the child and parents is required for a short time, but that it does not need to obtain PARENTAL RESPONSIBILITY, then an interim supervision order is sufficient. If the authority concludes that it must remove the child and acquire parental responsibility for a limited period of time, then it will ask for an interim care order. Interim orders can be used to construct an acceptable legal solution to all parties. For example, a child's grandparents may apply for a RESIDENCE ORDER on a child, with the court deciding that an interim supervision order made to the local authority is also necessary. This outcome ensures that the child remains within the family but gives the authority some powers of oversight.

Department of Health, *The Children Act 1989 Guidance and Regulations Vol. 1 Court Orders*, London: HMSO, 1991.

**internal market** arrangements for different units inside large public service organizations to buy and sell services from each other.

Throughout the 1980s the Conservative government reorganized many public services, so that parts of, say, the National Health Service took on the sole function of buying services from other parts of the same organization. The intention is to set up MARKET-like transactions inside the organization itself, whereby separate units buy and sell the service in question on behalf of clients or other members of the public. The aim of the reform is to compel the public services, such as local authorities and the health service, to behave as if they had to deal with market conditions. This, it is argued, encourages them to be more responsive to the public and to provide services with greater efficiency, which are the chief characteristics of any market. These large public service organizations were in particular need of such reforms, since they had previously provided their service under monopoly conditions and grown complacent and bureaucratic as a result.

In one form or other, internal markets have been introduced into school education, with the introduction of local management of schools, into local authority services such as refuse collection, by means of COMPULSORY COMPETITIVE TENDERING, and into the health service by establishing NHS hospital trusts and funding-holding general practitioners. PURCHASER/PROVIDER units within community care services are a form of internal market arrangement that has affected social services agencies considerably. In each case, the aim of the policy is to achieve greater efficiency and responsiveness of the service by introducing a sense of competition and the discipline of cost control.

The proponents of internal markets hoped that they would provide a third way between forcing public service organizations into open, external markets and the old style of central control and monopoly provision. Critics argue that the introduction of internal markets so far shows little prospect of making a difference, particularly in the health service. This is because the arrangements protect purchaser monopolies, have increased administrative work and in the end still produce a heavily rationed and unappealing service.

J. Le Grand and W. Bartlett, eds., *Quasi-Markets and Social Policy*, Basingstoke: Macmillan, 1993.

**intervention** a general term suggesting, in social work, a step or plan with a purpose initiated by a social worker or other welfare worker with or on behalf of a service user. The recipient of intervention might be an individual, a couple, a family or a wider group.

The term came into vogue in the 1970s, replacing the concept of 'treatment', which had strong associations with the medical model. Although the word 'intervention' is still used, it has tended to be replaced by other terms that are specific to particular social work transactions, such as CARE PLAN and 'initial investigation'.

**interview**   in social work, a purposeful exchange, usually face to face, between a social welfare worker and a service user or potential service user.

In some circumstances interviews may take place on the telephone or via a video link. It is useful to distinguish between a planned interview with a known person and an INITIAL INTERVIEW with an unknown person. Interviews may have an information-gathering, decision-making or therapeutic focus. The interviewer has the prime responsibility for ensuring that sufficient time and attention are given to the service user so that the purpose of the interview is achieved; LISTENING and COMMUNICATION skills are crucial to success. For initial interviews, open-ended questions (for example, 'How do you think we may be able to help you?') are especially useful, both in information gathering and in determining the nature of the problems. Closed questions (for example, 'How long have you been married?') help to gather information and narrow the focus of discussion. Interviews often begin with open and broad-based questions, moving on to more closed or focused questions as particular problems and concerns are identified. Planned interviews with known service users can sometimes proceed in the same way, but it may be that an interview schedule has been prepared to some purpose. For example, a juvenile justice worker might be trying to understand why a teenager offends. Thus the interview will be focused on offence behaviour, and such an interview could entail specific questions about the circumstances in which offences are committed.

Increasingly with very important set pieces, such as initial investigations in child protection work, or the assessment of children and their families where ABUSE is known to have taken place, formal interview schedules are habitually used, ensuring that the crucial questions are covered systematically. The Department of Health's assessment guide to protecting children is one example of such a schedule. Other sensitive areas, such as the interviewing of children thought to have been sexually abused, which is to be recorded on video, or techniques in family therapy, require specialized training. (See also JOINT INTERVIEW.)

A. Kadushin, *The Social Work Interview*, New York: Columbia University Press, 3rd edn, 1990.

**invalid care allowance**   a benefit paid to someone who cares for a severely disabled person. The carer must spend at least thirty-five hours caring for someone who gets the attendance allowance or DISABILITY LIVING ALLOWANCE CARE COMPONENT at the higher or middle rate.

Invalid care allowance can be claimed from age 16 and is normally payable only if claimed before reaching pensionable age. It cannot be paid if the carer earns £50 per week or more or is in full-time education. Take-up of invalid care allowance is thought to be low, and non-claimers who would gain include, for example, women with partners in full-time work. Although it is taken into account as income for means-tested benefits, it gives entitlement to a carer's premium, which increases the value of INCOME SUPPORT, HOUSING BENEFIT and COUNCIL TAX BENEFIT. Invalid care allowance became payable to married women only after the European Court required this under EC SOCIAL SECURITY DIRECTIVE 79/7. It is subject to further argument in the European Court because of the different ages at which men and women cease to qualify. Invalid care allowance overlaps with all income replacements benefits, such as INVALIDITY BENEFIT, UNEMPLOYMENT BENEFIT and WIDOWS PENSION.

**invalidity allowance**    an addition paid with INVALIDITY BENEFIT, the amount depending on the claimant's age at the time incapacity began. The allowance is reduced by any additional pension payable.

**invalidity benefit**    benefit paid to a person who has been incapable of work for twenty-eight weeks and getting either STATUTORY SICK PAY from their employer or SICKNESS BENEFIT.

Invalidity benefit, which includes additions for dependants, is paid as long as the incapacity for work continues, until the claimant reaches pensionable age (60 for women, 65 for men). By deferring retirement, the claimant can continue to receive invalidity benefit for a further five years beyond retirement age. During this time benefit is paid only at the same rate as the claimant's RETIREMENT PENSION but is not taxable. In November 1993 the government announced its intention to replace invalidity benefit from April 1995 with a new benefit called INCAPACITY BENEFIT. The government cited a huge increase in claimants, from 600,000 in 1978 to 1.5 million in 1993, as evidence that a number of people who were not really incapable of work were getting the benefit. However, any explanation for this increase should also include the growth of long-term unemployment over that period and a rise in the number of people deferring retirement for the tax advantages. See also INVALIDITY ALLOWANCE.

**investigative interviewing**    an INTERVIEW conducted with a child as part of an inquiry following concerns that a child may have been abused.

The term denotes that interviews with children are to be approached with an open mind in accordance with the three possible situations that the child faces: (1) the ABUSE has occurred and the child is speaking of it; (2) the abuse has occurred and the child is unable to speak of it or is denying it; (3) the abuse has not occurred and the child cannot speak of it. Investigative interviews are generally jointly conducted by a police officer and a social worker specifically trained in interview techniques in accordance with the *MEMORANDUM OF GOOD PRACTICE*. The interviews do not have to be recorded on videotape. However, if a criminal prosecution of an adult for an offence against the child is a possibility, a video recording is usually made unless the child is unhappy about being recorded on video. Further, the CLEVELAND INQUIRY recommended that children should not be subject to repeated interviews nor to probing confrontational DISCLOSURE interviews, as they are potentially damaging and represent a form of abuse themselves. Current practice interprets this as meaning preferably one interview, or at most two. Investigative interviews are particularly significant in cases of alleged SEXUAL ABUSE, because forensic evidence of assault is often ambiguous or absent. In cases of PHYSICAL ABUSE there is usually an injury present that is open to forensic analysis and thus makes the testimony of the child less crucial.

The process of investigative interviewing is problematic because of the difficulty of balancing a child-centred approach to communicating with children with a need to satisfy evidential requirements if the child is to be legally protected or a successful prosecution is to be mounted. Theoretically the burden of proof is less in CIVIL PROCEEDINGS than in CRIMINAL PROCEEDINGS. In practice, civil courts have applied a rigorous burden of proof when concerned with allegation of child sexual abuse, and the way the child's testimony is obtained is subject to close scrutiny. This approach is unlikely to change unless or until the Department of Health issues guidance on interviewing specifically designed to take account of the requirements of civil proceedings. Current guidance focuses on the requirements of criminal proceedings.

Home Office and Department of Health, *Memorandum of Good Practice*, London: HMSO, 1992.

**involuntary client**    a person who is compelled to be a recipient of a social work or medical service.

Typically people become involuntary clients as a result of a court order (for example, a PROBATION ORDER or CARE ORDER), or if they have been found guilty of particular offences or have been compulsorily hospitalized under mental health legislation. Although in some situations service users appear to lose all or most of their rights to SELF-DETERMINATION (such as under compulsory treatment in a hospital), in many circumstances they may well have some rights or some say in decisions. People on probation or COMMUNITY SERVICE ORDERS, for example, have to agree to the arrangements. It may be argued that this is no freedom to choose when the alternative is prison, although some do prefer the custodial sentence. For those compelled to be treated in a mental hospital, the element of compulsion is removed as soon as the service user is thought responsible for their actions.

A core objective of good practice is to work with people in a manner that respects their person and rights and promotes self-determination and EMPOWERMENT. Where compulsion is seen to be necessary these principles do not have to be abandoned. Self-determination, for example, is not a concept without limits, for one person's actions may infringe another person's liberty. Thus, to work in partnership with an involuntary service user may be an elusive aspiration, but it should be pursued nevertheless. To consult at every stage in the work with such people, and to provide them with good-quality INFORMATION and independent help in the form of, say, advocates, are important sources of empowerment for the involuntary service user that may counterbalance the unbridled power of the professional.

*J*

**job seekers allowance**    a planned replacement for UNEMPLOYMENT BENEFIT from April 1996, announced by the government in November 1993.

Job seekers allowance will be paid as a contributory benefit for six months only. After this it will become means-tested like INCOME SUPPORT; it is estimated that 90,000 people will lose entitlement.

**joint finance**   health authority funding for COMMUNITY CARE projects developed with SOCIAL SERVICES DEPARTMENTS.

Established in 1976, the purpose of joint finance resources is to act as a source of 'pump priming' for new schemes in the community. These are mainly schemes managed by local authority social services departments but may be run by the health authority or the voluntary sector. A number of problems have been encountered by joint finance as funding periods have come to an end. As the Audit Commission noted in 1986, at the end of the joint funding, responsibility transfers to the main agency, and local authorities have become increasingly reluctant to accept long-term commitments implied by such funding. With the pressure local authorities felt on their finances, they sometimes saw joint funding as a way for health authorities to pass on expensive responsibilities. However, while the government recognized some of the difficulties encountered in the area of joint finance, the 1989 white paper *Caring for People* reinforced central government commitment to its continuation as an important way in which resources could be transferred from the health authorities to social services departments.

Audit Commission, *Making a Reality of Community Care*, London: HMSO, 1986; Department of Health, *Caring for People*, London: HMSO, 1989.

**joint interview**   a formal meeting with one or more service users, conducted by two social welfare or justice workers.

Joint INTERVIEWS may achieve greater effectiveness than single-worker interviews. This may be the case in FAMILY MEDIATION or CONCILIATION work, so that each of the two workers may focus on a different parent, for example, to avoid the accusation of bias, and also to enhance the process through the two workers being able to compare notes. FAMILY THERAPY can also benefit from the joint approach. In addition, such interviews are increasingly used in initial child protection interviews, which are invariably conducted by the police, together with a social worker. The police are concerned to know whether a crime has been committed, the social worker whether a child needs protection. Where workers are threatened with VIOLENCE or AGGRESSION, joint working has clear merits.

**joint planning**   a statutory obligation placed on local authorities and health authorities to collaborate in planning care provision for their areas.

Local authorities and health authorities have had a statutory duty to plan service provision together since 1974. The National Health Service Act 1977 expanded on this by recommending that joint planning take place at all levels within the service planning process. However, there has been frequent criticism of the operation of such planning systems. The Audit Commission noted in *Making a Reality of Community Care* (1986) that joint planning arrangements were often too complex, largely due to the number of agencies involved. Given the geographical coverage of some local authorities and health authorities, joint planning meetings could involve both regional and district health authorities, as well as county and district local authorities. The number of agencies was often well into double figures, resulting in a complex series of meetings; in one case, the director of social services of one of the largest shire counties estimated that his staff had to attend 2,000 such meetings a year. With the white paper *Caring for People* (1989), the government stated its intention to emphasize joint planning agreements as a more flexible approach, to try to overcome the problems experienced. However, there is still a recognized need for local authorities and health authorities to work closely together in the development of services for client groups.

**judicial review**   an action based in the HIGH COURT whereby the legality of the decision-making process of a public body is reviewed.

The decisions of courts of law, central government departments and local authorities may all be subject to judicial review. The action is an assessment of whether decision-making procedure was followed correctly and not of the merits of a case. The applicant must satisfy a legal requirement of sufficient interest in the case, and to succeed in the action they must demonstrate that the public body acted illegally, improperly or unreasonably. The High Court has the power to remit the case back to the public body to make its decision in the correct way, but it cannot compel the public body to change its decision.

**just deserts**   the philosophy of sentencing, underpinning current government policy, that emphasizes proportionality of punishment; that is, sentences should reflect the nature and seriousness of the offence rather than the social characteristics or personal needs of the offender (see PRINCIPLES OF SENTENCING).

**justice**   a term that is indefinable without answering the questions 'justice for whom?' and 'justice within what context?'. In the context of criminal law and legal proceedings, the simplest definition might be 'the fair treatment of offenders and victims by people given the power and authority to punish'.

Such a definition of justice recognizes the existence of power relationships, but the phrase 'fair treatment' requires further analysis. It has been argued that offenders have a strong sense of justice in so far as they expect 'fair treatment' to be based on the following principles: cognizance – that is, efforts have been made to establish guilt; consistency – people of the same status committing the same offences should be treated the same; competence – those who pass judgement should be able to justify their right to do so; commensurability – punishment should fit the magnitude of the crime; and comparison – differences in treatment between offenders of different status should be reasonable and tenable.

Sociologically, there are three broad perspectives on 'criminal justice'. A conservative or traditional approach would argue that the British CRIMINAL JUSTICE SYSTEM comes close to dispensing justice most of the time. Our system of law and DUE PROCESS is regarded as rational, sophisticated and effective, giving appropriate weight to different PRINCIPLES OF SENTENCING and taking account of a wide variety of relevant information about the offence, the offender and, where appropriate, the victim. It is inevitable that mistakes are made from time to time, but there are sufficient checks and balances in the system to ensure that mistakes are remedied, and serious miscarriages of justice are, therefore, rare. A liberal approach would argue that the widespread existence of discretion in the system means that justice cannot be guaranteed and has to be negotiated. Achieving the ideal of justice requires individuals to interact or 'play parts' in the 'drama' of criminal proceedings. Decisions may be unduly influenced by non-rational, non-legal variables, such as discrepancies of age, class, race or gender, and between the offender and criminal justice personnel (see ANTI-DISCRIMINATORY PRACTICE). To achieve justice, the use of discretion must be monitored and constrained, and criminal justice personnel must be held more visibly accountable for their decisions. A radical approach would argue that what we choose to call 'justice' is no more and no less than the product of a system designed by those in power to maintain their position. 'Justice' is a rhetoric that persuades the majority of people that the criminal justice system exists for their benefit, while criminalizing the poorest and most vulnerable groups in society. From this perspective, there will never be true criminal justice without the achievement of broader social justice, which itself is dependent on reducing structural inequalities in society.

D. Matza, *Delinquency and Drift*, New York: Wiley, 1964.

**justice of the peace**   see MAGISTRATE.

**juvenile**   a term that refers to YOUNG OFFENDERS from the ages of 10 to 15 years and may refer to those aged 16 and 17.

A child younger than 10 cannot be subject to CRIMINAL PROCEEDINGS, as they are below the age of criminal responsibility. This means that they are deemed to be incapable of understanding the implications of committing a criminal offence. Children aged 10 to 13 are referred to in law as children, while those aged 14 to 17 are referred to as young persons. The CRIMINAL JUSTICE ACT 1991 created the YOUTH COURT, which extended the jurisdiction of the former JUVENILE COURT from an upper age limit of 16 to one of 17. At the same time, however, the Act also allowed the youth court to regard young persons of 16 and 17 years as adults (depending on their maturity and stage of development) for the purposes of sentencing. (See also JUVENILE/YOUTH JUSTICE).

**juvenile court**   a court that originated in 1908 (see CRIMINAL COURTS) to deal with children and young persons aged under 17 years, replaced under the CRIMINAL JUSTICE ACT 1991 by the YOUTH COURT.

The public were excluded from juvenile court proceedings, which were intended to be less formal than in an adult court. There were also restrictions on the punishments that could be imposed. The welfare of the young person was seen as paramount, and the court dealt with care proceedings for children in need as well as criminal proceedings for YOUNG OFFENDERS. During the 1980s, however, the government came to view the 'welfare' focus of the juvenile court as inappropriate; hence its replacement by the youth court under the 1991 Act. (See JUVENILE/YOUTH JUSTICE.)

**juvenile liaison officer**  a social worker or probation officer with special responsibility for consultation with the police about whether to caution or prosecute a YOUNG OFFENDER.

Juvenile/youth liaison committees meet regularly and consist of representatives of social services departments, the PROBATION SERVICE, the police and the Education Welfare Service. They originated with the Children and Young Persons Act 1969 to promote inter-agency cooperation in dealing with young offenders. A similar term is also sometimes used in relation to social workers who specialize in work in the YOUTH COURT.

**juvenile/youth justice**  refers to social work undertaken with offenders under the age of 18, in a social services or multi-agency setting, and to the philosophy, policy and practice of dealing with such offenders differently and separately from the adult CRIMINAL JUSTICE SYSTEM. The preferred term is now 'youth justice'.

The term 'youth' justice has come to be preferred to 'juvenile' justice since the introduction of the YOUTH COURT under the CRIMINAL JUSTICE ACT 1991. From the middle of the nineteenth century there has been a recognition that young people cannot be held as fully responsible for their actions as adults and that they should be protected from the full force of adult punishment (see THEORIES OF CRIME). At the same time, it has been acknowledged that young people commit a large proportion of all crime (the peak age for male offending being 18 years old and for female offending 15 years old). Half of all crime is committed by people younger than 20. Since 1908 YOUNG OFFENDERS have been dealt with in a separate court that is closed to the public and where proceedings are less formal than in an adult court (see CRIMINAL COURTS).

The history of juvenile justice has been one of tension between the JUST DESERTS model of sentencing and that of rehabilitation in which the young person's welfare is held to be paramount (see PRINCIPLES OF SENTENCING). Until the 1970s concern with the welfare of the juvenile offender was predominant, and explanations for juvenile crime were seen to lie in the poor home life or social environment in which the child grew up. The result was that many children were admitted to the care of the local authority to avoid being subjected to criminal proceedings, which were believed to be stigmatizing and unlikely to prevent further offending. The Children and Young Person Act 1969 attempted to reduce the powers of criminal courts and give more powers to local authority social workers in deciding how to deal with juvenile offenders. However, critics of the Act argue that it failed because courts did not have faith in social workers and consequently sent more young people than ever to detention centres and borstals. During the 1980s a return to a 'just deserts' model was advocated, whereby young people received proportionate punishment (rather than years in care), and their civil rights were protected by DUE PROCESS of law. It was argued that crime is a relatively normal part of adolescence and that most young people 'grow out of' crime, provided they are not dealt with inappropriately by the courts. Social workers increasingly provided programmes of groupwork and activities for young offenders on SUPERVISION ORDERS (known as intermediate treatment schemes) to offer courts alternatives to custodial sentences, and police cautioning increased. In the decade from 1981 to 1991 there was a 37 per cent decrease in the numbers of known young offenders relative to the population (more than could be accounted for by the population reduction in that age group), and numbers brought to court were quartered. It might be argued that only the 'hard core' were brought to court, but the numbers of young people sent to custody also declined dramatically, from over 7,500 in 1981 to fewer than 1,500 a decade later. Many people felt that juvenile justice was a penal success story. Despite this, there has been growing public concern about so-called 'persistent young offenders', and recent government statements suggest that the 'just deserts' model is being reinterpreted to mean tougher penalties, with more young people being locked away.

# K

**ketamine**  in its legal form, used as an anaesthetic by doctors and vets. Ketamine is commonly used illegally, often at 'raves', sometimes as an additive to ECSTASY, inducing varying feelings of numbness and irregular muscle coordination as well as HALLUCINATIONS.

Also known as 'special K', ketamine may be used in liquid, powder or pill form and either swallowed, sniffed, 'smoked' or injected. It is not classified under the MISUSE OF DRUGS ACT 1971 but is a prescription-only medicine, making supply or production illegal. Effects vary and can be unpredictable but may include temporary paralysis and a feeling of being 'out of the body' or, with heavy use, psychosis.

**key worker**  a named worker responsible for coordinating service arrangements for a person using residential or day care services and who usually forms an important relationship with that person.

Originally the key worker was a named worker to whom a child in residential care could turn to discuss their plans and problems. Now the role includes acting as a focal point for the coordination and communication about a particular social work case. The key worker should be a competent professional known to others participating in the case and should have skills in communicating and working with other identified professional workers. The key worker, especially in CHILD PROTECTION cases, has an important role and responsibilities and is perceived by professionals in other agencies as the key person who ought to have a grip on the issues and be pursuing them actively and effectively. The key worker advises all professionals involved in the case on the methods and processes of inter-agency contact; they record promptly, file all written communications and disseminate information to the relevant professionals; additionally, they keep under review the involvement of other agencies and actively seek information from other professionals.

**Kilbrandon Report** the report of the committee headed by Lord Kilbrandon that made recommendations in 1964 about how to deal with YOUNG OFFENDERS in Scotland.

The Kilbrandon Report addressed the issue of rising numbers of young offenders in the early 1960s and advocated setting up the system of CHILDREN'S HEARINGS in Scotland. The welfarist approach and philosophy of the report also heavily influenced the setting up of the Scottish social work departments in 1968. (See SOCIAL WORK (SCOTLAND) ACT 1968.)

*L*

**labelling (and labelling theory)** the process whereby people holding positions of power or influence sometimes attribute generalized negative characteristics to particular categories of individuals, tending to produce or amplify those behavioural characteristics attributed.

Powerful and influential groups to whom labelling may apply include the police, judges, the communication media and social workers. As the outcome of such a labelling process, the individuals or categories of people labelled (for example, as 'drug addicts' or 'the mentally ill') tend to live up to the negative label, thus tending to confirm, reinforce or amplify the behaviour that led to the initial label. In these circumstances, it may become difficult for a person to counteract or ever escape the implications of the application of a label (see STIGMA). The people or categories of people so labelled may acquire what sociologists refer to as a 'deviant identity'. DEVIANCE has been famously described as not a quality of the act that a person commits but rather a consequence of the application by other people of rules and sanctions.

At one level, the insight of sociologists with regard to labelling may appear relatively trite, seeming to assert little more than such commonplace or folk conceptions as 'Give a dog a bad name and it will tend to live up to its reputation.' Guided by the theoretical approach in sociology known as symbolic interactionism, however, labelling theory directs systematic attention to several features of human social behaviour: (1) the way our behaviour is highly influenced by the social expectations that others have of us; (2) that far from always successfully explaining deviant behaviour, some forms of 'scientific' (or positivistic) social science (such as would-be genetic explanations of criminal behaviour) can operate as part of the labelling process; (3) the widespread operation of 'labels' and labelling in modern societies, in which both individuals and agencies often operate on the basis of stereotypical conceptions of particular categories or groups of people (see STEREOTYPE); (4) that individuals can become caught up in an escalating process initiated by labelling that leads to an increasing exclusion from conventional social intercourse or even incarceration; (5) that institutional labellers, including social workers, and labelling state agencies, such as social work, possess considerable power to attach labels that can radically influence the lives of others.

Labelling theory can be seen as part of a distinctive social-interactionist approach to social problems. Criticisms can be directed at labelling theory, for example that it sometimes overstates the effects of labelling while ignoring the intrinsic features of some deviant behaviour. Nevertheless, an awareness of labelling theory and the widespread operation of labelling processes is useful to social workers, first because many clients of social work can be seen as adversely affected by the application of social labels, and second because social workers must be aware of how they themselves operate as labellers. A concern to offset the more negative effects of labelling processes can be seen as central to the orientation of much modern social welfare practice, with its aim of limiting discriminatory practices both within social work and in wider society.

H. S. Becker, *Outsiders: Studies in the Sociology of Deviance*, Glencoe, Illinois: Free Press, 1963.

**leading question**    a form of question used in INVESTIGATIVE INTERVIEWS that either suggests a required answer or is based on alleged facts that have not yet been proved. Rules of evidence do not permit information gained from leading questions to be placed before courts.

**learned helplessness**    the inability of a person to act in situations where they have learned previously that they will have no control over the outcome.

Learned helplessness has three components: an environment in which some important outcome is beyond a person's control; the already learned response of giving up; and the person's expectation that no voluntary action of theirs can control the outcome. Learned helplessness has been implicated as a contributory factor to DEPRESSION, since one aspect of depression is the giving up of attempts to control one's own life.

M.E.P. Seligman, *Helplessness, Development, Depression and Death*, New York: W.H. Freeman, 2nd edn, 1992.

**learning difficulty**    a frequently used term to indicate intellectual disability, for which LEARNING DISABILITY is now the officially approved term.

The term 'learning difficulty' superseded 'MENTAL HANDICAP' in the 1980s but has been criticized for being imprecise, since a learning difficulty may not be related to an intellectual disability. However, the term has the merit of being preferred by a number of SELF-ADVOCATES with learning disability. Thus a recent publication by the Central Council for Education and Training in Social Work utilizes the term 'learning difficulty' throughout – excluding in the title – in accordance with the wishes of contributors who were self-advocates.

P. Allen, H. Brown, P. Druce, J. Mersov, P. Mathias, Participation Forum, T. Scragg, P. Sills, D. Thomas, P. Wakeford and J. Wood, *Learning Together: Shaping New Services for People with Learning Disabilities*, London: Central Council for Education and Training in Social Work, 1992.

**learning disability**    the government-approved term for intellectual functioning that is more limited and is developing or has developed more slowly than is the case for most of the population. Expectations of people with learning disability are frequently too low, and their ability to learn and develop has often been adversely affected by unstimulating environments.

Historically, it was with the introduction of mass education in the second half of the nineteenth century that methods were developed that aimed to identify children who learned more slowly than average. This was the beginning of a movement in Western industrialized society to segregate people with learning disability. Large-scale institutions were developed, and people with learning disability were committed to them in substantial numbers. In recent decades these institutions and the poor-quality environments they generally provided have been recognized as contrary to the interests of people with learning disability, along with the process of LABELLING that accompanied access to services for such people. Current good practice generally encourages integration into the COMMUNITY, rather than segregation from it, and avoidance of labelling. People with learning disability express a preference for the term LEARNING DIFFICULTY, and the formerly prevalent phrase 'MENTAL HANDICAP' has been generally superseded because of its stigmatizing connotations. It has also been recognized that ASSESSMENT procedures for people with learning disability have deficits, including frequent cultural bias due to their being based on the experiences of middle-class white people. Assessment procedures, still the focus of debate and criticism, are now more varied than formerly and include a range of methods of assessing competence.

In recent decades the most influential philosophy as regards people with learning disability has been NORMALIZATION and its more recent form, social role valorization. These philosophies emphasize the need for people with learning disability to adopt socially valued roles in society so as to promote their acceptability. One problem with this approach is that it is essentially conservative and involves adhering to prevailing rules and customs in society, regardless of their desirability. However, normalization and social role valorization have had a number of positive consequences in Britain, including the placing of emphasis on five principles: community presence, community participation, choice, competence and respect. Services based on these principles aim to support people in the community, where they should take part in community life, have opportunities for making choices and gaining skills and be afforded respect. It is well recognized that services should be geared to individual need, and a system of individual review (individual programme planning) is widely known. This is a system of goal planning that involves regular meetings of all relevant parties, including the service user. Models of good practice exist in which services are local and based on individual need and use community provision that also serves the general population. However, many services remain underresourced while attempting to meet the widely differing and sometimes incompatible needs of large groups of service users. In this context, the need for service providers and purchasers to take into account the gender, ethnic group and sexual orientation of people with learning disability has only recently been recognized and is currently attracting more attention than formerly. Another positive development in services for people with learning disability is the SELF-ADVOCACY movement, in which service users represent their own views, both individually and collectively. CITIZEN ADVOCACY exists to provide independent representatives for people who cannot speak for themselves.

Social work with people with learning disability should support their aspiration to share in community life and to be given real choices. It should recognize the potential of people with learning disability to participate fully in generally available experiences, which may be positive, such as making relationships with other people and undertaking employment, or more negative, such as undergoing bereavement. Adults with learning disability need to be accepted as sexual human beings (although there are some legal constraints to this). However, it is also important that the possibility of their abuse by others is recognized.

In recent years hospitals for people with learning disability have been reduced in size, and some have closed. Their residents have been relocated, often to the communities from which they were admitted. A variety of living situations are possible for people leaving hospital and for those living in the community independently of their families. Some people live independently with minimal supervision, while others require the varied level of support available in small GROUP HOMES. Some service users live in supported lodgings or foster homes, while others may be accommodated in HOSTELS or occasionally in special villages or communities. Many people with learning disability continue to live with their families after they become adults. In all these circumstances it is the social worker's role to asses the needs of people with learning disability, to coordinate the provision of necessary support, to monitor the quality of care provided and to review the situation regularly in order to ascertain changing needs.

J. O'Brien, 'A guide to personal futures planning', in G.T. Bellamy and B. Wilcox (eds), *The Activities Catalogue: A Community Programming Guide for Youth and Adults with Severe Disabilities*, Baltimore, MD: Paul M. Brookes Publishing, 1986.

**learning theory**   a cluster of theoretical explanations that seek to explain how experience at a particular point in development affects subsequent behavioural and mental activities. Learning theory embodies such perspectives as BEHAVIOURISM, cognitive views of conditioning, observational learning and ecological explanation.

**leaving care**   the process, for young people aged 16 and over, of moving from the care of a local authority into independent or unsupported living.

In the mid-1980s about 8,000 young people left the care of local authorities in England and Wales. Children can stay in the care of local authorities until aged 18; in practice, most children leave care aged 16 or 17. Contemporary numbers are likely to have dropped, because under the CHILDREN ACT fewer children have been taken into the care of local authorities. To have a background in care is to be vulnerable in later life in a number of critical respects. People who have been in care are overrepresented, proportionately, among offenders who receive community sentences, prisoners, people with mental health problems, the homeless and the unemployed. Among black people who have been in care, the overrepresentation is even more marked. Explanations for this additional vulnerability include pre-care 'damage' (that is, factors associated with the child having to come into care), the negative experience of care itself and problems associated with being cast out into the world before being prepared for it. Researchers have come to the conclusion that the aspiration of care leavers to live independently at an early age has more to do with the organizational needs of social work agencies than with the emotional and developmental needs of these immature young people. Although the Children Act has given local authorities wider powers and duties in relation to care leavers, these new possibilities appear not to have appreciably altered this view.

> Few young people aged 18 are financially or materially independent. Indeed, the general thrust of government policy in recent years has been to make children more dependent upon their families for longer periods (benefits for under–25s have been considerably reduced on the assumption that they will live at home; similarly, the value of education grants has been eroded). Housing stock for single people has not improved in this period either, with single homelessness increasing dramatically. More importantly, few young people are emotionally ready for independent living at 18, even among those who leave home for socially valued reasons. Counselling services within universities testify to the numbers of young people who feel lonely and homesick. It is not surprising therefore that the average age at which people finally leave home in Britain is about 25, and this is sometimes achieved after a few false starts. Pointers to better policy and practice include a commitment to a less arbitrary age for leaving care. The decision should be made upon the basis of an assessment of a young person's readiness to live independently, in the context of known support services that are, rather than might be, available to them. The Children Act also gives local authorities the power to give financial support, a power that probably ought to be used regularly rather than exceptionally as it is now. Some departments have made substantial attempts to increase their support to care leavers with the provision of much-enlarged leaving care support teams covering counselling and emotional support, advice on money and benefit issues, accommodation services and support in relation to the pursuit of work. Many researchers have pointed out that the responsibilities of the Children Act fall on all local government departments. Although some housing departments regard care leavers as 'priorities', many do not; such inconsistency seems inexplicable. HOUSING ASSOCIATIONS are proving more imaginative and committed in this area of work.

>     M. Stein, *Leaving Care and the 1989 Children Act*, Leeds: First Key, 1992.

**legal aid**     aid available under the Legal Aid Act 1988 in both criminal and civil cases to a person who demonstrates that they need legal representation and cannot afford to pay for it.

Guidelines for granting legal aid include a serious risk of loss of liberty, job or reputation; language difficulties; complex legal points; and the need for expert cross-examination.

**lesbian issues**     see HOMOSEXUALITY.

**Lesbians and Gay Men in Probation**     a national support group for lesbian and gay probation officers. The group's primary purposes are to provide personal assistance to individual officers and to promote ANTI-

DISCRIMINATORY PRACTICE in relation to lesbian and gay people caught up in the CRIMINAL JUSTICE SYSTEM.

The group organizes training events and provides advice and counselling services, and it acts as a pressure group both within the PROBATION SERVICE and more broadly within the justice system.

**liability order**  an order made by a MAGISTRATES' court confirming an individual's liability to pay COUNCIL TAX. The order allows a local authority to use an attachment of earnings order or bailiffs to collect sums owed.

**libido**  energy arising from sexual drives, which can be directed into other activities, such as artistic creativity. The term is often interpreted as meaning 'life energy' and is a key concept in PSYCHOANALYSIS.

**life chances**  the social expectation that accompany a person's position within society. Such expectations are invariably influenced by social structure features such as SOCIAL CLASS, membership of an ethnic-minority group and GENDER, but very particular factors can also be important, such as a DISABILITY.

There are strong associations between social class and the experience of health, educational achievement and membership of particular occupations. The CULTURE OF POVERTY will, in many instances, severely constrain the chances of a person to achieve any measure of social mobility. To be black in Britain is to experience major DISCRIMINATION that will effectively debar or limit many people from particular social positions. Gender too can predispose a person to make or be prevented from making particular choices. In sum, life chances are not equal; opportunities are substantially affected by pre-existing social factors of a structural nature.

**life course**  the process of personal change, from infancy through to old age and death, brought about as a result of the interaction between personal and social events.

Growing interest in exploring and defining the concept of life course in recent years has been from two broad perspectives: first, the biological, which emphasizes stages in psychosocial development, the common process underlying the human life course (in this usage often referred to as the life cycle); second, the experiential, which emphasizes the importance of unique experience and significant life events, that is, the contrasts between lives rather than their similarities. While the biological model provides a framework, each individual life course is unique; individuals have the power to make choices, and each constructs their own biography within broad biological and social constraints.

Acknowledging the importance of both age and experiences when considering an individual's current concerns, a model has been proposed that describes the adult developmental process, not tied to age stages or to typical life experiences, but distinguishing concerns. It describes the establishment of self-identity, the establishment of relationships, the extension of community interests, the maintenance of position, disengagement and the recognition of increasing dependency. While this may be seen as a life course process, individuals may pass in and out of these areas of major concern, become stuck in one, cope well or badly, and experience crises and development as a result of the interactions within them. Social workers and educators particularly may find this and other models of the life course useful in interpreting reactions to crises at transition points, problems of adjustment, and failures of communication between family members, and in assisting individuals to gain insight, use their experiences developmentally and improve their social relationships.

**life sentence/imprisonment** following the abolition of the death penalty in Britain in 1965, the most severe punishment that can be imposed by the courts. It is the only indeterminate sentence (that is, without a fixed stated length) remaining in the CRIMINAL JUSTICE SYSTEM.

A life sentence is mandatory (compulsory) for the offence of murder and discretionary (one of a range of options) for a number of other serious offences such as manslaughter, rape, arson and kidnapping. There are about 3,000 life sentence prisoners in Britain, of whom about 80 per cent fall into the mandatory category. To reduce the level of uncertainty about the length of a life sentence (the only other previously remaining indeterminate sentence, of borstal for YOUNG OFFENDERS, was abolished in 1982), each sentence is accompanied by a tariff, which is the period of detention that must be served in order to satisfy the requirements of retribution and deterrence (see PRINCIPLES OF SENTENCING). This is set by the sentencing judge and is now stated in open court where the sentence is discretionary. In practice, it may be as little as four years or as long as thirty years. Life sentence prisoners are treated as a special group in the prison system and are subject to individual sentence plans. Once their tariff date is reached, they are subject to periodic reviews and assessed for release on the criteria of their behaviour in prison, their dangerousness and their risk to the public. They are eventually released by the Parole Board (for discretionary sentences) or the Home Secretary (for mandatory sentences).

**life story book** an account of a child's life, put together in terms and in media that can be clearly understood by the child. Such a document might contain written material, photographs, pictures, letters and even audio or video material.

The central purpose of a life story book is to give shape to a child's past, so that the child has a sense of their own roots and an understanding of what has happened to them. Such documents are thought to be critical in helping a child form and hold on to an identity. Life story books have been found to be extremely helpful to children who have experienced many, and often distressing, changes in their lives. Any trusted adult may be able to help a child construct their own life story book. Social workers, foster parents or a 'significant other' could all be appropriate. The process of constructing the book can also be critical in unlocking a child's emotions, so the process must not be hurried and in essence should be taken at the child's pace.

T. Ryan and R. Walker, *Making Life Story Books*, London: British Agencies for Adoption and Fostering, 1985.

**listening**   the ability to hear what someone is communicating completely and accurately.

Listening skills are generally held to have cognitive and social dimensions. First, cognitive skills enable the listener to understand what has been conveyed in both detail and substance and to convince the speaker that such understanding has been achieved. Second, social skills help and encourage the client to unburden themselves in a manner that makes it more likely that the whole story will be told. Key elements to these two related skills seem to be management of body posture and facial expressions, empathy, encouragement to the speaker, accurate listening to what is really being said, patience, summarizing and checking at intervals, and monitoring and evaluating the listener's own contribution.

J. McLeod, *Introduction to Counselling*, Buckingham: Open University Press, 1993.

**local authorities**   the democratically elected bodies responsible for providing public services at a local level.

The present local government system was established by the Local Government Act 1972 and implemented in 1974. This created a two-tier system of shire and metropolitan county councils as the upper tier, with district (including London borough) councils as the lower tier. Each tier of government has a council composed of elected local people who are part-time councillors, increasingly members of one of the main political parties. Serving the councils are full-time officials, including general administrators and professionals such as social workers and housing officers. Services are divided between the two levels, with services deemed to require a larger geographical and demographic component to work effectively being at county level. Those services that cater for more local needs are provided by the districts. For example, the large departments providing education and social services are provided by the counties in the shire authorities, while housing, refuse collection and street lighting are provided by the districts. The metropolitan counties operated slightly differently, as their districts had very large populations and were therefore deemed to be able to provide some of those services provided by the counties in the rural shire counties themselves, including education. However, these metropolitan counties, including the Greater London Council, were abolished in 1985 due to a mixture of administrative reasoning and political conflict. All their responsibilities were devolved down to the district authorities, so that in areas such as Greater Manchester, South Yorkshire and the West Midlands a single-tier system of district authorities is in operation.

Increasingly, central government has been changing the range of activities engaged in by local authorities. Many argue that this has entailed an attack on local government, reducing its role and increasing centralization. The government has aimed to reduce the role of local government, but it would argue that it has done this to reduce the role of the state in general and not to increase centralization. This will lead, in the government's view, to the creation of an ENABLING AUTHORITY to replace a system of direct provision of services by local authorities. As a result, the existence of a two-tier system has also come under criticism for unnecessary bureaucracy, too much conflict between tiers, a needless level of administration and a lack of democracy because of confusion among the electorate about which tier does what. In 1991 the government introduced proposals to abolish a tier of government and create single-tier authorities throughout the country. At the time of writing, a local government commission is engaged in examining each remaining two-tier council to determine the future geographical boundaries of the local authorities. This may result in the creation of two to five single-tier authorities to replace an old county with its eight or nine districts. The future of social services within such a framework may well be the subject of debate, since the size of some of the new single-tier authorities might mitigate against the efficient provision of care services.

G. Stoker, *The Politics of Local Government*, Basingstoke: Macmillan, 2nd edn, 1992.

**lone-parent family**   a family with one parent on their own raising dependent children.

Lone-parent families arise for different reasons but share similar difficulties. They include single mothers who have never married and mothers who have either separated, divorced or been widowed. Lone fathers form a small but evident percentage of all lone-parent families – approximately 8 per cent. Whatever the source of lone parenthood, over the last twenty years the number of lone-parent families has roughly doubled from about half a million to about 1.3 million. Altogether, nearly 2 million children are currently being raised by a lone parent, and lone-parent families now constitute some 20 per cent of all families with dependent children. Lone parents usually face financial hardship, having to rely primarily on INCOME SUPPORT, and only to a lesser extent on earnings, because employment compatible with looking after children is difficult to obtain and often poorly paid. Research indicates that lone fathers are usually better off financially, because they are more likely to be in full-time employment as well as receiving higher wages than women for comparable work. Maintenance is not a major source of income for many lone parents, on average accounting for no more than 7 per cent of their income, despite the government's recent CHILD SUPPORT initiatives.

The circumstances of lone-parent families have caused unease across the political spectrum. Commentators from the NEW RIGHT are concerned that they herald a breakdown in family integrity, and link them to the growth of an UNDERCLASS. Liberal and social democratic analysts point to the fact that because most lone parents are reliant on income support a great many children are raised in families on unacceptably low incomes. Interestingly, both the political left and the right have agreed that absent fathers must acknowledge responsibility for their children by contributing financially to their upbringing. A broad spectrum of SOCIAL POLICY analysts are calling for reforms in benefits that would allow lone parents on income support to supplement this by keeping the earnings from any part-time employment. Another element in social policy that would assist lone parents is a system of adequate and affordable child-care. The principal dilemma facing most lone parents (women) arises from the uncertainty in society at large over whether mothers ought to stay home to look after their children or work in order to provide them with an adequate standard of living. (See also FINER REPORT.)

L. Burghes, *One-Parent Families: Policy Options for the 1990s*, York: Family Policy Studies Centre and Rowntree Foundation, 1993.

**looked after**   the phrase used in law to describe a child being cared for by the local authority.

Under the CHILDREN ACT a child is looked after by the local authority if either they have been provided with ACCOMMODATION at the request of their parents or they are in the care of the authority. The whole point of the concept is to underscore that the responsibilities of the local authority are the same for any child, regardless of whether they have been voluntarily accommodated or the subject of a CARE ORDER or EMERGENCY PROTECTION ORDER. The primary duty of the authority is to safeguard and promote the welfare of children they are looking after, including to take decisions in their long-term interest. In planning the placement of a child it is looking after, the authority must consult all of those concerned with the child, as well as the child themselves, before a placement decision is reached. The Children Act also requires that the authority place the child as near to their home as practicable. The authority is responsible for drawing up a plan for the future of every child being looked after, including how long the placement will last, when that child will be reunited with their family and the amount of contact between child and family while on placement.

**loss**   the feelings and behaviours that accompany BEREAVEMENT, change and/or separation, and during the period immediately following bereavement or change.

Loss is an inherent part of many of the situations that social workers might work with. For example, children moving from home into a care environment, older people entering residential care, a person disabled by a road traffic accident, and a person experiencing insidious sensory impairment will all experience loss to a greater or lesser extent. However, not all loss is traumatic. Developmental loss associated with the process of growth, of moving from one life stage to another, involves changes in appearance, in status, and so on, but may not be experienced as painful. If appropriate supports and social facilitation are present, such losses may actually be life-enhancing. Traumatic loss is the form of loss that accompanies traumatic life events such as divorce, death or unemployment. Some losses carry a measure of control – for example, divorce or a change of job – and the strength of control may mitigate the effects of the loss. The feelings and sensations that typify loss vary according to a person's support systems, their personality and the strategies they may have developed in the past to manage life crises.

Prior to loss, there must be ATTACHMENT to a person, place or thing from which the separation occurs. Loss is closely linked to grieving, the latter being the process of recovery from loss. The emotions that accompany loss may include anxiety, insecurity, fear, unhappiness, bewilderment, loneliness, loss of self-esteem and hopelessness. There may be anger towards the dead person or towards others, for example medical staff. However, people may also feel relief, a sense of challenge or 'new life', depending on the nature of their relationship to the deceased or separated person.

The behaviours accompanying loss may include crying, yearning, searching, panic, withdrawal, passivity, apathy, restlessness, talkativeness, lethargy and motivational deficits. There may be a preoccupation with images or mementoes of the dead person, or alternatively a refusal to look at photographs, etc. Physical sensations may be present: changes in heart and/or breathing rate, muscle tension, appetite disturbance, sleeplessness, hallucinations, thought blocking, and monitoring the movements of others.

The wide variability of responses in loss reflects the variability of ways in which people cope with traumatic life events. A person could, in principle, exhibit all, none or any combination of emotional, behavioural and physical reactions to loss; but the majority of people are likely to experience a period of disengagement from social events and relationships. Recovery from loss is complete when the person experiences increased feelings of pleasure at the resumption of activities.

Effective social work practice with people experiencing loss should focus on permitting the person to explore the nature and extent of the loss. For example, following the death of her husband a woman may wish to talk about not simply the loss of her partner but the loss of income, of shared parenthood or grandparenting, of status, of friendship and possibly the loss of a home. Support with such practical issues as funeral arrangements, paying bills, shopping or form-filling is vital. The loss experienced by an older person entering residential care may involve support for decision-making, moving belongings, introductions to new people, enabling the person to say goodbye to familiar things in their home and neighbourhood, and offering emotional support as the person encounters the loss of home and independence. Black elders may experience loss and longing for a homeland they may never see again, and social workers should pay attention to the black elder's need to share memories and to reminisce with others from similar backgrounds.

Social work with loss should also seek to discover how people affected by it coped with traumatic life events in their past and how they make sense of life events. This can be effective in identifying with the person their strengths from previous situations that can be built on in this current period of loss. Alternatively, such work might indicate that a person is in need of more specialist help than a social worker can offer, such as PSYCHOTHERAPY and/or medical intervention.

C.M. Parkes, *Bereavement: Studies of Grief in Adult Life*, London: Tavistock, 1972.

**low pay**   income that barely permits individuals and families to meet the basic requirements of life. Conventionally, low pay covers the poorest section of the working population, although the population will vary according to the economic climate of a country and governing policies.

Low pay correlates closely with POVERTY, and with jobs that are low in security and fringe benefits and that have been associated with the employment of ethnic minorities and women. The given areas of concern for social workers and others are to ensure that appropriate finances are claimed (especially family credit and housing benefit) and that people are helped with debts (see MONEY ADVICE).

**low vision aids (LVAs)**   aids that improve visual functioning, designed for BLIND AND PARTIALLY SIGHTED people.

LVAs range from simple to 'high-tech' solutions and include spectacle correction, magnifiers, closed-circuit television, text enlargement programmes for word processors, large-print products, lighting and colour contrast. Advice on appropriate aids can be obtained from voluntary organizations of and for visually disabled people and from specialist workers in SOCIAL SERVICES DEPARTMENTS.

**LSD (lysergic acid diethylamide)** a synthetic HALLUCINOGENIC DRUG based on an ergot extracted from a rye grass fungus. LSD may be in capsule or tablet form or on a sugar cube but is mostly sold as tiny squares of paper (sometimes decorated) impregnated with minute quantities of the drug.

LSD is not physically ADDICTIVE but may be psychologically so. The usual way of taking it is to swallow it. Under the MISUSE OF DRUGS ACT 1971 it is classified as a class A drug, attracting penalties ranging from a fine to a LIFE SENTENCE for possession, supply or production. The effects of LSD, called a 'trip', vary, often depending on the state of mind of the user. Hallucinations usually consist of a distortion of the senses, with heightened colours and sounds. It is not unknown for users to think they can fly while under the effects, sometimes with fatal results. Although there is no evidence of direct physical harm resulting from LSD use, there are psychological dangers, usually in people with a tendency to mental illness. FLASHBACKS can occur as late as several months afterwards.

# M

**'magic mushrooms'** several varieties of wild fungi with HALLUCINOGENIC properties, perhaps the most common being the liberty cap; usually picked in the wild and eaten raw, which is not a criminal offence, but if processed in any way (dried, brewed or cooked) they become an illegal DRUG.

The act of isolating psilocybin, which the fungi contain, is a class A drug offence under the MISUSE OF DRUGS ACT 1971, with penalties ranging from a fine to imprisonment for possession and supply. Low doses of up to approximately twenty mushrooms produce a sense of euphoria and detachment, while bigger doses are liable to cause HALLUCINATIONS. These may be pleasant or frightening, with the risk of FLASHBACKS at a later date. In the absence of long-term research studies into the effects, the main danger seems to be the possibility of picking the wrong variety of fungi, some of which are poisonous.

**magistrate** also called a justice of the peace (or JP), a magistrate is an ordinary member of the public, without special qualifications, appointed by the Lord Chancellor to preside over the lowest level and civil CRIMINAL COURT, dealing with 98 per cent of criminal offences.

Magistrates sit in threes, known as benches. In 1992 there were about 29,500 magistrates, of whom 45 per cent were women and 2 per cent were from ethnic minorities. A magistrate is supposed to represent the local community; however, the overwhelming majority are recruited from what might be termed the professional and managerial classes. This raises the criticism that magistrates are out of touch and out of sympathy with the social circumstances of most defendants, who are drawn from the ranks of the working class and the unemployed (see ANTI-DISCRIMINATORY PRACTICE). A stipendiary magistrate (of whom there are between 70 and 80) is a professional lawyer who presides alone in some of the busier magistrates' courts. They have the same powers as a lay magistrate but tend to work more quickly.

**Makaton**   an artificial sign system of communication, used predominantly with people with learning disabilities who have limited or no verbal expression.

The vocabulary of Makaton is a limited number of signs from BRITISH SIGN LANGUAGE, used in English word order, with or without speech, to facilitate language development.

**mandated problem**   a problem that, by law, client and social worker must address.

The term is found in TASK-CENTRED WORK, an approach that in the main focuses on problems that the client regards as a priority. 'Mandated problem' are those exceptional matters that the social worker must bring up, whether or not the client considers them a problem. For example, the social worker must raise the problem of poor parenting standards with a client if those standards are likely to cause their child SIGNIFICANT HARM. The worker will attempt to frame the problem in a way that the client is willing to address. If the client then refuses to acknowledge this as a problem, no further task-centred work can be undertaken with that person, although the worker may have to pursue some compulsory intervention.

**manic depression**   defined by PSYCHIATRY as an 'affective disorder', that is, a type of PSYCHOSIS, involving responses of moods and emotions that depart from cultural expectations. Such behaviours are regarded as problematic.

Extreme MOOD SWINGS are the central experience of manic depression; for psychiatry these are the main 'symptoms' of the 'disease'. Involved in these swings are 'mania' and 'DEPRESSION', and either may be predominant for some time. 'Mania' is a powerful feeling of elation, which leads the person to 'speed up' all their responses and behaviour to an extreme degree. It involves the experience of 'flights of ideas', vigorous activity – often involving excessive drinking, spending or sexual activity, regardless of how different this may be from the person's usual values and behaviour – and a conviction that nothing can go wrong. These extreme feelings of elation thus have enormous consequences for the person themselves and for others. 'Depression' involves feelings of pessimism and hopelessness, sadness, guilt and low self-esteem. These feelings are likely to lead to the opposite behaviour to that following from 'mania', that is, loss of interest and enjoyment in life, slowness and inactivity, withdrawal and tearfulness. Poor memory and weak concentration, indecisiveness and disturbance in sleeping and eating (often the person does not eat) are also likely, and there may be delusions and auditory 'HALLUCINATIONS', expressing the guilt experienced by the person.

The mood swings described above can be understood perhaps as reactions to each other and thus to a degree can be experienced by many people. PSYCHODYNAMIC theory explains that 'manic' feelings can protect the person from feeling depressed, and depression can be a natural reaction to guilt and loss. However, it is the extremity of these feelings – and hence the person's extreme behaviour – that result in the definition of psychosis, because these responses fall outside the limits of what can be understood in the person's culture. There is evidence from recent research in psychiatry that there is a strong genetic influence upon the likelihood that an individual may develop manic depression; in as many as 70 per cent of identical twins, if one twin develops the condition, the other will too. The strength of this constitutional influence means that medication (lithium carbonate) given for the condition is particularly effective, but only if taken consistently. One difficulty for people with manic depression is that they may consider themselves 'well', when elation is approaching, and thus stop taking their medication. People are likely to develop this condition in their forties, and recovery is possible, but the existence of chronic social problems makes it likely to persist. Social work clients are, of course, particularly likely to experience chronic social problems, and thus are at risk of the condition becoming long-term.

The responses of people suffering from manic depression are likely to generate serious problems for themselves and for others. Their actions when elated can result in debt, violence in the home or in public places as a consequence of drinking, disruption to neighbours (for example, playing music loudly), sexually transmitted diseases, and accidents (the latter following perhaps from drinking or from the conviction that no harm can possibly befall the person, as when they may drive a car very fast). Excessive drinking is also strongly linked to child ABUSE and to DOMESTIC VIOLENCE and is therefore of particular significance for social work. Additional difficulties arising from the risk and antagonism thus generated include court proceedings, family breakdown, hostility and possible refusal of services by agencies if the person harasses them as part of their 'mania' (such as by writing frequent letters of complaint to councillors or housing department). Depression can put the person at risk of suicide, or, in extreme cases, death can result from malnutrition or from an accident caused by poor memory and concentration. Withdrawal may lead to poor self-care, and to neglect of children.

Many opportunities exist for social work involvement that can make for improvements in the situation of manic depressive people. Help to the family in understanding that the person acts thus from 'illness' rather than intention; help to the person (when recovering) and/or family in managing debts; liaison with angered agencies or neighbours to explain the situation and negotiate better relations; planning for child protection; support and access to legal help with court proceedings: all are ways in which the practitioner can assist. In relation to the person's inner world, much guilt is experienced when recovering after 'mania'-led actions, and the worker can help alleviate this using the 'sustaining' psychosocial approach that provides the person with a sense of personal value and security; they may also help the sufferer work towards a better future by discussing the implications of taking medication or other preventive steps the person may wish to take in the event of relapse. With depression, the worker is mainly concerned with identifying that the person has become depressed and assessing the risks (see MENTAL ILLNESS), along with alleviating any social problems and helping the family cope with the situation: again the 'sustaining' psychosocial approach is invaluable and can have a positive effect on the person's feelings of depression, perhaps increasing their motivation to use help.

In relation to both moods, and to the person generally, the practitioner will usually work in conjunction with the psychiatric services; they will thus need to develop the skills and awareness of issues relevant to MUTLTIDISCIPLINARY working and have a basic understanding of psychiatry. Manic depression is, among all serious mental health problems, perhaps the most responsive to medication, so the worker needs to be clear about what aspects of the person's difficulties can be helped in this way and which require social work intervention. For example, it is not helpful if the worker tries to 'cure' the condition using PSYCHOTHERAPY or behaviourism while ignoring the person's financial debts. Monitoring is another important part of the social work role in relation to people with these difficulties, that is, the ability to assess when medical intervention may be necessary, such as when the person is becoming depressed, and perhaps not eating, or starting to become elated.

A. Corob, *Working with Depressed Women*, Aldershot: Gower, 1987.

**marginal 'tax' rate**   the percentage of additional earnings lost because of new or increased deductions in a particular set of circumstances.

The marginal 'tax' rate refers to situations where people may be in receipt of MEANS-TESTED BENEFITS but are also in part-time work. There are circumstances where additional part-time earnings result in increased 'taxation' in relation to NATIONAL INSURANCE contributions, personal tax, loss of HOUSING BENEFIT, loss of COUNCIL TAX BENEFIT and possibly also loss of FAMILY CREDIT. Where all of these deductions are relevant, the marginal tax rate may be as high as 97 per cent (that is, 97 pence out of any additional £1 earned might be lost). If increased child-care costs or loss of FREE SCHOOL MEALS are included, then the marginal 'taxation' can exceed 100 per cent. (See also POVERTY TRAP.)

**marital problems**   problems arising between two people who are living in a committed relationship. This field of work covers people who are not married and includes both heterosexual and homosexual relationships. Work with such couples is often called couple COUNSELLING or couple therapy.

Our understanding of MARRIAGE in contemporary society is complex; and although cohabiting heterosexual couples and gay and lesbian couples may not be legally married by the law of the land, their relationships may be just as committed as those of married couples, and they may thus experience similar problems. Marital problems are difficulties that either or both partners choose to define as problems; the problems should not be defined by someone else except by agreement and discussion with counsellors as suggested new ways of looking at a difficulty. Social workers or counsellors need to take particular care therefore to encourage the partner(s) to describe as fully as possible, in their own terms, exactly what the problems are and what impact they feel they have on their relationship.

A common theme in marital problems is the breakdown in communication between partners, often resulting in needs not being met and expectations not being fulfilled. The ROLES played in the relationship by each partner may alter and develop over a period of time, and couples may not always realize that the shape of their relationship has been changing. Parenthood, for example, can reshape a relationship, as can new caring responsibilities for older dependants or when a woman resumes a career after a period of child-care. Poor communication may result in a deteriorating sexual relationship, with either or both partners becoming sexually unfulfilled. Some partners respond to these difficulties by seeking other sexual partners, and many who cannot resolve their difficulties separate and divorce.

A range of help is available to couples who are experiencing relational problems. Relationship counselling seeks to enable couples to communicate with each other about the problems they face, and to work towards solutions. For some couples the problems can be tackled and their relationship deepened; for others the solution involves disengaging from the relationship, ideally in as honest a manner as possible. Relate (formerly the Marriage Guidance Council) is a national organization that offers professionally trained counselling to couples in need of help. The organization's change of name indicates its commitment to work towards solutions that are in the best interest of the couple concerned (and of any children there may be). Counselling may be with both partners or with just one, depending on the willingness of each to engage in the process. Specific help with SEXUAL PROBLEMS is also available through Relate, which trains its own sex therapists; the main focus of their work is to enable and empower a couple to deepen the quality of their physical relationship by (re)learning how to relax and enjoy each other's intimate company, as a prelude to undertaking specific regimes and programmes designed to help them overcome sexual problems such as failure to achieve orgasm, premature ejaculation and general unresponsiveness. Couples who need help in greater depth may be referred to FAMILY THERAPISTS, psychologists, psychosexual counsellors or marital therapists. Couples who need specialist help during separation or divorce may be offered conciliation or FAMILY MEDIATION by the PROBATION SERVICE as part of its divorce court welfare work, especially if the care of children is a contentious issue. There are also independent mediation services provided by the VOLUNTARY SECTOR.

Social workers should also be aware of the needs and problems of couples in a relationship where either partner or both may have a physical DISABILITY. Special care needs to be exercised to ensure that as far as possible they can meet each other's emotional and physical needs, and that they are empowered to create an environment where their relationship can develop and flourish. Specialist advice to help people with physical disabilities overcome sexual difficulties is available through organizations such as Sexual Problems of the Disabled. There is a debate about society's and social workers' response to people with LEARNING

DIFFICULTIES who express a wish to live together and/or to be married. Social workers may be reluctant to face issues of emotional and sexual need and to explore ways of working in PARTNERSHIP to help people with learning difficulties overcome any problems they may have.

A frequent criticism of agencies that offer help to people with marital problems is that their workers are predominantly white and middle class and do not meet the needs of significant minority groups. There are common STEREOTYPED assumptions about Asian families, for example, that imply that counselling and support are not necessary because their communities are self-sufficient and care for each other. There is an increasing body of evidence, however, that Asian women whose relationships have broken down experience devastating social isolation. Social workers need to be aware of this growing problem. There are now some Asian mediation services in existence, and some counselling services actively recruit counsellors from ethnic-minority groups, but in general such services are scarce.

S. Litvinoff, *The Relate Guide to Better Relationships*, London: Vermilion, 1992.

**market**   a means through which products may be bought and sold. Markets are one, but not the only, mechanism for allocating goods and services in conditions where resources and personal incomes are limited but demand tends to be unlimited.

Two factors, supply and demand, are central to the functioning of a market. As consumers we have wants for goods and services but a limited income with which to obtain them. We have to make decisions as to which goods and services we should buy. Demand for a particular product arises from the extent to which consumers are willing to pay for it (if at all). In general, market theory holds that the higher the price for a product, the lower the consumer demand for that product will be. Supply is the quantity of a good or service available from its producers and in general depends on costs such as materials and labour; the lower the costs for producing the product in relation to the price obtained for it, the greater the supply of that particular item. To put it another way, the higher the price at which the product can be sold, the more resources producers will put into its production. Economists talk of the theory of the 'perfect' market. In reality, markets are frequently distorted by various pressures and are not necessarily stable. Supply of a particular product can remain in the hands of a few producers or even one. The latter case is called a monopoly, which can often result in the consumer paying an unjustifiably high price. Or the reverse can be true; too many producers produce an excess, or glut, so that quantities of goods remain unsold regardless of price; then producers suffer, since they often do not recoup their costs.

The use of a market to allocate goods and services assumes that consumers are placed in the best position to make the decision as to whether a particular good or service is worth paying for at a particular price, that is, the consumer is best placed to decide on the value of the goods or services. This finds expression in the notion that 'the consumer is sovereign' or 'the customer knows best'. In practice, there are important questions concerning the quality and accuracy of the information that consumers hold, and whether their decisions are affected by such external influences as advertising.

Increasingly economists, welfare specialists and politicians are speaking favourably of markets operating in health care and in community care. Advocates of market principles note the lack of choice in the provision of services because their supply is dominated, in effect, by public monopolies – the local authority and the National Health Service. They conclude that this fosters dependency, inasmuch as people do not try to provide for themselves but are forced to take what is on offer or go without the service. They view the introduction of the market mechanism into community care services as the only way to increase both choice, by encouraging other suppliers to come forward, and efficiency, by containing rising costs. The government has introduced changes designed to expand the influence of the market mechanism in determining allocation of both health and community care services. It has done this through the creation of purchasers, which assess needs and buy the services to meet those needs for a particular individual, and providers, which organize and sell the services required (see PURCHASER/PROVIDER SPLIT). These two distinct roles are now widespread within local government and are undertaken by different personnel in an attempt to change the culture and the way of thinking.

Evidence is mixed as to whether these reforms are achieving their stated objectives of increased choice and more efficient use of resources. Competition between suppliers is essential to a fully functioning market, and in health and community care services it is assumed to lead to greater choice for consumers and greater efficiency for purchasers. However, experience within the NHS suggests that, because of the obvious need to preserve continuity of service provision, purchasing bodies may increasingly adopt a partnership model – involving long-term contracts for a wide range of services – as opposed to a competition model, and thus blunt some of the reforms' objectives. In community care services the success of the reforms will depend on whether market mechanisms will in themselves increase diversity within the private sector. In some cases, however, user choice of community care services has not expanded; indeed, in some areas the particular service contracted for by the local authority was the *only* service available in that locality. In such situations, user choice is clearly not the only important criterion in shaping purchasing strategy.

J. Le Grade and W. Bartlett eds., *Quasi-Markets and Social Policy*, Basingstoke: Macmillan, 1993.

**market rent**   the phrase used to describe a rent officer's determination of a reasonable rent for a particular dwelling.

All assured tenancies (after 15 January 1989) have to be referred for a determination if HOUSING BENEFIT is claimed. Although housing benefit authorities should not blindly follow these 'market rents', they obtain no benefit subsidy if they pay above this level, except where the tenant falls into a protected group. (See RENT RESTRICTION.)

**marriage**   a socially acknowledged and legally ratified relationship or union between an adult male and an adult female. In Britain the officially recognized form of marriage is monogamy.

Marriage in traditional or preindustrial societies appears to serve kin interests and to be regulated by kin relationships. Marriage within capitalist or industrial societies is more likely to be a matter of choice between the two adults concerned, although choice seems to operate within a comparatively narrow range; that is, most people marry others of roughly comparable social status. In Britain individual choice seems to predominate, although there are situations where more traditional forms of marriage still occur – for example, among some Muslim and Sikh groups or in some parts of rural Wales. Marriage continues to be very popular, despite increasing DIVORCE rates; a high proportion of divorcees subsequently remarry. In 1988 only 63 per cent of marriages were between a bachelor and a spinster, whereas in 1971 the figure was nearly 80 per cent. COHABITATION before marriage is also increasing rapidly. Because so many marriages end in divorce, and so many people remarry, new families with children of previous relationships are often formed. These families are called step-families or reconstituted families. Many families face difficulties that do not lead to separation or divorce. Social workers and other therapeutic workers sometimes become involved in attempts to help such families (see FAMILY THERAPY).

D. Gittins, *The Family in Question*, London: Macmillan 1992.

**maternal deprivation**  a theory that has sought to demonstrate a connection between an unsatisfactory relationship between a child and its mother and difficulties for that child in later life.

Deprivation here may be understood either as the loss of a mother entirely, or as her absence for lengthy (if temporary) periods, or as a mother who acts distantly or indifferently towards the child. The originator of the theory, John Bowlby, conducted research that appeared to show that maternal deprivation can lead to juvenile delinquency and to behavioural disorders in later life. Bowlby's work has been read to imply that even short and temporary separations can have profound and lasting effects upon the child's later ability to function as a mature adult.

The debate on maternal deprivation seems to reappear vigorously from time to time. Some, for example, have argued that a preschool child attending a nursery or with a child-minder should be seen as experiencing maternal deprivation. More recent considered criticism of Bowlby's ideas has it that there are many important ingredients in a (separated) relationship between a child and their mother, including the age of the child, the quality of the relationship before separation occurred, the length of separation, the quality of substitute care and the quality of maternal care after child and mother are reunited (if this happens). Where a period of separation is relatively brief, where the child understands what is happening and why, and where a warm and loving relationship exists both before and after separation, it is unlikely that any harm will come to the child. A more negative experience on any of these criteria might increase the chances of later difficulties for the child. Feminists have argued that the theory is oppressive to mothers. They argue that in times of war or periods of economic expansion, men are content to encourage women into paid employment; in periods of recession, however, women are reminded of their domestic responsibilities and especially the duties of motherhood. The theory therefore seeks to control women directly and indirectly, the latter by avoiding the question of what the role of the father should be in relation to child rearing and what consequences for the child may result from paternal deprivation.

M. Rutter, *Maternal Deprivation Reassessed 2nd edition*, London: Penguin, 1981.

**maternity allowance**   a benefit paid to a woman off work while having a baby, for up to eighteen weeks, when STATUTORY MATERNITY PAY is not available, for example to someone who is self-employed.

Entitlement to maternity benefit is based on the claimant's recent NATIONAL INSURANCE contribution record. Benefit can be claimed at any time after the eleventh week before the expected confinement.

**maternity expenses payment**   a payment made from the regulated SOCIAL FUND to an applicant who is in receipt of INCOME SUPPORT, FAMILY CREDIT or DISABILITY WORKING ALLOWANCE and has just had a child or expects one within eleven weeks.

The payment is worth £100 in 1994 for each child. This part of the Social Fund was introduced before 1988, replacing provision in the Single Payment Regulations that allowed realistic payments to be made to meet the expenses of a new child.

**Matrimonial Causes Act 1973**   the main statute governing DIVORCE in England and Wales. There is now only one general ground for divorce, and this is that a marriage has irretrievably broken down.

To demonstrate to a court that their marriage has failed, the petitioner must show either that the other party has committed adultery, or that they have behaved unreasonably, or that they have deserted for at least two years, or that the couple have lived apart for two years and that the respondent agrees to the divorce, or that the couple have lived apart for five years (in which case the respondent's consent is not necessary). A petitioner may not seek a divorce within the first year of marriage. Judicial or legal separations are covered by the same legislation. A legal separation can be secured at any point in a marriage, on the same grounds as for divorce. Legal separations are sought by people who may have a moral or religious objection to a divorce. Legally separated people cannot remarry until they secure a full divorce.

> A 1993 government green paper concerning possible reform of divorce law proposes a waiting period of twelve months (currently many petitioners do not wait for the period of separation to elapse but secure a quicker divorce on grounds of adultery, desertion or unreasonable behaviour) during which there will be an expectation that couples will use MEDIATION to settle matters in relation to children, property and maintenance. In this proposed system, lawyers will play a less prominent role than at present, although they may still give advice on legal agreements. Mediation services, it is suggested, should be provided by an entirely new organization (clearly not the divorce court welfare section of the PROBATION SERVICE).

**meals on wheels**   the provision of meals to older or vulnerable people, either within their own home or in luncheon clubs in community facilities, by statutory or voluntary organizations.

Meals on wheels provision is increasingly offered by voluntary organizations like the Women's Royal Voluntary Service, often on a less generous basis (in terms of both cost and frequency) than before, because of cuts in public expenditure.

**means-tested benefits** benefits to which entitlement depends on personal circumstances, family structure and means (specifically income and capital).

To claim FAMILY CREDIT, for example, you must have one child, work sixteen hours or more and earn less than the amount prescribed by Parliament (then it is a matter of arithmetic). Means-tested benefits include INCOME SUPPORT, family credit, HOUSING BENEFIT, COUNCIL TAX BENEFIT, DISABILITY WORKING ALLOWANCE and HEALTH BENEFITS.

**mediation** see FAMILY MEDIATION.

**medical model** the understanding of a person's problem, behaviour or condition in terms of illness, diagnosis and treatment.

Social workers use the term 'medical model', often critically, to summarize what they consider to be the limited, even oppressive, interpretation that medical practitioners sometimes apply to a client's condition. Fundamental to this medical viewpoint is the concept of physical illness, which is then used to explain a number of behavioural difficulties or 'symptoms'. An illness requires diagnosis and treatment through medication; it involves the body or mind being attacked by an outside pathogen. Social workers often refer to the medical model in relation to people with mental health problems (see MENTAL ILLNESS), where medically trained psychiatrists may see a person's behaviour in terms of a physical illness requiring drugs to cure, whereas social workers may see the onset of the condition as more crucially a result of stress such as family pressures or poor housing.

***Memorandum of Good Practice*** the voluntary code of practice on interviewing children issued by the Home Office and Department of Health in 1992.

The memorandum is a guide to the video recording of interviews of child witnesses admissible in criminal proceedings under the CRIMINAL JUSTICE ACT 1988. The practice of videotaping interviews with child witnesses is usually confined to occasions when the child is the alleged victim of an assault by the accused. It is generally used when it is suspected that the child is a victim of sexual assault. There are upper age limits for the use of video-recorded interview. In cases of violent offences the child must be under 14 years at the time the recording is made, and under 15 at the time of the trial. In cases of sexual offences the child must be under 17 years at the time of the recording and under 18 at the time of the trial. Children older than these limits are expected to give oral evidence in court.   The memorandum is the indirect result of a series of civil cases heard in the HIGH COURT and the CLEVELAND INQUIRY that were critical of videotaped DISCLOSURE interviews with children submitted as evidence in care proceedings. Such interviews were originally conducted for clinical purposes and so did not take into account evidential requirements. The courts had recognized the potential value of video-recorded interviews with children in court proceedings, however. The Home Office subsequently convened an advisory group on video evidence, which produced its report in 1989.

The memorandum was produced to promote interviewing of children that satisfied general rules of evidence. It offers advice on how to prepare for and plan a video-recorded interview, how to conduct the interview and guidance on storage, custody and disposal of tapes. The aim of video recording interviews with children is to reduce frequent repetition of their accounts during the investigation process. It is recognized that giving evidence is stressful for children; the aim of videotaping interviews is to restrict the need for children to give oral evidence in court. The reforms of the CRIMINAL JUSTICE ACT 1991 allow for the video-recorded interview to replace the child's evidence in chief, that is, the first part of their evidence. The child must, however, be available for cross-examination and re-examination.

The success of video-based evidence is a matter of debate in legal and social work circles. Cross-examination is most difficult for children, and there is frequently a significant time delay between the making of the video recording and the criminal trial, which undermines children's ability to give sound evidence. It is questionable whether the memorandum's aim of balancing a child-centred approach with evidential requirements is achieved.

Department of Health and Home Office, *Memorandum of Good Practice*, London: HMSO, 1992.

**mental disorder**   a term used to cover a number of extreme dysfunctions of the mind. The MENTAL HEALTH ACT 1983 defines mental disorder as including MENTAL ILLNESS, arrested or incomplete development of the mind, or any other mental disability such as psychopathic disorder that results in persistent, abnormally aggressive behaviour.

**mental handicap**   a term for LEARNING DISABILITY that is utilized less frequently than formerly because it is widely regarded as having stigmatizing associations.

A number of SELF-ADVOCATES with a learning disability have expressed a dislike for the term, and some have stated a preference for the term LEARNING DIFFICULTY.

**mental health**   absence of MENTAL ILLNESS, in Western cultures, referring to an individual's personal and social well-being, meaning both inner experience and outer behaviour.

Western culture locates health conditions in 'body' or 'mind', hence giving rise to the concepts of mental and physical health. In other cultures this distinction may not be so important; but in most there is a concern with something similar, although the emphasis on inner experience or outer behaviour will vary. Ideas of well-being express the social values of importance in the person's culture and thus differ between cultures. For example, contributing to group harmony may constitute positive mental health in Eastern cultures, as opposed to individualism in the West. It is therefore likely that service users will hope to realize such values as a result of social work intervention, not only with MENTAL HEALTH PROBLEMS as such, but generally. The anti-racist worker consequently needs to be responsive to these value differences, both in their individual interventions and in the promotion of culturally sensitive services. Failure to do this may compromise the service user's cultural identity, which is a form of racism.

The World Health Organization has defined HEALTH in general, including mental health, as 'a complete state of physical, mental and social well-being, not merely the absence of illness'. This definition incorporates two different perspectives on mental health that are currently being debated and have major implications for service provision.

The first of these perspectives – mental health as the 'absence of illness' – is associated with Western PSYCHIATRY. From this perspective, any departure from the state of personal and social well-being constituting mental health is understood as a state of illness; that is, any inner experiences that are subjectively unhappy and any outer behaviours that contravene social values in particular ways are defined as mental illness. These experiences or behaviours are thereby regarded, as are all illnesses in Western (and some other) cultures, as 'bad' and 'abnormal', and accordingly mental health represents 'goodness' and 'normality'. This approach is widely practised in Western society and has implications for ANTI-DISCRIMINATORY values. As a 'normal', 'good' condition, mental health is regarded as superior to mental illness. This equation of superiority with positive mental health means that valued groups of people are likely to be regarded as more mentally healthy than devalued groups, while devalued groups are more likely to be seen as potentially or actually mentally ill and thus to be diagnosed as such and admitted to psychiatric hospital more often than valued groups. In addition, the illness diagnosis itself may, as a negative 'label', be highly stigmatizing to the person (see STIGMA). On the other hand, women, as an oppressed group, may appreciate the care and validation of their distress that they receive by being diagnosed as ill; thus the state of mental ill-health may not always be a devaluing experience. From the above perspective, mental health as a 'normal' state is also regarded, like physical health, as automatically present if illness is absent. Thus, no professional interventions of any sort are required to maintain mental health. If illness occurs, however, society will seek to eliminate it as a 'bad' and 'abnormal' state. Medical treatment is the main means of achieving this in Western cultures, because illness, including mental illness, is regarded as primarily physiological in origin. This means that, in this perspective, health is recovered after illness only through medical treatment. The significance here for social work is that there is no role for social workers in the promotion or maintenance of mental health.

The second of the above perspectives – defining mental health as 'mental well-being' – is more likely to be found in non-Western than in Western cultures, but it also is associated with both conservative and more radical approaches to mental health concerns in Western social work and health care thinking. From this perspective, most forms of mental distress or socially unacceptable behaviour may be understood as within the range of 'normal' human functioning, and therefore not to indicate the presence of the 'abnormal' state of illness, although in most cultures some experiences or behaviour will be defined in these terms. This position is adopted by 'anti-psychiatry' theories – especially in the ideas of Szasz, which have been linked to COMMUNITY CARE policy – and by radical social theory, which provides the theoretical basis for radical and anti-oppressive social work. Szasz defines most departures from the state of personal and social well-being conservatively as 'problems of living' that are an essential and 'normal' part of human life; in radical social theory they are understood as the products of oppressive social, economic and political conditions. From these viewpoints, then, mental health is regarded as a consequence of resolving these problems – for Szasz involving the individual in developing ways of coping with 'problems of living', and in radical social theory through the reduction of oppression in society. Both approaches consider mental health to be neither automatically present nor the product of medical treatment; rather, it depends on the powers of the individual and/or of the collective to achieve personal and/or social growth. This gives the key role in promoting positive mental health to social workers, service users and non-medical professionals, instead of to health professionals working within a medical model; hence community care policy gives priority to social care in the provision of services to people with mental health problems.

Social work approaches to promoting positive mental health are outlined in EMPOWERMENT theory and FEMINIST and ANTI-RACIST theories, and they involve enabling people to take control of their inner and outer lives collectively and individually. There are important implications here for anti-discriminatory practice, since the presence of mental health problems is regarded as 'normal' for the individual in their relations with society as a result of oppression. These problems are therefore not devalued as 'abnormal' and are not seen as the fault of the individual.

S. Fernando, *Mental Health, Race and Culture*, Basingstoke: Macmillan/Mind, 1991.

**Mental Health Act 1983** legislation that governs the assessment and treatment of people with MENTAL DISORDER, including the conditions under which a person can be compulsorily detained in a psychiatric hospital.

The Acts sets out four specific categories of mental disorder. Three of the four – mental impairment, severe mental impairment and psychopathic disorder – all share similar characteristics: incomplete development of mind, which may include significant impairment of intelligence and social functioning and is associated with abnormally aggressive behaviour or socially irresponsible conduct. The fourth and most important category, MENTAL ILLNESS, is left undefined in the Act. However, the Department of Health and Social Security in consultative documents issued at the time the Act was passed defined mental illness as having the following characteristics: (1) persistent interruption of intellectual functioning as indicated by a failure of memory, orientation, comprehension and learning capacity; (2) persistent alteration of mood to such a degree that it gives rise to the patient making a delusional appraisal of their situation; (3) the presence of delusions or other persecutory or grandiose beliefs: (4) thinking so disordered as to prevent the person from making a reasonable appraisal of their situation.

Section 2 of the Act provides for a person to be admitted to hospital for psychiatric assessment for up to twenty-eight days if they are suffering from mental disorder (that is, one of the categories above) to the extent that detention is justified and that they ought to be detained in the interests of their own health or safety or that of others. Compulsory admission for assessment can take place only on the recommendation of two registered medical practitioners. After the twenty-eight days have elapsed the person must either remain in hospital as an 'informal' – voluntary – patient or be detained for treatment under section 3. An order for the person's discharge may be made at any time during the course of the twenty-eight days. The person may seek their own discharge by making an application to a MENTAL HEALTH tribunal within fourteen days of their admission.

A person may be detained under section 3 of the Act for treatment on the grounds that they are suffering from mental illness, severe mental impairment or psychopathic disorder to the degree that it is appropriate for them to receive medical treatment *and* it is necessary for the health or safety of the person or others that they receive treatment that they would not otherwise receive unless detained. Again, the application for compulsory treatment requires the written recommendation of two medical practitioners.

The Act also allows for compulsory admission for assessment for seventy-two hours in cases of emergency. An emergency application may be made by a person's nearest relative or by an APPROVED SOCIAL WORKER and the written recommendation of a medical officer who is familiar with the person in question. The application cannot be renewed at the end of the 72-hour period.

The Act also allows for the appointment of a guardian for people over the age of 16 who are suffering from mental disorder to a degree justifying the appointment. The guardian is usually a local authority social services officer, who can require the person to live at a specified place, to receive specified medical treatment and to permit access by a medical practitioner or approved social worker. The value of guardianship has been the subject of considerable debate, since it contains no powers of enforcement and must rely on the cooperation of the person.

The Central Council for Education and Training in Social Work (CCETSW) and other commentators have noted, despite the 1983 Act's claims to uphold patients' rights, that detention under the Act has consequences that contravene the 1948 United Nations Universal Declaration of Human Rights. CCETSW points out that rights of citizenship are still further compromised for people coming under the provisions of the Act by the fact that denial of civil liberties, by all the implications of detention, such as segregation. It also results in a loss of social rights to work, housing, and so on. It goes on to explain that awareness of social workers and society generally concerning the disadvantage thus faced by people detained may be deflected by the fact that the restrictions placed upon them are defined as medical treatment. Social workers therefore need to be aware of the collective social needs of people detained under the Mental Health Act, besides the loss of their civil liberties.

Loss of rights is particularly great for members of devalued groups. Numerous studies have shown consistently that people of black African descent are detained in far greater proportions than members of other cultures, are more likely to come to the attention of the psychiatric services through the police, and receive more compulsory treatment. Studies have shown that this is likely to reflect racism on the part of psychiatric and social work practitioners (the ASW plays a major role in the decision to detain). Asian people, on the contrary, are detained in very low proportions, and this may be equally racist in denying people the right to treatment and protection. Women in all age groups, except the youngest, are detained in higher proportions than men, and older women at very high rates. Like black people, therefore, women and particularly older women seem to be regarded as having a high propensity to mental illness, through institutionalized sexism. The devaluation of these groups in society means that there is a serious lack of services provided for their mental health and social needs, both in terms of preventing a mental health crisis and as alternatives to compulsory detention.

Studies have drawn the attention of social workers to some of these needs, and anti-racist writers have outlined how projects run by black and ethnic-minority groups seek to fulfil such needs in minority communities. In general, it has been noted that alternatives to hospital are scarce for all groups, through lack of resources, and perhaps preventive services too, although a number of innovatory projects have been identified. Aftercare – legally to be provided on discharge from hospital, following assessment of need by a MULTIDISCIPLINARY team – is another area where resources are scarce. People discharged from compulsory admission are likely to need long-term support from the mental health services, and thus resource commitment is essential. Social workers who are not ASWs can be involved in aftercare planning and in the development of the preventive and crisis services outlined above.

*Department of Health Mental Health Act Code of Practice*, Second revised edition, London: HMSO, 1993.

**mental health problems**   problems identified, in Western cultures, with the 'mind'.

From the time of Descartes in the eighteenth century, 'mind' has been defined as the workings of a person's 'consciousness', including perception, thought and judgement, emotions and behaviour. Thus, in Western society mental health problems are located in both a person's inner thinking, feelings and experience and in their outer actions; and this means that the person's social as well as their psychological functioning is affected, as most behaviour takes place in a social context. Most cultures have a similar concern with this area of personal and social functioning but may not make such a strong distinction between 'body' and 'mind'; instead they may experience mental health problems holistically – as expressed in descriptions such as 'my heart is squeezed'. In white culture too, physical illness and aches and pains accompany these problems.

*Range of mental health problems.* Psychiatry and Western culture divide mental health problems into the following categories: stress, POST-TRAUMATIC STRESS (for example, among adult survivors of child SEXUAL ABUSE, NEUROSES or 'minor psychiatric disorders' (ANXIETY, DEPRESSION, EATING DISORDERS, HYSTERIA, obsessions, PHOBIAS, psychosomatic illness), PSYCHOSES or 'major psychiatric disorders' (DEPRESSION, MANIC DEPRESSION, SCHIZOPHRENIA), PERSONALITY DISORDER – including PSYCHOPATHY and seven other categories), and organic diseases of the brain (such as the DEMENTIAS). In the discussion of MENTAL HEALTH it is shown that mental health problems can be understood either as 'illness' or as psychological or social difficulties and distress. There is broad agreement that the 'major psychiatric disorders' and organic disease of the brain may be understood as 'illnesses', which is reflected in findings that most people with these conditions are referred to the psychiatric services. At the other end of the scale, stress represents psychological and social difficulties, and most sufferers are not referred. However, there is great disagreement over the classification of neuroses or 'minor psychiatric disorders' – known from the 'health' perspective as 'mental health problems' – and reactions to extreme experiences, and a substantial minority of people with these problems are referred. The 'health' perspective on all of these conditions is valuable in alerting the worker to the consequences of stigmatizing and devaluing people because they have an 'illness', although it is also important to be aware of the incapacitating and distressing experiences involved in all the above conditions, which those wishing not to stigmatize may underestimate.

*What are mental health problems?* These conditions are understood to have varying causes. At one extreme, stress is seen as the human and appropriate response to adverse circumstances. Defined as 'emotional-psychophysiological state', stress may involve discomfort on all these levels. At the other extreme, organic diseases of the brain have been found to have physical origins. The remainder of these conditions are more difficult to explain. They can be understood to possess the characteristics of 'illness', but only in the case of psychoses is there any evidence of a physiological component. With neuroses and personality disorder, PSYCHODYNAMIC theories suggest that causes may lie in early parent–child relationships, and LEARNING THEORIES see these problems as learned behaviour. It is of particular significance to social work, however, that social factors have been found to have strong links with neuroses and psychoses, in that people in disadvantaged circumstances, without confidants and experiencing low self-esteem, are more likely to experience these conditions on a long-term basis; and stress generated by life events can trigger their onset. Members of oppressed groups are therefore especially vulnerable, as a result of structural oppression. The explanation given by psychiatrists is that social factors may 'trigger' a 'predisposition' to the condition, but writers on EMPOWERMENT theory consider social disadvantage and oppression to be sufficient causes of depression and anxiety through the experience of LEARNED HELPLESSNESS and of psychoses as extreme distress.

*Consequences of mental health problems.* Although the risks of psychoses and organic disease (see DEMENTIA) are well known, there may not always be an appreciation of the consequences of less serious mental health problems such as the neuroses, stress and post-traumatic stress syndrome, personality disorder (see appropriate entries and also MENTAL ILLNESS).

*Responses to mental health problems.* Large numbers of social service clients experience mental health problems: perhaps 60 to 70 per cent, and 80 per cent of mothers of black children in care; yet workers are often not aware of these problems, unless they are the subject of the referral. Most of these people experience the less severe conditions, the neuroses of anxiety and depression, for which they are unlikely to be referred to the psychiatric services, and therefore they do not have a mental health 'label' to draw workers' attention to these problems. In other cases, perhaps where psychosis, personality disorder and even post-traumatic stress syndrome are involved, where the person has been referred to a psychiatrist, it has been shown that workers are ill-equipped to respond to these difficulties if the mental health problem is not the reason for referral. Practitioners are likely to react either by regarding mental health problems as 'normal' reactions to stressful circumstances – in which case it is believed that the problems will go if circumstances are improved – or by regarding them as mental illnesses and thus beyond social workers' skills, which concern social problems only. Workers may therefore ignore the problems or leave the psychiatrist to deal with them. In addition, workers are not immune to public stereotypes and thus may act in a discriminatory way towards people with mental health problems.

It is, however, possible within the social work role to respond to mental health problems in ways that take account of the range of difficulties involved – physiological, psychological and social. A 'bio-PSYCHOSOCIAL' approach to intervention with most of these problems has been recommended. This may involve understanding and working in relation to the use of medication to relieve the worst 'symptoms', and providing a 'sustaining' and valuing relationship without, at least initially, placing emphasis on problem-solving (for the person is not in possession of an accurate view of the situation or their capacities for action) but giving the support and confidence that can themselves reduce mental distress, and action to reduce social pressures. In the discussion of mental illness the steps the worker needs to take in responding to features of mental health problems that can be understood as 'illness' are explored, including working with health care staff, while in the entries on stress, psychoses, neuroses, post-traumatic stress syndrome, personality disorder and organic disorders the more specific contributions that social work can make to intervene with these conditions is explored.

W. Cockerham, *Sociology of Mental Disorder*, 3rd edition, London: Prentice Hall, 1992.

**mental illness** disturbance of mental functioning due to chemical, physiological, psychological, social or biological causes.

Mental illnesses are variable in duration, severity and prognosis, depending on the form they take. They are broadly divided into two categories: emotional disorders (often referred to as NEUROSES), such as ANXIETY and DEPRESSION, and the severe distortions of perception and thought in which hallucination and delusion are prominent (known as PSYCHOSES). There is recognition that emotional disorders scarcely can be considered as an illness, and that apart from mood-altering medication, such as anti-depressants, most forms of treatment for emotional disorders fall outside what medical doctors offer. The psychoses are rather different. Their impact on the sufferer and on people immediately in their environment is so enormous, and the impact of medication so pronounced, that treatment usually involves a period of hospitalization under the supervision of medically trained psychiatrists.

Examples of emotional disorders that social workers commonly come across when working with clients are anxiety, in which the person suffers from a general sense of fear and worry sufficiently severe to disrupt their quality of life; PHOBIA, in which the person suffers an overwhelming fear of specific objects or situations, preventing rational thought or action; obsessive compulsion, in which the person has recurring thoughts or pattern of behaviour so powerful that if resisted a feeling of intense anxiety results; and reactive depression, in which the person becomes depressed as a result of a specific event such as the death of a family member, an accident or a burglary. The treatment of emotional disorders does not usually involve medication, although sometimes minor tranquillizers are prescribed. Because the person is still capable of rational thought, treatment usually takes some form of PSYCHOTHERAPY such as COUNSELLING or COGNITIVE-BEHAVIOURAL THERAPY in which problems, sources of worry and ways of overcoming them are discussed over a number of sessions with a therapist. Specially trained social workers can undertake this work, especially when attached to mental health clinics and working in collaboration with other mental health professionals.

The psychoses are more severe and cause behaviour that is strikingly abnormal by any standard. They usually affect all aspects of a person's personality, while the individual has little or no awareness of their condition. There are several types of psychoses. Some have apparent causes, such as DEMENTIA, which results from degeneration of brain tissue. These are often called organic psychoses. Others, such as SCHIZOPHRENIA and MANIC DEPRESSIVE psychosis, have no known cause but produce powerful symptoms nevertheless; these typically include hearing voices, having delusional thoughts about identity, severe MOOD SWINGS and a complete lack of involvement in one's surroundings. Treatment very often involves a period of hospitalization and some medication.

The concept of mental illness is the source of much debate. In the nineteenth century some medical practitioners asserted that there was a similarity between the physical illnesses and the severe disruption of behaviour, thoughts and emotions that they observed in their patients. Just as a person who was physically ill suffered pain and disturbance of functioning, so a mentally ill person was seen as suffering in the mind, which resulted in disturbances to they way they thought and acted. Because they were ill they could not be held responsible for what they did and required treatment to become better. In this sense, the notion of mental illness allowed for the development of a more humane perspective than depicting sufferers as possessed by evil or as mad and dangerous, deserving punishment and incarceration. By looking at what was previously considered to be mad behaviour in terms of illness, the medical profession attempted to place its analysis on a scientific basis, to classify various forms of illness and to develop schemes of recognized symptoms, along with a process of diagnosis and means of treating these symptoms. Critics of the concept of mental illness argue that its terminology is in part a mere LABELLING of unpleasant or inconvenient behaviour with which other people cannot cope, and that this serves only to place the behaviour associated with mental distress into a medical framework which does little more than control the behaviour of the sufferer. They argue that parallels with physical illness are misplaced and serve to justify the administration of treatments, often in the form of DRUGS, that control the symptoms but do nothing to address underlying causes (see ANTI-PSYCHIATRY). In effect, a middle position now holds the balance of influence between the two views – that mental illness is not something that can be purely medically defined, but neither can it be reduced to a problem of unfair labelling. (See also MEDICAL MODEL.)

There are recognized links between mental illness and stress in a person's environment. Conflicts stemming from family relationships, excessive demands at work or school, or a recent bereavement may be implicated. There is also an established link between SOCIAL CLASS and formal psychiatric diagnosis, with higher rates of the psychoses in people who undertake menial and unskilled jobs, for instance, than in professional and managerial workers. Most importantly, there is a recognized association between ethnicity and diagnosed psychiatric disorders, such as the higher rates of schizophrenia diagnosed in black and Asian people. Members of ethnic minorities are also disproportionately admitted to psychiatric units for longer stays in hospital and with more active symptoms, compared with other groups. By contrast, it has been established that those diagnosed tend to be more isolated, have had greater contact with the police and are less likely to receive voluntary treatment and preventive treatments such as psychotherapy than is the case with non-ethnic-minority patients. Such evidence has led many commentators to assert that PSYCHIATRY is racist and a form of social control.

Social work with people with mental illness involves a number of tasks depending on the nature of the condition and the needs of the CLIENT and family. Necessarily there is a division of labour between the psychiatrist, who manages the treatment of the disorder and makes recommendations concerning discharge from hospital, and the social worker, who provides information and obtains key resources for a person when they live in the community. Despite much debate concerning the medical perspective on mental illness, this perspective still predominates, and it is within that perspective that tasks are allocated. One of the most important social work tasks is arranging community care for a person discharged from psychiatric hospital or to forestall hospitalization. This may involve assessing needs and purchasing services such as a place at a day centre and a place to live in a small GROUP HOME. It may involve coordinating day-to-day support for a person who finds it difficult to look after themselves following a psychotic episode. Or it may involve offering support to a family whose son or daughter will continue to live with them after a period of hospitalization. This work inevitably involves aspects of CARE MANAGEMENT and liaison with other professionals and organizations such as housing associations and psychiatrists. In essence, social work, while it cannot directly address the condition or illness itself, attempts to minimize its inevitable social effects such as isolation, and to initiate programmes that will improve skills and social functioning.

Other forms of social work have deliberately kept their distance from the MEDICAL MODEL and are built on non-medical views of mental disorder, aiming to offer intensive supporting relationships and counselling for people with mental distress rather than relying on medication to minimize that distress. This type of social work is found more often in small voluntary organizations such as drop-in centres, small group homes, support groups, or neighbourhood projects run by advocacy organizations such as Mind. Most social workers try to counter the STIGMA and suspicion attached to mental illness by explaining its real nature and joining in campaigns and community education initiatives.

(See also APPROVED SOCIAL WORKER, COMMUNITY PSYCHIATRIC NURSE, MENTAL HEALTH ACT 1983.)

W. Cockerham, *Sociology of Mental Disorder*, 3rd edition, London: Prentice Hall, 1992.

**mentally disordered offenders**    people convicted of criminal behaviour who are considered to be suffering from MENTAL ILLNESS.

The relationship between mental illness and criminal behaviour poses both ethical and policy dilemmas. The ethical dilemma concerns the extent to which a mentally disordered criminal can be held responsible for their actions (see THEORIES OF CRIME). The policy dilemma concerns the way such an offender should be treated or punished (see PRINCIPLES OF SENTENCING). It is a basic tenet of the British CRIMINAL JUSTICE SYSTEM that offenders should understand what they have done, be able to participate in their own defence and understand the implications of their punishment. If they are incapable of meeting any of these requirements, criminal proceedings should not take place, and they should receive psychiatric treatment instead. However, some people feel that this enables dangerous offenders to avoid just punishment, and courts sometimes refuse to accept that someone who has committed a very serious offence (for example, the 'Yorkshire Ripper') is mentally ill. Consequently, many offenders who might be considered mentally disordered are still sent to prison. Exact numbers are difficult to assess, but a recent study has suggested that up to a third of men in prison and a half of women in prison may suffer from some form of mental disorder.

> If an offender is considered fit enough to stand trial, a court may still accept that they suffer from mental illness or mental impairment under the MENTAL HEALTH ACT 1983. It then has a number of sentencing options, all of which require the recommendation of at least one psychiatrist. An offender may be placed on a PROBATION ORDER with a requirement to receive psychiatric treatment. Alternatively, they may be sent directly to hospital for a fixed reviewable period. If the offender is regarded as dangerous they may be committed to either a regional secure unit or one of the three high-security special hospitals at Ashworth, Broadmoor and Rampton. If the court decides, nevertheless, to send an offender to prison, it is possible for them to be transferred at a later stage to a hospital. (This is what happened to Peter Sutcliffe, the 'Yorkshire Ripper'.) It is widely accepted that provision for mentally disordered offenders is inadequate. The Reed Report (1992) reviews this provision and reiterates the principle that mentally disordered offenders should receive care and treatment from the health and social services in the community wherever possible.

**methadone**   a synthetic OPIATE available in liquid, tablet or ampoule form, in varying strengths, commonly used as a clean alternative in the treatment of people addicted to opiates (see also COMMUNITY DRUG TEAM).

Methadone is available on prescription only and is a class A drug under the MISUSE OF DRUGS ACT 1971, with a fine and/or imprisonment for unlawful possession or supply. Vehicle drivers may be at risk if they are apprehended and a sample of urine taken shows the presence of methadone; their driving licence may be withdrawn, and their vehicle insurance invalidated. Effects of methadone vary according to whether the person is a regular user of opiates or not. Like HEROIN, it is a sedative and could have fatal effects on someone unaccustomed to its use, depending on the amount used. However, the correct equivalent dose for a user with a high TOLERANCE to opiates will have the result of preventing WITHDRAWAL, enabling the user to maintain a normal lifestyle. People on a methadone prescription can work and bring up families without anyone knowing that they are addicted to opiates. The advantage of prescribing methadone over heroin in a treatment setting is that it is twice as long-acting and therefore does not need to be taken so often. In common with other opiates, methadone may cause users constipation, depression of respiration and a suppression of coughs. Because the liquid form is 50 per cent syrup, it may lead to tooth decay. It is not easy to come off methadone, and users need considerable support for some time after they have stopped.

**milk tokens**   free tokens that can be exchanged for milk, available to expectant mothers and children under 5 in families getting INCOME SUPPORT.

Each token can be exchanged for 7 pints of milk a week or, for a child under 1 year, for 900 grams of dried milk at a clinic. Tokens should be provided automatically by the Benefits Agency of the Department of Social Security to those who qualify.

**Minicom**   a portable text telephone used by DEAF people. Those who want to contact a text telephone user who do not have a Minicom can use Typetalk, the 24-hour national telephone relay service funded by British Telecom and run by the Royal National Institute for the Deaf.

**misdemeanour**   a historic term referring to a category of offences regarded as less heinous than felonies. This distinction, which still exists in the United States, was abolished in England and Wales by the Criminal Law Act 1967.

**mistrial**   a trial that is spoiled by a legally significant error (such as the disqualification of a juror). The term is also used in the United States to indicate an inconclusive trial (for example, where the jury cannot agree).

**Misuse of Drugs Act 1971**   the major piece of legislation in Britain concerning the use and misuse of drugs.

The Act lists numerous drugs, not all of which have medicinal purposes, and divides them into classes A, B and C, depending on how harmful the drug is perceived to be. Those in class A – for example, OPIATES, COCAINE and some HALLUCINOGENIC drugs – carry the most severe penalties, ranging from a fine to life imprisonment. It is illegal to possess, supply, produce or let premises to be used for the use of these drugs. Any drug that is prepared to be INJECTED is automatically put in class A. The vast majority of prosecutions (and the police may stop and search if they have reasonable suspicions) are for possession of CANNABIS. There is a considerable lobby in Britain of people who would like to see cannabis legalized, and many police forces now have a policy of CAUTION for first-time possessors of both cannabis and other drugs.

**mixed economy of care**   the provision of services from a variety of sources, including the statutory agencies and the private and voluntary sectors.

Many policy analysts, both inside and outside the Conservative government, believe that the provision of welfare services purely by the state sector reduces choice for individual users, undermines efficiency through monopoly, and benefits welfare professionals and local bureaucrats rather than those in need. An important core belief of Conservative ideology is that choice equals freedom and that by opening up the provision of care to a greater variety of providers more choice will be available to users of services, who will therefore experience greater freedom. The government has also argued that through the existence of what is largely a state monopoly there is inevitably more chance of inefficiency and waste. Some analysts see the state as being too insulated from the 'discipline of the MARKET', because it does not suffer the threat of bankruptcy that the private sector experiences, which in their view acts as a spur to efficiency. Thus, they argue that there is a need to open up the state sector to competition from the non-state sector and to introduce an INTERNAL MARKET through identifying PURCHASER/PROVIDER roles within SOCIAL SERVICES DEPARTMENTS. In addition, the private sector has complained that the criteria that local authorities use to register private residential accommodation are more rigorous than those used for their own in-house provision. Consequently, the government has increased competition through encouragement of the mixed economy made up of both the private and voluntary sectors.

> The development of the mixed economy of care should not be identified solely as a cost-saving exercise. The belief that the private and voluntary sector can provide care at a lower cost has played an important part in the policy. Privatization and competitive tendering are seen as ways of reducing public expenditure and the power of public-sector trade unions. The fiscal crisis of the state, emerging out of welfare commitments and the changing demographic structure, has put pressure on governments to seek ways of reducing the role of statutory provision. Local authority social services departments, however, still retain a core regulatory role and involvement through the purchase of services. The NATIONAL HEALTH SERVICE AND COMMUNITY CARE ACT places local authorities at the centre as enabling bodies that will purchase services from the private and voluntary sector in competition with their own in-house providers. The contractual relationship this will create between the state and the non-state sector is aimed at ensuring that users are provided for and that the level and quality of provision will be guaranteed and open to scrutiny.
>
> E. Papadakis and P. Taylor-Gooby, *The Private Provision of Public Welfare*, Brighton: Wheatsheaf, 1987.

**mixed race**    children of racially mixed parentage.

The central factor for mixed-parentage children is that of identification. The terminology used to describe such children 'mixed race', 'half-caste', 'halfbreed', 'half-coloured' – clearly demonstrates confusion and ambivalence. If mixed-parentage children are brought up and socialized in a white household and environment they can be, and often are, treated as white, with no reference made of their black parent, origins or history. The obvious danger here is that these children may eventually be rejected, because of their colour, by the white group with whom they have grown up and identify. Additionally, because some of these children may have had little awareness of, or personal contact with, black people, they may in turn be rejected by the black community. Such children or young people are then left in the limbo of searching for an identity in a society that can often be racially hostile and intolerant.

> Early research in Bradford looked specifically at the high rates of reception into care of mixed-parentage children and concluded that RACISM in the wider society and identity confusion compounded their problems. One study has referred to their 'special problems', suggesting that such children tend to be born in large numbers to 'socially inadequate mothers'. Unfortunately such pathology models may become influencing factors in social work practice; the extent of such a pathology fails to take account of the diverse experiences of these children. Past constructions of the mixed-parentage child are steeped in biological explanations

and fail to recognize the existence of large numbers of such children who have never come to the attention of the official agencies. In studies of the mixed-parentage child, issues of poverty and the realities of class and gender oppression have tended not to be discussed. Instead, any such problems are seen to be due to internally generated pathologies. Clearly, in Britain today, children of mixed parentage are likely to suffer from racist oppression. Resistance to that oppression can take diverse forms depending on the individual child. Social work practitioners should therefore seek to address the child's own experiences instead of generalizing.

V. Coombe and A. Little (eds), *Race and Social Work*, London: Tavistock, 1986.

**mobility allowance**   a benefit abolished in 1992 and subsumed into the higher rate mobility component of DISABILITY LIVING ALLOWANCE.

When first introduced in 1974, it was anticipated that 100,000 people would qualify for mobillity allowance. By 1992 some 678,000 people were receiving it. This discrepancy indicates official ignorance of the prevalence of disability in Britain.

**mobility component**   part of DISABILITY LIVING ALLOWANCE (see also MOBILITY ALLOWANCE).

**modelling**   essentially, learning by example, a therapeutic technique in BEHAVIOUR MODIFICATION.

The person being treated watches another person coping appropriately with an ANXIETY-provoking stimulus including anything from a social event to spiders. They thus learn the inappropriateness of their own reactions and more effective ways of responding. Many studies have confirmed that modelling is a speedy and effective treatment method.

**money advice**   advice for people with financial difficulties, typically including advice on how to maximize income, how to manage debt and how to budget, as well as the money adviser acting as the person's ADVOCATE with creditors and the courts.

Maximizing income can include helping people ensure that they have the best tax arrangements for their circumstances, that they are claiming all the state benefits to which they are entitled and that their wages or salaries are as high as possible. In addition, lump sums may be secured from charitable or other sources. The management of debt that has got out of hand entails working out detailed income and expenditure accounts. It is usual to distinguish between priority and non-priority debt (priority debts are those that could ultimately entail imprisonment, fines or loss of a service, goods or dwelling), although the consumer may have their own views on what is important. The next stage involves negotiating arrangements with creditors that are practicable for the consumer and are seen as sensible and fair by the creditors. In some cases it may be possible to challenge the legitimacy of debt (for example, is it really owed by the person, or is it their ex-partner's debt?) or get it apportioned. In other cases non-priority debts may be written off if the debtor has no long-term prospect of realistically dealing with them. Budgeting could entail giving advice about the relative costs of fuel and how fuel might be used more efficiently; information on cheaper sources of food or on the nutritional value of cheaper foods; advice about cheaper sources of credit; or help to the person in reflecting on the economic costs of their lifestyle. Frequently, budgeting includes advising consumers about how expenditure might be managed, where for example some bills are to be met weekly, some monthly and others at greater intervals. To be an effective debt adviser involves the ability to unravel complex financial matters, often with individuals who are themselves confused, anxious and embarrassed by their situation.

The middle classes have long used solicitors and banks to advise them about financial matters; however, the last twenty years have witnessed the growth of advice agencies prepared to help poor people with money difficulties. The Citizens Advice Bureaux (CAB) are pre-eminent among them, but in many areas NEIGHBOURHOOD and SOCIAL SERVICES DEPARTMENT offices as well as independent advice centres have developed money advice services. In 1992 debt became the largest category of inquiry dealt with by the CAB (social security problems were second). The economic context to these developments includes the growth of personal consumer credit, which in 1980 was £13,000 million and by 1989 had grown almost fourfold. During 1980, 22 per cent of those in the lowest income group used credit; by 1990 this figure had risen to 69 per cent. In the first two months of 1992 a record 280,000 personal debtors applied to be made bankrupt, an increase of 80 per cent on the year before. Figures from the Council of Mortgage Lenders show that in 1980 about 13,500 mortgages were between six and twelve months in arrears; by 1991 the comparable figure was 183,610, and more than half a million other borrowers had less serious arrears. Repossessions of mortgaged property rose from 3,000 in 1980 to more than 75,000 in 1991.

A rigorous analysis of debt and default debt has yet to be undertaken in Britain, but it is known that many people who develop problems do so as a result of unforeseen difficulties, such as unemployment, short-time working, divorce and separation, bereavement, sickness and the failure of businesses. Although there are examples of consumers whose behaviour could be construed as reckless, the vast majority seem to be those who cannot, rather than will not, pay. Indebtedness is mostly rooted in poverty, but the apparently foolhardy behaviour of some debtors still needs to be understood, and advice offered. Wider social forces such as the availability of credit, high and variable rates of interest and the general pressures to be a consumer are critical in this context.

Contemporary research into the access to credit for very poor people has consistently found that they are obliged to use moneylenders, 'loan sharks' and other credit agencies who charge extremely high rates of interest. Often social security claimants or residents living in particular areas will be denied access to normal sources of credit such as banks and finance houses. The CREDIT UNION movement, which aims to give poor people access to relatively cheap loans based upon savings societies, is well developed in some areas and not at all in others. The SOCIAL FUND, administered by the DEPARTMENT OF SOCIAL SECURITY, is another source of cheap loans, but the quota system with cash limits means that access cannot be guaranteed.

Most social workers now accept the connection between money problems and personal and social functioning. Stress caused by POVERTY is clearly acknowledged. Few social workers, however, develop expertise in this area of work, preferring to refer individuals to agencies like the CAB (which in many areas cannot cope with the volume of work). Yet consumers value practical help of this kind very highly. Some social services offices have their own money advice and welfare rights specialists, but these are uncommon. The part that social work has to play in ANTI-POVERTY STRATEGIES is as yet unclear and poorly developed.

M. Wolfe and J. Ivison, *Debt Advice Handbook*, London: Child Poverty Action Group, 1993.

**monitoring**   surveillance of a consumer of a social welfare or social work service or the general scrutiny of work to evaluate its effectiveness and efficiency.

In the first sense, monitoring applies to any situation where a person or family is watched in relation to some particular aspect of social functioning. For example, a child who has just started to attend school after a lengthy period of truanting may have their attendance monitored closely so that prompt intervention may be initiated in the event of further absences from school. Similarly, a family may be policed closely (perhaps with some form of help also being offered) following an incident of non-accidental injury to a child. Monitoring can also apply to standards within social welfare agencies. A general duty placed upon virtually all managers is to monitor the work of all those for whom they have line management responsibility. Elected councillors have this general duty on behalf of the public. There are an increasing number of people within social welfare agencies who have specific roles to play in monitoring processes: for example, ARM'S LENGTH INSPECTIONS and COMPLAINTS officers, lay visitors to prisons and police stations, and any manager with a quality assurance brief. The government has its own monitoring mechanisms, such as the SOCIAL SERVICES INSPECT-ORATE. Such monitoring seems to be preoccupied with value for money (efficiency), effectiveness (the evaluation function) and accountability (is work done according to standards laid down by the appropriate agency or government guidelines?).

**mood**   an emotional state that influences a person's thoughts and behaviour.

The basic division between good and bad moods refers to a number of different emotions. A good mood includes feelings of happiness, contentment, joy and cheerfulness. A bad mood can include feelings of irritability, depression, anxiety and anger. Social workers and social care workers frequently encounter people who have extreme moods – in which feelings of euphoria, excitement, anger or depression completely dominate their behaviour. These can arise from a variety of causes, such as SUBSTANCE MISUSE, MENTAL ILLNESS and BEREAVEMENT or other traumatic events.

**mood swings**   rapid changes between MOODS. Common examples are changes from feelings of elation to depression or from contentment to anger. Extreme mood swings can be a symptom of a MENTAL DISORDER.

**Moon**   a lesser-known form of tactile reading used by BLIND people, was devised by Dr William Moon.

Moon is based on a simplified form of the Latin alphabet and is easier to read than BRAILLE, although there is less literature available in Moon. Many older people find Moon quite easy to learn, and there is a new initiative to use Moon as a means of literacy for blind people with learning disabilities. Local authority social services departments have a duty to provide Moon teaching for visually disabled people.

**Motability**   the name of a voluntary organization set up to help people with disabilities to use their higher-rate MOBILITY COMPONENT. It offers lease hire or hire purchase of a new car in return for payment of the mobility component.

**motivation**   something that causes someone to do something. While motivation is easy to define in such global terms, however, it is harder to distinguish among potential motivators and identify the particular cause that could be said to have led a person to behave in a particular way.

One theory of motivation that has been influential is Maslow's 'hierarchy of needs', in which it is proposed that human needs can be placed in an order ranging from the most basic, such as thirst and hunger, to the highest, which is the need for self-actualization. According to this theory, a need further up the hierarchy becomes important as a motivator only when more basic ones have been fulfilled. It is true that explanations for behaviour can be seen to be of different types and may fall into different levels. At the most basic level, some behaviour, such as an eye-blink, is a reflex response to stimulus, such as a puff of air. But it is possible to override even a reflex; a person picking up a precious plate that is very hot is likely to try to put it down gently rather than drop it. At the next level, biological drives, such as hunger, can be seen to motivate behaviour. Once again, the dieter or the hunger striker demonstrates that one potential motivator can be countermanded by another, and so Maslow's hierarchy is not universally applicable. Beyond reflexes and biological drives, the identification of causes of behaviour becomes more problematic. Behaviourists have tried to identify secondary drives – those that, once fulfilled, could be used to satisfy a primary or biological drive. For example, money can be seen as a secondary drive that can be used to satisfy the primary drive of hunger. However, the argument becomes more circular when no obvious link between a piece of behaviour and a primary drive can be found. For example, when a child explores their environment, it adds little to say that the explanation for the child's behaviour is that they have a drive to explore.

The complexity of the subject of motivation can be seen from attempts to motivate people at work. Early researchers suggested that the way to motivate people to be more productive was to show them how to be more efficient and then pay them more for increased productivity. Later work showed, not surprisingly, that people differ; some are more affected by improvements in conditions at work, others by job satisfaction and yet others by job security. A key issue in social work is that of trying to establish how motivated service users are to try to change behaviour or circumstances that appear to be potentially within their control. Key questions are: can a person change, and do they want to change? To help service users in this regard, it is important to negotiate fully the nature both of the problems and of possible solutions. Motivation is more likely to be engaged if the person finds the issues relevant and the tasks achievable.

P. Evans, *Motivation and Emotion*, London: Routledge, 1989.

**mourning**   the process of adapting to the LOSS of an attachment figure, mainly, although not always, through death.

Grief accompanying a death is considered to be a departure from a state of well-being. Consequently, mourning is the process and period of restoring well-being. It has been suggested that mourning is a period of mental and physical activity during which a person accepts the reality of the loss, experiences the pain of grief, adjusts to an environment from which the deceased is absent and begins to invest their emotional energy in other people and activities. (See also BEREAVEMENT.)

W.J. Worden, *Grief Counselling and Grief Therapy*, London: Tavistock, 1982.

**multi-benefit assessment**   the computerized assessment, by some unitary authorities, of individuals' entitlement to all the MEANS-TESTED statutory and discretionary benefits and grants that they are responsible for administering, on the basis of one application.

Multi-benefit assessment has been developed as part of ANTI-POVERTY work and applies to such benefits and grants as HOUSING BENEFIT, COUNCIL TAX BENEFIT, FREE SCHOOL MEALS and house renovation grants. It is also used to advise on entitlement to Department of Social Security benefits such as INCOME SUPPORT and FAMILY CREDIT. It is hoped in this way to improve the take-up of benefits. Use of the same computer system would also afford an opportunity for sophisticated means tests to be used in the assessment of charges for local authority services.

**multidisciplinary work**   work undertaken jointly by workers and professionals from different disciplines or occupations.

In social work and in general social welfare provision, there is increasingly an expectation that services will be delivered collaboratively by several agencies or that a particular problem can be addressed only if professionals work together in the same organization or team. An example of the first approach is COMMUNITY CARE services involving collaboration between social services and health services in relation to vulnerable older people or those with chronic mental health problems. An example of the second is a CHILD GUIDANCE clinic, where social workers may be found in the same team as a psychologist, counsellors, psychiatrists, and so on. There are difficulties associated with multidisciplinary work. Sometimes professionals can disagree about the causes of and solutions to problems; they may have different objectives for their work; and there can be relational problems, for example because of differences in status, power and language. Multidisciplinary work requires effective decision-making and a clear allocation of roles and responsibilities.

**multi-infarct dementia**   DEMENTIA caused by disruption in the blood supply to the brain. The condition, which accounts for only 15 to 20 per cent of dementia, is observed as a series of minor 'strokes' that cumulatively result in an increase in mental impairment.

**Munchausen's syndrome by proxy**   a psychological condition in which the person feels compelled to engage in frequent contact with medical authorities such as hospitals and doctors. This is done 'by proxy' – by using someone else, almost always a child, as the person who requires medical attention rather than oneself.

A number of instances of CHILD ABUSE have been related to the syndrome, since the sufferer can actually harm the child in order to provide the reason for contacting the hospital or doctor. In extreme instances, protective action may have to be taken by the local authority.

# N

**National Assistance**   a scheme introduced by the National Assistance Act 1948, and forming part of the BEVERIDGE Plan, designed to provide a safety net for people with special needs or in situations not covered by the comprehensive scheme of social insurance introduced by the Labour government of 1945–50.

National Assistance became extremely complex as it attempted to meet the individual needs of recipients through additional weekly payments on top of the basic rates. It was replaced in 1966 by SUPPLEMENTARY BENEFIT, by which time weekly additions were paid to 60 per cent of claimants.

**National Association of Probation Officers (NAPO)**   the professional association and trade union representing all grades of probation officers and certain other PROBATION SERVICE employees.

Since NAPO was founded in 1912 it has provided a forum for the discussion of professional matters. It produces a monthly newsletter and the quarterly *Probation Journal*, holds annual conferences and also carries out trade union functions, negotiating pay and conditions of service on behalf of members. Since the 1970s NAPO has been viewed as politically radical, campaigning with other organizations on criminal justice matters and in the forefront of concerns about DISCRIMINATION against women, black people and lesbian and gay people. Closely allied to NAPO are two autonomous professional associations: the ASSOCIATION OF BLACK PROBATION OFFICERS and LESBIANS AND GAY MEN IN PROBATION.

**National Association of Social Workers in Education (NASWE)**   the professional organization for education social workers and education welfare officers. (There is also an education special interest group within the BRITISH ASSOCIATION OF SOCIAL WORKERS.)

NASWE represents its members' interests to the Department of Education, promotes good practice and, through a network of regional divisions, provides opportunities for training and professional development. It also publishes the quarterly journal *Education Social Worker*.

**National Health Service (NHS)**    the organization for the provision of state-funded health care. Established in 1948, the NHS aims to provide health care for all the population on the basis of need.

The original intention for the NHS was the provision of health care without reference to a person's ability to pay, based on the belief that expenditure would decrease as the population became healthier due to the benefits of the services provided. However, a number of significant problems emerged out of the original structure of the NHS. First, the service was centred on existing hospital provision, and there was therefore an uneven geographical distribution of resources. Second, demand for services proved to be greater than anticipated and expanded as new technologies emerged; this resulted in pressures on costs that led to the intention of providing free health care being undermined with the introduction of prescription charges shortly after the introduction of the service. Third, with the concentration on hospital services other areas of provision were overshadowed by developments in surgical and other interventionist procedures; the 'Cinderella' services included care for people with learning disabilities, mental health services and provision for older people.

The NHS became subject to an increasingly frequent series of reorganizations in order to tackle its problems, including the development of health authorities to replace hospital boards and a move to change the balance in resource distribution through the establishment of the Regional Allocation Working Party, which channelled resources towards underfunded areas. More recently, concerns with cost containment led to a major review of the service, resulting in the publication of a government policy statement, *Working for Patients*, in 1989. The most significant changes introduced by this review have included the following reforms: the introduction of an INTERNAL MARKET in which general practitioners and district health authorities purchase health services from hospitals, creating a PURCHASER/PROVIDER SPLIT within the NHS; the establishment of trusts in which hospitals and other services, including ambulance services and mental health hospitals, are managed independently of the health authorities; the introduction for some general practices of budgets that they have to manage themselves and from which they can purchase hospital services, screening services and sometimes the services of social workers and other carers. These changes have been criticized for potentially creating a two-tier system of health care in which resources are directed towards those hospital services with trust status and general practices that are budget- or fundholders. The government has argued that the changes will result in an improved service for patients in which the district health authorities and general practitioners act as 'champions' for the patient as customer. The internal market, according to this view, will help contain costs while promoting quality as money follows patients.

C. Ham, *The New National Health Service*, Oxford: Radcliffe Press, 1991.

**National Health Service and Community Care Act 1990**   an Act of
Parliament that makes additional provision for health authorities, such as
the establishment of NATIONAL HEALTH SERVICE trusts and the financing of
general practices, and additional powers concerning accommodation and
other welfare services provided by local authorities.

The government's proposals for COMMUNITY CARE in the next decade and
beyond rely on the continuing and developing partnership between local
authority social services departments and other agencies concerned with
health and social care. The philosophy underlying the Act is that of a user-
oriented service offering flexible and efficient matching of service to service
users' needs. The concept of partnership between social services
departments, the NHS, voluntary organizations concerned with health and
welfare, and independent, private and non-profit organizations is the key to
the success of the enactment of this legislation. The primary focus of the Act
is the reform of the organization and funding of social care.

The Act proposes six objectives for social services departments: first, to promote
the development of domiciliary, day and respite services to enable people to live
in their own homes wherever feasible and sensible; second, to ensure that service
providers make practical support for carers a high priority; third, to make proper
assessment of need and good case (care) management the cornerstone of high-
quality care; fourth, to promote the development of a flourishing independent
sector alongside good-quality public services; fifth, to clarify the responsibilities of
agencies and so make it easier to hold them to account for their performance; and
sixth, to secure better value for taxpayers' money by introducing a new funding
system for social care.

The Act proposes that service planning is rooted in an accurate assessment of
community care needs and individual care needs. The new role of care manager is
created to oversee some of the key tasks of this legislation and to ensure that
services are designed appropriate to need. Case (care) management should:
identify those people in the community in need; develop methods of referral that
ensure the accessibility of services for all in the community; plan and secure the
delivery of packages of care; monitor the quality of care provided; and review
service users' needs. The case (care) manager should ensure that services respond
flexibly and sensitively to need and allow a range of options for users. The
development of care packages should intervene in users' lives no more than is
necessary to foster independence and should be constructed with the active
involvement of service users, their carers and, where appropriate, an advocate.

Part III (chapter 19) of the Act specifies how community care services in
England and Wales are to develop. Part IV specifies the procedure for community
care in Scotland. These provisions are, in brief, as follows. The local authority is
liable 'to provide accommodation for persons aged 18 or over who are in need of
care and attention by reason of age, infirmity or other circumstances' (the local
authority may provide accommodation or purchase accommodation from others);
and it 'shall recover from each person for whom accommodation is provided
under the arrangements the amount of the refund which he is liable to make'
(allowing for recovery of all or part of the costs of residential care provided or
purchased by the local authority for service users). Section 3A(c) specifies the

liability of the local authority to make payments to service providers of all or part of the costs of providing social care. Section 43 allows for the exclusion of provision of accommodation in certain cases. Section 44 specifies a person's liability to pay for accommodation under Part III of the 1948 National Assistance Act. Section 45 allows for the 'recovery of sums due to local authorities where persons in residential accommodation have disposed of assets', and 'arrears of contributions' can be 'charged on interests in land in England, Wales and Scotland respectively', together with appropriate rates of interest. Section 46 specifies the devising of local authority plans for community care services; local authorities should draw up community care plans after wide consultations with all interested parties in the community. Section 47 specifies the duty of the local authority to carry out assessment of an individual's care needs 'where it appears to a local authority that any person for whom they may provide or arrange for the provision of community care services may be in need of such services', and 'having regard to the results of that assessment, [the local authority] shall then decide whether his needs call for the provision by them of any such services'; this section allows for the development of multi-agency assessments whereby the local authority can invite the district health authority and/or the local housing authority to take part in the assessment of community care needs for individuals. Section 48 allows for the registration and inspection of community care premises (residential and day) in order that those premises can be examined as to their fitness for the provision of care facilities; inspection officers can examine premises and records, request information, have access to information stored on computer, and interview residents and/or users; premises found to be failing in any of their social care activities may have their registration certificate withdrawn.

Community care is not a new concept. In 1959 the Mental Health Act attempted to implement community care strategies for people with mental health problems; and in 1968 Lord SEEBOHM noted that the intended new social services departments should accept a 'wider responsibility for the community and for the mobilization of community services'. In 1981 the government report *Care in Action* identified that in all major client (user) groups the main strategies for caring would involve a change in the balance of care. An increasing proportion of people would be cared for by domiciliary and day care services in their own homes, with a corresponding reduction in institutional services. The AUDIT COMMISSION noted in 1987 that there needed to be a major shift in service delivery from health to community-based services; but by 1985 domiciliary services were struggling to keep up with both the increase in numbers of older people in the community and also with the rapid discharge of older people from long-stay hospital wards. The 1982 BARCLAY Committee noted that the role of the social worker would change from one of service delivery by personal intervention to one of managing interventions by using community resources to provide support systems for vulnerable individuals. A community-based social work service means the organization of services at a local level, a recognizable contact point in neighbourhoods and a synthesis of domiciliary services with informal and formal caring services. All of this requires delegation of resources and decision-making. The National Health Service and Community Care Act attempts to achieve many of the above objectives, but the key to successful health and community services may be the joint planning of services, shared funding and visible accountability – all of which have been difficult to achieve in the past.

Department of Health, *Caring for People: Community Care in the Next Decade and Beyond*, London: HMSO, 1989.

**National Institute of Social Work (NISW)**   an independent institute concerned with the identification and promotion of good practice in social work.

The main objectives of the NISW are centred on the development of good practice through research, consultancy and training. Through the dissemination of good practice the institute aims to encourage social work agencies to be responsive to users, carers and their communities. The NISW contributes information and expertise to the development of social work policy and its implementation through a variety of approaches, including an information service for members and the development of in-house training programmes to improve the effectiveness of social work staff.

The NISW has a number of specialist units to help achieve its aims, including the following. Its Social Care Unit is intended to enhance good practice through consultancy, in-house training programmes and networking. Its Race Equality Unit provides advice, consultancy and support for the implementation of race equality policies. Its Education and Staff Development Unit provides a post-qualifying course, approved by the Central Council for Education and Training in Social Work, in staff development and training for future trainers, as well as other short courses for managers and practising social workers. The NISW also has an important Research Unit, largely funded by the Department of Health, that has worked on a range of issues including those relating to frail older people and residential care. The results of the research are disseminated through the institute's publications or through the sponsoring department by HMSO. The NISW publishes a regular series of papers on training, management and policy issues, as well as providing a library and information service.

**National Insurance benefits**   a phrase sometimes used to describe all non-MEANS-TESTED benefits, that is, contributory and non-contributory benefits.

**national standards**   a set of extensive government guidelines and requirements regulating practice in the PROBATION SERVICE and in the social services in relation to the supervision of offenders in the community and the preparation of PRE-SENTENCE REPORTS for criminal courts.

The national standards were issued jointly by the HOME OFFICE, the Department of Health and the Welsh Office in 1992 to coincide with the implementation of the CRIMINAL JUSTICE ACT 1991. Their stated objectives are to provide a clear framework of expectations and requirements for supervision, to facilitate professional judgement within a framework of accountability, to encourage the development of good practice and to ensure service delivery that is fair, consistent and without DISCRIMINATION. They are intended for use by sentencers, offenders and the general public, as well as by probation officers, social workers and other criminal justice agents. In short, they constitute the equivalent of a 'citizen's charter' for these aspects of the CRIMINAL JUSTICE SYSTEM. In relation to pre-sentence reports, the national standards set out expectations about both the process (impartiality, speed of preparation and depth of inquiry) and the content of reports (relevance of information, focus on offences, proposals for disposal).

In relation to supervision of offenders in the community on various court orders, the national standards highlight the need for supervision to commence promptly, for frequent appointments, for the drawing up of a supervision plan, for good record-keeping and for effective enforcement of the order, including breach proceedings. The national standards reflect the desire of the government to make the Probation Service accountable for the provision of a consistent and closely scrutinized service. Critics argue that they stifle initiative and creativity in work with offenders and erode professional autonomy.

**National Vocational Qualification (NVQ)** a qualification very closely related to particular areas of employment, based upon defined competences that are the result of functional analyses of jobs and occupations. Such qualifications are accredited by the National Council for Vocational Qualifications.

National Vocational Qualifications have been developed as a result of dissatisfaction on the part of employers and government concerning traditional training and education for a wide variety of occupations. The basic concern has been that traditional preparation for work has often not reflected contemporary needs of employers. Additionally, qualifications have mushroomed, often with a lack of clarity about their value within a generally accepted framework. To prepare for NVQs, occupations have been analysed to determine what workers in particular jobs actually do or are required to do; that is, a functional analysis is completed to reveal the specific competences required for particular jobs. Training packages are then devised (underpinning knowledge) to help people acquire defined competences. A competence can be demonstrated by reference to characteristic performance criteria. Although formal courses have been devised to meet the competences required for particular jobs, it has been recognized that people can acquire skills in other ways – for example, through practical, work or even life experiences. NVQs are currently awarded at five levels. Within the areas of social work, social care and social welfare the CARE SECTOR CONSORTIUM developed the first awards in SOCIAL CARE. More and more NVQs are now being developed to encourage joint training in the fields of social care and health, particularly in the light of COMMUNITY CARE initiatives. The DIPLOMA IN SOCIAL WORK is graded as level four.

Opinion is divided about the value of NVQs as educational and training packages. Supporters have it that people can have their skills recognized, that training has become relevant, that an overall framework has been established into which many levels of activities can be fitted and that a good deal of knowledge has become 'demystified'. Those who are sceptical about NVQs argue that education has become training, that it is excessively mechanistic and that people are not encouraged to think critically or imaginatively about what they do.

**nature–nurture debate** the debate concerning the extent to which individual characteristics can be attributed to the influence of biological, genetic or innate factors (nature) as distinct from the influence of environmental factors (nurture).

Much of the debate has centred around psychological factors such as PERSONALITY and intelligence, and it clearly may be perceived as having important repercussions for many aspects of SOCIAL POLICY such as compensatory education. If, for example, intelligence can be enhanced by having particular environments, then educationalists would want to create those environments for all children, regardless of their background.

Some psychologists argue that individual characteristics are fixed, and others argue that they can be changed. A further dispute concerns the extent of possible change, some believing that substantial change is possible while others have it that minimal change only is possible. Most agree that these issues are very difficult to unravel because most people (with the exceptions of identical twins, triplets, and so on) both are genetically unique and have a unique environmental experience too. There is also increasing recognition that a poor environment that gives rise to, say, certain health problems can affect the genetic characteristics passed from one generation to another.

**needs** the necessary requirements for maintaining life at a certain standard.

To have a need means requiring something in order to live a life to some agreed standard. This standard may be little more than subsistence living, such as provided by the nineteenth-century workhouse for its inmates. Or the standard may be higher and relate to a person's well-being or fulfilment in life. Debates over the concept of need always centre on the question of what this standard should be and who should define it. Often the standards for determining need are set by a mixture of influences, such as social consensus, Acts of Parliament, activist groups and professionals in the field. As a result, what constitutes need changes over time. A good example is provided by campaigns against DOMESTIC VIOLENCE and the need for physical safety and for safe places, such as a women's refuge (see WOMEN'S AID), where women and children can safely stay for a period. Such a need was scarcely recognized twenty years ago, although it is now widely accepted.

Needs, or what a person requires, are often distinguished in theory from 'wants', or what a person prefers or desires. In practice, however, defining what a person needs as opposed to what they want is fraught with difficulty. For example, a homeless person can be said to need shelter, but shelter can mean many things: a temporary bed in a hostel, a room in BED AND BREAKFAST accommodation, a permanently rented room, a rented flat or an owner-occupied house. What are the real needs of a homeless person and who decides?

In the attempt to resolve some of the conflicts over the definition of needs, a classification has been developed consisting of: *normative needs*, that is, needs as defined by a norm or standard set by professionals; *felt needs*, which individuals declare as their needs (the same as 'wants'); *expressed needs*, that is, felt needs turned into a demand through some action; and *comparative needs*, which are defined by the fact that others, living in the same conditions, have been recognized as having a similar need and receive a service.

Most people meet their needs through their own efforts, through family or friends, or through arrangements they make themselves. Social workers and social care professionals, however, often work with clients and service users who, for a variety of reasons, have many basic needs that they have not been able to meet themselves. Workers decide what these needs are through ASSESSMENT. They often have to consider a broad range of needs, such as physical care, the provision of shelter and food, cultural and religious sustenance, emotional and psychological needs arising from isolation or violent personal relationships, and social contacts. Very often clients in the same household have different needs that have to be met in different ways. Because needs are so much a matter of interpretation, it is essential that service users should participate in the process of deciding what their needs are, and that their wishes and preferences be taken into account. Welfare professionals have in the past often interpreted a person's needs in terms of the services that they could offer. Thus a frail older person might have been assessed as 'needing' a place in a day care centre or in a residential home, rather than the worker looking at what specific care needs they had and then deciding how these might best be met. The only way to overcome this is to consult closely with users, to include their wishes and preferences and to think how they might be most suitably met.

When social workers define need they do so on the basis of the definitions used by their agency and from formal guidance from the Department of Health. For example, when working with children and families in general social workers focus on the care and developmental needs of the children to ensure that each child's development is broadly in line with national averages. The needs of a child or family are assessed by a social worker and others before the family can receive services to help them look after that child. Typically these needs may include such factors as any lack of skills on the part of the child's parents, as well as any educational or health needs. When working with adults, practitioners concentrate on those needs that will allow the person to live as independently as possible. The Department of Health has outlined six broad areas of adult need that should be assessed: personal and social care; health care; accommodation; finance; education, employment and leisure; transport, mobility and access.

Needs can be met only if resources are there to enable this to be done. Because resources are so limited, social services professionals have often used a system of prioritizing needs and of developing criteria for eligibility; this invariably places greatest importance on the need to protect the health and physical safety of the client, and less importance on those needs that would improve the person's well-being but are not essential to their physical survival. At the same time, there are opportunities to widen the definitions of need. Groups of users are urging this across a number of services, including those for children and families, disabled people and people with MENTAL HEALTH PROBLEMS. Such groups can be involved in setting local policies on need, since COMMUNITY CARE reforms in particular envisage a growth of new services from the independent sector. (See also SPECIAL EDUCATIONAL NEEDS.)

B. Taylor and T. Devine, *Assessing Needs and Planning Care*, Aldershot: Arena, 1993

**needs-led assessment** ASSESSMENT that defines an individual's real NEEDS and not just their needs in terms of services that the local authority has to offer.

One of the common failings of local authority assessments before the introduction of COMMUNITY CARE reforms was that they viewed needs purely in terms of the services the local authorities had to offer. Thus a person with a LEARNING DISABILITY was declared as 'needing' a place in a training centre, regardless of whether the centre helped such people overcome their disability. The individual's need was defined in terms of the service available ('Mr X needs a place in a day centre'), rather than in terms that specified the needs of the individual ('Mr X needs to learn to recognize coins of different denominations' or 'Mr X lacks the skills to make basic purchases at his local shop and needs to acquire those skills'). The tendency to define need in terms of available services was heavily criticized as a way of protecting the interests of local authority staff; on this basis, the beds of residential units were filled, as were places at day centres, thus apparently demonstrating need for such establishments. One of the basic community care reforms aimed to make the assessment function independent of providing a service (see PURCHASER/PROVIDER), so that an independent judgement of need could be reached, taking into account the person's own view, instead of their needs being expressed simply in terms of existing service interests. For example, a frail, older person who is socially isolated may have a need for regular social contact that could be met by arranging regular outings with family or friends rather than by offering a place in a day centre.

Department of Health, *Community Care in the Next Decade and Beyond: Policy Guidance*, London: HMSO, 1990.

**neighbourhood offices** local authority service centres for relatively small geographical areas, usually of cities. The particular mix of services offered by these offices varies but typically includes housing, social services and environmental health.

Local authorities that have taken the decision to establish neighbourhood offices have done so because of a commitment to the decentralization of services and because they believe that anti-poverty strategies can be enhanced, such as through benefit take-up campaigns and money advice services offered locally. Temporary neighbourhood offices are also sometimes established to help an area deal with major urban renewal or redevelopment – for example, when housing is to be improved or demolished but local people will resettle in the area when the work is completed.

**network conference** a gathering of people, often family but including 'significant others', associated with a particular young person, meeting together in an attempt to solve accommodation and related problems of the YOUNG PERSON.

The idea of a network conference was developed from that of the family conference, a method of working adopted by New Zealand statutory child-care agencies in the mid- and late 1980s. Family conferences are rooted in Maori practices whereby extended families meet together to attempt to solve family problems. Such an approach, adopted by social workers, significantly increased the power of families to devise acceptable, and often novel, solutions to child-care issues. The same principles and procedures, with some adaptations, are being used with the problem of homelessness among young people. In this case, professional workers, in consultation with the young homeless person, convene conferences of family members and other people who are important to the young person (hence the use of the term 'network'). Network conferences are organized by workers who will provide key information (about possible resources for example) to the conference, which may help in devising solutions to the homeless person's problems; but it is the responsibility of the conference to try to find solutions. With its clear shift of power away from professionals towards individuals, families and significant others in the 'network', many see this way of working as an example of SELF-HELP and genuine PARTNERSHIP.

**neuroses**  a group of MENTAL DISORDERS with symptoms of long-term ANXIETY, nervousness, irritability, and constant worry about physical health.

Neurotic behaviour is quite common. Most people at some point in their lives show some forms of excessive worry, nervousness, anger or irritability, sleeplessness, or repeating the same thoughts over and over at times. All of these can be examples of neurotic behaviours when they do nothing to help resolve the problems or stresses facing us. In this sense, neurotic behaviour can be described as *maladaptive*, that is, an inadequate or inappropriate method of coping with the stress. The neuroses are extreme form of neurotic behaviour and are so designated at that point when they disrupt a person's capacity to lead a normal life, interfering with tasks and responsibilities, enjoyments and self-esteem, and leading to self-imposed regimes of isolation and repetitive behaviour and thoughts. The most commonly found neuroses are anxiety and DEPRESSION, which are thought to underlie most other neuroses, such as EATING DISORDERS, compulsive behaviour and HYSTERIA.

A. Butler and C. Pritchard, Social Work and Mental Illness, Basingstoke: Macmillan, 1981.

**New Right**  political, social and economic policies developed during the 1980s based on a belief that the MARKET is generally the best means of enhancing human well-being – because individual self-reliance is fostered by reducing state welfare services and benefits – and that state intervention should be kept to a minimum. The term also refers to people and organizations holding and practising these ideas and policies.

The term New Right is used to distinguish the policies of a group of economists, SOCIAL POLICY advocates and politicians who are on the right or conservative end of the political spectrum but depart radically from much of traditional conservative policy. From the end of the Second World War, British conservatives had largely supported the aims of the welfare state and thus were part of a broad political consensus that sought to develop it. The New Right advanced a radical set of ideas that broke with this consensus, believing that the market provided the most efficient way of producing and allocating goods and services and seeking to create conditions where markets could function without interference. It advocated widespread deregulation and privatization of state-owned industry, such as telecommunications and public utilities, which it thought had been hobbled in their economic performance by political considerations when under state control. It also favoured reducing public expenditure (except notably on defence) and introducing tax cuts to allow consumers greater choice. In the field of social welfare the New Right viewed the welfare state as responsible for creating a sense of dependency among claimants, arguing that claimants had little incentive to work because of the welfare benefits system. The New Right's view was that welfare institutions were bureaucratic, offered little choice and were often run to protect the special interests of the professionals employed by them. The introduction of market reforms was to be a means of overcoming all of these defects.

> Politically, the implmentation of New Right policies is largely associated with the Thatcher government in Britain and the Reagan and Bush presidencies in the United States; but similar policies of privatization and welfare state retrenchment can be found in many, if not most, industrialized countries. Although the New Right apparently had great impact throughout the 1980s, more sober assessments of its influence have recognized that welfare policies and institutions were not cut as severely as first thought and that the tax cuts of the late 1980s contributed, via excessive levels of consumer spending and debt, to the deep recession of the early 1990s.
>
> C. Pierson, *Beyond the Welfare State*, Cambridge: Polity Press, 1991.

**nicotine**  a stimulant found in tobacco, largely responsible for causing ADDICTION to cigarettes, both physical and psychological. Stopping smoking can cause temporary WITHDRAWAL effects that include nausea, weight gain, insomnia and irritability.

Nicotine is usually smoked in cigarette form, in cigars or in a pipe. It can also be sniffed as snuff or chewed, as with chewing tobacco. Although it is legal, its sale is restricted to people over 16 years of age. Effects include an increase in concentration and a decrease in fatigue and tension, along with physical influences such as an increase in blood pressure and heart rate, and urine retention. Long-term effects are well documented and include ulcers, coronary thrombosis, angina, high blood pressure, strokes and associated diseases of the heart and circulation. For those wishing to give up smoking, various nicotine aids such as patches and chewing gum are available as a means of gradually weaning users off the substance. 'Quit smoking' groups are sometimes available through the local health authority as an additional aid. RELAPSE is common with smoking, and users may make several attempts before being successful.

**night shelter**  temporary accommodation for homeless, usually single, people.

Such accommodation is invariably very basic, organized in dormitories and, as the name implies, unavailable for shelter in daylight hours. Meals and bathing facilities are often available too, and some night shelters have second-hand clothing stores. Night shelters are mostly offered by the voluntary sector, with religious organizations like the Salvation Army playing a prominent role. Staffing is often dependent upon VOLUNTEER effort. A limited number of night shelters have connections with longer-term housing projects that seek to help provide more stability in relation to accommodation for the rootless. (See also VAGRANCY.)

**non-contributory benefits**    benefits to which entitlement depends only on personal circumstances and not on any means test. Such benefits include CHILD BENEFIT, DISABILITY LIVING ALLOWANCE, attendance allowance, INVALID CARE ALLOWANCE and SEVERE DISABLEMENT ALLOWANCE.

**non-dependent deductions**    deductions from HOUSING BENEFIT, COUNCIL TAX BENEFIT and INCOME SUPPORT paid to cover housing costs that are made in respect of people living in the same household who are not the claimant's dependants (for example, grown-up children).

The amount deducted depends on the person's circumstances and on their earnings if they work.

**non-judgemental attitude**    a predisposition not to regard a person as guilty or blameworthy; the avoidance of thoughts that attach guilt or innocence to people or their behaviour.

This principle of social work practice is amenable to several interpretations. To some, it comes close to the idea of ACCEPTANCE, that is, seeing people as human beings and also as they actually are. To others, it means not judging, because we cannot ever know everything and therefore can never fully understand, rendering judgement inappropriate. Pragmatists would argue that the line between judgement and decisions about the need to intervene is often fine, because many behaviours are actually unacceptable to the public; this therefore in a sense requires judgements by social workers. (See also ETHICAL CODE, VALUES.)

**non-molestation order**    see INJUNCTION.

**normalization**    a concept (originating in Scandinavia and further developed in North America) that emphasizes the desirability for people with LEARNING DISABILITY to live a lifestyle as close as possible to the norms of the surrounding society.

Normalization has become associated with a recognition of the importance of choice, dignity and respect for people with learning disability and of the need for their integration with the rest of society. In terms of service provision this involves service users living in ordinary housing and being offered the opportunity to develop relationships with other members of society in the same way as anyone else. Normalization also acknowledges the need for people with learning disability to be treated in a way that is suitable for their chronological age (see AGE APPROPRIATENESS) and to be allowed to take risks and to speak for themselves.

Wolfensberger, who was responsible for developing and publicizing the concept of normalization, later refined it further using the phrase *social role valorization* (often referred to as SRV) to describe 'the creation, support and defence of valued social roles for people who are at risk of devaluation'. Wolfensberger and his team have also established methods of measuring how far services meet normalization criteria, and these are known as PASS and PASSING.

> Criticisms of normalization and SRV are frequently associated with the fact that these principles stress the importance of conformity to social norms. It has been pointed out that what is normal within a particular culture may be of questionable value to some people within that culture. A philosophy that stresses conformity to current social norms is essentially conservative and can be seen as operating to the detriment of the devalued groups to which people with learning disability may belong. This effect has been highlighted as regards black and ethnic-minority communities by some writers who have pointed out that service providers may take white values as the norm and impose them on service users for whom they are inappropriate.
>
> C. Baxter, K. Poonia, L. Ward, Z. Nadirshaw, *Double Discrimination: Issues and Services for People with Learning Difficulties from Black and Ethnic Minority Communities*, London: King's Fund Centre and Commission for Racial Equality, 1990.

**notification** an action on the part of medical practitioners who come into contact with people they believe to be addicted to certain named DRUGS. Medical practitioners are required to notify the chief medical officer at the Home Office of the ADDICTION.

The most usual notifiable drugs are heroin and cocaine. A specially printed form is used. The purpose of notification is twofold: first for statistical reasons, so that annual changes in the use of different substances can be noted; second, for general practitioners and other doctors to check whether or not a patient is already being prescribed medication from another source. In spite of this, some users of illegal substances are frightened of presenting themselves to services for help, as they think notification will mean, for example, that the police or social services will be informed. This is not so, and strict medical confidentiality applies to all information received.

**nurseries** facilities providing supervised day care for preschool children (normally aged under 5), run either by local authorities (usually by social services departments, although a few facilities are jointly run with education departments) or privately. Children may attend on a full-time or part-time basis.

A high proportion of nursery staff have qualifications in nursery nursing and increasingly they are required to work in collaboration with other social welfare workers such as social workers, health visitors and other medical staff. Local authority provision increasingly focuses upon children who are 'at risk' (that is, children who have been abused or neglected), have special needs (usually meaning some kind of disability) or are understimulated, or where there is some developmental delay, or because of the particular social and economic circumstances of parents. Care is therefore seen to be compensatory in some cases to help with a 'deficit' in a child's life. In others it may be to help 'rehabilitate' a child from care, while in yet others it could be to supplement the care provided by a parent or carer that is in some sense insufficient (such as with a parent who has a mental health problem). Private or voluntary nurseries may be run by employers (workplace nurseries), by community organizations and by private individuals as a business. Such provision is much more likely to be for the children of working parents. Private and voluntary nurseries are required to register with local authorities, which will inspect their provision and facilities at regular intervals.

Although the bulk of the work undertaken in nurseries is with children, some nurseries also attempt to work with parents and carers. Here the focus is on physical care, domestic skills, PLAY and the emotional needs of children. A few nurseries are located within FAMILY CENTRES, where much work is done directly with children, some with parents and children, and some with parents as individuals (that is, activities for the enjoyment of adults or for their needs apart from parenting needs).

The provision of nurseries in Britain is poor, with less than 2 per cent of the age group catered for, although there is considerable variation from area to area. In general, urban areas have more generous provision than rural areas, with some rural authorities having no provision at all. It is very difficult to estimate the extent of unmet need or demand, but it is considerable. Existing provision is often rationed to cope with known demand, and waiting lists are invariably very long. (See also TOY LIBRARY, UNDER–5S PROVISION.)

B. Owen, *Caring for Children*, London: Family Policy Studies Centre, 1988.

**nursing home**   a residential facility for the nursing care of people experiencing sickness, injury or infirmity.

Nursing homes must be registered with the secretary of state under the REGISTERED HOMES ACT 1984. It is an offence to operate a nursing home without registration, and the certificate of registration must be displayed in a prominent place. The Act, which replaces the Nursing Homes Act 1975, makes provision for the registration and inspection of residential care homes offering both living and personal care for four or more people. Nursing homes may offer specialized care, as do maternity homes, homes for elderly people and homes that offer medical treatment. Registration can be refused if the applicant is considered unfit to run the home or if the conditions of the home are unsatisfactory. A first-level nurse (state registered nurse or registered general nurse) must be in charge throughout the day, but if the authority so decides, and dependent upon the purpose of the nursing home, a second-level nurse (state enrolled nurse) may be in charge at night with a senior nurse on call. Registration can be refused if these conditions are not met.

The Registered Homes Act 1984 has been supported by a code of practice: *HOME LIFE*. This code specifies fourteen areas of good practice relevant to nursing homes, which include inspection, registration, furniture and equipment, services, food, facilities, provision of linen and laundry, and the disposal of waste materials. The guidelines also cover the control of infection and of drugs, fire safety, accident prevention, records, notification of death, and complaints. The code recommends that the environment should, as far as possible, be domestic in character and enable patients to retain their individuality and self-respect, with consideration of comfort, privacy, cleanliness and safety apparent. Long-stay residents of nursing homes should be encouraged to bring personal possessions into the home with them. Guidelines for the inspection of quality in nursing homes were issued by the Social Services Inspectorate in 1991 and laid a duty on directors of social services to set up and maintain specialized units for the registration and inspection of nursing and residential care homes.

*Home Life: A Code of Practice for Residential Care*, report of a working party sponsored by the Department of Health and Social Security and convened by the Centre for Policy on Ageing under the chairmanship of Kina, Lady Avebury, London: Centre for Policy on Ageing, 1984.

*O*

**object relations theory** the theory that an infant's relationships with family members have a continuing influence throughout life.

Object relations theory was developed by a group of British psychoanalysts in the 1940s and 1950s. Within PSYCHOANALYSIS 'object' refers to people other than ourselves, in the sense that they are the objects of our desires and sources of gratification as children. 'Object relations' then meant relations with those closest to us in infancy and early childhood, particularly mother, father and siblings. The object relations school expanded psychoanalysis in the sense that it emphasized the importance of these relationships themselves and moved away from the view that a child only uses the people close to them for their own gratification. The theory made a huge impact on the development of social work theory and could be said to have dominated theories in the 1950s of what social work should try to achieve. As a result of this influence, work with individuals focused on their damaged early relationships and how such relationships continued to affect their adult relationships by setting up expectations and patterns that were difficult to change. Only through the relationship formed between therapist and patient, between social worker and client, were the damaged contents of the person's early relationships to be re-examined and their power reduced. Object relations theory has continued to have influence in particular strands of social work and PSYCHOTHERAPY, notably in feminist counselling.

**occupational therapy** a rehabilitative profession concerned to help people recover from illness or to adapt to or cope with a disability.

Occupational therapy is one of the three rehabilitative professions recognized by the NATIONAL HEALTH SERVICE (with physiotherapy and speech therapy). It is equally represented in physical medicine and psychiatry.

Occupational services are also provided by SOCIAL SERVICES DEPARTMENTS. The occupation has a practical emphasis and is concerned with the problems and activities of daily living. In hospital settings with the focus upon physical problems, occupational therapy typically includes retraining for daily living skills (for example, washing and dressing), the prescription of therapeutic activities (for example, artwork, woodwork, group discussion) and provision of orthotics (for example, splints) and prostheses (for example, walking sticks and wheelchairs). In psychiatry occupational therapy is concerned with the provision of therapeutic activities, skills training for a return to the community and possibly some aspects of PSYCHOTHERAPY. Patients within the community receive occupational therapy from social services departments. A wide range of AIDS AND ADAPTATIONS to buildings to enhance daily living and the quality of life are the major concerns for this work. Close collaboration with social workers within adult teams is necessary for the effective ASSESSMENT of needs.

A. Turner, M. Foster and S. Johnson, *Occupational Therapy and Physical Dysfunction*, Edinburgh: Churchill Livingstone, 1992.

**offence**    a breach of the criminal law, infringing either statute law (Acts of Parliament) or common law (law that has developed through the centuries by judges' decisions in the absence of statute).

An offence may be described as summary, indictable or triable either way. Summary offences (such as motoring, minor assault and criminal damage) can be dealt with only in the MAGISTRATES' court. Indictable offences (such as murder, rape and robbery) can be dealt with only in the Crown Court. Most offences are triable either way, and their final venue depends on the choice of the defendant and/or the decision of the magistrates. (See CRIMINAL COURTS.)

**older people**    women and men who have usually retired from active participation in the labour force or have attained state pension age or both.

The term 'older people' is interchangeable with 'elderly', 'old persons', 'older adults', 'third age' and 'senior citizens', but it is the term favoured by Age Concern. There are considerable problems in defining the point at which people become 'older people'. Social, cultural, economic and health factors all categorize older people in differing ways. Conventional retirement ages can be misleading, and 'retirement' may erroneously be used to label women and men who continue to work in the domestic environment and/or change their occupation after the age of 60 or 65 years. It has been pointed out that definitions of older age present complex issues of how society views later life and AGEING. Attention is generally focused on the negative aspects of ageing, such as illness, poverty and incapacity, However, 85 per cent of people over 65 years are *not* housebound; 60 per cent of people over 70 do *not* report ill-health or disability; and 95 per cent of people over 65 do *not* report psychiatric disorder. Nevertheless, for 70 per cent of people over 65 older age is likely to be associated with poverty. Stereotypes of ageing rooted in notions of poverty and incapacity often confront older people with insensitive interactions, DISCRIMINATION and social inequality.

There is an increasing trend to view older people in the population as a social problem in terms of health and social security needs. This view reflects the increasing numbers of women and men now living to 60 years and beyond. Older people are seen erroneously, in terms of a 'burden of dependency' on society. Increases in life expectancy reflect improvements in health care and in the quality of life since 1945; hence, older people should be viewed not as dependants but as embodying successful social policies. The increased longevity of women and men has, however, contributed to a gender imbalance at ages 69 and above. Women live longer than men; at age 85, for every 100 men there are 325 women, and at age 75+, 80 per cent of women are likely to be single widowed or divorced. This means that ageist assumptions may combine with gender oppression for older women, adversely affecting their quality of life.

Both the diversity and the homogeneity of older people need to be acknowledged. What older people have in common is that they have significantly less income than others. They are denied the opportunity to earn more and are on the margins of the labour market. However, they experience greater freedom than younger people and take on the task of organizing their own lives. The diversity of older people's lives seems to reflect their class position, gender, prior occupation, health status, housing, financial resources, personal talents and personality. Family networks and responsibilities vary, as do attitudes and motivations. Social and family roles, status and access to choice also vary. Hence, the lives of older people are as varied as those of younger people.

The increasing numbers of older people, currently and projected into the next century, have implications for the social work task, for resource allocation and planning of social services, for increased use of primary health care and hospital facilities, and for the older person's family and care networks. The NATIONAL HEALTH SERVICE AND COMMUNITY CARE ACT 1990 specifies that older people requesting domiciliary or residential care services should be assessed according to need. Such requests may accompany their discharge from hospital or arise directly from a need for assistance at home. The extent of the assessment will vary, from details about mobility for a parking card, to a full multi-agency ASSESSMENT for a person who has major health and social care needs. Social workers are the people most likely to undertake assessments, although in particularly complex situations a care manager may be appointed. The latter may be a member of the health service, if an older person has health concerns. The multi-agency assessment will involve health and social services personnel. Following the assessment, the purchaser/provider arrangements of the 1990 Act mean that social services are likely to purchase the care services that an older person needs from independent, voluntary and/or non-profit care providers. The 1990 Act specifies that needs and services should be reviewed at intervals to ensure that allocated resources continue to reflect need accurately.

These complex social work tasks are undertaken in partnership with the older person, their carer and other concerned people, such as family members and possibly neighbourhood services. Social workers need a broad spread of skills and knowledge to carry out this work: counselling skills; knowledge of resources; knowledge of welfare benefits; coordination and liaison skills; assessment skills;

knowledge of relevant legislation; and a commitment to the values of partnership and choice embodied in the 1990 Act.

J. Bond and P. Coleman, *Ageing in Society: An Introduction to Social Gerontology*, London: Sage, 1990.

**ombudsman**   a government official who investigates COMPLAINTS of maladministration made by members of the public against benefit authorities, including, for example, complaints about delays in dealing with claims.

The ombudsman does not investigate any matter where there is a right of appeal. If the ombudsman finds that there has been maladministration, they will recommend action by the authority, including an apology and possibly compensation. There are two ombudsmen concerned with benefit administration. The Parliamentary Commissioner for Administration investigates complaints against the various executive agencies of the Department of Social Security; these complaints should be made through a constituency Member of Parliament, who will normally seek solutions direct from the agency in the first instance. The Commissioner for Local Administration investigates complaints against local authorities; these complaints should first of all be made directly to the authority, but if still dissatisfied the complainant can then approach the ombudsman.

**one-parent benefit**   a benefit paid on top of CHILD BENEFIT in respect of the first or only child, paid only to a person who is living with the child and is not living with a spouse or anyone else as husband or wife.

If the person is recently separated, one-parent benefit is not paid for the first thirteen weeks unless a legal order is obtained.

**open adoption**   an ADOPTION in which the natural parents retain some involvement in the life of their child during and after adoption.

Historically, adoption was based on the complete anonymity of the adoptive parents, and the child's natural parents knew nothing about the family that adopted their child. The term 'open adoption' covers a number of changes in the adoption process that in one way or another break down this anonymity. This can happen in several ways. The birth parent can be actively involved in hearing about and choosing the adoptive parents through written profiles and face-to-face meetings with them, or there can simply be an exchange of non-identifying information between the two sets of parents. Most commonly an open adoption enables some form of link to be retained between the adopted child and their natural parents after the adoption is completed. Legally this is now possible in England and Wales, since a court can make a CONTACT ORDER in favour of the natural parents at the same time as granting the ADOPTION ORDER on the child. Such contact might involve letters, the exchange of gifts or face-to-face meetings.

The practice of open adoption is increasingly favoured as a result of numerous studies that have highlighted the destructive impact of the secrecy and anonymity surrounding adoption. For the adoptive child this meant knowing nothing of their family identity. The secrecy and evasiveness often required to keep the child from finding out anything about their origins is thought to have frequently been the source of behavioural and emotional difficulties for the child. Similarly, studies of the mothers of adopted children have indicated that they frequently suffered lifelong distress as a consequence of their decision. The practice of open adoption is designed to limit these painful consequences, to allow the child to retain a sense of identity and family origin and to facilitate communication between parent and child after the latter has reached maturity.

A. Mullender (ed.), *Open Adoption: The Philosophy and Practice*, London: British Agencies for Adoption and Fostering, 1991.

**open system**   a system that does not have rigid or closed boundaries and can therefore exchange information, concepts, resources and energy with the environment around it, allowing it to adapt to changes in the environment that ensure its survival (see SYSTEMS APPROACH).

**operant conditioning**   learning strategies in which the person or animal must act on a stimulus to obtain a reinforcement. The reinforcement increases the likelihood of the behavioural strategy occurring again.

Operant conditioning has its theoretical origins in Thorndike's 'law of effect' (1898), which states that behavioural responses that achieve a satisfactory effect are likely to occur again, while those responses that elicit a discomforting effect are less likely to be repeated. B.F. Skinner (1904–90) is the psychologist credited with the development of theories of operant conditioning during the twentieth century.

**opiates**   a group of sedative DRUGS derived from the opium poppy and used medicinally in the treatment of extreme pain, as cough suppressants and for diarrhoea. Most are prescription only, but some mild forms are available over the counter in combination with other constituents.

Examples of opiates include HEROIN, opium and morphine. Opiates can be both physically and psychologically ADDICTIVE. People who are addicted to them will use any form of the drug that is available, often resorting to BLACK MARKET adulterated supplies. Opiates that are synthetically produced are called opioids and include METHADONE, pethidine and dipipanane.

**organization theory**   a form of theory that attempts to understand how organizations work with respect to their internal structures and processes, both formal and informal, and their external relations.

In relation to social welfare agencies, policy-makers have been concerned to answer several related questions. First, how can services be organized and delivered most effectively? Second, what structures will be most supportive of workers in what are widely recognized as stressful occupations? Third, how are social welfare agencies to relate to service users? Fourth, how are social welfare organizations to relate to each other? SOCIAL SERVICES DEPARTMENTS have experimented a lot in the last few decades. Three kinds of models have emerged. Departments using 'functional' arrangements are organized into sections based on setting – typically fieldwork, residential and day care services. Other functional sections might comprise research, inspection, staff development, and so on. Departments increasingly structure services around 'client group', with the integration of all residential, fieldwork and day care services for each client group in one section of the organization. Finally some have a 'geographical model', dividing up the organization into smaller units, which then usually employ either the functional or client group models. In practice, hybrids of various kinds are often devised. Research seems to indicate that client group models work best, because all resources for a case are contained within one section of the organization. Such a model, however, is not without its difficulties; how are services to be organized, for example, when two client groups are involved in one case?

> Most social welfare workers have a clear preference for flat hierarchies; that is, they appear to want few levels or tiers within the organization. Such arrangements give them access to decision-makers and make plain where the responsibilities for decisions actually lie. Similarly, they want direct access to support staff without having to go through intermediaries. For example, a worker with a case of child SEXUAL ABUSE will wish to consult with the department's adviser without complex referral systems to that adviser. 'Chains of command' vary a lot within welfare and justice agencies. Some agencies operate as collectives or with one manager only (often in the VOLUNTARY SECTOR); others may have as many as seven or eight levels (typically some social services departments), with many somewhere in between (probation departments often have only three or four tiers).
>
> Service users will wish to have reasonable access to services. Agencies should pay attention to the siting of offices in relation to populations and to public transport routes. Many social services departments have devised outposts for isolated communities, and in large densely populated areas NEIGHBOURHOOD OFFICES may offer the first point of contact with several local government departments. Policies to promote access frequently include the provision of transport by the social welfare agency.
>
> With the efficient coordination of services as the objective, it is clearly advantageous for welfare and justice agencies to have the same area boundaries. With some functions this has proved possible, but with others both boundaries and forms of accountability vary significantly. Some organizations are accountable to local government, others increasingly to central government or to QUANGOS. Where these organizations also have different boundaries, coordinating mechanisms are required. Not surprisingly, the service user, required to deal with two or more agencies, can be confused.
>
> *Social Work Departments as Organizations: Research Highlights*, Aberdeen: University of Aberdeen, 1987.

**organized sexual abuse**    the systematic SEXUAL ABUSE of a number of children by several adults acting in a planned, coordinated way; often linked to paedophile rings and/or (less substantially) to 'Satanic' or 'ritual' CHILD ABUSE.

**ouster orders**    an order issued by county court that can require a spouse, a partner or somebody associated with the spouse or partner to leave the matrimonial home; an exclusion order issued by magistrates courts has similar powers.

An ouster order can be issued both by a MAGISTRATES' court and by a county court. The order has as its objective the protection of people (usually women) and their children who have experienced VIOLENCE or harassment.

**outreach**    any attempt to take a service to people who need it and who would otherwise probably not use the service.

Many social welfare agencies offer their services in a relatively passive way; their presumption often is that their service is generally well known and that those who wish to use it will do so. Similarly, it is argued that those who do not use the service do not need it or do not wish to use it. These assumptions are now known to be false. Many services if offered on an outreach basis considerably increase their usage and often bring to the service people who are different from more habitual users (sick people, people with DISABILITIES and members of ethnic minorities, for example).

Outreach workers have long been employed by the youth service to work with young people who would otherwise probably not use the service (see YOUNG PERSON, YOUTH WORK). Such work is especially useful in relation to the young single homeless, to those involved with SUBSTANCE MISUSE and to those involved in, or who have the potential for involvement in, delinquent activity. ADVICE work is another context that has demonstrated the benefits of outreach work. Campaigns to persuade claimants to apply for a benefit that they are entitled to but do not know about (or are reluctant to claim or are unsure about how to claim) have much higher TAKE-UP rates when advice workers leaflet an area with accessible information or undertake to contact each household or both. Health services have also improved their uptake of service, especially around critical issues like immunization in relation to an epidemic of a serious disease and HIV/AIDS (see also COMMUNITY DRUG TEAMS). It should be remembered that poor or vulnerable people experience relative powerlessness. In this regard services have to demonstrate their relevance to people who often sorely need them but lack the will or understanding to use them. Such services have a major role to play in relation to PREVENTIVE WORK, because they have the capacity for identifying problems at an early stage of development. (See also DOMICILIARY SERVICES.)

**overlapping benefit**    a term that refers to the general principle of social security that individuals should not be entitled to receive more than one income replacement benefit, for example RETIREMENT PENSION, at any one time. Where a person is entitled to more than one such benefit, such as WIDOWS BENEFIT and INVALID CARE ALLOWANCE, they can receive only the higher of the two.

If a person (usually a woman) claims an income replacement benefit in their own right, then their spouse will not be eligible to claim a dependant's increase in respect of them, unless the amount of the increase is greater than the other benefit payable.

**overpayment**    benefit paid in excess of a person's entitlement.

Overpaid social security benefits are recoverable if they occur because the claimant has misrepresented or failed to disclose a material fact. This includes innocent misrepresentation but not a responsibility to disclose facts that the claimant is not aware of at the time. The overpayment is not recoverable if caused in some other way, such as through a failure of the DEPARTMENT OF SOCIAL SECURITY to act on information. Before repaying overpaid benefit it is worth claimants checking the particular circumstances against existing case law as well as checking the calculation of the overpayment. These rules do not allow for the recovery of overpaid INCOME SUPPORT resulting from late payment of another social security benefit, such as unemployment benefit. A special rule allows recovery in these circumstances. Recovery can be made by deduction from any social security benefit except child benefit, and maximum rates of deduction are laid down by law. Overpayments of housing benefit and council tax benefit involving actions by the local authorities (called EXCESS BENEFIT) are treated differently, being always recoverable unless they result from official error and the claimant could not have realized they were being overpaid. Most local authorities recover without proper consideration of the circumstances, even where the overpayment results from their delay in acting upon information held by them. Decisions to recover benefits overpaid by the Department of Social Security or local authorities are subject to appeal.

# *P*

**paranoia**   a mental disorder in which the sufferer holds the unshakable conviction that they are being persecuted by others.

Intense and persistent paranoia is often diagnosed as a type of SCHIZO-PHRENIA. In this form the sufferer believes or perceives, where others would be unlikely to do so, that there is a direct threat in their environment. It can take the form of persecution or revolve around a perceived injustice or belief that they will sustain a physical attack. Anger, argumentativeness and aggression are all possible behavioural consequences.

**parental responsibility**   defined in the CHILDREN ACT as the rights, duties, powers, responsibilities and authority that in law parents have in relation to their children.

The term is used in sections 2, 3 and 4 of the Children Act to emphasize that parents have inescapable responsibilities when bringing up children and should not view the relationship with their children as based solely on PARENTAL RIGHTS. Parental responsibility is automatically conferred on both parents of a child as long as those parents were married at the time of the child's birth. If the parents were not married at the time of the birth, the mother of the child automatically acquires responsibility, but the father does not and can acquire responsibility only through a court order or by agreement with the mother. A parent who has parental responsibility for a child cannot lose it except through ADOPTION. However, it can be shared, delegated by a parent or acquired by others who are not the child's parents. For example, foster parents who have looked after a child for a period of time can acquire parental responsibility through a RESIDENCE ORDER, and the local authority itself acquires parental responsibility when it holds a CARE ORDER on a child. In both instances the parents do not lose parental responsibility but have to share it with the foster parents or local authority.

> Knowing who does or does not have parental responsibility for a particular child is extremely important for social workers and other care professionals working with families. Although the Children Act does not define what the specific responsibilities are, people with parental responsibility have an important role in decision-making concerning a child who is being LOOKED AFTER by a local authority and have certain rights to maintain CONTACT with a child unless there are compelling reasons why they should not do so.

**parental rights** the rights, powers and duties that a parent holds in relation to their child.

The concept of parental rights derived originally from property law, namely that children were the property of their father, who, until the mid-nineteenth century, almost always prevailed in any contest for custody. The term came to embrace aspects of the care and control of the child as well, but it later fell into disfavour as a more child-centred perspective in law became dominant. In GILLICK v. *West Norfolk and Wisbech Area Health Authority*, for example, the House of Lords emphasized that parental power to control a child existed not for the benefit of the parent but for the benefit of the child. The CHILDREN ACT has replaced the concept of parental rights with PARENTAL RESPONSIBILITY, which emphasizes what the old concept did not, namely that parents have certain obligations and responsibilities towards their children that they must meet and cannot easily evade even if they need to ask for help from the local authority with this task. Within social work the concept of parental rights was often viewed as contrary to children's rights, and it was considered that if a child's welfare was to be protected the local authority had to take over parental rights from the parents. What were assumed to be opposing sets of interests provided a justification for compulsory intervention in a family's life. There is now greater realization within the profession that children's rights and parental rights are intertwined and coincide rather than oppose each other.

**parliamentary select committees** committees of Members of Parliament that scrutinize the implementation of government policy, including social services and social work issues.

In 1979 after an experiment in widening the role and number of parliamentary committees, a series of select committees was established to shadow each of the main central government departments. Each committee is composed of appointed MPs who have expressed a particular interest in the work of that committee. Membership is weighted in proportion to the relative strengths of the main political parties in the House of Commons, thus giving the majority party the largest number of committee places. However, these committees are seen as being the servants of Parliament and as a result they work across party lines and make serious efforts to ensure an agreed report.

Parliamentary select committees have important powers that add significantly to Parliament's ability to scrutinize the actions of the government. These powers include the ability to summon ministers, civil servants and members of the public to give evidence, which enables them to question the opinions of outside experts, including local government councillors, officials and social work staff. Their investigations can take them out of the House to visit organizations in the furtherance of their inquiries. This broadens the scope of Parliament to examine issues more widely and in more detail than in the traditional debate on the floor of the House. The nature of parliamentary debates and their formal structure do not permit detailed examination of ministers and do not include non-MPs. Select committees can examine issues in detail over some weeks, and this can result in lengthy questioning of ministers and others.

Reports of the committees are published along with, in most instances, the full transcripts of hearings and the written reports of witnesses. As with the main parliamentary debates, the hearings of select committees are recorded for television and radio. Select committee reports are, however, only advisory; all too frequently the government takes only limited notice of them. The response to these reports may take place verbally on the floor of the House when the report is debated, or the government may publish a reply. Reports by the Social Services Select Committee have provided important material on both COMMUNITY CARE and the care of children. In addition, evidence has been provided on the needs of formal and informal carers, although most information is provided by organized pressure groups, such as BRITISH ASSOCIATION OF SOCIAL WORKERS and Mencap, rather than individuals. So the existence of these committees allows a more public expression of the detailed views of these organizations to Parliament than would otherwise be the case.

In 1991 the structure of some committees was altered, and the Social Services Select Committee was abolished in favour of two new committees: the Select Committee on Health and the Select Committee on Social Security. This change was brought about through the reorganization of the Department of Health and Social Security into separate departments of Health and of Social Security.

**parole**   the period of discretionary conditional release from PRISON under licence, for which prisoners are now eligible under the CRIMINAL JUSTICE ACT 1991 if they have served at least half of a sentence of four years or more.

The period of parole lasts until the three-quarters point of the sentence, when release under supervision becomes automatic (see also EARLY RELEASE).

**participation**   the involvement of service users in decisions that affect them.

The term 'participation' is used widely to refer to different levels of involvement by clients in decisions affecting them. Because of this, it is easy to have misunderstandings as to what is authentic participation, where the CLIENT has had real influence. For example, professionals from a social work agency may regard a client attending a meeting about them as participation, while the client may think it nothing of the sort since they neither could understand what was going on nor had a chance to contribute to the decisions. To achieve greater precision in the use of the word, a number of ways of classifying degrees of participation have been worked out. One of the most influential is Arnstein's 'ladder', which summarizes seven different types of participation. Finding the appropriate level of participation for clients is not easy. On the one hand, the profession's deep-rooted paternalism – in which the practitioner as expert defines both the purpose and the manner of the work to be undertaken – allows for little participation in deciding what is to be done. This approach is clearly counterproductive, because the nature of social work and social care decisions often requires negotiation between practitioner and client to decide what level of service should be provided. To be successfully carried through, work frequently depends on client motivation, which will be low if the client has made no contribution to the decisions that affect them. On the other hand, many social work decisions are extremely difficult to make, requiring the use of expensive resources or legal powers, so it is impossible for clients to have complete and solo control over the deciding of outcomes.

> The push toward increasing the level of client participation has come principally from groups of users extending across the range of social work and social care. ADVOCACY and SELF-ADVOCACY groups, spanning children and families, people with MENTAL DISORDER and people with DISABILITY, have all pressed for greater rights of participation. As a result, social work agencies are attempting to increase client participation in even the most sensitive areas of work. For example, after much debate and resistance, parents of children thought to be abused are encouraged to participate in the CHILD PROTECTION CASE CONFERENCE on their child. What the actual degree of user involvement in decision-making should be, and what form it should take, are both important issues that have received considerable attention. To guarantee some degree of real participation requires: (1) the availability of INFORMATION in a language and form that users can understand; (2) users' access to independent sources of advice and representation; and (3) users' attendance at, contribution to, and influence on the outcome of meetings, both formal and informal, where decisions are made.
>
> S. Croft and P. Beresford, *Citizen Involvement*, Basingstoke: Macmillan, 1992.

**partnership** a working relationship between care professional and service user in which the latter has some influence in deciding what is to be done and how.

The concept of partnership is now widely used to denote a social work approach more closely linked to the wishes and aspirations of those for whom services are provided. It attempts to leave behind an out-of-date paternalistic method in which social services professionals on their own decided what was in the best interests of CLIENTS. To work in partnership requires a considerable change of approach and attitude on the part of practitioners. In effect, it gives greater informal powers to service users, because no genuine partnership can be formed unless there is some distribution of power – even if not equal distribution – between the partners.

A number of principles may be outlined that underpin practice based on partnership: first, investigation of problems should be with the explicit consent of the potential user; second, there are only two legitimate bases for social work involvement in an individual's life, either because the law says so or because the user has agreed; third, social work services should be based on the views of all relevant family members and carers; fourth, services should be accessible to all, particularly in terms of race, gender, age, culture, language, and services adapted in response to group needs; fifth, users should have the greatest degree of choice of services as possible. Working with service users on a partnership basis is explicitly called for in the Department of Health guidance to practitioners for the CHILDREN ACT. One of the main aims of this Act is to have social services practitioners help parents carry out their responsibilities towards their children, not by making decisions for them but by offering supportive services that the parents themselves want. To work in partnership, families should be told about the worker's role and powers, share in deciding which problems need addressing, and know what is said or written about them. They should be able to give consent to or refuse any social work intervention except where the social worker is obliged by law to act. In key areas of work with children, such as in placing a child away from home, the decision is expected to be taken with consultation with parents, and a plan for the child's future should be jointly drawn up. While parents will not expect to be equal partners, they will expect to have all the INFORMATION they require for informed decisions, and to remain deeply involved in the life of their child even while the child is away from home. (See also PARTICIPATION, TASK-CENTRED WORK.)

C. Newton and P. Marsh, *Training in Partnership: Translating Intentions into Practice in Social Services*, York: Rowntree Foundation, 1993.

**pass and passing** methods of determining a service's quality by measuring how far that service meets criteria associated with NORMALIZATION.

The techniques of pass and passing are proposed by their authors as suitable for assessing services for people from any devalued group, but are most commonly employed with regard to people with LEARNING DISABILITY. They focus on how far services enhance two main areas affecting service users: their social image and their personal competence. Pass and passing are similar; however, passing includes only measures of normalization, while pass includes additional criteria associated with service quality. Workshops are utilized to train people in these assessment techniques.

W. Wolfensberger and S. Thomas, *Passing Program Analysis of Service Systems' Implementation of Normalization Goals*, Ontario: Canadian National Institute of Mental Retardation, 1983.

**passport benefits** a phrase used to describe benefits or concessions that automatically accrue with receipt of a particular benefit. For example, income support is a passport to housing benefit, council tax benefit, free school meals and health benefits.

**patch work/patch system** a way of delivering social welfare and especially social work services within a particular geographical area.

Patches might be worked by a single worker, by a small group of workers or by whole teams. This way of working was especially popular with GENERIC teams, that is, where a social work team undertook all the work within a designated geographical area. More recently genericism has given way to relative specialisms, and this has discouraged or diluted the development of patch working. A patch would normally be small enough, first, for professional workers to become familiar with the other welfare agencies in the area, thus encouraging close collaborative work where needed, and, second, for workers to be able to identify and work with informal networks. Some patch systems, like that in Normanton in Yorkshire, relied heavily upon both VOLUNTEERS and DOMICILIARY care workers; these workers seemed to combine the roles of family aides, HOME HELPS and SOCIAL WORK ASSISTANTS. The experiment raised interesting questions about the numbers of professional social workers needed on a patch if their efforts are augmented by both ancillary workers and volunteers.

**PCP (phencyclidine)**    a general anaesthetic and HALLUCINOGEN that may be sniffed, smoked, eaten or injected. Also known as 'angel dust' or 'crystal', it is available in liquid, tablet and powder form, although its use in Britain is uncommon.

PCP no longer has any medical uses but is used in veterinary medicine. It can be taken for its hallucinogenic properties, but other effects can include DEPRESSION, violent behaviour and paranoia. It is classified as a class A drug under the MISUSE OF DRUGS ACT 1971, with penalties for possession and supply.

**peer group**    a group of people with the same social standing or status. Although peer groups are thought to be especially influential among young people, the term has general application to other age groups.

Peers may be a specific group (such as colleagues in a social work organization) or a wider group (such as the social work profession in general). Both groups can act as reference points for individuals, enabling them to make judgements about how they are faring in some particular respect. Judgement by peers is regarded as a crucial part of being a professional, in relation both to education and training and to disciplinary matters.

**penal practice**    see PENOLOGY.

**penal theory**    see PENOLOGY.

**penology**    an aspect of CRIMINOLOGY concerned with the theories, policies and practices of punishment. Its primary focus tends to be on CUSTODIAL SENTENCES and PRISONS, but it is also concerned with alternative forms of punishment, such as COMMUNITY SENTENCES.

**pensionable age**    the earliest age at which RETIREMENT PENSION can be paid (women 60, men 65).

**performance measurement**    a management method for quantifying output or some aspect of the performance of an organization or service.

Performance measurement is increasingly used in the public sector as a way of trying to improve efficiency and effectiveness. Central government is seeking to introduce such measures throughout most public-sector activities. The main problem in the public sector has always been the lack of a simple measure of success in the attainment of its objectives. The private sector has had the ready-to-hand measure of profitability, but the public sector frequently operates in areas where profit is an inappropriate indicator. In addition, many areas of provision may also be seen as having multiple objectives for which a simple indicator would provide little useful information. Consequently, the government is encouraging the development of performance measures by LOCAL AUTHORITIES that will enable them to identify success in the attainment of stated objectives. It believes that this will improve the efficiency of local authorities and also increase their accountability to the public. If there are specific objectives with key measures, preferably quantifiable, then the public will be able to see clearly whether the local authority is efficient and effective in its use of public money.

The AUDIT COMMISSION has played a key role in identifying performance measures for local authorities in a wide range of services, including the personal social services. The method adopted is to identify a series of objectives and then to ask questions about the processes used to attain them. These questions should relate to the identification of specific targets: for example, the number of children in care per thousand population and the direction this figure is moving in, whether up or down. Other questions may concern the number of shared rooms in a residential home or the staff-to-resident ratio. Such questions should be related very carefully to the policy objectives specified for the area of service in question and the targets for that service. A service can be broken down so that specific problems may be identified either over time or on a comparative basis. The existence of quantitative measures allows a local authority to compare the performance of different service providers to see if some are performing well or badly. The authority may also be able to compare its own service provision with that of other similar authorities. More particularly, such measures allow managers to improve service delivery by identifying more discrete areas of service where problems may exist, and act as triggers for further analysis of policy implementation problems.

However, there are problems with the development of performance measures. To some extent, there is suspicion among public-sector employees and trade unions that such measures will inevitably be linked to the development of performance-related pay. Comparisons with other local authorities or even within an authority are difficult to use, because of differences in socioeconomic factors. Also, there are major difficulties in developing reliable output measures on the quality of service provision. Input measures, such as staffing levels and financial inputs, are comparatively easy and therefore tend to dominate. To establish appropriate quantifiable output measures for issues such as quality of life and user satisfaction is much more complex and fraught with difficulties. Even so, performance measurement is increasingly utilized in service provision, and efforts will continue to improve its sensitivity.

Audit Commission, *Performance Review in Local Government: A Handbook for Auditors and Local Authorities*, London: HMSO, 1986.

**permanency planning**  planning the provision of a secure, permanent home for a child LOOKED AFTER by the LOCAL AUTHORITY.

The concept of permanency planning was developed in the 1970s and early 1980s as a way of counteracting the uncertainty and drift that many children experienced in the care of the local authority. The thinking behind it stemmed from the fear that many children would move in and out of care frequently and suffer because they would not develop dependable long-term relationships with either their parents or substitute care-givers. This led to the conclusion that children in the care of the local authority should either be reunited with their family or be placed with foster parents on a long-term basis, where they would have a chance to form such relationships.

Difficulties arose over how the basic idea of permanency planning was interpreted. At the time, it was widely regarded as requiring a quick resolution of the issue of whom the child would live with. Many local authorities introduced time limits of three or six months, during which they would attempt to reunify the child in care with their family. If this was not successful, the authority would look for a permanent placement for the child with foster parents, often on the understanding that the foster parents would eventually adopt the child and thereby sever all links with the natural family. In retrospect this was a simplistic view that ignored the fact that the local authorities themselves were extremely poor at facilitating the reunification of children with their natural families (see CHILD RESCUE, CONTACT). By the late 1970s permanency planning became little more than a justification for compulsorily removing children from their own families, terminating contact between the child and family members and placing the child either for ADOPTION or for long-term FOSTER CARE.

Only later did powerful research accounts emerge to discredit this rigid and one-sided interpretation. They demonstrated that children in long-term care of the authority enjoyed anything but a 'secure' future, with placement breakdowns and moves between foster homes occurring frequently. It is now more widely recognized that often the most effective 'permanent' home for a child is with members of the child's own family, even if this means living for periods with other relations such as grandparents or in ACCOMMODATION provided by the local authority. Children are also seen as more adaptable than previously thought and capable of forming close relationships with more than just one set of parent figures. Rather than being detrimental to family life, properly planned periods away from home that meet specific needs of the family can assist in the long-term stability of that family rather than undermine it.

J. Thorburn, *Child Placement*, Second edition, Aldershot: Arena, 1994.

**personality**  those aspects of an individual's character that remain relatively permanent across different situations.

There is a debate over the degree of permanence and how to describe an individual's personality. At one extreme, some theorists have argued that an individual differs so much between situations – for example, with friends, family or at work – that there is no element that is constant. The ways of describing personality range from classifying people according to type, such as an AUTHORITARIAN PERSONALITY, or according to a set of traits, such as neurotic and extrovert, to the ideographic approach that you should not try to classify people but treat them as individuals. A further debate concerns whether the structure of personality has unconscious elements; psychoanalysts such as Freud and Jung have suggested that some parts of personality are unconscious.

> Numerous methods have been employed to assess personality, ranging from clinical interviews to paper-and-pencil tests, and the method adopted reflects the theoretical position of the designer. Psychometricians such as Cattell and Eysenck utilize questionnaires containing explicit questions about a person's behaviour. These questions have been selected partly to reflect the specific structures that the questionnaire designer believes constitute personality and partly through a statistical technique called factor analysis, which helps to identify the most useful questions to address such structures. An alternative approach, employing a projective test, is to give people ambiguous pictures that they are asked to interpret. The reasoning behind this approach is that a person will project aspects of themselves, some of which may be unconscious, through the interpretations which are given. Examples of such tests are Rorshach's ink blot test and McClelland's 'thematic apperception' test. Two questions that anyone wishing to employ a test should ask are: how valid is the test, and how reliable is it? A valid test is one that measures what it was designed to measure, and this is usually checked against criteria such as the clinical judgement of a psychiatrist. A reliable test is one that produces the same assessment of an individual from one occasion to another. The validity and reliability of a personality test are usually reported in the manual that accompanies it.
>
> S.E. Hampson, *The Construction of Personality: An Introduction*, London: Routledge, 1988.

**personality disorder**　a MENTAL DISORDER evident in a general and persistent pattern of maladaptive behaviour.

There are no defining characteristics of a personality disorder, but an individual may be regarded as having such a disorder if they experience general problems of communicating with others, and of developing and sustaining relationships, that can be traced to behaviour rather than social factors. A brief description of the variety of personality disorders illustrates that these behaviours are at the extremes of or just outside the spectrum of what is generally acceptable behaviour: dependency (dependent personality disorder); shallowness of feeling, inability to interpret emotional cues, lack of insight (schizoid personality disorder); avoidance (avoidant personality disorder); suspiciousness (paranoid personality disorder); compulsive behaviour (compulsive personality disorder); and attention-seeking and manipulative behaviour (histrionic or hysterical personality disorder). Antisocial personality disorders may be frequently seen by social workers as CONDUCT DISORDER in children. The profile of this covers lying, stealing and truancy in young children, developing into drug and alcohol abuse, violent sexual behaviour and criminality.

> Personality disorders are generally distinguished from the mental illnesses (PSYCHOSIS and NEUROSIS) by the absence of distress. These problems can often be traced to the early relationship with parents and other significant figures in the environment. Thus the presence of hostility or aggression, and a lack of expressed love, human warmth and acceptance, provide messages to the child about themselves, about personal interactions and about the world in general.

**person-centred counselling**  an approach to counselling that enables the client to develop feelings of worth.

Person-centred counselling was largely developed in the work of Carl Rogers, whose terminology and concepts strongly influenced social work in the 1950s. Rogers believed that the self developed from the interaction of organism and environment. For example, a child has musical talent (organism), but parents see athleticism as of prime importance and interact with the child on that basis (self). In this case the discrepancy between organism and self may generate anxiety. Rogers viewed the organism as striving to maintain, enhance and actualize the self. For healthy development the organism and the self need to be in harmony. However, the organism seeking to actualize may do things that are discouraged by others, bringing disapproval and possible withdrawal of affection. Thus Rogerian theory can be seen as describing how children acquire moral standards.

The organism strives to achieve potential, Rogers suggested. This striving is the root of motivation for human beings. People may be limited by their hereditary and social environment, but this does not stop them from seeking self-fulfilment. From this striving emerges an awareness of 'I' and 'me', that is, the self. The self encompasses what a person does and what they are, and the maintenance of this phenomenal self becomes the individual's priority.

Rogers sees the development of the individual in terms of how one is evaluated by others and dependent on a number of factors: *positive regard*, that is, approval by others; *positive self-regard*, the child being able to give themselves what they previously needed from others; *conditions of worth*, conditions attached to regard, such as approval and attention requiring particular courses of action; and *unconditional positive regard*, genuine love and respect regardless of the child's actions. The individual also seeks to maintain a *consistency* between the self and experience. Experiences that are not consistent with a self-view are generally ignored. However, such inconsistencies may appear as a *threat* to the view of the self. Threats may be ignored, distorted or gradually taken into the self-view. The last strategy may bring about change in a person's behaviour as it brings change in the phenomenal field. All of these activities may occur without the individual being aware of them.

Rogerian theories have their roots in the work of Jung, with its reliance on the meaning of events as a motivator for behaviour, and the person-centred approach to therapy has as its basic premise the meaning of behaviours and events for the person concerned. The therapist's strategy is to enable the client to recognize their feelings and behaviours in order to resolve the distortions in perception that are causing them distress. The therapist uses empathic understanding, genuineness and unconditional positive regard to facilitate feelings of worth and personal growth in the client. The aim of therapy is to bring about change in the way a person sees the world, and changes in behaviour will follow.

Person-centred therapy has become increasingly popular in the last forty years, and Rogers is seen as third only to Freud and Skinner in terms of the influence of his theories. Perhaps because person-centred therapies do not prescribe specific techniques – rather, they imply an overall approach, which appears easy to learn – they also promise improvement in a shorter time than analytically derived therapies.

M. Cook, *Levels of Personality*, Eastbourne: Holt, Rinehart & Winston, 1984.

**phenomenology**  a humanistic approach to understanding people that emerged in the 1950s as a third force in PSYCHOLOGY, emphasizing people's ability to develop self-understanding. Phenomenology is based on the view that human behaviour is purposeful, governed by perceived meanings, and that people have choice.

While it has its roots in the work of several writers in the first part of this century, phenomenology developed rapidly after 1945. The most influential exponent of phenomenological explanations of the person has been Carl Rogers (1901–87). Phenomenology involved a move away from psychoanalytical and behavioural traditions and paid attention to the conscious aspects of the individual. Its basic theme is that behaviour is determined by the way the person perceives and understands events around them, that is, by their phenomenal field. It follows that changes in behaviour link to changes in perception. Phenomenology places emphasis on the concept of self, defining the self as everything a person sees as belonging to them: thoughts, characteristics, competency, anxieties, and so on. This perspective views people as conscious of the motives for their behaviour and aware of behavioural outcomes. The phenomenological movement is diverse, embracing a number of approaches to understanding the person; it is a group of perspectives rather than a 'school of thought'. These perspectives might be humanistic, existential or holistic, but the common theme is one of focusing attention on the whole person, in their social setting.

**phobias**  understood widely by the medical profession as NEUROSES and very closely linked to the condition of ANXIETY (also a 'neurosis').

As neuroses, phobias can be further regarded as MENTAL ILLNESS, and thus the person with a phobia may be referred to the psychiatric services and correspondingly may be regarded and treated negatively in society because of this label (see LABELLING THEORY). Given the understanding that phobias are forms of mental illness, the person experiencing a phobia is most likely to approach or be referred to their general practitioner. They may then be treated as are people with other neuroses, receiving medication from their GP, but if the problems are long-term they may be referred to the psychiatric services (see PSYCHIATRY).

Professionals with particular training for treating phobias are clinical psychologists, but the social worker has a number of important possible roles in relation to the problem. Phobias can often arise when the person is suffering anxiety; a phobia can be understood as anxiety directed at a particular target, such that the subject when faced with that object is likely to experience a panic attack. This is very frightening and unpleasant, often leading to fears of illness, because there are powerful physiological symptoms, and thus the person will go to great lengths to avoid facing that object. Such a difficulty will affect the person's life in greater or lesser degrees according to the focus of the phobia. At one end of the scale might be agoraphobia, whereby all open spaces, and indeed most situations, provoke this response; and at the other might be phobia of spiders. The former would therefore profoundly interfere with daily living, while the latter would be both occasional only, and with few implications for the person's life and functioning.

*Social work involvement.* The social worker is likely to be involved in only those cases of phobia where there is an impact on the person's coping ability and thus on their life and that of others. This will very often be in situations of family conflict, typically where a woman cannot fulfil her family responsibilities of child-care and household management because of her phobia(s); as studies have shown, the community is very intolerant of neuroses, and relatives/friends of the person experiencing these are likely to expect them to 'pull themselves together'. STIGMA and criticism thus experienced can lead to further difficulties, such as depression. The usual GP intervention is to medicate, especially with women, and this may lead to additional problems – drowsiness, for example – that increase the risk of accidents to self and/or others, including children.

Women are more likely to experience phobias than men, and perhaps this is so for black people too. An explanation of this may be found in the likelihood that these groups will be vulnerable to anxiety – the underlying state from which phobias can arise – through experiences of insufficient nurturance in childhood (for white women due to their socialization into meeting the needs of others; for black people as a result of racism reducing parental resources). Other accounts are offered by BEHAVIOURISM, which regards a phobia as the result of response conditioning. PSYCHODYNAMIC theories may also explain phobias as the result of projection of unacceptable painful feelings on to an aspect of the environment.

*Intervention.* BEHAVIOUR THERAPY involving desensitization techniques is an approach to phobias commonly used by clinical psychologists, and social workers are not trained in these particular skills. However, more general approaches employed with DEPRESSION and anxiety may be appropriate: anti-racist and feminist EMPOWERMENT, anxiety management, COGNITIVE THERAPY, assertiveness training. It is important with all these approaches, or in its own right, to remember the general 'sustaining' approach of PSYCHOSOCIAL THEORY, which values the person and relieves anxiety and distress, thus facilitating their working towards resolving the problems by any of the above methods. The person may also be on medication, or be seeing the GP or psychiatrist, which means that the social worker needs to liaise with these professionals. Additionally, intervention with long-term social difficulties such as housing and finance is important in preventing chronicity. Intervention in relation to family conflict, stigmatization, isolation and child-care concerns is also important, taking full account of different cultural and other differences in need. If the focus of the referral is the child-care situation, the best outcomes will be achieved by intervening in appropriate ways with the anxiety problems, in addition to any more child-centred strategies.

A. Butler and C. Pritchard, *Social Work and Mental Illness*, Basingstoke: Macmillan, 1981.

**Physeptone** a brand name for METHADONE.

**physical abuse** non-accidental injuries inflicted on a person by another person. The abused person is usually in a subordinate position to the abuser.

The VIOLENCE involved in physical ABUSE often results in problems that require medical attention and can typically include fractures, bruises, burns, concussion and variable injuries to the head, abdomen and genitals (the list is not exhaustive). Historically it is the physical abuse of children that has preoccupied both the public and social welfare agencies (see CHILD ABUSE), but more recently the abuse of vulnerable adults has received some recognition, as well as spouse abuse (SEE DOMESTIC VIOLENCE, ELDER ABUSE). The physical abuse of people is thought to be widespread in many societies and in all social classes. Some writers would include neglect as a form of physical abuse, at least if intention on the part of the abuser could be established; others prefer to maintain a distinction. If neglect is included, then failure to feed somebody properly, failure to provide protection from hazards and failure to secure appropriate medical care might all be included under the general term of 'physical abuse'.

There are cultural and religious differences that suggest wide variations in what might be considered to be physical abuse. The physical chastisement of children by parents would probably be regarded as acceptable by many people in many societies. Some, however, would regard such chastisement as technically an assault, although one that most law enforcement agencies would not pursue unless it was severe. There have also been changes within societies. A hundred years ago a beating with a cane by a parent would probably have been acceptable to most people; now it would bring a visit by a social worker and at least a warning to the parent. Recently the European Court decided that corporal punishment in schools was no longer permissible.

Some cultures still practice forms of mutilation of skin, facial features or sexual organs. Although circumcision, for example, has many critics in industrialized societies, it is still one of the most frequently performed operations, sometimes conducted in ritualized ways in public places. In the extreme, infanticide is still practised in many societies with unwanted children (especially girls), with the active collusion of government bodies. In Brazil many street children have been murdered by the police in the last decade. Tolerance of the physical abuse of children is generally widespread in societies where human rights are not valued.

The belief that children (and wives or female partners, and perhaps older people within the family) are the property and responsibility of the family – or, more specifically, the 'powerful' man – is widespread; this creates an environment where vulnerable children and adults may not be protected. This belief is also associated with varying definitions of the public and the private. Many societies regard the family in particular as the private sphere. Those societies that seem to have made some progress in challenging abusive behaviour have had also to uphold individual human rights at the cost of PARENTAL RIGHTS and the power of men over women. (See also CHILD PROTECTION, EMOTIONAL ABUSE, SEXUAL ABUSE.)

W. Stainton Rogers *et al.*, *Child Abuse and Neglect: Facing the Challenge*, London: Batsford in association with the Open University, 1989.

**physical disability** a DISABILITY deriving from an impairment that is physical rather than intellectual.

Sometimes a further distinction is made as regards sensory disabilities, which comprise visual impairment and deafness. (However, some DEAF people prefer to be regarded as a cultural minority rather than as disabled people.) The social construction of disability argues that such distinctions may be counter-productive, because all disabled people are adversely affected by restrictions imposed on them by society. Thus all disabled people are affected by social oppression. For a more detailed discussion, see DISABILITY.

**pin-down** a method of control, involving use of compulsory baths, special clothing and systematic isolation, that was adopted by several children's homes in Staffordshire in the late 1980s and came to be regarded as dehumanizing and degrading.

The practice of pin-down gave rise to the Levy–Kahan Report commissioned by Staffordshire Social Services Department. The report perceived the regime as humiliating and the behaviour of staff as intimidating to children and young people considered to be already damaged and vulnerable. The policy was defended by some staff because they felt that they needed to be able to control children who were apt to abscond. If children could not be contained, they argued, they could not be helped. Absconding children were often at large for months and might never return to the social services for help. Once on the run, it was argued, such children are frequently forced into dangerous or immoral situations. Although these difficulties were acknowledged by the inquiry, the practice of pin-down was found to be wholly unacceptable. More positively as a result of pin-down, the CHILDREN ACT brought about a review of control mechanisms within children's residential facilities.

A. Levy and B. Kahan, *The Pindown Experience and the Protection of Children*, Stafford: Staffordshire County Council, 1991.

**placement (1)** a period spent in a social welfare agency by a student as a part of their education and training to achieve a social work or other qualification.

A wide range of social welfare qualifying courses require students to undertake at least one placement as an integral part of their studies. Such arrangements are to be found in the training courses of social workers, probation officers, nursery nurses, community workers and health visitors. Placements may be observational but more usually entail supervised practice. Supervisors are expected to be experienced practitioners, often with a practice teaching qualification. Their task is to assess the student's competence to practise, and so they need to work closely with educational institutions in relation to the practice curriculum. Although students may have a common educational experience in college, placements may vary considerably in setting, client groups and methods. Ensuring that students are competent to practise against these varying situations can be difficult. Placements may be undertaken in either voluntary or statutory settings, with the private sector also beginning to offer placement opportunities on a small scale. For social workers, the Central Council for Education and Training in Social Work is insisting that social work agencies themselves become accredited, a process that should ensure common and improved standards in relation to practice teaching.

**placement (2)** the finding of suitable care for a child being LOOKED AFTER by the local authority, or where ACCOMMODATION is being provided.

Placement care is usually with foster parents, adoptive parents or residential facilities; but it may be with relatives of the child (see PERMANENCY PLANNING).

**placement planning**    a number of essential steps in planning PLACEMENTS for children, laid down by the CHILDREN ACT and by related guidance from the Department of Health.

Historically, social work placed little emphasis on planning for children, but rather put faith in the strength of relationships between child and residential staff or foster parents as the primary means by which major life decisions for the child would be taken. Plans, certainly written plans, were not deemed necessary for such objectives. Even as social workers became more involved in protective work with children, and it became increasingly clear that a child rarely remained with a single set of carers long enough to reach decisions on the child's long-term future, child-care plans, if they existed at all, were rudimentary. This lack of planning was critically highlighted in a summary of research published by the Department of Health (1986) as a chief reason why children were often the subject of erratic decision-making by local authorities.

The Children Act 1989 and the related DoH guidance now require placement planning to encompass the following. *Inquiry*: the views of the child, parents and other members of the family must be obtained, as to whether a placement is required and if so what sort of placement (for example, whether residential or short-term with foster carers); relevant information must also be collected, with the consent of the family, from other agencies and professionals involved, such as the schoolteacher, health visitor, doctor or child psychologist. *Consultation*: the Act requires consultation with the child, parents and any other people with PARENTAL RESPONSIBILITY or whom the authority thinks are important to the child. Consultation should be explained and completed before the placement decision is made. The child's views must be sought in a way appropriate to their understanding of the situation; these views, which may differ from the parents', particularly with an older child, should be discussed at any formal meeting of professionals and recorded in writing. Both the child and their family need to be given all relevant information regarding the choices before them, together with explanations about what each involves. Having consulted, the authority must give due consideration to these views, but it is not obliged to follow them. All aspects of the consultation must be recorded in writing. *Assessment*: the needs of the child – including those relating to their health, development, education, disability (if any) and religious and cultural background – are identified (see ASSESSMENT).

*Decision-making*: the social worker, in collaboration with the child and family wherever possible, now considers what kind of placement is most fitted to meeting the child's needs and whether or not any child-protective measures are required. This decision-making entails defining the child's needs in terms of general objectives, listing and appraising the specific options available for achieving these and deciding on the preferred option.

A written placement plan, based on the information collected and decisions taken, involves both the objectives – what the needs of the child are – and what services are to be provided, including placement, to meet these. It will include, at a minimum, what sort of accommodation is needed; what other services for the child or other members of the family are to be provided; what services other professional organizations such as the health authority or local education authority will provide; and the likely duration of a placement. The most important element of the plan will entail arrangements for ensuring the continuing involvement of the parents and other relations in the life of the child while on placement, particularly CONTACT and when and how the child is to be reunited with their family. In the formulation of written plans for children's placement, the format devised by Bristol University and the Dartington Social Research Unit are highly recommended for practitioners.

Department of Health, *Children Act: Guidance and Regulations Vol. 3 Family Placements*, London: HMSO, 1991.

**placing, assessment and counselling teams (pact)**     teams of specialists who provide assistance to disabled people on issues concerned with employment and retraining.

Located within the employment services, pacts have absorbed duties previously provided by disablement resettlement officers, the disablement advisory service and the employment resettlement service. There are approximately seventy pacts nationwide. (see also DISABILITY.)

**play**     a complex set of processes undertaken by both adults and children that involve exploration and learning in many contexts and situations.

Play may be unstructured or 'free-form', as with a child playing without adult intervention in an unfamiliar situation, or highly structured, as with a well-known game with agreed rules. Play serves many purposes, including the development of motor or physical skills, the development of the intellect and the development of the person both emotionally and socially. Social workers and other social welfare workers are mostly concerned with the issue of play with respect to children and young people (although play may have therapeutic role with mentally ill people, with REMINISCENCE THERAPY with older people and with other client groups too). Here play is regarded as a key process in socialization; without it, children will be developmentally inhibited. The ability to play is thus perceived as a significant indicator of a child's HEALTH in its broadest sense. If a child is seen as in need of help, programmes of play can be devised to promote particular skills that are seen to be lacking or poorly developed. Nurseries, NURSERY schools and specialist units for play therapy are facilities where help may be available for children with such needs. Play is also a very useful tool for social workers and therapists working with abused children; it can provide a medium for revealing and understanding what has happened to a child and for therapeutic work with children who have been damaged by their experiences. (See also TOY LIBRARIES, UNDER-5s PROVISION.)

J.R. Moyles, *Just Playing?*, Buckingham: Open University Press, 1989.

**plea bargaining**     a process whereby a defendant in the Crown Court changes an original plea of not guilty to one of guilty in the hope of securing a less severe sentence than they might have received had they pursued a trial and eventually been found guilty by a jury.

Judges frequently award 'discounts' on sentences to defendants who save the court time and spare witnesses from having to give evidence. The process of bargaining takes place through barristers and is never discussed openly in court. The aim is to discourage 'frivolous' trials and to reward honesty on the part of defendants who know they are guilty. However, there is always a danger that defendants who believe they are innocent will feel under pressure to plead guilty inappropriately (for example, to avoid publicity or to get the case over quickly). (See CRIMINAL COURTS.)

**police**   the main civil organization devised to maintain law and order, using at least some military methods. The primary tasks of the police are to investigate alleged criminal acts, to gather evidence for the CRIMINAL JUSTICE SYSTEM and to charge (in some cases to arrest and detain) alleged offenders.

A substantial and increasing amount of social work is undertaken jointly with the police or in close liaison with them. In CHILD PROTECTION, the greater proportion of initial child investigations are conducted jointly by social workers and police officers. The police also have power to remove children on EMERGENCY PROTECTION ORDERS. In some authorities, juvenile bureaux have been established, comprising seconded social workers, probation officers, youth workers, teachers and police officers, who collectively work to investigate juvenile offence behaviour and to provide cautioning schemes, diversion and sometimes REPARATION schemes too. Decisions are made within bureaux (and within juvenile liaison committees elsewhere) as to whether juveniles are to be prosecuted or not. Social workers often play the role of appropriate adult where the police are interviewing juveniles suspected of offences (see POLICE AND CRIMINAL EVIDENCE ACT 1984). The police organize attendance centres and in some areas are involved with OUTREACH work in the youth services.

An increasing area of work affecting the police is that of investigating alleged incidents of DOMESTIC VIOLENCE and, in the most progressive forces, having an active involvement in the initial work to protect women and children and to restrain and possibly charge abusing men. A further area of work concerns detaining people who are exhibiting symptoms of MENTAL HEALTH PROBLEMS in public places, pending their assessment by social work and psychiatric services.

**Police and Criminal Evidence Act 1984**   an Act codifying POLICE powers in relation to suspected offenders and thus defining more sharply than before the rights of citizens in relation to the police.

The Act sets out clearly the powers and obligations of the police in relation to stopping and searching, entering premises, arrest, detention at a police station and interviewing. It also sets out the machinery for investigating complaints against the police, lays down rules for the admission of certain types of evidence in criminal trials and has introduced in statutory form the concept of COMMUNITY involvement in policing. For social workers and probation officers, the most important aspect of the Act is probably that relating to the role of the appropriate adult, and this is covered in the codes of practice issued by the Home Secretary. Social workers and (less frequently) probation officers may act as appropriate adults in relation to either juveniles or mentally disordered people who are arrested and interviewed by the police. In the absence of parents or close relatives, they are required to be present throughout the proceedings, not just to observe but also to offer advice, help communication and make representations where appropriate.

**police protection** provision under the CHILDREN ACT whereby a police officer may remove a child to suitable accommodation or ensure that they remain in a safe place such as a hospital if they have reasonable cause to believe that the child might otherwise suffer SIGNIFICANT HARM.

A child may remain under police protection for a maximum of seventy-two hours. During that time the child's parents and others should have reasonable CONTACT with the child if it is in the child's best interests. Having taken a child into police protection, the police officer concerned must notify the child's parents and the local authority, ensure that the child knows what is happening and take steps to find out what the child's wishes and feelings are. If it is appropriate to seek an EMERGENCY PROTECTION ORDER the police officer may do so on behalf of the local authority, even without the authority's knowledge; more usually the police will notify the local authority, which in turn will apply for the order from the court.

**Poor Law** a system for dealing with POVERTY and UNEMPLOYMENT laid down in 1598 during the reign of Elizabeth I. With various amendments, notably the Poor Law Amendment Act 1834, the Poor Law remained the law of England until the introduction of the welfare state in 1948.

The introduction of the Elizabethan Poor Law Act arose from genuine concern to help the poor and from concern to control the masses of unemployed people roaming the country in search of work. Under the system, parishes (later local authorities) were empowered to raise local taxes to support sick, old, disabled and unemployed people. Those in need could apply to their parish of origin for assistance. Concerns that the system might be abused by malingerers led to the introduction of a system of 'outdoor' and 'indoor' assistance. The 'deserving poor' – the sick, old, disabled and genuinely unemployed – could apply for 'outdoor relief', that is, payments or goods and/or parish work outside the poorhouse. The able-bodied unemployed and malingerers were obliged to enter the poorhouse (later known as the workhouse) and to earn their keep. The system operating after the 1834 reform Act became an aberration of the Elizabethan system in that it refused to acknowledge unemployment as anything other than a personal failure. The system became more punitive, and the stigma attached to entering the workhouse became greater; distinctions between the 'deserving' and 'undeserving' poor became less clear.

> The underlying philosophy of the poor laws was that of deterrence; people had to be discouraged from getting something for nothing and so were encouraged to obtain an income by selling their labour either inside or outside the workhouse. A guiding principle was that of 'less eligibility'; that is, parish (later state) relief

should not be so generous relative to prevailing living standards that people were attracted to it from paid work. The most significant aspect of the Poor Law system was that it operated within a framework of charity and not rights. The notion of rights took root during the early twentieth century and came to fruition with the introduction of the welfare state.

**positive action**    measures permitted by the RACE RELATIONS ACT 1976 and the SEX DISCRIMINATION ACT 1975 to help members of ethnic minorities and women achieve more equality (in comparison with white people and men respectively) in relation to seeking employment or promotion.

British law does not permit DISCRIMINATION at the point of selection for employment or promotion. Positive action measures mostly concern training opportunities targeted at women and members of ethnic minorities. Such training might include special attempts to equip and encourage women to apply for jobs in areas of employment hitherto dominated by men, such as in engineering. Similarly, it might be demonstrated that black people are a substantial proportion of the population within a particular area but are practically unknown within a local authority department. Training in these circumstances might be to familiarize black people with an area of work or occupation relatively unknown to them and to help them acquire the specific skills necessary to secure a job. Other measures might include networking, that is, telling particular community groups that an organization really does want to recruit more people from ethnic minorities. The use of particular newspapers and advertisements in various languages would send strong signals to particular communities about the seriousness of an organization's equal opportunities policies. It is also possible to appoint a black person or a woman to a post (where they are competing with a white person or a man respectively) if they are considered to be equally competent to do a job and women or black people are under-represented at that level within the organization. A limited number of posts can also be 'reserved' for black people and for women where the job could be said to offer a personal service that only somebody of that ethnicity or gender could reasonably be expected to provide. Thus a woman and only a woman should be considered for a job in a rape crisis centre, and only a black person for a job as Afro-Caribbean advice worker.

**post-traumatic stress syndrome**    refers to a person's reactions following an 'extraordinary' or 'catastrophic' experience that shatters their sense of invulnerability to harm.

Stress itself describes the state of discomfort arising in a person's emotions and mental and physical state when they are struggling to cope against overwhelming odds. The experiences leading to post-traumatic syndrome, in order to shatter the person's sense of invulnerability to harm, would involve a major betrayal of trust. This may mean the betrayal of trust in a particular human being (the experience of child SEXUAL ABUSE has been identified in the literature as an outstanding example of this in society); or the betrayal of trust in the government or an official agency, such as the police, if such an agency attacks the person's basic human rights through, for example, torture or imprisonment without trial; or the betrayal of trust in society through serious crime against the person, such as rape, assault, mugging or breaking into their home, especially while the person is present. Devalued groups in society – black people, women, older people, disabled people, and gay and lesbian people – are particularly likely to be the victims of crime and abuse from the general population, and may be treated unjustly by professionals and officials; so members of these groups are more likely than others to experience post-traumatic stress syndrome.

The feature shared by all the above experiences is that trust in a parent, in official agencies and in other people in society may be very fundamental and taken for granted as a reality to depend upon. Children trust their parents to protect them from harm in every area of life, as they have little power to do this for themselves. Members of society expect the government and official agencies, such as the police, to be active in protecting, or at least not compromising, their basic human rights, and people have a measure of trust in others also not to infringe the latter. It may be that a person has never been able to trust parents, official agencies or other people; but even so, being the victim of harm from any of these sources may still shatter the person's sense of safety and security to the degree that they have no other source of safety to which to retreat. It is the very fundamental nature of these sources of security that makes harm from any of them such a devastating experience, one that is said by some writers to be very difficult to recover from.

Professional abuse from a doctor, therapist or social worker – whether it involves sexual or other forms of malpractice – may also fall into this category, if the harm is significant, because of the expectation, from professional ethics, that the professional will protect the client's interests first. Other forms of trauma betraying trust would include personal disasters, such as a house fire or involvement in a serious accident, and major disasters that again destroy or shatter the person's taken-for-granted experience of safety in their home or car or in a public place such as a football stadium.

All the above experiences, which are likely to lead to post-traumatic stress syndrome, are familiar to social workers, including the experiences of torture and other human rights violations by refugees coming from abroad. However, practitioners are particularly likely to encounter clients who have experienced childhood sexual abuse (and perhaps other forms of child abuse) and crime, while the dangers of professional abuse also need to be borne in mind. It is therefore important to understand the effects that these experiences can have and helpful forms of intervention.

Writers on post-traumatic stress syndrome have identified two different stages of this condition: post-traumatic stress reactions, which refer to the person's immediate or short-term responses to the trauma, and post-traumatic stress disorder, referring to the longer-term responses. Post-traumatic stress *reactions* can include HYSTERIA, involving perhaps loss of memory and even consciousness, restlessness, impaired concentration and coordination, impulsiveness, weeping, confusion and perhaps psychotic experiences such as hallucinations or delusions (see PSYCHOSES). Soldiers experiencing 'shell shock' in the First World War exhibited these symptoms. The fact that psychotic symptoms are sometimes experienced may lead the worker to conclude that the person is mentally ill, or may have led to a referral for assessment under the MENTAL HEALTH ACT 1983. Workers should be aware that such symptoms may arise from other causes and assess the person's circumstances fully. Post-traumatic stress *disorder* is a continuation of these symptoms into the longer term, along with chronic disturbance of sleep, ANXIETY, DEPRESSION and impulsiveness. Lack of concentration and co-ordination, impulsiveness and perhaps even impaired vision or hearing may lead to accidents; in addition there is a risk that hallucinations, 'flashbacks' of the experience, impulsiveness and depression may result in suicide attempts.

In the very long term, adult survivors of childhood sexual abuse are highly likely to suffer the MENTAL HEALTH PROBLEMS of depression, self-harm, anxiety and low self-esteem. SUBSTANCE MISUSE is also highly likely. People suffering other severe traumas may well experience similar difficulties long-term. It is important to be aware, however, that the original trauma, especially if it occurred in childhood, may be repressed from memory; but change and crises in the person's current life may trigger the memories, and this may result in all the original post-traumatic stress reactions.

CRISIS INTERVENTION alone is not sufficient to relieve the distress of the post-traumatic stress syndrome, either after the original trauma or if memories of it are triggered in later life. Long-term help is always needed, and this may often be most effective in a long-term group. This is especially so for survivors of childhood sexual abuse, where the one-to-one client–worker relationship may so painfully remind the person through transference of the abuse situation that distress, distrust and dissociation act against any benefits the therapy might provide. The main benefit that groupwork can bring is to help the person, through exploration of what has happened, develop greater self-esteem. One of the major long-term effects of trauma, and especially of violence or abuse to the person, is a feeling of guilt and unworthiness, as if the person had themselves wanted such treatment.

When working, either in a group or performing other social work duties with the person, reliability and consistency are essential if the person's trust is not to be betrayed again. Nevertheless, the person may very early perceive the worker as untrustworthy, through transference, and this needs to be understood by the worker, not taken personally, and perhaps acknowledged and worked with in whatever depth is appropriate within the particular client–worker relationship. A further consideration in work with people experiencing post-traumatic stress syndrome is the likelihood that the psychiatric services, or at least the general practitioner will be involved, and thus the worker needs to liaise with these services constructively (see MENTAL ILLNESS, MULTIDISCIPLINARY WORKING).

C. Kenney, *Counselling for the Survivors of Sexual Abuse*, Social Work Monographs, Norwich: University of East Anglia, 1989.

**poverty** a state of existence whereby people are inhibited from participation in society because of a serious lack of material and social resources.

Most writers distinguish between absolute and relative poverty. The former refers to conditions that will not sustain physical life, the latter to a lack of resources to obtain the types of diet, participate in the activities and have the living conditions and amenities that are customary, or at least widely encouraged and approved, in the society to which a person belongs. In this case, the person's resources are so seriously inferior to those commanded by the average individual or household that they are, in effect, excluded from ordinary living patterns, customs and activities. Attempts to draw a poverty line, below which people could be said to be living in absolute poverty, have in practice incorporated culturually specific standards; thus, social security benefit levels do not simply address physical survival (they are many times the subsistence income of some Third World peoples, for example) but include at least provision to meet some social needs too.

Early studies conducted by Booth and Rowntree in the 1890s in Britain revealed widespread absolute poverty, which has now virtually been eradicated. Using eligibility for social security as a guideline, the contemporary picture would suggest that one in five people live in relative poverty. This approximation does not include many who might claim benefit but who do not, nor indeed those whose quality of life is only marginally better than that of the social security claimant (see POVERTY TRAP). Particularly vulnerable groups include the chronically sick and disabled, old people, the unemployed (especially the long-term unemployed) and LONE PARENTS. Recent studies have suggested that race and gender have strong associations with poverty. Women are more likely to be lone parents, carers, unemployed or in part-time work than men, and proportionately there are more old women than old men. Studies have also analysed the distribution of resources within families where there is an adequate income, to reveal that the woman's share is disproportionately small. Members of ethnic minorities similarly are more likely than other people to be unemployed or to be in low-paid work.

In the main, people blame the poor for their poverty. Media coverage of poverty issues presents a fairly constant set of negative images of poor people as lazy and welfare-dependent. These views do not accord with the evidence, which reveals that many are actually in work, but that it is poorly paid. Variations in levels of unemployment are better explained by the vagaries of capitalism than by any fecklessness on the part of poor people. The vast majority, made up of children and old people, could not in any event be expected to be economically active. Attempts to offer alternative views, focusing upon the substantial amounts of unclaimed benefit and the behaviour of some of the bigger 'fish' who defraud governments of taxation, seem to have been generally unsuccessful. The belief that the poor are responsible for their own difficulties is persistent. In the public domain the idea of the CYCLE OF DEPRIVATION, and among sociologists the theory of CULTURE OF POVERTY, seek to explain the persistence of poverty by reference to ideas and behaviours transmitted from one generation to another. Critics of these views point to the major changes that have occurred when governments have pursued policies that seek to redistribute wealth – the clear implication being that poverty is a structural feature of society and not a question of individual behaviour.

Poor people form the largest group of consumers of social services. Poverty is a major source of stress, and although it cannot be regarded as a simple causal factor (because many who live in poverty manage to escape major personal and family difficulties), it has strong associations with MENTAL HEALTH PROBLEMS, with crime, with family problems including CHILD ABUSE and with ill-health. The role of social workers in trying to alleviate the poverty of consumers of social work services is full of ambiguity. Many still do not see such work as part of their brief, preferring to perceive it as the responsibility of other agencies. Often such social workers align themselves with therapy, or at least regard helping with relationships as their major focus. Others may limit their assistance to, for example, help with second-hand clothing, or a grant for a holiday. Few social workers have poverty 'centre stage' or indeed are required or permitted to develop an effective ANTI-POVERTY STRATEGY. Such an approach might entail income-maximization programmes, MONEY ADVICE, housing improvement programmes and programmes to facilitate the involvement of poor people in employment (for example, adult education services, nursery provision, and work and food cooperatives). Many such ventures would require at least a COMMUNITY focus and methods rooted in the approaches of COMMUNITY DEVELOPMENT and community action.

P. Townsend, *Poverty in the United Kingdom: A Survey of Household Resources and Standards of Living*, Harmondsworth: Penguin, 1979.

**poverty trap**   the situation of people when the gains they make from increased income, typically earnings from employment, are exceeded by losses through increased payments of tax and National Insurance and reductions in MEANS-TESTED BENEFITS.

The reform of means-tested benefits in 1988 reduced the extent of the POVERTY trap. Although MARGINAL TAX RATES of 87 per cent are commonplace (that is, only 13p of extra income for every additional £1 received), it is only when someone with school-age children comes off INCOME SUPPORT by increasing their earnings or hours of work that a poverty trap arises. In practice, the phrase 'poverty trap' is used to describe any situation where it is difficult for a person to make significant improvements in their disposable income by working or increasing their earnings.

**practice teacher**   a person who supervises social work students during practice PLACEMENTS as part of qualifying courses.

Partnerships between educational institutions and social work agencies such as SOCIAL SERVICES DEPARTMENTS, the PROBATION SERVICE and appropriate voluntary agencies. Students now spend, on average, half of their courses on placements under the supervision of practice teachers. Although there remain some parallels with the student supervisor/study supervisor roles familiar to Certificate of Qualification in Social Work and Certificate of Social Service programmes (the predecessors of the Dip.SW), there are some important differences. Previous models of supervision embraced the idea of an apprenticeship, with students working alongside the supervisor in one social work setting to develop their skills, knowledge and expertise. Practice teachers have a wider managerial role; this includes working in close partnership with college tutors, contributing to teaching within colleges, joint marking of practice-based assignments, and ensuring that students use a wider range of resources to develop their competences if the agency within which they are primarily located is not fully able to meet their learning needs. An additional form of practice teaching recently developed includes the 'long-arm' model, whereby a practice teacher regularly visits a student on placement and works closely with a day-to-day supervisor who is not a practice teacher. Together with college tutors, practice teachers have overall responsibility for the management of an educational experience.

In the key document (Paper 30, 2nd edn), the Central Council for Education and Training in Social Work (CCETSW) has set out the knowledge base, social work values and core skills of social work that are fundamental to competent practice and thus to qualifying at Dip.SW level. The document also describes how competence in social work practice is to be assessed, and this assessment is central to the practice teacher's task. Many social work programmes have devised complex assessment documents to give shape to the practice teacher's evaluation of a student. Central to this process is the identification of evidence to demonstrate that a student has indeed understood the knowledge and value base of social work and that they can apply it effectively in practice. In this regard, increasing emphasis is placed on the direct observation of the student's work by the practice teacher.

Nowhere is this more important than in the area of ANTI-RACIST and ANTI-DISCRIMINATORY issues. Social workers do not practise in a vacuum. Their own values are likely to affect the way they work. They also need to be aware of the various oppressions affecting many service users. Students therefore have to develop an understanding of the impact of SEXISM, RACISM, 'disablism', HOMOPHOBIA and AGEISM pervading British society. Practice teachers have a key role to play in developing the students' practice skills in these areas; and a student should not be regarded as competent without them.

Major attempts have been made to improve the quality of practice teaching by a much longer basic training and a regulation stipulating that practitioners must have at least two years' post-qualifying experience of social work before they can become practice teachers. Practice teachers are accredited by the CCETSW after the completion of a now lengthy training course or the presentation of portfolio work testifying to the quality of their practice teaching with previously supervised students (CCETSW document 26.3). It is the aim of the CCETSW to ensure that by 1995 every Dip.SW student should be supervised by an accredited practice teacher within an accredited social work agency.

**premiums** part of a person's APPLICABLE AMOUNT and so serving to increase the amount of INCOME SUPPORT that they can receive. Premiums are paid for families, lone parents, pensioners, people with disabilities and carers.

**prescribed industrial disease** a disease that gives rise to benefits under the INDUSTRIAL INJURIES SCHEME and is listed in detail in regulations showing the 'prescribed disease or injury' and the occupation that causes it.

**pre-sentence report** a report prepared by probation officers (or social services social workers) to assist a court in determining the most suitable method for dealing with an offender. Under the CRIMINAL JUSTICE ACT 1991 pre-sentence reports (PSRs) replaced SOCIAL INQUIRY REPORTS.

Courts are required to obtain PSRs before passing certain sentences, such as CUSTODIAL SENTENCES and some COMMUNITY SENTENCES. However, they often ask for reports in other cases. There is an assumption that the defendant has already pleaded, or been found, guilty. In the Crown Court, reports sometimes have to be prepared before a trial for practical reasons, and this presents a problem. It has been argued that it is unethical to write a report that advises on sentencing when the defendant has not yet been found guilty of the offence. The content of PSRs is laid down in NATIONAL STANDARDS and normally includes information about the offence, especially its seriousness, and the offender's attitudes and circumstances; it concludes by proposing possible appropriate sentences. The main difference between a social inquiry report and a pre-sentence report is that the former traditionally placed greater emphasis on the personal and social circumstances of the offender, while the latter is primarily concerned with the seriousness of the offence and the offender's attitude towards it.

> Preparation of court reports is one of the primary occupations of the PROBATION SERVICE, and nearly a quarter of a million reports are prepared every year. It usually takes probation officers three to four weeks to prepare reports, although they can be written more quickly if this is considered essential. Probation officers normally interview a defendant twice, often with one interview at the defendant's home in order to assess their circumstances. In their reports, probation officers gather relevant personal information, which is then verified as far as possible, assess the defendant's attitude to the offence and discuss possible sentences. Some sentences, such as PROBATION ORDERS and COMMUNITY SERVICE ORDERS, require the offender's consent, so it is important that the offender understands what is involved. Probation officers have to try to ensure that they conduct the interviews and write the reports in a way that accords with ANTI-DISCRIMINATORY PRACTICE. They should take account of the fact that black people and women may experience DISCRIMINATION in the CRIMINAL JUSTICE SYSTEM. Some probation officers ask colleagues to read their reports (a process known as gatekeeping) to help them identify any discriminatory language or comments.

**presenting problem**   the problem that a CLIENT or the person referring a client states as the reason for needing a social work service.

In the past, there was often a professional presumption that the presenting problem was not, or might not be, the 'real' problem; only the professionally trained practitioner could pick out the real problem. This was a presumption in particular of those approaches to social work that placed great importance on family relationships and unresolved conflicts from the client's past. This perspective devalued problems to do with housing, money or child-care that frequently lay behind a person's approach to a SOCIAL SERVICES DEPARTMENT in the first place. There is currently a wider acceptance among social workers and related professionals that the presenting problem forms the basis of work if that is the problem that matters to the client, and that a social worker proceeds to other problems only through discussion with, and with consent of, the client and others who matter to that person, such as family members or carers (see TASK-CENTRED WORK).

**pressure groups**   a range of organizations that may try to influence central or local government policy-making.

Pressure groups have become a significant part of the British political scene since the Second World War. The range of such groups is extraordinarily varied and often difficult to classify. However, some writers have tried to develop a dual classification along a variety of lines. One such writer identifies pressure groups as either interest groups or cause and promotional groups. Under this classification, groups are identified by use of a number of criteria. *Interest* groups are seen as having a limited membership, existing to promote the interest of the membership, having a long life span and being political only at the margins. For example, trade unions and professional associations such as the BRITISH ASSOCIATION OF SOCIAL WORKERS (BASW) may be characterized as interest groups. The BASW has a membership limited to qualified social workers, acts to defend and promote their interests, aims to exist as long as the profession exists and is more concerned with negotiating with employers than with entering the political arena. The other form of group, *cause or promotional* groups, may have the following characteristics: they have open-ended membership; they promote the interest of others rather than those of their own membership; their life span often last no longer than the issue they are concerned with; and they may act primarily in the political arena, to change government policy on a particular issue.

Many organizations that may be identified as cause or promotional groups do not reflect all the above criteria, however, although they are certainly not interest groups as defined above. While groups such as pro- and anti-abortion campaigners can be identified as cause groups, organization such as Mancap and the National Society for the Prevention of Cruelty to Children are less easily placed. Yet it can be argued that the latter have a largely open membership policy, are concerned with the interests of others than their members, and are frequently engaged in trying to influence policy on issues affecting those interests. Both these types of organization play an important role in the development of policy in relation to social services and social work activities. While interest groups such as the BASW are obviously directly involved in social work issues, other interest groups such as the British Medical Association and Unison may become part of the policy-making process affecting social workers, sometimes cooperating with the BASW and sometimes in conflict with it. Cause groups such as Mencap also affect the policy process in this way but may also be involved alongside social workers through their role in providing voluntary or charitable services, including residential accommodation and advice to parents of children with LEARNING DISABILITIES. The existence of such groups is an essential part of policy-making and implementation in a modern welfare state.

G. Stoker, *The Politics of Local Government*, Basingstoke: Macmillan, London, 2nd edn, 1992.

**preventive detention** see EXTENDED SENTENCE.

**preventive work/prevention** any work that seeks to stop a potential problem emerging or an existing problem becoming more acute.

The concept of prevention has specific meanings in medical practice in many contexts. Health services differentiate between primary, secondary and tertiary prevention. The first refers to efforts made to keep diseases from occurring with such projects as immunization and sanitation programmes and public health schemes around diet and nutrition. The second refers to efforts to stop a disease that has erupted in a locality from spreading; the remedies might include some of the measures identified above but could also, for example, list some social practices that might help in the prevention. The third refers to attempts to assist people who have had a disease to recuperate and not to fall foul of the disease again. In social work there is less clarity about the way the term is used, although there are some obvious parallels to the medical model. For example, in a geographical area identified as having the social ingredients associated with delinquency, work might usefully be done to increase opportunities for young people, with educational programmes or the location of new industries in the area. Similarly, for young people who have committed minor offences, diversionary programmes or schemes to improve social skills might prevent the development of criminal careers. For those who have, however, spent years in criminal activity including spells in prison, useful preventive work might be done to reduce the chances of further offending, with assistance focused on jobs, accommodation and social support.

> Many people working in social welfare services, especially in social work, argue that the increased range of statutory duties placed upon them, together with cuts in public expenditure, has resulted in a decreased capacity for preventive work. Thus in some circles prevention has come to mean either non-statutory work or the permissive parts of social legislation. In relation to the CHILDREN ACT, for example, LOCAL AUTHORITIES have powers to help young people after they have left care. Such preventive work is carried out to widely varying standards by social services departments, despite the known vulnerability of young people LEAVING CARE.
>
> P. Marsh and J. Triseliotis, *Prevention and Reunification in Child Care*, London: Batsford, 1993.

**primary carer**   a person with the main responsibility of providing care for another, usually thus experiencing restriction in their own life. The person cared for may be physically disabled, have a mental illness or DISABILITY, or be ill or frail due to old age.

Approximately 1.7 million CARERS in Britain live in the same household as the person they care for; 1.4 million carers spend at least twenty-four hours a week in caring activities. Three-quarters of these people look after an old person, and about half are themselves above retirement age. Carers are usually women and men in their fifties but may be as young as 10, and spouse carers may be 70-plus. Caring is a developmental sequence over a time period – from 'semi-care', when the person cared for can be left alone at night, through part-time care, when they need full-time care but the carer can attend to their own affairs, to full care, when it becomes impossible to leave the cared-for person alone. The primary carer is likely to be a close family relative, and up to 70 per cent of carers are likely to be daughters or daughters-in-law.

> The primary carer, the person with the major responsibility for and tasks of caring, is the focal person for the implementation of COMMUNITY CARE services. They are the person most likely to experience the physical and emotional strain that can be associated with caring, although many carers choose to care and gain great satisfaction from caring for loved ones. The differences for men and women

primary carers have been noted. Men are less likely to be pressured to give up their paid employment than women, are more likely to receive support from relatives and social services and are more likely to be offered residential care for the cared-for person at an early stage. Women are often expected to give up well-remunerated work with associated pension rights to care for family members and are offered more short-stay residential and day care support than men – but as a means of helping them to carry on longer. The NATIONAL HEALTH SERVICE AND COMMUNITY CARE ACT provides entitlement to a full ASSESSMENT for primary carers; this is a right for all carers, whether they are men, women or children.

C. Hicks, *Who Cares? Looking after People at Home*, London: Virago, 1988.

**principles of sentencing** the collective term used to describe the explanations and justifications given for the imposition of punishment on people who break the criminal law.

It is usually argued that there are two broad philosophies of punishment, known as retributivism and utilitarianism. Put simply, retributivism (which can be traced back to ancient legal systems) maintains that the punishment of wrongdoing is a moral right and duty, an end in itself and an essential component of a civilized society. The obligations on the punisher are to ensure, first, that the person to be punished is correctly identified (that is, that guilt is established) and, second, that the punishment is proportionate to the seriousness of the crime (that is, that it is not excessive). Utilitarianism (whose most eloquent exponent was the philosopher Jeremy Bentham, 1748–1832) maintains that punishment is itself an evil that can be justified only if it brings about a greater good, namely the reduction of wrongdoing. Punishment in this view is a means to an end, not an end in itself. The most obvious distinction between the two philosophies is that utilitarians have to demonstrate that punishment (or sentences) work, while retributivists have only to demonstrate that punishment is deserved. The main criticism of utilitarianism is that it takes insufficient account of the relationship between punishment and the seriousness of the crime, while the main criticism of retributivism is that it takes insufficient account of the effect of punishment.

From the two broad philosophical approaches of retributivism and utilitarianism, a number of principles have developed that provide frameworks for sentencing. These are as follows.

'*JUST DESERTS*'. This phrase is the modern equivalent of the term 'retributivism'. It implies that the main purpose of sentencing is to denounce the crime and 'visit retribution' on the criminal to the extent that they deserve it. (Retribution must be distinguished from revenge, which is disproportionate punishment and has no place in any philosophy of justice.) The crucial considerations are the seriousness of the crime and the culpability of the criminal, that is, the extent to which they can be held responsible for their actions. There is scope to consider aggravating and mitigating factors in so far as they relate to the offence and the offender's part in it, but wider considerations of the offender's circumstances are less relevant. The government white paper *Crime, Justice and Protecting the Public* (1990) sets out the philosophy underpinning the CRIMINAL JUSTICE ACT 1991 and states that its aim 'is to ensure that convicted criminals are punished justly and suitably according to the seriousness of their offences; in other words that they should get their just deserts' (para. 2.1).

*Deterrence.* This was the original concern underlying utilitarianism. It implies that the main purpose of sentencing is to deter people from committing crime. There are two elements in this principle: individual deterrence and general deterrence. Individual deterrence refers to measures intended to impress on the offender that the personal consequences of their actions in the form of the punishment received make it 'not worth' committing crime again. The most commonly used individually deterrent sentence is the fine, but any sentence that restricts offenders' liberty or inconveniences or shames them may have a deterrent effect. General deterrence refers to measures intended to set an example to other people in the hope of deterring them from committing crime. For example, a bout of criminal damage in a particular locality may result in an 'exemplary' prison sentence to demonstrate that local people have 'had enough'. One objection to deterrent sentences is that they may be disproportionate to the seriousness of the offence in order to 'make a point'. A more fundamental criticism is the underlying assumption that crime is committed as a rational choice, with the offender weighing up the possible consequences of their actions before deciding to offend. Although this may be true in some instances, it is by no means the only explanation for offending. Much crime is impulsive or stems from what most people would view as irrational thoughts or feelings.

*Protection and incapacitation.* Another utilitarian principle related to deterrence is that of protecting the public from further harm from the offender. Rather than relying on the rational judgement of the offender that 'crime does not pay', a safer way of ensuring that no further crime is committed is to reduce the opportunity for crime by restricting the offender's liberty. The ultimate example of such a sentence is, of course, the death penalty. Imprisonment is less effective, since prisoners may escape, and they will, in any case, be released at some point. Giving someone a COMMUNITY SERVICE ORDER, sending them to a PROBATION CENTRE or even subjecting them to ELECTRONIC MONITORING may seem mild measures in comparison, but the principles of restriction and surveillance are basically the same. The extent of the restriction has to be decided according to the seriousness of the offence, and this means that the retributive principle of proportionality also has to play a part.

*Compensation and reparation.* Just as deterrence may be either individual or general, so the retributive principle of 'making good' harm done can include both the individual victim and wider society. Compensation (predominantly financial) is usually made to the individual victim of a crime. REPARATION is a broader concept that involves the offender in doing something socially useful and morally uplifting (such as community service), thereby demonstrating their remorse and willingness to put back something into society.

*Reform, rehabilitation and correction.* The bringing about of fundamental changes to the personality, attitudes and behaviour of an offender, so that they no longer commit offences – not because they fear the possible consequences but because they appreciate that crime is wrong – has long been a utilitarian aim of sentencing. The distinction between reform and rehabilitation is not an easy one. Reform tends to imply a change of attitude or beliefs, whereas rehabilitation tends to imply a change of circumstances (personal, social or medical) leading to a change of behaviour, although the two concepts are very closely related. The term 'correction' has been imported from the United States. For some people, it has unacceptable overtones of coercion, but it has been interpreted as a 'noncommittal' word that we are wise to adopt because it implies appropriate humility about the state of our knowledge about the reasons why people stop committing crimes. In the past, people have viewed crime as a symptom of sin (which only religious conversion will remedy) or of disease (which only medical science will cure) or of an emotionally deprived childhood (which only psychotherapeutic casework will resolve) or of poverty (which only social and political action will alleviate). While all these explanations might provide some insight into understanding some crime, none provides a full explanation; many people now believe that such an explanation is neither possible nor desirable.

People commit crimes for many reasons (see THEORIES OF CRIME). They also stop committing crime for many reasons, and the sentence they receive may be only one of several influential factors. It would also be a mistake to assume that sentencing is always a rational activity, based on the above principles. Sentencers' decisions may be influenced by many factors, not all of which might be considered 'relevant'. Sentencers' own backgrounds, political persuasions, occupations and prejudices can result in sentences that appear inconsistent or unfair. Some commentators argue that sentencing practice is devoid of agreed aims and objectives and impervious to attempts at evaluation. The Court of Appeal attempts to rectify miscarriages of justice in the lower courts, but some people believe that we should have a sentencing council to give clear guidance to courts about the sentences they should impose for particular crimes.

N. Walker, *Why Punish?*, Oxford: Oxford University Press, 1991.

**prioritizing problems** a stage of TASK-CENTRED WORK in which CLIENT and practitioner draw up a list of the client's problems and decide which two or three of these are the most pressing and which the client would most like solved.

With some complicated problems it may be that sub-problems have to be tackled in a particular sequence – the solution to one problem may then unlock a subsequent problem. In selecting problems to work on, the MOTIVATION of the client is a key factor.

**prison** since the abolition of the death penalty in 1965, imprisonment is the most severe penalty available to the courts in England and Wales.

Maximum prison sentences are laid down by Acts of Parliament, but within those limits courts have discretion about the length of sentences, although MAGISTRATES' courts cannot send anyone to prison for more than six months for one offence or a total of twelve months for more than one offence. Ninety per cent of prison sentences are given by Crown Courts. (See CRIMINAL COURTS.) Men's prisons are categorized according to their functions and levels of security. There are 35 local prisons (which house prisoners immediately after they have been sentenced), 52 closed training prisons (housing high- and medium-security-risk prisoners), 19 open training prisons (housing low-security-risk prisoners), 17 remand centres (for prisoners awaiting trial or sentence) and 22 YOUNG OFFENDER INSTITUTIONS (for prisoners aged 15–21 years). Some prisons serve more than one function. There are 12 female prisons, some of which also incorporate remand centres and young offender institutions, categorized only as either closed or open. The average prison population was about 46,000 in 1991–2, having reached 48,600 in 1989. Of these prisoners, just under 1,600 are women. Sixteen per cent of the male prison population and 26 per cent of the female prison population are known to be from ethnic-minority communities. Twenty-two per cent of the total prison population is untried or unsentenced (that is, on remand). The prison population in England and Wales is one of the highest in Western Europe in relation to the general population.

One of the major criticisms of prisons has always been the levels of overcrowding, especially in the local and remand prisons, many of which are Victorian buildings. The government has responded to prison overcrowding in two ways: by engaging in a vast prison-building programme, and by introducing legislation restricting the powers of courts to send people to prison. The CRIMINAL JUSTICE ACT 1991 (implemented in October 1992) required a court to send people to prison only if the seriousness of the offence warranted it; other offences and previous records could be considered only in a very limited way. The evidence after the first six months of the Act's implementation was that it had succeeded in reducing the prison population to around 43,500. However, vociferous criticism (especially from sentencers) resulted in the government amending the Act within a year to allow courts greater discretion to consider all offences before them as well as previous convictions. The prison population has subsequently begun to rise again.

Prisons as they now exist are a relatively modern form of punishment. In medieval times they were used for detention before trial (compare modern remand), not for punishment as such, which was invariably physical. During the sixteenth and seventeenth centuries houses of correction and workhouses developed with the general purpose of containing the vagrant poor and the unemployed. Among these were some petty offenders, but more serious offenders were more likely to receive the death sentence or to be transported to North America. During the eighteenth century, however, two factors influenced the increased use of imprisonment as a punishment in its own right. First, the independence of the United States made it necessary to find alternatives to transportation (although Australia was still available). Second, a more enlightened attitude to the criminal law resulted in a reduction in the number of offences that attracted the death penalty. At this time, prisons were regarded as places of deterrence and retribution (see PRINCIPLES OF SENTENCING), but by the end of the nineteenth century they had become places for reform and rehabilitation. Emphasis was placed on religious instruction, education, training and psychiatric treatment for prisoners, the purpose being 'to encourage and assist them to lead a good and useful life' (Prison Rule number 1). During the second half of the twentieth century, however, the gap between the rhetoric of rehabilitation and the reality of the conditions and regimes in most prisons has become very clear. Ideologies of 'treatment and training' have been replaced by more modest goals such as those formulated in the 'mission statement' of the Prison Service: 'Her Majesty's Prison Service serves the public by keeping in custody those committed by the courts. Our duty is to look after them with humanity and to help them to lead law-abiding and useful lives in custody and on release.'

A number of radical analysts of prison history have linked the emergence of imprisonment with the needs of industrial capitalist society. For example, it has been argued that prison serves various social functions: first, containing people who are unproductive or disrupt the normal processes of production; second, minimizing the influence of such people by denying them responsibility for their daily lives; third, symbolically stigmatizing such people and allowing those not in prison to distance themselves by creating a 'them and us' division; fourth, diverting attention from other socially harmful acts committed by people with power and wealth in society, by focusing on a narrow group of criminals from the lower classes who constitute the majority of the prison population; and fifth, reassuring people that 'something is being done' about law-and-order problems.

The prison system is constantly faced with a number of serious problems that are frequently described as 'crises'. They may be summarized as problems of security (preventing escapes while avoiding undue oppression of the compliant majority), of conditions (the squalid and deteriorating accommodation in many prisons and the poverty of many prison regimes, which have inadequate work, education and association), of authority (the poor state of prison staff morale and industrial relations), of control (maintaining discipline among prisoners and preventing riots) and of legitimacy (the growing fear among some sections of the public that the whole prison system may be unjust). Following the serious disturbances at Manchester Prison in 1990, Lord Justice Woolf and Judge Stephen Tumim produced a report that argued that it was vital to strike the correct balance between security, control and justice in prisons. Among their recommendations (only a few of which have so far been implemented by the government) was one that most prisons should be 'community prisons', catering for a wide variety of prisoners from the locality.

The Criminal Justice Act 1991 introduced a new system for the early release of prisoners. In place of the old system of remission (after two-thirds of the sentence) and parole (discretionary release after one-third of the sentence or six months, whichever is the longer), the Act provided that half of all sentences should be served in custody. Thereafter, more systematic and less discretionary arrangements for release pertain. On the one hand, the new system assures courts that prisoners will serve at least 50 per cent of their sentences in custody; on the other, prisoners have clearer information about their rights.

The PROBATION SERVICE has had a presence inside prisons since 1966 – although there has always been a degree of opposition within the service to working in what some consider to be a professionally hostile environment. Initially concerned with routine 'welfare' matters, this role has been increasingly taken over by prison officers, through 'shared work' schemes, and probation officers have become more involved in therapeutic work. They run a variety of groups addressing such issues as offending behaviour, anger management and sex offending. In women's prisons they also run groups for survivors of sexual abuse. They contribute to sentence planning and write reports when early release is being considered. Probation officers from prisoners home areas also maintain contact through letters and visits and often work with prisoners' families. They supervise some prisoners on licence when they are released. Thus the Probation Service provides what is known as a 'throughcare' service to prisoners.

One of the most significant recent developments in relation to prisons has been that of privatization. The arguments in favour of privatizing prisons are both ideological (that it is compatible with a market economy) and pragmatic (the need to build more prisons quickly and maintain them cost-effectively, to hold prison management more accountable and to make prison staff working practices more flexible). The arguments against privatization are similarly ideological (that punishment is a direct responsibility of the state) and pragmatic (that private security staff are not competent to contain and care for prisoners, and that private prisons will have a vested interest in maintaining a high prison population). The government has set itself the target of privatizing 10 per cent of the prison estate, or twelve prisons. This will include five newly built prisons and seven existing prisons, as yet unnamed.

M. Cavadino and J. Dignan, *The Penal System: An Introduction*, London: Sage, 1992.

**prison welfare** officially an outdated term but remaining in common usage to refer to the work of the PROBATION SERVICE inside PRISON establishments.

Probation officers are seconded to work in probation departments in prison and are accountable to Prison Service management, despite remaining employed by the Probation Service. They have worked inside prisons since 1966, although there has always been opposition within the service to working in what some consider to be a professionally hostile environment. Initially concerned with routine 'welfare' matters, this role has been increasingly taken over by prison officers, through 'shared work' schemes, and probation officers have become more involved in therapeutic work. They run a variety of groups addressing such issues as offending behaviour, anger management and sex offending. In women's prisons they also run groups for survivors of sexual abuse. They contribute to sentence planning and write reports when early release is being considered. They help prisoners to maintain links with their families and the Probation Service in their home areas.

**private law** those aspects of family law that do not involve the state, including the local authority. Most private law proceedings that concern social workers involve matrimonial disputes.

The CHILDREN ACT contains some important private law orders called SECTION 8 ORDERS, which resolve practical matters to do with children caught up in matrimonial disputes. That Act also created a unique flexibility for courts that can draw on any of the private law orders in proceedings for a CARE ORDER if it thinks this would promote the child's welfare.

**probation board** see PROBATION COMMITTEES.

**probation centre** a building approved by the secretary of state and run by the PROBATION SERVICE to provide programmes of organized activities for offenders made subject to PROBATION ORDERS with requirements to attend such programmes.

Under the CRIMINAL JUSTICE ACT 1991 a probation order requiring attendance at a centre is a COMMUNITY SENTENCE that meets the sentencing aim of restricting an offender's liberty. It is normally used for serious offences that are close to being serious enough to warrant imprisonment. Offenders are normally required to attend for up to sixty days and if they fail to do so may be subject to BREACH PROCEEDINGS. The first probation centres (known initially as day training centres and later as day centres) were established in 1973. In the past, some centres have admitted offenders on a voluntary basis, but programmes are now confined to offenders on court orders. Most activities in centres are for groups of offenders, ranging from being intensively therapeutic (for example, work with SEX OFFENDERS) to providing constructive leisure pursuits. Offenders are expected to address their offending behaviour, which means facing up to the consequences of their actions, trying to understand why they commit offences and looking for realistic ways to stop offending. Offenders also receive help with personal problems affecting their offending and can learn social skills to improve the way they function in their daily lives (including adult literacy, assertiveness training, anger management and ALCOHOL education).

Most probation centres are attended predominantly by white young men, who constitute the majority of serious offenders coming before the courts. In accordance with ANTI-DISCRIMINATORY PRACTICE, there is concern that better provision should be made for black people and women so that centres are perceived by probation officers and by sentencers as being appropriate disposals, thus avoiding CUSTODIAL SENTENCES for these offenders.

**probation committees**  local committees consisting of magistrates, judges, local authority representatives and independent people, which have responsibility for the management of the fifty-six local probation services in England and Wales, including the appointment of probation officers. They are to be replaced by probation boards.

**probation order**  a COMMUNITY SENTENCE requiring an offender to be supervised by a probation officer for up to three years.

Under the CRIMINAL JUSTICE ACT 1991 a probation order may be made on any offender over the age of 16, although the juvenile equivalent, a SUPERVISION ORDER, remains an available option for 16- and 17-year-olds. A probation order can be imposed only with the consent of the offender. The probation order has a long history, dating back to the Probation of Offenders Act 1907. It was originally intended to be an alternative to a sentence and remained so, technically, until the Criminal Justice Act 1991. Its traditional purpose was to offer advice, assistance and friendship to offenders, in the belief that they could thus be reformed or rehabilitated (see PRINCIPLES OF SENTENCING). More emphasis is now placed on restricting offenders' liberty, although under the Criminal Justice Act 1991 the objectives of a probation order still include the rehabilitation of the offender, as well as protecting the public and preventing reoffending. The conduct of probation orders is governed by NATIONAL STANDARDS.

Under a probation order, the offender signs a contract that, while on probation, they will keep in touch with their designated probation officer through regular office appointments and visits at home. They must also notify their probation officer of any change of address or employment. If they fail to meet these requirements they may be subject to BREACH PROCEEDINGS. Since 1948 it has been possible for courts to add conditions to a basic order, requiring an offender to live at an approved residence or to undergo psychiatric treatment. More recently, courts have been able to require an offender to attend programmes of activities at a PROBATION CENTRE for up to sixty days (or longer for SEX OFFENDERS).

Advocates of the traditional probation order extol its flexibility as a sentencing option. They argue that it can be used for both relatively minor and serious offences and can be tailored to the particular needs of an offender. However, it has been hard for the probation order to shake off its image in the eyes of courts as a 'soft option', suitable only for less serious offences. After the introduction of COMMUNITY SERVICE in the 1970s, the use of the probation order declined dramatically. In response, the PROBATION SERVICE emphasized its value as an alternative to custody for serious offences. Since the Criminal Justice Act 1982, the use of the probation order has increased from about 24,000 per year for men to 36,000 in 1991. By contrast, orders for women have declined from about 12,000 to 8,000. This may be explained by the success of probation officers in persuading courts that most offences committed by women are insufficiently serious to warrant supervision.

Probation orders can now be combined with community service orders in the form of COMBINATION ORDERS. The rationale for this is to provide courts with an additional community sentence that offers help to the offender while also exacting REPARATION.

**Probation Service**   the major organization in England and Wales for dealing with offenders in conditions of freedom. (In Scotland the Probation Service ceased to exist as a separate organization when it was incorporated into the new social services departments in 1968.)

Probation officers supervise adult offenders placed on probation by the CRIMINAL COURTS and some YOUNG OFFENDERS under 18 years who are made subject to either PROBATION ORDERS or SUPERVISION ORDERS (although social services departments also supervise some juvenile offenders). Probation Service staff also supervise offenders placed on COMMUNITY SERVICE ORDERS and staff APPROVED PROBATION HOSTELS and BAIL HOSTELS. They provide what is called a 'throughcare' service for offenders sent to PRISON, which includes staffing a probation office in each prison and supervising prisoners on EARLY RELEASE or PAROLE. Probation officers prepare PRE-SENTENCE REPORTS on offenders to help courts arrive at the best sentencing decision. In civil matters, they provide reports for the county courts and the FAMILY PROCEEDINGS COURTS to assist in decisions about children's residence and contact with their parents following divorce. There are fifty-five probation areas in England and Wales (mostly coterminous with counties), employing around 7,000 probation officers, 1,800 ancillary workers, 4,500 clerical and administrative staff and 700 non-probation-officer staff in approved probation and bail hostels. Just under half of all probation officers are women, but less than 3 per cent are black.

The Home Secretary is responsible to Parliament for the work of the Probation Service, whose interests are dealt with by the Home Office Criminal Department. The Home Office provides 80 per cent of the Probation Service's funding, the other

20 per cent coming from local authorities. In each probation area there is a PROBATION COMMITTEE, consisting of magistrates, judges, local authority representatives and independent people, with responsibility for the management of the local probation service, including the appointment of probation officers. These committees are to be replaced by PROBATION BOARDS, which will have fewer members and will exercise less detailed but more strategic and policy control over the service.

Each probation area has a chief probation officer (CPO), with overall responsibility for the direction and delivery of service in that area. Responsible to the CPO are deputy (DCPO) and assistant (ACPO) chief probation officers, who usually have responsibility for particular aspects of service (for example, training and prisons) and/or geographical parts of the area. Senior probation officers (SPOs) are in charge of teams of probation officers (POs) covering a geographical 'patch' or a specialism such as courts, community service or a PROBATION CENTRE. Most teams include a probation service assistant (PSA), who is not professionally qualified, as well as clerical and administrative staff. Attached to many teams are probation service voluntary associates (VAs), ordinary members of the public who assist probation officers in such tasks as befriending and transporting clients. In the past, probation areas have enjoyed relative autonomy to develop their own policies and practice, but the service has become increasingly centralized, particularly since the publication by the Home Office in 1984 of the Statement of National Objectives and Priorities. Since that time, central government has sought to standardize practice across England and Wales, and probation officers now work within the framework provided by the national standards, which set out the expectations and requirements of all aspects of supervision.

There is considerable disagreement about the extent to which the Probation Service can be regarded as a social work organization. In order to be appointed as a probation officer it is necessary to have a professional social work qualification (the Certificate of Qualification in Social Work, the Certificate of Social Service or the Diploma in Social Work); but the Home Office green paper *Supervision and Punishment in the Community* (1990) argues that more emphasis should be placed on the service's role as a criminal justice agency. A brief account of the history of the service will illustrate how this debate has come about.

The Probation Service has its roots in the work of the nineteenth-century police court missionaries, first employed by the Church of England Temperance Society in 1876 to 'reclaim' offenders charged with drunkenness or drink-related offences. The Probation of Offenders Act 1907 gave MAGISTRATES' courts the right to appoint probation officers, whose job was to advise, assist and befriend offenders placed under their supervision. Such a measure was officially deemed to be imposed instead of a court sentence – and remained so until the CRIMINAL JUSTICE ACT 1991 finally made the probation order a legal sentence! The Criminal Justice Act 1925 made it obligatory for every court to appoint a probation officer, and during the first half of the twentieth century the work of the service expanded to include work with juveniles and families, as well as with adult offenders. Part of that work included dealing with matrimonial problems, and it was through this aspect of the work that the role of the divorce court welfare officer developed. By the mid-1960s the service had also taken responsibility for the welfare of prisoners, both inside prison and on release. During this time, the evangelical mission of the service developed into a secular professional social work service to the courts. The distinctive professional skill that probation officers developed was that of the SOCIAL INQUIRY REPORT. This was a social work assessment of an offender in their social environment, with a specific purpose of assisting courts to make sentencing decisions.

Although there had always been a degree of tension in the role of the probation officer between caring for the offender and controlling their criminal behaviour, these two aspects of the work were viewed as part and parcel of both the psychoanalytic casework and the paternalistic 'common-sense' advice that combined to characterize the typical probation officer of the early and mid-twentieth century. However, despite its social work base, the Probation Service saw itself as distinct from other social work specialisms, and for that reason in England and Wales it did not follow Scotland's example of joining the social services departments newly created in 1971 after the SEEBOHM REPORT. Ironically, however, at this time the service agreed to accept generic social work training for probation officers, eventually replacing the separate Home Office training.

The Criminal Justice Act 1972 introduced community service orders, which involved probation officers in supervising offenders undertaking unpaid (often manual) work, with little obvious social work content in the relationship. It proved a popular sentence with courts and resulted in a dramatic decline in the use of probation orders. With the tide of national politics turning towards an explicit 'law-and-order' agenda and some writers advocating the creation of a 'community correctional service', the emphasis on punishment and strict 'alternatives to custody' increased. With the new Conservative government in 1979 there began a fundamental review of the identity and ethos of the service. Many commentators sought ways of reconciling the increasingly conflicting demands to care and control, some of them arguing for the service to jettison its pseudo-medical claims and concentrate on helping offenders stop offending, others advocating a radical socialist approach to probation work. The latter view was widely embraced within the NATIONAL ASSOCIATION OF PROBATION OFFICERS, the professional association and trade union for probation officers.

Throughout the 1980s central government control of the service increased. Alongside the rise of a managerial ethos that stressed 'economy, efficiency and effectiveness' emerged a penal philosophy of 'punishment in the community' based on JUST DESERTS rather than REHABILITATION (see PRINCIPLES OF SENTENCING). The dilemma facing the government was that of stemming the soaring PRISON population while ensuring 'value for money' from the Probation Service and not appearing to be 'soft' on crime. Its aim, in the green and white papers that preceded the Criminal Justice Act 1991, was to strengthen the credibility of community punishments by subjecting both offenders and probation officers to greater scrutiny and making both more accountable to the courts.

The historical role of probation officers to 'advise, assist and befriend' is still widely (and nostalgically) quoted within the Probation Service, but it has been suggested that contemporary probation officers are more likely to be committed to challenging the attitudes and behaviour that lead offenders to commit crime and to cause distress to their victims.

T. May, *Probation: Politics, Policy and Practice*, Buckingham: Open University Press, 1991.

**problem family** a term widely used in the post-Second World War period in British social work agencies to describe families thought to have persistent problems that either were impervious to help or required constant support.

The concept of the problem family was closely associated with the idea of a CYCLE OF DEPRIVATION. Problem families were thought to have their roots in other problem families – the problems were transmitted from one generation to another through the process of socialization. Although the term is no longer used by social welfare professionals, the idea is still thought to be alive both in the public consciousness and implicitly in some social work practice. There are strong associations with the idea of the UNDERCLASS and the 'SCROUNGER'. Critics of the term argue that 'families with problems' is a more defensible idea, especially if the 'problems' are defined. The same critics have also suggested that the long-term support thought necessary for 'problem families' was actually a form of casework that cultivated in such families a form of dependence upon social work agencies.

**process recording** a detailed account of a piece of work conducted in a social work or social welfare setting.

Process recording may be a verbatim account of an interview or of a critical part of an interview. It may also include, in parallel, an account of the worker's reasoning or decisions in pursuing, for example, one particular line of inquiry rather than another. Thus the recording may include the aims and objectives of the interview or transaction, an evaluation of content and outcome, and an assessment of the effectiveness of the social work process. This kind of detailed recording is especially useful in social work training with student social workers and with workers in the early stages of their careers. Some see such detailed work as fruitful with very difficult cases too, especially where people are hostile or obstructive, or where they find it difficult to express themselves. Process recording can be used with individual cases, with families and with GROUPWORK.

**profession** a group or body, of some social standing, claiming expertise in an area of work.

Features thought to characterize a profession include lengthy training in relation to some clearly demarcated area of knowledge and skill, the idea of public service or even altruistic practice, impartial service regardless of client, uniform (that is, competent) service regardless of practitioner, and a code of ethics or conduct. The classic concept of the profession, based upon the medical and legal professions in the nineteenth century, included a scale of fees and a commitment to independence, the latter implying that none could possibly judge the individual professional except a peer or colleague.

The process of professionalization seems to involve a sequence of developments. A particular skill or area of knowledge emerges in response to changes in economic and social activity; people gather together to exchange ideas and to develop the new territory; if the 'field' has commercial or social potential, the group will increase in number; the members seek to define and set boundaries on the new activity and by so doing seek to distinguish it from associated activities;

decisions are made about who can be a member and later a 'practitioner'; and the final stages involve controlling the qualifying process and the conduct of members. The state will incorporate the training of professionals into the mainstream of higher education if the activity is regarded as sufficiently important, although professional organizations will still have some measure of autonomy.

There is no doubt that social work has emerged as an occupation in the way described above. Most commentators, however, question whether social work is or can be a fully fledged profession, preferring to regard it as a 'quasi-' or 'semi-profession'. They point, first, to the roots of social work in voluntary activity and to the continuing debate about how much social work requires genuine expertise and how much of it might be undertaken by communities, in SELF-HELP activity and by volunteers. Second, they point to the lack of agreement among social workers about the knowledge and value base of the occupation. Social workers, even within the same team, may adopt quite different styles of practice based upon differing views of the social work task. Third, social workers operate within a bureaucratic context. They are part of hierarchies and far from exercising autonomy they are clearly accountable to a line manager on a day-to-day basis. Additionally, given that many important decisions concerning social work activities are actually made by lawyers, doctors and other professionals, the claim to full professional autonomy is flawed.

Critics of the idea of profession have pointed to the self-interested behaviour of professional bodies. They may speak the language of public service and of a commitment to high-quality practice for all, but their tactics often restrict entry to the profession, discriminate against women and members of ethnic minorities and seek to maintain if not improve high salaries. The social class origins of the established professions are principally from the same social groups. Given these general criticisms of professions, some social workers have questioned the desirability of adopting the idea of the profession as the occupational goal. If the average social worker does accept structural inequality as the major explanation for the social problems that they have to deal with, then maybe, they argue, the occupation should aspire to a strong trade unionism. Trade unions too are interested in competent, high-quality services.

T. Johnson, *Professions and Power*, Basingstoke: Macmillan, 1972.

**prohibited steps order**   a court order under the CHILDREN ACT that prevents a parent or any other person specified in the order from taking, without the consent of the court, a particular action that could be taken in meeting PARENTAL RESPONSIBILITY (see SECTION 8 ORDERS).

Examples of possible prohibited steps orders are an order preventing the removal of a child from the United Kingdom, an order preventing a child undergoing certain surgery or an order preventing a change in the child's schooling.

**psychiatry**   the medical approach to the understanding and treatment of MENTAL HEALTH PROBLEMS.

Psychiatrists are qualified medical practitioners with a specialist postgraduate training in psychiatry and PSYCHODYNAMIC theory. They operate traditionally from the hospital base.

*Impact of psychiatry.* Psychiatry applies the MEDICAL MODEL, taken for granted in Western culture as the most scientific and effective approach to physical health problems, to mental health problems. Central to the medical model is the idea that 'disease entities' exist in the person as the cause of the symptoms of illness. These 'disease entities' are named in the diagnosis given to the symptoms. One example of this in psychiatry is the diagnosis of SCHIZOPHRENIA. 'Disease entities' can be understood as developments in the physical make-up of the individual that are defined as 'abnormal' or pathological by medical science, and in the case of physical 'diseases' these developments can be detected by scientific procedures (for example, the presence of a virus in blood cells). However, in the case of mental health problems, although there is some evidence suggesting the genetic predisposition to PSYCHOSIS and NEUROSIS, this evidence is not conclusive (see MENTAL ILLNESS).

Although, therefore, physical 'disease entities' have not been found in relation to mental health problems, the symptoms of psychoses are activated by biochemical processes in the nervous system. It has been found that the physical treatments of drugs and ELECTRO-CONVULSIVE THERAPY can affect these processes with many who have these conditions, with the result of reduced symptoms. The impact of these treatments was striking in the 1950s and onwards, enabling the majority of people with psychotic conditions in psychiatric hospitals to be discharged after short stays only. This meant that psychiatry could claim effectiveness in using the medical model with mental health problems. The Mental Health Act 1959 (see MENTAL HEALTH ACT 1983) consequently treated mental health problems as equivalent to physical health problems, making the decision (on the part of psychiatrists and social workers) to admit someone compulsorily to hospital as the result of a psychiatric decision that the person was too ill to be responsible for their own safety and for the safety of others. However, because no 'disease entities' have been found, these physical treatments can only control, and do not cure, psychotic symptoms; also, more recent COMMUNITY CARE studies show that people with the most severe symptoms are least likely to be helped by medication. A result of this is that there are people in the community with uncontrolled symptoms who, as a result, may be unable to cope with settled accommodation and daily living; subsequently they may become homeless and suffer a poor quality of life, and they may also offend and end up in PRISON or secure hospitals.

The emphasis on the use of drugs by psychiatry and the compulsory powers that psychiatrists ultimately hold have led Szasz from the ANTI-PSYCHIATRY position, and a number of other radical writers, to regard psychiatry as a form of social control, restricting the rights and liberty of people who do not conform to the expectations of society. Anti-racist writers make this point strongly in respect of black people, who are far more likely than white people to be treated restrictively, by drugs and compulsory detention.

*Pathways to the psychiatrist.* It is important for the worker to understand who is referred to the psychiatric services, and by what routes. About 250 people in every 1,000 in the population have recognizable psychiatric problems; about 230 of these consult a general practitioner with these problems; only about 140 are recognized by the GP as having psychiatric difficulties; and only 17 are referred to the psychiatric services. Many more 'drop out' once referred – at least one-third do not keep their initial appointment. This means that any help that psychiatrists can give reaches only a very small proportion of those who may be in need. The people who get referred are those with severe symptoms, and usually with a psychotic diagnosis, although about a fifth have a neurotic diagnosis (usually DEPRESSION). They will have had the symptoms for a long time and are likely to have serious social problems, possibly challenging behaviour, and may be at risk of suicide. People who see psychiatrists therefore have the most serious difficulties – although it could also be said that they are the people society considers to be most in need of control.

An important point about the people referred is that men, once given a psychiatric diagnosis by the GP, tend to be referred in high proportions, while women are less likely to be referred; the same pattern is found for younger as opposed to older people. This may suggest the mental health problems of women and older people are treated less seriously than those of men and younger people. Black people are admitted to hospital in high proportions, come to the attention of psychiatrists to a disproportionate extent through the police and the courts and are more likely than white people to be placed in secure provision. Asian people, by contrast, may not be receiving a service to the extent it is needed, as they are less likely than white and black people to be referred to a psychiatrist. Members of lower socioeconomic groups who are referred to the psychiatric services with psychoses are the most likely to become 'long-term patients', that is, likely to relapse frequently, thus needing hospital admission, and possibly needing medication and other help from the psychiatric services on a more or less permanent basis. This group is not large – perhaps a quarter of the 10 to 20 per cent of outpatients admitted to hospital – but require specialized social work besides psychiatric help, and may also have physical disabilities.

*Psychiatry and COMMUNITY CARE.* Community care policy, which has in recent years become law under the NATIONAL HEALTH SERVICE AND COMMUNITY CARE ACT, has as a central objective: the reduction of institutional care and the location of the main focus of care in the community. Consequently, psychiatric hospital beds have been massively reduced in number. The majority of people referred to psychiatrists therefore receive care in the community, in a variety of settings. People with long-term, chronic conditions may reside in GROUP HOMES or HOSTELS, and a wider range of people may attend day care or community mental health centres; others may receive visits from social workers and COMMUNITY PSYCHIATRIC NURSES at home. Important in these services is the communication between the different professionals; often the social worker is involved in a MULTIDISCIPLINARY team responsible for the people needing psychiatric services in a particular area. The team makes decisions about the care of particular individuals, and about the roles of each professional in delivering that care, and often a psychiatrist is the head of the team. The social worker's approach to mental health problems has been shown in many studies to be different to that of the psychiatrist; and this, along with the higher status of the psychiatrist in relation to the social worker, raises many issues for the worker to deal with if they are to work effectively within the requirements of community care policy.

Central Council for Education and Training in Social Work, *Improving Mental Health Practice*, London: CCETSW, 1993.

**psychoanalysis**   a theoretical perspective of the development of the individual based on the view that the early life experiences of a person interact with 'basic human nature' to create the adult PERSONALITY.

Psychoanalysis is both an explanation of the development of the personality and a therapeutic process in the treatment of neurotic disorder. Psychoanalytic theory emphasizes the *unconscious* aspects of the individual, that is, those aspects of the personality that are below a person's level of awareness but which have effects on behaviour, thoughts and feelings. In 1895 Freud and Breuer introduced the concept of the unconscious as an active force within the individual, containing basic drives, conflicts and discomforting material, the existence of which is unknown to the person. This inadmissible material does, however, have a powerful impact on a person's activities and on the way the person interacts with the world around them. Early psychoanalytic explanations also referred to the presence of a preconscious – material that is accessible but not immediately available – and the conscious, that is, behaviours, thoughts and feelings that the person is aware of.

In 1900 Freud presented the key concepts of psychoanalysis: the notion of mental structure; infantile sexuality; defence mechanisms; repression; the meaningfulness of unexplained behaviours.

*Mental structure.* The *id* is the most primitive part of the personality and is wholly unconscious. It is explained as the basic structure that the infant is born with; it has no control over its actions and seeks to gratify the basic drives of hunger, thirst and sex. The *ego* begins to develop soon after birth as the infant interacts with the world around them. The ego is the control centre and is both conscious and unconscious. It is guided by reality and attempts to meet the needs originating in the id by negotiation with the person's environment; for example, love and work are socially acceptable ways of meeting the id's needs for sex and aggression. The *superego* is the internal judge, that is, the internalized value base of parents and society. It punishes and praises in accordance with those internalized rules.

*Infantile sexuality.* Psychoanalysis proposes that the development of the id, ego and superego is in conjunction with an individual's progression through a number of stages in their early years, referred to as the *psychosexual* stages of development. Human biology interacting with environmental factors, such as parental discipline, determines a healthy or otherwise progression to adulthood. For healthy psychosexual development the individual must progress in ways that optimize gratification and control through the *oral* stage (0–12 months), *anal* stage (12–30 months), *genital* (or phallic) stage (30 months to 5 years), *latency* stage (5–12 years) and *sexual* stage (adolescent years). Throughout these stages, both boys and girls develop sexual attraction to the opposite-sex parent and wish to displace the same-sex parent. Freud termed this the Oedipus complex in boys and the Electra complex in girls. Psychoanalysis argues that the resolution of these conflicts and development through the psychosexual stages are a complicated process involving the conscious, the unconscious, longings, fears, insecurity and anxiety. The conflicts are finally resolved by the child identifying with the same-sex parent.

*Defence mechanisms.* Throughout these stages of early life the anxiety experienced may be so intolerable that the material (memories, thoughts and feelings) is 'pushed' into the unconscious. The individual can use any number of strategies to protect the ego from anxiety, collectively referred to as mechanisms of defence. Psychoanalysis sees two of the major defence mechanisms, *regression* and *fixation*, as interlinked. If a person receives too little or too much gratification in any of the psychosexual stages, they may become fixated in that stage; that is, anxiety in later life may be managed (defended against) by regression to that stage of childhood in which the person is 'stuck'. Freud saw fixation and regression as mechanisms for enabling a person in adult life to manage stress. Anna Freud later identified and explained further the concept of defence mechanisms – for example, that denial is the refusal to acknowledge anxiety-provoking material in the environment, and reaction formation involves substituting an unacceptable emotion for one less anxiety-provoking, such as love for hate.

*Repression.* An ego defence mechanism in which the ego 'pushes' 'discomforting impulses, thoughts, feelings or memories' into the unconscious. This reduces anxiety and protects a person's self-image. The process is unconscious and in this it differs from suppression, which is the conscious avoidance of anxiety-provoking material. Psychoanalysis argues that residual sexual feelings for a parent are repressed as the boy or girl passes through the final psychosexual stages of growth. It is considered that the ego uses energy from the id to block (repress) anxiety-provoking material.

*Meaningfulness of material.* Psychoanalysis has its roots in biological determinism, implicit in the view that all behaviour is caused and has meaning for the person themselves. The cause may lie deeply repressed in the unconscious and be unknown, but actions, behaviour, thoughts and feelings are directed by the unconscious drive of the id and the repressed material. Psychoanalysis believes that seemingly inexplicable behaviour can be explained and understood. To arrive at the cause may require a long period of analysis.

PSYCHOTHERAPY. Psychoanalysis as therapy relies on the technique of *free association*. The patient says whatever comes into their mind while under instruction from the psychoanalyst to report their thoughts without reservation. The aim is to give patients an insight into their NEUROSIS by examining the contents of the unconscious through exploration of thoughts, fantasies, dreams, slips of the tongue, mistakes, beliefs and attitudes. The psychoanalyst may or may not attempt an interpretation of the material, but the basic premise of treatment is that capricious behaviour can be explained by reference to events in a person's history. Psychoanalysis can thus reveal the motive underlying the behaviour. Psychotherapy is a prolonged and expensive form of treatment, whose efficacy has been questioned. Eysenck has suggested that, in such a lengthy treatment, symptoms are likely to remit spontaneously, regardless of any treatment. Gregory, reviewing some of the evidence for and against the value of psychotherapy, concluded that statistical research evidence confirms that 'psychotherapy in general works and its effects are not entirely due to non-specific effects such as arousal of hope nor to spontaneous recovery'.

Psychoanalysis since its early years has aroused criticism and acceptance almost in equal measures. Some of the first critics, such as Alfred Adler and Carl Jung, were themselves originally psychoanalysts. FEMINIST approaches to PSYCHOLOGY are critical of such explanations as the psychosexual stages while acknowledging the importance of early life experiences. Others have questioned whether all human behaviour can be understood as the expression of sexual and aggressive drives. Psychoanalysis was extremely influential in social work training and practice in the postwar decades in Britain; it has been substantially replaced by more pragmatic approaches to personal and social problems, but it is still influential in PSYCHIATRY.

G. Pearson, J. Treseder and M. Yellowly, *Social Work and the Legacy of Freud*, Basingstoke: Macmillan, 1988.

**psychodynamic approach**   an approach to social work that uses some of the main concepts of PSYCHOANALYSIS.

Social work theory and practice were heavily influenced by psychoanalytic ideas in the 1940s and 1950s. They particularly took up the concept that children develop through a number of stages and the notion that if this development is incomplete children's behaviour can become 'fixated', remaining stuck at a certain level, or 'regress', returning to that of an earlier stage of development. The psychodynamic approach also viewed the adult PERSONALITY as a product of childhood development. Adults suffered anxiety when childhood relationship conflicts had not been fully resolved. Adults deal with anxiety by employing a number of defence mechanisms such as regression, denial (refusal to accept that something is a problem or causes distress) or projection (an unacceptable feeling such as hatred or anger is attributed to another person).

Social work theorists developed a model using psychodynamic concepts but in a way more applicable to relatively fluid and less intensive relationship between social worker and CLIENT. They saw clients' problems and distress as arising from childhood needs and drives (often as a result of poor relationship with parents) that persisted into adulthood because they had not been adequately dealt with at the time. The client experiences distress arising from poor ego functioning – that is, an ego that has not mastered living in the day-to-day world. Social workers used a number of techniques to help clients. Among these were: *diagnostic understanding*, understanding the precise origins of a client's distress; *ventilation*, allowing the client to express feelings; and *corrective relationship*, whereby the relationship with the social worker enabled the client to compensate for previously unsatisfactory relationships. Above all, by exploring and giving insight into the origins of conflict the practitioner helps the client to become aware of how to change.

The psychodynamic approach was widely criticized in later decades for lacking a way of addressing the social origins of problems. Indeed, a number of psychodynamically oriented theorists did introduce a social dimension into their analysis. Even so, the main legacy of the approach was a deep impact on social work terminology, which in its crudest terms was used to describe clients in a patronizing way. Behaviour could be described as 'infantile' or refusal to accept a social worker's point of view as 'denial'. There was also the tendency to examine a client's current difficulties as reflections of deeper problems of unsatisfactory relationships and to overlook the very real dilemmas of current relationships or environmental pressures. (See also CASEWORK, LOSS, OBJECT RELATIONS THEORY.)

F. Hollis and M. Woods, *Casework: A Psychosocial Therapy*, New York: Random House, 1981.

**psychology**   the scientific study of behaviour and of mental processes, such as perception, memory, social interaction and thinking.

Psychological theories have had considerable influence on social work practice. The application of such theoretical frameworks can improve practice and enhance the worker's understanding of the service user and of themselves. Psychology is now an integral part of social work training programmes. Social psychology, behaviourist theories, interactionist approaches and psychoanalytic insights are the core topics often included in the social work syllabus.

The central theme of social work is a commitment to humanely and socially based strategies to enable people to deal more effectively with the concerns and stresses of everyday life in ways that maintain dignity and self-esteem. Social workers when working with service users may need to act as counsellor, advocate, mediator and resource seeker. These complex tasks require a sophisticated approach to understanding how people react to such situations. Psychology can offer conceptual and theoretical insights that impact on the social work task to the benefit of all participants. Social work may use any one or more of a number of therapeutic strategies with service users that have their roots in psychological research: GROUPWORK, COUNSELLING, psychotherapy, BEHAVIOUR MODIFICATION, social interaction work, FAMILY THERAPY, SYSTEMS theory, crisis intervention, disaster responses, and working with the DYING and bereaved. The difficulty for social workers is that psychological knowledge is developing rapidly, and hence a reliance on particular frameworks may ultimately mean that the worker is using an outmoded approach. Thus, to use psychology appropriately in social work requires a flexibility of approach, an updating of knowledge, an evaluation of psychological theory and a willingness to review and change the way social work uses psychology. A useful example of this is that in the 1960s Freudian insights were considered of major importance in workers' one-to-one approach to problem-solving, whereas in the 1980s and 1990s phenomenological theories have come to offer a greater understanding of the individual and their social frameworks. Social workers may only use a small number of psychological insights, but these should be rooted in sound knowledge. Social workers' belief that their own therapeutic efforts can bring about change has been rooted in a commitment to a psychological framework for much of their work. Clearly much social work attempts to address problems rooted in structural oppression; social workers in this respect are required to look beyond the individual to the social structures that shape them. Social psychology helps to some extent in this respect, but the link between broader social structures and individual functioning is properly the province, mostly, of SOCIOLOGY.

M. Herbert, *Psychology for Social Workers*, Basingstoke and London: Macmillan and British Psychological Society, 1981.

**psychopathy**   a persistent disorder of mind that results in abnormally aggressive or seriously irresponsible conduct.

Psychopathy is one of eight 'PERSONALITY DISORDERS' in the International Classification of Diseases (others include 'inadequate personality' and 'depressive personality'). It is classed as a 'NEUROSIS' and therefore as a form of 'mental disorder' (see MENTAL ILLNESS); this has particular implications for the MENTAL HEALTH ACT 1983, in that psychopathy is therefore a condition subject to compulsory admission to hospital. Up until the early twentieth century psychopathy was considered as an inborn impairment of the person's moral faculty, similar to the idea of impaired intelligence. In the 1950s it was defined as a 'conduct disorder' of an antisocial or a social nature, operating from an early age and difficult to influence. Although psychopathy is officially classed as a disease, however, no 'disease entity' as the underlying cause of a set of symptoms has been identified. The Butler Report (1975) said that the diagnosis is easily used with any form of antisocial behaviour; it was formerly often used to admit people using DRUGS and ALCOHOL to hospital compulsorily, but this was stopped by the Mental Health Act 1983. People with diagnoses of psychopathy are, however, still admitted to hospital compulsorily in significant percentages.

*The experience of psychopathy.* The behaviour associated with psychopathy arises from an inability to take in and respond to much from the environment, which may be due to physiological causes or attitudes developed in early childhood. Some organic diseases, such as DEMENTIA or AIDS, can also give rise to these difficulties. There is poor perception and anticipation of events, along with feelings and behaviour inappropriate to the demands of the situation, as the latter are not perceived. Hence what follows is aggression, intolerance of frustration, lack of concern for others and disregard of social obligations; people do not clearly know what they are doing. One person after committing a violent crime said he found it 'confusing'. These experiences result in behaviour that threatens not only the interests of others but also those of the subject themselves, because of the difficulty in anticipating and in responding appropriately. In this important way, psychopathy is different to crime; the subject with a diagnosis of psychopathy is more likely to be detected, cannot restrict their antisocial behaviour, commits incomprehensible offences, does not respond to help or punishment, has little apparent loyalty to other people, and commits a greater number of offences and more violent offences than offenders without a psychiatric diagnosis. Some writers have identified four different types of psychopathy, including a range of antisocial behaviours from 'difficult' behaviour to serious offences to the person. Women are rarely diagnosed as psychopathic, because the behaviour is much closer to that identified with the male or 'macho' stereotype. This means that women displaying such behaviour are much more likely than men to be hospitalized and labelled as dangerous, because they are perceived as so 'abnormal'.

*Social work and psychopathy.* The diagnosis of psychopathy is linked to a number of other problems commonly encountered by social workers: DOMESTIC VIOLENCE, EVICTION and CHILD ABUSE; truancy and delinquent behaviour on the part of children of parents with a diagnosis of psychopathy; work with mental illness; offending and marital problems in the probation sphere; ASW (approved social work) and aftercare; ASW with mentally disordered offenders, in or discharged from special hospitals and secure units; job loss, shortage of money, problem drinking and rejection by the social services. It is important when working with a client with this diagnosis or condition that the practitioner is aware of their own stereotypes of 'dangerousness' that they may be applying to the person; workers should seek instead for positive aspects of the person to relate to, also treating the person with genuine respect. This is most effectively done by exploring with the person the actual circumstances of their antisocial behaviour. Failure to value and understand the person in this way will mean that the worker does not adequately assess their needs and/or the risk they present to self and/or others; also, the person will experience LABELLING and rejection, leading to further antisocial reactions towards the worker and others, and with negative consequences for themselves.

There are many problems in the person's life, referred to above, that the worker can help with. The worker also plays an important role in assisting the family, who are likely to suffer great emotional distress; and spouses may need assistance in the decision to leave their partner. Statutory work – in connection with child abuse and use of the Mental Health Act – are possible too. It is very difficult to work with the person towards significant change in behaviour, but it is possible; social work writers indicate that a sustaining, valuing and consistent relationship with the client – understanding the person's behaviour as the result of their difficulties rather than as a personal attack on the worker, and thereby continuing to accept rather than reject the person – is beneficial to the person. Along similar lines, a study of people with a diagnosis of psychopathy discharged into the community from a special hospital showed that a 'fraternal' rather than 'authoritarian' relationship led to better coping in the community.

P. Huxley, *Social Work Practice in Mental Health*, Aldershot: Gower, 1985.

**psychoses**   a group of incapacitating MENTAL DISORDERS that severely disrupt thinking, speech and behaviour.

Psychoses are understood broadly in Western cultures as different forms of MENTAL ILLNESS; the majority of cases are referred to the psychiatric services, as they represent the main concern of PSYCHIATRY. Psychoses include DEPRESSION, MANIC DEPRESSION and SCHIZOPHRENIA. Their main distinguishing feature is that the person's responses appear to be inappropriate to their circumstances as defined by that person's culture and social groupings. These responses may take the form of 'hallucinations', 'delusions', 'mood disorder', inaccurate judgements and/or unintelligible behaviour. Substantial numbers of people with these conditions recover, and the acute symptoms of many who do not can be controlled, in varying degrees by psychotropic medication – particularly successfully in the case of manic depression. For many people with schizophrenia, however, 'chronic' symptoms of apathy, slowness and loss of motivation can continue long-term, despite medication; and it should always be remembered that the side effects of the medication itself are severe.

*Origins of psychosis.* There is considerable debate over whether the psychoses are an illness or not. In favour of the 'illness' view, psychiatry has relied considerably upon evidence from twin studies, and studies conducted with relatives of people with diagnoses of psychosis, to show that there are strong hereditary – and hence biological – influences on the likelihood of an individual developing a psychotic condition. Identical twins have a 45 per cent chance of developing schizophrenia, and a 70 per cent chance of developing either depression or manic depression. These figures contrast significantly enough with the 2 to 3 per cent chances of a member of the general population developing a psychotic condition to show that being born in the same family as someone with a psychotic condition has an influence upon the likelihood of developing the latter. However, it has never been shown conclusively that the reasons for this lie more in physiological than environmental family factors. Recent research has furthermore shown that these studies may not have been reliable, at least in respect of schizophrenia – although other evidence is presented for the possibility that a general physiologically based sensitivity may be found among people who develop psychotic conditions. Nevertheless, psychotropic drugs are fairly effective at least in blocking symptoms, thus making it possible for many people with psychotic diagnoses to live in the community. Other factors important in the development of a psychotic condition include social disadvantage; those with the most deprived socioeconomic backgrounds and circumstances will be most likely to experience a psychotic condition long-term, and the 'symptoms' will be more severe. Also, life events and stress are important in the onset and relapse of psychotic conditions. Psychiatrists argue that these stressors will 'trigger' a biological 'predisposition' to the condition. Writers with an anti-racist perspective have pointed to the importance of fully assessing the pressures arising from RACISM in the situation of a black person to consider if these do not wholly account for the person's distress, without needing to impute the presence of 'illness'. Similarly, recent research has shown that stress can directly give rise to psychotic symptoms. In contrast to these views, which regard psychoses as definite illness states resulting from biological and/or social conditions, LABELLING THEORY and some ANTI-PSYCHIATRY approaches suggest them to be no more than learned behaviour.

*Impact of psychoses*. About 0.3 per cent of the population are admitted to hospital each year with psychotic diagnoses, and among this group are small numbers (about 0.06 per cent of the population) who experience persistent severe symptoms not affected by medication, which may result in challenging behaviour. A third of those admitted, especially those with a diagnosis of schizophrenia, suffer severe chronic conditions with frequent relapses; a further quarter will be less disabled but still relapse. Only about a third of the people admitted with psychotic diagnoses will recover. Those who do recover are most likely to have diagnoses of depression, to live with a partner and to have been employed for significant periods of time in their lives. A model has been drawn up of the problems experienced by someone with a psychotic diagnosis, and the social work response can be related to these problems, as follows.

*Primary problems* are those problems associated with the 'symptoms', such as HALLUCINATIONS, and the functioning affected by these. People with 'acute' symptoms suffer fear, distress and physical discomfort as a result of these symptoms. Also, the inappropriate perceptions, feelings and beliefs involved in these symptoms can make such people liable to present risk to self and/or others. Those suffering persistent acute symptoms, beyond the control of medication, are, if discharged from hospital without adequate support, highly likely to become homeless (see MENTAL HEALTH ACT), as they cannot cope with day-to-day living, and their behaviour is not acceptable to informal or formal carers. They may often offend, although the offences are usually trivial (see MENTALLY DISORDERED OFFENDERS). Those with long-term chronic conditions may relapse and in the chronic state are still likely to be unable to cope with day-to-day living in varying degrees, especially as many in this group (and in the groups suffering persistent acute symptoms) have come from disadvantaged backgrounds and have never acquired daily living skills.

*Secondary problems* are connected with the person's psychological reactions to the effects of the illness, such as loss of confidence and apathy. Confidence and motivation can be lost as a result of battling against distressing inner experiences – the 'acute symptoms' – and from the forbidding consequences of the illness described under tertiary problems, which leave the individual with little sense of self-worth or belief in a future. Additional implications of experiencing psychosis are that the person may misuse alcohol or drugs (see SUBSTANCE MISUSE) to relieve the discomfort of their symptoms. One study found 56 per cent of patients in psychiatric hospital had misused drugs.

*Tertiary problems* arise through the societal reaction to the person's condition. Societal reaction to psychoses can take place on two fronts. First, difficulties in behaviour and functioning may present stresses for family, friends and actual or potential employers, and thus may result in tensions, rejection and unemployment (the latter in turn leading to poverty, poor housing and deprivation). Children can be seriously affected, through neglect as a result of parental psychosis, thus involving the worker in CHILD PROTECTION work; and the experience of the latter is sufficiently disturbing to lead the children themselves to develop mental health and/or behaviour problems, such as delinquency and truancy. Additional social and legal problems can result if the person is misusing drugs and/or alcohol. Second, tertiary problems for the person can arise also from lack of appropriate service provision. People with chronic psychoses who become homeless, offend, and/or use drugs are particularly unlikely to have their needs taken account of by the services.

*Social work response.* Thus there are a number of different ways in which the worker can assist the person with psychoses: first, in liaising with the psychiatric services over treatment of primary problems and relating to the person through the sustaining psychosocial or CLIENT-centred approach; second, in helping alleviate secondary problems through the provision of supportive services; and third, in family work, advocacy and development work in respect of tertiary problems. With devalued groups – such as women, black people and OLDER PEOPLE – their specific needs in all three areas must be addressed. Social stereotypes of mental illness serve to label the person pejoratively, even though they may be capable of functioning in acceptable ways, and this will lead to the same results of exclusion, tension, rejection and subsequent deprivation, including the possibility that children will be taken into care without justification as a result of labelling. These problems are especially likely if the person is also a member of an oppressed group, and research has shown that black people, particularly black women, are far more likely than white people to be defined as psychotic and given diagnoses of schizophrenia. There may be little that the worker can do about the primary problems, although it is critical to liaise effectively with medical and other staff (see MEDICAL MODEL, MULTIDISCIPLINARY WORKING, PSYCHIATRY) and to have an understanding of the impact of drugs (see DRUGS, MENTAL ILLNESS). With secondary problems it has been shown that use of the psychosocial approach, offering acceptance and valuation, and moving at the person's own pace, can relieve distress, particularly helping with low self-esteem. With tertiary problems there is a great deal the worker can do. An assessment is a critical first step, to ascertain actual difficulties in functioning and any challenging behaviour, along with reasons for these; potential for rehabilitation can usually be judged from whether or not skills have been present prior to the illness. Assessment of the extent of 'labelling' in the person's environment is equally important. Where real difficulties in functioning are identified, services and resources need to be fitted to the person's needs, enabling them to function at their best and enjoy the maximum quality of life within the limitations of their own difficulties and available resources. It is important that these limitations are taken account of, or the person can be distressed and RELAPSE. This heightened vulnerability also means that the more intensive forms of help – such as psychotherapy, cognitive therapy and even behaviour modification if the pace is too fast – are experienced as highly stressful by the person, and thus may result in relapse; with depression they can also result in suicide. Thus great care needs to be taken by the worker in the interventions used and especially when the person is experiencing severe symptoms. This would apply to the use of empowerment theory; although general application of empowerment principles is essential, intervention on this basis would need to incorporate a very accurate assessment of the stressors affecting the person and the actions they feel comfortable with, alongside the 'sustaining' approach of psychosocial theory.

Throughout social work involvement, the 'sustaining' approach in psychosocial theory needs to be employed both to provide a channel for the service user to express needs and feelings and to offer support and valuation. This approach is essentially non-pressurizing but at the same time provides the basis on which other interventions can be selected and employed.

A. Tilbury, *Working with Mental Illness*, Basingstoke: Macmillan, 1993.

**psychosexual development** see PSYCHOANALYSIS.

**psychotherapy** systematic psychological approaches undertaken by a therapist to help people suffering from MENTAL HEALTH PROBLEMS, difficulties in relationships, behavioural problems and other problems of living.

Psychotherapy may be practised with individuals, with people in relationships including families, and with groups, although there is no agreed conception of what it is. Psychotherapists may be social workers, counsellors, psychologists, psychiatrists or other social or medical professionals. The length of training to become a psychotherapist thus varies enormously. There are also many different theoretical approaches to psychotherapy, based on different and sometimes competing analyses of both the nature of human beings and the means by which individual and relational problems may be solved or ameliorated. For example, some schools of thought stress the importance of understanding an individual's past, whereas others place great emphasis on current circumstances. Some therapists have it that effective work may take many years, whereas others argue that useful work must of necessity be brief. Some take a holistic approach, attempting to understand the whole person; others are content to focus upon a particular aspect of behaviour; and so on. (See also BEHAVIOURISM, COGNITIVE-BEHAVIOURAL THERAPY, GESTALT, PSYCHOANALYSIS, TRANSACTIONAL ANALYSIS.)

**punishment in the community** the basis of the government's new approach to sentencing, outlined in the white paper *Crime, Justice and Protecting the Public* (1990).

The concept of punishment in the community is perceived to be a more positive replacement for that of 'alternatives to custody' and is intended to reduce the role of imprisonment as the central plank of penal policy. An emphasis on restrictions on liberty provides a connecting thread between COMMUNITY SENTENCES and custody.

**pupil referral units**   provision made under the EDUCATION ACT 1993 for the education of children not able to attend school, either because they are too ill or because they are permanently excluded and no other school is willing to take them in.

This form of provision is not mandatory, in that local education authorities may choose to deal with severely ill or excluded children in other ways. But where units are established they are now to be called pupil referral units and managed as schools.

**punishment**   see PRINCIPLES OF SENTENCING.

**purchaser/provider split**   the designation of posts within SOCIAL SERVICES DEPARTMENTS as either a purchaser of services or a provider of services.

As part of the central government's guidelines for the implementation of COMMUNITY CARE the DEPARTMENT OF HEALTH requires local authority social services departments to introduce an INTERNAL MARKET as a way of encouraging greater efficiency and gearing up to compete with the private and voluntary sectors. The approach is one adopted in other service areas where COMPULSORY COMPETITIVE TENDERING (CCT) has been introduced. While CCT has not yet been adopted for the social services, the DoH is looking for much greater utilization of the private and voluntary sectors in line with the concept of local authorities becoming ENABLING AUTHORITIES rather than direct providers. As a result, the aim is to introduce an internal market by separating staff who plan services and assess need from those staff who provide services such as residential care.

> One approach to the purchaser/provider split may be a situation where the CARE MANAGER who assesses need and acts on behalf of the consumer of the service will then become a budget holder. As a purchaser they will look for the best service for their client. The local authority in-house service will compete with other providers from the private and voluntary sector for the contract from the purchaser. The belief is that this will encourage the provider unit to become more efficient in order to compete, but also there will be greater choice, thus encouraging the development of a MIXED ECONOMY OF CARE. The purchaser will be able to exercise choice rather than being directly linked to a specific provider unit simply because they are both part of the same social services department. The AUDIT COMMISSION has argued that in general such arrangements can lead to 20 per cent savings on costs of services even when the in-house team wins the contract. In the commission's view, it is not the question of ownership that is at issue but rather the fact of competition. The purchaser/provider split allows for greater competition without necessarily resulting in the local authority losing out to the private and voluntary sector in all cases.

> However, there are some problems identified with this approach, particularly in relation to the role of social workers. A study by the management consultants

Price Waterhouse for the DoH looked at the organizational changes required. The result of this study was the development of three possible options for restructuring. In the case of the role of social workers, Price Waterhouse admitted that there were problems in identifying a purchaser or provider role because of the range of activities required of social workers in community care. As assessors of need, social workers could be identified as purchasers, in that they would play a role in ensuring that needs were met by a variety of provider organizations; but in their role as counsellors, they act as providers of a service to clients. The report made no specific recommendation on how this problem might be resolved. A future consequence of this change may be that provider units could find it an advantage to search out ways of opting out of working directly within the local authority, and this would also facilitate the government's enabling policy while continuing to ensure employment for those they used to employ.

Department of Health and Price Waterhouse, *Implementing Community Care: The Purchaser, Commissioner and Provider Roles*, London: HMSO, 1991.

# Q

**quango** a form of government agency used to provide services or carry out other duties determined by government.

The term, which is North American in origin, is subject to some dispute as to what it means. Originally an acronym for 'quasi-autonomous non-governmental organization', it referred to voluntary and non-profit organizations that had become dependent on grants and funding from government and were thus seen to be linked into government policy implementation; questions were asked about their independence. In Britain the term more frequently became associated with agencies established by government departments, among the best-known examples being the Commission for Racial Equality and the Equal Opportunities Commission; for this reason the term sometimes refers to 'quasi-autonomous *national* governmental organizations'.

Question marks about the role of quangos were raised in the early 1980s when the Conservative government was committed to the idea of reducing the role of government. An ex-civil servant, Sir Leo Pliatsky, produced a report on the extent to which quangos were being used, with the aim of reducing their role. The main questions about quangos concerned some of the following issues: abuse of patronage by ministers who had the posts in quangos in their gift; questions of accountability, in that members of quangos are non-elected appointments; the level of expenditure by quangos; and the use of quangos to depoliticize important issues.

The attack on quangos was not sustained, however, for while a range of these bodies were abolished or amalgamated, new ones were created. This was mainly because governments have found that they are very useful bodies, able to be set up at minimal costs, with appointees often paid a minimal stipend or employed on a voluntary basis. Quangos take the political heat out of a subject by removing issues such as equal opportunities from the main party political arena. They also allow the appointment of experts to consider issues outside of the traditional civil service hierarchies. As a result, after a brief period of decline, quangos are now as prominent as ever.

**quota scheme**   a statutory requirement introduced under the Disabled Persons (Employment) Act 1944 that organizations and companies employing twenty or more people should include registered disabled people as at least 3 per cent of the workforce.

The quota scheme was introduced as a means for disabled people to obtain and keep employment. In practice, most organizations ignore its provisions and fail to seek the necessary formal dispensation required of them by the scheme. Indeed, the whole scheme lacks 'teeth', other than being able to embarrass some organizations. Disabled people feel very strongly that such legislation does not seriously address the ANTI-DISCRIMINATORY issues in relation to disabled people and employment. They would prefer to have a scheme that in some sense corresponds to sex and race anti-discrimination provisions with their more effective sanctions.

*R*

**'race'**   a term used to describe groups considered to be biologically distinct. The biological characteristics thought to typify such groups were believed to be constant or unalterable unless 'races' intermingled. The term has effectively been discredited by physical scientists and social scientists.

Most sociologists are no longer prepared to use the term 'race' except in inverted commas, thus demonstrating that they do not accept the biological distinctness of ethnic (the preferred term) groups. 'Race' is clearly a socially constructed concept, which both currently and historically has been used to justify exploitative behaviour on the part of powerful groups. (See RACISM.)

**Race Relations Act 1976**   the major piece of British legislation that seeks to promote good relationships between ethnic groups and to combat racial DISCRIMINATION. The Act repealed the previous, more restrictive legislation of the 1965 and 1968 Race Relations Acts.

The Act established the COMMISSION FOR RACIAL EQUALITY to oversee its operation, and provided definitions of direct and indirect racial discrimination, and of victimization. Direct discrimination is defined as 'treating one person less favourably than another on grounds of colour, race, ethnic or natural origin, in the provision of goods, facilities and services, employment, housing and advertising' (for example, always offering jobs to white candidates where black candidates have comparable qualifications). Indirect discrimination arises where certain requirements or conditions can be met differentially by different groups but where such differences are not justified (for example, a requirement to have particular English-language skills where an ethnic group's first language is not English and it can be demonstrated that these skills are not necessary for a particular job). Victimization occurs when a person is treated negatively because they have complained or intend to complain about their treatment under the law.

> Evidence concerning the operation of the Act in relation to individual complaints is disappointing. Few formal complaints are actually made (about 800 each year), and of these less than 10 per cent are successful. Levels of compensation are low (on average £1,200 in 1991), and the process is often lengthy. More importantly, tribunals can recommend the reinstatement of a person who has been dismissed but cannot require such reinstatement. In practice, then, complainants may lose their job, receive poor compensation after a long and emotionally draining experience, and run the risk of being labelled a troublemaker, with the consequent danger of not being re-employed. Most complainants do not win.

> The Act empowers the Commission for Racial Equality to investigate alleged discrimination and to order organizations to change their policies and practices if they are found to be illegal. The issuing of non-discrimination notices to organizations has had useful outcomes, particularly in the public sector. In relation to local authorities the Act (s. 71) requires that policies to eliminate racial discrimination and to promote equality of opportunity in all respects be pursued. The evidence in this regard is mixed (see EQUAL OPPORTUNITIES POLICIES, POSITIVE ACTION).

**racial or race equality councils**  voluntary organizations, previously known as community relations councils, constituted to promote good 'RACE' relations within particular areas.

Race equality councils are registered charities. Financial support for the councils is usually from local authorities and from the Commission for Racial Equality, with some funding from special projects sponsored by central government departments such as the Home Office and further financial support from local industries and affiliates. Councils have as their principal objectives: first, the implementation of policies designed to promote good community relations, together with the elimination of racial DISCRIMINATION in the private, voluntary and public sectors; second, education and information services for the public; third, support and advice for ethnic communities; and fourth, support for individuals experiencing discrimination.

**racism**  ideas, attitudes, behaviours and policies that discriminate against ethnic groups, nations and other social collectivities, where the discrimination is justified on the basis of a supposed biological superiority of the oppressing group (see also DISCRIMINATION).

Racism may be a matter of individual belief (personal racism) or of official policy, either by design or default (institutional racism). It seems to rest upon a number of basic assertions: first, that there are distinct racial groupings; second, that the differences between racial groupings in terms of culture and behaviour are to be explained by biological characteristics; third, that these biological characteristics can be arranged to demonstrate the relative inferiority of other racial groups in relation to white Europeans, especially Aryans. The origins of racism appear to be rooted in the colonial experience; colonial powers needed a set of beliefs to justify their economic and cultural exploitation and oppression of many groups throughout the world. Such beliefs embraced a range of ideas from paternalism to genocide. Racism would seem therefore to be the invention and practice of white Europeans. Conflicts between nations and ethnic groups have been widespread throughout history, often characterized by mutual prejudice between groups; it is the biological basis of racism that distinguishes it from mere prejudice. The attempts to establish distinct racial groups with distinct cultures scientifically have now been discredited, although racist ideas are still very much alive in Europe and in other societies with substantial European origins. Because the ideas are discredited, many writers now refuse to use the word 'RACE' (preferring 'ethnic group' or 'origin' – such as in the expression 'a child from mixed origins'), or they use the term only with inverted commas: 'race' rather than race.

Some writers have argued that racism can apply only to black (that is, 'non-white') people, whereas others would include anti-Semitism and attitudes to particular ethnic groups, such as Irish people. Clearly, the treatment of Jewish people by the Nazis was influenced by a set of beliefs that included the view that Jews were somehow less than human. On a lesser scale, the 'Irish' joke, which depicts Irish people as stupid, also appears to be inspired by an attitude that infers that Irish people are somehow genetically less intelligent than the 'white Anglo-Saxons'. If racism is rooted in notions of biological inferiority, then anti-Semitism and anti-Irish attitudes must be seen as racist. Yet black people's visibility as other than white precipitates an immediate and everyday racism that seems to be different from anti-Semitism and anti-Irish attitudes, although they have a common root.

In the context of social welfare services, racism can take many forms, involving personal or institutional racism or both. Racism can occur, for example, when responsibility for tackling racism is placed on black workers alone. Tackling racism should clearly be the responsibility of all workers, and especially white workers – who, after all, live in and, in a general sense, espouse white culture, which spawned racism. Racism can occur when the legitimacy of others' cultural needs is ignored, or when the racism of clients is overlooked and not challenged. Another common form of racism is to assert that all clients receive equal treatment, without recognizing that a service should take into account the effects of racism and the very uneven starting points that racism creates for different groups within racist societies. (See also ANTI-DISCRIMINATORY PRACTICE, ANTI-RACISM, ETHNICALLY SENSITIVE PRACTICE.)

J. Rex, *Race and Ethnicity*, Buckingham: Open University Press, 1986.

**radical social work**   an attempt to achieve a major rethink of social welfare and of social work theory and practice – either by emphasizing the degree to which personal problems are shaped by such oppressive forces as class division and racial DISCRIMINATION, or by emphasizing the role of the MARKET in social welfare provision.

Britain has witnessed two loose movements regarded as radical in the field of social work over the last two decades or more. The first, springing from an unorganized socialist movement in the 1970s, held that the welfare state offered an important mechanism for sustaining and improving the conditions of poor and vulnerable people. This movement was united in the belief that social problems are socially constructed and in the main to be explained by structural inequality, notably social class. By contrast, earlier methods employed by social workers implied a view of problems as rooted in personal inadequacy or pathology, or perhaps in family dysfunction, rather than in poverty or differential life chances. Major ingredients of this movement were 'consciousness raising' (explaining to users the structural origins of their problems), user involvement in the decision-making process, and COMMUNITY WORK and GROUPWORK as legitimate methods to neutralize the dangers of CASEWORK, which tended to lay the blame for problems on individual weaknesses. It also placed greater emphasis on legal rights (including the right to free welfare services) and the creation of progressive political alliances of community and residents' groups, user groups, trade unions, pressure groups and political parties. This movement has been criticized for its omissions in relation to race and gender stratification in particular, and for its lack of awareness of the problems of other oppressed groups, including people with disabilities, old people and gay men and lesbians.

The second movement, rooted in the NEW RIGHT of the 1980s, has sought to be radical in an anti-welfarist stance. The New Right is committed to the market, individual enterprise and initiative, and to a view that public spending should be curtailed. The New Right has attacked welfare provision because it interferes with the free working of market forces. It sees families as the principal source of moral responsibility and therefore of welfare, except where the market has encouraged the growth of welfare within a vigorous private sector. Although the notion of a welfare safety net has not been entirely eroded, it has been much reduced.

M. Langan and P. Lee, *Radical Social Work Today*, London: Unwin Hyman, 1989.

**rationing** controlling the allocation of services and other resources to ensure they are used as effectively as possible.

Both social services and the NATIONAL HEALTH SERVICE ration the resources they have at their disposal, with the intention of producing the maximum effect. Whether they succeed or not, and whether the methods devised for controlling the allocation of resources are fair, are subject of intense debate. For example, should resources be used to benefit the greatest number of people, or those, far fewer in number, who need them most?

There is general agreement that rationing has been taking place for a long time but has not been recognized as such. For example, in the National Health Service waiting lists for particular types of operation are a way of controlling the use of such medical resources as hospital beds and surgeons' time. The existence of waiting lists therefore is a way of rationing. Following changes in the health service and the government's pledge to guarantee speedier treatment for all patients, managers have had to devise more formal ways of rationing medical resources. To this end, they have ranked illnesses according to their severity and have stated rules as to who is and who is not eligible for treatment. Some of these have stirred considerable controversy, such as when a patient who smokes heavily is denied a heart bypass operation on the grounds that the treatment would be wasted until they stopped smoking.

Social service agencies also have had to develop priorities as to people they regard as in the greatest NEED. As an example, highest priority is given to children who are in need of some protective action on the part of the local authority, whereas far lower priority is accorded to families whose children may be in need but are not in any immediate danger. This is a form of rationing that determines that a small number of children and their families receive intensive resources in social work time, family placements and other support services, while the much larger number of children in need and their families receive little or nothing in support services.

**reactive depression**   feelings of hopelessness, sadness, tearfulness and ANXIETY that arise in response to particular circumstances, such as death of a close family member. Such symptoms may be milder than in clinical or endogenous DEPRESSION.

A person experiencing reactive depression may recover spontaneously within a year of the trigger event, although the condition may become long-term if there are chronic problems such as financial pressures or housing difficulties. Studies of women who were depressed following specific events in their life have shown that lack of a confidant, loss of mother before the age of 11, lack of paid employment and caring for young children are all factors associated with prolonging such depression. The person with reactive depression may, in many cases, be receiving help, usually medication, and the social worker may therefore need to liaise with the general practitioner to judge the effects of the medication. A small number of sufferers may have been referred to the psychiatric services. The worker may offer grief COUNSELLING as one way of helping the person to find an alternative response to the loss they have suffered.

**reality orientation**   a therapeutic approach to maintaining memory and thinking in older people who are experiencing impairment of mental functioning.

Reality orientation uses spoken and written reminders of past and current events to enable people to maintain contact with daily life. It has developed into a philosophy of care rather than simply a set of facilitating strategies.

**reasonable parent test**   the minimum standard of care that can reasonably be expected of parents of a particular child.

To obtain a CARE ORDER on a child, a local authority must demonstrate to the court that the SIGNIFICANT HARM the child has suffered, or is likely to suffer, is attributable to the care given to the child by their parents. It has also to be shown that the care is not up to the standard of what it would be reasonable to expect a parent to provide for that child – the reasonable parent test. In other words, if that standard were all that could be reasonably expected of hypothetical parents, the grounds for a care order would not exist.

**reassessment**   the process of looking anew at a case in the light of developments, new information or a new emphasis to be given to old information.

Some social work ASSESSMENTS are uncomplicated, with needs identified in a straightforward way without differences of view between worker and service user. In many cases, neither worker nor service user can be clear about the nature of the problems or about the best plan of INTERVENTION. In these circumstances short-term plans may be necessary that may solve the difficulties but may not. Any competent social welfare worker will be prepared to reassess their work and, in the same vein, to view past work as unsuccessful. In a sense, the best work involves constant reassessment and a willingness to see old problems in a new light. The social work process usually entails an invitation to formally evaluate work in progress at regular intervals, and this kind of reassessment is often called a CASE REVIEW.

**recidivism**   an alternative term to 'persistent offending'. A recidivist is a person who repeatedly commits (usually relatively minor) offences and is likely to be punished disproportionately severely as a result of accumulating a lengthy list of previous criminal convictions.

A very high proportion of people in PRISON are recidivists, and this contributes greatly to prison overcrowding. In an effort to reduce the prison population and adopt a JUST DESERTS approach to sentencing, the CRIMINAL JUSTICE ACT 1991 restricted the powers of courts to take previous convictions into consideration when passing sentence. However, as a result of vociferous opposition, this particular aspect of the Act was amended in 1993 to enable courts to return to their previous practice of utilizing a TARIFF approach to sentencing, taking account of both offence seriousness and previous criminal record.

**recording**   the process by which a social welfare agency maintains an account of its dealings with a service user. Such a record may be kept in written files or increasingly on computers.

The selection and recording of relevant information about service users and their families are a central task for social welfare agencies and especially for social work agencies. Recording may be understood as an expression of accountability for the practitioner to their agency, but it is also crucially a means by which there can be accountability to the service user and, beyond them, to the general public and the profession. Recording can also constitute evidence in a court of law. It is generally agreed that the overriding principle for ethical and effective recording is the service user's best interests. Good practice to the service user requires clear and purposeful recording. Competent recording facilitates an accurate account of what has actually happened and an understanding of why it has happened. This process will enhance an evaluation or a review of progress in the work. It will also help colleagues if they have to take the work on, in the absence of the responsible worker. Additionally, recording is often used by social work agencies to gather critical information about their own activities for research or monitoring purposes.

There are many interesting practice issues and dilemmas in relation to recording. Access to personal files on the part of the service user, a principle established in law with the Access to Personal Files Act 1987, can in many instances be problematic. Should, for example, a family casefile be open to scrutiny by all members of that family? It may be agreed as a basic right of civil liberties that service users should see their own records; but workers may need at times to protect other people's privacy and safety, and their sources of information. Similarly, the business of writing an account of an individual's or family's problems that is truthful and faces up to the considerable difficulties that some service users have but does not damage or label people in discouraging ways and may be shared with all the relevant people is patently very difficult. A related matter, which can assist in this process, is writing the record with the service user; some regard this as a major change in orientation in dealings with service users. To inform people that they may see their record if they wish is a relatively passive commitment to greater access. But to take the record to them, to invite their scrutiny and to record with them is clearly going significantly further.

Fashions have changed in relation to the fullness or brevity with which records are kept. In some critical and sensitive work, great detail helps to reveal hidden patterns; in other work areas, a detailed account of daily events is unnecessary. The depth of recording and analysis depends upon the objectives of the work. In all circumstances, however, it is important to distinguish facts from opinions; and where an opinion is ventured, the supporting evidence should always be listed to reveal the worker's thinking and analysis.

British Association of Social Workers, *Ethical and Effective Recording*, London: BASW, 1984.

**recovery order**   a court order under section 50 of the CHILDREN ACT that compels any person who is in a position to do so to return a child who has been unlawfully removed from the care of a local authority.

A recovery order also applies to a child under an EMERGENCY PROTECTION ORDER or in POLICE PROTECTION. It authorizes a constable to enter and search premises, using reasonable force if necessary. The order is designed to stamp out the harbouring of children and young people who have absconded from the care of the local authority.

**reduced earnings allowance**   see INDUSTRIAL INJURIES SCHEME.

**re-entry order**   an ORDER issued by a court ordering a person to be admitted to accommodation in which they are entitled to live.

This order is invariably issued in cases where DOMESTIC VIOLENCE has occurred and one person has been excluded as a result of an incident (see also NON-MOLESTATION ORDER, OUSTER ORDER).

**referral**   the process by which a social welfare agency is formally notified that a potential CLIENT or user may require access to its services.

A referral can be made by the person requesting the service or by some third party, typically members of the person's family, friends or neighbours, or by a professional within the social welfare or socio-legal systems. Some organizations label the initial contact with a user, or a person referring the would-be user, as an 'inquiry'. If the social service agency considers the inquiry suitable and that a service can be offered, then a referral is accepted. Whether a referral is accepted and becomes a live case or not can be unpredictable. Clarity of referral information, the outcome of the initial ASSESSMENT, the power and influence of the referrer, and the coherence of agencies' policies in service delivery are all major determinants as to whether a person who is the subject of a referral becomes a client.

**reframe**  to develop a different viewpoint or opinion regarding the same set of circumstances or events.

Reframing is used in FAMILY THERAPY, in which family members are helped to understand the actions, attitudes or behaviour of another family member in a more positive light. The term is also used widely in social work, in relation to practitioners and users alike, to mean to come to a new understanding about a person's behaviour or to reformulate a problem in a new way.

**Registered Homes Act 1984**  legislation providing for the registration, conduct and inspection of RESIDENTIAL CARE homes for adults.

The Act specifies how a range of residential homes offering care to more than four adults are to be registered and inspected. These include homes for those who because of old age, disability, mental disorder or drug dependency need residential care. The Act requires all such homes to be registered with the local authority, which vets each application according to a set of standards governing physical accommodation, financial viability and, most importantly, standards of care; the latter are scrutinized carefully and in detail (see *HOME LIFE*). The local authority is able to set conditions of operation for particular homes and can cancel registration if the standards or conditions are not met. The Act also covers nursing homes, which offer health care within a residential setting, allowing them to be dual registered and thus to provide elements of residential care at the same time.

**regression**  see PSYCHOANALYSIS.

**rehabilitation**  derived from the Latin word meaning restoration, the term has been used to describe the renovation of land or property, and the reform of offenders.

Most commonly used in social work and medicine, 'rehabilitation' describes activities aimed at the restoration of patients to their fullest physical, mental and social capacity. It is used as an umbrella term and is applied to people experiencing temporary or permanent DISABILITY in later life, as well as to those born with a disability. In the case of the latter group, the term 'habilitation' would be more appropriate. As long ago as 1943 the Tomlinson Committee recognized that rehabilitation was more than a medical problem; subsequently the Tonbridge Report (1972) and the Mair Report (1972) endorsed this view by identifying a need for a MULTIDISCIPLINARY approach. Both reports criticized the lack of information and cooperation of services, and Mair stressed the need for medical leadership.

Despite recognition of the social, as well as the medical, dimensions of disability and rehabilitation, many disabled people would argue that rehabilitation has been dominated by a medical approach, with a concentration on physical functioning as judged against an 'able-bodied' concept of 'normality'. Many disabled people might argue that rehabilitation services are important in helping them restore or develop physical, intellectual and social functioning, but rehabilitation of disabled people will not overcome the physical and attitudinal barriers to disability that exist in society.

A. Mair, *Report of the Subcommittee of the Standing Medical Advisory Committee*, London: HMSO, 1972.

**Rehabilitation of Offenders Act 1974**   an Act that allows a person not to disclose a criminal record (for example, when applying for a job) under certain circumstances.

Offences are deemed to be 'spent' after a certain time period has elapsed. The length of time depends mainly on the nature of the penalty. For example, an offence punished by a sentence of conditional discharge becomes 'spent' at the end of the discharge period (usually one or two years). An offence punished by imprisonment of more than two and a half years, on the other hand, may never be regarded as 'spent'. For young people under the age of 18, the rehabilitation periods for adults are halved. Certain jobs, however, such as social work or any work with children, are exempted from the Act and require applicants to disclose any criminal record.

**relapse**   in the case of people ADDICTED to various DRUGS, a reversion back to the habit after a period of being drug-free.

Relapse is common with any habit, and in any work with drugs users the possibility needs to be discussed so that techniques can be developed to deal with it if and when it occurs.

**remand**   a process whereby CRIMINAL COURT proceedings are adjourned after an initial appearance by the defendant so that prosecution and defence cases can be properly prepared, or for the preparation of PRE-SENTENCE REPORTS or medical reports.

A defendant may be remanded on BAIL provided they have an address, can be trusted to reappear in court when required and are not likely to interfere with prosecution inquiries or commit further offences. Under the amendments to the CRIMINAL JUSTICE ACT 1991 it is now a separate offence to commit offences while on bail. In some courts probation officers run bail information schemes to provide verified, factual and favourable information about defendants so that courts can make fully informed decisions in relation to bail. The PROBATION SERVICE also runs BAIL HOSTELS to provide accommodation for defendants who would otherwise be refused bail. If the prosecution nevertheless persists in its objections to bail, or if the offence is very serious, it is likely that the defendant will be remanded in custody (that is, to PRISON). Young men under 15 and young women under 17 cannot be remanded to prison, and the preferred option for all YOUNG OFFENDERS is to remand them into the care of the local authority if bail is not considered appropriate.

Remand prisoners who have not yet been to trial have special privileges (such as daily visits) and must be assumed to be innocent. However, the benefit of any such privileges tends to be negated by the unsettled nature of the remand population in a prison and the generally impoverished regime. The only other possible advantage of being remanded in custody is that time served in this way is deducted from any prison sentence eventually given. Remand prisoners must be produced in court periodically during the adjournment period – an ancient protection against abuse or even 'disappearance'. The escorting of remand prisoners to court by prison staff is time-consuming and expensive; the service has now been partially privatized and is carried out by a security firm in some parts of Britain.

**reminiscence therapy**   the process of recalling the past, a technique of memory-revival usually used with older people who have experienced memory loss.

Reminiscence work with OLDER PEOPLE has developed in the last ten years and is an important strategy for aiding them, particularly in groupwork settings such as residential or day care. Reminiscence work is a form of oral history-sharing that involves the older person with their peer group and with carers. It is easy to instigate, yet the outcomes are a rewarding and enriching experience. For example, all members of a small group of older people may be asked to bring a small object to the group that has significance for them and then to tell the group the story of that object, such as a brooch or an ornament. This in turn stimulates memories in other group participants, and a rewarding diversity of conversation topics is stimulated that may have immediate relevance to group participants. Reminiscence work thus creates 'communities' of memories that maintain and re-establish a person's place and role within the COMMUNITY.

Shared memories renew a sense of rootedness and connectedness to others that help to anchor the person with memory difficulties in a social setting. Conventional or pre-existing relationships may change for a little while as the older person shares, with their carer, times from the past, giving the older person control over conversation topics. It has been shown that reminiscence group participants arrive early for sessions, greet others with enthusiasm and anticipate the events with pleasure – often wearing their best clothes and jewellery for the sessions, indicating that the group has the status of an event in the older person's life. However, for some people reminiscence is painful, and the unavoidable recall of loss that accompanies later life may mean that sessions can be distressing for all concerned. Workers need to be genuine and skilled in supporting older people through sad memories. Involvement in reminiscence groups has been seen to help residents new to group living and to aid their transition from home and their integration into group life. It has been suggested that groups become 'safe places for sharing both joyful and sad recollections', giving participants an enhanced sense of the value and significance of their past life and enriching their relationships with contemporaries and workers.

F. Gibson, 'Reminiscence groupwork with older people', *Groupwork*, vol. 5, no. 3, 1992, pp. 28–40.

**remission**   prior to the CRIMINAL JUSTICE ACT 1991, the amount of time discounted from a PRISON sentence (on the presumption of good behaviour) in order to calculate a prisoner's release date. Normally, this constituted one-third of the original sentence.

Remission was distinguished from PAROLE, since the latter referred to discretionary early release, while the former came to be regarded virtually as a prisoner's right. Remission could be lost as a result of the commission of disciplinary offences in prison. The term is now obsolete and has been replaced by arrangements for EARLY RELEASE.

**rent allowance**   a payment of HOUSING BENEFIT to a tenant of a private landlord or housing association.

**rent rebate**   a payment of HOUSING BENEFIT to a tenant of a local authority.

**rent restriction**   action taken by a local authority in assessing a claim for HOUSING BENEFIT from a private tenant. Where the authority decides that the accommodation is unreasonably expensive or unnecessarily large, it must restrict the amount of housing benefit payable by working it out on a reduced rent.

People aged over 60 and those who are long-term sick or have dependent children should not have their rent restricted unless there is cheaper suitable accommodation available and it is reasonable to expect them to move. The incentive to restrict rents is provided through the benefit subsidy arrangements. Local authorities get no subsidy from central government if they pay benefit over a MARKET RENT level fixed by a rent officer: they get just 60 per cent subsidy for high rents paid to people in the protected groups.

**reparation**   the process of making good, returning things to their original state or making amends.

In social work or probation practice, reparation involves confronting VICTIMS and seeking to do something directly or indirectly about the consequences of an offence. A simple example might be the replacement of a window that has been broken in a case of criminal damage. Directly and personally compensating somebody for their loss where returning things to their original state is not possible may also constitute reparation (for example, a sum of money or something in kind). Work undertaken in the community may also be seen as reparation. Some workers in the justice system perceive reparation as a key component to genuine reform because it entails understanding the effects of criminal behaviour on victims and the wish to make amends. Reparation is not always suitable, especially with crimes against the person, where the trauma for the victim may be extremely difficult to manage.

**reporter**   an independent official in the youth justice system in Scotland who determines whether YOUNG OFFENDERS should be referred to CHILDREN'S HEARINGS or instead have voluntary arrangements to ensure that any needs are met and they do not reoffend.

In making their decision the reporter takes into account the social and personal needs of the child or young person, as well as the nature of the offence.

**reporting officer**   a person with a social work qualification who reports independently to a court in prospective ADOPTION cases regarding certain matters, including whether the natural parents' consent to the adoption has been fully and freely given.

The reporting officer is usually a member of a panel of GUARDIANS *AD LITEM* and reporting officers administered by the local authority or another welfare agency in each area. Panel members are independent of all other services and free to comment on cases on the basis of their professional judgement alone.

**research**   social research is the conduct of systematic study in order to describe social behaviour or to test theories about social behaviour.

Reasons for undertaking research can differ considerably, and research studies can be of different types. They can be: *descriptive*, involving the study of a pattern of social behaviour or changes in patterns of social behaviour; *explanatory*, explaining differences in patterns of social behaviour among different groups; *evaluative*, that is, the assessment of a particular programme or outcome; *exploratory*, making an initial study of a social behaviour or setting; or *scientific* – the testing of a particular hypothesis. Whatever the purposes of undertaking research, the heart of the process is the research problem, usually defined both empirically and in relation to specific theoretical issues or concerns. Research projects can be derived from an empirical question – such as the extent and different types of need among young single parents – or from a theoretical issue, such as whether men and women have differently constructed moral needs, or both. Researchers must also choose which settings to undertake their investigations in; the selection of particular settings will, of course, alter the results. Research into the social background of young homeless people usually takes place in hostels, in squats and on the streets, and only very infrequently in homes where they are temporarily lodged. Selection of these settings for research often underestimates, for example, the number of young women who are homeless.

In essence, research design is made up of the research problem, the research setting and the selection of a particular methodology, comprising all the methods a researcher feels they require to understand the particular issue they are studying. Among the many methods a researcher might choose are: in-depth INTERVIEWING (individual or group), interviewing using questionnaires, self-completion questionnaires, participant observation, structured observation, experimental design, natural experiment, statistical analysis (using official statistics collected by an agency, local authority or central government) or documentary analysis. As this list shows, a great range of techniques can be used. For interviewing, researchers can decide to use in-depth interview techniques, collecting the 'narrative' of the person interviewed (perhaps using a minimal list of topics that they will ask each respondent); or they can decide to use a very structured questionnaire for a face-to-face interview or for a postal survey. Observation methods can range from participant (such as sitting in a wheelchair and observing reactions to you) through to structured observation (such as having a checklist of behaviours addressed to wheelchair users). Experimental design ranges through organized experiments (for example, only one group of older people receive home helps) to natural experiments (home helps are withdrawn from one group of people living in one local authority and not in another).

In the past, many researchers made a distinction between *qualitative* research methods, such as in-depth interviewing and participant observation, and *quantitative* research methods, such as structured questionnaire interviewing and observation using checklists. Increasingly, however, there is recognition of a need for researchers to employ a range of research methods. Researchers often conduct in-depth individual group interviews before or alongside a statistical survey in order to illuminate the experience of a particular group within the survey. Secondary analysis of government data sets can also lead to qualitative research work, and the latter will discover issues that require to be explored through statistical analysis and large-scale survey research.

A major growth area of social research has been the secondary analysis of government information collected by the General Household Survey, the Labour Force Survey, the Family Expenditure Survey and the Census. In particular, the General Household Survey of 10,000 households annually has been used for research into the health or income of different groups of people living in private households in Britain. The Census is, of course, an extremely important source of information because it includes both private households and communal accommodation. However, the 1991 Census is flawed; compared with the 1981 Census, more than half a million people could not be accounted for, over and above the usual shortfall. In particular, there was an unlikely shortfall among young men compared with young women. It is highly probable that the desire to avoid paying the community charge ('poll tax') distorted the results in 1991.

Alongside the government-funded surveys, grant-funded surveys are now also important sources of information about the whole population. One well-known source in social work is the research into children and young adults conducted through the New Child Development Survey (NCDS) of children born in one week in 1958. The British Social Attitudes survey has been run by Social and Community Planning Research (SCPR) for over ten years and includes two volumes on international social attitudes, comparing Britain with other countries in Europe, North America and Australia. In the last few years a new initiative has begun to study micro-social change in Britain, led from Essex University. All of these data can be accessed for secondary analysis by researchers in the fields of social work, SOCIAL POLICY and SOCIOLOGY.

As part of their methodology, researchers adopt different strategies to help them gain insight into their topic. In the *case study* approach, researchers gather many different sources of data achieved through different research techniques such as interviewing, statistical/documentary analysis and observation. In the *comparative* approach, researchers often use a similar method to compare two different settings, such as CASE CONFERENCES held by different area teams. In a *historical* approach, researchers try to chart the changing situation of different social groups, such as young people in the 1960s compared with young people in the 1990s. A *longitudinal* approach, such as the NCDS or the micro-social change study, would follow the same group of people over a twenty- or thirty-year period. The Social Work Research Unit at Stirling University has produced a summary of its research into social work; this shows how many of the methods described here have been applied by researchers in the field of social work. Increasingly, the effectiveness of social work is being evaluated.

Social Work Research Centre, University of Stirling, *Is Social Work Effective? Research Findings from the Social Work Research Centre, University of Stirling*, Stirling: Scottish Office, Economic and Social Research Council and University of Stirling, 1994.

**residence order**   a court order under section 8 of the CHILDREN ACT that specifies with whom the child is to live. It is used primarily in matrimonial disputes, replacing the concept of custody.

The aim of the residence order is to reduce tension between divorcing parents, because neither party any longer 'wins custody'; the issue is now merely one of the court's deciding where the child or children should live. Whatever the court's decision, both parents retain PARENTAL RESPONSIBILITY and are expected to continue to take part in decisions regarding the child. It is possible for the court to grant a residence order to each parent, with the child living alternate weeks with each. The residence order can also be used in other FAMILY PROCEEDINGS and can be applied for by people who are not parents and who do not hold parental responsibility for the child. For example, a grandparent may apply for a residence order on their grandchild in care proceedings as an alternative to the local authority's application for a CARE ORDER or SUPERVISION ORDER. Or they may apply for a residence order some time after a care order was made at a previous hearing; if their application is successful, the care order is automatically discharged. As another example of the order's flexibility, FOSTER CARERS may apply for a residence order on a child who has been living with them for more than three years.

Whenever an applicant is granted a residence order, it automatically gives parental responsibility for the child to the person who has applied, if they do not have it already. It thus provides a means by which grandparents or other members of the child's extended family, and indeed foster carers, become included in decisions regarding the child. Children may also apply for a residence order on their own behalf and have done so when they want to live with a person other than their parents. There are no specific grounds for the residence order other than the WELFARE CHECKLIST in the Children Act and the consideration that making the order should be better for the child than not making it. The local authority cannot apply but can support others such as foster carers to do so.

**residential care**   care services provided for people living in residential homes.

Residential care embraces a number of services, some formal, some informal, that are provided for people who have left their own home and moved to particular establishments in order to receive those services. Some of these services are basic requirements for survival, such as regular bathing to ensure physical cleanliness, meals, help with getting dressed. Other services help people overcome isolation by providing contacts with members of staff or other residents or by facilitating continued contact with family and relations. Still other services may address specific emotional needs such as counselling or group therapy. What distinguishes residential services from DOMICILIARY care (services provided in a person's own home) and COMMUNITY CARE (services provided in the community) is that in order to receive them a person moves into a specially organized residential establishment in which they live for a period of time, perhaps permanently. These establishments vary greatly in size from large homes for OLDER PEOPLE of perhaps thirty or more residents to small CHILDREN'S HOMES of perhaps only a half a dozen. There are also homes for people who have previously lived in an institution such as a psychiatric hospital who are getting used to living outside that institution but are not yet ready to fend for themselves, and small GROUP HOMES for adults with LEARNING DISABILITY who cooperate in preparing meals and purchasing food and other household items, and who learn to plan their own recreation and vocational training. The kind of care that each establishment has to offer depends on the needs of the residents who live there.

Many commentators have observed that certain features of residential care have a great impact on the people who live in residential establishments. People living together with the same difficulties are highly visible, and this tends to set them apart in the eyes of the community in which they live. The way care services are provided and the attitudes of staff working in the home have also been shown to deprive people of choice. Many residential regimes have allowed little flexibility in how residents arrange their room with personal effects, for example discouraging residents from bringing with them mementos from their family home. They have also discouraged independence, such as by not allowing residents to cook for themselves. The care in such establishments was in the past marked by rigid bedtimes and meal times, creating an atmosphere that seemed in the interests more of the staff than of the residents themselves. But with increased emphasis on choice and on CLIENTS' rights and initiative now reflected in many aspects of residential care, practice has recently been looked upon more positively. For example, parents of children who are being LOOKED AFTER by the local authority often feel more encouraged to keep in touch with their child when that child is in a children's home than if placed with foster parents. Older people, particularly frail people with several serious physical limitations, may feel more secure than when in their own home; and in an atmosphere of greater individuality they are now more likely to be able to personalize their rooms in ways that would not have been possible even ten years ago. The positive evidence concerning the way the best residential care is valued by residents and their relatives was extensively reported in the WAGNER REPORT.

**residential rehabilitation**    REHABILITATION in places of residence where people experiencing problems with ALCOHOL and DRUGS can stay for up to eighteen months to help them with their problem of misuse and associated difficulties.

Domestic rehabilitation units vary considerably in philosophy, some being of a Christian nature, others not, with widely differing programmes available; some are very formal and hierarchical, others loosely structured. It is important to match the client to a programme that they can cope with, to avoid failure. Sometimes it takes a person three or four attempts at a rehabilitation unit before they succeed. RELAPSE is fairly common. The funding for residential rehabilitation units is now the responsibility of social services departments through the NATIONAL HEALTH SERVICE AND COMMUNITY CARE ACT. It is normally the responsibility of the social worker in COMMUNITY DRUG TEAMS to arrange funding.

**residential work**    social work undertaken within units where people live, either permanently or temporarily.

Residential provision has many purposes: an alternative home, therapy, RESPITE CARE, custody, diagnosis and assessment, or some combination of these purposes. From workhouse to orphanage, from ASYLUM to PRISON, residential work to some social end has existed for some considerable time. In general terms, residential provision for many client groups has contracted in the last few decades; some has changed in character, and virtually all residential services have been closely examined. The review of residential provision has been motivated partly by its substantial cost and partly by fundamental criticisms of some residential services.

In relation to children, long-stay CHILDREN'S HOMES have virtually vanished. This change has come about principally because children's experience of long-term residential care has been very negative – in effect, allowing children to drift without effective care plans. There was a virtual absence of strategic policy for children's residential services, alongside substantial staff turnover. Staff within such services were invariably unqualified and, although often very committed to the children, felt themselves to be undervalued by their employers. The concept of 'houseparent' gives a clue to the way they were viewed – as carers, and carers can be 'ordinary' people without any special expertise but with an ability to meet the basic physical and, to a lesser extent, emotional needs of children. In the recent past, a number of highly publicized accounts of children being abused by their carers have further diminished the number (see PIN-DOWN). Other residential provision for children, such as observation-and-assessment centres, has also attracted criticism, because of the problem of trying to assess children when they have been removed from their normal environment. If a family cannot cope with a child any more, such arrangements may still be necessary, but they are now regarded as a measure of last resort.

For old people, the growth of local authority residential homes (Part III of the National Assistance Act 1948) has been reversed, partly by the growth of private provision and partly with a renewed commitment to COMMUNITY CARE services. Cuts in public expenditure have also contributed to this change. Some commentators have questioned the need for social work services at all in many contemporary residential facilities for old people, arguing that nursing care applies for some and that the residence is an alternative to a home in the community for people who, in the main, have no more problems than anybody else.

For people with long-term mental health problems and those with LEARNING DISABILITIES who previously might have been long-stay hospital patients, residential provision is being developed in sometimes imaginative ways. A range of residential services are available in some areas that reflect the ability of people to live more or less independently. GROUP HOMES and HALFWAY HOUSES are examples of such provision, with HOUSING ASSOCIATIONS particularly active in this area.

Residential provision is increasingly specialized and focused. Examples are BAIL HOSTELS as alternatives to remand in custody, units to help prepare children for LEAVING CARE, RESPITE CARE for a range of client groups to give carers a break or a holiday, SECURE ACCOMMODATION for children who are a danger to themselves or others, and residential facilities with a very particular therapeutic focus – for example, programmes for sex offenders. Alongside such developments, the status of RESIDENTIAL WORK is increasing as workers are seen to offer very specialized skills. In the light of the number of incidents of child abuse in residential homes, the government has also committed itself to a greater proportion of qualified social work staff in residential work.

R. Clough, *Residential Work*, London: Macmillan, 1982.

**resource centre**  a central point where information, equipment, advice and sometimes training are available to a particular interest group. Resource centres tend to be specialist – for example, TOY LIBRARIES, services for disabled people and teachers' centres.

**respect for persons**  a well-established value in social work, which holds that all people are entitled to respect because of their humanity.

It follows from this principle that respect should not be contingent on any role an individual might perform, nor on any trait of character this might display. Some authors have considered respect for persons to be the core value in social work, from which other VALUES can be derived. However, in the regulations for the Diploma in Social Work, the Central Council for Education and Training in Social Work simply lists 'respect' among a number of values to which qualifying social workers are expected to be committed, and gives equal weight to all the values listed.

**respite care**  care for vulnerable people, provided either in their own home or more usually in a RESIDENTIAL or DAY CARE setting, that supplements the care provided by the main CARER – usually a family member or friend.

There is now recognition that good practice in respite care provision should ensure a stimulating and enjoyable experience for the service user, as well as an opportunity for the main carer to have a break. The pattern of care depends upon need and available resources. It may be for a few weeks a year to permit habitual carers to, say, take a holiday; or it may be for a few hours a day or a week. Patterns of respite care may increase as a problem increases in severity, as with a dying person. Usually respite care is provided in residential facilities – services include short-term care beds in hostels, hospitals and small homes, as well as care provided in the homes of specially recruited and trained families. In addition, respite may be provided in a service user's own home by the employment of support staff for this purpose. Most respite services are hard pressed and are unable to give as much support to carers as they or the carers would wish. Charges are levied for some of these services, and there are local variations in rates. Entitlement to benefit may be affected by respite care; if a service user spends a total of twenty-eight days away from home, they must then spend twenty-nine days at home before more respite care away from home is provided, in order not to lose benefit. Concerns about the appropriateness, quality and availability of some respite care have been raised, particularly in the case of service users from black and ethnic-minority groups. (See HOSPICE CARE.)

C. Baxter, K. Poonia, L. Ward and Z. Nadirshaw, *Double Discrimination Issues and Services for People with Learning Difficulties from Black and Ethnic Minority Communities*, London: King's Fund Centre and Commission for Racial Equality, 1990.

**retirement**   the transition from waged participation in the labour market to non-waged status.

Until recently, for most people retirement was a rapid process at age 65 for men and (currently) 60 for women. The disengagement from waged occupation entailed changes in daily activity, social contact and standard of living. Retirement often has considerable psychological and emotional consequences as the individual may lose a sense of usefulness. Because it affects so many areas of an individual's life, it ought to be carefully planned for.

**retirement age**   the age at which RETIREMENT PENSION is paid, regardless of other circumstances. For women this is currently 65 and for men 70 years of age (cf. PENSIONABLE AGE).

In 1993 the government announced plans to raise the retirement age for women to 65. This will be phased in between 2010 and 2020. Women born before April 1950 will not be affected.

**retirement allowance**   see INDUSTRIAL INJURIES SCHEME.

**retirement pension**   the benefit payable to people over PENSIONABLE AGE, which is 60 years for women and 65 years for men. It can be paid even if a person continues to work. Alternatively, retirement can be deferred for up to five years, when RETIREMENT AGE is reached (women 65, men 70).

Deferring retirement for up to five years increases the value of the pension when claimed. There are four types of retirement pension. The category A pension is based on the claimant's contributions over their working life and can include additions for dependents. The category B pension is based on contributions paid by a spouse or sometimes a former spouse: typically it is paid to a married woman who has either no or only reduced entitlement to a category A pension. It can be paid only once the contributor has retired. The category C and D pensions are non-contributory and for people age 80 or over. See also ADDITIONAL PENSION, GRADUATED PENSION, STATE EARNINGS RELATED PENSION SCHEME.

**reunification**   returning children to their family after they have been LOOKED AFTER by the LOCAL AUTHORITY for a period of time.

The conclusion of much research in the 1980s was that children who were looked after by the local authority away from home for a period of time easily lost touch with their family. The longer the period of separation, the greater the likelihood that the child would remain in the long-term care of the authority. To successfully reunite a child looked after means consciously planning for their return from the very beginning of the PLACEMENT. To do this the social worker and foster parents or residential care staff facilitate CONTACT such as visits and exchange of letters and gifts. The intention is to keep the parents and family involved in the life of their child and allow them to make as many decisions affecting their child as possible.

The concept of reunification therefore has to do both with the planned return as well as with the actual return of the child to members of their family. The family is understood in the extended sense; the child may be returned to relatives such as grandparents or adult siblings, for example. For many years the word 'rehabilitation' was used to denote this process of returning the child home, but this implied that parents had to overcome certain personal defects and thereby 'earn' their child's return. This approach has now been firmly discarded. 'Reunification' acknowledges a far greater responsibility resting with the local authority social worker, who often has to work intensively with parents in setting up plans, and facilitating home visits, to ensure the child's return home takes place quickly and effectively.

S. Millham, R. Bullock, K. Hosie and M. Haak, *Lost in Care*, Aldershot: Gower, 1986.

**review**   see CASE REVIEW.

**rights**   a claim to treatment, benefits or protections that an individual can make on the basis of a law, code of practice or declaration.

There are several kinds of rights. *Political and civil rights* both protect a citizen of a particular country from the arbitrary use of power by state authorities and entitle that person to undertake certain positive actions that enable them to exert some influence, however nominal, in the political process and in influencing public opinion. *Social and economic rights* lay claims to publicly provided goods and services; these rights are not dependent on whether an individual is eligible for them or in some way is deserving. *Human rights* claim a universal status and are usually framed in global terms pertaining to all peoples. *Procedural rights* lay claim to giving people a fair hearing before any decision is made regarding a social benefit or service, such as setting a level of an individual's income support, meeting the special educational needs of a child with a learning disability or taking a child into local authority care.

Those political and civil rights that protect a citizen against abuse of state power include the right of free speech, the right to vote, the right to trial by jury, the right to personal security and the right not to be discriminated against on the basis of race (see DISCRIMINATION). Such rights were established in law, often as the consequence of considerable struggle, from the seventeenth century onwards in Britain. They are not universal, nor can they be assumed to be permanently irreversible, as recent discussions about the right to silence of the accused in criminal trials indicate.

Social and economic rights include the right to medical care, the right to social security, the right to vocational training and the right to housing. The concept of social and economic rights does not enlist the same consensus as political and civil rights. There is fierce argument as to whether they should exist as rights at all. In general, commentators from the NEW RIGHT think that, because such claims involve a call on resources such as money and the time of those who would deliver the services or benefits, they cannot be considered as rights, because the resources needed to provide them may not always be available and the concept of right as an unconditional, automatic entitlement would be undermined. Others at the political centre and on the left argue that the difference between civil rights and social rights is not as great as it seems, because they both depend on a sufficient level of resources being available. The right to personal security, for example, requires an effective police force, and the right to a fair trial requires court time and the provision of legal aid.

The best instances of global human rights provision are found in United Nations declarations regarding, for example, the right to work, education, social security and health care. Nations may have such rights enshrined in their laws, but most do not. In practice they are often ignored even by countries that have assented to particular UN conventions. However, they continue to exert influence by their claim to universality and through the work of many organizations, both governmental and non-governmental, such as the UN Commission on Human Rights and the World Court.

Procedural rights have a broad political consensus behind them. Increasingly they are seen by the public as the most effective way for individuals to guard against arbitrary decisions by government bureaucracies, including those of the local authority. This trend has important implications for social work and social care. The right of a person to participate in the process of defining their own needs, the right to be told about the worker's role and powers in a specific situation, the right to give explicit consent or to refuse intervention (except where the worker has statutory protective duties), the right of people to receive information in their first language, the right to written agreements as the basis of any service provided – are all powerful examples of procedural rights affecting how welfare professionals undertake their work with users.

N. Biehal, M. Fisher, P. Marsh and E. Sainsbury, 'Rights and social work', in A. Coote, *The Welfare of Citizens*, London: Rivers Oram Press, 1992.

**risk** the chance that the health or development of a person may be damaged by certain conditions or actions of others.

Care professionals use the phrase 'at risk' to indicate that a client is exposed to some source of harm and that possibly some protective measures should be taken. These sources of harm to a client may be external, such as assault by someone else, or arise from the client's own habits, such as not feeding themselves. For example, a 'child at risk' is regarded as vulnerable to physical or sexual ABUSE by one or more people or to other sources of harm through parental neglect. What is rarely stated is the probability that the child will suffer some harm. This is the drawback to the phrase; it is used widely but with little agreement over the actual chance that a client deemed at risk will come to some harm. Care professionals also use the word in the sense of 'risk-taking', which means making a conscious decision to put something at stake in order to make possible a worthwhile gain or benefit for the client (see RISK ANALYSIS).

**risk analysis** assessing the chances of some harm occurring to a client or other person.

RISK analysis means carefully weighing the chances that particular forms of harm will happen to a client or be caused by them in a given situation. Analysing the degree of risk is necessary, for example, when discharging from hospital a person with a mental illness who has previously been violent, when returning a child home who has been physically abused by their parents, or when leaving an elderly confused person who refuses to turn on the heat in the winter in their home. In each instance, the practitioner has to try to gauge the chance of harm occurring against the benefits. It is often necessary to accept a certain level of risk, because to try to minimize risk has its own costs and can be detrimental to the interests of the client. Although the risk could be reduced or eliminated in each of the cases above, to do that would require taking action that would be highly restrictive for the person concerned and might itself present different risks to the client's health or development. The person with mental illness, if not released, could become institutionalized, the child placed long-term with foster parents would suffer from loss of family contacts, the older person if removed to a home could become severely disoriented.

> With risk analysis, the care professional must be clear as to the specific benefits and harms that may result from proposed action. Increasingly this is a joint task, discussed with the CLIENT and the client's family and carers. After both the benefits and harms are itemized, some attempt must be made to judge the probability or likelihood of each occurring. One of the most difficult examples of risk analysis concerns the level of danger to a physically or sexually abused child if left at home. To undertake risk analysis it is important to know precisely what the nature of the abuse was, whether or not it was committed by a member of the family and what the likelihood is of it happening again. Both the severity of the abuse and the probability of it happening again are important considerations. Often the analysis will be difficult, since it must try to balance the possibility of immediate harm against the long-term harm the child could suffer if removed from home for a lengthy period of time.

**role**   expectations and obligations to behave in a particular way, arising from a recognized social position or status. Roles may carry with them specified rights as well as obligations.

People can play many roles – for example, roles of parent, worker and neighbour. People may be seen as belonging to role sets, that is, all the people associated with the playing of a particular role. Some people have many role sets; others have fewer, perhaps even as few as one (or none in the case of hermits or recluses). Roles can conflict in two ways. First, there can be conflict within a role; for example, a team leader might be expected, by members of the team, to protect them from further pressure if they are already working to capacity, but the same team leader could be expected by senior management to get workers to work harder if there are many unallocated cases. Such role conflict is referred to as intra-role conflict. The second kind of role conflict refers to conflicts between roles, that is, inter-role conflict; an example might be a person having to work long hours (role of worker) who is very worried about their children (role of parent) but feels unable to alter their situation to meet the obligations of both roles.

Roles can also usefully be seen as ascribed or achieved. Here sociologists look at the issues of whether roles are given and are unchanged (as in some traditional societies) or might be developed in later life. Some interesting problems, for example, of how first-generation Asian children adapt to both traditional expectations of them from their families and those of their peers can be usefully analysed using role theory. Similarly, some roles might be considered to be tightly defined (specific) and others to be of a more general nature (diffuse); this typology of roles can be helpful looking at the range of responsibilities that may be built into a role. A shift from a tightly defined role to something more diffuse, or the same process in reverse, can have interesting repercussions for the parties involved with the role-player.

ROLE THEORY has useful applications for social work and allied occupations in its attempts to make general sense of particular social problems or situations (say, women's roles in modern Britain) and in its potential for helping to understand individual problems, say, within social groups and families. FAMILY THERAPY is an area of work that has developed and applied role theory. (See also SICK ROLE.)

**role-play**    a device or method used in the education and training of social workers and allied professionals in which participants take on specified ROLES and act out a scene or situation.

The central purposes of role-play exercises are to help students grasp imaginatively the experience of people with problems and to help them develop their skills as workers in situations where mistakes are of little consequence. Typically, students are provided with a short case history and some indication of the personalities and personal styles of the characters in the situation. Students are then asked to develop the story in a manner that is consistent with the initial scenario. Other students can take on the roles of various workers, and students may be given the opportunity to try differing roles in the same situation. The direct observation of role-plays by trainers can provide immediate and useful feedback to students. Such devices have been found useful in developing skills for direct work with children and families, and courtroom and COUNSELLING skills.

**role theory**    the theoretical view that a major part of observable day-to-day behaviour is simply people carrying out their social ROLES.

The theory understands role as a set of expectations with regard to the actions appropriate to a social position. For example, the role of social worker carries a set of behavioural expectations prescribed by legislation, employers and professional ethics. Role theories place a strong emphasis on understanding the individual within their social networks and organizations. Thus the concept of role is useful in explaining why a person's behaviour changes when they change social position. Hence if a person's social position is known, it should be possible to predict their behaviour. The theory maintains that attitudes and beliefs are shaped by the role a person occupies; a person brings their attitudes into line with the expectations of the role. For example, a soldier would be expected to develop strong attitudes of patriotism. It follows that a change in role should lead to a change in attitudes.

Role theory argues that people spend much of their lives participating in organizations and groups, within which they occupy distinct positions, formally or informally assigned. Roles attach to those positions defined by expectations of behaviour, or norms. Role theory suggests that in general people conform to behavioural norms and to the expectations of others, and an individual is evaluated by others on their level of conformity to norms.

The theory has its origins in the language of the theatre; that is, people play parts in everyday life in ways that resemble actors' performances. The difference is that social roles are learned so effectively that a person *becomes* the role, such as daughter, son, soldier or doctor. People identify themselves as the role, having learned and internalized the script (expectations) through SOCIALIZATION processes. Thus roles are a key part of a person's social identity. The theory has been summarized in terms of part of people's self-concept being based on how they think others see them, and these perceptions in turn being partially based on the roles people occupy. Some commentators have criticized role theory for seeming to imply that people are endlessly compliant to the expectations of those around them, and for suggesting that people receive information about role performance during socialization and interaction processes and then willingly set out to meet those expectations. Thus role theory, it is claimed, ignores the impact of individual determinants of behaviour: motivation and personality.

M. Barton, *Roles*, London: Tavistock, 1965.

**Rossi index**  an index calculated as the retail price index less certain housing costs, normally used to uprate income-related benefits; named after Secretary of State for Social Security Hugh Rossi, who introduced the differential in 1980.

# S

**schizophrenia**  a MENTAL ILLNESS in which the sufferer has severe disorganization of thinking and behaviour.

The symptoms of schizophrenia include HALLUCINATIONS such as hearing voices, delusions such as the sufferer believing they are an important historical figure, and 'thought disorder' in which the ideas expressed are unintelligible to others in the person's culture. Behaviour based on these experiences often appears bizarre and does not form an appropriate response to circumstances. People with schizophrenia also have an emotional flatness or lack of rapport in their contacts with other people. These symptoms and experiences may last for only a short period – described as an 'acute episode' – and can be alleviated for most people by medication; but substantial numbers of people with this diagnosis also experience long-term 'chronic symptoms' of withdrawal, apathy, inactivity and poor motor control, along with periodic relapses into more 'acute' episodes. Altogether, schizophrenic experiences are highly disabling and stressful; studies have reported that people with these difficulties suffer long-term ANXIETY and DEPRESSION. The acute symptoms may have harmful consequences for the sufferer, and/or for others living with them, through their inability to care for themselves and occasional outbursts of physical or verbal aggression.

In most societies people with a diagnosis of schizophrenia constitute 1 per cent or less of the population. There is variation, however, because psychiatrists do not fully agree on the range of symptoms identifying the condition, and it has been argued that people with the diagnosis differ so widely in the 'symptoms' they experience that there may be no such thing as a single condition of schizophrenia. The people likely to experience, or be diagnosed with, the condition in Western societies tend to be of lower socioeconomic status, and black people are more likely to receive this diagnosis than white people. These differences may reflect assumptions or stereotypes on the part of psychiatrists and society generally that certain groups are more likely to develop schizophrenia than others, and there is evidence for this in relation to black people particularly.

What are the causes of schizophrenia? There is some evidence that people who have other family members diagnosed with schizophrenia are more likely to develop this themselves. But this could be due to genetic factors or to common environmental influences, and after 100 years of research no conclusive evidence has been found that any single physiological process is responsible for the condition. Social factors such as stressful family interactions and life events have been shown to have some influence on relapse; social disadvantage is also linked to chronic schizophrenia.

People are most likely to develop schizophrenia in their late teens or early twenties. People diagnosed as having schizophrenia and the pubertal form hebephrenia are highly likely to be referred to the psychiatric services. A substantial proportion will be in long-term contact with these services. In Western society, although over a quarter of people given this diagnosis recover fully after the first 'episode' of illness, a further two-thirds are chronically ill in varying degrees of severity, and about 10 per cent persistently suffer severe symptoms.

The social worker may be involved in a variety of ways with people diagnosed as suffering schizophrenia. These include arranging accommodation in, for example, a GROUP HOME, work to maximize the quality of life for the person with chronic schizophrenia, and work with the family in understanding the condition. Stressful life events and/or family interactions can lead to relapse. The practitioner works to prevent this by reducing the likelihood of stressful events occurring (for example, ensuring that rent is paid to avoid eviction), by working with the family or setting up self-help groups for families, helping to create less stressful family interaction. Social workers are also involved in MULTIDISCIPLINARY crisis centres that attempt to resolve crises arising for mentally ill people in the community.

Long-term work with a person with a diagnosis of chronic schizophrenia involves setting up contacts, support and activities with the individual that enable them to cope with everyday life. It is important that the specific abilities and vulnerabilities of the person concerned are fully taken into account in this provision, as overstimulation or excess pressure is likely to lead to relapse, and understimulation leads to depression and apathy. Ongoing relationships with the client and other professionals – such as the psychiatric services, which are usually involved – facilitate this preventive and ameliorative work considerably.

The long-term effects of schizophrenia include other elements of mental distress for the person – lack of confidence, depression and anxiety – and can also lead to exclusion by society. Because it is hard for them to obtain and, often, to cope with employment, the schizophrenic person is more likely to live in poverty, with poor housing and few social contacts. STIGMA also results; the person is rejected by society and often by former friends and relatives. If the person lives with their family, these close relatives too are affected by these difficulties. The worker needs to try to relieve these pressures as far as possible, as family tensions may otherwise ultimately lead to relapse and/or family break-up.

R. P. Bentall, ed., *Reconstructing Schizophrenia*, London: Routledge, 1990.

**school refusals**　the term applied to those children who refuse to attend school over long periods of time.

Some of these children might once have been called 'school-phobic', but this is not a particularly helpful term unless their anxiety relates specifically to the school experience. Other children refuse school for emotional and behavioural reasons or to call attention to distress and trauma caused by ABUSE or other family difficulties. Some can receive education only through special provision, home tuition or special units; others may be helped back to at least some level of school attendance by close working relationships between parents, schools and social work agencies. School refusal is not, in itself, a SPECIAL EDUCATIONAL NEED, though such children clearly suffer educational disadvantage. Opinions vary as to whether such behaviour should be seen as deviant, in quasi-medical terms, or as an entirely normal reaction where education does not meet the child's needs. (See TRUANCY.)

**school transport**　refers to the statutory duty of local education authorities to provide transport to school for children who live more than two miles from their designated school (primary) or three miles (secondary).

If parents choose an alternative school, they are responsible for providing transport themselves. This is sometimes a contentious issue for children who are LOOKED AFTER some distance away from their home. The LEA may not feel that it is responsible for transport to a school in the child's home area. If the social services department/parents wish the child to continue attending the same school as before, rather than transfer to the school serving their current address, they may have to finance the transport themselves.

**Scottish Office**　the central government department responsible for social work provision in Scotland.

The Scottish Office is divided into five core departments covering most of the main internal policy issues affecting Scotland. The Scottish Home and Health Department (SHHD) is the main department responsible for the development of the NATIONAL HEALTH SERVICE in Scotland. Social work is organized within the Scottish Education Department (SED) under a semi-independent organization, the Social Work Services Group (SWG). This emerged as a result of the centrality of child-care to social work activity and the work of the SED; but it has created difficulties for the development of COMMUNITY CARE in Scotland, even though there has been a Minister for Health and Social Work since 1979. The 1989 white paper *Caring for People* made some effort to improve the situation in Scotland by providing the local authorities with more responsibilities in the area, including that of needs assessment. However, there was no move to give the SWG a greater role in directing policy, and it was left with a predominantly advisory role.

J.D. Hunter and G. Wistow, *Community Care in Britain*, London: King's Fund Centre, 1987.

**Scottish Vocational Educational Council (SCOTVEC)**   an industrial lead body that sets occupational standards and awards qualifications in vocational training.

**'scrounger'**   in common usage the word used to insult a person who claims benefit. The term may be directed at someone thought to be claiming fraudulently, who continuously asks for more from the benefit system or who is happy to rely on benefits rather than be self-supporting.

The rather wide meaning of the term intimidates some potential claimants; the only certain way to avoid being a scrounger is not to claim.

**sculpting**   a technique used in experiential work to help individuals depict their thoughts and feelings about their family, their social work team or other collections of people. The technique entails individuals moving people around so that they assume particular relationships and attitudes and postures in relation to each other.

The configurations produced by sculpting are regarded both as revealing an individual's feelings about particular people and as potentially diagnostic about family, team or group functioning. Sculpting techniques can be used in such activities as FAMILY THERAPY, team-building exercises or SUPERVISION.

**second adult rebate**   a rebate payable on COUNCIL TAX that allows a reduction of the tax payable if the liable person has no partner and is not charging rent, and if all the other adults in the dwelling have a low income.

The rebate exists because council tax is based on the principle that each dwelling accommodates at least two adults able to pay. If all the other adults receive INCOME SUPPORT the rebate is worth 25 per cent of the tax bill.

**section 8 orders**   the collective name given to the four court orders described in section 8 of the CHILDREN ACT and used mainly in matrimonial proceedings: CONTACT ORDER, PROHIBITED STEPS ORDER, RESIDENCE ORDER and SPECIFIC ISSUE ORDER.

**secure accommodation**   a residential unit for children that maintains locked doors and windows and permits only limited and closely supervised movement of residents inside and outside the premises.

To place a child in secure accommodation requires the authority to obtain a SECURE ACCOMMODATION ORDER. Considerable debate surrounds the use of secure accommodation and whether more such units are required. Such establishments are usually run by local authorities, although the government has invited voluntary child-care organizations to run additional units in order to meet what it regards as a national shortage.

**secure accommodation order**   a court order under section 25 of the CHILDREN ACT that authorizes the local authority LOOKING AFTER a child to place them in accommodation restricting their liberty.

The order may only be made if three criteria are met: (1) if it appears that the young person has a history of running away; (2) if they are likely to do so from other types of accommodation; and (3) if in running away the young person would be likely to suffer SIGNIFICANT HARM or injure themselves or others.

**Seebohm Report**   The report of the committee set up under Sir Frederic (later Lord) Seebohm and published in 1968. The committee was established in 1965 to examine the then fragmented state of social work services, which had been the focus of increasing criticism.

At the time of the Seebohm Committee's investigation and report, services for OLDER PEOPLE, the HOMELESS and people with physical DISABILITY were delivered by LOCAL AUTHORITY welfare departments; services for children and families were the responsibility of children's departments; and services for people with MENTAL ILLNESS and LEARNING DIFFICULTIES were provided by health departments. The report proposed bringing these different services together into one large SOCIAL SERVICES DEPARTMENT and argued that the diverse social work tasks could be combined into the role of an all-purpose or GENERIC social worker. The report was optimistic about what it thought social work could achieve. Since the institutions of the welfare state had solved most of the major social problems, it expected social work to provide assistance to the small number of people who experienced problems in adapting to life and who perhaps needed emotional support or help in raising their children or in claiming benefit. Such a service should be non-stigmatizing and should be available from one local authority department.

The hopes of the report were not realized. Social problems such as homelessness and POVERTY were not eradicated but increased, and social work's capacity to assist individuals facing major social or personal difficulties was seen to be limited. The report's major legacy was the construction of large local authority social services departments, which in the following decades received a measure of criticism as impersonal and bureaucratic.

**self-advocacy**   involves service users in speaking for themselves and the development of processes that encourage this.

The self-ADVOCACY movement is particularly well established in the field of LEARNING DISABILITY, where groups of service users come together in self-advocacy groups to develop their skills and confidence in this area and to act as a pressure group for improvements in services and in society. Self-advocacy groups are varied in type and may be either service-based (for example, in a day service setting) or independent (for example, as part of the People First movement, which is international). There is some debate about the role of members of staff in such groups, but the importance of advisers is recognized. However, service users must have control over the groups. Self-advocacy has also had an impact on services for people with mental health problems. As with people with learning disability, the role of 'survivors' of hospital and other services has been important.

K. Simons, *Sticking Up for Yourself: Self-Advocacy and People with Learning Difficulties*, York: Rowntree Foundation, 1992.

**self-determination**   the making of decisions for oneself without influence or interference from others.

In social work practice, CLIENT self-determination refers to fostering service user choice, seeking to minimize dependence upon others (especially social workers) and encouraging personal autonomy. Self-determination is also constrained by social circumstances (a poor person cannot choose to be rich), personal limitations (somebody with ALZHEIMER'S DISEASE may find it difficult to form a view), agency resources (accommodation for many vulnerable groups is simply not available) and the needs or wishes of others. The promotion of self-determination is a key social work task in all settings and with all client groups. (See also EMPOWERMENT, ETHICAL CODE, VALUES.

**self-help**  a process by which individuals, groups or organizations work together with the objective of mutual aid or benefit. The focus of such activity could entail a wide range of experiences including personal and COMMUNITY problems.

If EMPOWERMENT is the process by which individuals or groups are encouraged to become more powerful, then self-help can usefully be seen as a form of empowering. Self-help activity necessarily usually involves avoiding the status of a CLIENT or user of a social work service. Other critical defining characteristics include equality of status among members, shared decision-making by individuals within the group or organization, CONFIDENTIALITY with regard to the group's or organization's activities and a common focus, interest or problem on the part of members.

Self-help encompasses a very wide range of activities, including self-sufficiency, community living, worker participation in industry and industrial cooperatives. In relation to social, health and community concerns, the list is very long indeed and includes carers' and relatives' groups, groups focusing upon some form of therapy and groups for people experiencing major problems of STIGMA. One of the best-known of the large 'anonymous' self-help groups is Alcoholics Anonymous, but many more have followed this model. Over the last decade there has been a mushrooming of groups concerned with the needs of carers – for example, relatives of people with Alzheimer's disease and relatives of schizophrenics. A major commitment to self-help has developed from the community worker's perspective. COMMUNITY DEVELOPMENT and community action have both had substantial ingredients of self-help, principally because such activities have often rested upon a belief that the normal channels for getting things done are not working and that direct action is required by the people most affected by the problem. In some instances such groups have received some support from social service agencies, but in others they have managed their affairs without any external assistance from the helping professions. Some social and community workers believe that an acceptable way of working is to help establish self-help groups and then, at some later stage, to encourage the groups to 'go it alone'. Many community and interest groups have started in this way. Purists, however, would have it that this form of professional 'contamination' is unacceptable and that such intervention prevents a genuine form of self-help emerging. It is argued that, even where the professional withdraws at an early stage and where their contribution has been minimal, they many nevertheless fundamentally determine how the group conducts its affairs. There is an obvious danger that this will be so when the 'professional' holds the purse strings for the costs of the groups' activities, as with many carers' groups.

Some commentators have been concerned that the growth of self-help groups may be a response to cuts in public expenditure. In this respect self-help may be perceived as a part of voluntary activity and perhaps a substitute for what was previously a professional welfare service. Others have argued persuasively that social work and other services have encouraged clients' dependence on professionals. Seen in this way, self-help may be a healthy antidote to professional power. The key to this debate may be in discussions about what should be guaranteed by the state and how such services are to be delivered.

R. Adams, *Self-Help, Social Work and Empowerment*, Basingstoke: Macmillan, 1990.

**service manager**   a middle manager in a local authority SOCIAL SERVICES DEPARTMENT responsible for day-to-day management of an entire service area, such as for older people or disabled people.

Service managers are described as operational managers, as opposed to those above them in the hierarchy, such as principal officers, who have a strategic and policy-making role.

**severe disablement allowance**   a non-contributory and non-MEANS-TESTED benefit paid to a person who has been incapable of work for twenty-eight weeks but does not qualify for INVALIDITY BENEFIT.

If the allowance is first claimed before age 20 and claimed continuously, there are no further qualifying rules. If it is claimed at age 20 or after, the claimant must also be assessed as 80 per cent disabled. This assessment is based on the INDUSTRIAL INJURIES SCHEME, which ascribes percentages to particular injuries. Young people can claim at age 16 even while they remain at school if they are in special education. Other likely recipients are people who become disabled after a period out of the job market, that is, not working or signing on as unemployed, and married women who paid a reduced stamp while working. Severe disablement allowance was first introduced in the 1970s as 'non-contributory invalidity pension'.

**severe learning difficulty**   defined in the United Kingdom as affecting children with an intelligence quotient (IQ – see INTELLIGENCE TESTING) from 20 to 50 (cf. the World Health Organization's classification of IQ 20 to 35).

Categorization of severe learning difficulty by IQ has all the problems generally recognized as associated with IQ testing. Since the Education Act 1981, the emphasis has been upon the assessment of children's SPECIAL EDUCATIONAL NEEDS and the issuing of STATEMENTS that may identify additional resources required. Children with severe learning difficulty may be placed in mainstream schools with support, but more usually attend special schools. Social workers' liaison with special schools can improve the service that children and their care-givers receive.

**Sex Discrimination Act 1975**   an Act of Parliament that seeks to eliminate DISCRIMINATION in relation to GENDER in respect of employment, education, the provision of housing, goods, facilities and services, and advertising.

Specifically in relation to employment and advertising for jobs it is also illegal to discriminate on grounds of marital status.

The Sex Discrimination Act of 1986 has increased the scope of the earlier Act. The 1975 Act distinguishes between direct and indirect discrimination. The first might cover situations where, for example, an interview panel asks a woman about her intentions to get married and have children. The second would cover issues like length of experience. Because women on average spend less time in paid employment, they usually have less work experience than men. Good practice in these circumstances would be to express the requirements for a job in terms of the skills and knowledge needed; a woman might then compete on level terms. Victimization, where somebody is punished or dismissed because they intend to complain under the Act, is also illegal. Women who feel aggrieved and cannot solve their grievances informally or through an organization's formal procedures can take their problem to an industrial tribunal. Research has demonstrated that few such cases actually get to court. Although some women settle matters out of court, the majority do not seek redress at all; and of those who do, few are successful. Until recently financial penalties for discriminating employers, for example, were low (a maximum of £11,000), but a recent European Commission directive has forced British tribunals to abolish the upper ceiling on claims for compensation. In the last two decades there has been little evidence to indicate that the Act has improved matters for women in the areas of concern addressed by the legislation.

**sex education**   all secondary schools must provide sex education within a moral framework that focuses on personal responsibility and respect for others. Primary schools may also do so if the governors wish.

Parents have the right to withdraw their children from all sex education lessons (though not from the biological elements of the National Curriculum). There is no requirements on parents to consult the child about such a decision, even when the child is over 16. There is some confusion about the rights of older children to receive advice from school staff about their sexual behaviour. In general, the Department for Education (DfE) does not recognize the concept of the 'mature minor' in the way the Department of Health does. Many school staff are reluctant to do anything that appears to encourage or condone sexual activity among young people under 16 unless they are given explicit permission to do so by parents. DfE guidance suggests that parents should always be informed if schools believe the child to be breaking the law. All guidance from the DfE assumes that sex education relates only to heterosexual activity.

**sexism**   the negative and unjustified treatment of any person by virtue of their sex or GENDER. Sexist behaviour is regarded as discriminatory and may take personal or institutional forms.

Although men may be subject to DISCRIMINATION, it is women who experience discrimination on a major scale both within Britain and worldwide. In social work there are many examples of sexism in terms both of employment practices within social welfare organizations and of services.

The majority of employees in social welfare agencies are female, yet management is predominantly male. In social work departments in the pre-SEEBOHM period, women occupied a greater proportion of senior posts. In terms of equality of opportunity and employment practices, there is little evidence of progress for women. Services are clearly institutionally sexist on a grand scale. The failure of social welfare agencies to grasp and deal with the problem of violence against women can be understood only in terms of male explanations for such violence continuing to dominate both policies and practice. Social services for vulnerable people of all kinds who require care rest very clearly on an almost unquestioned assumption that women will care. In relation to mothers, social work practice often seems unable to look beyond the woman as parent, to perceive the individual with individual needs. Women often face multiple problems in relation to their caring responsibilities – poverty, social isolation, poor housing and second-class citizenship – and yet still seem to attract blame for not being able to cope. The problems of black women are, of course, compounded by their additional experience of RACISM.

> Different analyses and perspectives have been developed to attempt to understand the nature and origins of sexism. Some feminists perceive the problem to be rooted in an almost universal patriarchy, that is, that women are everywhere oppressed by men. This oppression takes the form of ideologies, policies and the social fabric within which men and women conduct their personal relationships. That men occupy positions of power throughout society is unquestionable, and such occupancy is a primary source of oppression. Other feminists locate the problem within an analysis of capitalism and critically in the roles they play as part of the reserve army of labour (to be taken up and put down by the economy as and when needed) and as bearers and carers of the future labour force. Some have sought to embrace both theories to achieve some kind of synthesis. It has been recognized that each theory leads to quite different anti-sexist strategies (see ANTI-SEXISM), although there is some common ground. (See also ANTI-DISCRIMINATORY PRACTICE, DOMESTIC VIOLENCE, EQUAL OPPORTUNITIES POLICIES, EQUAL PAY ACT 1970, SEX DISCRIMINATION ACT 1975.)
>
> L. Dominelli and E. McLeod, *Feminist Social Work*, Basingstoke: Macmillan, 1989.

**sex offender**   a person who commits a sexual offence, in itself sufficient grounds for a CUSTODIAL SENTENCE. The CRIMINAL JUSTICE ACT 1991 allows courts to pass a longer prison sentence than is the norm if it considers that a sexual offender poses a serious risk to the public.

Sex offenders are overwhelmingly male. There has been recent interest in women who sexually abuse children, but no evidence as yet suggests that numbers are significant. Some sex offenders are referred to as Schedule 1 offenders under the Children and Young Persons Act 1933, but strictly speaking the schedule covers any serious offence against children, not just those of a sexual nature. If an offender falls into this category, special precautions must be taken by probation officers and social workers to ensure that he does not have any inappropriate contact with children (for example, through work or place of residence).

In the past, it has been argued that imprisoning sex offenders does nothing to prevent them reoffending on release. The only PRISON that catered specifically for such offenders until recently was the psychiatric prison at Grendon Underwood in Buckinghamshire. At many other prisons, sex offenders are victimized as 'nonces' by other prisoners and have to be segregated for their own protection. However, most prisons now provide a special programme of treatment in which offenders are challenged to accept responsibility for their behaviour and to demonstrate their willingness to change. Similar programmes are also run in the community by the PROBATION SERVICE at PROBATION CENTRES. If the court decides to send a sex offender to a special programme at a probation centre, it may extend the length of that programme beyond the normal sixty-day maximum.

Working with sex offenders provides particular challenges and can be very stressful. Workers can be angered and distressed by accounts of offences, and such work raises questions about basic social work VALUES. For example, how far can workers be expected to remain non-judgemental towards and accepting of an offender? On the other hand, is there a danger that constantly confronting an offender with the unacceptable nature of his behaviour may become little more than 'legitimized nonce-bashing'? Despite these concerns, community-based programmes appear to have good success rates, and a substantial body of knowledge has now been established about the treatment of sex offenders.

**sexual abuse**   the involvement of a person or people of any age in sexual activity against their wishes, or where they do not adequately comprehend the activity, or where it is unlikely that they could give informed consent to the activity.

The phenomenon of sexual ABUSE is thought to be present in many societies and in all social groups. The evidence consistently suggests that abusers are invariably male and that the abused are primarily female, although boys constitute a smaller but nevertheless significant group of abused. Recent evidence has revealed that women too can be abusers, but abuse perpetrated by females is rare. Sexual abuse is now accepted as a frequent component of DOMESTIC VIOLENCE. There is also increasing evidence that rape and sexual assault are much more common in many societies than previously supposed, both between married and cohabiting couples and in other relationships, and where the parties are not known to each other. However, the major preoccupation of social workers and health professionals in the last decade has concerned child sexual abuse.

There are additional important dimensions to sexual abuse in relation to children. The Standing Conference on Sexually Abused Children described the issue in the following terms: 'Any child below the age of consent may be deemed to have been sexually abused when a sexually mature person has, by design or by neglect of their usual societal or specific responsibilities in relation to the child, engaged or permitted the engagement of that child in any activity of a sexual nature which is intended to lead to the sexual gratification of the sexually mature person(s). This definition pertains whether or not this activity involves explicit coercion by any means, whether or not it involves genital or physical contact, whether or not initiated by the child, and whether or not there is a discernible harmful outcome in the short term.' Clearly child sexual abuse involves many kinds of behaviour, such as non-contact sexual activity (voyeurism, provocative speech, exposure), actual contact including fondling and masturbation, various forms of sexual penetration as well as sexual exploitation such as prostitution and pornography.

Most child sexual abuse is between two people, but it is possible for there to be more than two people involved. Again, usually the perpetrator is an adult, but sometimes both perpetrator and victim are children. The perpetrator may be adolescent and the victim a younger child, sometimes much younger; or conceivably the victim and perpetrator are the same age, but the victim is at an earlier developmental stage. Sexual abuse of almost any kind is more likely to be committed by a person known to the victim than by a stranger. Early studies suggested that the incidence of child sexual abuse was very low; but more detailed research has since revealed that the problem is on a much greater scale. The principal sources of information are statistics collected by various social work agencies that reflect upon the agencies' own work, and the disclosures of adults about abuse experienced in their own childhood. A recent study in Britain indicated that at least 10 per cent of young people over the age of 15 had experienced abuse of some form at an earlier stage in their lives; 77 per cent reported that they had not experienced abuse; and the remaining 13 per cent refused to comment. Other studies in Britain and the United States have suggested much higher figures.

The dominant explanations of abusive behaviour have changed significantly over the last few decades. Individual pathology (the belief that it is an individual fault in some sense) and family dysfunction (the view that there must be something fundamentally wrong with the way family members related to each other) were the major explanations until the 1970s. Such ideas still have wide currency in public circles and in some treatment regimes. One particular persistent theme at this time was implicitly to blame mothers either for not discharging their sexual obligations to their partner or for not managing to protect their children from abuse (implying that they had colluded with the abuse). Such theories have been rigorously criticized by feminists, who perceive sexual abuse in almost any form as an expression of male power and patriarchal institutions. Far from accepting the argument that sexual abuse is an aberration on the part of a small number of individuals, feminists have it that sexual abuse is an expression of the widespread abuse of power by males and that, in some sense, all men are implicated.

Treatment programmes in many places are now beginning to focus upon the offence behaviour of perpetrators, to emphasize their responsibility for the behaviour and to help them develop coping mechanisms for dealing with their attraction, for example, for young children. Few treatment programmes claim that perpetrators are cured, but the claim is that many can control their problem. Almost all workers involved with sexual offenders believe that such programmes are more effective than imprisonment. The PROBATION SERVICE is active in this field.

The major difficulties in working with the problem of child sexual abuse are those of secrecy, denial and incredulity. The major impediment to the protection of children who have been sexually abused has been the disbelief of those working in the field, including social workers, health professionals and the police. Although more abuse is perhaps being disclosed than ever before, clearly much more could be done preventively to help children disclose earlier or to prevent abuse taking place at all. (See also CHILD PROTECTION, CLEVELAND INQUIRY, EMOTIONAL ABUSE, PHYSICAL ABUSE.)

R. Coulborn Faller, *Child Sexual Abuse*, Basingstoke: Macmillan, 1989.

**sexual problems and issues** problems and dilemmas faced by social workers, therapists and counsellors in advising CLIENTS and service users in the matter of sexual behaviour and sexual identity.

Sexual problems and issues are a major area of work for social welfare workers that is often not acknowledged and for which professional preparation is as yet piecemeal. The issues include contraception, sexual behaviour and health risks, confronting unacceptable sexual activity and COUNSELLING around issues of sexual identity.

Work relating to contraception includes advising and providing services for prisoners, children in care and people with LEARNING DIFFICULTIES. Much of this work involves key dilemmas. For example, should contraception be offered to children under the legal age of consent, and should contraception be provided in PRISON establishments when the Home Office's official policy is that sexual activity should not take place there at all? Similarly, what kinds of advice ought people with learning difficulties be given about sexual behaviour, and is compulsory sterilization ever justified?

The second area of work refers to general advice about sexual behaviour and health-related matters. The focus of such work might be educational and preventive or it might be concerned with the consequences of sexual activity such as HIV/AIDS counselling. The third area includes work with SEX OFFENDERS and with child SEXUAL ABUSE. Dealing with sex offenders in the community has become a major focus of work in recent years. Similarly, identifying child sexual abuse and helping children, or adult survivors, to work through their difficulties is also an important and growing area of work.

Counselling people in relation to problems of sexual identity and of social responses to those problems – for example, with children in care who feel themselves to be gay or lesbian – is a sensitive and difficult process. Similarly, the consequences for people 'coming out' (publicly acknowledging their homosexuality) can be substantial. Social workers may also become involved in official reports on the future care of children when families break up and one parent decides to live with another person of the same sex.

In all these areas of work there are major dimensions of ANTI-DISCRIMINATORY PRACTICE.

J. Milner, *Social Work* and *Sexual Problems*, Birmingham: Pepar, 1986.

**sharps safe** a container for the collection of used needles and syringes.

When two-thirds full, the container should be sealed and incinerated at an officially designated place. Health authorities or drug counselling agencies will advise on disposal. All such containers should confirm to BS6 standards.

**sheltered accommodation** units of dwellings designed for vulnerable people where some measure of help is available from a paid warden who lives on the premises or nearby.

Most sheltered accommodation is purpose-built for OLDER PEOPLE. People with LEARNING DISABILITIES also live in such units, although the term GROUP HOME is sometimes used for this client group. Sheltered accommodation was thought to be potentially a primary service for old people. Research has revealed that although some old people move to sheltered accommodation when they become frail or less able to look after themselves independently, many do so in anticipation of future vulnerability. Wardens also prefer to have a 'mixed' group of older people, that is, some vulnerable and others relatively robust. Such findings have suggested that people in sheltered dwellings may not be significantly different from those living in their own homes in the community. Given these findings, some argue that sheltered housing may not be 'the way forward' that it once appeared to be and that a strong case can be made for supporting people in their own homes with community services such as home helps, meals on wheels and peripatetic warden schemes.

**sibling abuse**   the inflicting of harm – sexual, physical or emotional – by a brother or sister upon another brother or sister.

Although most ABUSE occurring within families is perpetrated by adults on minors, there are a significant minority of cases where the abuse is inflicted by one minor upon another or by a young adult brother or sister upon a younger sibling. Children with disabilities are thought to be especially vulnerable to sibling abuse, as are siblings within step-families.

**sickness benefit**   a benefit paid during the first twenty-eight weeks of sickness when STATUTORY SICK PAY from an employer is not available, for example for self-employed people.

Entitlement to sickness benefit is based on contributions paid or credited in the last two years before claiming. After twenty-eight weeks the claimant can receive INVALIDITY BENEFIT.

**sick role**   a ROLE that can be entered by a sick person in which sickness becomes a special status, with positive and negative implications for the person concerned.

The concept was developed in the 1950s by the US sociologist Talcott Parsons, who suggested the following elements in the sick role: (1) the sick person is exempted from many usual social responsibilities; (2) it is accepted that the sick person may be unable to fend for themselves; (3) the sick person is expected to strive for health; (4) the sick person is expected to seek professional advice and treatment.

The sickness role may sometimes be adopted or maintained by people who may wish to escape the burden of social obligations. In these circumstances, professional agencies such as those of medicine and social work may be seen as performing a social control function in determining 'true' fitness and unfitness and thus the legitimacy of occupation of the sick role.

**significant harm**   the degree of harm to a child that it is necessary to establish to obtain protective orders under the CHILDREN ACT.

The intention of the Children Act is to ensure that a local authority would remove a child compulsorily from their family only as a last resort, when there is no other means to protect the child. Only when the child has suffered serious harm would such a measure find favour with the courts.

Section 31 of the Children Act defines two types of harm: *ill-treatment*, which includes PHYSICAL, SEXUAL and EMOTIONAL ABUSE, and the *impairment of* HEALTH or development, which includes the effects of neglect and deprivation on the child's physical, intellectual or social development. The definition obviously includes traumatic injury such as might result from deliberate cigarette burns or assault that causes bone fractures. It also includes types of harm at the hands of adults that are harder to define, such as repeatedly subjecting a child to sources of terror, keeping a child locked up or depriving them of even minimal amounts of food.

The crucial question for practitioners is, what level of harm is 'significant'? Department of Health guidance suggests that 'significant' means considerable, noteworthy or important. It also states that the significance of harm suffered by a child can lie either in the seriousness of the harm itself or in the effects of the harm. A physical injury such as a severe beating inflicted by a parent does not have to have longer-term effects on the physical or mental health of the child to be significant. Conversely, a physical injury – for example, to a child's genitals inflicted when they were being sexually abused – may be more serious in its emotional and long-term consequences. Whether a particular harm is significant depends on certain factors such as the age of the child and the length of time for which the child has suffered the harm. Overly harsh physical punishment administered to a 6-month-old child leading to severe bruising would be significant, whereas the same amount of force would not necessarily be significant for a 10-year-old. A 3-year-old child wandering streets late at night could be likely to suffer significant harm, whereas a 10-year-old would be less vulnerable and less likely to suffer significant harm.

As a form of harm, the impairment of health or development includes the effects of neglect and deprivation such as a very young child being left on their own for great lengths of time, persistent weight loss and the failure to grow over a long period of time. In addition, harm in this sense may be measured in relation to the child's overall development, including their intellectual or social development.

In general, social workers view the harm suffered by a child as increasing in significance if it is repeated and occurs within the context of constant parental anger, indifference or outright rejection. To establish whether the harm is significant to the particular child, the effects of the ill-treatment or neglect must be considered in detail, particularly if the case is to come to court. This is done by describing the extent of injuries inflicted by parents or other members of the family, or the extent of the neglect, such as persistently low levels of nutrition, and how the child's health and development have suffered as a result. If the harm is to the child's health and development the Children Act requires that its significance be established by contrasting the harms that the child has suffered with a hypothetical similar child, that is, a child of the same weight, age, size and physical attributes or disabilities.

The most difficult of all forms of harm to identify is emotional or psychological abuse. Constantly criticizing the child, always blaming them for things and prolonged episodes of shouting or screaming at the child may or may not do significant harm. Severe rejection of the child, refusal to speak to them over a long period of time and long periods of enforced isolation, depending on the age of the child, probably would be significant harm. In terms of an application to court in such cases, much would depend on the behaviour and reactions of the child; if the child showed severe behaviour problems, the harm, though not physical, could be significant. Undoubtedly, the attempt to establish this as significant harm would require a psychologist's expert opinion. (See also CHILD ABUSE, THRESHOLD CRITERIA.)

M. Adcock, *et al.*, *Significant Harm: Its Management and Outcome*, Croydon: Significant Publications, 1991.

**simple assessment**   the relatively straightforward ASSESSMENT of NEED to determine the extent to which a person requires COMMUNITY CARE.

Following Department of Health guidelines, most local authorities have divided their assessments of need into at least two categories: simple and complex. Simple assessments are undertaken when a person's needs are relatively straightforward and a single service is likely to be provided, such as home care or a place at a day centre. Even so, collecting information for simple assessments requires a range of information on the person's health, housing, income level, and social and family contacts. This information is usually coordinated by a local authority social services officer such as a COMMUNITY CARE WORKER or CARE MANAGER.

**social care**   assistance given to people to maintain themselves physically and socially. This type of care is usually provided in residential and day care centres or by domiciliary staff at home; it is distinguished from other forms such as health care and the care given by one member of a family to another.

Social care includes a certain level of physical and personal care, such as assistance in toileting, bathing and coping with incontinence. It also typically includes social support by helping people in maintaining contact with family and friends, developing social skills and skills for independent living such as food preparation, and making social contacts both inside and outside their home or residential establishment. Social care tasks include other such functions as collecting and giving information (for example, in contributing to the ASSESSMENT and CARE PLANS for individuals), arranging admission to and DISCHARGE from residential units, and dealing with AGGRESSION or CHALLENGING BEHAVIOUR. Many observers have noted that the distinction is blurring between social care tasks and the work undertaken by staff traditionally employed in certain health care settings such as NURSING HOMES and long-stay hospital wards for older people and people with severe learning difficulties. Residential staff in all settings are having to work across a broader range of tasks that embrace aspects of both health care and social care.

S. Sillars, *Caring for People, A Workbook for Care Workers*, Basingstoke: Macmillan, 1992.

**social class**   commonly defined either as a stratum within society based upon a classification of occupations or as a system based upon the distribution and ownership of property in society.

The idea of social class includes not simply economic dimensions (ownership of property, security, income and other benefits) but the social relationships that are dependent or contingent upon the economic dimensions. Although there are variations between sociologists on how they view the relationship between economic issues and other aspects of life, all agree on the overwhelming importance of the economic. The difference seems to be about whether the economic variables determine or simply strongly influence other aspects of life. Sociologists have been able to demonstrate a very close association between membership of a social class and other behaviours within other areas of social life; for example, class correlates closely with educational achievement, with criminal activity, with the experience of HEALTH (both mortality and morbidity), with the structure of communities and with LIFE CHANCES generally. There are also strong associations between the experiences of poor people and those of black people, although the dynamics of 'RACE' and class are by no means straightforward. The bulk of social work service users are from the working class. Such a phenomenon has to be understood as having both controlling and caring functions, partly because some service users are unwilling recipients of social work intervention and partly because some want to have contact in order to try to secure additional resources or services to meet their problems.

There is no overall ground for supposing that social work has been able to seriously embrace ANTI-DISCRIMINATORY PRACTICE in relation to poor people. Most of the social work effort has appeared to be marginal or, at best, to be able to re-establish the status quo. Indeed, many commentators have perceived social work as essentially oppressive in its practices and in its association with the state apparatus. Others are more optimistic (see also EMPOWERMENT, RADICAL SOCIAL WORK).

M. Simpkin, *Trapped within Welfare*, Basingstoke: Macmillan, 1979.

**Social Fund** a public fund that provides lump-sum payments towards one-off expenses.

The Social Fund consists of two very different parts. The 'regulated' fund provides MATERNITY EXPENSES PAYMENTS and FUNERAL EXPENSES PAYMENTS as of right in these two closely defined circumstances. The fund's expenditure in this area is determined purely by demand and not by the judgements of individual Social Fund officers. The 'discretionary' fund provides COMMUNITY CARE GRANTS, BUDGETING LOANS and CRISIS LOANS. For this expenditure each district of the Benefits Agency has a set budget from which such payments can be made, and its expenditure is therefore limited by its budget. The discretionary Social Fund was introduced in 1988 along with INCOME SUPPORT. It replaced 'single payments', paid as part of supplementary benefit and worth £360 million in 1985/6, with community care grants, currently worth £60 million, and repayable loans, worth £141 million.

The Social Fund is criticized on three main grounds: first, the budget limit which requires Social Fund officers to ration payments; second, the extensive use of discretion by fund officers; and third, the absence of an independent appeal mechanism. The law on the discretionary Social Fund is provided by the secretary of state's directions, which broadly outline the circumstances in which a payment can be made. Fund officers who make decisions must follow the directions and take account of guidance, local priorities and the local budget. Despite an already suppressed demand for grants, only 25 per cent of community care grant applications are successful. When an applicant is refused they may ask for an internal review; this includes an interview at the local office, at which a representative acting for the claimant may attend. A further review is provided by Social Fund inspectors at the Independent Review Service, but this is conducted in writing only; the inspectors check that previous decisions comply with the law, including the secretary of state's directions. Frequently, the inspectors refer cases back for further consideration. This involves a lengthy process to deal with a claimant's needs, which are often immediate and essential.

**social inquiry report**   see PRE-SENTENCE REPORT.

**socialization**   the process whereby people learn the cultural norms of their society and the ROLES they play. In other words, they learn how members of their society expect them to behave and what ATTITUDES they are expected to hold.

As with many other areas, there is debate over the degree to which aspects of a person, such as GENDER identity, are determined by our genetic make-up rather than by experience. Socio-biologists argue that many of our ways of behaving have evolved, and thus we are born with many behavioural patterns predetermined. Cross-cultural research suggests that there is greater diversity than this view should permit. The mutualist view holds that socialization is produced by an interaction between the qualities with which a child is born and the behaviour of the people with whom the child interacts.

There are a large number of sources of the information that a person gains about their culture – that is, socializing influences – some of which conflict. The first influence in this process will be care-givers, such as members of the immediate family. Once a child starts to be cared for by people outside the family, such as CHILD-MINDERS or teachers, they are exposed to new influences – not only from new adults but also from children of other families. A distinction is made between a person's PEER GROUP – those who are in a similar situation, such as fellow schoolchildren – and their reference group, that is, those people with whom a person identifies. If these groups do not coincide, there can be conflict as people meet pressures from their peer group to conform.

The media provide a further source of information about behaviour. This has led to fears that the norms of one culture may swamp those of another, a process sometimes called cultural imperialism. As a reaction to this, some societies have argued that the showing of films and television programmes from certain foreign countries should be rationed, and that inhabitants of the country should be deliberately exposed to media that reflect the indigenous society's norms. An additional fear arises from the effect that exposure to violent or pornographic media can have, particularly on the young. Researchers disagree over the effect of such influences, some claiming that there is a detrimental effect, others that there is insufficient evidence on which to base a decision. Nevertheless, social learning theorists have demonstrated that children learn behaviour patterns from watching adults.

Socialization does not cease when a person becomes an adult. The roles a person plays when adult can help to mould their behaviour. Here the pressures are not simply from people in the same occupation but also come from other members of society who have a view about how it is appropriate for a person in a given role to behave, or from STEREOTYPES about how such a person is likely to behave. (See also NATURE–NURTURE DEBATE.)

M. Hewstone, W. Stroebe, J.P. Codol and G.M. Stephenson (eds), *Introduction to Social Psychology*, Oxford: Blackwell, 1988.

**social policy**   government policy in the area of welfare, and the academic study of its development, implementation and impact.

The area of government policy covered by the generally accepted concept of social policy encompasses education, health, housing, social security, including transfer payments such as pensions, and the personal social services. This is a wide range of policy issues but one that relates closely to the ideas embodied in the welfare state. While government played a partial role in many of these areas prior to the Second World War, the idea of an activist welfare state has come to be seen as a product of the postwar period. However, important aspects of the welfare system and social policy were in place in the early years of the twentieth century, including pensions, some hospital care and state education. The commitment to full employment from the Labour government after the war and consequent legislation to support that aim resulted in a major acceleration in the development of a comprehensive system of social policy and welfare.

The academic study of social policy developed initially as part of the longer-established study of government policy associated with political science and public administration. Consequently, the field of study was originally that of social administration, which centred on the empirical examination of policy and the issues it was concerned with. This tradition is still central to the discipline, providing important information and analysis, such as by using evidence of government expenditure patterns to test assumptions about the nature of government policies. Important developments in the study of social policy have directly confronted this tradition, however. These approaches have emerged from a wide range of political perspectives and have resulted in a re-evaluation of social policy both theoretically and in its practical development. There are three main groups of critics: the NEW RIGHT, associated with 'public choice' theory; socialist theories, particularly Marxist; and feminist.

The New Right has been the most influential group in practical terms, due to its influence on Conservative governments since 1979 both in the UK and abroad. The essential criticism of this group has been that the main beneficiaries of the welfare state have not been those in need, or the clients of welfare services, but rather the welfare professions, including clinicians, social workers and bureaucrats. The New Right argues that in the areas covered by social policy the tendency has been for budgets and services to increase as a result of bureaucrats seeking to expand their departments to enhance their status, rather than to serve the needs of client groups.

Socialist critics have argued, from a different angle, that the welfare state has been concerned mainly to ensure the existence of a pool of labour to aid the accumulation of capital, and to ameliorate the conditions of the working class to blunt its potential as a revolutionary social force. While welfare provision is essential to tackle the problems caused by market failure and inequality, under capitalism the needs generated are such that the economy cannot meet those needs due to their extent and to prevailing priorities for expenditure.

Recent feminist writings have been concerned to show how the assumptions on which the welfare state has been built embody patriarchal attitudes to the role of women and to the position of the traditional family at the centre of society, which reinforce structural inequalities. These inequalities particularly disadvantage women through the structure of benefits, pensions and other aspects of welfare that reinforce the gender-based division of labour. Other examples frequently quoted include the consequences of moves towards community care, which place a greater reliance for the provision of care on the family and other voluntary carers. Such a change in policy tends to assume that women will take on a greater share of the caring role.

The above does not exhaust the full range of approaches that have emerged over recent years in the area of social policy. As interest in the development of government policy has widened, so too has the impact of the different social sciences with their contrasting disciplines. The challenge to the welfare state provided by Thatcherism in the practical realm of social welfare provision has inevitably encouraged a response from those concerned with the academic study of social policy.

J. Hills (ed.), *The State of Welfare: The Welfare State in Britain since 1974*, Oxford: Oxford University Press, 1990; F. Williams, *Social Policy: A Critical Introduction*, Cambridge: Polity Press 1989.

**social security**   a term used to describe financial assistance funded and regulated by the state. In Britain most social security benefits are directly administered by one of the DEPARTMENT OF SOCIAL SECURITY executive agencies, the BENEFITS AGENCY. But housing benefit and council tax benefit are administered by local authorities.

Although the BEVERIDGE REPORT is often credited with the birth of the social security system in the United Kingdom, its origins can be traced to the latter part of the nineteenth century. Friendly societies offered financial protection through collective effort over 150 years ago, while the first state schemes were introduced by the Liberal government of the day under National Insurance Act 1911. This Act provided sickness benefit and medical treatment for all manual workers and unemployment benefit for some groups of workers. The same Liberal government introduced the Old Age Pensions Act 1908, which provided a means-tested pension for people over 70; this marked a shift away from the discretionary POOR LAW by providing benefits as a right. The current social security system includes three types of benefit. CONTRIBUTORY BENEFITS are still based broadly on those introduced by the Beveridge Report to cover maternity, unemployment, sickness, widowhood and retirement. NON-CONTRIBUTORY BENEFITS include child benefit and one-parent benefit and a range of benefits relating to disability introduced in the 1970s. MEANS-TESTED BENEFITS were substantially overhauled in 1988 in an attempt to contain costs and simplify administration. In 1992/3 social security expenditure was £74 billion, representing 12.3 per cent of gross domestic product (GDP), or 30.8 per cent of government expenditure. Half of this expenditure is met from National Insurance contributions and the other half from general taxation. Although benefit provision has continued to develop in some areas, in the fifteen years since 1979 the government has begun to withdraw significantly in others. The value of the State Earnings Related Pension Scheme has been reduced, while people have been offered incentives to opt out into private pensions. Statutory sick pay and statutory maternity pay administered by employers have replaced sickness benefit and maternity allowance for most employees. Individuals may describe themselves as 'getting social security' when they are getting income support, perhaps as a top-up to unemployment benefit or retirement pension.

**social security appeal tribunal**  a tribunal that hears appeals against decisions made by adjudication officers of the DEPARTMENT OF SOCIAL SECURITY, which includes most decisions about social security benefits.

The tribunal has three members: the chairperson, who is a lawyer, and two 'wing members', who are lay people. A claimant may speak for themselves or be represented, for example by an advice worker. A claimant's chance of success is hugely improved by attending the tribunal hearing in person.

**social security commissioner**  an appointed official who decides appeals from SOCIAL SECURITY APPEAL TRIBUNALS and DISABILITY APPEAL TRIBUNALS. The commissioner looks at the tribunal's decision to see if there has been an error in law, and either gives a new decision or refers the case to a fresh tribunal. Since most errors in law concern inadequate reasons and findings of fact, the most common outcome is to refer the case back. Commissioners' decisions set legal precedent that has to be followed. All decisions are available to the public, and the most important ones are published.

**social services committees**  the committees of elected representatives in LOCAL AUTHORITIES who are responsible for local social services policy.

Local authorities responsible for social services are at present the shire county councils and the metropolitan district councils. They have a statutory requirement to provide personal social services, and a group of nominated elected councillors comprise the social services committee to oversee the work of the SOCIAL SERVICES DEPARTMENT. The committee is accountable to the whole council for the running of the department and for the development of policy within the limitations imposed by central government legislation. The committee does not technically make decisions on social services but makes recommendations to the full council for approval. In reality, most committees are looked to for expert decision-making, with most policy recommendations being passed by the full council. In many authorities, before the committees recommendations reach the full council they are considered by a policy and resources committee, which assesses the policy in the light of overall council priorities and resource constraints. Central government also has an interest in these decisions and now requires the development of a COMMUNITY CARE PLAN by each authority. The secretary of state may intervene to overrule the council if advised that the plan is unrealistic or out of line with government policy.

Members of the committee are elected representatives, usually with an interest in the area of social services. They are put forward by their respective parties, and committee membership is allocated in line with the relative strength of the different parties on the whole council. This gives the majority party in the council an automatic majority but also gives minority parties a full say. Prior to recent legislation, the majority party could form a committee made up exclusively of their supporters. During meetings senior full-time officers sit with the chair of the committee to give advice on policy and management issues and also on the constraints imposed by central government legislation and finance. For some areas of specialist activity, committees utilize subcommittees and working parties. These comprise members of the committee and often appoint non-elected experts to give advice, sometimes allowing them to vote on issues within the subcommittee. However, these seconded individuals do not normally have a vote on the full committee when it meets to discuss any recommendations from the subcommittee. The members of the committee are councillors and therefore, in general, part-time politicians. They bring to debates about social services and social work issues more general and political priorities, which may lead them into conflict with full-time officers and professional social workers. However, these different criteria can often bring a new light to bear on an issue and prevent a more narrow professional viewpoint from dominating decision-making. As elected representative they also have the important task of trying to balance the needs of individual service users with the wider concerns of the local electorate. Local government is largely about ensuring the public accountability of the actions of full-time public officials and service professionals.

P. Daniel and J. Wheeler, *Social Work and Local Politics*, Basingstoke and London: Macmillan and British Association for Social Work, 1989.

**social services departments**   the organizational structure for the delivery of personal social services in LOCAL AUTHORITIES.

Personal social services departments are the primary deliverers of social services. They are the largest employers of social workers and are the main providers of care for the main client groups. Departments are composed of full-time and part-time officials. They are accountable to elected representatives from the local authority who comprise a SOCIAL SERVICES COMMITTEE. The responsibilities of the departments include care for people with LEARNING DISABILITIES, MENTAL HEALTH PROBLEMS and PHYSICAL DISABILITIES, and for OLDER PEOPLE and children. These responsibilities are now largely determined by the NATIONAL HEALTH SERVICE AND COMMUNITY CARE ACT and the CHILDREN ACT.

The present structures of social services departments are the result of the reorganization of local government under the Local Government Act 1972, which established the county and metropolitan councils, and have been influenced by the SEEBOHM committee which recommended the creation of unified social services departments to replace a more fragmented and client-based structure. Organizationally, these departments are structured along a number of lines. Until recently the major organizational arrangement was on the basis of fieldwork and residential work, with some decentralization down to local area divisions. More recently, pressures to create specialist posts have resulted in CLIENT-based approaches for the delivery of services to children and adults, or to older people, children, health and disability. Such organizational arrangements can have important consequences for the provision of services and have the potential to lead to conflict between different sectors of the departments.

After education, social services are the largest spenders of local government finance and one of the largest employers. Until the National Health Service and Community Care Act the only statutory requirement for local authorities was that they had a social services director and a social services committee. This situation led to a very wide degree of differentiation between departments, with differing structures and working practices depending on the part of the country officers worked in. However, since that Act, these departments now require the existence of an ARM'S LENGTH INSPECTORATE, which reports to the director of social services. In addition, efforts have to be made to identify PURCHASER/PROVIDER roles throughout the departments.

Within departments, social workers are the predominant professional group and as such are also dominant within the management structure, with directors and their deputies often qualified social workers. However, this does not rule out disputes between managers and those social workers who have direct contact with clients. The central issue is that of resource constraints and their impact on the provision of services. Managers within the departments have a responsibility to ensure that public money is used with probity, and they are increasingly concerned with value for money. For this they are accountable to the social services committee and to central government through the district auditor, an employee of the AUDIT COMMISSION. Pressure is increasingly exerted on local authorities, including social services departments, to introduce more commercial management techniques, such as PERFORMANCE indicators, to help ensure value for money.

L. Challis, *Organizing Public Social Services*, Harlow: Longman, 1990.

**Social Services Inspectorate (SSI)** an agency of the DEPARTMENT OF HEALTH that inspects SOCIAL SERVICES DEPARTMENTS and provides professional guidance on the development and implementation of departmental policy.

Established in 1985, the SSI developed from the Department of Health and Social Security's (DHSS) Social Work Service (SWS), which had been in existence since 1971. The SWS had been created as a result of the changes emerging out of the SEEBOHM REPORT and in particular the movement of children's services from the HOME OFFICE to the DHSS. The creation of large, unified personal social services departments at local level, it was believed, also required some monitoring and guidance from the centre. The SSI, while composed largely of professional social workers, is part of the DoH, and these officers are therefore civil servants. Consequently, its role is both that of a source of professional consultancy and guidance and that of a central DoH 'policeman'. It has been pointed out that the role of the SWS was from the start more than developmental, because it also had a 'scanning and monitoring' role.

Further reinforcement of the monitoring role of the SWS came about with the change in its name to the Social Services Inspectorate. The change reflected the developing concern within central government departments for improvements in the management of services as opposed to a concern with good professional practice, although this was still a core concern. As with the AUDIT COMMISSION, the SSI became concerned with improving efficiency and effectiveness as well as with the provision of professional social work advice. Sometimes working with the HEALTH ADVISORY SERVICE, the ssi examines the practices of a social services department at the request of the local authority. In some reports, the SSI has emphasized the need for more specialist social workers. In addition, it has been critical of the unwillingness of some local authorities to utilize the private and voluntary sectors as service providers. This latter point is in line with its role of communicating government policy to social services departments.

The white paper *Caring for People* (1989) emphasized a more interventionist role for the SSI under the new COMMUNITY CARE policy initiative. As a result of this change of emphasis, the SSI began to provide more explicit guidance to local authorities in the run-up to the implementation of the community care legislation in April 1993. In particular, a series of publications on quality issues and quality assessment have been issued that include methods and materials for use by departments. A series entitled *Caring for Quality* has been produced covering residential care for various client groups and guidance on quality issues in home care services. The direction of these guidelines is best summed up in the introduction to the SSI publication *Caring for Quality in Day Services* (1992), which states that the document 'encourages agencies to reflect on the future development of day services in their roles as providers, purchasers and enablers, and offers guidance on how best to provide positive packages of day services'. Such a statement reflects the DoH's policy on the role of social services departments as enablers and highlights the guidance on identifying a separation between purchaser and provider. To emphasize further the dual role of professional advice on policy development on the one hand and monitoring and inspection on the other, the SSI reorganized its formal structure in 1992. There is now an explicit division of responsibility within the agency, with an inspectorate formally separate from the policy wing.

P. Day and R. Klein, *Inspecting the Inspectorates*, York: Rowntree Trust, 1990.

**Social Services Select Committee**   a committee of Members of Parliament that scrutinizes the implementation of government policy on social services and social work issues.

In 1979 after an experiment in widening the role and number of parliamentary committees, a series of PARLIAMENTARY SELECT COMMITTEES was established to shadow each of the main central government departments. These committees are composed of appointed MPs who have expressed a particular interest in the work of the committee. Membership is weighted in proportion to the relative strength of the main political parties in the House of Commons, thus giving the majority party the largest number of committee places. However, these committees are seen as being the servants of Parliament and as a result they work across party lines and make serious efforts to ensure an agreed report. The committees have important powers that add significantly to Parliament's ability to scrutinize the actions of government. These powers allow committees to summon ministers, civil servants and members of the public to appear before them, enabling them to question the opinions of outside experts, including local government councillors, officials and social work staff. Their investigations can take them out of the House to visit organizations in the furtherance of their inquiries. As such this broadens the scope of Parliament to debate issues that the traditional debate on the floor of the House of Commons limits; the nature of these debates and their formal structure do not permit detailed examination of ministers and do not include non-members. Select committees can examine issues in detail over some weeks, with lengthy questioning of ministers and others.

Select committee reports are usually published along with the full transcripts of hearings and the written reports of witnesses. As with the main parliamentary debates, committee hearings are recorded for television and radio. The reports are only advisory, however, and all too frequently the government takes only limited notice of them. The response to these reports may take place verbally on the floor of the House when the report is debated, or the government may publish a reply. Reports by the Social Services Select Committee have provided important material on both community care and the care of children. In addition, evidence has been provided on the needs of formal and informal carers, although most information is provided by organized pressure groups, such as the BRITISH ASSOCIATION OF SOCIAL WORKERS and Mencap, rather than individuals. So the existence of these committees allows a more public expression of the detailed views of such organizations to Parliament than would otherwise be the case.

**social skills training**   a teaching procedure designed to increase competence in social interactions.

Training people to be more effective in a variety of social situations uses particular methods drawn from social learning theory, which holds that people learn by watching the specific behaviours of another person. On this general principle a set of training methods has evolved. First, the social skill to be learned is described, and instruction is given as to an appropriate performance. This often involves the instructor MODELLING or demonstrating the skill. Second, the trainee rehearses the skill with the instructor or other trainees and receives comments on how well they accomplished it. Third, the trainee practises the skill in more complex ROLE-PLAY that simulates real-life situations. As they do this the instructor may coach the trainee as to what is the most appropriate or effective response. Throughout the training some form of reinforcement is used, such as praise or recognition of what has been accomplished. Fourth, the trainee is given homework by setting the skills to be performed in live situations outside of the training. Care professionals often engage in social skills training with diverse groups of people such as YOUNG OFFENDERS, people with LEARNING DISABILITY and or people who lack social confidence. The social skills taught are often quite specific – for example, initiating and sustaining conversation, being interviewed, making a purchase from a shop, and how to be more assertive. In training in such areas a greater emphasis is placed now on the understanding of what makes for an effective social response and on cultural values than on the simple repetitive rehearsal of a skill, which often characterized social skills training in the past.

J. and M. Collins, *Social Skills Training and the Professional Helper*, Chichester: John Wiley, 1992.

**social work**   the paid professional activity that aims to assist people in overcoming serious difficulties in their lives by offering care, protection or COUNSELLING.

From the inception of social work, there has been controversy over what it is. Essentially, the argument has been between those who believe it is an activity that actively seeks to change social structures that oppress certain groups of people, and those who believe it should assist individuals to adapt to their circumstances and that if those people are unwilling or unable to conform to existing social norms or standards – for example, in their behaviour or methods of raising children – it must use its legal powers to compel them to do so.

Social work evolved from the work undertaken by various charitable organizations in the last quarter of the nineteenth century. From its beginnings, it was based on personal contact between a largely volunteer force offering practical assistance, advice and support, and people such as abandoned or neglected children, the elderly and infirm, destitute families and the homeless who seemed to be casualties of rapid industrialization. Social work thus formed part of a broader pattern of social concern and social reform that arose as the effects of urbanization, POVERTY and deprivation on the lives of the urban poor were better documented. These early volunteer social workers were attached to hospitals, courts and prisons. Others, perhaps attached to charitable housing projects, visited people in their homes. Their legacy remains in the methods that they developed, which the profession has used to this day: systematic interviewing, record-keeping and devising rudimentary plans for improvement. They also devised the basic distinction between the 'deserving' and 'undeserving', or the helpable and unhelpable, which had lasting influence within the profession.

By the middle part of the twentieth century social work had added a strong psychological perspective to its work. Under the influence of PSYCHOANALYSIS, social workers began to pay more attention to early family experiences, unconscious motivation and the roots of inconsistent or irrational behaviour. The practical consequence of this was to emphasize the relationship between social workers and the individuals and families with whom they worked. Through this relationship CLIENTS would find compensating experiences and learn strategies for overcoming their difficulties. While social work never completely abandoned its concern with the effects of poverty, it came to place great emphasis on the psychological inadequacies of clients.

In the late 1960s and 1970s social work, at least in part, began to focus on social deprivation and how the wider structures of society contributed to and even caused the problems of service users. RADICAL SOCIAL WORK practice in this period was intent on providing expressions of solidarity with the working class – for example, in work with unemployed centres, in joining with groups of users in community and neighbourhood action, in welfare rights work and in advice centres. When working with individual clients, radical social workers tried to heighten their awareness of the social origins of their difficulties.

Each phase in its development left its mark on social work, but each also tended to generate a number of critics both inside and outside the profession. In effect, social work came to be many different things, with large – at times grandiose – objectives, to an extent that a single summary of what it entailed became impossible. Attempts to define social work became increasingly general, such as that of the BRITISH ASSOCIATION OF SOCIAL WORKERS in 1977: 'Social work is the purposeful and ethical application of personal skills in interpersonal relationships directed towards enhancing the personal and social functioning of an individual, family, group or neighbourhood, which necessarily involves using evidence obtained from practice to help create a social environment conducive to the well-being of all.'

Because social work found it difficult to explain itself and seemed as a profession unsure of its role, it became vulnerable to attacks throughout the 1980s as political forces mobilized against the concept of the welfare state.

Contemporary social work has had to shed some of its more grandiose objectives and to accept that its activities and tasks will be more prescriptively defined by legislation and government than previously, as well as by vastly more assertive groups of users and their lobbies. It has proven to be effective in assisting people overcome problems where it can: (1) help users define problems clearly and translate these into specific objectives; (2) agree with users clearly focused tasks as small steps to reaching these objectives; (3) mobilize the support and resources of people who are significant to the user as well as the user's own resources; (4) reach agreed goals, usually jointly written down and in terms the user understands, together with active user involvement in decisions that have to be taken.

Counselling, an area of work that attracts so many social workers to the profession in the first place, forms a diminishing but still significant part of the work. This therapeutic expertise has been challenged from both inside and outside the profession and has been curtailed in areas where it was appropriate, such as child guidance and hospitals. A more managerial set of tasks has taken the place of intensive face-to-face work with users. For instance, CARE MANAGEMENT, in which the social worker concentrates on the ASSESSMENT OF NEED and the purchase of services, has done much to alter the nature of social work. It is arguably the greatest single source of change in social work for the last fifty years. Heightened public concern over protection, whether in relation to psychiatric patients released from hospital or perceived draconian social work action in removing children unnecessarily from their families, has prompted the government to be more prescriptive in directing social workers how to handle these matters and has compelled most local authority SOCIAL SERVICES DEPARTMENTS to commit considerable resources in this direction.

The Central Council for Education and Training in Social Work (CCETSW) has recently released a basic statement in an attempt to explain clearly what social workers do. It perhaps offers the best, if an unexciting, summary of social work tasks in the last decade of the twentieth century. According to the CCETSW statement, social workers (1) assess the needs of many kinds of people, (2) plan and deliver services and (3) review results. The first area of work includes identifying signs that a child or adult may be at risk of ABUSE; assessing the strengths of a family and identifying which services a family might need to help support a vulnerable child or adult; assessing the need for practical help such as housing, welfare benefits and health care; assessing the sentencing recommendation appropriate for a particular offender; and assessing a person with mental health problems. The second area – service planning and delivery – may involve the social worker in buying in and managing services or themselves providing services. These services can include care, support and counselling of individuals, families and groups; support and protection for people facing abuse or in distress; implementing legal powers such as protecting a child at risk; and helping children and others living in institutional care to plan for their future. The third area – review – involves seeing whether the objectives agreed with the user have been met and making improvements or searching for alternative approaches if they are needed.

C. Hanvey and T. Philpot eds., *Practising Social Work*, London: Routledge, 1994.

**social work assistant**    a person who works within a field social work team and carries their own caseload but does not usually hold a social work qualification. The word 'assistant' is largely a misnomer.

Generally the work of a social work assistant is less complex than that undertaken by a qualified social worker and does not involve decisions restricting a person's liberty or the initiation of protective measures such as taking a child into care. Many local authorities have recognized the valuable experience of long-serving social work assistants and as a result have encouraged them to pursue a social work qualification. In other cases, assistants have become COMMUNITY CARE WORKERS. As a result of both processes, assistant posts have begun to disappear in the last few years.

**Social Work (Scotland) Act 1968**    legislation that established the modern social work service in Scotland.

The Act was a product of a time of optimism, even euphoria, about what social work could achieve for the communities it served. The Act built on the recommendations of the KILBRANDON REPORT on YOUNG OFFENDERS but went further to establish a comprehensive social work service for all prospective client groups, including adult offenders (by bringing probation work into the new social work departments). Even more than the SEEBOHM REPORT, which was its contemporary, the Act set up the 'single door' for families and individuals seeking social work assistance. The Act's guiding principle was found in section 12, which placed the duty on the new social work departments to promote the welfare of all individuals within the communities they served by making available advice, guidance and assistance (in cash or in kind) appropriate to the area. In this sense, the values and organizational culture established within the social work departments were more closely linked to the welfare of the communities they served than was the case with the SOCIAL SERVICES DEPARTMENTS set up in England and Wales a few years later.

**sociology**    the study of social structures and the different life experiences of individuals within those social structures.

Sociology is, alongside PSYCHOLOGY, one of the defining academic disciplines of social work. Social work operates within a context of law and social policy, but the disciplines of psychology and sociology have produced theoretical frameworks that have sought to make sense of the relationship between the individual and the social world. If psychology has informed the practice of social work with individuals and groups, then sociology has provided an understanding of the social context in which that practice is undertaken (including the basis of a radical critique of some practice) and of differential LIFE CHANCES, affected principally by the SOCIAL CLASS, GENDER and 'RACE' of the individual.

The early sociologists who established this new science of society – namely, Marx, Durkheim and Weber – were preoccupied with questions such as, how does society change?, how is stability maintained?, what are the bases of power in society and how are they legitimated? All three thinkers were also interested in the issue of social inequality and its structural determinants. A particular major interest of Durkheim concerned deviance in society and how individuals who do not share the social norms of the majority can be affected by their marginality. All these concerns have been regarded as 'grand theory', with the objective of trying to understand the mechanisms by which whole societies function.

Subsequent theorists have sought to understand individual experience within social structures. The interaction between biography and history, or character and social structure, is accepted as a complex relationship. Most individuals born into the same social conditions seem to be constrained by those conditions in ways that seem to reveal patterns, but others are not so constrained. Sociologists have made two points here: first, that individuals are not simply determined by social forces outside themselves, but can act to change or limit the effect of those social forces in some circumstances; second, that apparently similar social conditions can mask major differences of experience for people within the same family (to be the first child and to be a girl can be a very different experience from that of a second child who is a boy). There is recognition of the uniqueness of individual experience, on the one hand, but also acceptance of the relatively persistent patterns within society. How the particular can be understood in the context of the general continues to be the challenge of sociology.

Within the last two decades the perspectives of 'race' and gender have become very important to sociological analysis. Many sociologists have accepted that they had previously conducted research in a manner that overlooked the experiences of women and of black people. New perspectives have thus opened up to add new dimensions to old sociological preoccupations. The analysis of advanced capitalist society, for example, has developed new concerns from the perspectives of women and black people in both the industrialized countries and, in the analysis of neo-colonialism, in the Third World.

Virtually every aspect of social life has been scrutinized by sociologists. Social workers have been able to draw upon studies that throw some light on the many social problems with which they have to deal. Social work training frequently uses the idea of the social construction of problems (given that individuals may need particular help too) that would appear to be suggested by a sociological analysis. Social workers work individually and are therefore invited to look inwards to relational problems and not outwards to broad social conditions that affect many service users. Because social workers also feel powerless in the face of POVERTY, UNEMPLOYMENT and HOUSING PROBLEMS, they emphasize what they feel they can achieve and run the risk of losing sight of the structural issues. It is not surprising, therefore, that sociologists have also turned their attention to the role played by welfare provision, including social work services, within societies like Britain. This analysis has revealed both empowering and liberating aspects to the role of social worker, as well as more worrying oppressive practices. (See ANTI-DISCRIMINATORY PRACTICE, CASEWORK, EQUAL OPPORTUNITIES POLICIES, RADICAL SOCIAL WORK.)

A. Giddens, *Sociology*, Cambridge: Polity Press, 1993.

**solvents**   the fumes of various volatile substances that can be inhaled to give intoxicating effects. The list of products is considerable and includes glue, aerosols, cleaning fluids, paint, nail varnish, lighter fuel and petrol.

The peak age for using solvents for their effects appears to be about 14 years, although the majority of this use is short-term experimentation and is not repeated. The very small percentage of people who go on to use solvents on a regular basis probably have some underlying problem that needs to be addressed. Solvents have a similar effect to being drunk, whereby problems may be temporarily forgotten. (See SUBSTANCE MISUSE.)

**special educational needs (SEN)**   local education authorities are required under Part III of the EDUCATION ACT 1993 to identify children with such needs, including children with learning difficulties, specific learning difficulties (dyslexia), emotional, behavioural and physical difficulties, and sensory and speech impairments, and make appropriate provision for them.

Special educational needs are not to be confused with 'children in need' under the CHILDREN ACT, although some children with SEN also come into this wider definition. For nine out of ten children with SEN, special educational provision is made at the local school level out of the school's own budget. Only one in ten such children has a 'statement' designed to ensure their statutory right to provision. Some of these are placed in special schools, but by no means all. The Education Act 1993 established a tribunal to which parents can appeal if there are disputes about the local education authority's action, and defined timetables within which ASSESSMENTS should be completed. It also contains enforcement powers against parents who fail to cooperate in the process, although these are rarely used. Where the child's welfare is at stake, action under the Children Act 1989 would be more appropriate. (See EDUCATIONAL PSYCHOLOGIST.)

**specific issue order**   a court order giving directions for settling a particular question that has arisen between parents or others with PARENTAL RESPONSIBILITY for the child concerned.

The order is one of four SECTION 8 ORDERS under the CHILDREN ACT. In effect, it gives the court power to settle a dispute over some aspect of raising a child, such as medical treatment or education, through stipulating what is to happen. Local authorities may apply for the order if they obtain leave from the court to do so. They could, for example, obtain an order directing that a child they are accommodating should have a particular medical operation.

**squatting**   to live in a dwelling without the permission of the landlord or owner.

Many people regard the problem of HOMELESSNESS as a political problem, because in Britain it is estimated that there are more dwellings than households. These excess dwellings may be a second home for some people, void dwellings of local authorities awaiting repairs before being relet, properties that are empty pending redevelopment or renewal, and properties empty for a variety of other reasons (ex-army camps, for example). In the face of such apparent wasted resources, squatters' movements have appeared from time to time. Homeless families and single people, sometimes desperate for shelter, have taken direct action by occupying such properties. On occasions, they have succeeded in persuading an owner to let them stay in a property for a negotiated period. More often disputes occur between owners and squatters, sometimes of a violent nature and leading to the forcible eviction of squatters. Legally a court order is required to evict squatters, but on occasions owners have hired their own 'informal' bailiffs. Squatters can also be accused of trespass or criminal damage if they have had to use force to gain entry.

Landlords have sometimes agreed to 'short-life tenancies', whereby a habitable property awaiting demolition is rented to a tenant on a temporary basis – although 'temporary' has been known to be as long as five years. Some HOUSING ASSOCIATIONS have put a lot of effort into the renovation of short-life housing. The installation of a decent bathroom, basic heating and some new windows can make a basically sound dwelling habitable for a family for a temporary period and may be preferable to BED AND BREAKFAST accommodation, although clearly this is not a long-term solution to homelessness.

**standard spending assessment (SSA)**   a method of calculating local government spending levels based on a range of information and criteria and used to make decisions about the allocation of central government grant to LOCAL AUTHORITIES.

The standard spending assessment is used by central government to calculate what it believes to be an appropriate level of spending on services by local government. According to central government, such spending should be in line with overall targets for public expenditure as a whole. The SSA is a successor to a system called the grant-related expenditure assessment (GREA), which was introduced by the government in the Local Government, Planning and Land Act 1980. The information is provided by local authorities themselves and covers all service areas. The assessment allows central government to assess the allocation of grant on the basis of its determination of local need. In this way the government can present local authorities with a breakdown of where the grant should be spent.

In addition to their primary function, the GREA and the SSA have been used to implement expenditure constraint on local authorities. In particular, in cases where central government believes an individual local authority to be overspending, then a system of tapered grant or penalties can be used to control the authority. This has also allowed the government to establish a system for determining which authorities will be penalized through the imposition of council tax capping, in which the ability of the local authority to raise funds through local taxation is controlled. The AUDIT COMMISSION has argued that this change in the role of SSAs has created problems for local authorities. In particular, it noted that the level of SSA from one year to the next is subject to a degree of instability due to changes in the levels determined by government as controls for different services. For example, in one authority the level of SSA was reduced by 15 per cent in 1990/1 and increased by 30 per cent in 1991/2 before being reduced again the following year. This problem was not so acute when local taxation provided a large percentage of finance for local expenditure; but with changes in financing since the abolition of the community charge, local taxation comprises only between 15 and 20 per cent of local authority finance, with a proportionately larger amount allocated through central government grant and therefore subject to changes in SSA. With these changes SSAs create major difficulties for local authorities in attempting to plan service provision, because of uncertainties over the level of grant.

Audit Commission, *Passing the Bucks: The Impact of Standard Spending Assessment on Economy, Efficiency and Effectiveness*, London: HMSO, 1993.

**State Earnings-Related Pension Scheme (SERPS)**   a scheme providing an additional pension based on individual contributions that is paid to people claiming RETIREMENT PENSION but only paid with the latter if the contributor has 'contracted in', thereby paying a higher rate of National Insurance contributions.

From the scheme's inception, employers were allowed to contract out, provided they paid a guaranteed minimum pension. Also known as ADDITIONAL PENSION when paid with invalidity benefit and widows pension, SERPS started in 1978. The benefits payable have been eroded in a variety of ways since 1988, and the government now encourages individuals to contract out into personal pensions.

**statementing**   the formal process whereby a local education authority must prepare a statement of the SPECIAL EDUCATIONAL NEEDS, and how these are to be met, of any schoolchild aged between 2 and 19 identified as having such needs. LEAs are required by the Education Act 1981 to identify and assess children who may have special needs.

A key principle of statementing is that parents have the right to be involved in the process and have their views taken into account. In principle, statementing should ensure an appropriate education for all children with special educational needs, including 'gifted children'. In practice, lack of resources has meant that many authorities cannot meet the full demand for ASSESSMENT, and statementing has become selective. The process can be very protracted.

**statutory maternity pay**   a legal minimum rate of pay, paid by employers, during maternity leave for eighteen weeks beginning between the eleventh and the sixth week before the expected week of confinement. Many employers pay more than this statutory minimum.

To be eligible, a woman must have been working for her employer for at least twenty-six weeks and earn at least the lower earnings limit (£57 in

1994/5). Women who have been working sixteen hours or more for two years, or eight hours per week or more for five years, get a higher rate of pay for the first six weeks. Women who do not qualify for statutory maternity pay may be able to get MATERNITY ALLOWANCE from the DEPARTMENT OF SOCIAL SECURITY. Disputes about entitlement can be referred to the BENEFITS AGENCY of the DSS.

**statutory sector**    a term describing those SOCIAL WORK agencies that by law, or statute, are obliged to provide certain services.

In practice, 'statutory' is another term for LOCAL AUTHORITY social work services, which by law must take certain actions to protect a child or to assist in detaining a person in psychiatric hospital. Voluntary social work agencies do not have such responsibilities and under the law may not exercise such powers even if they wish to. The fact that local authority social workers may exercise their considerable powers when working with CLIENTS often presents them with uniquely difficult decisions. Probation services are, of course, also statutory.

**statutory sick pay**    a legal minimum rate of pay, paid by employers, during sickness. Some employers pay more or even full pay during the early weeks of sickness.

Statutory sick pay is paid to an employee for the first twenty-eight weeks of sickness. It is paid at one of two rates, depending on normal earnings, but is not payable to people who earn less than the lower earnings limit (£57 in 1994/5), to those who are over PENSIONABLE AGE or to those who have contracts of employment of less than three months. A person who does not qualify can claim SICKNESS BENEFIT instead. If an employee is dissatisfied with a decision of their employer about their entitlement they can refer it to the BENEFITS AGENCY of the DEPARTMENT OF SOCIAL SECURITY.

**stereotype**    a set of biased, inflexible assumptions about an individual or group, based on physical appearance or characteristics, or social attributes or roles. These include sex, ethnicity, age, physical capacity, class, marital status, kinship, language, nationality, religion and sexual orientation.

Stereotypes differ from typifications in that typifications are flexible sets of assumptions based on individual life experiences. Typifications are open to modification through the acquisition and assimilation of additional life experiences; they are useful as building blocks to help people make sense of their social experiences and assist in the formulation of expectations of behaviour. Stereotypes, by contrast, are formulated through dominant political, social and cultural value systems and promoted by various institutions (such as through cultural traditions, religion and the media) controlled directly or indirectly by a dominant social group. They are used to justify privilege or to discriminate against individuals and groups in society in terms of access to resources or employment opportunities. Social workers often work with people who have been unfairly stereotyped, such as LONE PARENTS and people with learning disability, and they may have to counter the effects of such negative stereotyping by others.

**stigma**   a characteristic or attribute that conflicts with the expected norms or STEREOTYPES assigned to an individual or group and is therefore viewed as undesirable.

The term 'stigma' originates from the ancient Greek word for a sign branded on a person to signify something bad about them, for example that they are a traitor. The concept is now used to describe the process whereby people are allocated social identities based on stereotypes. When we first have contact with a person, we anticipate what that person is like from information that we have about them. Inferences are drawn from the person's visible characteristics, such as sex, ethnicity and physical capacity. As knowledge is acquired about that person, further assumptions are made on the basis of their name, accent, religious belief, sexual orientation, class, economic status and other invisible attributes. An attribute becomes a stigma when it is spuriously linked with undesirable behaviour or unvalued experiences: for example, an assumption that being a black man means that the person is a threat to the social order, or that being female means that the person is physically weak. It is possible for some attributes to be ascribed as acceptable or desirable for some individuals but not for others; for example, it is socially acceptable for men to grow facial hair, but facial hair is stigmatizing for women.

> Dominant political, social and cultural values play key roles in the operation of stigma, as they help to formulate individual value systems and reinforce the stereotypes of what is desirable for individuals and groups within society. Stigma strikes at the core of individual identity, because stigmatized people either believe messages about themselves as inferior or have consciously to reject the process of stigmatization and challenge the stereotype assigned to them. The concept of stigma is useful in understanding the operation of DISCRIMINATION at all levels – from internalized racism and sexism, and so on, through individual prejudice to direct and indirect institutionalized discrimination. The process of stigmatization is particularly relevant to social work, because the use of a social work service is commonly perceived as a stigmatizing experience for service users.
>
> E. Goffman, *Stigma: Notes on the Management of Spoiled Identity*, Harmondsworth: Penguin, 1968.

**stimulants ('uppers')**   particular DRUGS that speed up bodily functions, particularly of the brain and central nervous system. Examples include caffeine, tobacco, AMPHETAMINES, ANABOLIC STEROIDS and COCAINE.

**subsistence level**   a standard of living thought sufficient to sustain life in a minimal way.

The idea of subsistence level has been used to define a minimum standard for people living in abject poverty in developing countries where life is constantly hazardous, but also a minimum standard capable of supporting an individual in HEALTH. These variations in the way the concept is used reflect the relative nature of POVERTY. Subsistence levels determined by government policies and even by poverty relief agencies usually reflect the prevailing standards within a particular society. Thus when Victorians such as Charles Booth attempted to arrive at an objective poverty line (subsistence level), his calculations were based upon standards that prevailed in late nineteenth-century England, and those were much higher than standards thought necessary for minimal life in many, if not most, other societies at that time.

**substance misuse**   the non-medical use of substances that when taken into the body can substantially affect psychological and physical functions. Substances commonly misused may include legal and illegal DRUGS (amphetamines, cocaine, opiates, cannabis, LSD, Ecstasy), ALCOHOL and prescribed drugs such as tranquillizers and barbiturates.

Figures for drug and alcohol misuse have increased over recent decades. Alcohol use has increased by 74 per cent since the 1950s, and heroin users registered with the Home Office have increased many times in the same period. Also, illegal drugs and alcohol are used by more and more young people and at increasingly young ages. People using illegal drugs are usually (though not exclusively) aged 20–35 and increasingly poor, unemployed, living in disadvantaged areas with poor housing and facilities, and often involved in criminal activity to sustain their habits. Alcohol users who develop problems from its use are often older, male and with families, but those with very severe problems are usually unemployed and socially isolated. Substance misuse by women, black people and older people is more hidden, because these groups do not approach helping agencies (fearing stigma, racism and/or their children being taken into care), and because agencies do not recognize these groups have substance misuse problems or cater for their particular needs. Studies have shown that there may be extensive use in these groups, but resulting in different problems and needs compared to those of the white male user; it is important that services take account of these differences.

Drug and alcohol misuse results in a range of serious problems for users themselves, their family and the wider society. In understanding these problems it is important to realize there are three different types of drug and alcohol misuse – experimental, recreational and dependent use. There is no necessary progression to dependency, but people experience problems with each type of use. Experimental use can lead to intoxication and death – for example, small numbers of young people taking too large a dose of Ecstasy have died – and also to accidents, through lack of control of usage due to unfamiliarity. Recreational use means controlled use in situations where the user knows that harm is minimized. However, the physical and psychological effects of the substance still take their toll. PSYCHOTIC and/or NEUROTIC symptoms may arise – short- or long-term with LSD and amphetamines; moderate use of alcohol can affect the functioning of most organs in the body, and intoxication with any substance impairs functioning for several days, and may lead to accidents.

Dependent use means that the person finds it very hard to exist without the substance; and if the person is poor, crime or prostitution may be the only way of financing their habit. Criminal charges and imprisonment are likely consequences. Dependent use of a substance also leads to longer-term mental and physical health problems, along with problems of poor housing, homelessness, self-neglect and loss of relationships.

Social workers would have a duty to intervene in all these areas of difficulty if the person was referred. In addition, there is a strong likelihood with alcohol misuse that children may be physically or sexually abused; in large proportions of CHILD PROTECTION cases, studies have shown there to be parental alcohol misuse. Neglect of children is also possible with substance misuse of all kinds, and especially when use is dependent. Thus child-care and child protection work should take full account of the issues of substance misuse if intervention is to be appropriate.

The risk of HIV/AIDS is also increased, not only through injecting substances but through the greater vulnerability to infections resulting from malnutrition and self-neglect. Social work has a responsibility to respond to the COMMUNITY CARE needs of people with HIV/AIDS in collaboration with the health service and other agencies.

There have been attempts to reduce substance misuse on a number of fronts. First, legislation making the possession and sale of illegal drugs criminal offences is intended to reduce the supply of drugs and deter use. Only specially licensed doctors are allowed to prescribe illegal drugs and opiates, and users have to be notified to the Home Office. Second, treatment programmes in general have been health-based, with drug and alcohol dependency units located in psychiatric hospitals, and more recently COMMUNITY DRUG TEAMS and community alcohol teams funded by health authorities. The authority of licensed doctors to prescribe illegal drugs is one aspect of treatment, intended to keep the user away from the risks of the illicit market. However, government policy, expressed in the various reports of the Advisory Committee for the Misuse of Drugs, recommends that social work should play an important role in treatment. This arose through the idea, still influential, that substance misuse was the result of the person's inability to manage their lives, due to social or psychological pressures, and the social worker was expected to make a major contribution to the work of the medical team by helping the person to cope independently. 'Treatment' thus included REHABILITATION. One important rehabilitation route has been residential rehabilitation in residential care homes provided by voluntary agencies. Social services now have the responsibility of finding these (and other) RESIDENTIAL CARE services under the community care legislation.

The third approach to reducing substance misuse involves PREVENTIVE WORK. In the 1980s the Advisory Committee for the Misuse of Drugs recommended that prevention be directed both at the risk of the person engaging in substance misuse and at the harm associated with misuse. Social work has been expected to deal with the former through the generic community work of addressing the sources of stress that bring about coping difficulties and subsequent substance misuse. There are opportunities for such work to be funded now by the Home Office drugs prevention team. A particular focus of harm reduction strategies since 1988 has been to seek to minimize the spread of AIDS and HIV resulting from injecting substances. Emphasis has therefore been placed upon providing easy access to clean needles and prescriptions of substitute, non-injection drugs. Other targets for harm reduction include the major problems presented by users for themselves and the wider society, through criminal activity to finance drug use, also unemployment, and distress and disruption in family and social relationships. The relative stability involved when a person receives drugs by prescription alleviates some of these problems and brings the user into contact with the services, where they may quickly receive support and referral if they are ready to try to stop using substances. In the case of people misusing drugs or alcohol, social work is involved in harm minimization through the community care legislation, which requires social services to include the needs of drug and alcohol users in their plans.

The fourth approach consists in the important role of social work in both prevention and treatment aspects of working with substance misuse. Traditionally, social workers have regarded the problems as more within the province of psychiatry than of social work, and they have been deterred from engaging with these issues through negative social STEREOTYPES of people misusing different substances. The Central Council for Education and Training in Social Work has, however, published guidelines for social workers that emphasize dealing with stereotypes, developing understanding of the problems and possible intervention approaches, and learning the skills of appropriately recognizing substance misuse patterns. The guidelines also encompass some of the important components of assessment and intervention, and of determining risks and needs.

R. Griffiths and B. Pearson, *Working With Drug Users*, Aldershot: Wildwood House, 1988.

**sudden infant death syndrome**   the death of an infant from no apparent cause, commonly known as 'cot death'.

While medical research has still to determine what precisely causes the swift and wholly unexpected death of an infant, it has highlighted preventive measures that can help reduce the risk: infants should be placed on their back or side when sleeping and not on their stomach; and they should not be allowed to get too warm – parents should use lightweight blankets, adding to them or taking them away according to room temperature. Cot death seems to occur mostly to infants between 1 month and 5 months old.

**suicide**   an intentional act of commission or omission on the part of a person that results in the same person's death. A suicidal act of commission might include self-hanging, taking an overdose of drugs or inhaling carbon monoxide fumes; an act of omission would include failing to take a life-maintaining medicine.

Statistics about suicides are notoriously unreliable and almost certainly under-represent the actual suicide rate. There are often very difficult decisions to be made by, among others, coroners and doctors about the cause of death, and strong social pressure exists, where there are doubts, to record causes other than suicide. Suicides affect all social classes. Rates are higher for men than for women, and among older people, those without children, the divorced and the widowed. Significant loss of social status is a precipitating factor. There are cultural differences too, with pre-industrial societies usually having much lower suicide rates. Behaviour can vary a lot historically, with times of war, for example, leading to a lower incidence of suicide if group cohesiveness rises.

To determine whether an act is genuinely suicidal entails examining the problem of intent. Suicide attempts are sometimes inadvertently discovered, whereas mock-suicidal behaviour often entails careful planning in the expectation that the person will be discovered. All such behaviour must be taken very seriously, including mock-attempts, because such acts are inherently risky and mock-suicides usually represent profound unhappiness and major personal problems. Suicidal behaviour, if known of, usually brings about intervention from the STATUTORY services. Social work effort tends to concentrate upon the social problems that may underpin, for example, an ANXIETY state or DEPRESSION, or upon attempting to alter a person's perception of themselves.

**supervision**   the overseeing of the work of social care staff, social workers and student social workers by either a practice teacher or line manager (usually a team manager) or a consultant.

The role of supervisor includes three elements: first, to ensure that workers account for their work (the managing or administrative function); second, the professional development of workers (the educative or teaching function); and third, the personal support of workers in times of difficulty (the supportive or enabling function). The form and content of supervision vary according to the needs of the worker, the nature of the work and the abilities of the supervisor.

Qualified practitioners in any of the established professions (law, medicine, and so on) would maintain that supervision is necessary during training; thereafter the need to 'consult' with specialists would be sufficient. This pattern tends not to apply to social work and SOCIAL CARE. There is continuing uncertainty about the status of social work as a profession and thus of the ability of even experienced and qualified practitioners to work independently. The location of much social work within bureaucratic local authorities, together with the stressful nature of the work, may also account for the widespread use of supervision, at least within fieldwork teams, for even the most experienced practitioner. Within day care and residential settings supervisory practices vary, with many workers continuing to receive scant support.

The predominant form for supervision continues to be the one-to-one relationship of supervisor and supervised. It is possible for experienced practitioners to be supervised by inexperienced managers, and it is common for women workers to be supervised by male team managers and black workers by white supervisors. Interesting alternative methods and arrangements for supervision continue to be rejected in favour of line management. A major initiative from the Social Care Association has, however, led to some limited experimentation on the part of some employers in supporting workers under stress, including independent counselling services that are gender- and 'race'-sensitive. A more recent trend has added appraisal of staff competence to the supervisor's role – either for the purpose of NATIONAL VOCATIONAL QUALIFICATIONS or for in-house staff appraisal systems. This has tended to dilute the supportive role of the line manager as supervisor by adding to it a watchdog function that does not always sit easily with the support function.

C. Payne and T. Scott, *Developing Supervision of Teams in Field and Residential Social Work*, Parts I and II, London: National Institute of Social Work, 1982 and 1985.

**supervision order (1)**   in criminal proceedings, a sentence that places a child or YOUNG PERSON aged 10 to 17 under the supervision of a local authority social worker or a probation officer for a period of up to three years.

The order may include additional requirements, such as a programme of activities (intermediate treatment), night restrictions or residence.

**supervision order (2)**   a court order under section 35 of the CHILDREN ACT that requires a local authority social worker or probation officer to act as supervisor to the child or children named in the order.

The court may make a supervision order only when a child has suffered, or is likely to suffer, SIGNIFICANT HARM and that harm is attributable to the standard of parental care (see THRESHOLD CRITERIA). Although the grounds for making a supervision order are exactly the same as those for a CARE ORDER, it is the less intrusive of the two, since the local authority does not acquire PARENTAL RESPONSIBILITY for the child. In this sense, the court will see it as preferable to a care order, as long as it is assured that the powers under the order are sufficient to protect the child and safeguard their welfare. Under a supervision order the supervisor has a duty to advise, assist and befriend the child; in practice, this often means giving guidance to parents on, for example, matters of discipline. The supervisor may have the child medically or psychiatrically examined only after seeking the court's approval and then only with the child's consent. The supervisor may also direct the child to live at a specified place for a period of up to ninety days and to participate in designated activities. These provisions are aimed at young people in their teems who may be required to attend certain activities or courses of instruction; they would apply particularly to young people who are likely to suffer significant harm through being beyond parental control. The supervisor also has powers to take all reasonable steps to see that the terms of the order are put into effect. Within the terms of the order the court may appoint a 'responsible person' – often a parent or another adult in the family – with that person's consent. The responsible person must take all reasonable steps to ensure that the terms of the order and the directions of the supervisor, such as a curfew, are met. A supervision order lasts for one year but can be extended to a maximum of three years. It can be varied or discarded by application of any of the parties involved such as the local authority, the child or the parent.

M. Freeman, *Understanding the Children Act*, Basingstoke: Macmillan, 1994.

**supplementary benefit**   a scheme introduced in 1966 to replace NATIONAL ASSISTANCE and designed to reduce the number of people receiving additional weekly payments.

The revised scheme included automatic additions for pensioners and other long-term recipients but not for the unemployed. However, extra discretionary allowances could be paid in 'exceptional circumstances' or for 'exceptional needs', and by 1974 over a third of claimants were entitled to an additional weekly payment. In the face of ever increasing expenditure, the scheme was revised in 1980, and the system of discretionary extras was replaced with a much narrower range of legal entitlements governed by regulations. Although the number of additional payments reduced initially, expenditure soon began to rise again, partly because of welfare rights activity including large-scale take-up campaigns run by some local authorities. This formed part of the pressure for the review that resulted in the Social Security Act 1986 and the introduction of INCOME SUPPORT in 1988.

**survivor**  a term now sometimes used in preference to 'victim', especially in relation to women who have experienced SEXUAL ABUSE, rape or DOMESTIC VIOLENCE.

Derived from the vocabulary of assertiveness training, the term implies that a woman who has had the strength actively to survive such an ordeal should be respected and admired rather than treated as a powerless and passive object of pity (and sometimes contempt).

**syringe exchange scheme**  a system that enables DRUGS misusers to swap old needles and syringes for new.

Syringe exchange schemes have spread throughout Britain in the last ten years as a response to HIV/AIDS. Schemes may be offered by pharmacies or drugs agencies, whether statutory or voluntary. Schemes usually work on the basis of 'new for old', with injectors bringing back used equipment in a SHARPS container. The service is confidential, perhaps with initials and numbers of syringes returned and given out collected for monitoring purposes. Such schemes are usually free. The giving of clean needles, syringes and sharps containers is part of an overall HARM MINIMIZATION programme designed to prevent the spread of the HIV virus.

**systems approach**  the undertaking of social work based on analysis and activation of the human systems around the CLIENT.

A system is a set of objects that are interdependent and interrelated so that they function as a single unit. We often refer loosely to systems in contemporary life, such as sound systems or computer systems, to indicate a grouping of components that produce something through the relationships between them that they could not produce on their own. Systems display a number of characteristics: The parts are *reciprocal*; each is related to every other, so that a change affecting one will change the whole. Their *structure* endures over a period of time, because systems can adapt to changes in the surrounding environment; a system copes with environmental change by receiving inputs such as information from the environment, processing that information and producing an output that enables it to adapt. Systems have a *boundary* that marks off where each system ends and the environment begins; the boundary may be open, allowing the system to interact with its environment, or closed, preventing influences, information or changes in the environment to affect its internal working. Systems strive for *equilibrium*, that is, some balance in their relationship to their environment, so that they may survive with their fundamental nature intact.

In the 1970s some social work educators turned to systems theory as a basis for developing a single social work approach, or 'unitary method', that would be applicable to all social work settings. The concept of systems was applied to the way people interacted with one another. It was theorized that people depend on human systems in meeting needs. People were part of informal systems such as family, friends and colleagues, as well as formal systems such as clubs and trade unions, and societal systems such as schools and employing organizations. Problems arose for people when their systems had broken down or were failing to produce sufficient resources to allow the system to continue working as before. The role of the social worker in this approach is to identify the different systems of which the client is a part (the CLIENT SYSTEM), such as family and employing organization, and to analyse how the interaction of the parts of those systems cause problems. The social worker's task is to make the client system function again by modifying the interactions between people and resources within the system. Such thinking had the benefit of requiring the social worker to see the client as a product of wider forces and to move away from the traditional concentration on the individual client. A client's problems might well be generated by relationships within their system, so that one had to look beyond the individual to make change occur.

As a theory, systems thinking in the form of the unitary method was criticized for its difficult terminology, lack of practical guidance to social workers and tendency to exclude radical changes as options. It has, however, continued to influence social workers' understanding of families. Placing a client in relation to the various systems, now often simply understood as networks, often diagrammatically, is now a commonly used tool to allow both social worker and client to understand the range of supports present and those areas where they may have to be created. The systems approach has also provided a basis for seeing families as self-regulating systems that function according to rules established through a process of trial and error. Social workers and family therapists emphasize the capacity of family systems to adapt and change as their environment changes. Families that are closed systems, that resist change and do not evolve, become 'stuck' in patterns that often place the entire blame for this on individual family members. The use of ECOMAPS is another widespread technique drawn originally from systems thinking. A whole school of FAMILY THERAPY has developed around the basic insight that family problems are a product of the relationships between all the family members and that change requires changing how all the family members behave in relation to each other, rather than pinning blame on a single delinquent member. (See also ECOLOGICAL APPROACH.)

D. Howe, *An Introduction to Social Work Theory*, Aldershot: Wildwood House, 1987.

# T

**take-up**   the number of people claiming a benefit as a proportion of those eligible to claim it. Take-up of benefits is a matter of concern, since benefits provide at best a minimal standard of living. In particular, anyone failing to claim MEANS-TESTED BENEFITS is likely to be living in POVERTY.

Universal benefits with simple, well-known and non-stigmatizing rules are claimed by the vast majority of people who are eligible. CHILD BENEFIT, for example, is claimed by 98 per cent of people who are eligible. By contrast, many potential claimants feel that means-tested benefits are stigmatizing, and the rules are often complex and confusing. For example, the rather obscurely named FAMILY CREDIT is claimed by only about 60 per cent of those eligible, even though it has been quite intensively promoted since it was first introduced five years ago. Take-up rates of means-tested benefit are estimated using data from benefit administrators and from the Family Expenditure Survey. Data from 1989 suggested the following take-up rates: INCOME SUPPORT, 75 per cent (67 per cent of eligible pensioners claiming, 81 per cent of eligible non-pensioners claiming); family credit, 57 per cent; HOUSING BENEFIT, 83 per cent. In total, it is estimated that £1,600 million in means-tested benefits is unclaimed every year. The take-up rates of other benefits have never been systematically estimated, but it is likely that non-contributory benefits for people with disabilities, such as DISABILITY LIVING ALLOWANCE, attendance allowance and SEVERE DISABLEMENT ALLOWANCE, are significantly underclaimed because of their complexity, the offputting nature of the claiming process and the isolation of many potential recipients. General take-up campaigns by local authorities to encourage claims for DEPARTMENT OF SOCIAL SECURITY benefits were widespread during the 1980s and often enormously successful. More recently campaigns have relied more on targeting likely claimants.

**targeting**  a term originally borrowed from the world of advertising ('to target') by welfare rights workers to describe the intention to deliver information about particular benefits to those individuals or groups most likely to be eligible to claim them.

Because of the plethora of underclaimed benefits (see TAKE-UP), each with their own set of rules, it is difficult in general campaigns to impart enough specific information to enable individuals to be sufficiently confident about their potential eligibility to make a claim. By finding ways of targeting information it is possible to address the potential claimant more directly and to give fuller details to allow a more informed choice to be made. Examples of targeting information would include writing to people receiving domiciliary services about attendance allowance or DISABILITY LIVING ALLOWANCE, or writing to people who are registered blind about the lower-rate MOBILITY COMPONENT. Since the mid-1980s the word 'targeting' has been used by the government to justify an increased reliance on means-tested benefit – for example, 'targeting the most needy' – and to imply that universal provision is a waste of public expenditure. Thus a reduction in services may be described as 'better targeting'.

**target system**  the system of people or organizations that social work intervention aims to change in order to produce solutions to a CLIENT's problems.

The target system may be the same as the CLIENT SYSTEM, that is, the client's own family or immediate social network; or it may be quite different. An example is a young person who regularly truants; the school becomes the target system within which the social worker attempts to effect some change to make the school more attractive to attend.

**tariff (1)** a concept used in sentencing decisions that prior to the CRIMINAL JUSTICE ACT 1991 involved consideration of both the seriousness of an offence and the extent of a defendant's previous criminal record.

The Criminal Justice Act restricted a court's power to consider previous convictions and thus modified the use of the term to that of linking sentencing option to offence seriousness – though subsequent amendments to the Act may serve to strengthen the concept again.

**tariff (2)** a term used specifically in relation to life imprisonment, which refers to an informal agreement between the sentencing judge and the Home Office about the approximate length of time that a particular offender should spend in PRISON.

**task-centred work** a particular approach to social work that places strong emphasis on solving problems that the CLIENT considers important through completion of a series of small tasks.

Task-centred work is one of the very few approaches to social work developed by social workers themselves. It originated in the United States in the 1960s as a response to increasing criticism that long-term CASEWORK was both time-consuming and ineffective for a substantial proportion of clients. The approach is based on three key principles: first, that the social worker and user together tackle problems that the user has defined as the most important; second, that these problems are resolved through a series of small steps or tasks; and third, that the work is short-term, usually completed within three months.

Task-centred work proceeds through a number of stages. The first stage is *problem selection*. This is achieved by the social worker and user listing all the problems facing the user. From the list of problems the user and social worker agree on which are the two or three most important problems to resolve. The selected problems are written down in language that is clear to the user, and expressed in as much detail as possible. For example, a problem such as 'Janice is socially isolated' is general and vague; a better way of framing the problem would be 'Janice has no opportunity to meet people during the week because she has to look after her 18-month-old twin daughters. She has no car and finds the bus service too infrequent to be of use.' It has been suggested that practitioners should use the 'five *W*s' to help with problem specification: who, what, where, when and why. The social worker's role is to facilitate this process of problem selection but not to impose their views as to which is the most important. There is one exception to this rule; the worker may have to insist that, because of a responsibility in law such as protecting a child, a particular problem must be addressed by the user whether or not the user considers it a priority. If the social worker is unable to convince the user that the problem – say, a parent's habit of going out in the evening and leaving a young child unattended – is important to address, it means that no further task-centred work can take place, at least in respect of that particular problem. In practice, overriding the user's priorities in this way rarely happens.

The second stage is *goal setting*, that is, moving from what is wrong to what is needed. The goal is what the user wants as a way to resolve the selected problem.

Goals should be realistic and achievable in a short time. Choosing goals often involves negotiation between worker and user in order to reach agreement on their feasibility or desirability. If the social worker cannot agree that a particular goal is realistic for the user, this observation is also recorded and reasons are given. As with problems, the goals are written down in the user's own words and in as much detail as possible, so that everyone can agree when they have been reached. This has the merit of forcing social workers to think as specifically as possible about the user's goals. They have been notoriously vague in goal setting. 'We will work to reduce Janice's social isolation' is too woolly and does not include any way of satisfactorily measuring when the goal has been achieved. 'I want to visit my friends more often' is better but still unclear. 'Janice wants to visit her mother at least once a week and to meet with her best friend two evenings a week in her local pub' is better yet. The goal as expressed is less grandiose but clear and attainable.

The third stage of task-centred work is *the setting of tasks*. Tasks are the small steps that the user, the practitioner or both undertake in order to move towards the defined goal. Tasks are jointly negotiated in a session between practitioner and user, and recorded, and a timetable for their completion is drawn up. They are often everyday activities and may seem obvious or mundane. This is their strength; they are small and achievable, but each relates to the others, often as part of a sequence. As with problems and goals, tasks are written down in a way that makes it clear whether or not they have been completed: 'Janice will ring the local bus company and note down exactly when buses call at her local bus-stop'; 'Janice will ask the driver to help her aboard with her pushchair'; 'Janice will find out what evening classes are available and will consider which one she might want to attend.' The work should emphasize the user's tasks. The whole point of task-centred work is to enhance the user's capacity to solve problems and through that to gain some control over their life. It makes little sense therefore for the practitioner to undertake tasks that the user could, with preparation or rehearsal, undertake for themselves. Individual task can be set for completion before the next meeting between practitioner and user. Or they can be completed during sessions; typically session tasks rehearse with the practitioner an activity that the user wants to undertake, such as attending a job interview or writing a letter.

The fourth stage is *reviewing*. At every session, user and practitioner review whether or not the tasks set at the previous session have been completed. Both will have a written copy of what those tasks are, what they require for completion and when they should be completed. If there is little apparent progress towards the selected goals, it may be that they are inappropriate or unrealistic after all, or that user motivation is low. Whatever the reason, it may be necessary to renegotiate a new set of goals and a new time frame. But task-centred work is always short-term work, using deadlines as a spur to activity; redefining the timetable too often inevitably undermines the work.

Task-centred work fits in closely with concepts of PARTNERSHIP and the user's PARTICIPATION in decisions that affect them. It places emphasis on written agreements as to what work will be undertaken and by whom. The increasing requirement for partnership with users in all phases of social work makes the approach a model of considerable relevance. It is one of the few models of social work that encourages users to determine what they wish to work on, rather than having to work on problems that the practitioner considers most important. It also places emphasis on user motivation, responsibility and enhancing problem-solving capacity. A significant body of research into work with a range of user groups has established task-centred work as one of the most effective of all approaches to social work.

P. Marsh and M. Doel, *Task-Centred Work*, Aldershot: Arena, 1992.

**team**   a group of people working together to deliver a service.

Within social welfare occupations teams vary considerably in size, complexity, management structure and purpose. In social work organizations, teams may comprise GENERIC workers who carry responsibilities for all client groups within a designated area, but such teams are increasingly rare. Typically fieldwork teams are now divided into adult services (covering principally mental health, DISABILITY and OLDER PEOPLE) and children's services. Within these two broad categories of teams there are often relative specialisms; thus for children there may be juvenile justice teams and teams concerned with fostering and adoption. Often there are also specialisms within teams; for example, within adult teams there are likely to be workers who have interests in mental health and others whose expertise lies with LEARNING DISABILITY.

A distinction may be drawn between a team and a network. Teams are characterized by a common goal, shared working and a high degree of consensus about how the job is to be done. Networks, by contrast, are loose entities where people work independently and where there may be substantial differences in practice from one worker to another. RESIDENTIAL WORK teams are typical of the first category. Clearly such workers are exposed to each other's practice and clients; in these circumstances several workers may have primary responsibility for one case. Fieldwork teams comparatively have their workers operating much more independently, although there may be circumstances where a case is held jointly (such as with an aggressive or potentially violent service user). Teams can be MULTIDISCIPLINARY in nature. Thus in mental health settings psychiatrists, social workers, psychiatric nurses and psychologists work together, each with their own particular focus. In hospital settings psychiatrists are likely to be seen as the managers of the 'case'; in the COMMUNITY, the social worker is more likely to play the KEY WORKER role. Teamwork is enhanced by an effective team manager; few teams operate without a line manager. Effectiveness seems to be related to clear and appropriate policies, active staff support and SUPERVISION systems, and a WORKLOAD MANAGEMENT scheme that ensures both worker protection and good-quality service delivery.

A. Hey, 'Organizing teams – alternative patterns', in M. Marshall, M. Preston-Shoot and E. Wincott (eds), *Teamwork: For and Against*, London: British Association of Social Workers, 1979.

**terminal care**   the approach to caring for people dying of a diagnosed incurable disease that embodies symptom control, pain relief, and psychological and social support for the DYING person and their relatives and loved ones.

Terminal care encourages dying people and the significant people in their lives to live in active and fulfilling ways and to participate in decisions about the management of the disease. The focus of attention is the emotional, spiritual and practical care of the dying person and their close relationships. This holistic approach has its origins in the HOSPICE movement founded by Cecily Saunders in 1967 at St Christopher's Hospice. Terminal care occurs in a number of settings. The hospice may offer short-term inpatient care on a respite basis or longer-term care as death approaches. Multidisciplinary teams – doctors, nurses, social workers and occupational therapists – also use the hospice as a base for offering terminal care to patients in their own homes or in community resources. In addition, hospice teams may offer symptom control with the care of the dying in general hospital wards. Experiences from the hospice movement have in recent years led to the establishing of palliative care strategies in hospitals, COMMUNITY CARE and residential and own home settings. Palliative care teams work alongside the patient's own primary health care workers, the general practitioner and district nurse. The distinction between hospice care and palliative care is becoming increasingly blurred. Further support to the terminally ill is offered by nurses from the Cancer Relief Macmillan Fund, who usually work from community settings in close liaison with the primary health care services.

Patients cared for by the hospice and to a lesser extent by palliative care teams are most likely to have a diagnosis of terminal cancer. Both care strategies have been reluctant to offer care to people and their relatives where the diagnosis is Alzheimer's disease or where a person is in the latter stages of AIDS (see HIV/AIDS). While the hospice movement particularly is considering its services for AIDS patients, much of the terminal care of people dying from AIDS-associated illness is undertaken by friends, relatives and buddies. Buddies are people who befriend and support those with AIDS. People with AIDS experience multiple losses in addition to the diagnosis of terminal illness – friends, other family members and their sexual partner may have already died from AIDS – and a buddy may be their only social support. Terminal care of people with ALZHEIMER'S DISEASE is usually in the person's own home, supported by health and social services personnel and resources.

The social worker's role is a key one in the planning of care for dying people. The patient's own concerns and wishes, and the facilitation of patient choices in care plans, is the worker's overriding concern. The person also has a right to choose where they die and to be supported in this choice, although clearly the social worker will have regard for the concerns of others affected by this choice. The social worker's emphasis should be a maintenance of the dying person's rights, as these can all too often be eroded by the demands of medical and social care. Institutional arrangements in hospitals are often a barrier to patient choice. The control of choice may be in the amount of information available to a dying person; such information can be controlled by relatives, family and loved ones. The social worker should be informed as to the availability of care resources, knowledgeable in benefit provision, sensitive to possible care needs of other family members, including OLDER PEOPLE and children, and skilled in building confidence and trust.

Caring for dying people is stressful. Social work must therefore take account of the needs of the carer for respite. For example, children's hospices were established to provide relief for parents recognizing the stress that a dying child places on a family. Children's hospices are usually small and as homelike as possible, even to the provision of pets.

B.A. Backer, N.R. Hannon and N.A. Russell, *Death and Dying: Understanding and Care*, New York: Delmar, 1994.

**theories of crime and deviance** the collective term for the various explanations offered for social rule-breaking in general and criminal lawbreaking in particular.

Theories of crime and deviance vary in the extent to which they emphasize personal, cultural, social or structural factors. They assist us in understanding why people commit crime, but they do not necessarily provide prescriptions for what should be done about crime. Although there are links between theories of crime and PRINCIPLES OF SENTENCING, it is usually argued that solutions to crime reside in the attitudes and conditions in society as a whole rather than in the policies and practices of the CRIMINAL JUSTICE SYSTEM.

The earliest systematic attempt to provide an explanation of crime emerged in the late eighteenth and early nineteenth centuries as a response to earlier barbaric, repressive and arbitrary legal practices. The *classical school of CRIMINOLOGY* was based on a number of key beliefs about human nature and society, drawn from the philosophical movement known as the Enlightenment. All individuals were believed to be self-seeking and greedy by nature and therefore liable to commit crime. Nevertheless, there was believed to be a consensus in society as to the desirability of protecting private property and personal welfare. In order to prevent a 'war of all against all', individuals freely enter into a social contract with the state to preserve the peace within the terms of this consensus. All individuals are rational and equal in the eyes of the law. The individual has free will and is responsible for their actions; mitigating circumstances or excuses are therefore inadmissible. (Closely allied to these beliefs were the sentencing principles of proportionality and deterrence.) Crime was therefore viewed as a matter of choice – a deliberate attempt to undermine the social contract.

Classical criminology, however, was subject to some fairly obvious criticisms. Because of differing mental capacities, not all people could be held to be equally responsible before the law. Some allowance had to be made for the very young, the 'feebleminded' and the insane. It was also apparent that material inequalities existed in society that meant, first, that the impact and effects of punishment would differ and, second, that crime might be a rational response to inequality or poverty. Neoclassical explanations of crime, therefore, began to take account of the personal circumstances and characteristics of the criminal. Many people believe that neoclassicism is still the predominant view in the criminal justice system today.

With the development of medical science during the nineteenth century, there was increasing interest in the possible existence of a 'criminal personality' that could be identified by biological or mental abnormalities. This school of thought was known as *positivist criminology*. Its basic tenets were that crime was induced or determined by factors of birth or environment; these could be studied scientifically, so that crime could be predicted and prevented by the treatment rather than the punishment of criminals. Some of the best-known positivist theories of crime include the apparent discovery of physical stigmata on criminals and the apparent preponderance among criminals of particular body builds or types, particular chromosomal make-ups, low intelligence and extrovert personalities susceptible to poor conditioning. Such theories lead to the ascendancy of rehabilitation as a sentencing principle. They have been widely criticized, however, on technical grounds (that the so-called scientific findings are unreliable), on sociological grounds (that they provide a very narrow explanation of crime that ignores issues of power and inequality) and on political grounds (that the 'treatment' required to 'cure' a criminal personality may be out of all proportion to the seriousness of the offence, thus infringing civil liberties and notions of 'just deserts'). Despite this, the belief that criminal activity is learned, or a matter of conditioning that can be unlearned, has enjoyed a revival over the past decade with the cognitive and behavioural approaches adopted by the PROBATION SERVICE. These have involved offenders (often in groups) analysing their offending behaviour, identifying factors that trigger criminal responses and expanding their social skills to handle situations in more socially acceptable ways.

*PSYCHODYNAMIC theories of crime* focus on the early emotional experiences of offenders. Criminal activity is seen as an attempt to compensate for childhood (especially maternal) deprivation and for an inability to resolve – as a healthy person would – the internal emotional conflicts of growing up. Crime is viewed as disturbed, attention-seeking behaviour that requires an individual psychotherapeutic response. In the mid-twentieth century such theories were seen as particularly relevant in understanding juvenile crime, but their influence has declined with a return to JUST DESERTS.

*Social organization theories* developed in the United States from the 1920s onwards and were the first attempt to provide sociological explanations of crime. Theories of 'social space' were concerned with the influence of what would now be called town planning or building development on the attitudes and behaviour of city dwellers. The constraints of poor housing and decaying inner-city residential areas were highlighted as contributory factors to the development of a socioeconomic 'pecking order' and subcultures that condoned the commission of crime. Closely related to the 'social space' theories were those concerned with 'social (lack of) opportunity'. With increased affluence in society, people trapped at the bottom of the social structure are frustrated by the vision of success and wealth alongside the absence of legitimate opportunity for them to achieve those goals. The response to this may be the development of delinquent subcultures or a proclivity to 'drift' in and out of crime.

*Social reaction and social control theories* are less concerned with why people commit crime in the first place than with how criminal behaviour is perpetuated as a result of social responses to the criminal. Social reaction theory argues that official responses to crime (such as heavy policing and severe sentencing) serve to label and stigmatize a criminal and thus make it more difficult for them to reintegrate into the community as a law-abiding citizen. Consequently, the criminal is likely to seek the company of other criminals and fulfil the negative predictions made about them. In this way, deviance is amplified, and there is a danger of moral panics being constructed by the media, which reinforce stereotypical reactions and play on public fears about the escalation of crime. Social control theories develop this idea further (and also hark back to classical criminology) by arguing that, if it were not for the strength of our socialization and our fear of getting caught, most people would commit crime at some point in their lives. Whether or not we commit crime depends on the extent to which we feel we have an investment in remaining law-abiding; the strength of this feeling may vary over time and in different situations. Being labelled and stigmatized as a criminal may be a decisive factor in continuing rather than discontinuing a life of crime.

The major criticism of all these theories is that they fail to take account of the power structure and conflicts in society. *Conflict theories* argue that it is impossible to separate individual criminals (or even local environments and responses) from the way the criminal law and the criminal justice system have been constructed and are maintained to serve the interests of powerful groups in society. Defendants are overwhelmingly drawn from the ranks of working-class and unemployed people, but some of the most serious crime (particularly financial crime) is committed by the rich and powerful. Serious class and racial conflicts are dealt with as matters of narrow criminal justice, rather than as issues of broad social justice. Similarly, *feminist explanations* of crime have underlined the fact that both crime and criminal justice are overwhelmingly male enterprises and that this requires analysis of gender power relations within society.

Theories of crime and deviance provide different levels of explanation, and many people feel that they are not all necessarily mutually exclusive. Professionals working with offenders frequently adopt an 'eclectic' approach that combines elements of structural, cultural and biographical explanation.

A. Jones, B. Kroll, J. Pitts, P. Smith and J.L. Weise, *The Probation Handbook*, Harlow: Longman, 1992.

**theory** a set of propositions or hypotheses that seek to explain phenomena.

Theory usually implies that sets of assumptions have been formalized, published, debated and tested in some way. For example, personality theories have been defined as a 'collection of assumptions and concepts about how best to regard people and study them'. Theory provides a structure or model through which reality can be observed and predictions about events may be made. It is a way of organizing information so that it can be transmitted and added to. The concepts implicit in theories attempt to describe reality, but the theoretical concepts, the explanations, are not reality. Theories organize knowledge in a form that makes it usable and communicable, ensuring a common understanding and making for reliability and usefulness. Theories should have utility, that is, they should explain what they are intended to explain; if they do not, they may have limited application and be discarded. In social work 'good' theories offer a framework to aid an explanation of behaviour.

In the area of social welfare it is usual to distinguish between first, theories 'borrowed' from the social sciences which have been adopted by social welfare workers; second, theories which seek to explain the nature and functions of welfare provision within societies; and third, theories which have been developed by those working in social work and allied fields.

There are many examples of the first group of theories because social work and social welfare services have relied very heavily upon the insights of social science especially sociology, psychology and political science. Sociology has provided evidence of persisting patterns of inequality within society; has provided explanations of social forces which have extended our understanding of both social change and social stability and has developed interesting and suggestive ideas about the nature of deviance. Psychology has in the main looked at individual and interpersonal processes helping us to understand how individuals develop over the course of a lifetime; how they think, feel and perceive the world; and of how relationships and group dynamics are to be understood. Political science, for its part, seeks to understand the nature of power and of how it is distributed and regulated throughout society. All the social sciences are trying to make sense of how the behaviour of individuals is to be understood in the context of wider social forces. Some theories focus upon the large canvas of society seen as a whole, some upon smaller entities of relationships, families and communities. All theorizing in their attempts to identify the principal ingredients of whatever they are studying and endeavouring to understand how those ingredients behave in relationship to each other. (see for example, SOCIAL CLASS, MATERNAL DEPRIVATION, LABELLING, PRESSURE GROUPS, PSYCHOLOGY, SOCIOLOGY).

The second set of theories seek to explain the nature of welfare provision within society. Many writers have compared the differing manner in which welfare functions are delivered within many societies. Varying ideas about the nature of the state's responsibilities as against those of individuals and families have been noted. In general the role of ideology in the formation of welfare provision has been regarded as most important. At a micro level social work has sometimes been regarded critically as an agent of social control and as a form of oppression as well as a helping profession. The theoretical analysis of the social work function has therefore sought to identify these ingredients of oppression and by so doing to minimize them where possible. (see MARKET, NEW RIGHT, RADICAL SOCIAL WORK, ANTI-DISCRIMINATORY PRACTICE).

The third set of theories, generated by social work academics, have been much more limited in range and indeed some would argue that they are more methodological than theoretical. These 'theories' include TASK-CENTRED methods, SYSTEMS THEORY, COUNSELLING and CRISIS INTERVENTION. All four of these approaches lend themselves to differing theoretical interpretations. Thus, the problems defined in the task-centred methods might be differentially identified in negotiations between a worker and service user depending upon the ideas about the origins of problems which inform their views. Similarly systems theory can be used conservatively or radically depending upon which ingredients are thought to be most important to a person's situation (that is, systems theory can be used in conjunction with socialist view of society as well as a conservative view). Counselling too takes many competing theoretical forms and the manner of intervention into crises can depend very much upon other perspectives held by worker and client. A feminist, for example, might work in a very different way with a woman who has been raped or the victim of DOMESTIC VIOLENCE, from another worker with more traditional views of a woman's role in society.

Many practitioners and students are worried about thinking theoretically. They might prefer to think about themselves as practical people without a need for

theory. Such people do, of course, think theoretically, although they do not usually acknowledge the theory in their practice. Yet a good theory is essentially practical.
M. Payne, *Modern Social Work Theory*, Basingstoke: Macmillan, 1991.

**threshold criteria**   the grounds for granting a CARE ORDER or SUPERVISION ORDER to a local authority under section 31 of the CHILDREN ACT.

The threshold criteria are that a child is suffering, or likely to suffer, SIGNIFICANT HARM and that this harm is attributable to the standard of care given by the parents or to the fact that the child is beyond the parents' control. A very young child left to wander streets at night, an infant losing weight because of lack of food and a child suffering fractures as a result of parental assault are all examples that meet the criteria. The grounds are referred to as threshold criteria because, even if they are established in court in respect of a particular child, the court, before making a care or supervision order, must consider other grounds as well, including the points in the WELFARE CHECKLIST and the principle that making the order must actually benefit the child in ways that would not happen if the order were not made.

**throughcare**   a term used to indicate a continuity of supervisory interest in a prisoner both during and after a PRISON sentence.

The term was adopted in response to criticism of the term 'aftercare', which used to form part of the title of the PROBATION SERVICE (formerly the Probation and After-Care Service). It was felt that 'aftercare' reflected, all too accurately, the attitude of many probation officers that work with prisoners (especially during a sentence) was a low priority or an 'afterthought'. The supervision of prisoners and liaison between probation officers inside and outside prison are governed by NATIONAL STANDARDS. Probation officers are now involved in sentence planning and review as well as in writing reports for home leave applications and for EARLY RELEASE decisions. When prisoners are released, probation officers supervise their licences. They also offer help and support to the families of prisoners.

**time out**   the placing of a child for a short while in an area where they receive no attention.

Time out is used as a mild form of punishment within a programme of BEHAVIOUR MODIFICATION. In full, it means 'time out from positive reinforcement'. When a child engages in unwanted behaviour they are immediately removed to a neutral place for a short period of three to five minutes. While there, the child has nothing to do and receives no attention for that period. Time out is used only in carefully anticipated situations, such as of refusal to comply with a request, and where positive reinforcement has failed.

The child in time out must be monitored at all times. This approach is inappropriate with children older than 9, since often the child has to be physically removed to the neutral place. On occasion, the concept has been grossly misused by residential regimes and converted into a harsh practice of deprivation and isolation over a considerable period of time. In this form, it has nothing to do with the original meaning of the term. (See also PIN-DOWN.)

**tolerance**   the way the body adapts to the presence of a substance or
   DRUG being taken so that more and more is required to give the same
   effect.

The same drug taken by different people will have varying effects
depending on how accustomed they are to taking it. This unpredictability is
dangerous, making overdose a possibility, especially if the purity of the
drug is higher than expected or if there has been a break from taking the
drug. (See SUBSTANCE MISUSE.)

**toy library**   a facility for people to borrow toys for their children. Such
   facilities are often attached to NURSERIES, nursery schools, playgroups or
   specialist facilities for young children.

The general purpose of toy libraries is to help poor families have access to
toys that a low income would normally not allow and, in the case of some
specialist units, the use of toys specifically chosen to help stimulate a child.
This may be with reference to a general understimulation or to an identified
problem or need, including a DISABILITY.

**tracking**   means by which social workers keep in touch with service users
   in order to monitor their behaviour and to encourage them to avoid
   difficulties. The concept has particular application for work in the
   JUVENILE/YOUTH JUSTICE system.

Practically, young offenders, and offending adults in some circumstances
(see ELECTRONIC MONITORING) are required to report regularly in the course of
a day to a social worker or a support worker. The purpose of such exchanges
is to help juveniles who are in situations where they seem to be offending
frequently. Such close monitoring may deter them from getting into
situations of temptation by means of frequent contact and encouragement
from positive influences.

**trait**   a stable predisposition in a person to behave in a particular way, such
   as impulsively or secretively.

Traits are intrinsic to the person and are not part of the environment,
although observed behaviour may be an interaction of traits with
environmental factors. Traits are presumed to be a constant within an
individual; they may be mental or physical, inherited or learned. Traits
cannot be observed directly; their presence can be deduced only from
observable behaviours.

**Transactional Analysis**   a theory that sees interactions between
   individuals as one of the fundamental ways in which people express and
   seek confirmation of their PERSONALITIES.

Devised by Berne in the 1960s, the language of Transactional Analysis is
derived from United States slang. According to the theory, the structure of
each person's personality is comprised of a 'parent' and 'adult' and a 'child'
ego state. In any interaction one of these ego states is in control for each
person and addresses one of these ego states in the other person. As long
as the two participants share the same assumptions, the interaction can

continue. Thus, if a wife's 'parent' talks to her husband's 'child' about his drinking habits, the interaction can continue as long as the husband accepts the basis of the interaction and his 'child' replies to his wife's 'parent'.

Transactions can take a number of forms, the most destructive of which are games. Games involve two or more people who are willing to adopt certain rules. The pay-off of a game is to confirm individuals' views of themselves, to protect them from some truth and from establishing true intimacy with others. For example, the game 'If it weren't for you' could be played by a couple whereby a woman states that if her partner had not prevented her, by his demands, she would have been a famous writer. In this way, the woman never has to confront the possibility that if she had tried to write she might have been a failure. As long as the partner accepts responsibility the game can continue. An additional element in this system is that an individual can view themselves, those they interact with and other people either as OK or as not OK. In this way, a depressive view would be 'I'm not OK but you are OK and they are OK', while an arrogant view would be 'I'm OK, you're not OK and they're not OK', and a prejudiced view would be 'I'm OK, you're OK but they're not OK'. Berne suggested that parents determine the attitude that their children will have towards themselves. The aim of transactional analysis is for individuals to recognize the games in which they habitually become involved, to stop playing them and to come to a view whereby they, those close to them and others are all OK. In this way, people should break away from the images of themselves that have been handed down to them by their parents.

E. Berne, *Games People Play: The Psychology of Human Relationships*, Harmondsworth: Penguin, 1966.

**transfer summary** an account of work undertaken to date, including problems solved and tasks yet to be tackled, usually completed by a social worker when a case is to be taken over by another worker.

The worker receiving the transfer summary may be either in the same team or in another area, if the service user moves from one area to another. Transfer summaries offer an opportunity for social workers to take stock or to evaluate the work completed to that point. (See also CASE REVIEW/SYSTEM, REASSESSMENT.)

**transracial adoption** the placing of children of one 'RACE' (or of 'MIXED RACE') with the families of another 'race', so that, legally, the adopted children are to be regarded as if they were born to that family.

In practice transracial ADOPTION amounts to the placing of black children with white families; the converse has rarely, if ever, taken place. Since British society regards all non-white people as effectively black, what follows utilizes that distinction. The practice of transracial adoption emerged from a number of developments in the 1970s: first, changes in the abortion law; second, increased availability and usage of contraception; and third, major changes in social attitudes towards unmarried mothers and single parenthood. These three related developments had the effect of reducing the supply of 'healthy white babies' for adoption. Significantly, as a result of changing attitudes to adoption too, this was a time when the demand for adoptable babies was in fact growing, especially among middle-class couples. A dwindling supply of suitable babies and at the same time a growing demand for them brought to light the situation of many black babies who were languishing in care, who had previously been regarded as unadoptable (along with children with disabilities and older children). Not only were black children considered 'hard to place'; suitable black families were thought 'hard to find'. Early attempts to recruit black adopters were remarkably unsuccessful, leading to the misplaced conclusion that the idea of adoption was 'alien' to certain cultures. From these circumstances, and from the prevailing 'assimilationist' views on race of the period, the practice arose of placing black children with white families.

Until the mid-1960s the majority of ADOPTION AGENCIES operated in accordance with a strict 'matching' policy whereby the 'race' of the child was the focal issue. The concern in many policy documents of adoption societies was that children should be presentable as the biological offspring of the couple. In this context, much attention was also given to matching the religious background of the child's family of origin to that of the adopters. In the 1970s major and wider struggles took place to determine how community relations were to be handled in Britain in the future. Opposing forces on the one hand sought the total assimilation of immigrant groups into the 'host society' and on the other supported the idea of cultural pluralism. The former position implied that 'race' in a sense did not matter, or at least should not. This broadly assimilationist view underpinned the commitment to transracial adoption. The problem of the child's identity was reduced in importance; if assimilationist policies were pursued, we would all be white in the end (so long as strict immigration policies were enforced, at least in relation to New Commonwealth citizens).

In the late 1960s a small group of black social workers provided the first critique of transracial adoption. They argued that the 'black community' might not survive because it was being 'robbed' of its most precious resource, its children. How, they asked, could the 'black community' feel any measure of pride in itself if advantage (for children taken into care) was being defined as being brought up by white families? Their second concern was the effect of transracial adoption on the psychosocial development of black children. This point raises the issue of whether white adoptive parents can grasp the problems that blacks have to face in a racist society such as Britain. Can white parents of black children create in them a pride in their blackness, in effect a positive black identity? Can such parents equip them with the necessary coping and survival skills to help them deal with racism and disadvantage? In the same vein, will such children be able to take on the social and cultural characteristics that will enable them to move freely in the 'black community'? Finally, the remaining preoccupation of the social workers was to challenge the assumption that blacks would not adopt. They were fundamentally critical of the unsuccessful methods employed to try to attract would-be black adoptive parents.

Research has been divided on the issue of whether black children adopted by white couples can meet the standards implied by the critique from the BLACK PERSPECTIVE. Some research has apparently indicated that many black children brought up by white adoptive parents are broadly well adjusted, have succeeded reasonably well at school and are able to sustain good peer relationships. Critics of this research have suggested that these children have a 'defensive' form of self-esteem, that their sense of self-worth is unlikely to stand the test of a lifetime of racism in Britain and that these children are white in all respects (including their consciousness) except their skin. The phrase 'black skins but white masks' has been widely used about these children.

In relation to the search for black families for the adoption of black children, new approaches explored by the London Borough of Lambeth in 1980 proved encouraging. The recruitment of black social workers to help identify, train and support black families who were interested in adoption was but one ingredient in Lambeth's success, but an important one. Other factors included combating racist attitudes in other workers, discarding stereotyped notions of the normal family, and the ability to use 'black networks' in imaginative ways. These experiments have now been repeated elsewhere in Britain with at least some success.

By the mid-1980s the placement of most black children for adoption took place 'in race'; that is, the children were placed with families of the same ethnic origin. Key difficulties remain. Not a few social services departments still do not have rigorous policies in relation to adoption and 'race'. There are circumstances where black or 'mixed-race' children have been in long-term placements with white foster parents and where PERMANENCY has been sought with black adopters. The bonds established between white families and their black foster children can be strong; criteria must be established to determine whether in these circumstances it is in the children's best interests to be moved. Similarly, it cannot be assumed that black families necessarily have the best attitudes and values to adopt a black child. Recent discussion documents from the BRITISH ASSOCIATION OF SOCIAL WORKERS and the government suggest that a more flexible practice in relation to 'same race' adoptions should be pursued by social work agencies; but black social workers and others have been very critical of what they see as an attempt to undermine the progress made in the last decade.

S. Ahmed, J. Cheetham and J.J. Small (eds), *Social Work with Black Children and their Families*, London: Batsford, 1986.

**truancy**   illicit absence from school by children of compulsory school age; the term is often used to describe all forms of 'unauthorized absence'.

Children do not break the law by staying away from school; only parents can commit an offence (EDUCATION ACT 1993, section 199). Many people would adopt a generally punitive approach, regarding truancy as a symptom of either poor parenting or the child's being 'beyond control'. Recent research, however, suggests that children truant primarily in response to issues within the school: subjects they do not like, unpopular teachers, bullying, or broadly negative experiences or labelling that the child is right to resist. It is usually helpful to distinguish between 'blanket truancy', when children miss whole sessions or days, and 'post-registration truancy', when children leave lessons or the school building during the day. (See EDUCATION SOCIAL WORK, EDUCATION SUPERVISION ORDER, SCHOOL REFUSAL.)

P. Carlen, D. Gleeson, J. Wardhaugh, *Truancy: The Politics of Compulsory Schooling*, Buckingham, Open University Press, 1992.

# U

**underclass**  a term used both to describe and to explain the over-representation in the CRIMINAL JUSTICE SYSTEM of defendants who live on state benefits and are unemployed, homeless and/or without stable family relationships.

The term is used by conservative politicians to argue for the existence of a class of people who are morally and criminally deviant as a result of being raised in fatherless families with a 'welfare state' mentality. Thus, in adulthood, such people are unwilling to work for a living and expect to take from, rather than contribute to, the good of society. Left-wing critics either refuse to use the term because of its judgemental connotations or insist that it should be used only in a descriptive and not an explanatory manner. According to this view, while many poor, unemployed, homeless people commit crime, this is the result of social inequality and injustice. There is no evidence to support the idea that such people have different moral values or aspirations from other people. Given the opportunity, they would also appreciate a home, a job and a settled family life. (See ANTI-DISCRIMINATION, CULTURE OF POVERTY.)

**under-5s provision**  day care facilities for preschool children, including day NURSERIES, CHILD-MINDERS, nursery schools or nursery classes in primary schools, playgroups and other provision (nannies, au pairs, nurseries in FAMILY CENTRES).

The CHILDREN ACT places a duty on local authorities to 'facilitate' day care provision for preschool-aged children. It also requires authorities to review such provision, including voluntary and private facilities, every three years. Acceptable standards have to be maintained; and to help providers reach and sustain these standards, authorities can provide training and guidance. In comparison with many European countries, Britain's under-5s provision is poor and unevenly developed from one area to another. There is a clear lack of strategic thinking at both national and local levels. Comprehensive policies are needed to address the issues of child-care needs and EQUAL OPPORTUNITIES, employment and social security rights. In Britain there are a bewildering variety of complex regulations about how child day care provision is to be regarded, costed and charged for. There is also great inconsistency in criteria for access to such provision. Urgent requirements are the development of good-quality under-5s provision on some scale, improvements in the employment conditions for workers (especially pay) and financial help for the costs of child-care for single parents.

B. Cohen, *Caring for Children*, London: Family Policy Studies Centre, 1988.

**unemployability supplement**  a supplementary benefit paid to people incapable of work because of an industrial accident or disease before April 1987. Since then INVALIDITY BENEFIT is paid on a non-contributory basis when the incapacity is due to an industrial accident or disease.

**unemployment**   a condition of being without paid work and of being available for such work.

Actual rates of unemployment are widely disputed because of the varying ways in which availability for work is officially acknowledged. Many people are not counted because they do not register with government agencies such as job centres; for example, women who are not entitled to any welfare benefits in their own right often do not use 'the system'. Unemployment may be redefined as working on employment training schemes. Sick and disabled people can also in some circumstances not have their wish to secure employment taken seriously. Some may be working part-time when they wish to work full-time.

The social consequences of unemployment include POVERTY, ill-health, low morale and contingent personal and family difficulties. The longer the period of unemployment, the more chronic is the poverty. In these circumstances, savings become depleted, household goods wear out and cannot be replaced, and comforts have to be given up. Unemployment is also associated with default debt, as reduced income fails to meet financial commitments incurred while the person was still in work. Not surprisingly, therefore, unemployment often leads to ill-health as morale diminishes and personal relationships become strained. The BLACK REPORT found a very strong link between health and unemployment that could even have repercussions from one generation to the next if prolonged.

Social welfare workers mostly attempt to help with the social and personal consequences of unemployment. Thus ADVICE workers assist with benefit entitlement and debt that has got out of control; health and social workers deal with emotional, relational and family problems. SOCIAL SERVICES DEPARTMENTS can directly create employment through sheltered workshops for people with learning difficulties. Otherwise efforts of social and community workers are confined to attempts to get unemployed people involved in COMMUNITY projects, which are perceived as useful in their own right and also as helpful in maintaining the morale of unemployed people. There is also the possibility that new skills might be learned that may subsequently be helpful in securing a job in the future. ADULT EDUCATION programmes can be integral to these efforts.

**unemployment benefit**   a benefit paid to a person who is unemployed, 'signing on' as available for work and actively seeking work. Entitlement is based on contributions paid and credited in the last two years before claiming.

Benefit is paid for up to fifty-two weeks, after which a person can requalify only by working for thirteen weeks. Since the late 1980s the government has introduce administrative arrangements to test 'availability' and 'job-seeking activity'. A claimant is disqualified from benefit for a maximum of twenty-six weeks if they are dismissed from their job for misconduct or leave voluntarily without just cause. Many cases of dismissal or of people leaving employment voluntarily include circumstances that justify only a short period of disqualification or none at all. In practice, a maximum disqualification is almost always imposed in the first instance, and claimants have to appeal to have their disqualification reviewed and to begin receiving their benefits. Unemployment benefit is not paid for any period covered by wages in lieu of notice. By contrast, redundancy payments do not affect entitlement.

> Unemployment benefit is a daily benefit paid for six days in the week (not Sunday or other normal rest day); a claimant can work and forgo benefit on individual days but can lose the benefit for days on which they do not work if a pattern of part-time work develops or if their earnings exceed the lower earnings limit within a period of seven days. In December 1993 the government announced its intention to abolish unemployment benefit from April 1996 and replace it with a new JOB SEEKERS ALLOWANCE based on contributions for the first six months and means-tested thereafter.

**unforeseen aggravation**  see INDUSTRIAL INJURIES SCHEME.

**uniform grants**  local education authorities have the power to assist with the purchase of distinctive school uniforms and necessary clothing (for example, sports kit). Many authorities make no payments, while others make payments at the start of secondary school.

**unit fine**  a method introduced by the CRIMINAL JUSTICE ACT 1991 (implemented in October 1992) of calculating the most commonly used sentence so as to equalize its impact on both rich and poor defendants.

A defendant was fined a number of units according to the seriousness of the offence, but the value of each unit is dependent on the defendant's disposable income. As a result of vociferous criticism from sentencers and some wildly anomalous decisions, the unit fine was abolished in September 1993 and replaced merely by an exhortation to take account of defendants' means when deciding on the amount of a fine.

**unmet need**  a NEED identified by ASSESSMENT that is then not met, usually because the resources do not exist.

The purpose of recording unmet need for all assessed service users is to keep track of the shortfall in resources. There has been considerable debate between central government and LOCAL AUTHORITIES as to whether the latter should compile this sort of information. In practice, most authorities do so in order to argue for more resources.

**Utting Report**  commissioned in 1991 by the Department of Health in the aftermath of PIN-DOWN, a report into the management, purpose and direction of CHILDREN'S HOMES after a decade of increasing incidence of ABUSE, problems of control and persistent reliance on inexperienced staff.

The report, officially entitled *Children in the Public Care*, is usually known by the name of its author, William Utting, who was head of the SOCIAL SERVICES INSPECTORATE at the time. It made a number of recommendations regarding the management, practice and resourcing of children's homes. Among these were a call for increased numbers of staff to be qualified social workers, that each staff member should have an individual development programme, and that social services departments should manage residential child-care within their overall strategy for children's services and apply the same management principles concerning information systems and quality assurance that they do to other areas of their service.

Sir William Utting, *Children in the Public Care, a Review of Residential Child Care*, London: HMSO, 1991.

$$V$$

**vagrancy** the practice of living without permanent accommodation or of having no fixed abode.

The term is often associated with wandering, although vagrants in fact often confine themselves to particular areas. Usually vagrants are single, but families too might be vagrant. Vagrants' lifestyles may vary substantially, involving sleeping rough, using NIGHT SHELTERS, taking on temporary work with tied accommodation, and spells, often brief, of living with family or friends. Housing workers, social workers and, to some extent, probation officers have increasingly argued that the 'problem' of vagrancy should be viewed not as personal pathology or inadequacy but as an issue of homelessness. Night shelters should therefore be seen as only a first step in trying to secure permanent accommodation for the single and mobile homeless. A recognized additional problem for vagrants is that of securing an income from the BENEFITS AGENCY. The process is usually lengthy, with benefit being given on a day-by-day basis. There are strong associations between vagrancy and a background in care and MENTAL ILLNESS.

**value judgement** an assessment or statement based upon one's own ETHICAL CODE or norms about the worth of a person, group or whole community, particularly about their actions or beliefs.

The very idea of having some form of social work system embodies value judgements, for it presupposes that there are certain people who need some form of support, punishment, treatment or restraint. There will be many disagreements between people about the social and moral significance of certain kinds of behaviour. Much social policy rests upon a consensus of belief, that is, value judgements. Much social work intervention is justified by reference to some value or other; there is simply no avoiding them. The task in education and in policy formation is to reveal one's own assumptions (that is, value judgements) and to be able to defend them as reasonable and just.

**values** a belief that something is good and desirable. It defines what is important, worthwhile and worth striving for.

The activity of social work is value-laden. It is not a technical activity operating in an ethical vacuum; its objectives and practices are very much influenced by the views that people have about how society ought to be organized and how social relationships ought to be regulated. These considerations clearly imply that values refer to both the personal and the political.

Social welfare organizations contain workers with a wide range of beliefs and attitudes. The same social work team may contain people committed to explanations about the origins of social problems that are rooted in a critique of capitalism, and others who view the same problems as a failure of families to socialize their children appropriately, for example. Such analyses may have differing values at their root (say, a view of society based on the sharing of resources, as against another view that perceives inequalities as both inevitable and desirable), and differing values in their consequences (such as regarding how offenders should be treated or punished). Social workers have nevertheless developed a value base that most practitioners feel able to endorse; these principles for practice include: a repudiation of all forms of negative DISCRIMINATION; developing an awareness of the interrelationship of the processes of structural oppression, race, class and gender; understanding and counteracting the impact of stigma and discrimination on grounds of poverty, age, disability and sectarianism; demonstrating an awareness of both individual and institutional racism and ways to combat both through anti-racist practice; developing an understanding of gender issues and demonstrating anti-sexism in social work practice; and recognizing the need for, and seeking to promote, non-discriminatory and anti-oppressive policies.

While most practitioners would feel able to endorse these guiding principles, an analysis of, say, encouragement to practice in an anti-sexist manner can lead to different analyses in the hands of different people. For example, is the goal of an anti-sexist practice complete equality between men and women, or is the aspiration effectively much more modest? Similarly, in relation to ANTI-POVERTY STRATEGIES, how unequal a society can we tolerate in our practice aspirations? Agreement on the above general formulations of value issues masks considerable problems about what they actually mean in terms of ultimate goals and the behaviour of social welfare workers.

At a different level, social work and social welfare organizations subscribe to what are in effect moral principles concerning the worker–CLIENT relationship, including a commitment to ACCEPTANCE, NON-JUDGEMENTAL ATTITUDES, client SELF-DETERMINATION and a need to offer CONFIDENTIALITY. All these guiding principles are in fact problematical in practice. Client self-determination, for example, has to be limited at least by other people's rights; confidentiality cannot always be guaranteed, especially when another person may be at risk. Values in practice can therefore be codified but are invariably constrained or limited by either another principle or another person's rights.

The key tasks for workers in the field of social welfare would appear to be: (1) to determine what our values actually are and what they are based upon, to bring them out into the light of day and to acknowledge their true nature; (2) to decide whether they need to be adjusted or perhaps rejected, to ask whether they are consistent and whether we are happy with the consequences of their being adopted; (3) to think through the problems of how our values will cope or relate to people who hold alternative or indeed contradictory values. See also ETHICAL CODE.

Central Council for Education and Training in Social Work, *Requirements for the Diploma in Social Work*, London: CCETSW, Paper 30, 1990; M. Horne, *Values in Social Work*, London: Community Care/Wildwood House, 1987.

**ventilation**   the expression of strong feelings to some purpose beyond personal display.

In COUNSELLING, therapy and many other situations people may need to express powerful feelings, often previously suppressed, before being able to make progress in tackling their problems. One of the skills required by workers is to recognize this need and to help the service user fully to express their feelings. It may be that ventilation will achieve a measure of catharsis; that is, a person may benefit directly from getting their feelings out into the open and acknowledged by themselves and perhaps by their helper. Ventilation may therefore be immediately helpful as well as contributing to the 'movement' in a problem that might otherwise have been stuck.

**victim**   a person injured, harmed or even killed by the direct action of a third party or indirectly as a consequence of their actions.

Concern for victims of crime has increased in recent years, following accusations that the CRIMINAL JUSTICE SYSTEM pays too much attention to the needs of offenders. In the past, there has been a tendency for victims to feel, at best, neglected and, at worst, blamed for their plight. The government white paper *Crime, Justice and Protecting the Public*, which preceded the CRIMINAL JUSTICE ACT 1991, begins: 'Too many people in England and Wales are hit by crime. Being a victim of crime and being frightened by crime stunts many lives.' The government provides limited funding to VICTIM SUPPORT schemes, which offer emotional support and practical advice to victims of crime referred by the POLICE. The police have been given special guidance on their treatment of women who are victims of sexual assault and DOMESTIC VIOLENCE. The government has also published a Victims' Charter (1990), which offers advice to victims about the treatment they should receive. A number of voluntary organizations exist to offer help to victims (or survivors) of personal violence.

The BRITISH CRIME SURVEY indicates that patterns of victimization differ according to the offence and according to age, gender and lifestyle. Most burglary victims live on poor council estates. Young men are the most likely to be victims of violence or robbery, especially if they go out frequently, drink heavily and engage in 'boisterous' group activity. Women are more likely to be victims of theft, sexual assault and domestic violence. Serious assaults are far more likely to be committed by someone known to the victim than by a stranger. Probation officers make the point that offenders are often victims too. Many men and women in PRISON have been physically or sexually abused as children, or have themselves been victims of theft and burglary.

Some victims complain that they are never informed about the progress of the offender through the courts or the outcome of the prosecution. Others have felt under pressure to cooperate with REPARATION or mediation schemes, whereby they meet with the offender in a situation that sometimes seems to be more for the benefit of the offender than for the victim. Yet others experience traumatic ordeals when they are required to give evidence in court. The Criminal Justice Act 1991 makes provision for child witnesses to give evidence on videotape in some cases. Courts attempt to take account of the needs of victims by making offenders pay compensation. In 1991, 102,700 offenders were ordered to pay compensation (averaging £161) in MAGISTRATES' courts and 10,100 offenders were ordered to pay compensation (averaging £882) in Crown Courts. Applications to and awards from the Criminal Injuries Compensation Board (CICB) (available to victims of crimes of violence) more than doubled between 1981 and 1991, but only half of all applications are processed within a year. There are also a number of rules (such as if the victim has a criminal record or in some way contributed to the incident) that enable the CICB to refuse or reduce compensation.

**Victim Support** an independent charity whose volunteer workers offer help to VICTIMS of crime.

Victims are referred to the charity by the police or other agencies or by themselves. Victim Support is made up of a network of local groups and it receives limited funding from the Home Office.

**violence** purposeful behaviour intended to hurt or damage others, defined widely in social work to include not only physical assault but also AGGRESSION, threatening behaviour, intimidation, and racial and sexual harassment. Violent acts should be seen as varying combinations in the abuse of physical, psychological and sexual power.

Most theorists regard violent behaviour as learned rather than arising from instincts. Social welfare agencies have become concerned with violence first in terms of internal relationships between employees, second in the context of staff–service user relationships and third in relation to direct work with violent clients where the concern is to help them develop coping mechanisms and to avoid violent behaviour.

Many organizations within the field of health and social services have now recognized that employee relationships can sometimes be very unhappy. In particular, relationships between superiors and subordinates can be affected by attempts to bully or harass, with sexual or racist motives common components of such behaviour. Other motivations may include religious discrimination, HOMOPHOBIA or simply an attempt to get someone to leave an organization. Enlightened services have developed grievance procedures to cover these kinds of behaviour, so that staff can complain if they are harassed. Anti-harassment campaigns can usefully be relaunched from time to time to ensure that the anti-harassment culture is constantly renewed and thus kept high on the agenda.

Over the last two decades the issue of CLIENTS' violence towards social welfare staff has come to the fore. It is now recognized as widespread, affecting all kinds of staff (including reception and ancillary workers) and sometimes significantly affecting how the work is done. Some social work staff have actually lost their lives; many have been injured or intimidated to the point that they felt unable to continue working; and many more have testified to the great stress involved in working with violent and aggressive service users. Social work and allied occupations now work, in the main, in situations where it is possible to speak of their anxieties in the expectation that practical and emotional support will be offered and that, importantly, they will not be made to feel that their competence is in question. This climate of trust within teams and workplaces, which is clearly necessary, is as important to men as it is to women.

Many social welfare agencies have recently developed policies and procedures concerning staff safety when dealing with violent or potentially violent clients. Such policies usually involve: first, attempts to help staff assess the risks to themselves; second, suggestions about how violence might be prevented or minimized; third, advice on how to handle violent incidents; fourth, ideas about how staff might be supported after a violent incident. The assessment of risk can usefully include systems for noting known violent clients so that workers are forewarned about potential difficulties. Men and boys between the ages of 14 and 45 constitute the group with greatest risk, although violence may come from any quarter. Clearly some social work 'set pieces' – for example, the compulsory removal of children from home, or a mental health 'section' – are also likely to lead to high emotion and to the potential for violence. Risk sometimes has to be estimated more immediately, such as in interviews where clients exhibit signs of agitation or expressive behaviour that begins to be threatening.

Attempts to prevent violence can involve tactics at many levels. Consistent policies that avoid differing practices among staff can be critical, for example, in working in a children's home. It is often helpful for staff to work in pairs in anticipated crisis situations. Similarly, careful thought about where a testing encounter is to take place could defuse a difficult interview. The layout of a room, the location of exits and the means for summoning help might all be critical. Avoidance of officious behaviour, together with a quiet, assertive and clear manner, is now generally accepted as more likely to calm than enrage.

If violence occurs, decisions have to be made rapidly about flight or containment in the light of the worker's assessment of risk, their willingness to use self-defence and containment techniques, and perhaps the involvement of others (the proximity both of help or of further danger from additional clients). Post-violence support should minimally involve medical attention and reports, a debriefing to try to understand what has happened, decisions concerned with immediate and future work with the offending party, possible criminal prosecution of the offender and personal support and counselling for the injured worker. Management should monitor violent incidents very closely. Analysis of the frequency and nature of such incidents might highlight, for example, the need for additional staff, different practices and staff training needs.

Programmes to help violent people develop alternative ways of dealing with situations that have in the past led to violence have been devised by both medical and various social work agencies. Approaches vary but typically include SOCIAL SKILLS TRAINING and ANGER MANAGEMENT and avoidance. Often individual COUNSELLING based upon a detailed analysis of what situations precipitate difficulties for particular clients is also offered, with many such analyses including discussions of problems around SUBSTANCE MISUSE and ALCOHOL consumption. (See also ABUSE, DOMESTIC VIOLENCE, SEX OFFENDER.)

C. Lupton and T. Gillespie, eds., *Working with Violence*, Basingstoke, Macmillan, 1994.

**voluntary/independent sector**  following government discussion (1990) and decision (1992) papers entitled *Partnership in Dealing with Offenders in the Community*, the PROBATION SERVICE is required to commit a percentage of its annual budget to developing links with voluntary and independent organizations in the COMMUNITY to undertake work that complements the service's statutory duties.

The main areas in which partnerships might be involved include CRIME PREVENTION, support for VICTIMS, ACCOMMODATION, supervision projects and voluntary befriending. Partnerships have been particularly successful in provision for YOUNG OFFENDERS, and examples include work with National Children's Homes, Barnardo's and the Rainer Foundation. In the area of crime prevention, the services of Crime Concern, an independent consultancy charity, have been used; projects have also been developed with the National Association for the Care and Resettlement of Offenders (NACRO). NACRO is one of a number of voluntary organizations whose main objective is to campaign for penal reform; others include the Howard League and the Prison Reform Trust. All these organizations aim to educate the public by providing an information service about the CRIMINAL JUSTICE SYSTEM, publishing journals and commissioning RESEARCH, as well as undertaking political lobbying.

**volunteers**   people who work for a statutory or voluntary organization without pay. Volunteers sometimes deliver a social welfare service or help in indirect ways so that others may deliver the service. Such activity is considered altruistic.

Volunteers can enact many roles, including those of befriending the vulnerable, offering support in relation to very tangible tasks such as driving or keeping financial accounts, or directly delivering the service as with advice bureaux and ADVOCACY schemes. A major contribution made by many volunteers is to the management committees of voluntary organizations. The scale of the contribution varies too – some people helping for a few hours a week and others working almost full-time.

Much social work and social welfare provision has its roots in voluntary activity. Over the past century in Britain, professional social work services have grown and in the main have been located in the STATUTORY SECTOR. The responsibility to discharge the duties of social welfare provision enshrined in law is mostly placed upon local government or statutory health authorities. The contribution of the VOLUNTARY SECTOR to social welfare remains considerable, however. Many voluntary organizations in fact employ only paid professional workers – sometimes to deliver, on the basis of an agency agreement, a service on behalf of a local authority (for example, social work services to DEAF people). Others have a mixture of the paid and unpaid, and yet others rely wholly on unpaid volunteers. There is also considerable variation in the extent to which organizations train, support and supervise their volunteers. Some are rigorous in their training programmes (the Citizens Advice Bureaux, the Samaritans and the PROBATION SERVICE, for example); others have yet to develop explicit policy on these issues.

The role of the volunteer is a matter of partisan debate, a debate located in the question of what responsibilities properly belong to the state, what to the COMMUNITY and what to the individual or family. The period between 1945 and 1975, with some fluctuations, was characterized by the growth of statutory provision. Since that time there has been encouragement for families to look after their own and for voluntary effort to replace statutory provision. There is thus considerable ambiguity in the role of the volunteer, with some seeing it as an indication of SELF-HELP and of a caring community, while others are concerned at the erosion of the minimum standards that should be guaranteed by the state.

**voucher**   a document entitling the holder to purchase services to a certain value when given in exchange.

Providing vouchers is a way of giving purchasing power to those who could not afford to buy the services of their choice. It is also a way for a government to privatize services that it used to provide (see MARKET). For example, if the government wished to have every parent buy their child's education, it could provide vouchers up to a certain limit that would enable all parents whether rich or poor to do so. The concept of vouchers has been the focus of heated political debate, generally along left–right lines.

# W

**Wagner Report**   the government report on RESIDENTIAL CARE services by the review committee chaired by Lady Wagner.

The Wagner Committee was set up by the government in 1985 to review residential services at a time when residential care was not only in a state of flux because of impending COMMUNITY CARE reforms but also demoralized because it was perceived by professionals and public alike as a low-status, residual service of last resort. The Wagner Report, subtitled *A Positive Choice*, intended to change that perception and through its recommendations establish residential services as part of a continuum of care in the community. It wished to see residential care as a service that people would actively choose to use because it met their needs in a way they wanted. The report focused on the rights and needs of individuals as a way of ensuring that active choice was possible. Users should have full information on the residential care options in their area as well as a number of realistic options to choose from, and they should be able to try establishments on trial. Once individuals had made a choice, it was important to protect their rights to complain about poor-quality service and to carry out those activities they were capable of such as handling their own money. Individual capacities were not to be undermined. Other Wagner recommendations sought to ensure quality by adherence to a national set of standards and by regular inspection. The report also wished to raise the status of residential work by ensuring that all managers were professionally qualified social workers and through improvement in the pay and conditions of staff.

While the Wagner Report's recommendations were not implemented in full by the government, much of its thinking, particularly on standards and the rights of users, found its way into official guidance. Uniquely, a Wagner Development Group continued to meet after the report was published and to publicize its conclusions around the country. In this way, its objective of changing the public and professional views of residential services was achieved.

G. Wagner, *Residential Care: A Positive Choice*, London: HMSO, 1988.

**Warner Report** the report published in 1992 by the committee of inquiry set up by the Department of Health following the imprisonment of child-care staff for CHILD ABUSE in Leicestershire.

Chaired by Norman Warner, former Director of Kent Social Services, the committee's aim was to examine the selection, development and management of staff working in CHILDREN'S HOMES. Its report, *Choosing with Care*, urges a more rigorous staff selection procedure. Among its key recommendations are: job specifications and person specifications issued for each post and directly related to the stated purpose of the children's home; advertisements for posts offered externally; a short list of at least three candidates to be made up for each vacancy; each short-listed candidate to visit the home prior to interview; and written exercises and preliminary interviews to form part of the selection process. The report also made many recommendations concerning the management of children's homes. These included regular supervision and appraisal of all staff, ensuring children know of the complaints procedure, and an encouragement to staff to report any concerns outside their line of management if their immediate superior seems unconcerned. The committee also recommended that all staff should have a personal development contract covering their own training. Most controversially, the report called for a new diploma in the group care of children, a recommendation based on the view that the current DIPLOMA IN SOCIAL WORK cannot give sufficient attention to this complex and fraught area of work.

*Choosing with Care, Report of the Committee of Inquiry into the Selection, Development and Management of Staff in Children's Homes*, London: HMSO, 1992.

**welfare checklist** the seven points that courts must bear in mind when considering making an order under the CHILDREN ACT.

The seven points of the checklist are: (1) the wishes and feelings of the child, taken in the light of their age and understanding; (2) the child's physical, emotional and educational needs; (3) the effect of any change of circumstances on the child; (4) the age, sex and background of the child (which inevitably includes the child's racial, cultural and religious background); (5) the harm that the child has suffered or may suffer; (6) how capable each of the parents is at meeting the child's needs; (7) the range and powers of the court under the Children Act itself. The importance of the checklist is immense. It acts as a reminder to the court that it must above everything else consider any order it might make in the light of the child's welfare (except the EMERGENCY PROTECTION ORDER, to which the checklist does not apply); and for the first time in child law it itemizes, however broadly, what welfare means. In particular, a court must not make an order under the Act, even if the grounds for that order exist, unless it has also taken into account the effect of making that order on each of those aspects of the child's life contained in the checklist. Although the welfare checklist is expressly for the court to consider, social workers and other professionals appearing in court in connection with an application for an order must also bear its contents in mind when presenting their arguments.

**welfare report** a report prepared by a member of the FAMILY COURT WELFARE SERVICE (or local authority social services department) at the request of a court, considering any matter relating to the welfare of a child under the provisions of the CHILDREN ACT.

The most commonly requested reports relate to the arrangements for children following DIVORCE. The role and status of such reports have been matters of much debate and the subject of numerous practice directions from the Family Division of the HIGH COURT. There is a clear professional distinction between conciliation, where parents are enabled to reach agreement about arrangements, and the preparation of a welfare report, when disagreement continues and court orders have to be made. In the latter situation, court welfare officers are required to investigate and assess proposed alternative arrangements for residence and parental contact, taking account of the views of the child where appropriate, and to recommend to the court which arrangements appear to be in the child's best interests.

A. Sanders and P. Senior (eds), *Jarvis: Probation Service Manual*, PAVIC, 5th edn, 1993.

**welfare state** the organizing, financing and provision of welfare benefits and services by government.

The term 'welfare state' is used to describe the combination of benefits and services intended to increase the well-being of citizens and provided either directly or indirectly. The welfare state also seeks to relieve poverty and reduce inequality by guaranteeing a minimum level of financial assistance through SOCIAL SECURITY or UNEMPLOYMENT BENEFIT. While state involvement in housing, education and social insurance occurred in Europe throughout the last half of the nineteenth century, the welfare state as it was constructed in Britain between 1944 and 1949 was unusually comprehensive and supported by a well-articulated philosophy that viewed it as a natural progression in social development. In Britain the welfare state became closely associated with the publicly financed services run by large institutions such as the NATIONAL HEALTH SERVICE, local authority housing and state schools.

For some thirty years after the Second World War the continued expansion of the welfare state was taken for granted by a broad consensus across the political spectrum. Expenditure on services and benefits took a greater share of the gross national product each year until the mid-1970s, when the government began to focus on the increasing costs of welfare. The architects of the welfare state had always linked its benefits and services to the presumption of full employment, for men if not for women; most households, it was assumed, would have a relatively well-paid wage earner. In the mid-1970s the destabilizing effects of a sharp rise in the price of oil and the rapidly changing nature of the economy made full male employment difficult to sustain or achieve. Unemployment soared, as did inflation. At the same time, the broad consensus supporting the welfare state also began to weaken. Electorates became less willing to fund services and benefits through taxation, while politicians and commentators from the NEW RIGHT argued that welfare benefits were too generous and created a disincentive to work and a dependency on the state. Governments hostile to the welfare state were elected in both the United States and Britain.

However, sober assessment of the retrenchment of welfare policies that both governments adopted indicates that the welfare state has survived, if in somewhat different form. Not until its second term did the Thatcher government attempt to cap social security spending by reducing any increase in benefits to the cost of living (previously they had been up-rated more generally with the increase in the standard of living). Other government reforms throughout the 1980s and 1990s changed the institutional arrangements of the welfare state by limiting the direct provision of welfare by state institutions. They did this by trying to separate purchasers of services from providers (see PURCHASER/PROVIDER SPLIT) and by allowing schools and hospitals to manage themselves rather than be managed by local or health authorities. In effect, this introduced MARKET-like reforms into some welfare provision, channelling public money into welfare services provided through an increasing number of private and voluntary organizations, rather than by public institutions and local authorities as in the past. Most analysts note that, while the form of the welfare state has changed, moving towards a greater role for private and voluntary organizations, government financing has not been cut as severely as first thought, and public support for the welfare state overall remains high. (See also ANTI-POVERTY STRATEGY, BEVERIDGE REPORT, NATIONAL INSURANCE BENEFITS, UNEMPLOYMENT BENEFIT.)

H. Glennerster and J. Midgley (eds), *The Radical Right and the Welfare State*, Hemel Hempstead: Harvester Wheatsheaf, 1991.

**Welsh Office**   the central government department responsible for most internal affairs in Wales.

Responsibility for social services was transferred to the Welsh Office in 1971. This responsibility was linked to that for the health service in Wales in the Health and Social Work Department. As a result of this development, an attempt at establishing a coherent policy in respect of social services and health was embarked upon in 1976. The most notable success is the development of a fully evaluated 'all-Wales strategy' for people with learning disabilities. The existence of an integrated department for health and social services has enabled the Welsh Office to overcome some of the departmentalism that has inhibited coordination of policies in England and Scotland. Responsibility for developing COMMUNITY CARE policy has also rested with social services rather than health services personnel, and this has allowed a social work perspective to develop rather than a medical model of care. For this reason, the section of the white paper *Caring for People* (1989) on Wales is dominated by a record of achievement by the all-Wales strategy. However, the white paper formally ended specific joint funding provision by the health authorities, and responsibility has been placed more firmly with local authorities.

D.J. Hunter and G. Wistow, *Community Care in Britain*, London: King's Fund Centre, 1987; Welsh Office, *Proposed All-Wales Policies and Priorities for the Planning and Provision of Health and Social Services from 1976/1977 to 1979/1980*, Cardiff: Welsh Office, 1976.

**widowed mothers allowance**     a benefit paid to a woman who is widowed, based on her late husband's contribution record, as long as she has a dependent child living with her.

If the claimant is aged at least 45 when her widowed mothers allowance stops, she will go on to WIDOWS PENSION. Widowed mothers allowance stops if the woman remarries or cohabits.

**widows payment**     a one-off lump-sum payment (of £1,000 in 1994) to a widow, based on her late husband's contributions.

**widows pension**     a benefit paid to a woman who is widowed, based on her late husband's contribution record.

The full pension is paid if the claimant is aged 55 either when first widowed or when her WIDOWED MOTHERS ALLOWANCE stops. It is reduced by 7 per cent for every year under 55, and nothing is paid to women who first qualify when under 45. Widows pension stops if the woman remarries or cohabits.

**withdrawal**     the physical reaction to the loss of a DRUG that has been taken for long enough for the person to become addicted in some measure. Symptoms can include cramps, diarrhoea, shivering and nausea. In extreme cases convulsions and death may result.

**Women's Aid**     a federation of refuges for women seeking to leave or have respite from violent partners. The women's aid movement, established in 1975, is a voluntary SELF-HELP movement run by women for women.

Women's Aid is prepared to accept any woman experiencing difficulties with a violent or abusing partner. The women themselves define what is an intolerable situation; there is no 'objective' test set by the movement. The clear aims of Women's Aid in relation to women and children who have experienced violence are to help them recover from the trauma and to encourage them to take control over their own lives. The movement also has broader educational and campaigning aims in relation to social welfare and justice systems as well as the public. These are to inform about the problem of DOMESTIC VIOLENCE and the inadequacy of current policies and provision for the protection of women and children. The movement has grown rapidly in Britain. In 1975 there were 30 refuges, but by 1987 this number had grown to over 200. The under-resourcing of women's aid in general and the remarkable lack of support from local authorities in particular have dogged the movement and made it financially vulnerable. Current provision is still far short of that recommended by the Domestic Violence Select Committee in 1975.

**workload management**     systems for determining and managing the quantity and quality of work of an individual worker and teams of workers.

Two systems of workload management are typically used; the first rests upon estimates of time allocated to identified task (for example, it is estimated that case A requires 5 hours a week, case B 10 hours, case C 8 hours, groupwork 6 hours, team meetings 3 hours, duty 7 hours, a training day 7 hours, and so on). Thus a worker might anticipate how their next month is to be spent. The second system is similar except that standard allowances (either points representing time or actual time slots) are given to, say, a PRE-SENTENCE REPORT, a SUPERVISION ORDER, a CHILD ABUSE investigation, a day in court and other set pieces. Systems vary in their complexity, depending upon their objectives. Some systems are also used to help management determine the range and duration of work. The principal objectives are to help protect workers from overload and thereby sustain quality in work, and to help management determine where resources are to be allocated. Workload management can also be an aid to supervision and, if information is shared, to team functioning.

**written agreement**   a statement written and agreed jointly by client and social worker setting out the aims and tasks to be undertaken in any future work.

Written agreements are key tools in contemporary social work. They are designed to ensure that there is no misunderstanding over the scope and intention of any planned social work intervention and to highlight areas of cooperation between practitioner and client. They should set out clearly what specific tasks are to be undertaken and by whom. The content of any written agreement is arrived at through negotiations and should always be framed in the client's own words or in words that are readily understandable by all concerned. When working with children and families, Guidance to the Children Act requires that a written agreement be drawn up before a child is placed in ACCOMMODATION; in particular such agreements will specify the length of time, the frequency and manner of contact between the child and its parents and the role the parents will play in the life of the child when it is accommodated.

Michael Preston-Shoot, 'Written agreements: a contractual approach to social work', in C. Hanvey and T. Philpot, eds, *Practising Social Work*, London: Routledge, 1994.

**young offender**   see JUVENILE/YOUTH JUSTICE.

**young offender institutions**   penal establishments for offenders aged between 15 and 20, formerly known as youth custody centres, which were in turn preceded by detention centres and borstals.

The aim of these institutions is to keep all YOUNG OFFENDERS separate from adults to avoid hardened criminal influence; but in practice this applies only to men, since all female establishments combine young and adult offenders. There is a substantial body of research that casts doubt on the effects of such institutions on the subsequent criminal careers of young offenders.

**young person**   generally refers to a person between the ages of 14 and 17, that is, the four years before a person reaches the age of majority.

The definition by age is found in the largely repealed Children and Young Persons Act 1969, which also defines a child as under 14. However, the important CHILDREN ACT has dropped this distinction and refers to all people aged under 18 as 'children'.

**youth court**   the court for offenders aged 10 to 17, introduced by the CRIMINAL JUSTICE ACT 1991 to replace the former juvenile court (see PROBATION ORDER, COMMUNITY SERVICE ORDER, COMBINATION ORDER) on 16- and 17-year-olds.

The juvenile court dealt with both criminal and care matters, but with the implementation of the CHILDREN ACT the youth court now deals only with criminal cases. Proceedings in the youth court tend to be less formal than in an adult court. The public are excluded, and the press are prevented from reporting names and addresses of defendants. (See CRIMINAL COURTS, JUVENILE/YOUTH JUSTICE.)

Sentencing options available to the youth court that are not available to an adult court are a SUPERVISION ORDER, ATTENDANCE CENTRE ORDER and detention in a YOUNG OFFENDER INSTITUTION (for offenders aged 15 and over). The youth court has an additional power to remand a young person into the care of the local authority rather than to PRISON, although the latter course is still available in respect of boys aged 15 or over. The absence of sufficient secure local authority accommodation for difficult young people is a matter of concern.

In dealing with YOUNG OFFENDERS, the government white paper *Crime, Justice and Protecting the Public*, which preceded the Criminal Justice Act 1991, made clear its view that 'crime prevention begins at home' and that parental responsibility was a key feature of government policy. Children under the age of 10 cannot be brought before a criminal court, as they are deemed in law to be unreliable in their understanding of the difference between right and wrong. If their behaviour is beyond parental control they may be placed in the care of the local authority. For a child over the age of 10, the youth court has powers to require parents to attend court, to pay fines on behalf of their child and to be bound over (that is, to consent to forfeit a sum of money in default of an agreement) to take proper care of and exercise control over their child. While the overriding principle in sentencing in the juvenile court was the welfare of the child, the youth court is required to balance welfare and proportionality. This means that greater consideration is now given to the seriousness of an offence, in line with sentencing in adult courts.

A further requirement of the youth court is to take account of the maturity and stage of development of young offenders, particularly those aged 16 and 17. This means that youth courts may treat 16- and 17-year-olds as either juveniles or adults for the purposes of sentencing. Little guidance has so far been given to courts to help them define and assess maturity objectively, and there is some concern that the concept may result in prejudiced judgements of teenagers' circumstances and abilities. For example, it is feared that a young person living with supportive parents and in full-time education may be treated as a juvenile and dealt with more leniently than a homeless, unemployed young person or a young mother. The latter may be treated an adult, although it may be questionable whether they are actually more mature.

**youth culture or subculture**   a system of VALUES, ATTITUDES and behaviours shared by a group of young people and different from those exhibited by other young people or people in general within a particular society.

Sociologists have examined the idea that there are youth subcultures in Britain. The characteristics thought by some to typify a youth subculture include a degree of classlessness, particularly in relation to leisure habits, a measure of opposition to adult values and behaviour and, most important, the replacement of the family by the peer group as the key set of social relationships. Critics of this analysis have argued that for most young people class, race and gender continue to be the most important defining characteristics rather than age. They add that society is remarkably good at reproducing itself, and in this respect attitudes and values are frequently shared by generations. Where differences are discernible, they are thought, with some exceptions, to be transitory.

Social workers and others working with adolescents and young people have it that particular PEER GROUPS can be an extremely important influence upon the behaviour of individual young people. In practice, it may be difficult to distinguish between the influence of a youth culture as distinct from a more immediate peer group. It may be that a peer group is a subculture, but it is also possible, indeed usual, for the subculture to be much larger than the peer group. In some circumstances (with some offence behaviour, for example) social work with young people has to acknowledge the importance of the group in relation to an individual's behaviour and work with the group if particular problems are clearly rooted in group dynamics. Gangs, for example, can provide exclusive group membership with tightly prescribed roles and in some cases the expectation of very distinctive behaviour. Members of such groups may clearly be culturally different from other young people, but such all-embracing social groupings are rare. The values and attitudes of particular youth groups may best be understood by reference to other social phenomena such as class or race. The class origins of rockers or skinheads, for example, may be a better explanation of their behaviour than intergenerational relations. Similarly, Rastafarianism among the young in Britain may, in part at least, be understood by examining racism and relations between ethnic groups rather than through age-related explanations.

**youth custody**   generally refers to the imprisonment of YOUNG OFFENDERS under the age of 22 years in a YOUNG OFFENDER INSTITUTION.

During the 1980s the term 'youth custody centre' replaced the term 'borstal', but both terms are now obsolete. Under the CRIMINAL JUSTICE ACT 1991 young offenders are subject to at least three months' compulsory supervision by a probation officer or social worker when they are released from custody, whatever the length of their sentence (see EARLY RELEASE).

**youth work**   a wide range of services concerned with children and young people within the age range 10 to 21 (although many would regard these age boundaries as entirely arbitrary), focusing upon social, recreational and educational needs and the resolution of particular problems such as homelessness and unemployment.

Youth services witnessed rapid expansion in Britain in the 1960s in both the VOLUNTARY SECTOR and the STATUTORY SECTOR. The core of these services was the youth club, offering mostly recreational provision. Clearly perceived by successive governments as a way of diverting potentially disaffected youth through constructive leisure, most localities had a youth club providing sports and leisure activities, with some weekend and holiday provision. Many clubs would additionally offer some kind of social education programme, especially the voluntary clubs located within churches. The content of social education would vary enormously depending upon the host organization, although all contended that preparation for citizenship and for adult roles was central to the task. Some youth workers were trained as social workers or had undertaken courses in teacher training colleges; a very large proportion, however, were volunteers or untrained sessional workers. An early innovation, in recognition of the fact that many young people did not attend clubs, was the unattached youth worker; such workers were to engage with 'street-corner society', especially those young people considered to be 'at risk' of criminal activity or in moral danger. The major objective in this work was more closely akin to social work, that is, to identify problems and to engage with the young people in solving them.

In the face of recent cuts in public spending, the youth club 'movement' has declined. Services for adolescents and young people have, however, developed in other ways to meet targeted needs. Within the field of juvenile justice, specialized provision is widely available to deal with young offenders in relation to diversionary programmes as well as punishment in the community (see COMMUNITY SERVICE ORDER). Other provision, mostly in the voluntary sector, has as its focus HOMELESSNESS among the young. This is a growing problem that has only recently met with any kind of official recognition, at least for children leaving local authority care. Similarly, SUBSTANCE MISUSE among young people has seen the development of advisory and counselling services, again mostly in the voluntary sector, but with limited statutory provision from health and social services. A similar picture exists in relation to pregnancy advisory services and gay and lesbian helplines. General youth COUNSELLING services are offered in some localities, but provision is uneven. In educational contexts, paradoxically, the most comprehensive services occur in higher education and the least satisfactory in secondary schools, where research indicates the greatest need. Although some teachers are very good at the pastoral role, many are not, and in any event many children and young people will not consult with teachers.

Although some services are proving responsive, many have been criticized for ignoring the needs of the young from ethnic minorities, girls and young women, young people with disabilities and particularly gay and lesbian young people. These discriminatory practices are long-standing. In relation to recreational provision, for example, it is rare for youth clubs to offer programmes for girls; rather, the assumption is that they like to be where the boys are. Similarly, research clearly indicates that problems such as homelessness are especially acute among young black people, yet services to advise and befriend them are even more poorly developed than for young whites.

The absence of coordinated policy in relation to youth in Britain, at local and national level, is cause for concern. The central plank of current government thinking is to locate responsibility for young people clearly within their families. There is, in addition, a reluctance to accept that many young people cannot and should not live with their families because of irreconcilable difficulties. Even with the CHILDREN ACT, which places responsibility upon all local authority departments to promote the interests of children and young people, there is little evidence of interdepartmental cooperation.

T. Jeffs and M. Smith, eds., *Youth Work*, Basingstoke: Macmillan, 1987.